Why Do You Need this New Edition?

If you're wondering why you should buy this new edition of *Odyssey*, here are 10 good reasons!

1 **Increase Your Confidence and Skills through Practice.** To gain confidence and develop mastery in any activity you attempt in life, you need to practice. *Odyssey's* unique "Portfolio" feature gives you a space to showcase your writing achievements in four different formats: Best Work, Essay Answer, Timed Writing, and Reflection.

2 **Improve Your Critical Thinking.** Consistent and regular practice makes you a better judge of your subject and audience. The "Challenge" activities promote critical thinking through the application of writing principles.

3 **Learn to Identify Plagiarism—and How to Avoid It.** Because of the ever-increasing availability of material online, *Odyssey* renews its emphasis on the dangers of plagiarism. Chapter 4 introduces the concept and Chapter 14 extends the discussion with more detailed explanations of how to quote directly, paraphrase, and summarize another individual's work. Chapter 15 shows specifically how to acknowledge your sources using the *Modern Language Association* (MLA) and *American Psychological Association* (APA) formats. A new sample essay also includes a sample Works Cited list to show documentation in context.

4 **Develop Your Own Prewriting Style.** In this edition, you learn to combine prewriting techniques in order to come up with one that best suits your personal style and fulfills your specified writing goals.

5 **Remember That Writing Is Recursive.** New examples in Chapter 3, "Composing," now more clearly illustrate each element of a complete paragraph and essay (from thesis statement, to topic sentence, to supporting details and transitions), as well as each recursive stage of the writing process (prewriting, composing, revising, editing).

6 **Get Creative.** Get creative with the "Discovering Connections" activities that, through photographs, inspire you to write. This new edition now features images from reality television to world travel. Add variety and style to your writing by studying the new material on different sentence types and classes in Chapter 17.

7 **Combine Modes to Best Persuade Your Readers in an Argument Essay.** To argue persuasively, you need to mix your modes. In Chapter 15, learn in detail how to combine modes effectively in order to persuade effectively; a new sample essay now clearly demonstrates multiple modes in action.

8 **Learn What Good Writing Looks Like.** See what good writing looks like and read the model paragraphs and essays that now cover such high-interest topics as innovative computer games, YouTube, traditional and distance-learning courses, and athletes with prosthetic legs competing in the Olympics.

9 **Recognize the Connection between Writing and Reading.** The book concludes with an anthology of six professional and seven student readings, with five of the readings newly chosen for this edition. Each reading provides opportunities for critical thinking, active reading, discussion, and writing.

10 **Go Beyond the Page.** MyWritingLab (www.mywritinglab.com) prompts at the end of each chapter take you to Pearson's dynamic online learning system for additional writing practice.

PEARSON

A Conversation with

William J. Kelly

Q. *What is the biggest stumbling block for new or developing writers?*

A. By far, it is just plain fear.

Q. *How can new or developing writers overcome their feelings of inhibition and anxiety as they face the blank page or computer screen?*

A. It may sound simplistic, but one of the best ways is to try to lessen expectations of the finished product. I'm not suggesting that anyone plan to write ineffectively. But many people become intimidated when their initial efforts do not match what they think the finished product should look like, and as a result they become discouraged. A better idea, then, is to assume that the first words you write won't yet be in their best or most complete form. They will serve as the foundation you need to fulfill the promise of your ideas.

Q. *Do you think that everyone can learn to express ideas clearly in writing?*

A. Absolutely. If people can think and say their ideas so that others can understand them, they can write them.

Q. *What is the most important lesson you'd like students to take away from this book/course?*

A. The most important lesson is this: People have difficulty with writing not because they lack ability but because they lack practice. Be patient and keep writing. You will get better. You won't be able to avoid it. The truth is that I was not a good student in high school. I had the ability. In fact, I had been an honor student up until the end of the ninth grade. But after that, I made the ridiculous, conscious decision not to work at my studies anymore. Instead I turned my attention to athletics and socializing. In my senior year, I applied to two local colleges. Fortunately for me, one of them took a chance and admitted me. At that point, I was ready to turn my attention to academics once more, but after my three high school years of self-imposed academic inertia, I struggled greatly. It wasn't until the second semester of my sophomore year in college that I began to reach the level of my true capability again. Throughout my teaching career, I've tried to remember what that struggle was like, how it felt to want to do something but to be unable to reach it immediately. I learned that if I was patient with myself, if I was persistent, if I learned from my mistakes, I could succeed. This lesson forms the foundation for my teaching and this book.

Q. *Is there anything else you would like to say to students who are about to begin using this book?*

A. I don't believe that a book has to be tedious to be rigorous. Students who lack knowledge or haven't had practice with writing need a text that talks to them simply, directly, conversationally, with a tone that is encouraging, respectful, and lighthearted. That's what I want you to find here.

Odyssey

From Paragraph to Essay

Sixth Edition

William J. Kelly
Bristol Community College

Deborah L. Lawton
Bristol Community College

Longman

Boston Columbus Indianapolis New York San Francisco Upper Saddle River
Amsterdam Cape Town Dubai London Madrid Milan Munich Paris Montreal
Toronto Delhi Mexico City São Paulo Sydney Hong Kong Seoul Singapore Taipei Tokyo

Dedication

To Matthew

To Michelle—
My life is better than I could have ever dreamed—because of you.

Editor in Chief:	Craig Campanella
Acquisitions Editor:	Matthew Wright
Director of Development:	Mary Ellen Curley
Development Editor:	Lai T. Moy
Marketing Manager:	Thomas DeMarco
Senior Supplements Editor:	Donna Campion
Media Editor:	Stephanie Liebman
Production Manager:	Eric Jorgensen
Project Coordination, Text and Art Design, and Electronic Page Makeup:	Elm Street Publishing Services
Cover Design Manager:	Wendy Ann Fredericks
Cover, Contents, and Part-Opening Photo:	© FogStock LLC/Index Stock Imagery, Inc.
Photo Researcher:	Clare Maxwell
Senior Manufacturing Buyer:	Dennis J. Para
Printer and Binder:	Courier Corporation/Kendallville
Cover Printer:	Phoenix Color Corporation

For permission to use copyrighted material, grateful acknowledgment is made to the copyright holders on p. 558, which is hereby made part of this copyright page.

Library of Congress Cataloging-in-Publication Data

Kelly, William J. (William Jude), 1953–
    Odyssey: from paragraph to essay/William J. Kelly; Deborah L. Lawton—6th ed.
      p. cm.
    Includes index.
    ISBN 0-205-73982-2–ISBN 0-205-73983-0
    1. English language–Rhetoric–Handbooks, manuals, etc. 2. English language–Grammar–Handbooks, manuals, etc. 3. Report writing–Handbooks, manuals, etc. I. Lawton, Deborah L. II. Title.

  PE1408.K475 2010
  808'.042–dc22

                                     2009039694

2 3 4 5 6 7 8 9 10—CKV—13 12 11

Longman
is an imprint of

www.pearsonhighered.com

ISBN-10: 0-205-73982-2
ISBN-13: 978-0-205-73982-0
(Student Edition)
ISBN-10: 0-205-73983-0
ISBN-13: 978-0-205-73983-7
(Annotated Instructor's Edition)

Detailed Contents

PART 3
Moving On to the Essay   163

PART 4
Developing Sentence Sense   249

PART 5
Understanding Subjects and Verbs   313

PART 6
Keeping Your Writing Correct   373

PART 7
Connecting: Responding to Reading   507

Appendix Tips for ESL Writers   543

Preface

The word *odyssey* comes from *The Odyssey*, the epic poem about the wondrous, fantastic travels of the legendary hero Odysseus, first sung by the Greek poet Homer in the eighth century B.C. It is after this great journey that this book is named. Writing is an odyssey, a voyage of self-expression through the world of ideas. It begins with a few ideas scribbled on paper or typed across a computer screen. You tap into your creativity and draw on stored reserves of experience ank knowledge as well as your interactions with others. Gradually, your original ideas evolve and grow. The end result of this journey is a piece of writing that expresses your thoughts in simple, clear, complete, and correct terms. Think of *Odyssey* as a guidebook for all the voyages—and all the promise—that writing involves.

Three fundamental beliefs about writing form the foundation of *Odyssey*:

- **Practice leads to confidence and competence.** The more you write, the more comfortable and confident you will become with the process. As your confidence grows, so will your competence as a writer. Therefore, the single best way to learn to write is by writing.
- **Writing well involves sound critical thinking and creativity.** In order to create an effective paragraph, essay, or even blog post, you need to understand your subject and to analyze it from different perspectives. Evaluating your audience is also key to knowing how best to write about your topic. At the same time, you must articulate key ideas about that subject in an orginal voice that can capture and engage your readers.
- **Good writing combines correct form and inspiring content.** You succeed as a writer when you express your ideas clearly, in full detail and in accordance with the rules of standard American English. Knowing when to add variety to your writing by combining different sentence types, using figurative language, or inserting humor when appropriate will inspire your readers and keep them interested.

Odyssey emphasizes these three fundamental principles and provides you with the guidance you need to achieve writing success in school and beyond the classroom. In this sixth edition, we have built on this foundation and further enhanced favorite features to help you achieve a greater mastery of writing.

What's New in the Sixth Edition?

Across the country, scores of two-and four-year colleges have increased their emphasis on portfolis, standardized testing, on-demand writing, timed writing tests, and the proper acknowledgment of sources in more advanced writing assignments requiring research. The sixth edition of *Odyssey* addresses these growing trends by offering comprehensive guidance for how to achieve your best writing under such circumstances. Renewed emphasis has been placed on the following:

- **Recognizing the recursive nature of the writing process.** Chapter 3, "Composing," has been completely revised to include a more comprehensive definition of the writing process and each recursive stage; new examples now more clearly illustrate each element of a complete paragraph and essay (for example, thesis statement, topic statement, supporting details, and so forth), as well as each stage of the writing process (prewriting, composing, revising, editing) in action.

- **Understanding plagiarism and how to avoid it.** With the ever-increasing availability and sources of material online, *Odyssey* renews its emphasis on the dangers of plagiarism, providing you with updated guidelines for learning how to identify and avoid it. Chapter 4 introduces you to the concept, and Chapter 14 extends the discussion with more detailed explanations of how to quote directly, paraphrase, and summarize another individual's work. Chapter 14 also briefly covers common documentation styles, and Chapter 15 shows specifically how to acknowledge your sources using the *Modern Language Association* (MLA) and *American Psychological Association* (APA) formats. A new sample essay also includes a sample Works Cited list to show documentation in context.

- **Combining modes to best persuade your readers in an argument essay.** In "Writing an Argument Essay: Using Mixed Modes" in Chapter 15, you learn in detail how argument essays must rely on mixed modes in order to persuade effectively; the chapter also includes a new sample essay that clearly demonstrates multiple modes in action.

- **Prewriting as an essential first step in the writing process.** Prewriting is one of the essential first steps in the writing process. Without solid prewriting techniques, you would be hard-pressed to come up with specific topics around which to focus your writing. Therefore, Chapter 2 now presents two new sections that cover writing in a response journal and developing a prewriting technique that fits your personal style. In a new section titled "Employing a Response Journal," you learn the value of and difference between the informal journal, used to write whatever comes to mind, and the response journal, used to respond to specific questions about assigned readings. In "Choosing the Prewriting Technique for Your Personal Style," your learn about the benefits of combining prewriting techniques to come up with the best ideas to fulfill your specified writing goals.

- **Understanding sentence types and classes.** Part of being an effective writer is learning to add variety to your writing. There are several techniques, but the most basic is recognizing and knowing when and how to use different types and classes of sentences. Chapter 17 defines, explains, and exemplifies the functions of declarative, interrogative, imperative, and exclamatory statements, as well as simple, compound, complex, and compound-complex sentences.

Favorite Features

Favorite features of *Odyssey* that have, for the past five editions, encouraged comprehension and practice, boosted confidence, promoted critical thinking, and inspired creativity continue these same aims in the sixth. To motivate you on your journey toward writing excellence, *Odyssey* offers numerous models of excellent writing in both paragraph and essay form throughout the book. Part 7 emphasizes the connection between reading and writing through a brief anthology of essays written by both student and professional writers.

Encourages comprehension and practice. *Odyssey* lives up to its promise of offering ample opportunities for writing comprehension and practice.

- **Comprehension and Practice Exercises.** These activities and exercises check your understanding of the writing process, grammar, usage, or mechanics and provide practice in applying these elements. Most are in continuous discourse form—brief examples written in complete sentences with an opening, supporting details, and a closing—so they also model good writing.

- **Timed Writing Activities.** College students regularly face challenging timed writing tasks, including essay questions and entrance and exit assessments. *Odyssey* provides specific strategies for dealing with timed writing situations (Chapter 16) and numerous opportunities for practice (the timed writing activities in the six portfolios).

- **Quick Study Activities.** Appearing toward the end of Chapters 16–31, these writing models illustrate specific weaknesses so that common writing errors are discussed and illustrated in appropriate context. They also provide several topics for paragraph development and include opportunities for true collaborative work.

- **Chapter Quick Checks and Summary Exercises.** These exercises, found at the end of each chapter in Parts 4, 5, and 6, deal with all the concepts from a particular chapter in a single drill. Chapter Quick Checks are composed of ten items each and are intended to prepare you for the longer twenty-item Summary Exercises, which can be used to assess your mastery of the chapter material.

- **Chapter RECAPs.** These charts, appearing at the end of each chapter, provide definitions of new terms in the chapter as well as visual summaries of key concepts.

- **ESL Appendix and Notes.** Specifically designed for English as a second language students, but useful for native speakers as well, the Appendix and marginal Notes cover the trouble spots of standard American English that everyone should know how to identify and correct.

Boosts Confidence. Lack of confidence can negatively affect your ability to learn the writing skills you need to succeed in college and beyond. These features not only help you master basic and complex writing skills, they also remind you that you are more than capable of achieving success.

- **Portfolios.** These unique portfolios conclude the first six parts of book and provide the opportunity to focus on:
  1. *Best Work,* a successful piece of writing completed for the previous section of the book.
  2. *Essay Answer,* response to one of two engaging essay questions.
  3. *Timed Writing,* an assignment that fulfills one of two challenging writing tasks, completed in a set period of time.
  4. *Reflection,* a demonstration of mastery of as well as comfort level with the material presented in the section preceding the portfolio.

- **Getting Started Q&A.** All writers—whether experienced or novice—have questions, fears, and concerns about writing. Each chapter opens with questions most frequently asked (but sometimes not often voiced) by students about the writing process, grammar, usage, and mechanics; answers focus on and reinforce the essence of the chapter.

Promotes critical thinking and inspires creativity. *Odyssey* not only provides you with the tools you need to improve your basic writing skills, but also enhances your critical-thinking abilities. With continued practice, you become not only a better writer, but also a better judge of your subject and audience. While *Odyssey* emphasizes the communicative function of writing, it also reminds you that writing is very much a creative activity that, while challenging, is ultimately rewarding.

- **Challenge Activities.** Appearing in each chapter, these activities promote critical thinking and encourage application of various principles of writing, grammar, usage, and mechanics, often through the creation of brief writings. And, because writers need feedback, the Challenge activities offer the opportunity for meaningful collaborative work with classmates. A distinctive icon identifies these tasks.
- **For Further Exploration Writing Assignments.** These writing assignments, which provide opportunities for both individual and collaborative work, appear at the end of every chapter and provide several topics for paragraph writing (Chapters 1–13) and essay writing (Chapters 14–31) Topics have been updated to include such high-interest subjects as Facebook, Twitter, and other social networking sites; national public service and civil disobedience; BlackBerries and other smart phones; text messaging; computer gaming; and global climate change
- **Discovering Connections.** Located in the writing process and rhetorical modes chapters (1–15), these writing assignments use photos to help inspire creative paragraphs and essays using everything students have learned in the chapter. Eight of the 23 photo prompts are new to better reflect students' interests, experiences and knowledge.

Models and exemplifies the writing process. Annotated facsimile examples, peer responses, and instructor's comments, and sample paragraphs and essays throughout the book provide a unique window into key stages of the paragraph and essay writing process.

Emphasizes the writing-reading connection. An anthology of six professional and seven student readings (five of which are new) provides opportunities for critical thinking and active reading as well as for discussion and writing.

Organization of the Text

Odyssey's organization fosters cumulative learning. The four chapters of **Part 1, Starting Out,** cover the essential elements of the writing process and the primary purposes of writing (Chapter 1). It then moves on to the importance of generating ideas through prewriting (Chapter 2)—using one of the six techniques presented or a combination of several. Strategies for developing a technique that best fits your personal style are also featured. Chapter 3 discusses and illustrates the entire composing stage of writing, tracing the creation of a paragraph from topic sentence to completed first draft while emphasizing the difference between writer-centered and reader-centered ideas. Chapter 4 explains each step of the revision stage and then puts the process into action, illustrating how revision can turn the solid first draft from Chapter 3 into an even more effective final draft.

Part 2, Using the Patterns of Paragraph Development, covers the traditional rhetorical modes or organizing strategies. Chapters 5 through 12 explain and illustrate the specific characteristics of narration, description, example, process, definition, comparison and contrast, cause and effect, and division and classification while also emphasizing the purpose or aim in the resulting paragraphs. Chapter 13 covers argument not as a mode but as a purpose, and one for which writers use a combination of modes to fulfill.

The three chapters in **Part 3, Moving On to the Essay**, apply the principles of paragraph writing presented in Parts 1 and 2 to writing an essay. Chapter 14 features each phase of the writing process (from prewriting to final, polished draft) through a single, annotated essay. Chapter 15 discusses ways to use the rhetorical modes to develop entire essays, and now features a new argument essay that includes a sample Works Cited page to illustrate documentation in action. Chapter 16 presents simple, clear, logical steps to perform well on specific types of writing, including essay exams, timed writing assessments, and summaries.

The four chapters in **Part 4, Developing Sentence Sense**, focus on writing correct sentences and avoiding the three most serious sentence errors: fragments, comma splices, and run-on sentences. The four chapters in **Part 5, Understanding Subjects and Verbs**, cover subject–verb agreement as well as different aspects of verb use. The seven chapters comprising **Part 6, Keeping Your Writing Correct**, deal with other aspects of usage and mechanics. Specific topics include working with nouns, pronouns, and modifiers; maintaining correct parallelism and spelling; using commas and other punctuation; and capitalizing words properly.

Part 7, Connecting: Responding to Reading, is a brief anthology of fifteen readings, including six pieces by professional writers such as Amy Tan, Judith Ortiz Cofer, and Bob Greene and seven by students, each accompanied by questions that promote critical thinking, discussion, and writing.

The book concludes with an appendix, **Tips for ESL Writers**, which is intended for nonnative speakers of English, but is also useful for native speakers. This simple and direct appendix covers selected aspects of grammar and usage that students find most confusing.

Book-Specific Ancillary Materials

- *Instructor's Manual and Test Bank* includes a wealth of teaching suggestions. Also included are a diagnostic test, tests for each chapter in Parts 4 through 6, a comprehensive Mastery Test, and sample syllabi.
- *The Pearson Developmental Writing Package* Pearson is pleased to offer a variety of support materials to help make teaching developmental English easier on teachers and to help students excel in their coursework. Many of our student supplements are available free or at a greatly reduced price when packaged with *Odyssey*, Sixth Edition. Contact your local Pearson sales representative for more information on pricing and how to create a package.

Acknowledgments

A number of people deserve our thanks for their guidance, direction, inspiration, and support as we completed this Sixth Edition of *Odyssey: From Paragraph to Essay*. First among them are John M. Lannon, University of Massachusetts, Dartmouth (retired); Robert A. Schwegler, University of Rhode Island; and Paul Arakelian, University of Rhode Island, whose ongoing friendship and encouragement mean so much.

We also want to acknowledge a number of people at Bristol Community College (BCC). We are particularly grateful to our students for all that they have taught us over the years. Thanks also to our colleagues at BCC for their continuing interest in our work, including Catherine Adamowicz, Debbie Anderson, Denise DiMarzio, David Feeney, Michael Geary, Tom Grady, Jeanne Grandchamp, Farah Habib, Penny Hahn, Betsey Kemper-French, Diana McGee, Linda Mulready, Jean-Paul Nadeau, Joanne Preston, and Howard Tinberg, for their kind words and genuine interest in our work. In addition, we want to thank Jack Warner, Chief Executive Officer and Chair of the South Dakota Board of Regents of Higher Education, for his encouragement and his friendship. We are especially indebted to Paul F. Fletcher, Professor Emeritus of English and retired Dean for Language, Humanities, and the Arts at BCC. Through his own example, Paul taught us about respect and compassion for students and colleagues and about excellence in teaching.

We also salute our reviewers, whose careful analysis greatly informed this edition of *Odyssey*. These insightful professionals include Kathleen Beauchene, Community College of Rhode Island; Nancy F. Bullard, Florida Community College at Jacksonville, North Campus; Gwendolyn E. Bunch, Midlands Technical College; Alisa Cooper, South Mountain Community College; Angela Hebert, Hudson County Community College; Jean-Paul Nadeau, Bristol Community College; and Christine Tutlewski, University of Wisconsin-Parkside.

The talented team at Pearson Longman deserves accolades for making this edition of *Odyssey* so attractive. Thanks to Editor-in-Chief Craig Campanella for his ongoing support and interest in us and our work. Thanks also to Acquisitions Editor Matthew Wright for his support and enthusiasm as well as his determination to make *Odyssey* the best book of its type—and for his patience as we completed our work. We are especially grateful to Development Editor Lai T. Moy for her tireless efforts to ensure that what we have written says what we intended it to say. In addition, Eric Jorgenson, Production Manager, and Sue Nodine, Project Editor for Elm Street Publishing Services, have done a superb job of transforming the manuscript into its final form.

Deb Lawton would like to thank her friends and colleagues who have encouraged and inspired her, and who have, above all, listened: Kathleen Hancock, Karen Dixon, Penny Hahn, Liz Alcock, and Cynthia Brenner. They have shared their stories and given her the opportunity to do the same. Above all, she would like to thank her extended family for their love and continuing support. She is most grateful to her daughter, Amy, and her husband, Kevin, with whom she shares her memories and hope for the journey ahead.

Bill Kelly would first like to thank his parents, the late Mary R. and Edward F. Kelly. The lessons they taught Bill and his brothers remain with him to this day. In addition, he offers thanks to his parents-in-law, Flo and Leo Nadeau, and to his sons-in-law, Timothy Matos and Jeremy Wright, for their continued and consistent support. Words don't exist to express how deeply he loves his daughters, Nicole C. Matos and Jacqueline M. Wright, and how profoundly grateful he is to be their father—and to be the grandfather of Alexander Owen Matos. But most of all, he offers thanks to his wife, Michelle Nadeau Kelly, who some thirty-eight years ago stepped into his life and transformed it. Her love and support have made his happiness—as well as his teaching and the rest of his work, including this book—possible.

WILLIAM J. KELLY
DEBORAH L. LAWTON

About the Authors

William J. Kelly earned his Ph.D. in English from the University of Rhode Island. He also received an M.A. in English from Rhode Island College and a B.A. in English from Southeastern Massachusetts University (now the University of Massachusetts, Dartmouth). A classroom teacher since 1975, he began his career teaching junior high school and high school English in the Fall River (MA) Public Schools. In 1984, he joined the English Department at Bristol Community College and within five years was promoted to full professor. In addition to his teaching at BCC, he enjoyed a three-year stint writing a weekly newspaper column and has presented numerous teacher training workshops and graduate courses in the teaching of writing. In 1997, the Carnegie Foundation for the Advancement of Teaching and the Council for Advancement and Support of Education (CASE) named him Massachusetts Professor of the Year, the first and only time a community college professor in the state has received this prestigious award. He is the author of several other texts, including Pearson Longman's *Discovery: From Sentence to Paragraph; Simple, Clear, Correct: Paragraphs; Simple, Clear, Correct: Essays; Strategy and Structure: Short Readings for Composition;* and *Intersections: Readings for College and Beyond.* A runner for more than forty years, he is also an avid handball player. He and his wife, Michelle, Assistant Professor of Psychology at Bristol Community College, live in Fall River. They are the parents of two daughters, Nicole C. Matos, Assistant Professor of English at the College of DuPage, and Jacqueline M. Wright, a musician and conductor, currently pursuing further graduate studies in flute performance.

Deborah L. Lawton has been an advocate of the community college mission and student success for all of her professional life. As an educator, she has held positions in academic administration and student affairs, in addition to more than twenty-five years as a teacher of writing and literature. She is currently Associate Professor of English and Coordinator of the Liberal Arts and Sciences program at Bristol Community College, where she has worked since 1977. A community college graduate, she holds an A.A. in Liberal Arts from Greenfield Community College in Greenfield, Massachusetts, a B.A. in English from the University of Massachusetts, Amherst, and an M.A. in English from Western Michigan University. While Assistant Dean for the Division of Language, Humanities, and the Arts at Bristol, she attended and successfully completed the Massachusetts Community College Leadership Academy. With William J. Kelly, she is co-author of Longman's *Discovery: From Sentence to Paragraph.* When not reading essays or advising students, she breeds and shows border terriers. She lives in Swansea, Massachusetts, with her husband, Kevin, and daughter, Amy.

PART 1

Starting Out

CHAPTER 1
Ensuring Success in Writing

GETTING STARTED ...

 Q Why does it seem harder to *write* something than to *say* the same thing? What can I do to make writing as comfortable for me as speaking?

 A Writing presents you with challenges you don't normally face when you speak. For instance, you don't need to worry about things like correct spelling or punctuation when speaking. And, if what you say aloud doesn't make sense, your listener can ask you questions. Perhaps the best way to become more comfortable with writing is to learn what's involved when you write—the stages of **the writing process.** These stages apply regardless of whether you are writing a paper for one of your classes, a blog posting, an e-mail, an online profile, a status report, or a letter of application.

Overview: Understanding the Importance of Good Writing Skills

In many ways, *odyssey,* a word that means an extended, adventurous journey, may be the ideal term to describe what happens when you write. On this odyssey, you discover the power of and connections between your ideas. You also learn to express your ideas more effectively and to develop improved usage, spelling, and punctuation skills. When you convey your good ideas clearly, directly, and correctly in the classroom, you will earn top grades. Do the same thing at work, and you will earn the respect of your colleagues and supervisors, ensuring your success as a professional. It's that simple.

Navigating This Chapter On this part of your odyssey, you will discover the basic elements of writing:

- the three stages of the writing process—prewriting, composing, and revising
- the four interacting components of writing—writer, reader, message, and means
- the purposes of writing—to inform, to entertain, and to persuade

Recognizing the Stages of the Writing Process

A successful piece of writing is much more than the final *product,* the words you see on a piece of paper. It is a process, one that consists of three stages: *prewriting, composing,* and *revising.*

The first stage of the writing process is **prewriting**. Think of prewriting as rehearsal, exploration, planning, or warm-up. No one would expect a musician, artist, or athlete to perform at top level without preparing in some way. The same is true of a writer. You need to plan first. When you prewrite, you generate ideas on a subject that you can then develop into a piece of writing. Any activity that enables you to examine a subject more closely can be a good prewriting technique. Thinking, reading a book or magazine, reading an electronic message board or a Twitter posting, observing behavior, or talking in person or online with others can all be effective prewriting methods. You can also choose from a number of more formalized, structured prewriting activities, which are fully discussed and illustrated in Chapter 2, "Generating Ideas through Prewriting."

The next stage of the writing process is **composing**. During composing, you transform the ideas generated during prewriting by expressing them in correct sentences and then arranging them in a complete version or **draft**. Your ultimate goal is to communicate your full meaning to someone else—your reader. Chapter 3, "Composing," explains this part of the writing process.

The third stage of the writing process is **revising**. Think of revising as reseeing. When you revise, as Chapter 4, "Refining and Polishing Your Draft," illustrates, you reexamine and then return to the earlier stages of the writing process, each time creating a more effective draft until you arrive at your final draft.

The following figure illustrates the process:

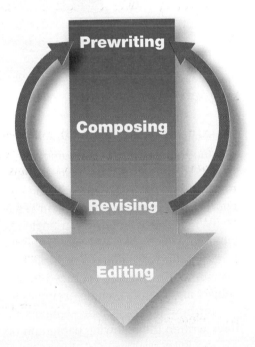

As the smaller arrows on the sides of the figure show, you begin with prewriting, move to composing, and shift to revising. The process leads back from revising to prewriting and continues through composing and through revising to editing. Although the next three chapters focus on the writing process one stage at a time, keep in mind that writing doesn't move in one direction as a step-by-step, linear process. Instead, it is *recursive*. In other words, as you write, you move back as well as forward through the process in order to make a piece of writing as effective as possible. For example, if you notice that an initial draft needs more detail to make your point clearer and easier to understand, you return to prewriting to generate new ideas and then move again to composing to develop those ideas into supporting sentences.

Understanding the Dynamics of Writing

Writing involves four interacting components: (1) a **writer,** the person expressing ideas; (2) a **reader** or *audience,* the person or persons receiving the ideas; (3) a **message**—the writer's **topic** and supporting ideas about the topic; and (4) the **means;** the expressive form the message takes—in this case, written language. The following communications triangle illustrates the interaction among these four components:

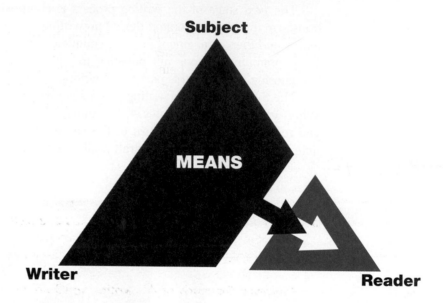

In this figure, the shaded portion on the left represents the *message*—what you understand and want to communicate to your *reader.* Your goal, as the arrows indicate, is to use the *means*—written language—to communicate the examples, explanations, and details encapsulating what you know, therefore completing the connection between you and your reader.

When you write, as the triangle also shows, a division always exists between you and your reader. You have a specific degree of knowledge about your subject, a level of understanding and insight that your reader probably doesn't have. To overcome this division, you need to anticipate your reader's questions about your subject and then to include examples and details that will answer those questions.

So how do these four elements interact in a piece of writing? Imagine you have written the following paragraph on the subject of life in a big city:

> From my experience, a big city is more like a series of interconnected towns. For example, just about everything anybody could need is available within walking distance in my neighborhood. This area covers only about six blocks, but it contains several coffee shops, pizza places and other restaurants, bodegas, and small grocery stores. In addition, the area includes a small playground for children, its own branch library, and a small park with five benches and two picnic tables. But it's the people in the

neighborhood who make my neighborhood special. The familiar faces on the streets, in the shops, and on the subway make the neighborhood seem like an extended family. Most residents live in apartment complexes that can house fifty or more families. As a result, people get to know their neighbors and the shop owners and workers well. If you go into Izzy's, a small diner at the very center of the neighborhood, on a Friday or Saturday night, the tables and booths will be filled with people from the neighborhood. On most days, it all seems so comfortable that I forget that my neighborhood is just a small part of an enormous city.

In terms of the elements of the communications triangle, you've written the piece, so you are the *writer.* Your *message* is the information you have included about your view of life being in a big city more like life in a small town. The *means* of communicating your ideas is written language—the words, examples, and details you have included. Finally, your *reader* is the person or persons to whom you are directing this information.

Focusing on the Reader

As a writer, you need to concentrate primarily on your reader. If your writing doesn't communicate to a reader, then it's not effective. It's that simple.

Sometimes you will know exactly who your reader is. For example, if you are writing a thank-you letter following a job interview, you know that the reader will be the person who interviewed you.

However, for much of the writing you'll do, your reader won't be so clearly identified. In these cases, you must envision a reader. It may be an actual person, someone you know slightly but not well. You should avoid envisioning someone close to you because you share too much common knowledge. Unless you assume that you are writing to a relative stranger, you may omit information necessary to communicate with your actual readers.

Sometimes you may find it easier to focus on the **average reader.** Think of yourself *before* you learned detailed information about your subject. The average reader is just like you were. What kinds and degree of information did you need to know? The average reader needs the same type of examples and details.

Imagine that you have just purchased a sweatshirt with the insignia of your favorite college football team. You begin to wonder how much money colleges and universities make from the sale of goods bearing their names and the emblems of their athletic teams. After discussing the issue with your marketing professor and doing a little research on the Internet, you learn the astounding truth: The sales of merchandise with the names and logos of top collegiate teams like the Texas Longhorns, Michigan Wolverines, and Notre Dame Fighting Irish generate millions of dollars for the colleges. The sale of items bearing the familiar Longhorns insignia of the University of Texas, currently the most popular logo, brings as much as $8 million to the school every year. Typically, a significant amount of the money schools receive—in the case of the University of Texas, half—goes directly to the athletic department, with the rest used to support academic programs.

ESL Note
See "Unity," page 555, and "Think about Audience Expectations," "Strive for Clarity," and "Reinforce Your Point with a Concluding Paragraph," pages 556–557, for more about the needs of the audience.

These details—especially the information about the staggering amount of money that licensing brings these schools and the way the money is distributed—give you a greater understanding of this subject. They are therefore exactly the examples that the average reader would need in order to understand this issue as you now do.

The more personal, unusual, or complex your subject is, the more important it is for you to address the needs of the average reader. A topic may seem easy or ordinary to you, but that's because of the background knowledge you've already developed about it. Such a subject won't be so familiar to most readers, however. To help reduce this unfamiliarity, you, as the writer, should provide the kinds of details and examples that enabled you to understand the subject in the first place.

COMPREHENSION AND PRACTICE 1.1

Considering the Stages and Dynamics of Writing

1. Why do writers move back and forth through the stages of the writing process as they develop a piece of writing?

   because they prewriting first is like a clean up then they composing the writer express them in a correct sentence arranging in a complete draft then they revise.

2. How do you overcome the barrier in terms of the level of knowledge that separates writer and reader?

   the readers 2 a person or person who the writer give the information the writer has to communicate on the readers

3. Why is focusing on the average reader often a better choice than writing for a close relative or friend?

   bac, is more isier to give information necessary to a strange reader

4. Look again at the paragraph about life in the big city on pages 4–5. What level of understanding about this subject does the writer believe the reader has?

   has a lot of details also the readers can picture the town.

CHALLENGE 1.1   Exploring the Writing Process

1. How do you feel about writing? On a separate sheet of paper, briefly explain what you like about writing—and what you don't.

collaboration

2. Now compare your response with a classmate's. On the following lines, briefly summarize what the two of you have in common regarding writing.

   _____

   _____

   _____

collaboration

3. Working with a classmate, make two columns on a separate sheet of paper. In one, list at least four things that strong writing skills would enable you to do. In the second, list at least four problems that you or others would face because of weak writing skills.

4. Consider everything you understand about *social networking sites* or *YouTube*. On the following lines, list three details you have thought of that you feel most readers would know, and explain why you think they would know these things.

   _____

   _____

   _____

Examining the Purpose behind Your Writing

When people write, they fulfill three main **purposes** or aims: *to inform, to entertain,* or *to persuade.* A paper explaining the effects of lead poisoning in children, for example, would inform. So would a paper spelling out how to edit a digital photograph.

A paper about a positive experience—attending a concert or sporting event—would clearly entertain. A story about the breakup of a relationship would also entertain because it would arouse your reader's interest and emotions.

A paper suggesting that world powers should work together on developing alternative energy sources would be persuasive. So would one asserting that drivers should face mandatory road testing once they reach the age of sixty. As a college writer, you'll frequently be called upon to prepare persuasive writings or *arguments,* which can be particularly challenging. Chapter 13 is devoted entirely to developing an effective argument paragraph, and a section of Chapter 15 explains ways to write an effective argument essay.

Often your purposes in writing overlap, with one purpose dominating. An informative paper on lead poisoning might also entertain if it draws in the reader by describing specific cases. It might also be persuasive if it claims that more research money should be devoted to discovering ways to reverse the effects of the poisoning. Still, one purpose will dominate, so always identify that purpose. Remember, purpose influences the information you include and also the style and tone you adopt.

For example, imagine that your instructor asks you to write a paper that outlines some of the difficulties a first-semester college student might encounter. The primary purpose is to inform. If you instead write a paper in which you assert that college students today have greater opportunities to explore careers than ever before, the paper won't fulfill the primary purpose. Moreover, it won't meet the needs of your reader, who expects a different focus and content.

Understanding the Important Relationship between Writing and Reading

One of the best ways to improve as a writer is to read more. When you read, whether it is an essay, a textbook chapter, a message board posting, a magazine article, a blog, and so on, you immerse yourself in the world of words. As Part 7, "Connecting: Responding to Reading" (pages 507–542), indicates, active reading enables you to uncover the significance or importance of what a writer is saying.

But just as important, active reading puts you in the position to notice the way other writers present their ideas. You'll begin to notice how they arrange their sentences, how they structure documents, and how they start and end them. Once you begin to identify different writing strategies, you'll be in the position to use those strategies yourself. In other words, you'll develop a **writing awareness** that will result in more effective papers.

COMPREHENSION AND PRACTICE
1.2

Considering the Roles of Reading and Purpose in Writing

1. How does understanding the purposes underlying a piece of writing help you as a writer?

   Makes me understand that I need write with more details the way a reader can understand and live what I write.

2. How would you explain the relationship between reading carefully and improving as a writer?

   reading slow to be able to understand and write clear with details to make the reader easear to understand.

3. Read the following paragraph:

   A successful and controversial innovation in television programming is reality TV. On reality shows, people, sometimes ordinary folks and sometimes celebrities, interact in specially arranged situations and locales. MTV is sometimes credited with beginning this trend with *The Real World*, which featured a number of young people from diverse backgrounds sharing a house and trying to get along with each other. Reality TV hit the mainstream with *Survivor*, which involves teams of people of different ages and backgrounds living in some deserted area. The participants, competing for a huge cash prize, engage in staged events while trying to avoid being voted off the island. Other reality shows, such as *Celebrity Rehab, Dancing with the Stars*, and *The Celebrity Apprentice*, turn the camera on current or former celebrities as they interact with the public and with each other. Some critics complain that reality shows often exploit personal weaknesses and highlight bad behavior. But at least for now, the popularity of reality shows means they will be around for a while.

a. What is the *primary* purpose of this paragraph? What details and examples in the paragraph led you to this answer?

> talk about the controversial about the tv programming reality show. the tv shows some ppls critics and complain about the show—

b. Does it fulfill other purposes as well? Explain your reasoning on the following lines.

_____

_____

_____

CHALLENGE 1.2   Focusing on the Importance of Reading and Purpose in Writing

1. Of all the different documents you've read in your life—novels, print or on-line articles, plays, essays, blogs, children's books, textbooks, personal profiles, and so on—which one do you best remember? On a separate sheet of paper, identify this document and what you think the writer did to make the text stand out for you.

2. Take another look at the paragraph on life in the big city on pages 4–5. On a separate sheet of paper, identify its main purpose and any secondary purposes, explaining what examples and details led you to these conclusions.

collaboration

3. Working with a classmate, choose two of the following three subjects:

- a proposal to raise the driving age to eighteen
- text messaging
- a popular vacation destination

Now, list details and examples you might include in a paper on this topic that fulfills each of the following purposes:

a. to inform

_____

_____

_____

b. to entertain

_____

_____

_____

c. to persuade

_____

_____

_____

FOR FURTHER EXPLORATION Topics for Writing

Focus on one of the following writing topics. Consider the subject, deciding what someone else might need in order to understand what you are thinking, and write down these examples and details. At the same time, identify and write down what you expect your primary purpose would be. Save this work for possible later use.

- a modern innovation that you would never want to live without
- a funny incident that happened to you or that you witnessed
- the different ways the Internet affects—positively and negatively—your life

DISCOVERING CONNECTIONS Developing a Paragraph

For this assignment, consider the picture and then respond to one of the following questions (or another that the picture inspires). Using the material in this chapter to guide you, jot down what you think an average reader would need to know in order to understand your thoughts. At the same time, write down the primary purpose you expect your paper to fulfill. Save your work for later use.

A. Does this image inspire you to go on an odyssey to a place far away from home in terms of country, culture, and heritage? Where would you choose to go? Why?

B. This sculpture is likely thousands of years old. What do you think it represents? Does it make you think of history in general and what the past can teach us about the present—or the future?

RECAP Ensuring Success in Writing

Key Terms in This Chapter	Definitions
the writing process	the series of stages in writing: prewriting, composing, revising, and editing
prewriting	when you generate ideas to develop into a piece of writing
composing	when you select and then express in sentence and paragraph form some of your prewriting ideas
draft	a complete version of a paper
revising	when you create new drafts through reexamining, improving, and polishing your initial version
writer	the person expressing ideas through the written word
reader	the audience to whom a paper is directed
message	the supporting examples, details, and explanations that represent your understanding of the topic
topic	the subject of a paper
means	the written language used to express ideas
average reader	a device to help you meet the needs of a reader that involves envisioning your level of knowledge before you learned what you now know about a subject
purpose	the intent or aim of a paper
writing awareness	a recognition as you read a document of devices and strategies that other writers have used

What You Need to Know to Write Effectively

- The stages of the writing process: **prewriting, composing,** and **revising.**

- How the four elements of writing—**writer, reader, topic,** and **means**—interact.

- The importance of focusing on the **reader.**

- The **purpose** of any writing assignment:

  to *inform*—as in a paper explaining how a movie special effect is created
  to *entertain*—as in a paper recalling the first time you drove a car
  to *persuade*—as in a paper asserting that recycling should be mandatory throughout the United States

Using Odyssey Online with MyWritingLab

For more practice understanding the writing process, go to
www.mywritinglab.com.

CHAPTER 2
Generating Ideas through Prewriting

GETTING STARTED ...

 Q What can I do to overcome my anxiety of dealing with that blank page or computer screen?

 A Identifying the correct prewriting technique—or combination of techniques—appropriate for your own writing style will definitely help you feel less overwhelmed and intimidated. So will reminding yourself that the final version of anything always starts out as something far less complete and polished. Keep your focus on what is important at this stage—developing the details and examples that you will shape as you work through the rest of the writing process.

Overview: Seeing Prewriting as a Way to Explore Ideas

As Chapter 1 discusses, writing is an odyssey through the world of ideas. On this excursion, you develop your writing skills, and you also develop your creativity and powers of analysis. Through writing, you discover the significance of your ideas and explore the connections among them. This chapter will explore the most creative stage of writing: **prewriting**.

Navigating This Chapter On this portion of your odyssey, you will learn how to use the following prewriting techniques:

- freewriting
- brainstorming
- clustering
- branching
- idea mapping
- maintaining a journal

Understanding Prewriting

Prewriting is the first stage in the writing process, during which you discover what you think and know about a topic and then generate details and examples that will express and illustrate your understanding. A number of common activities can also serve as informal prewriting techniques, including thinking; talking with others online or in person; reading an article, a book, a blog, or a Twitter posting; or watching a video or multimedia presentation.

Another informal, but intentional prewriting technique involves asking and answering a series of *Discovery Questions:*

- What do I already know about this subject?
- Why would someone else want to know about this subject?
- What kinds of details and examples made it easier for me to understand this subject?
- What's the most interesting aspect of this subject?

The answers to these questions can help to form a framework for writing. Prewriting also includes a number of more structured techniques, such as *freewriting, brainstorming, clustering, branching, idea mapping,* and *maintaining a journal.* This chapter offers you the opportunity to try them all out. That way, you'll know which technique—or which combination of techniques—is best for you.

Freewriting

Freewriting is a no-holds-barred prewriting technique that involves writing down all your ideas on a subject for a set period of time—typically ten minutes. To freewrite, simply write everything that comes to your mind, even if it contains errors, drifts from the original subject, or doesn't immediately make sense. Don't stop, even if you feel blocked. Instead, write something like, "I can't think" or "I'm stuck here," or find a rhyme for the last word you've written until a new idea comes to mind. The strength of this method is its ability to help you overcome inhibitions and concerns and get your ideas flowing.

If you do all your writing on a computer, you will discover that it is an excellent tool for freewriting. First, set up your program to double-space your document. If you'd like, darken the screen so that you cannot see what you write. This may make you feel less inhibited. Now you can simply type away on your keyboard for ten minutes. When you are finished, print out what you have written.

A freewriting on a subject such as *connecting through the Internet* might look like this:

> Time spent on the Internet—an hour a day? Maybe even more? Facebook is always my first stop, always updating and checking in with my friends—some of them are in other parts of the country. One of them is in Iceland! YouTube! I love YouTube—watch all kinds of stuff people post, silly videos, portions of shows and movies, it's almost addictive. Hulu is a newer one—downloaded video clips. Whenever there's something big in the news, somebody posts video from a phone or one of the Flip video cameras. People also post pictures and video on Facebook and MySpace. Some people have lost out on jobs because their pictures showed them partying, etc. and somebody in the company checked! Invasion of privacy? You have to use your head about stuff you post. My pictures are pretty ordinary, though—and so are most of

> *the people I connect with. Some sites for professional people—LinkedIn is the one they showed us in College Success Seminar—Xing, too—looked like a cool way to connect with other people in your field. And jobs! Who knows better about jobs in a field than people who are already doing the job?*

Keep in mind that at this point in the writing process, promising ideas will likely be in a very rough form. Still, they have the *potential* to become part of a good piece of writing later on, once they are developed more fully and supported by other related details and examples. After you prewrite, always take a few moments to highlight, underline, or ⟨circle⟩ your best ideas. That way you can easily find them later if you decide to develop them more fully.

COMPREHENSION AND PRACTICE

2.1

Trying Freewriting

1. Now it's your turn. On a separate sheet of paper, freewrite for ten minutes on one of the following topics: *transportation complaints, ambition, money.*

2. Identify the most promising ideas in the freewriting by highlighting, underlining, or circling them.

3. Of the ideas you have identified, which one has the most potential for development? List it on your paper, and then generate three additional details about it.

Brainstorming

Brainstorming is a far less expansive technique than freewriting. To brainstorm effectively, concentrate on a subject and then make a list of every idea directly connected to that subject. A set time limit isn't necessary, although some people prefer to establish a time frame, say, fifteen minutes. Remember, though, that you list only ideas directly related to the subject. After brainstorming, you may have fewer notes on paper than you do when you freewrite, but the ideas you generate are likely to be more obviously connected.

You can also brainstorm with your computer. If you wish, darken the screen so that you cannot see what you write. Then type your list, letting your mind lead you easily from one idea to another. When you are finished, print your list.

After you brainstorm, you should highlight, underline, or circle ideas that you think have potential as writing topics.

Take a look at this brainstorming on the subject of *camping vacations:*

Camping Vacations

✓ cheap compared to staying in a hotel

✓ borrow or rent a tent and sleeping bags

✓ food cooked outdoors tastes great

✓ swimming, fishing, hiking

✓ many campsites have individual electrical and water hookups

✓ trailer camping and SUVs—popular choice but really different from tent camping

✓ even some small RVs cost more than a luxury car or SUV

✓ everything in these RVs—microwaves, TVs, showers, air-conditioning—more like a hotel

✓ great to wake up with the sun warming the tent

✓ aroma of the pine trees is great

✓ some people are such pigs—leave litter everywhere

✓ state and national camping areas—good maintenance and security

As this example shows, once you complete a brainstorming, you should identify the most promising ideas by highlighting, underlining, or circling them.

An added advantage of brainstorming is that the list of ideas can sometimes serve as an informal **outline** or a plan for presentation for your first draft. Brainstorming is also an excellent technique when you are working with a partner or a group. Other people's ideas will spark your own creative thoughts, and soon you will find that the ideas come more quickly.

COMPREHENSION AND PRACTICE 2.2

Trying Brainstorming

1. Now try brainstorming. On a separate sheet of paper, brainstorm on one of the following topics: *your earliest memory, stereotypes, personal responsibility.*

2. Go through your brainstorming, and highlight, circle, or underline the ideas that are especially promising.

3. What single idea in your brainstorming seems most suited for further discussion? List it, and add three details you could use to develop the idea.

Clustering

Clustering is a visual prewriting technique that shows connections among the ideas you develop. Rather than starting from the left of the page and moving to the right, this approach allows you to move in multiple directions. Related points appear next to each other, regardless of the order they come to you. Clustering is probably easier to do on paper, although some computer programs enable you to create a clustering electronically.

To create a clustering, write a general idea in the middle of the page and circle it. As you think of a related idea or detail, write it down and circle it. Then draw a line to connect the new idea to the idea from which it developed. Continue this process until you have thoroughly examined the subject. The result is a series of ideas and examples, with lines showing how they relate to each other. You can then highlight or underline the ideas that hold the most promise.

Look at this clustering on the subject *bad habits:*

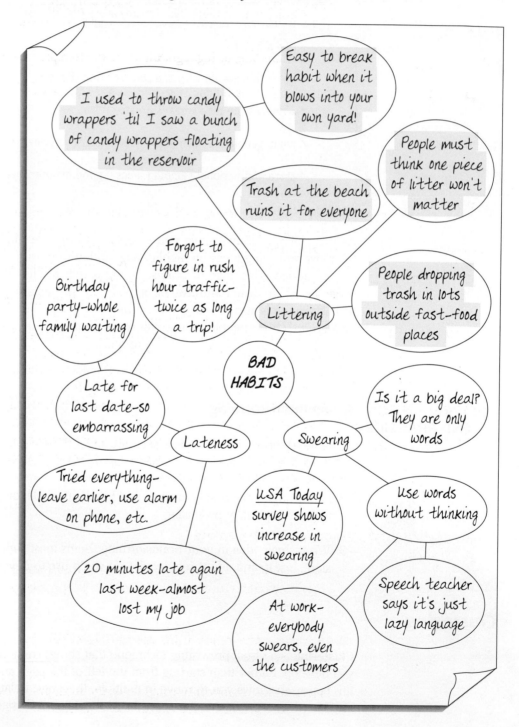

As this example shows, clustering allows you to move from one good idea to another while emphasizing the various connections among the ideas. By highlighting, circling, or underlining the strongest points, you create the foundation for an effective piece of writing.

COMPREHENSION AND PRACTICE 2.3

Trying Clustering

1. Now try clustering. On a separate sheet of paper, create a clustering on one of the following subjects: *crowd control, humor, weather complications.*

2. Circle, underline, or highlight the ideas or examples that interest you the most.

3. What single idea holds the most potential for development? Write that promising idea, and add three details about it.

Branching

Like clustering, **branching** is another form of visual prewriting. In this case, several groupings of related items spread from left to right across a page. Think of an informal outline, only turned on its side. Branching probably works best with pen or pencil on paper, but if you are experienced with graphics programs, you can use one to create a branching on your computer.

To create a branching, first list your topic on the left side of a piece of paper. Next, write ideas inspired by this topic to the right of it, and connect them to it with lines. As these new ideas lead to related thoughts and ideas, add these to the right again. Working from left to right across the page, let your ideas branch out, with lines showing relationships. Once you complete the branching, highlight, underline, or circle any promising ideas for later development.

Look at the branching on the subject of *competition* on page 18. As you can see, branching leads you from one aspect of a topic to other, more specific aspects. As an added advantage, each branch holds an arrangement of related ideas. This focused organization allows you to concentrate on one area of your topic now and save the other areas for development later on.

COMPREHENSION AND PRACTICE 2.4

Practice with Branching

1. Now give branching a try yourself. On a separate sheet of paper, complete a branching on one of the following topics: *power, invaluable social skills, staying in shape.*

2. Highlight, circle, or underline the portions of your branching that might be further developed.

3. What section in your branching holds the most promise for development? List it, and then add three details about this idea or section.

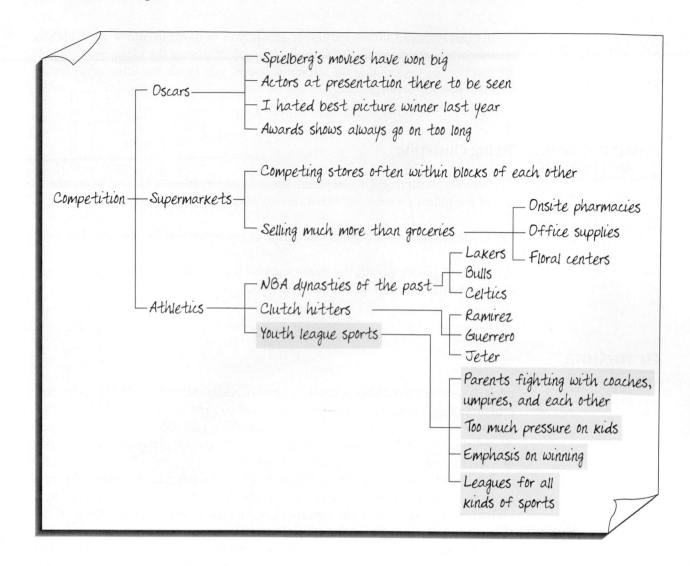

Idea Mapping

Idea mapping is a freewheeling prewriting technique that attempts to stimulate multiple aspects of your creativity. When you idea map, you write words *and* create images such as icons, scribbles, sketches, and symbols. According to the theory underlying this technique, the words you include flow from the areas of your brain responsible for logic and analysis. The sketches and doodles you create arise from the areas of your brain responsible for creativity.

With this strategy, start anywhere on the page, writing a word or drawing a picture representing the general topic. Then let your mind range freely on the subject, recording your associations in images or words, as seems natural. After you finish, identify the ideas and images that have the most depth and meaning to you, and then highlight or circle them.

An idea map on the subject *frustration* is shown on page 19. The final step in idea mapping is to translate key images into words. For example, you might translate the scribbled sketch of the traffic light this way: "All the road construction makes the streets near the college seem more like a parking lot." You

might convert the rough drawing of the computer to something like this: "Last night my computer crashed again. This time, I lost almost all my documents." The written version of the image can then serve as an idea to be used in a paper.

COMPREHENSION AND PRACTICE 2.5

Trying Idea Mapping

1. Look at the scene you see from your vantage point in the classroom, and create an idea map of your thoughts and feelings about the scene. Or, if you prefer, complete an idea map on one of the following subjects: *advertising, a perfect weekend, deadlines.*

2. Highlight, circle, or underline the ideas in your map that you feel you can develop further. Remember—translate key images into words.

3. What particular image or idea on your map holds the greatest potential for later development? Write it down, and add three details about it.

Maintaining a Journal

A **journal** is a place in which you can explore different subjects through informal writing. Writing in your journal every day is one of the best ways to make writing seem as natural as talking and thinking. In many ways, a journal entry is like one of the many conversations—in-person discussions, online chats, text messages, and so on—that you have every day. The difference is that, at this point anyway, you are simply talking to yourself.

How you set up your journal is up to you. It can be a notebook that you devote entirely to this purpose or a separate section of a notebook you use for other purposes as well. You might also maintain your journal on a computer. Think of your journal as an idea book or personal blog. Simply flip to a page or click open a document, list the date and title of your entry, and start writing.

Spend at least 10 to 20 minutes exploring your feelings about your topic—for example, an issue or person in the news, a concern, or a day-to-day experience that is important to you. After you complete each entry, reread what you've written, highlighting, circling, or underlining any ideas that you might want to develop into more formal writing later. Regardless of what you choose to write about, you can be sure of one thing: This extra practice will pay off in terms of improved writing.

When you don't already have a subject to write on, focus on one of the following topics:

urban legends	dieting	ideal vacation destinations	true justice
creativity	impolite behavior	the best profession	nightmares
legalized gambling	roller coasters	a day at the mall	pet problems
favorite study spot	faith	discrimination	cheating
personal security	a fashion disaster	hearing versus listening	bullying
ways to waste time	the power of music	entertaining advertising	courage
dating adventures	questioning authority	difficulties with a boss	testing worries
stressful experiences	a special keepsake	practical jokes	plastic surgery
natural disasters	abuses of power	secret ambition	physical fitness

Here is a sample journal entry on the subject *space exploration:*

I still think it's wild that NASA managed to send those robot rovers all the way to Mars, and rovers were able send back all that information. They had to travel for months, millions of miles—and that was just to get to the neighborhood! After that unbelievably long journey, those rovers worked like they were just big remote control cars—amazing! The pictures they sent back were also amazing, reddish rocks and dust all over the place. And the scientists have confirmed that there is ice beneath the surface, and with water, there could be life. But here's the thing that makes me wonder. These space missions eat up money that we could be using back here on earth. Is finding out whether there could be life on Mars more important than rebuilding roads and bridges and improving

health care and schools here on earth? It's really hard because humans have al-

ways been explorers, but how can you put space exploration ahead of issues like

poverty and hunger that directly affect some people?

Don't be concerned if an entry isn't complete or correct at first. You will get to be a better writer by writing, and journal entries are great opportunities to become even more comfortable with writing.

Employing a Response Journal

A **response journal** records your reactions to and assessments of specific topics. Although a response journal is good for examining day-to-day events, it is especially valuable for your academic work. Write in your response journal at least once a week and record a brief reaction to what was covered in your various classes. The preparation of these entries alone is certainly great writing practice. In addition, when you write about something, you gain a greater understanding of it.

Consider this entry in reaction to a podcast posted on the Web page of an economics class:

The podcast we had to listen to for class really made me think. A finan-

cial writer named David Bach was discussing the way people don't pay atten-

tion to the money they spend on nonessential small purchases. He calls this

"The Latte Factor," after those expensive coffee drinks that people order.

Bach said that people buy things like bottled water, fast food, and snacks on

their way to work or school. If you add up the money you spend on a daily

basis for these things, you'll find that it sometimes totals $5 or $10 or more.

Add up a week's worth, and you'll be shocked, especially when you realize

that you could buy some of those items at a supermarket much more cheaply

and then bring them from home. I thought about what I had spent on coffee

and lunch that day—it was almost $9. If I had just brought a sandwich or

salad from home, I would have had $5 still in my pocket, or in my bank ac-

count. I can hardly wait for the class discussion about Bach's Latte Factor

next week.

This journal entry recounts the details presented during the podcast, but it also explores the significance of the information. If you write a weekly journal entry on each of your courses, you can expect to have a greater understanding of the class topics.

<table>
<tr><td>

COMPREHENSION AND PRACTICE 2.6

</td><td>

Trying Journal Writing

1. Now try journal writing yourself. On a separate sheet of paper, write a page on one of the following topics: *teamwork, fame, dishonesty.*

2. Reread your journal entry. Circle, underline, or highlight the material you would like to explore in greater detail.

3. What section holds the most promise? Why? On your paper, briefly explain.

</td></tr>
</table>

Choosing the Prewriting Technique for Your Personal Style

When it comes to prewriting, there is no such thing as one size fits all. Not everyone prefers the same prewriting techinique, so you should choose the one that best suits your individual style of working and organizing.

You may even find that your choice of prewriting technique changes for different writing tasks. For example, if you need to break down or simplify a topic before you can deal with it, you might turn to branching. If you need to explore an idea to identify a specific focus, you might select freewriting.

In addition, you may discover that you prefer a **hybrid** prewriting technique—one that combines more than one approach. You could start with brainstorming, for example, and then switch to clustering to examine an idea that stands out from the others. Or you could use the *Discovery Questions* on page 13 in conjunction with freewriting, letting the answers to the questions shape the direction of your exploration. There is no wrong way to prewrite. The approach—or combination of approaches—that works for you is always the correct choice.

Considering Your Writing Rituals

No two people follow the same routine when they write. It's an idiosyncratic act. Just think of the rituals you follow when you write. For instance, when you have a choice, what time of day do you prefer to write? Do you have a favorite location? Do you need silence and isolation, or is a public area—a coffee shop, cafeteria, or common area of a library or dorm—a better match for you? Do you work from start to finish on a computer, or do you start out with pen and paper and then switch once you have generated some preliminary work? If you start out writing by hand, does the type of paper and pen (or pencil) make a difference to you?

The point to keep in mind is that answers to questions like these represent your own optimum conditions for writing. When you have control over the circumstances, always plan your work so that you write under these optimum conditions. The whole process will go more easily that way.

Taking Time to Check in

The goal of prewriting is to establish a foundation for your piece of writing. Once you have completed this preliminary stage, you should take a few minutes to *check in,* that is, to see whether the direction you want to follow makes sense. Checking in is a simple process. Just share your ideas with a classmate, friend, or family member in person or online, explain your plans, and ask a few basic questions:

- Can you see where I am going with this?
- Does the approach I want to take seem reasonable to you?
- Besides what I've indicated, are there other things I might do to develop support—for instance, read a particular book or document, see a movie or video, interview somebody?
- Am I overlooking anything obvious?

This kind of check in can help you see if your initial concept for writing holds merit, allowing you to make adjustments before you invest any more time.

COMPREHENSION AND PRACTICE 2.7

Analyzing Your Prewriting Choice, Personal Writing Rituals, and Checking in

1. You have now had the opportunity to try all the prewriting techniques discussed in this chapter. On the following lines, list the technique—or combination of techniques—you prefer and discuss why you think this choice works for you.

   I prefer the freewriting technique because is the only way I can write down all my ideas them revise without foregth what I want to write

2. What are your writing rituals? On a separate sheet of paper, take 10 to 15 minutes to address this subject in a journal entry. Then share your entry with a classmate. See what rituals—if any—you have in common.

3. Consider again the list of check-in questions above. Working with a classmate, develop two additional questions that could help identify whether initial plans for writing make sense and list them on the following lines.

   _____

   _____

FOR FURTHER EXPLORATION Prewriting

1. Focus on one of the following topics. Using the prewriting technique—or combination of techniques—best suited to your writing style, examine the possibilities that the subject holds.

   - things you should throw away
   - technology you depend upon
   - a lost friendship

collaboration

2. Examine your prewriting material, highlight, underline, or circle the key ideas, identify a focus, and create a draft paragraph of at least seven to ten sentences.
3. Exchange your draft with a classmate. Using the material in this chapter as a guide, evaluate the draft you receive. Note any ideas that should be explored more fully, and return the draft to the writer.
4. Revise your draft, eliminating any problems identified by your writing partner.

DISCOVERING CONNECTIONS Prewriting

For this assignment, use your favorite prewriting technique to explore this picture and one of the following questions (or another the photo inspires). Consider the purpose you might fulfill, and then, using the ideas you have developed, prepare a draft paragraph of at least seven to ten sentences. Save your work for later use.

A. Now that we have so many options for recording and communicating information, including voice technology, do you think schools should still be teaching printing and handwriting? Would anything be lost if children were simply taught keyboarding instead?

B. During your lifetime, is there a letter or note that you should have written and sent but for some reason didn't? To whom do you now wish you had written? What issue was involved and what kept you from writing? What keeps you from writing now?

RECAP Generating Ideas through Prewriting

Key Terms in This Chapter	Definitions
prewriting	the initial idea-generating stage of the writing process
	Prewriting techniques include freewriting, brainstorming, clustering, branching, idea mapping, and maintaining a journal.
freewriting	writing freely about a subject for a set period of time without stopping or worrying about correctness or completeness
outlining	establishing a plan for presentation in list form
brainstorming	focusing on a subject and listing all related ideas that come to mind
clustering	writing and circling an idea in the middle of a page, developing and circling related ideas around it, and drawing lines to connect related clusters of ideas

Key Terms in This Chapter	Definitions
branching	listing a subject on the left side of a page, writing ideas inspired by that subject to the right, and connecting the branching ideas with lines
idea mapping	writing words and drawing images about a topic in a random manner across a page and then translating the images into words
maintaining a journal	writing several times a week in a separate notebook to explore or discover new ideas, respond to points raised in classes, or explore issues important to you
response journal	maintaining a series of informal writings in response to subjects raised in various academic classes
hybrid technique	combining more than one prewriting technique

Using Odyssey Online with MyWritingLab

For more practice with prewriting, go to www.mywritinglab.com.

CHAPTER 3
Composing: Creating a Draft

GETTING STARTED ...

 I've done my prewriting, and I now have good ideas about the subject that make sense—to me, anyway. What do I do to make sure I get my ideas in a form that will make sense to a reader?

You are already halfway there. Good ideas form the foundation of an effective piece of writing. Building on that foundation means taking the time to identify what someone else—your reader—would need in order to understand your good ideas and then expressing those ideas in full detail and correct sentence form.

Overview: Understanding Composing

Chapter 2 discusses the first stage in the writing process, showing you various techniques for generating preliminary ideas. This chapter focuses on the next stage of your odyssey: **composing**. During this part of your journey, you focus on a specific point or aspect of your general subject. Then you organize your most promising, relevant ideas into a coherent message.

During composing, you also begin to pay attention to *correct form*, expressing your good ideas in correct sentence structure. Sentences vary in type and length, but they must always:

- contain a subject and a verb
- express a complete thought

When you write, your primary goal is to communicate your ideas clearly to your reader. No matter how good your ideas may be, your reader will not understand them unless you express them in correct sentences that support, explain, or illustrate your topic, as these examples show:

NOT A SENTENCE The touch screen on my new phone already heavily scratched. [*The verb is missing.*]

SENTENCE The touch screen on my new phone **is** already heavily scratched.

NOT A SENTENCE Once the plane landed safely. [*The unit doesn't express a complete thought.*]

SENTENCE Once the plane landed safely, **the relieved passengers cheered.**

For more on how to express your ideas in complete sentences, see Chapter 17, "The Sentence," pages 250–264, Chapter 18, "Fragments," pages 265–278, and Chapter 20, "Comma Splices and Run-on Sentences," pages 291–309.

Navigating This Chapter In this chapter, you will develop the skills you need to transform your best prewriting ideas into sentences and then to organize those sentences into a complete draft paragraph that meets your reader's needs. This part of your odyssey will introduce you to the two components that make up an effective paragraph:

- the topic sentence
- the supporting sentences

Recognizing the Structure of a Paragraph

A **paragraph** is a series of sentences that work together to develop one main idea. With longer, multiparagraph documents like **essays**, each paragraph represents a building block of words and thoughts. As you expand your discussion, increasing its level of detail, you move from paragraph to paragraph, each one covering a different aspect of the larger subject. (For more on the essay, see Chapters 14 and 15.) These kinds of paragraphs can consist of as few as three sentences, depending on the level of topic complexity and the needs of the reader.

Sometimes, however, a paragraph stands alone, functioning like a miniature version of an essay, but with a more limited scope than an essay has. This kind of paragraph contains several items of support for its main idea, and generally runs between seven and ten sentences (approximately 150–250 words).

The following figure shows how a paragraph is arranged:

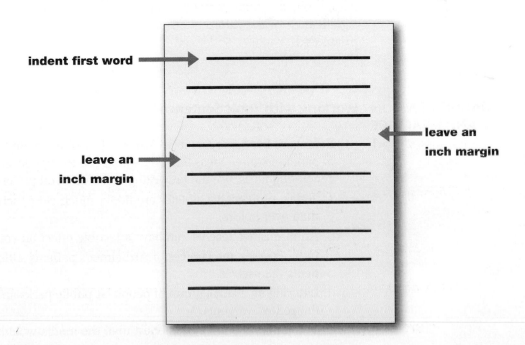

ESL Note
See "Writing Paragraphs," especially the section on unity, on pages 555–556.

As this figure shows, the first sentence in a paragraph is *indented* about a half-inch from the left margin, with each subsequent sentence flush to the left margin. In multiparagraph documents, this indentation indicates a new paragraph, and serves as a visual cue that the writer has moved from one idea to another.

Here's a sample paragraph that illustrates how you should structure the *content* or message of a paragraph:

> **Last year, my aunt was a victim of identify theft, and she is still trying to straighten out her life**. She first became aware of the problem when she received her credit card bill. She had been charged for all kinds of expensive items that she hadn't purchased, including two laptop computers and a large-screen plasma television. Altogether, the bill was for almost $10,000. When she called the credit card company, a supervisor mentioned identity theft and suggested that she check the status of her credit. When she requested a credit report, she almost had a heart attack. The report indicated that she was delinquent on payments for thousands of dollars on several credit cards she had never even applied for. She then called the police, and they told her to call her bank right away. It's a good thing that she did, because just that day, the bank had received a notice of change of address and a request for a debit card in her name. If she hadn't called, her bank account would have been empty in a couple of days. The amount of damage that an identify thief can do to a person's financial life is just unbelievable.

The first sentence of this paragraph—the **topic sentence**—states the main idea. The topic sentence answers the reader's unstated question, "What's the point?" The other sentences—making up the **body** of the paragraph—support the topic sentence with specific details and examples. Together, the supporting sentences communicate to the reader the seriousness of identify theft. With a stand-alone paragraph, the final sentence—called the **closing sentence**—reemphasizes the significance of the information presented, bringing the paragraph to an appropriate end.

COMPREHENSION AND PRACTICE
3.1

Working with Topic Sentences

1. Below are five topic sentences. Choose two of them, and on a separate sheet of paper, list three ideas that you would use to support each. If you need help generating ideas, use the prewriting technique you prefer.

   a. Today, professional athletes are under much closer scrutiny by the media than ever before.

   b. An insensitive teacher can have a terrible effect on young children.

   c. In most cases, the families of Alzheimer's patients suffer more than the patients themselves.

   d. Littering by a small group of people at public parks and beaches can ruin things for everyone.

   e. The public is often more honest than the media would have us believe.

2. The following paragraphs lack topic sentences. Read each passage, and then, on the lines after it, write a suitable topic sentence.

a. Millions of people of all ages are affected by these severe headaches, which cause throbbing pain, nausea, sensitivity to light and sound, and sleep problems. Often, the intense pain and discomfort of a migraine headache occurs with little warning, leading to lost days at work or school. Sometimes, sufferers know a migraine is coming because about half an hour or so beforehand, they experience an aura. This phenomenon may involve a shimmering light around an object or other visual disruption, including temporary loss of sight. The lucky ones experience the aura without the intense headache following. Regardless of the type of migraine, however, once it hits, sufferers find it impossible to function normally.

_____ Migraine headache. are affected
by _____ severe headaches sleep prch

_____

b. Rent costs me $750 a month, a big chunk of my pay. In addition, I have to pay for my utilities: heat, electricity, and telephone. That's usually $175 a month. Then I have to pay for food. Between the groceries I buy and the few meals I eat out, food costs me $400. My school expenses are enormous, too. I receive some aid, but I'm still responsible for $1,000 per semester plus the cost of books. At the end of the month, I have about $10 left.

_____ My expenses and utilitys
responsiblety _____ allpensed
As my

c. Many of my jobs involve cutting lawns and raking. These stops are fairly standard, and each takes me about an hour or two to complete, depending on the size of the property. I also have to dig up and reseed any problem spots in the lawns. On some jobs, I also tend gardens. This means regular watering, weeding, and fertilizing of the flowerbeds and turning the mulch. On some days in the spring and summer, I work ten hours straight. Once I finish my degree, I hope to concentrate on marketing and managing the business and hire some employees to provide customer service.

_____ cutting lawns and raking.

_____

_____

CHALLENGE 3.1   Considering Topic Sentences and Supporting Details

1. The following passage consists of two paragraphs run together. After reading the entire passage, put a / at the point where the first paragraph ends. Then, on the lines that follow, explain what leads you to believe that the second paragraph begins at that point.

> Last summer, when a small circus set up in a nearby town, I witnessed a scene that was once commonplace across the United States. First, the twenty members of the circus crew spread out the yellow-and-white-striped canvas, half as long as a football field. They hammered enormous spikes into the ground and tied off one end of the tent. Next, they laid the main tent pole flat on the ground, with the center of the tent attached to the top of the 35-foot post. At several key points across the site, they placed a number of smaller posts that would spread and support the heavy canvas. Once this step was completed, the workers pounded in several more spikes along each side and tied these sections off. Then came what everyone was waiting for: the elephants/ The handlers harnessed the elephants to the center pole, and they quietly urged the enormous animals on. The canvas seemed almost to come to life as it slowly rose. After five minutes of work, the pole was up, and the handlers moved the elephants to the supporting posts and repeated the steps. Once all the posts were in place, the crowd applauded while the elephants enjoyed their reward, an extra bale of hay and a shower.

_____

_____

_____

collaboration

2. Look again at the paragraph on page 28 about identity theft. Working with a classmate and using a separate sheet of paper, explain how the rest of the sentences in the paragraph support or explain the topic sentence.

3. Choose one of the following topics. On a separate sheet of paper, list five ideas that could support it. Try your hand at writing a paragraph, putting your ideas into sentence form. Save the paragraph for possible later use.
   a. the perfect night out
   b. a dangerous outdoor activity
   c. cyberculture

Identifying an Effective Topic

When you prewrite, as the previous chapter illustrates, you examine a subject in order to identify a focus and generate ideas that will illustrate, explain, and support that focus. Imagine, for example, that you have been asked to consider communication in the 21st century. You immediately think of the way people connect through the Internet and freewrite on the subject. Here is that freewriting (which also appears in the previous chapter):

> Time spent on the Internet—an hour a day? Maybe even more? Facebook is always my first stop, always updating and checking in with my friends—some of them are in other parts of the country. One of them is in Iceland! YouTube! I love YouTube—watch all kinds of stuff people post, silly videos, portions of shows and movies, it's almost addictive. Hulu is a newer one—downloaded video clips. Whenever there's something big in the news, somebody posts video from a phone or one of the Flip video cameras. People also post pictures and video on Facebook and MySpace. Some people have lost out on jobs because their pictures showed them partying, etc. and somebody in the company checked! Invasion of privacy? You have to use your head about stuff you post. My pictures are pretty ordinary, though—and so are most of the people I connect with. Some sites for professional people—LinkedIn is the one they showed us in College Success Seminar—Xing, too—looked like a cool way to connect with other people in your field. And jobs! Who knows better about jobs in a field than people who are already doing the job?

This freewriting highlights a number of ideas that could potentially become supporting points. You are now set for the next step: to translate your main idea into an effective topic sentence.

Writing a Clear, Specific Topic Sentence

Once you have decided on your main point, the next step is to develop a topic sentence that effectively expresses it. A typical topic sentence accomplishes two things: (1) It states the topic clearly, and (2) it suggests the direction or tone of the paragraph, often by revealing the writer's attitude toward the topic.

An effective topic sentence needs to be simple and direct. Don't simply announce your intent by writing, "I am going to write about _____" or "This paragraph will cover _____." Instead, express your point so that it answers your reader's implied question, "What's your point?"

Take another look at the topic sentence from the paragraph about identify theft on page 28:

                                       —topic—   —writer's attitude or reaction—

EFFECTIVE   *Last year, my aunt was a victim of identify theft,* **and she is still trying to straighten out her life**.

This topic sentence is effective because it answers the reader's implied question. The topic is identity theft, and the writer's attitude or reaction expresses how disruptive this act can be.

An effective topic sentence is also clear and specific. Consider this version of the topic sentence about identity theft:

WEAK   My aunt had her identity stolen, and it was bad.

ESL Note
See "Strive for Clarity,"
page 556, for more on
the importance of clear
writing.

This topic sentence is too vague to communicate the main point effectively. The sentence doesn't indicate when the theft took place or why it was bad.

The freewriting on connecting through the Web contains a number of promising details about social networking sites. Therefore, an effective topic sentence would focus on this aspect of the main subject:

                                                     —topic—

EXAMPLE   In a matter of only a few years, *social networking sites on the Internet*
              —writer's attitude or reaction—
have exploded in number and popularity.

This topic sentence is effective because it is clear and specific and because it answers the reader's implied question, "What's the point about social networking sites?"

As these examples illustrate, you'll generally place the topic sentence first in a stand-alone paragraph. That way, your reader will know immediately what the paragraph is about and in what direction it is heading. When a paragraph is part of a longer piece of writing, however, the placement of the topic sentence will depend on the reader's needs and the specific function of the paragraph. In an introductory paragraph for an essay, for instance, sometimes the best place for the topic sentence is at the end, with the other sentences building the reader's interest. In other cases, the topic sentence of a supporting paragraph might appear in the middle of the paragraph, with a sentence or two leading up to it and a sentence or two following it to explain or illustrate the specific point raised.

COMPREHENSION
AND PRACTICE

Analyzing Topic Sentences

3.2 In each of the following topic sentences, circle the topic, and underline the writer's attitude or reaction to it. Use the example as a guide.

EXAMPLE   The (many costs of owning a car) make an automobile a luxury some students cannot afford.

1. Most people don't spend enough time planning for their future.

2. Poor highway design is a major reason for auto accidents.

3. Both major political parties in the United States seem out of touch with the average person.

4. Not all top high school athletes are poor students.

5. The fierce winter weather is particularly hard on the poor and elderly.

COMPREHENSION
AND PRACTICE

Turning Topics into Topic Sentences

3.3 Below are five topics. On a separate sheet of paper, turn each topic into a topic sentence by adding an attitude or opinion about it. Use the example as a guide.

EXAMPLE   melanoma, the most serious type of skin cancer
Melanoma, the most serious type of skin cancer, continues to increase because of our love affair with sunbathing.

the using of text mess when you drive is the cause of

1. an increase in the number of fatal auto accidents

2. special effects in movies

If you study contability you can
3. investing in the stock market

4. a better understanding of world geography

5. an increase in the minimum wage *can ca'*

COMPREHENSION
AND PRACTICE

Revising Topic Sentences

3.4 The following topic sentences are general and vague. On the lines provided, rewrite them, making sure they clearly focus on a specific topic and express a definite attitude.

1. I enjoy physical activities.

   I like to be in shape, that way I enjoy physical activities.

2. Being laid off is bad.

   When a person works hard to improve his or her life being laid off is bad

3. Ultimate fighting is popular.

4. Television programming isn't challenging.

   Today on our tv channel alot of television programming isn't challenging because they're full of violence action.

5. Science is interesting.

   Today too alot of life saver is basicos alot os science study, we can se that science is interesting.

CHALLENGE 3.2   **Evaluating and Developing Topic Sentences**

collaboration

1. Here are several potential topic sentences. Working with a classmate, label the effective topic sentences with an *E* and the weak ones with a *W.*

   _____ E   a. Working in a nursing home has helped me learn the true meaning of dignity.

   _____ W   b. Abandoned dogs and cats worry city officials.

   _____ W   c. My uncle's best decision ever was to get his general equivalency diploma (GED).

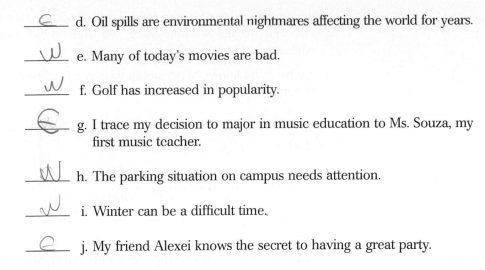

____C____ d. Oil spills are environmental nightmares affecting the world for years.

____W____ e. Many of today's movies are bad.

____W____ f. Golf has increased in popularity.

____E____ g. I trace my decision to major in music education to Ms. Souza, my first music teacher.

____W____ h. The parking situation on campus needs attention.

____W____ i. Winter can be a difficult time.

____C____ j. My friend Alexei knows the secret to having a great party.

collaboration

2. With the same classmate, select one of the topic sentences that you identified as weak.

   a. On a separate sheet of paper, rewrite it. Be sure it focuses clearly on a *specific* topic and expresses a definite reaction.

   b. On the same paper, develop at least three supporting sentences for this topic sentence.

3. Prewrite on the topic of *superstitions*. Then, after identifying the most promising ideas, on a separate sheet of paper, write a draft topic sentence for this topic.

Providing the Best Support for the Topic Sentence

After you have developed a clear, specific topic sentence, you need to develop additional sentences that will support, illustrate, or explain it. Start by evaluating which ideas from your prewriting will offer the strongest support.

Consider again the topic sentence on connecting through the Internet:

EXAMPLE

In a matter of only a few years, *social networking sites on the Internet* **have exploded in number and popularity**.

Now let's review once more the highlighted ideas from the freewriting:

Facebook is always my first stop, always updating and checking in with my friends—some of them are in other parts of the country.

People also post pictures and video on Facebook and MySpace.

Some people have lost out on jobs because their pictures showed them partying, etc. and somebody in the company checked!

YouTube! I love YouTube—watch all kinds of stuff people post, silly videos, portions of shows and movies, it's almost addictive.

Hulu is a newer one—downloaded video clips.

Whenever there's something big in the news, somebody posts video from a phone or one of the Flip video cameras.

Some sites for professional people—LinkedIn is the one they showed us in College Success Seminar—Xing, too—looked like a cool way to connect with other people in your field.

And jobs! Who knows better about jobs in a field than people who are already doing the job?

Next, try to figure out the best way to present these ideas. To do so, you have to:

- establish an effective arrangement
- express the ideas in correct, complete sentence form

COMPREHENSION AND PRACTICE 3.5 ### Analyzing the Relationship between Topic Sentence and Body

1. Read the following paragraph and underline the topic sentence:

The most beautiful sight I have ever witnessed was a <u>sunset two years ago at Horseneck Beach.</u> I had a weekday off from my summer job at the hotel reservations center, something that rarely happened, so I headed to the beach at about noon. During most of the day, the sky was full of clouds, but the temperature was a comfortable 80 degrees. At about 7 P.M., just after I had packed up all my stuff, the sky suddenly cleared, and the bright sun emerged low in the sky. Instead of heading home, I decided to take a walk to the end of the beach. As I reached the point where the Westport River flows into the bay, I looked out across the water to see a stunning rose-colored sun. For the next twenty minutes I watched as the softly glowing sun seemed to melt into the water. I had never seen anything so wonderful, and I probably never will again.

2. On the lines that follow, explain the connection between this topic sentence and its supporting sentences.

the supporting sentences describes the
the day on the Horseneck beach.

Deciding on the Most Effective Arrangement

Once you select the details and examples that will best support your topic sentence, you need to identify a logical, effective way to arrange them. Taking the time to sort out your ideas and establish a tentative order is an important step in creating an effective piece of writing. Remember—your final decisions about how to present the details should always depend on your subject and the needs of your reader.

The three most common methods of arrangement include:

- **chronological order**—presentation based on time
- **spatial order**—presentation based on location of one item or individual relative to others
- **emphatic order**—presentation based on the relative importance of the supporting details and examples.

(For more complete details on these methods of arrangement, see Chapter 4.)

The topic sentence on connecting through the Web talks about the rapid growth of social networking sites. The prewriting material contains three general categories of information related to the main point: personal networking sites, video sharing sites, and business-associated sites. The sites for professionals are growing in importance and popularity, as are video sharing sites, but personal networking sites are by far the most prevalent and most popular. Therefore, *emphatic order*—starting with business-associated sites to catch and encourage the reader's interest, moving to video sites, and concluding with personal networking sites— would be a good choice for this paragraph.

Here is an informal outline showing the categories presented in emphatic order:

Topic Sentence: In a matter of only a few years, *social networking sites on the Internet* **have exploded in number and popularity**.

1. Business-Associated Sites—LinkedIn, Xing

2. Video Sharing Sites—YouTube, Hulu

3. Personal Social Networking Sites—Facebook, MySpace

Concluding Sentence

CHALLENGE 3.3 Arranging Supporting Details in Your Writing

1. Imagine that you had written the following topic sentence: *Credit cards make it easy to spend more than you really want to.* On a separate sheet of paper, prewrite to develop at least six details that you could use to support this statement.

2. Exchange your list with a classmate. On the list you receive, evaluate the order of the details and make any suggestions that you think would help the writer develop a better paragraph. Return the list to the writer.

collaboration

3. After considering your reader's comments, make any changes you feel are necessary. Put this list aside for later use.

Making Your Material Reader Centered

ESL Note
See "Think about
Audience Expectations,"
page 556, for addi-
tional details about ad-
dressing the needs of
the reader.

If your reader is to understand your ideas, you must express those ideas fully and in complete sentences so that they are **reader centered**. For the most part, prewriting ideas aren't in correct sentences. They are **writer centered**, that is, raw and unpolished, making sense to you but not necessarily to another person.

To understand the difference between writer-centered and reader-centered material, think of your notes for one of your classes. In a psychology class, for example, you might have written the following notation:

WRITER CENTERED   Personality types/Jung—way you behave?

These words mean something to you because you wrote them during class while your instructor explained the material, and you participated in the class discussion that followed. However, a reader who was not in that class would no doubt have trouble interpreting your notes.

Now, look at this reader-centered version of the same material:

READER CENTERED   Carl Jung's theories about personality types raise some questions about the way we behave.

As you can see, this version expresses the ideas more thoroughly and in complete sentence form. With the ideas spelled out this way, even a reader unfamiliar with psychology can understand what the note actually means.

Another step to make your writing more reader centered is to *amplify*. When you amplify, you provide additional, specific examples and details to support your ideas. As a way to cue yourself to amplify, you might even consider including the expressions *for example* and *for instance*. When you write one of these expressions, you make a commitment to your reader to provide additional, specific details about the information.

Consider the reader-centered example about personality types, but this time with the additional supporting information:

EXAMPLE   Carl Jung's theories about personality types raise some questions about the way we behave. **For example, some people prefer to work independently, while others prefer the company of co-workers. These preferences are connected to a person's personality type, which is identified by an instrument called the Myers-Briggs Type Indicator.**

As you can see, the idea becomes even more reader centered once the information introduced by *For example,* shown in boldface, is added. Even when you don't use *for example* or *for instance,* make sure to supply information to support or explain the point you are making.

Now consider this writer-centered detail from the prewriting on connecting through the Internet:

WRITER CENTERED   Some sites for professional people—LinkedIn is the one they showed us in College Success Seminar

As written, this information merely *suggests* the significance of this detail and doesn't state it explicitly. It also can't communicate its full meaning to a reader because it is not written as a complete sentence.

Now consider how much clearer and more effective this same detail is in the following reader-centered version:

READER CENTERED   LinkedIn is a successful social networking site that enables working professionals to connect with fellow professionals, raise and answer questions within their fields, and track career possibilities.

CHALLENGE 3.4   Evaluating and Developing Reader-Centered Sentences

collaboration

1. Make a copy of a page of notes you took for another class. Exchange this copy with a classmate. On a separate sheet of paper, try to change the writer-centered notes you receive to reader-centered sentences.

2. Return the notes and your reader-centered version to the writer. Review the papers returned to you and circle any detail that your reader failed to understand. Explain the point you meant to communicate.

3. Take another look at the prewriting material you developed on superstitions for Exercise 3 in Challenge 3.2 (page 35), and for which you developed a topic sentence. On a separate sheet of paper, identify and transform the three strongest writer-centered details into reader-centered sentences.

collaboration

4. Exchange your reader-centered sentences with a classmate. On the page you receive, put a + if a sentence is now reader centered and a ✓ if a sentence is still writer centered. Suggest a way to improve any sentence marked with a ✓, and then return the page to the writer. Save your own work for later use.

Using a Reader Evaluation Checklist

ESL Note
See "Think about Audience Expectations," page 556, for additional details about addressing the needs of the reader.

The secret to writing success is to meet the needs of your reader. In most cases, you can assume that your reader knows a little bit about many subjects but not necessarily a great deal about most subjects. Using a **reader evaluation checklist** is one way to make sure that your supporting information meets the needs of your reader.

To use the reader evaluation checklist below, simply insert the name of your topic in the blanks, and then write your answers to the questions.

✔**READER EVALUATION CHECKLIST**

☐ What does the average reader need to know about _____?

☐ What does the average reader already know about _____?

☐ What information would help the average person better understand _____?

☐ What did I find the hardest to understand about _____ at first?

☐ What helped me to figure out _____?

☐ What's the best example or explanation I can give the average person about _____?

As you answer these questions, you will also focus on the examples or explanations that your reader will need to see your point.

COMPREHENSION AND PRACTICE
3.6

Analyzing Your Reader's Needs

1. On the lines below, list three subjects that you know a great deal about and then three subjects that you wish you knew more about.

I know a great deal about ...
a. what I want to talk
b. description
c. How I feel about

I wish I knew more about ...
a. what you understand
b. you like
c. _____

2. Choose one item from each column in number 1, and then answer the following questions.

a. What details would help you communicate to a reader what you know about the subject you understand well?

what they want to know about my story, If they like the story or not.

b. What details would help you understand more about the subject you want to explore?

If I knew what I am talking about, and If I live that moment.

CHALLENGE 3.5   Evaluating How Well a Paragraph Meets a Reader's Needs

collaboration

1. Working with a classmate, assess the following paragraph. Use the questions below the paragraph as guidelines.

> Coffee bars are popular in cities and towns throughout the country. In big cities, one major chain seems to have coffee shops all over the place. The shops serve several varieties of coffee and food, and they offer a pleasant atmosphere. Some coffee bars have begun to include features and activities to make patrons feel comfortable and enable them to communicate and work as they enjoy their favorite coffee. Today it's hard to imagine life without these places.

   a. How effective was the writer in providing information about this subject that the average reader might not know?
   b. What did the writer assume the average reader already knows?

2. On a separate sheet of paper, make suggestions to the writer of what could be added or adapted to improve this paragraph.

Developing a Complete Draft

As you develop your initial version of your paragraph, remember that it doesn't have to be perfect. (The next chapter will show you how to revise—to refine and polish—your writing.) At this point, focus your energies on stating your ideas completely and clearly. In fact, think in terms of creating two initial versions of your document: a *rough draft* and a **first draft.**

ESL Note
See "Strive for Clarity," page 556, for more on the importance of keeping your writing complete and clear, and "Reinforce Your Point with a Concluding Paragraph," page 557, for more on bringing your writing to an effective close.

The rough draft is the first complete version, and it is for your eyes only. Whenever possible, prepare this draft on a computer. The various spelling and grammar tools on a computer make it easier to eliminate major problems. Always double-or triple-space your draft so that you will have room to add any corrections by hand. If you can't use a computer, write on every other line of a piece of paper.

Once this rough draft is complete, take a brief break and then scan it for any obviously awkward or unclear spots and any noticeable errors in form. Correct those and you'll have your first draft. Of course, make sure your first draft is clean and readable, because this version will be read and evaluated by someone else.

Here's a completed draft of a paragraph about making connections on the Web. The key ideas from the original freewriting are underlined:

Connecting: Only a Click Away

The topic sentence expresses the main idea and the attitude about it.

In a matter of only a few years, social networking sites on the Internet have exploded in number and popularity. LinkedIn is a successful social networking site that enables working professionals to connect with fellow professionals, raise and answer questions within their fields, and track career possibilities. YouTube is the premier place

The supporting details and examples are expressed in complete, correct sentence form.

for users to upload and share video content, both original creations and

The closing sentence restates the significance of the main idea and the supporting ideas.

snippets from professional performances. Facebook and MySpace are popular, especially among young people. Members of these networks can post personal profiles, including photos and videos and blogs and other multimedia content. They can view the pages of other members, and, subject to approval, communicate and interact with them. Some people have posted embarrassing pictures on their sites that caused them to lose out on jobs later on. The growth of these social networking sites has made it possible for people across the country and around the world to relate to people with similar interests.

As you can see, the original writer-centered prewriting ideas from pages 35–36 are now reader-centered supporting sentences. The material has also been amplified, with additional supporting ideas, all expressed in sentences, offering further clarification and explanation of the key points. The information is arranged in emphatic order, as indicated on page 37, and the final sentence serves as a conclusion, repeating the importance of the topic sentence and supporting sentences. The result is an effective first-draft paragraph.

COMPREHENSION AND PRACTICE 3.7

Analyzing a First Draft

1. On the following lines, explain what you like most about the first-draft paragraph on social networking sites.

_____

_____

_____

2. On the following lines, list any examples in this first draft that need improvement.

_____

_____

_____

CHALLENGE 3.6

Creating a First Draft

1. For Exercises 3 and 4 of Challenge 3.4 (page 39), you transformed prewriting material on superstitions into reader-centered sentences. Now, using the paragraph about connecting on the Internet (pages 41–42) as a model, use this material to create a complete draft version of a paragraph.

collaboration

2. Exchange your draft with a classmate. On the paper you receive, put a + next to the topic sentence if it is clear, specific, and effective. Put a ✓ next to any example or detail about which you'd like to know more. Return the paragraph to the writer.

3. Consider your classmate's suggestions, and then make any necessary changes to your paragraph.

FOR FURTHER EXPLORATION Composing a First-Draft Paragraph

1. Focus on one of the following topics, using the prewriting technique—or combination of techniques—that you prefer to generate some preliminary ideas, considering what purposes you might fulfill as you write about it:

   • the biggest mistake you have ever made
   • class clowns
   • the one thing that all people need

collaboration

2. Evaluate your prewriting material, identify a focus, and create a draft paragraph of at least seven to ten sentences.
3. Exchange your draft with a classmate. Using the material in this chapter as a guide, evaluate the draft you receive. Note any problems with topic or supporting sentence development, and return the draft to the writer.
4. Revise your draft, eliminating any errors identified by your writing partner.

DISCOVERING CONNECTIONS Drafting a Paragraph

Take a look at this photo and then consider one of the following questions (or another that it inspires). After you prewrite, consider the purpose you might fulfill, and create a draft paragraph of at least seven to ten sentences, following the steps outlined in this chapter. In particular, concentrate on making your paragraph reader centered. Save your work for later use

A. The matador may be considered courageous—or foolish—for facing a half-ton, charging animal. Why do you think some people are willing to take such chances with their lives?

B. As it has been practiced in Spain, bullfighting leads to the eventual, violent death of the bull. Many animal rights activists argue that this sport is inherently cruel and should be banned. Do you agree or disagree? Why?

RECAP Composing: Creating a Draft

Key Terms in This Chapter	Definitions
composing	the stage of writing during which you focus on a topic and provide supporting ideas drawn from your prewriting material
paragraph	a series of sentences that work together to develop one main idea
essay	a multi-paragraph writing covering a topic in extended detail
topic sentence	the sentence stating the main idea, or topic, of a paragraph and setting the tone or direction for the writing The topic sentence expresses the topic, limits it to a manageable size, and usually reveals the writer's attitude or reaction to the topic. 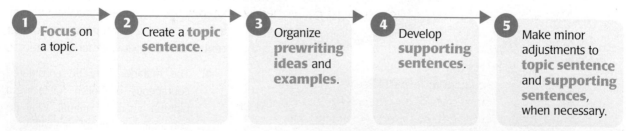
body	series of sentences supporting the topic sentence
closing sentence	the sentence that restates the significance of the paragraph
chronological order	organization based on time sequence
spatial order	organization on basis of location
emphatic order	organization on the basis of importance or significance
reader-centered writing	ideas expressed thoroughly and in complete sentence form so that they make sense to the reader
writer-centered writing	raw, unpolished ideas that provide enough clues to make sense to the writer but not necessarily to the reader
reader evaluation checklist	a series of questions designed to help writers ensure that their supporting information meets their readers' needs

EXAMPLE
┌─────────topic─────────┐
The new biography of former President Carter is
┌─ attitude or reaction ─┐
fascinating reading.

The Process of Composing a Draft Paragraph

1 **Focus** on a topic.

2 Create a **topic sentence**.

3 Organize **prewriting ideas** and **examples**.

4 Develop **supporting sentences**.

5 Make minor adjustments to **topic sentence** and **supporting sentences**, when necessary.

Using Odyssey Online with MyWritingLab

For more practice composing, go to www.mywritinglab.com.

CHAPTER 4
Refining and Polishing Your Draft

GETTING STARTED ...

Q I've already spent a lot of time on this paper, and I don't really understand what good can come of working on it anymore. Why should I spend any more time on my paper when it's already as good as I can make it?

A Yes, your initial draft was as good as you could make it—at that time. You worked hard, and when you work hard, you get tired and are less likely to see potential areas for improvement. But haven't you ever had a discussion and then, after the discussion was long over, remembered something else you wish you had said? Writing is likewise a *recursive* act, a process that you will cycle through, sometimes several times, until your paper is as good as it can be. After a little time away from your draft—and with some reactions from a reader or two—you will probably see several ways to adjust or improve things, making a good paper even better.

Overview: Understanding the Revising Stage

One sure truth about writing is that you won't write a masterpiece on the first try. A good first draft is only the beginning, and if you stop at this point, that draft will never fulfill its potential. Once you have completed a solid draft, you must *revise—* or refine and polish—your draft. This chapter explains how revising your writing will turn something good into something even better.

Revising actually involves three interrelated steps: reassessing, redrafting, and editing. **Reassessing** means checking for *unity, coherence,* and *effective language.* It also involves seeking feedback from an objective reader. **Redrafting** means rewriting to eliminate any problem spots and adding needed material. Writing is recursive, so you will likely reassess and redraft more than once to achieve the results you want. This sixth edition of *Odyssey,* like the previous editions, features significant adjustments, thanks to reassessing and redrafting. **Editing** takes you in a slightly different direction, away from content to form. When you edit, you proofread and employ computer spelling, grammar, and style tools to make any last-minute changes and eliminate any remaining errors. Editing ensures that your paper is as correct in form as it is complete in content.

Navigating This Chapter On this leg of your writing odyssey, you focus on refining and polishing your initial draft so that it most effectively expresses what you mean through the following stages of revision:

- reassessing
- redrafting
- editing

Reassessing: Re-Seeing Your Work

With your first draft completed, you will probably feel that you've taken your paragraph as far as you can. Put your first draft away for a day or two—*create a distance*—and you will no doubt find areas that still need work. When you *re-see* your draft with a fresh eye, you'll be better able to reassess it for *unity, coherence,* and *effective language.*

Maintaining Unity

ESL Note
See "Unity," page 555, for more on the importance of ensuring that all the information you include is directly connected to your main idea.

If your reader is to understand your point, you need to keep your writing *unified,* which means that all examples and details relate directly to your main idea. When you reassess for **unity**, you eliminate any material that is not clearly connected to your subject.

Take a look at the following paragraph about a stressful experience—a road test for a driver's license. As you read, identify which information is not relevant to this topic.

> Getting my driver's license was the most stressful experience I have ever faced. During my final road lesson that morning, I had no problems. In fact, my instructor told me that it was the best of my six training sessions. But as soon as the inspector from the Registry of Motor Vehicles stepped into the car, I could feel my heart racing. Stress contributes to the number of people who suffer heart attacks each year in the United States. Bad diet is one of the major factors leading to heart problems. Heredity is another major cause. By the time the inspector sat down and put on her seat belt, I could feel my shirt becoming damp. When she told me to start up the car, for a moment I couldn't even think of what to do. After a couple of seconds, I remembered to turn the key. For the next ten minutes, I felt like I was watching someone else pull out into traffic, turn left and right, complete a three-point turn, and parallel park. After I parked the car back at the Registry parking lot, the inspector turned to me and said that I had passed. At that point, I was exhausted, but I was happier than I had ever been.

If you identified the fifth, sixth, and seventh sentences, you are correct. They deal with heart attacks, which are related to stress, but this information is irrelevant to the specific experience of getting a driver's license. Once you eliminate these sentences, the paragraph is unified.

COMPREHENSION AND PRACTICE

4.1

Eliminating Unrelated Sentences

1. Check the following paragraph for unity. Circle any sentences that do not belong with the others.

Last summer, I had a great experience working as a soccer coach for the day camp at a local Boys and Girls Club. I was in charge of the indoor soccer games for the youngest group of campers, ages five to seven. In many countries, soccer is called football. During the first week of camp, I assigned the fifty kids to different teams and had practice games. They didn't really understand how to play the game, so I spent the first two weeks teaching them basic things like passing and playing defense. Soccer is the world's most popular sport. So far, professional soccer has not been especially successful in the United States. For the rest of the summer, I was able to watch the children as they improved and learned to love soccer. At the end of the summer, all the players gave me a plaque naming me "Most Valuable Coach." I never would have guessed that a simple summer job could be so rewarding.

2. Use the following lines to explain why the sentences you've circled do not belong.

because the writer is talking about his experience working as a soccer coach last summer, not about soccer and his introduction to the world.

CHALLENGE 4.1 **Focusing on Unity**

collaboration

1. Below is a topic sentence, followed by several possible supporting ideas. Working with a classmate, choose at least three of the ideas and, on a separate sheet of paper, identify why you think these ideas, developed fully, would be directly relevant to the topic sentence.

For most people, life regularly presents the chance to perform little acts of selflessness.

- being polite
- checking on old or infirm neighbors
- becoming a foster parent

- being a positive role model for younger family members
- squeezing time from your schedule for extracurricular activities at school

collaboration

2. Discuss one item from the list that you don't think is as connected as the others to the topic sentence, and, on the same paper, explain why this detail isn't sufficiently related.

3. Choose one of the ideas you have identified as relevant, and, on the lines that follow, express that idea in a complete sentence that supports the topic sentence.

_____

_____

_____

Providing Coherence

ESL Note
See "Strive for Clarity," page 556, for more on the importance of keeping your writing coherent.

To communicate your ideas to your reader, the information you include must be **coherent,** that is, easy to follow. When you reassess your writing for coherence, make sure you have provided plenty of *transition* to keep ideas flowing smoothly and an effective *order of presentation* of your sentences.

Transition   A list of good ideas is not enough to qualify as an effective piece of writing. Instead, you must make the connections among your good ideas clear for your reader through the use of *transition.* To provide transition:

1. Repeat key words and phrases or rename them with pronouns.

2. Substitute **synonyms,** words that have similar meanings, for key words.

3. Insert transitional expressions to connect ideas.

The repetitions and substitutions provide a thread of continuity that keeps the main idea uppermost in the reader's mind. Look at the italicized words in the following sentences.

EXAMPLE   *The manager* came out of *the movie theater* to talk to *the crowd* waiting to get into the *building. She* told *the angry people* that a smoke alarm had gone off. *Her* staff was checking to make sure the *facility* was safe.

In the first sentence, the synonym *building* substitutes for *the movie theater.* In the second sentence, *She* takes the place of *The manager,* and *the angry people* renames *the crowd.* In the third sentence, *Her* refers to *She,* and another synonym, *facility,* replaces *building.*

Perhaps the most useful technique for showing the relationships among sentences is adding **transitional expressions** to connect ideas. Here is a listing of common transitional expressions. Note the italicized words in the sentences following each list. These words provide a sense of connection between the ideas expressed.

Common Transitional Expressions to Show Cause and Effect

accordingly	consequently	indeed	particularly
after all	for example	in fact	specifically
as a result	for instance	of course	therefore
because	for one thing	overall	thus

EXAMPLE Interest in alternative energy has risen dramatically over the past few years. *As a result,* sales of photovoltaic panels have increased.

Common Transitional Expressions to Add, Restate, or Emphasize

again	finally	in conclusion	on the whole
also	first (second, last, etc.)	in other words	too
and	further	moreover	to sum up
besides	in addition	next	

EXAMPLE Last week, people in the central part of the state faced intense temperatures and high humidity. *Finally,* a cold front brought three days of much-needed rain.

Common Transitional Expressions to Show Time or Place

above	beyond	lately	soon	until
after	currently	now	then	when
as soon as	earlier	once	there	whenever
before	here	presently	to the left (or right)	where
below	immediately	since	under	

EXAMPLE The golden retriever raced toward the open gate. *When* its owner shouted, the dog came to a dead stop.

Common Transitional Expressions to Compare or to Contrast

although	despite	in the same way	similarly
and	even though	likewise	still
as	however	nevertheless	though
both (neither)	in contrast	on the other hand	whereas
but	in spite of	regardless	yet

EXAMPLE Small stores can't compete with the prices of the giant home improvement centers. *However,* they can provide more personalized service.

As you can see, the italicized words in each of these example sentences signal the connection between ideas.

Consider the boldfaced and italicized words in the following paragraph on time management:

> **Good time management** is the key to success in college. Setting up **an hour-by-hour breakdown** is the first step. *As* you make your **time plan,** don't forget to include time for meals and for **nonschool activities** *such as* **exercise.** *Once* you establish your **schedule,** you *then* need to follow **it** closely. *For example,*

if you set aside Mondays from 12 to 2 for **study time in the library**, make sure to follow through on **your commitment**. *Once* you begin to follow **your schedule** carefully, you will find the quality of your work improving.

As you can see, transition holds this paragraph together. For example, **an hour-by-hour breakdown, time plan,** and **schedule** appear in place of **Good time management. Exercise** refers back to **nonschool activities**, and **your commitment** is used in relation to **study time in the library**. In addition, a number of transitional expressions, including *as, such as, once, then,* and *for example,* emphasize the connections between the points.

COMPREHENSION AND PRACTICE 4.2

Working with Transition

1. Read the following paragraph. As you read, circle all transitional expressions and underline synonyms or pronouns that rename other words in the passage.

When I want to relax, I get in my car and take a ride to Phoenix Park next to the Rodman River. Once I get there, I head to the benches on the riverbank. The ones I prefer are at the far end of the property. Because the parking lot is almost a quarter of a mile back from this area, I can hear the flowing water washing against the rocks along the shore. Problems seem to melt away as soon as I close my eyes and listen to the water.

2. Choose two of the transitional expressions you have underlined and, on the following lines, explain how these expressions help to keep ideas in the paragraph unified.

and – help put to action together.

Because – reason.

CHALLENGE 4.2   **Focusing on Transition**

1. Write a draft paragraph of seven to ten sentences about what you do to relax.

2. Exchange your draft with a classmate. On the paper you receive, underline any transition you find. At the same time, put a ✓ at any spot where you feel transition is still needed and then return the paper to the writer.

collaboration

3. Check your reader's evaluation and make any necessary changes to your paragraph.

Organizing Sentences Effectively   Another crucial aspect of coherence is *organization.* As you reassess, make sure that you've arranged your ideas effectively because order affects the ease with which your reader can understand your point. Three common methods of organization include *chronological order, spatial order,* and *emphatic order.*

Using Chronological Order   **Chronological order** is order of time, and you should employ it whenever you are recalling a series of events as they occurred in sequence.
Look at this paragraph about dealing with jury duty:

> Being called for jury duty proved to be a waste of time for me. When I arrived at the courthouse at 8:30 A.M., I joined about twenty other people in the main courtroom. The court clerk then addressed us, explaining our duties as jurors. After the clerk was done, we watched a brief video about proper conduct in the courtroom. Next, the clerk told us to wait in that room until we were summoned. Sitting with nothing to do wasn't easy for me because of a problem I was having at work. Two days before, my boss had given me a huge new project with a tight deadline. I had been working like mad from that point on. Now I had to watch the minutes tick by. After about forty minutes, another court officer came into the room, told us that we were dismissed, and thanked us for our time. At that point, I picked up my jacket and headed to the door, thinking about my lost morning.

In this paragraph, chronological order and transitional words help the reader keep the events straight. *When* the writer arrived, she went into a courtroom and *then* the court clerk addressed them. *After* the talk was over, they changed rooms, and *next* they were told to wait. *After* some time passed, the prospective jurors were told that they could leave, and *at that point* the writer thought about the time she had wasted.
Incidentally, as a writer, you will sometimes intentionally break the sequence of events by using a *flashback.* This device involves presenting information that occurred *before* the event under discussion in order to clarify or emphasize some point. In this paragraph about jury duty, for example, you probably noticed that sentences 7, 8, and 9 concern a situation at work that occurred before the day of jury duty. In this case, the flashback underscores how much of an inconvenience a day as a juror can be. The secret to using a flashback effectively is to provide sufficient transition so that your reader recognizes that you have switched the order of events.

COMPREHENSION AND PRACTICE 4.3

Considering the Uses of Chronological Order

1. List three types of subjects that would be best organized in chronological order—for example, an explanation of a date or party that went badly.

When,

Next

First

2. Choose one of the subjects you listed in Exercise 1 and, on the following lines, list at least three steps in that sequence of events.

when I start my job, first I
read the job ticket . Next I I start
my M.P.

CHALLENGE 4.3 Focusing on Chronological Order

collaboration

1. Read the following paragraph. Then, working with a classmate, note where transition would help the flow of the paragraph. On a separate sheet of paper, rewrite the paragraph, inserting appropriate transitional expressions.

> One of my best childhood memories is of my first trip to New York City with my godmother when I was 12. We arrived at Penn Station at 8 A.M. and after checking our subway map, we began our adventure. We took the subway down to Battery Park to board the ferry to the Statue of Liberty, where we spent an hour. My aunt and I boarded the subway to head uptown to Central Park. We walked for a while along the different paths of this beautiful park, and we went across the street to the Museum of Natural History. We were really hungry. We went to the cafeteria for a quick lunch. We went into the museum and for the next two hours viewed the different exhibits, including my favorite ones, the dinosaurs. We got back on the subway and rode down to see the Empire State Building. It was 4 P.M., and we had to go back to Penn Station for the train to take us home. I've been back to New York City, but my first trip is the one I remember best.

2. Imagine that you had written this paragraph and have now decided to revise it to include a flashback. On a separate sheet of paper, indicate what kind of information you might include, why you would include such information, and where in the paragraph it would appear.

Using Spatial Order   When you need to explain where one object, place, or person exists in relation to other objects, places, or people, you rely on **spatial order.** This method of arrangement helps a reader visualize a particular scene. Spatial order enables items, locales, and individuals to be viewed in an organized, natural way: top to bottom, left to right, near to far.

Look at this paragraph about a newly decorated apartment:

> The biggest transformation I have ever seen in a space was my Aunt Monique's last apartment. When I first saw the place, it was in terrible shape. The wallpaper throughout was torn and stained, with piles of trash in each room. When I walked through the front door a month later, the change was unbelievable. The living room was now painted off-white, with a stenciled pattern along the edge of the ceiling. Next to the living room was the kitchen, now decorated with pastel-colored striped wallpaper. Above the new sink and counter, a flowering plant hung. Under the counter were new cabinet doors.

Through the door at the far corner of the kitchen was her bedroom. On the floor in front of her bed was a small blue area rug, with matching blue curtains decorating the window next to her bed. It was hard to believe that this apartment was the same place I had seen just a month earlier.

In this paragraph, spatial order helps the reader more accurately envision the apartment. After the renovation, the living room walls were newly painted, with stenciling *along the edge* of the ceiling. The kitchen, *next to* the living room, was also newly wallpapered, with a plant hanging *above* the sink and counter and new cabinet doors *under* the counter. The bedroom, which was *through the door* at *the far corner of the kitchen*, was also newly decorated and painted. The curtains on the window *next to* her bed matched the small area rug *on the floor in front* of the bed. As these italicized words illustrate, spatial cues make the scene easier to visualize.

COMPREHENSION AND PRACTICE 4.4

Reviewing Spatial Order

1. On the following lines, list at least five landmarks of some kind—stores, offices, signs, traffic lights, and so on—near your home.

   from my house to my school first you take your loft go all straight, you have to pass to light, then take you rish in a city poll, go all straisht im your rish you will see the BCC school.

   walgreen
   co laundry & t

2. On a separate sheet of paper, make a list of at least five transitional expressions that would be appropriate to suggest the location of these places in relation to each other (for example, *next to*).

   next to, near to, left, right, straisht

3. On the same sheet of paper, use spatial order to explain where your home is located in relation to three of the five landmarks you have listed.

CHALLENGE 4.4 **Focusing on Spatial Order**

collaboration

1. Ask a classmate to give you a verbal tour of a room with which the classmate is very familiar on campus, at work, at home, and so on. As your classmate describes this room, sketch its layout on a separate sheet of paper. Switch roles and then exchange sketches.

2. On a separate sheet of paper, assess the accuracy of your classmate's sketch. In your view, what aspects of spatial order affected your classmate's comprehension of your description?

Ordering for Emphasis Another way to organize your ideas is order of emphasis, also called **emphatic order** or order of significance. Emphatic order is the method used to organize the paragraph on social networking sites, developed in the previous chapter and revised in this one. Emphatic order, as the paragraph on connecting on the Web shows, involves moving from strong or significant examples (networking sites for professionals) to stronger or more significant examples (sites for video sharing) to the most important or significant examples (sites for personal networking). In this way, the examples or details build to a high point and sustain the reader's interest, much the way a story or play does.

Now look at this paragraph about concerned parents of juveniles who have committed crimes:

> The parents of juveniles convicted of crimes like vandalism, shoplifting, and auto theft should be held legally responsible for the actions of their children. For one thing, kids generally have no permanent income and are not in the position to make restitution. More important, juveniles aren't always aware of the full significance of their actions, but their parents are, and it is their job to make sure they teach their children. Furthermore, knowing that their parents will be drawn into the legal issues may cause kids to rethink becoming involved in illegal activity. Most important of all, parents are supposed to shape and monitor the behavior of their children. Nobody ultimately has greater influence over children than their parents. If parents don't wield that influence over their children, then the parents should pay the price.

The paragraph begins with a significant reason for holding parents legally responsible for the criminal actions of their children: children lack the means to make any financial restitution. The paragraph follows this reason with a more significant one: parents understand the seriousness of these incidents more than their children do, and it is therefore their job to communicate this to their kids. An even more significant reason follows after that: fear of their parents' reaction may convince kids not to become involved in criminal activity. The paragraph concludes with the most significant reason of all: parents have the ultimate influence over their children, and therefore they should bear the responsibility if their children break the law. As you can see, emphatic order sustains the reader's interest as it accentuates the point of the topic sentence.

COMPREHENSION AND PRACTICE 4.5

Working with Emphatic Order

1. Consider the following topic sentence:

> A course in public speaking should be required for all college students.

Decide whether you are in favor of this statement or against it, and then, on a separate sheet of paper, generate at least four reasons to support your stand. On the lines that follow, list your supporting reasons in *emphatic order,* moving from strong to stronger to strongest order.

first speaking is very important everywhere

second students need know use appropriate words when they will do any speach or talk with someone

Its important to know talk in front of others in case you have a interview.

_____

_____

_____

_____

_____

_____

2. Read the following paragraph and as you do, underline transitional expressions and phrases that help to illustrate the degree of importance of each point in the argument.

American public schools should adjust the current school calendar and hold classes year-round. A schedule calling for ten-week sessions of school followed by two-week vacation periods makes more sense. For one thing, this arrangement allows for a concentrated period followed by a rest period. As a result, students and teachers avoid the fatigue they face under the traditional calendar. In addition, the ten-week sessions would help with matters of discipline and order in the schools. For instance, more frequent breaks from school would minimize tensions among students. More important, though, adjusting the schedule would eliminate the long break in summer. When farming had a larger presence in the United States, the long summer break was necessary so that children could work. In today's world, however, the long summer break creates child-care problems for working parents. Even more important, the long break away from the classroom means students have a greater opportunity to forget what they have worked so hard to learn. Nobody would ever disagree that education is vital to success. Therefore, we should follow a calendar that will give students the best opportunity for sustained learning.

CHALLENGE 4.5 **Working with Emphatic Order**

1. Here are three topic sentences on controversial issues:

   a. People who participate in cyberbullying should face criminal and civil penalties.

   b. Police should be able to pull over and search cars without a search warrant if they believe they contain illegal weapons or drugs.

   c. Once they reach age sixty-five, drivers should face yearly road tests in order to renew their licenses.

   Choose one of the statements, decide whether you are in favor of or against it, and generate at least four supporting reasons. Then, on a separate sheet of paper, write a draft paragraph of at least seven to ten sentences in which you include the topic sentence and use emphatic order to present at least three of the supporting examples you have generated.

collaboration

2. Exchange your paragraph with a classmate. Evaluate the paragraph you receive, making sure the supporting examples are arranged in emphatic order. If you think any part of the presentation should be adjusted, make a note in the margin of the paper and return it to the writer.

3. Consider the suggestions your reader has made and make all necessary adjustments to your paragraph.

Choosing Effective Language

Your choice of words plays a direct role in how effectively your ideas come across for your reader. Therefore, when you reassess, make sure that you use **effective language**—in other words, language that is *specific* and *concise*.

ESL Note
See "Confusing Words," page 553, for a discussion of words that may present particular problems for you, and "Strive for Clarity," page 556, for more on the importance of keeping your writing clear and specific.

Keeping Your Writing Specific To help your reader picture things as you picture them, you must keep your language *specific,* that is, detailed and to the point. If you want to communicate your exact vision to your reader, you need to make all general terms specific. For example, instead of *economical car,* identify a particular type and brand of vehicle: *a brand-new, metallic blue Honda Civic Hybrid.* This way, your reader will have no question of what you mean.

Keeping your writing specific is particularly important when you deal with abstract concepts or ideas. Expressions like *irresponsible* or *charismatic* are *abstract terms.* They *suggest* a broad array of possible meanings to a reader, but the concepts or ideas they name have no physical shape or equivalence. Therefore, when you use an abstract word, your audience might draw a different meaning from the one you intend.

The way to avoid difficulties with abstract terms is to support them with concrete examples. If you use *highly talented* to describe a person, include a *concrete* example to explain what you mean, as this example shows:

EXAMPLE

┌ abstract term ┐   ┌   concrete supporting example   ┐

Jacqueline is a *highly talented* musician. *In high school, she placed first in every*

regional and state solo flute competition. Her breath control is so strong that every

note is clearly audible, even during long, complicated pieces.

Consider the specific details in the following paragraph about a special childhood play area:

> When I was young, one of my favorite spots was in the back of a closet at my grandmother's house. This closet was in the small second bedroom next to her living room. She kept all the toys and games for her grandchildren there, and I thought of it as my private hideaway. The paint on the door was shiny white, and it had been repainted so many times that I really had to tug on it to pull it open. Right at the front of the closet, hanging from a rod that ran across the width of the closet, was a row of my grandfather's clothes. My special spot was at the very back of the closet, so I had to push through this forest of clothes to get there. Then I would pull the string to put on the light, sit against the back wall underneath the rows of storage shelves, and be in my own four-foot-by-four-foot paradise. Even on the hottest day of the summer, this area was always cool, and I would happily read or color in there for hours. When I helped my grandmother move to a smaller apartment a few years ago, she and I laughed about all the times she had to come knocking on the closet door to find me.

Information like the exact location of the closet *(in the small second bedroom next to her living room)* and the description of the closet door *(shiny white,* and *it had been repainted so many times that I really had to tug on it to pull it open)* no doubt help you visualize the area. In addition, specific details about the inside of the closet *(this forest of clothes, the rows of storage shelves,* and *my own four-foot-by-four-foot paradise)* and the activities involved *(would happily read or color in there for hours)* bring this special place alive.

Keeping Your Writing Concise   When you revise, you also need to make sure your writing is *concise*—brief but clear. One way to keep your writing concise is to eliminate deadwood. *Deadwood* is words and expressions that have no value and add no real meaning. For example, nonspecific words like *a lot, definitely, extremely, quite, really, somewhat,* and *very* may make your writing longer, but they do not help you communicate your message. They are even less effective when they are combined with weak, vague terms such as *good* or *bad.*

At the same time, concentrate on choosing the best word or two to express your meaning. The English dictionary is filled with words of precise meaning and almost endless variety. Don't write *really, really hot and humid* if you have a single word like *sultry* that provides the exact description you need. Take a look at the following two lists. The list on the left contains needlessly wordy phrases and expressions and the one on the right contains alternative phrases and expressions that are brief but to the point.

Convert these wordy expressions …	*into these concise words*
due to the fact that	because
a large number of	many
in the near future	soon

Convert these wordy expressions ...	*into these concise words*
prior to	before
completely eliminate	eliminate
come to the realization that	realize
with the exception of	except for
in order that	so
at the present time	now
take action	act
the month of January	January
give a summary of	summarize
mutual cooperation	cooperation
make an assumption	assume

As you read the following paragraph, identify areas that you think need to be made more concise:

> My job last summer as a flagger for a construction company was harder than I really expected it to be. When I first heard about the opening, I figured that earning $7 to direct traffic around construction sites would be very easy. I soon found out how wrong I was. On the first morning in the month of June, I reported to the site at 8:15. Due to the fact that I needed to be highly visible to oncoming traffic, the boss handed me a hard hat, a safety vest, and a large orange flag. My station was next to the excavation in the road, and for the next four hours I had to stand in the extremely blazing sun directing traffic with my flag. Minutes seemed like hours as I stood there, sweating and breathing in dust. By lunchtime, I felt that I had been on the job for a week instead of four hours. That's when I came to realize that I was in for a long summer.

You probably noticed that several sentences need to be made more concise. In the first sentence, *really* can be eliminated, as can *first* and *very* in the second sentence and *extremely* in the sixth. *The month of June* in the fourth sentence can be shortened to *June,* and *Due to the fact that* in the fifth sentence can be changed to *Because.* Finally, *came to realize* in the last sentence can be shortened to *realized.*

Here's the same paragraph, this time with the changes:

> My job last summer as a flagger for a construction company was harder than I expected it to be. When I heard about the opening, I figured that earning $7 to direct traffic around construction sites would be easy. I soon found out how wrong I was. On the first morning in June, I reported to the site at 8:15. Because I needed to be highly visible to oncoming traffic, the boss handed me a hard hat, a safety vest, and a large orange flag. My station was next to the excavation in the road, and for the next four hours I had to stand in the blazing sun directing traffic with my flag. Minutes seemed like hours as I stood there, sweating and breathing in dust. By lunchtime, I felt that I had been on the job for a week instead of four hours. That's when I realized that I was in for a long summer.

This version expresses the same idea, but thanks to the changes, it is more direct and concise.

COMPREHENSION AND PRACTICE

4.6

Working on Specific, Concise Language

1. On a separate sheet of paper, take each of the following general words and transform them into concrete, specific terms.

   a. a vacation spot

   b. a national monument

   c. a sports team

2. On the lines that follow, make each of the following sentences more concise.

   a. A large number of tourists travel to New England during the months of October and November.

   A large number of tourists travel to new
   England during october and november.

   b. The weather forecast calls for really cold temperatures in the near future.

   the weather forecast falls for cold temperatures
   in the future

   c. Michelle eventually came to the realization that cutting class definitely had the potential to create problems for her.

   Michelle realize that cutting class had the
   potential to create problems for her.

CHALLENGE 4.6 **Focusing on Effective Language**

collaboration

1. Read the following paragraph. Then, working with a classmate, underline the details that you agree are too general. On a separate sheet of paper, create details and write versions of these sentences that are more specific.

My first job, as a member of the staff at Mac and Al's Diner, was really fun. As a high school student, I worked every weekend for a long time. On Friday nights, I worked very long hours. On Saturdays and Sundays, I worked a lot of the day. I never knew what to expect when I went to work. Sometimes I'd be the dishwasher, and other times the boss would have me do other things. The people I worked with were very nice. Many of the customers came in a lot, so they seemed like family. One couple originally met at the diner, so when they got married, they invited everyone to the wedding.

2. On a separate sheet of paper, complete the following topic sentence by filling in the blank:

   The thing that I liked best about my first job was _____.

   Do some prewriting to generate ideas to support this topic sentence. Then, on the same piece of paper, create a draft paragraph of seven to ten sentences on this subject.

collaboration

3. Exchange your draft paragraph with a classmate. As you read the draft you receive, pay particular attention to the language, making note of any general or abstract words and expressions that need to be made more specific. Return the draft to the writer.

4. Consider any spots that your reader thinks should be more specific and make any adjustments in language that you agree are necessary.

Getting Feedback from an Objective Reader

An especially helpful step in reassessing is feedback from an objective reader. Anybody who will read your work and then respond intelligently and honestly to it—a classmate, a family member, a friend—is a potential reader.

To make the task easier for your reader, provide the following reader assessment checklist. This series of questions will guide your reader through an evaluation of your writing. More important, the answers will help you to see how effectively you communicate.

✓READER ASSESSMENT CHECKLIST

☐ Do you understand the point I am making? (topic sentence)

☐ Do I stick to that point all the way through? (unity)

☐ Are all my ideas and examples clearly connected and easy to follow? (coherence)

☐ Are the words I've used specific and concise? (effective language)

☐ What changes do you think I should make?

Here again is the first-draft paragraph about connecting on the Internet:

In a matter of only a few years, social networking sites on the Internet have exploded in number and popularity. LinkedIn is a successful social networking site that enables working professionals to connect with fellow professionals, raise and answer questions within their fields, and track career possibilities. YouTube is the premier place for users to upload and share video content, both original creations and snippets from professional performances. Facebook and MySpace are popular, especially among young people. Members of these networks can post personal profiles, including photos and videos and blogs and other multimedia content. They can view the pages of other members, and, subject to approval, communicate and interact with them. Some people have posted embarrassing pictures on their sites that caused them to lose out on jobs later on. The growth of these social networking sites has made it possible for people across the country and around the world to relate to people with similar interests.

Here is a sample peer response to this paragraph:

> I like your paper--it does a good job explaining the different online sites for connecting with people. The topic sentence is good because it lets you know what the paragraph is about. Your sentences are mostly unified and coherent. The seventh sentence, the one about the embarrassing pictures on Facebook or MySpace, seems to go off in a different direction. Maybe you should get rid of it. I think a little more transition would help, especially when you move from one type of networking site to the next. I like the stuff about YouTube, but would it be a good idea to mention some specific network shows you can see? Also, I don't know much about business sites like LinkedIn, so maybe more specific information about them would be a good idea. I think the language you use to explain the sites is one of the best parts of your paragraph. It is simple, so even somebody who has never heard about social networking sites can understand what you are explaining. I hope my suggestions help.

As you can see, comments like these can be very helpful in pointing out what is already good in a draft and zeroing in on problem spots remaining.

COMPREHENSION AND PRACTICE

4.7

Evaluating the Feedback Process

1. On the following lines, explain what you find most difficult about evaluating another writer's paper and why you find this part hard.

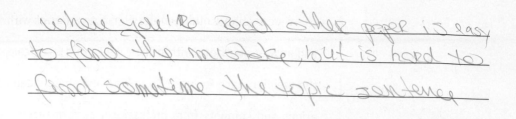

where you're read other paper is easy
to find the mistake, but is hard to
find sometime the topic sentence

2. On the following lines, identify the question on the reader assessment checklist (page 60) that you think is most important to help writers improve their
papers, and explain why, in your view, this question is more important than
the others.

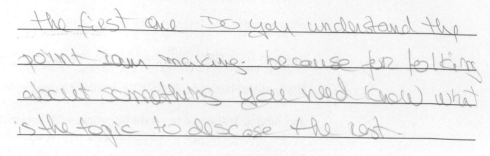

the first one Do you understand the
point iam making. because for talking
about something you need (now) what
is the topic to descuse the rest

CHALLENGE 4.7   **Working with the Reader Assessment Checklist**

collaboration

1. So far, you have completed a number of draft paragraphs. After consulting
with your instructor, choose one of these drafts and make a copy of it.
Exchange your paper with a reader who has not previously seen it. Complete
the following steps with the draft you receive:

   a. Put a + next to the topic sentence if it provides a clear direction. Put a **?**
   next to it if the main point isn't clear.

   b. Check the paragraph for unity and coherence. Underline any portion of a
   sentence or any complete sentence that disrupts the unity of the paragraph, and put a ✓ at any point where additional transition would help.
   Also, note any problem with the order of sentences, indicating how you
   think things should be changed to improve the paragraph.

   c. Check the paragraph for effective language. Circle any general or abstract
   words and overly wordy phrases and expressions. Write suggested substitutes above the circled words and phrases.

2. Return the draft to the writer. Save your draft and your reader's comments
for later use.

Redrafting

ESL Note
See "Strive for Clarity,"
page 556, for more on
the importance of
amplifying.

After you have identified what still needs work in your writing, the next step is redrafting, or writing a new version or draft of your paper. As you work through
later drafts, you will correct any flaws you've discovered. In addition, you will fill
any gaps in content. As pages 38–39 in Chapter 3 indicate, to do this you
amplify. In some cases, you provide additional, specific details and examples, and

in others you change the wording of these details and examples so that your reader can better visualize or understand them.

Take a look at this first-draft paragraph dealing with medical advances:

> Research has led to dramatic changes in medical treatment. Technological innovations have helped to turn ideas from science fiction into fact. In addition, researchers continue to develop new devices and treatments designed to prolong life.

Apply the reader assessment checklist to this paragraph and you will quickly uncover its strengths and weaknesses. The paragraph is largely unified, coherent, and organized, but right now, it is far too general and it lacks supporting details and examples. Amplifying by supplying information that answers the kinds of questions a reader might have about this subject will fill these gaps. For instance, what *specific* changes in medical treatment have occurred? What *particular* innovations have made the impossible real? What *exactly* are medical researchers working on now?

Now consider this amplified version of the same paragraph:

> Research has led to dramatic changes in medical treatment. **For example, serious surgical procedures such as heart and brain surgery are now commonplace.** Technological innovations have helped to turn ideas from science fiction into fact. **Today, burn victims enjoy faster healing because of the development of artificial skin. Replacement knees, hips, and knuckles mean that people suffering from degenerative joint conditions can now regain greater mobility.** In addition, researchers continue to develop new devices and treatments designed to prolong life. **Prototypes of a completely self-contained artificial heart, powered by a rechargeable battery the size of a book, already exist. Within the next few years, researchers hope to make available a number of other body parts, including artificial kidneys and retinas.**

As you can see, the new information, shown in boldface type, clearly improves the paragraph. This new material specifies the progress that medical researchers have achieved as well as the changes that are on the horizon.

Redrafting is different with every paper you write. With some papers, you'll need to make changes and adjustments in several areas. With other papers, you may have to concentrate to a greater degree on one particular point. No matter what you need to add, delete, or correct, however, remember that your goal in redrafting is always the same: to improve your writing.

COMPREHENSION AND PRACTICE 4.8

Amplifying for Effectiveness

1. The sentences below are too general to be effective. On the lines that follow each, add details or examples—in complete sentence form—that amplify the information.

a. That party was exciting. For example,

that party was exciting, I meet a lot of new people, also has a lot of food and drinks

b. My neighborhood is interesting. For instance,

_____

_____

c. My high school had problems. For example,

_____

_____

2. Choose one of the sentences you have just amplified. On a separate sheet of paper, write three additional supporting sentences, making sure that they are amplified so that they answer questions your audience might have.

CHALLENGE 4.8   **Employing the Reader Assessment Checklist to Identify Weaknesses**

collaboration

1. Read the following paragraph:

> One thing that college students can be sure of is that their money won't stay in their wallets very long. For one thing, they have to pay tuition, which costs a lot. Financial aid and scholarships help, but many students still struggle to pay for other things. Different living expenses add up to quite a bit, and transportation is a big issue. Students also have to pay for supplies they need for their classes. College may be an investment for the future, but when it comes to paying for it, most students are much more worried about the present.

Now, working with a classmate, prepare an evaluation of the paragraph on a separate sheet of paper, using the reader assessment checklist (page 60).

2. On the same paper, make a list of at least five details that would help to improve the paragraph.

Avoiding Plagiarism

If you support your own ideas with ideas or details from some other source, you need to tell your reader where you found this supporting information. Otherwise you would be guilty of **plagiarism**—taking someone else's work and passing it off as your own. Plagiarism is literary theft, and the penalty can range from a failing grade for the document to failure in the class to dismissal from school. It doesn't make any difference whether the act is accidental or intentional. When you fail to acknowledge your source for any reason and in any subject area, you are guilty of plagiarism. Therefore, it's vital that you know how to avoid the problem in the first place.

Fortunately, the solution is fairly simple. Whenever you come across material in another source that would help you make your point, you can include it in one of three ways.

1. As a **direct quotation:** presenting it word for word as it appears with quotation marks around it.

2. As a **paraphrase:** expressing the point in your own words and including an explanation or interpretation.

3. As a **summary:** presenting a greatly reduced version of the original in your own words.

Regardless of how you present information that you take from another source, you must let your reader know in two spots in your paper where you originally found the information. The first time is in a set of parentheses immediately following the information you have included, and the second time, in a more detailed form, is at the end of your paper. This process is referred to as *acknowledging and documenting your sources.* For more on how to acknowledge your sources using one of the standard methods of documentation, see Chapter 15.

Editing

Once you have eliminated the weaknesses in content in your draft, you are ready for the final step in revising: *editing.* Good content alone isn't enough to make a piece of writing effective. It must also be free from mistakes in form—errors in grammar and usage, spelling, and punctuation. In other words, it must follow the rules of standard written English. Errors in form are serious because they distract your reader from your content. Instead of concentrating on your message, your reader instead focuses on these problem spots, thus overlooking the overall quality of your work.

Think of editing as the final cleaning up and polishing, which you accomplish through *proofreading*—close reading to root out any remaining mistakes. The secret to effective proofreading is timing. Plan so that you proofread your paper when you are rested. That way, fatigue and familiarity with the content won't cause you to see what you *meant to write* rather than what you *have actually written.* When you are tired, for example, you may see *receive* even though you've actually misspelled it as *recieve.*

Developing a Personal Proofreading System

The following Proofreading Checklist addresses the errors in form that give writers the most trouble:

✓ PROOFREADING CHECKLIST

ESL Note
See "Sentence Basics,"
pages 543–544;
"Agreement," pages
546–548; "Spelling,"
page 552; "Strive for
Clarity," page 556; and
"Revise to Correct
Errors," page 557; for
more on dealing with
these problem areas.

☐ Have I eliminated all sentence fragments? *(frag)* (Chapter 18)

☐ Have I eliminated all comma splices? *(cs)* (Chapter 20)

☐ Have I eliminated all run-on sentences? *(rs)* (Chapter 20)

☐ Is the spelling *(sp)* correct throughout? (Chapter 29)

☐ Is the verb tense *(t)* correct throughout? (Chapters 22, 23, 24)

☐ Do all subjects agree with their verbs? *(subj/verb agr)* (Chapters 17, 21, 25)

☐ Do all pronouns agree with their antecedents? *(pro/ant agr)* (Chapter 26)

Of course, this checklist doesn't cover all the errors writers make. For example, you may have trouble with some other aspect of writing such as double negatives (Chapter 27) or apostrophe use (Chapters 29 and 31), neither of which appears on the checklist. Therefore, the best thing to do is to develop a *personal proofreading system* by tailoring the checklist: eliminating or adding categories so that it concentrates on the problems you find most difficult.

By the way, don't worry if you don't yet understand why some of these errors occur. Other chapters in this book will explain how to watch for and eliminate them. The Sentence Skill Locator on the inside back cover also indicates where in the text to look for help.

Teaming up with a proofreading partner is another way to eliminate errors in your paper. Once you have proofread your paper, exchange it with another reader. This proofreading partner will not be as invested or involved with the writing as you are and so may be better able to find any remaining errors. You can perform the same duties for your partner. The result will be better papers for both of you.

Using Computer Tools to Your Advantage

If you are using a computer to do your writing, you have additional proofreading tools: the spelling and grammar checkers. These features check your spelling and usage against the computer's dictionary and usage guide and then offer alternatives or solutions to correct these errors. Click on one of the options, and the program will insert the selection in place of the problem it detected.

Don't trust computer tools to find all your errors, however. Computer programs don't read and reason as humans do—at least not yet. If you write *quiet* when you mean *quite* or *principal* when you mean *principle*, the spell-check feature might not pick up on the error since both words in each pair are correctly spelled. Also, these tools are not always reliable with matters of subject–verb agreement and sentence fragments. Sometimes they misread the subject, choosing a noun or pronoun near the verb rather than the word that is actually serving as the subject. In addition, because the subject of an imperative or command sentence is implied (*Clean the surface completely before any application of the adhesive*), the software may incorrectly identify the group of words as a fragment.

Take full advantage of the spelling and grammar checkers available, but always do one final proofreading, slowly and carefully, to make sure that the computer program didn't miss any errors.

COMPREHENSION AND PRACTICE 4.9

Employing a Proofreading Checklist

1. Of the areas of concern noted in the proofreading checklist on page 65, which one has given you the most trouble in the past? Why do you think you have difficulty with this area?

_____

_____

_____

2. Proofread the following paragraph. Correct the errors you find. In the margin beside each error, write the abbreviation from the proofreading checklist on page 65 to identify the type of error (*frag, sp,* and so forth).

> The hardest thing I ever has to endure was my parents' divorce. I was ten when it happened, I had always thought I had the perfect family. A few days before Christmas, my mother sat down in front of my brother and me and told us that my father was moving out to live with another woman. Every kid wants to have someone they can look up to, and for me that used to be my father. But when I saw how sad my mother looks, I hated my father I wished he would just disappear. He kept calling the house to talk with me, but I wouldn't talk to him. Two years later, after the divorce was final. I met him by accident downtown. When he seen me, he started to cry and said he was sorry. I couldn't forgive him then I can't forgive him now. He ruined my prefect family.

Now check your answers against the corrected version on page 71.

CHALLENGE 4.9   **Editing to Complete a Final Draft**

1. For Challenge 4.7 (page 62), you and a classmate exchanged draft paragraphs you had been working on. You used the reader assessment checklist (page 60) to evaluate the draft relative to the topic sentence, unity, coherence, and effective language and returned the paper to the writer. Now take this paragraph and redraft it to eliminate the weaknesses you and your reader have identified.

collaboration

2. Exchange your redrafted paragraph with a classmate who has not previously seen it. Using the proofreading checklist (page 65) to guide you, edit and proofread the draft you receive. Put a ✓ before anything you believe to be an error. Then return the paragraph to the writer.

3. After considering your reader's evaluation, make any necessary corrections to your paragraph.

Seeing the Results of Revision

ESL Note
See "Writing Paragraphs," pages 555–556, for more on revising a paragraph.

So what happens when you follow the revising guidelines presented in this chapter? Here again is the first-draft version of the paragraph on connecting on the Web that appeared at the end of Chapter 3 (pages 41–42), with specific suggestions for improvement:

Connecting: Only a Click Away

In a matter of only a few years, social networking sites on

1.

the Internet have exploded in number and popularity. LinkedIn

is a successful social networking site that enables working

2.

professionals to connect with fellow professionals, raise and

answer questions within their fields, and track career possibilities.

1.

YouTube is the premier place for users to upload and share

2.

video content, both original creations and snippets from professional

3.

performances. Facebook and MySpace are popular, especially

among young people. Members of these networks can post

personal profiles, including photos and videos and blogs and

other multimedia content. They can view the pages of other

members, and, subject to approval, communicate and interact

with them. Some people have posted embarrassing pictures on their

sites that caused them to lose out on jobs later on. The growth of

these social networking sites has made it possible for people across

the country and around the world to relate to people with similar

interests.

1. Some transition here would help.

2. A specific example or two would help illustrate this point. Amplify.

3. This sentence isn't directly related to the topic—eliminate it.

Here is the revised version of the same paragraph. The changes made during reassessing and editing have been highlighted. As you examine it, note the **format**—the arrangement of the words on the page. This paragraph follows the guidelines of the Modern Language Association (MLA) (see Chapter 15). These guidelines call for *double-spacing* the entire document. In the upper-right corner, insert your last name and the page number, also called a **running head.** If you are using a computer, insert the running head into the header of the document by using the drop-down menu to open the header field. The computer program will then repeat your last name and the successive page number on each subsequent page. In the upper-left corner of the page, include a four-line heading: Your full name appears on the first line, followed by the name of the course on the second line, then the instructor's name on the third, and the date you submit the paper on the fourth. Hit the *Return* key twice, center the title, and hit Return twice again. Then, after indenting, begin the paragraph.

ESL Note
See "Unity," page 555, and "Think about Audience Expectations," page 556, for additional discussions about focusing on the reader.

Vincent 1

Jaime Vincent

English 010.40—Basic College Writing

Dr. Kelly

October 15, 2010

Connecting: Only a Click Away

In a matter of only a few years, social networking sites on the Internet have exploded in number and popularity. For example, LinkedIn is a successful social networking site enabling working professionals to connect with fellow professionals, raise and answer questions within their fields, and track career possibilities. Through LinkedIn and other sites like Xing, people can develop contacts across the country and around the world with specialists in their particular lines of work. An ever-increasing number of social networking sites serve other purposes or other audiences. For instance, YouTube is the premier place for users to upload and share video content, both amateur productions like video blogs and clips from TV shows, movies, rock concerts, and so on. Hulu, another video site, enables viewers to watch movies and current network shows like *The Office* plus classic TV shows like *Bewitched.* Finally, Facebook and MySpace are among the best-known electronic meeting spaces in the world, especially among young people. Members of these networks can post personal profiles, including photos, videos and blogs, and other multimedia content. They can also view the pages of other members, and, subject to approval, communicate and interact with them. The growth of these social networking sites has made it possible for people across the country and around the world to relate to people with similar interests.

The weaknesses identified during reassessing have been addressed during redrafting. Thanks to the amplified supporting material and added transition, this version of the paragraph is clear proof of the power of revision, as the following instructor's comments indicate:

> *Congratulations—you have done a fine job revising your paper. You have made a number of improvements since I saw the first draft a week ago. I especially like the specific examples you've added. Now in addition to just telling the reader about sites like YouTube and LinkedIn, you use specific details to show how these sites function. The new material about Hulu and Xing helps, too. So does the transition you've added. All in all, this is an excellent first paper.*

FOR FURTHER EXPLORATION Developing a Final Draft Paragraph

1. Focus on one of the following topics, using the prewriting technique—or combination of techniques—that you prefer to generate some preliminary ideas, considering what purposes you might fulfill as you write about it:

   - an experience with severe weather
   - myths, misconceptions, or stereotypes associated with physical beauty
   - true heroism

2. Evaluate your prewriting material, identify a focus, and create a draft paragraph of at least seven to ten sentences.

3. Exchange your draft with a classmate. Using the material in this chapter as a guide, evaluate the draft you receive, considering unity, coherence, and effective language, and then proofread carefully. Prepare a written response for the writer using the sample peer response on page 61 as a guide. Return the paragraph along with your response to the writer.

4. Revise your draft, addressing any problems your writing partner identified.

collaboration

DISCOVERING CONNECTIONS Drafting and Revising

Consider this photo and then reflect on one of the following questions (or another that the photo inspires). Think in terms of the purpose you might fulfill and create a draft of at least seven to ten sentences. Referring to the material in this chapter as a guide, reassess your draft in terms of unity, coherence, and effective language, and then create a final-draft version.

A. What are some threats facing the world's oceans today? What steps can we as individuals take to make sure that future generations will be able to enjoy the beauty captured in this scene?

B. Imagine that it's your job to prepare a paragraph to accompany this photo for a travel agency brochure and Web site. How would you describe this scene to accentuate and enhance the natural beauty and interest people to visit?

Corrected Version of Comprehension and Practice 4.9, Number 2

t & subj/verb agr   The hardest thing I ever ~~has~~ *had* to endure was my parents' divorce. I was ten

cs   when it happened⸴ I had always thought I had the perfect family. A few days

before Christmas, my mother sat down in front of my brother and me and

told us that my father was moving out to live with another woman. Every

pro/ant agr   ⟨kid⟩ wants to have someone ⟨~~they~~⟩ *he or she* can look up to, and for me that used to be

t/rs   my father. But when I saw how sad my mother ~~looks~~ *looked*, I hated my father⸴ I

wished he would just disappear. He kept calling the house to talk with me,

frag   but I wouldn't talk to him. Two years later, after the divorce was final⸴ I met

t   him by accident downtown. When he ~~seen~~ *saw* me, he started to cry and said he

rs   was sorry. I couldn't forgive him then⸴ *, and* I can't forgive him now. He ruined my

sp   ~~prefect~~ *perfect* family.

RECAP Refining and Polishing Your Draft

Key Terms in This Chapter	Definitions
revising	the stage of writing during which you refine and polish a draft Revising means (1) reassessing, (2) redrafting, and (3) editing.
reassessing	looking closely at a draft to find and correct errors and weaknesses
redrafting	creating a new version of a piece of writing by correcting problems and incorporating new material
editing	polishing and proofreading a piece of writing to eliminate errors in grammar, spelling, and punctuation
unity	the quality achieved in writing when all sentences relate to the main idea
coherence	the quality achieved in writing when sentences hold together well Coherence comes from logical order and connections that show how ideas interrelate.
synonyms	words with similar meanings
transitional expressions	words that connect ideas and show relationships between them
chronological order	organization in sequence on the basis of time
spatial order	organization based on location of parts in relation to a whole
emphatic order	organization based on order of significance, or importance
effective language	language that communicates well because it is specific (detailed) and concise (brief but clear)
amplification	the addition of specific details and examples
plagiarism	appropriating someone else's work
direct quotation	presenting information word for word within quotation marks as it appears in an original source
paraphrase	presenting information from a source in different words with an interpretation or explanation
summary	presenting information from a source in a greatly reduced form
format	the arrangement of a document on a page
running head	the writer's last name and the page number, positioned in the upper right corner of each page of a document

The Process of Revising

1 → Reassess

Check for
- Unity.
- Coherence.
- Effective language.

Seek feedback from an objective reader.

2 → Redraft ←

Add new material.

Improve existing material.

Delete irrelevant material.

3 Edit

Proofread for errors in
- Spelling.
- Grammar.
- Punctuation.

Using Odyssey Online with MyWritingLab

For more practice revising, go to www.mywritinglab.com.

> **portfolio • noun** (pl. **portfolios**) … **2** a set of pieces of creative work intended to demonstrate a person's ability. ORIGIN Italian *portafogli*, from *portare* 'carry' + *foglio* 'leaf'.

—*Compact Oxford English Dictionary*

One method used to assess success in many fields is to evaluate a *portfolio* of work. A **portfolio**, as the definition explains, is a collection of specific pieces of work done in response to different assignments or tasks. Together, the pieces offer a snapshot of progress at a point in time. A typical writing portfolio may include various types of documents, such as

- previously written and revised work

- writings in response to another document or artifact—an essay, a film, a photo, a piece of art or music, and so on

- a piece of timed writing

- a reflective or self-examining writing

To mark your progress up to this point, create the following portfolio.

BEST WORK   Select a previously completed piece of writing that you feel is your best work so far.

ESSAY ANSWER   Read Amy Tan's "Fish Cheeks" (pages 513–514), and write a brief answer (around 200 words) to one of the following essay questions:

- In your view, what is the actual reason that the young girl is so upset to discover that her family is entertaining the minister's family for Christmas Eve? What details in the story lead you to this conclusion?

- In the seventh paragraph, the mother tells her daughter, "'You must be proud you are different. Your only shame is to have shame.'" What do you think this advice means? Do you agree with the mother? Why or why not?

TIMED WRITING   In thirty minutes, complete a writing of at least 200 words on one of the following topics:

TIMED WRITING

- Motivation is the key to success in most fields, but staying motivated is easier said than done sometimes. What do you find is the best way to get started and remain interested in a task? Why do you think this process works?

- Have you ever made a decision and then, a day or so later, wished that you had made another choice? Tell that story, discussing the situation and explaining why you changed your mind.

REFLECTION   As Chapters 1 through 4 point out, writing is a process during which you develop, draft, evaluate, and refine your ideas. At this point, what part of the writing process do you find easiest? Why? What stage do you find most difficult? Why? In a paragraph of seven to ten sentences, address these questions.

PART 2

Using the Patterns of Paragraph Development

CHAPTER 5
Narration

GETTING STARTED ...

 Q I want to write about an experience that I had. How can I make the story of what happened to me clear and easy for my readers to follow?

 A You should use *narration*, the organizing strategy through which you relate a series of events. Identify your experience—or an experience that you witnessed someone else have—and then write about it as fully as you recall it and in the order in which the events happened.

Overview: Understanding the Modes, Purposes, and Importance of Telling Your Story

If you've looked through the table of contents or ahead in this book, you've seen words such as *description, example, process, definition, comparison and contrast, cause and effect,* and *division and classification.* These are the **modes,** the organizing or developmental strategies or techniques that you can use to express your point on a subject. Each of these organizing strategies enables you to approach and cover a topic in a different way.

As Chapter 1 (pages 7–8) shows, you write to fulfill one of three purposes: to *inform,* to *entertain,* or to *persuade.* The organizing strategies are the devices you use to fulfill those purposes. This chapter and the seven that follow examine the modes one by one. As you read this material, you will learn and practice the characteristics of each developmental strategy. When you do, keep this point in mind: Most writing relies on a combination of modes to communicate ideas to readers. One mode will dominate and one or more of the others will support it. The longer a piece of writing is, the more likely this will be the case.

Narration, the focus of this chapter, is the mode that people use to tell stories, from "Once upon a time ... " fairy tales to personal experiences to autobiographies and memoirs. You use narration whenever you relate a series of events or incidents, for instance, a story about a date gone wrong or the discovery of a family secret; these types of stories tend to *entertain.* Beyond the classroom, you would use narration for personal blogs and e-mails, or police and accident reports.

Navigating This Chapter This chapter will explore the basic requirements for writing an effective narrative paragraph:

- providing a topic sentence that establishes a context
- explaining the events in the story in chronological order
- recognizing the most effective point of view
- ensuring a thorough presentation

Writing a Clear Topic Sentence That Establishes a Context

ESL Note
See "Sentence Basics"
on pages 543–544 and
"Word Order" on pages
545–546.

In order to help readers understand the point of a narrative paragraph, the writer must provide a topic sentence, which establishes a context for the sequence of events that follows. In other words, it sets the scene and orients the reader for the story the writer is about to tell. As Chapter 3 showed, a typical topic sentence pinpoints both the *topic* and the *attitude* or *reaction* to the topic. In the narrative paragraph, the topic is the incident, or story. Your reaction is the "spin," or slant, you put on the events you relate.

Look at the topic sentence in this narrative paragraph from *Bird by Bird* in which author Anne Lamott discusses her father:

> I'm sure my father was the person on whom his friends relied to tell their stories, in school and college. I know for sure he was later, in the town where he was raising his children. He could take major events or small episodes from daily life and shade or exaggerate things in such a way as to capture their shape and substance, capture what life felt like in the society in which he and his friends lived and worked and bred. People looked up to him to put into words what was going on.

The first sentence is the topic sentence, and it prepares the reader for the focus of the rest of the paragraph. It states that her father was the one whom acquaintances counted on to present their experiences, and the other sentences explain why.

Relying on Chronological Order

Since narration is the mode that focuses on a series of events, how effectively you present the sequence will influence how your reader understands it. With narration, *chronological order* is often the ideal choice. As Chapter 4 (page 51) explains, this method of arrangement involves presenting the series of incidents in the order in which they happened. Consider the following narrative paragraph from John Monczunski's essay "Cornered," in which he discusses an encounter with a stranger who, he fears, intends to harm him:

> Then the spell breaks. Two blocks ahead, a solitary figure emerges from a building. He wheels around and begins walking toward me. When I see him my stomach knots. I am not sure if he is even aware of me, but I know I do not want to meet him. I decide on a tactical evasive maneuver and cross to the other side of the street. The man counters my move. Apparently he is intent on meeting me and he reestablishes our collision course. We mirror each other's movements all the while slicing the gap between us. His long-distance telegraphed intentions add to my unease. Am I paranoid or prudent?

Monczunski makes it easier for his reader to understand the experience by relating it in the order in which it occurred. First, he notices the man leave a building, turn and walk toward him. He then crosses the street to avoid the man, but the man crosses the street as well and continues heading toward him.

Sometimes writers employ a **flashback**, an incident deliberately presented out of sequence, often to give the reader some important background information. Imagine, for example, you were writing about how you finally overcame terrible stage fright in your public speaking course. You had originally developed the stage fright in the first grade when you forgot your lines in the spring play. Including this flashback in your paper would make it easier for your reader to understand how difficult overcoming your anxiety was.

COMPREHENSION AND PRACTICE
5.1

Considering Topic Sentences and Chronological Order

1. Read the following paragraph by Helen Keller from her autobiography, *The Story of My Life,* in which she discusses learning some basic signs of communication without understanding their significance:

> The morning after my teacher came she led me into her room and gave me a doll. The little blind children at the Perkins Institute had sent it and Laura Bridgman [the first deaf and blind person to be educated in the United States] had dressed it; but I did not know this until afterward. When I had played with it a little while, Miss Sullivan slowly spelled into my hand the word "d-o-l-l." I was at once interested in this finger play and tried to imitate it. When I finally succeeded in making the letters correctly I was flushed with childish pleasure and pride. Running downstairs to my mother I held up my hand and made the letters for doll. I did not know that I was spelling a word or even that words existed. I was simply making my fingers go in monkey-like imitation. In the days that followed I learned to spell in this uncomprehending way a great many words, among them *pin, hat, cup,* and a few verbs like *sit, stand,* and *walk.* But my teacher had been with me several weeks before I understood that everything has a name.

On the lines below, briefly explain how Keller's topic sentence sets the direction and context for the supporting sentences

_____

_____

_____

2. Choose one of the supporting sentences and briefly explain how it specifies the point made in the topic sentence.

_____

_____

_____

3. On the lines that follow, briefly explain how chronological order helps you understand what Keller experienced.

_____

_____

_____

Choosing the Most Effective Point of View

Any time you tell a story, you select a **point of view,** the perspective from which you relate the experience. Often when you use narration, you will write from a *first person point of view,* that is, as you participated in or experienced the event. With first person point of view, you use *I, me,* and other words that refer to yourself. Other times, you will write from a *third person point of view,* that is, as an observer rather than as a participant. Because you focus on others with third person narration, you use *he, she, her, they,* and so on.

Consider this narrative paragraph from "They All Just Went Away," an essay by writer Joyce Carol Oates:

> I must have been a lonely child. Until the age of twelve or thirteen, my most intense, happiest hours were spent tramping desolate fields, woods, and creek banks near my family's farmhouse in Millersport, New York. No one knew where I went. My father, working most of the day at Harrison's, a division of General Motors in Lockport, and at other times preoccupied, would not have asked; if my mother asked, I might have answered in a way that would deflect curiosity. I was an articulate, verbal child. Yet I could not have explained what drew me to the abandoned houses, barns, silos, corncribs. A hike of miles through fields of spiky grass, across outcroppings of shale as steeply angled as stairs, was a lark if the reward was an empty house.

It's clear from Oates's use of *I, my,* and *me* that she was a participant in the event and therefore writes from the first person point of view.

Now, consider this paragraph from Peter Griffin's biography of Ernest Hemingway, *Less Than a Treason.* It describes Hemingway's first encounter with flying.

> Ernest first saw the plane from the window of the taxi he and [his wife] Hadley took to the field. It was a silver biplane with a tiny cabin with portholes, and a seat for the pilot in the rear. Ernest bought the tickets at a counter in the plane shed, and had them checked by an attendant who stood just ten feet away, by the door to the field. Then, with cotton stuffed into their ears, Ernest and Hadley climbed aboard the plane and sat one behind the other. The pilot, a short, little man with his cap on backwards, shouted contact, and the mechanic gave the propeller a spin.

In this case, Griffin's use of *Ernest, Hadley,* and *them* shows that he is a witness to the event and therefore uses the third person point of view.

Providing a Thorough Presentation

With any type of writing, your reader depends on you to make the situation clear. Your thorough knowledge of the topic can result in two main problems: including too little specific information and becoming sidetracked. Because you know the story so well, there is a natural tendency to leave out details that a stranger would need to understand the story. At the same time, you may be inclined to include details of another experience that is indirectly related, which can confuse your reader. To ensure that you provide enough information without getting sidetracked, focus your narration on your reader's needs and your purpose in writing it.

Notice the degree of detail and the specific focus in the following passage by journalist and columnist Bob Kerr about his experiences as a Marine in Vietnam:

> Every Christmas now, somewhere in the giving frenzy, I think about the beautiful little girl in Cam Lo village, near Quang Tri. She had great big eyes and a joyous laugh, and we couldn't help watching her as she waited by the side of a Marine truck for her turn to reach up and receive one of the brightly wrapped packages sent by Americans to children in Vietnam. She carried her package to the shade of a tree, tore it open, and took out … a pair of white figure skates. She held them up, clearly mystified by the metal blades stuck to what appeared a perfectly good pair of shoes. She dragged them along the dirt street. A Navy corpsman who was treating villagers in a makeshift clinic looked over and said, "Don't those bozos back in the world know anything about this place?"

ESL Note
See "Strive for Clarity," page 556, for more on the importance of coherent writing.

Kerr makes sure to tell his story fully, including specific details about the location, the little girl's face and mannerisms, and her reaction to the gift. At the same time, he keeps his focus on this scenario, avoiding any shift in his subject.

Providing Transition for Narrative Paragraphs

When you write a narrative, you will find certain transitional expressions helpful to show the sequence of events. Some of them are listed here.

Transitional Expressions for Narratives

after	during	later	soon
before	first (second, etc.)	meanwhile	then

COMPREHENSION AND PRACTICE
5.2

Considering Point of View and Thorough Presentations

1. Read the following paragraph from "Ruby Bridges and a Painting," Robert Coles's personal account of when Ruby Bridges became the first African-American child to attend a desegregated New Orleans school in 1960:

> A fateful coincidence changed my life in the fall of 1960—and gave me, eventually, an unforgettable acquaintance with a Norman Rockwell painting. I was on my way to a medical conference in New Orleans when suddenly a police barricade confronted me and others trying to make our way toward that cosmopolitan city. All of us were told that because a nearby school was being desegregated by federal court order, we were not going to be allowed further travel—a blockade had been established to give the police control over some of the city's neighborhoods. Suddenly, unexpectedly, I had a lot of time on my hands. I could have turned around and returned to Biloxi, Mississippi, where I then lived as an Air Force physician, in the military under the old doctors' draft law. Instead, I walked a few blocks, and soon enough I was in the presence of a large crowd of men, women, and children, who were not only milling around but occasionally uniting in a shouted refrain: "Two, four, six, eight, we don't want to integrate!"

On the following lines, briefly explain how, in your view, the impact of this paragraph would be changed if it were presented in third person point of view rather than first person.

_____

_____

_____

_____

2. In your view, which of the details included by Coles does the most to make the experience come alive for the reader? On the following lines, identify this detail and explain why you have chosen it.

_____

_____

_____

_____

CHALLENGE 5.1   **Considering Purpose in Narration Paragraphs**

collaboration

This chapter features several sample narrative paragraphs. The names of the authors of these paragraphs, with the appropriate page numbers, are listed below. Working with a classmate, take another look at the paragraphs. Then, on the lines below the names, list the primary purpose and any secondary purposes for each paragraph.

1. Anne Lamott, page 77

_____

_____

_____

2. John Monczunski, page 77

_____

_____

_____

3. Joyce Carol Oates, page 79

_____

_____

_____

4. Peter Griffin, page 79

_____

_____

_____

5. Bob Kerr, page 80

_____

_____

_____

FOR FURTHER EXPLORATION Narration

1. Choose one of the following topics and, selecting one of the strategies that you practiced in Chapter 2, prewrite on that topic. Let your mind revisit the events of that episode:

   - the first time you voted in a presidential election
   - a trip to the "big city"
   - a time you were caught in a lie
   - a school, team, club, or family reunion

2. This chapter features several sample paragraphs:

   - a discussion of a father's special quality (Anne Lamott, page 77)
   - the story of an unwanted encounter with a stranger (John Monczunski, page 77)
   - the adventures of a child exploring on her own (Joyce Carol Oates, page 79)
   - the account of Ernest Hemingway's first flight (Peter Griffin, page 79)
   - the recounting of a poor child in subtropical, war-torn Vietnam receiving an incongruous gift: ice skates (Bob Kerr, page 80)

For this assignment, think of an experience you have had or witnessed similar to the events discussed in one of these paragraphs. Prewrite on the experience, identify a specific focus, and create a paragraph of at least seven to ten sentences in which you use narration to discuss the event. Use the material in this chapter to guide you through this process.

DISCOVERING CONNECTIONS Narration

For this assignment, examine this photo and respond to one of the following questions (or another that the picture inspires). Using the material in this chapter as a guide, develop a paragraph of at least seven to ten sentences that draws on the power of narration. Remember to pay close attention to chronological order and appropriate point of view.

A. Did you take music lessons as a child? If so, what instrument did you play? Was the experience positive or negative? Or, if you didn't have lessons, how do you think having had this experience would have affected and shaped you?

B. Observe the happy smile on the adult's face and the focused expression on the young boy's—what do you think is going through their individual minds? Have you ever spent time with an adult who truly inspired you? What did you do together?

✔ NARRATIVE PARAGRAPH CHECKLIST

☐ Does the topic sentence establish a context?

☐ Is the material arranged in chronological order?

☐ Is the point of view used to present the paragraph appropriate?

☐ In your judgment, the best part of this paragraph is _____. Explain.

☐ Which detail or example would be even better if it were expanded? Why?

RECAP Narration

Key Terms in This Chapter	Definitions
modes	organizational or developmental strategies
narration	the writing technique used to relate a series of events or incidents
flashback	a past event deliberately presented out of sequence to provide background information
point of view	the perspective a writer uses to tell a story
	Using *first person point of view* makes the writer a participant *(I, me, my, mine)*.
	EXAMPLE Suddenly, I heard a car stop outside my window.
	Using *third person point of view* makes the writer an observer *(she, he, they, him, her, his, them, their, it, its)*.
	EXAMPLE The old woman stood up and reached for her cane.

Writing a Narrative Paragraph

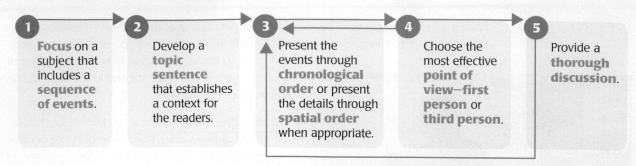

1 Focus on a subject that includes a **sequence of events**.

2 Develop a **topic sentence** that establishes a context for the readers.

3 Present the events through **chronological order** or present the details through **spatial order** when appropriate.

4 Choose the most effective **point of view—first person** or **third person**.

5 Provide a **thorough discussion**.

Using Odyssey Online with MyWritingLab

For more practice with narration, go to www.mywritinglab.com.

CHAPTER 6
Description

GETTING STARTED ...

 Q The experience was so vivid—it was like it was full of electricity. How can I capture that sense of energy and life for my reader when I write about it?

 A Whenever you need to record in words the vivid sensations you have seen or witnessed, rely on *description*. Through description, you re-create and animate subjects so that a reader can feel the same energy and life. First provide a specific topic sentence. Then present sensory details that objectively and subjectively describe the subject in spatial order or some other appropriate arrangement.

Overview: Creating a Picture in Words

When you write, think of your words as a camera lens through which your reader views your world. To bring into focus the scenes of your life for your readers, use **description.**

Descriptive writing effectively captures a particular setting, individual, experience, or object in words. A paragraph detailing the experience of speeding along on a motorcycle would call for description. So would a writing about the frenzy of last-minute holiday shoppers, or one dealing with a schoolyard full of children on the first day of school. Beyond the classroom, you might use description to write book and movie reviews, brochures about a new product, or patient progress reports.

Navigating This Chapter This chapter will explore the basic requirements for writing an effective descriptive paragraph:

- providing a topic sentence that previews your description
- drawing upon sensory details
- relying on both objective and subjective description
- considering spatial order

Previewing the Focus of Description through the Topic Sentence

To ensure that your descriptive paragraph will create a vivid impression of an object, person, or place in the reader's mind, begin with a topic sentence that previews what will be described and suggests your point of view. That way, your reader can make sense of the specific details and examples that follow.

Consider the italicized topic sentence in this paragraph from "The Inheritance of Tools" by Scott Russell Sanders in which the memories associated with the smell of sawdust make him think of his relationship with his father.

As the saw teeth bit down, the wood released its smell, each kind with its own fragrance, oak or walnut or cherry or pine—usually pine because it was the softest, easiest for a child to work. No matter how weathered and gray the board, no matter how warped and cracked, inside there was this smell waiting, as of something freshly baked. I gathered every smidgen of sawdust and stored it away in coffee cans, which I kept in a drawer of the workbench. When I did not feel like hammering nails, I would dump my sawdust on the concrete floor of the garage and landscape it into highways and farms and towns, running miniature cars and trucks along miniature roads. Looming as huge as a colossus, my father worked over and around me, now and again bending down to inspect my work, careful not to trample my creations. It was a landscape that smelled dizzyingly of wood. Even after a bath my skin would carry the smell, and so would my father's hair, when he lifted me for a bedtime hug.

The italicized topic sentence suggests to the reader that the paragraph will focus on memories. The body of the paragraph then offers details and examples from the author's childhood that involve the aroma and texture of sawdust.

Using Sensory Details

Vivid experiences create vivid memories. Think for a moment of the aroma of a bakery the last time you walked into one, or the way your heart pounded the last time you rode on a roller coaster. **Sensory details**—what you perceive by seeing, hearing, tasting, smelling, and touching—enable you to communicate these experiences to your reader. To write sensory details, choose concrete language that draws on the five senses.

Look at this paragraph from writer Richard Rodriguez's "Aria: A Memoir of a Bilingual Childhood," which features sensory details:

There were many times like the night at a brightly lit gasoline station (a blaring white memory) when I stood uneasily hearing my father talk to a teenage attendant. I do not recall what they were saying, but I cannot forget the sound my father made as he spoke. At one point his words slid together to form one long word—sounds as confused as the threads of blue and green oil in the puddle next to my shoes. His voice rushed through what he had left to say. Towards the end, he reached falsetto notes, appealing to his listener's understanding. I looked away at the lights of passing automobiles. I tried not to hear any more. But I heard only too well the attendant's reply, his calm, easy tones. Shortly afterward, walking toward home with my father, I shivered when my father put his hand on my shoulder. The very first chance that I got, I evaded his grasp and ran on ahead into the dark, skipping with feigned boyish exuberance.

As you can see, the passage contains a number of sensory details. When Rodriguez notes the brightness of the lights, the sound of his father's voice, and the shiver he felt, he fills the paragraph with a vivid of sense life.

COMPREHENSION AND PRACTICE

6.1

Considering Topic Sentences and Sensory Details

1. Read the following paragraph from "Total Eclipse" by Annie Dillard in which she describes experiencing the great darkness of a total solar eclipse:

> The second before the sun went out we saw a wall of dark shadow come speeding at us. We no sooner saw it than it was upon us, like thunder. It roared up the valley. It slammed our hill and knocked us out. It was the monstrous swift shadow cone of the moon. I have since read that this wave of shadow moves at 1,800 miles an hour. Language gives no sense of this sort of speed—1,800 miles an hour. It was 195 miles wide. No end was in sight—you saw only the edge. It rolled at you across the land at 1,800 miles an hour, hauling darkness like plague behind it. Seeing it, and knowing it was coming straight for you, was like feeling a slug of anesthetic shoot up your arm. If you think very fast, you may have time to think, "Soon it will hit my brain." You can feel the deadness race up your arm; you can feel the appalling, inhuman speed of your own blood. We saw the wall of shadow coming, and screamed before it hit.

On the lines that follow, briefly explain how the topic sentence prepares you for the details that follow.

_____

_____

_____

_____

2. In your view, which sentence in Dillard's paragraph provides the strongest support for her topic sentence? What makes you come to this conclusion?

_____

_____

_____

_____

3. On a separate sheet of paper, list the sensory details from this paragraph and briefly explain the role they play in the paragraph.

Relying on Objective and Subjective Description

Descriptive writing can be objective or descriptive. **Objective description** concerns actual details and sensations. **Subjective description** focuses on the impressions those details and sensations create. Rarely is a paper completely objective, as a lab report generally is, or completely subjective, as a journal entry might be. Most descriptive writing contains both.

Consider the details in this paragraph from E. B. White's essay "Once More to the Lake," which concerns a trip he took with his young son to a vacation spot of White's youth. Here, he focuses on the lake itself, remarking on how unchanged it seems from his own childhood:

> We caught two bass, hauling them in briskly as though they were mackerel, pulling them over the side of the boat in a businesslike manner without any landing net, and stunning them with a blow on the back of the head. When we got back for a swim before lunch, the lake was exactly where we had left it, the same number of inches from the dock, and there was only the merest suggestion of a breeze. This seemed an utterly enchanted sea, this lake you could leave to its own devices for a few hours and come back to, and find that it had not stirred, this constant and trustworthy body of water. In the shallows, the dark, water-soaked sticks and twigs, smooth and old, were undulating in clusters on the bottom, against the clean ribbed sand, and the track of the mussel was plain. A school of minnows swam by, each minnow with its small individual shadow, doubling the attendance, so clear and sharp in the sunlight. Some of the other campers were in swimming, along the shore, one of them with a cake of soap, and the water felt thin and unsubstantial. Over the years there had been this person with the cake of soap, this cultist, and here he was. There had been no years.

White employs both objective and subjective description to capture the scene at the lake. The number and type of fish, how he and his son killed them, the still and clear waters, the sunken sticks and twigs, and the other people in the lake are all examples of objective description. The words used to discuss how they caught the fish—*briskly, in a businesslike manner*—constitute subjective description, as do the descriptions of the weather at the time—*merest suggestion of a breeze*—and the lake itself—*utterly enchanted sea, constant and trustworthy body of water,* and *the water ... thin and unsubstantial.* Unlike the objective details, these subjective ones express abstract characteristics or qualities, ideas that lend themselves to different interpretations.

Using Spatial Order

ESL Note
See "Strive for Clarity,"
page 556, for more
on the importance of
coherent writing.

As Chapter 4 indicates, writers often rely upon *spatial order* to organize descriptive writing. Spatial order locates the described elements logically in relationship to each other. It directs the reader's attention, for example, from left to right, from near to far, or from top to bottom. Spatial order helps your reader to visualize the details of the scene as they actually exist.

Consider the order of details in this paragraph from *The Diving Bell and the Butterfly,* in which Jean-Dominique Bauby describes how his father looked on their last visit:

> Hunched in the red-upholstered armchair where he sifts through the day's newspapers, my dad bravely endures the rasp of the razor attacking his loose skin. I wrap a big towel around his shriveled neck, daub thick lather over his face, and do my best not to irritate his skin, dotted here and there with small dilated capillaries. From age and fatigue, his eyes have sunk deep into their

sockets, and his nose looks too prominent for his emaciated features. But still flaunting the plume of hair—now snow white—that has always crowned his tall frame, he has lost none of his splendor.

Here, Bauby's use of spatial order brings his father's face into clear focus. The description follows a logical order. He first discusses his father's neck, then moves his way up his father's face to describe his eyes, and finally ends up zeroing in on the hair at the top of his head.

Providing Transition for Descriptive Paragraphs

When spatial order is used to organize a descriptive paragraph, transitional expressions that show location help your reader. A few of these transitions are shown here.

Transitional Expressions Showing Location

above, below	in front of, behind	toward, away
close, far	next to, near, between	up, down

COMPREHENSION AND PRACTICE 6.2

Focusing on Objective and Subjective Description and Spatial Order

1. Read the following paragraph from "Final Cut," an essay by Atul Gawande in which he describes a room where an autopsy is to take place:

> Not long ago, I went to observe the dissection of a thirty-eight-year-old woman I had taken care of who had died after a long struggle with heart disease. The dissecting room was in the sub-basement, past the laundry and a loading dock, behind an unmarked metal door. It had high ceilings, peeling paint, and a brown tiled floor that sloped down to a central drain. There was a Bunsen burner on a countertop and an old-style grocer's hanging scale, with a big clock-face red-arrow gauge and a pan underneath, for weighing organs. On shelves all around the room there were gray portions of brain, bowel, and other organs soaking in formalin in Tupperware-like containers. The facility seemed run-down, chintzy, low-tech. On a rickety gurney in the corner was my patient, sprawled out, completely naked. The autopsy team was just beginning its work.

On a separate sheet of paper, make two lists, one of the subjective details and one of the objective ones. Then, on the lines that follow, explain whether you think the objective details or examples or the subjective ones do more to capture what the dissecting room was like and why you feel this way.

_____

_____

_____

2. On the following lines, explain the role you think spatial order plays in Gawande's paragraph.

_____

_____

_____

CHALLENGE 6.1   **Considering Purpose in Description Paragraphs**

collaboration

This chapter features several sample description paragraphs. The names of the authors of these paragraphs, with the appropriate page numbers, are listed below. Working with a classmate, take another look at the paragraphs. Then, on the lines below the names, list the primary purpose and any secondary purposes for each paragraph.

1. Scott Russell Sanders, pages 85–86

_____

_____

2. Richard Rodriguez, page 86

_____

_____

_____

3. E. B. White, page 88

_____

_____

_____

4. Jean-Dominique Bauby, pages 88–89

_____

_____

_____

FOR FURTHER EXPLORATION Description

1. Select one of the following topics. Then, following one of the strategies that you practiced in Chapter 2, prewrite on that topic. Consider sensory details and location of parts of the scene (or person).

- a distinctive, renowned, or unique restaurant, deli, bakery, or bar
- the feeling of speaking in front of a group of strangers
- what you see in a painting or photograph or hear in a song
- a normally busy place, now deserted

2. This chapter features several sample paragraphs:

- a description of memories associated with the aroma of sawdust (Scott Russell Sanders, pages 85–86)
- the story of a youngster's embarrassment at a parent's lack of knowledge (Richard Rodriguez, page 86)
- the recounting of a special place enjoyed by parent and child (E. B. White, page 88)
- the description of the face of a special person (Jean-Dominque Bauby, pages 88–89)

For this assignment, consider a similar scene or situation that you have experienced or witnessed. First, prewrite on this subject and identify a specific focus along with key supporting ideas. Then, create a paragraph of at least seven to ten sentences in which you use description to re-create the scene for your reader. Use the material in this chapter to guide you as you write.

DISCOVERING CONNECTIONS Description

For this assignment, consider this photo and one of the following questions (or another that the picture inspires). Then, using the information in this chapter to guide you, create a paragraph of at least seven to ten sentences in which you employ description to help your reader visualize the scene. Make sure you consider such key aspects as sensory details, objective and subjective description, and spatial order.

A. Pictured here is the Millennium Wheel (also known as the London Eye), located in London, England; it is the largest Ferris wheel in Europe. Using objective and subjective details, describe what you see here, and then imagine what the experience might be like if you were to visit this tourist attraction in person. If you've seen it before, what did you feel? What was the day like?

B. Now think about some of the travels you've experienced in your life. Of all the places you've visited, which has left the deepest impression upon you? Why? Try to recall the experience with as much vivid detail as possible.

✓DESCRIPTIVE PARAGRAPH CHECKLIST

☐ Does the topic sentence preview the description?

☐ Does the paragraph use sensory details? List them.

☐ Does it make effective use of both objective and subjective description? Write an *S* above every use of subjective description and an *O* above every use of objective description.

☐ Is it effectively arranged in spatial order or some other order? Explain.

☐ In your judgment, what is the best part of this paragraph? Explain.

☐ Which detail or example would be even better if it were expanded? Why?

RECAP Description

Key Terms in This Chapter	Definitions
description	the writing technique used to paint a picture in words of a scene, individual, object, or experience
sensory details	information perceived through sight, sound, taste, smell, and touch
objective description	writing that focuses on actual details and sensations
	EXAMPLE The restaurant featured wood-paneled walls and candlelit tables.
subjective description	writing that focuses on the impressions that details and sensations create within the writer
	EXAMPLE The atmosphere in the restaurant was warm and cozy.

Writing a Descriptive Paragraph

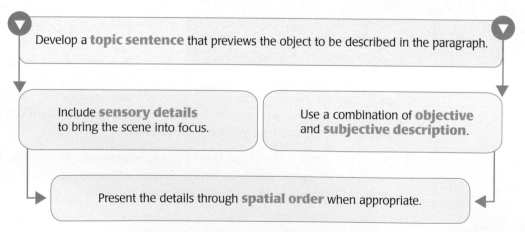

Develop a **topic sentence** that previews the object to be described in the paragraph.

Include **sensory details** to bring the scene into focus.

Use a combination of **objective** and **subjective description**.

Present the details through **spatial order** when appropriate.

Using Odyssey Online with MyWritingLab

For more practice with description, go to www.mywritinglab.com.

CHAPTER 7
Example

GETTING STARTED ...

Q I want to make sure that anyone reading my paper understands my subject the way I do. What's the best way to make sure I do this?

A Whenever you want someone to understand something the way you do, use *example* as your organizing strategy. An illustration or two can increase the odds that your reader will understand your point or message. Rely on specific and relevant examples that support your topic sentence, and try to arrange them so that they have the greatest impact on your reader.

Overview: Illustrating Your Point

You've probably said it hundreds of times yourself as you explained something: "For example, ... " We use examples to ensure that our points or statements are fully understood. In writing, **example** refers to the use of specific instances to illustrate, clarify, or back up a point.

As a writing technique, example is invaluable. Well-chosen examples help make a point powerfully. A paragraph outlining types of fads could be developed through example. A paragraph about college challenges might also use example. Beyond the classroom, you would use examples in a job application letter to prove why you are the ideal candidate for the position. In another scenario, you might write a blog about the pros and cons of various social networking sites.

Navigating This Chapter This chapter will explore the basic requirements for writing an effective example paragraph:

- providing a topic sentence that clearly states the point you will illustrate
- choosing examples that are specific
- selecting examples that are relevant
- employing an effective arrangement

Providing a Topic Sentence That States the Point You Will Illustrate

In an example paragraph, the topic sentence identifies the general idea that the examples will then clarify and illustrate. It should clearly state the point to be illustrated.

Read this paragraph from Leslie Heywood's article "One of the Girls," in which she discusses women and sports:

There are some great Nike ads out there that are a gateway to my vanished world, where I used to win races and everyone knew. In the black-and-white images, dreams, possibilities beckon to girls, welcome them into the world. Sports can give us that place, but a lot of work needs to be done before we've finished that race. Female athletes fight the same unrealistic images everyone fights, and researchers are only beginning to understand the relationship between those images and the "female athlete triad"—eating disorders and exercise compulsion, amenorrhea [abnormal stopping of menstruation]—that had me training until my bones fractured, my tendons ripped, and I stuck my fingers down my throat or simply didn't eat to stay lean. Nobody's been quite loud enough in saying that the female athlete triad is almost surely connected to all the old negative ideas about girls—girls trying to prove beyond a shadow of a doubt that they are not what those ideas say they are: weak, mild, meek, meant to serve others instead of achieving for themselves.

As you can see, the topic sentence (in italics) indicates the focus of the paragraph, her experiences as an intensely competitive athlete. The sentences that follow then provide specific examples of how the lives of top-flight runners like Heywood often differ dramatically from the photos in the Nike advertisements. When you write, keep in mind that, like Heywood, you may need to supply more than a single sentence to make each of your supporting examples clear for your reader.

Providing Specific Examples

Specific means detailed and particular. **Specific examples** give enough information so that your reader understands their meaning and significance. Generally, the more specific the information you supply is, the more convincing your examples are.

Imagine you are writing a paragraph about problems in today's schools, such as students' poor reading skills, lack of discipline in the classroom, students' personal difficulties, and unmotivated teachers. Supplying statistics or specific background about each of these examples would help your reader understand the problems. Simply stating that all of these things are problems would be less helpful and convincing.

Take a look at the following paragraph from the introduction to Eric Schlosser's *Fast Food Nation:*

Over the last three decades, fast food has infiltrated every nook and cranny of American society. An industry that began with a handful of modest hot dog and hamburger stands in southern California has spread to every corner of the nation, selling a broad range of foods wherever paying customers may be found. Fast food is now served at restaurants and drive-throughs, at stadiums, airports, zoos, high schools, elementary schools, and universities, on cruise ships, trains, and airplanes, at K-Marts, Wal-Marts, gas stations, and even at hospital cafeterias. In 1970, Americans spent about $6 billion on fast food; in 2001, they spent more than $110 billion. Americans now spend more money on fast food than on higher education, personal computers, computer software, or new cars. They spend more on fast food than on movies, books, magazines, newspapers, videos, and recorded music—combined.

Here, Schlosser provides a number of specific examples to support his main idea: that fast food is an inescapable part of today's world. These examples include the many places where fast food is available as well as the astounding amount of money Americans spend on it in the twenty-first century—$110 billion in a single year, up from $6 billion in 1970. Other examples point out a specific variety of other items that Americans spend less money on than fast food, including books, cars, college, and entertainment.

COMPREHENSION AND PRACTICE

Considering Topic Sentences and Specific Examples

7.1

1. Read this paragraph from "The Marginal World," an essay by environmentalist and writer Rachel Carson in which she discusses an area at the edge of the sea:

> The flats took on a mysterious quality as dusk approached and the last evening light was reflected from the scattered pools and creeks. Then birds became only dark shadows, with no color discernible. Sanderlings scurried across the beach like little ghosts, and here and there the darker forms of the willets stood out. Often I could come very close to them before they would start up in alarm—the sanderlings running, the willets flying up, crying. Black skimmers flew along the ocean's edge silhouetted against the dull, metallic gleam, or they went flitting above the sand like large, dimly seen moths. Sometimes they "skimmed" the winding creeks of tidal water, where little spreading surface ripples marked the presence of small fish.

On the lines that follow, explain the connection between the topic sentence and the supporting sentences.

_____

_____

_____

_____

2. On a separate sheet of paper, make a list of the specific details that Carson supplies.

3. On the lines that follow, identify the specific detail that you think provides the strongest support for Carson's main point.

_____

_____

_____

_____

Ensuring That Your Examples Are Relevant

Relevant means appropriate and connected. **Relevant examples** are directly associated with the topic. For a paper on frustrating household chores, examples such as dusting, vacuuming, and washing windows would be relevant. These tasks are all frustrating because they must be repeated so frequently. However, an example about sweeping up at your place of work would not be relevant. Although this task may indeed be frustrating, it is an employment duty, not a household chore.

Take a look at the following paragraph from "Gray Area: Thinking with a Damaged Brain," an essay by Floyd Skloot in which he discusses ways that his thinking has been affected by a brain virus:

ESL Note
See "Writing Paragraphs" on pages 555–556.

> I am so easily overloaded. I cannot read the menu or converse in a crowded, noisy restaurant. I get exhausted at Portland Trailblazers games, with all the visual and aural imagery, all the manufactured commotion, so I stopped going nine years ago. My hands are scarred from burns and cuts that occurred when I tried to cook and converse at the same time. I cannot drive in traffic, especially in our standard-transmission pickup truck. I cannot talk about, say, the fiction of Thomas Hardy while I drive; I need to be given directions in small doses rather than all at once and need those directions to be given precisely at the time I must make the required turn. This is, as Restak explains, because driving and talking about Hardy, or driving and processing information about where to turn, are handled by different parts of the brain, and my brain's parts have trouble working together.

Skloot's topic sentence indicates that the focus of the paragraph is how parts of his day-to-day life now overwhelm him. The examples that follow are all relevant because they detail a number of ordinary things that now "overload" him.

Providing an Effective Presentation

Once you've chosen the specific, relevant, and varied examples to fulfill the purpose of your document, you need to present this information so that it will have the most impact. Deciding on a method of arrangement always requires some careful thinking about your aims and the needs of your audience. No single right way to arrange a series of examples exists. One common method that you might find particularly useful, however, especially when your aim is to convince an audience of a point of view, is *emphatic order*. This method presents less important examples first and the most important ones later. Examples become increasingly convincing, with the very best—the final point your reader will remember—saved for last.

Take a look at the following paragraph about hand gestures from a psychology text by Carol Tavris and Carole Wade:

> Even the simplest gesture is subject to misunderstanding and offense. The sign of the University of Texas football team, the Longhorns, is to extend the index finger and the pinkie. In Italy and other parts of Europe this gesture means a man's wife has been unfaithful to him—a serious insult! Anita Rowe, a consultant who advises businesses on cross-cultural customs, tells of a newly hired Asian engineer in a California company. As the man left his office to lead the first meeting of his project team, his secretary crossed her fingers to wish him luck. Instead of reassuring him, her gesture thoroughly confused him: In his home country, crossing one's fingers is a sexual proposition.

Emphatic order helps Tavris and Wade make their point that serious consequences can result when simple gestures are misunderstood. The first example—that a gesture familiar to some U.S. sports fans indicates infidelity in some European countries—is surprising. More surprising is that an even more common gesture—crossed fingers indicating a hope for good luck—represents a proposition in some Asian

countries. Moving from a strong example to a stronger one underscores how innocent actions can send a far different meaning than the one intended.

Providing Transition for Example Paragraphs

ESL Note
See "Strive for Clarity,"
page 556, for more
on the importance
of coherent writing.

Consider using the following words when you write an example paragraph. These
transitional expressions will help you emphasize the significance of the illustrations
and details you include.

Transitional Expressions for Example Writing

after all	for instance	indeed	moreover	particularly
for example	in addition	in other words	of course	specifically

**COMPREHENSION
AND PRACTICE
7.2**

Considering Relevant Examples and Appropriate Order

1. Read the following paragraph from Henry Petroski's *To Engineer Is Human:
   The Role of Failure in Successful Design,* which discusses unacceptable failures
   in product design:

   > As the consequences of failure become more severe, however, the fore-
   > sight we must give to them becomes more a matter of life and death.
   > Automobiles are manufactured by the millions, but it would not do to have
   > them failing with a snap on the highways the way light bulbs and shoelaces
   > do at home. The way an automobile could fail must be anticipated so that,
   > as much as possible, a malfunction does not lead to an otherwise avoidable
   > deadly accident. Since tires are prone to flats, we want our vehicles to be
   > able to be steered safely to the side of the road when one occurs. Such a fail-
   > ure is accepted in the way light bulb and shoelace failures are, and we carry
   > a spare tire to deal with it. Other kinds of malfunctions are less acceptable.
   > We do not want the brakes on all four wheels and the emergency braking
   > system to fail us suddenly and simultaneously. We do not want the steering
   > wheel to come off in our hands as we are negotiating a snaking mountain
   > road. Certain parts of the automobile are given special attention, and in the
   > rare instances when they do fail, leading to disaster, massive lawsuits can re-
   > sult. When they become aware of a potential hazard, automobile manufac-
   > turers are compelled to eliminate what might be the causes of even the most
   > remote possibilities of design-related accidents by the massive recall cam-
   > paigns familiar to us all.

   On the following lines, briefly explain how the examples Petroski includes are
   relevant to his main point.

   _____

   _____

   _____

2. On a separate sheet of paper, identify the order Petroski uses to present his
   ideas and how this method of arrangement affects the impact of his paragraph.

collaboration

CHALLENGE 7.1 **Considering Purpose in Example Paragraphs**

This chapter features several example paragraphs. The names of the authors of these paragraphs, with the appropriate page numbers, are listed below. Working with a classmate, take another look at the paragraphs. Then, on the lines below the names, list the primary purpose and any secondary purposes for each paragraph.

1. Leslie Heywood, pages 93–94

_____

_____

_____

2. Eric Schlosser, page 94

_____

_____

_____

3. Floyd Skloot, page 96

_____

_____

_____

4. Carol Tavris and Carole Wade, page 96

_____

_____

_____

FOR FURTHER EXPLORATION Example

1. Select one of the following topics. Then, employing one of the strategies you practiced in Chapter 2, prewrite on that topic. Concentrate on useful, effective illustrations or examples.

   - shortcomings in today's high schools
   - duties as a pet owner
   - ways to cut personal expenses
   - ways to improve the quality of life in your neighborhood, town, or city

2. This chapter features several sample paragraphs:

   - a close examination of pressures faced by young women (Leslie Heywood, pages 93–94)
   - a discussion of Americans' love affair with fast food (Eric Schlosser, page 94)

- the consequences of a serious injury (Floyd Skloot, page 96)
- the ways that signs and gestures can be misinterpreted (Carol Tavris and Carole Wade, page 96)

For this assignment, think of a condition, situation, or locale like those portrayed in these paragraphs. Do some prewriting on this subject, identifying a specific focus and key supporting ideas. Create a paragraph of at least seven to ten sentences in which you rely on example to explain and illustrate your subject for your reader. Use the material in this chapter as a guide.

DISCOVERING CONNECTIONS Example

For this assignment, tackle one of the following questions or another that the photo suggests. Using the information in this chapter to guide you, write a paragraph of at least seven to ten sentences in which you include specific and relevant examples to give your reader a full view of the point you are making.

A. The zebras in this picture all look exactly the same and are all doing exactly the same thing. Now consider the deep-seated human tendency to be just like everybody else. Why do you think people find comfort in this kind of sameness? What does it take to break away, to be truly original?

B. Does this image make you dream of traveling to the Serengeti or some other wilderness area to observe and experience nature unspoiled by humans, where beautiful and powerful wild animals live as they have for thousands of years? What aspects of such a trip would excite you the most? How do you think it would affect your life?

✓EXAMPLE PARAGRAPH CHECKLIST

☐ Does the topic sentence clearly state the point to be illustrated?

☐ Does the paragraph provide specific examples? Underline any example that you feel needs to be made more specific.

☐ Are all the examples relevant? Put an * next to any example that you feel is not directly connected to the main idea of the paragraph.

☐ Are the examples effectively arranged?

☐ In your judgment, what is the best part of this paragraph? Explain.

☐ Which detail or example would be even better if it were expanded? Why?

RECAP Example

Key Terms in This Chapter	Definitions
example	the writing technique that uses specific instances to illustrate, clarify, or back up the point being made
specific examples	illustrative material that is detailed and particular
	EXAMPLE In the center of the room was *the old, dusty, mahogany roll-top desk.*
relevant examples	illustrative information that is appropriate and directly connected to the topic
	EXAMPLE The *household chores* I find most annoying are *dusting, vacuuming,* and *washing windows.*

Writing an Example Paragraph

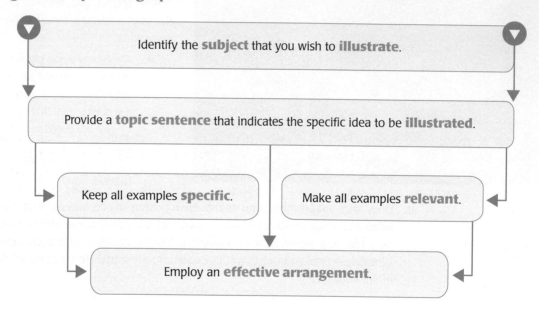

Identify the **subject** that you wish to **illustrate**.

Provide a **topic sentence** that indicates the specific idea to be **illustrated**.

Keep all examples **specific**.

Make all examples **relevant**.

Employ an **effective arrangement**.

Using Odyssey Online with MyWritingLab

For more practice with exemplification, go to www.mywritinglab.com.

CHAPTER 8
Process

GETTING STARTED ...

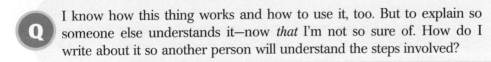

Q I know how this thing works and how to use it, too. But to explain so someone else understands it—now *that* I'm not so sure of. How do I write about it so another person will understand the steps involved?

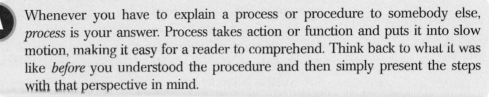

A Whenever you have to explain a process or procedure to somebody else, *process* is your answer. Process takes action or function and puts it into slow motion, making it easy for a reader to comprehend. Think back to what it was like *before* you understood the procedure and then simply present the steps with that perspective in mind.

Overview: Explaining How It Happens or How to Do It

Whenever you explain how something occurs or how to do something, you are using **process.** There are basically three types of process writing. One type, called *process analysis,* explains, for example, how tornadoes form or how certain foods contribute to cholesterol problems. A second type, called *process narrative,* explains such procedures as organizing a weekend park cleanup or performing a chemistry experiment. The most common type, often called *how-to writing,* usually appears as, for example, instructions for filling out a financial aid form or assembling a futon frame. Beyond the classroom, process will help you prepare product manuals or profile pages on social networking sites.

Navigating This Chapter This chapter will explore the basic requirements for writing an effective process paragraph:

- including a topic sentence that clearly states the procedure or technique
- using the imperative mood (*you*) when it's appropriate
- dividing the process into simple, logical steps
- relying on linear order

Including a Topic Sentence That Clearly States the Process

An effective topic sentence for a process paragraph must focus on something that can be adequately explained in a brief space. It must clearly state the specific process—procedure, technique, or routine—that the other sentences in the paragraph will later explain.

Take a look at the relationship between the topic sentence and the supporting sentences in the following paragraph from a book on solving children's sleep problems written by Richard Ferber, M.D.:

> Bedtime means separation, which is difficult for children, especially very young ones. *Simply sending a toddler or young child off to bed alone is not fair and may be scary for him.* And it means you will miss what can be one of the best times of the day. So set aside ten to thirty minutes to do something special with your child before bed. Avoid teasing, scary stories, or anything that will excite your child at this time. Save the wrestling and tussling for other times of the day. You might both enjoy a discussion, quiet play, or story reading. But let your child know that your special time together will not extend beyond the time you and he have agreed upon, then don't go beyond those limits. It is a good idea to tell your child when the time is almost up or when you have only two or three more pages to read, and don't give in for an extra story. Your child will learn the rules only if you enforce them. If both you and he know just what is going to happen, there won't be the arguments and tension that arise when there is uncertainty.

Ferber's topic sentence (shown in italics) indicates that the paragraph concerns bedtime for children, specifically how difficult it can be. The rest of the paragraph lays out a procedure that will make a difficult time far easier for both parents and children.

Using the Imperative Mood: *You*

With instructions, it makes sense to address the reader directly, using the **imperative mood**, often called the *command.* When you use the imperative mood, the subject is not stated but *understood* to be the person reading the piece. When you write, "Close the kitchen window," you are actually saying, "*You* close the kitchen window."

Note the use of the imperative mood in this paragraph from a textbook on study skills by James F. Shepherd, which concerns identifying a person's level of concentration:

> When you begin to study, make a note of the time. Then, when you first become aware that your attention is not focused on studying, record the time again. Compare the two times and make a note of how many minutes you studied before you lost your concentration. Next, spend a few minutes doing something other than studying; you might stand up and stretch or look out the window. When you begin to study again, make another note of how long you concentrate.

The use of imperative mood in this paragraph means that Shepherd *directly* relates the instructions for maintaining concentration to you as the reader. In fact, the subject is the word *you,* even though it isn't always stated.

COMPREHENSION
AND PRACTICE
8.1

Considering Topic Sentences and Imperative Mood

1. Read the following paragraph, an explanation from a Web site called videojug.com on how to make a serve in tennis:

> When serving, you start each game behind the baseline, to the right of the center mark. Have your front foot at an angle but have your back foot running approximately parallel to the baseline. This will, quite naturally, place you sideways on to the court. Your aim is to put the tennis ball into the service box diagonally opposite. If you're new to the game, just aim for the middle of the box.

On the following lines, briefly explain how the topic sentence prepares the reader for the discussion to follow.

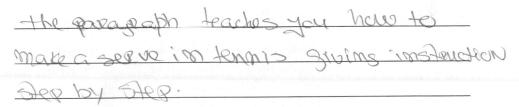
the paragraph teaches you how to make a serve in tennis giving instruction step by step.

2. On a separate sheet of paper, make a list of the steps involved in this process.

3. How does the use of the imperative mood help make this process clear for a reader? Briefly explain on the lines that follow.

this process is not clear enough for a reader need more details

Dividing the Process into Simple, Logical Steps

The key to successful process writing is to break down the process into small, manageable steps and then to spell out these steps in detail. For example, although blood circulation through the human body is a highly complex process, you can describe it fairly accurately in four basic steps: (1) The heart pumps oxygenated blood to body tissues through the arteries and capillaries. (2) The veins carry the blood back to the heart. (3) The heart pumps the blood to the lungs to be oxygenated again. (4) The blood returns to the heart to be circulated through the body again. Breaking the process down into discrete steps, each with its own function, makes the complex process easier to understand.

Consider how the steps are presented in this paragraph from Simon Winchester's book *The Professor and the Madman: A Tale of Murder, Insanity, and the Making of the Oxford English Dictionary:*

> The volunteers' duties were simple enough, if onerous. They would write to the society offering their services in reading certain books; they would be asked to read and make wordlists of all that they read, and would then be asked to look super-specifically, for certain words that currently interested the

> dictionary team. Each volunteer would take a slip of paper, write at its top left-hand side the target word, and below, also on the left, the date of the details that followed. These were, in order, the title of the book or paper, its volume and page number, and then, below that, the full sentence that illustrated the use of the target word. It was a technique that has been undertaken by lexicographers to the present day.

This paragraph explains the process in distinct, easily understood, detailed steps. As a result, a reader can understand the process that eventually produced the massive multivolume dictionary that is among the most well-known and most often used reference works of all time.

Relying on Linear Order

Effective process writing often depends on **linear order,** or the arrangement of steps in the order they occur. Writing about the process of taking a photograph with an SLR digital camera in manual mode would call for linear order: (1) adjust the focus; (2) change the setting to allow the proper amount of light through the lens; (3) push the shutter button to take the picture. Unless the steps are performed in this order, the photograph would probably not turn out well.

Consider the linear order of steps in this paragraph concerning a technique called pure contour drawing from Betty Edwards's *Drawing on the Right Side of the Brain:*

> Do not turn around to look at the paper. Observing your hand, draw the edges you see one bit at a time. Your eyes will see and your pencil will record bit by bit the changing configuration of the contour. At the same time you will be aware of the relationship of that contour to the whole configuration of complex contours that is the whole hand. You may draw outside or inside contours or move from one to the other and back again. Don't be concerned about whether the drawing will look like your hand. It probably won't since you can't monitor proportions, etc. By confining your perceptions to small bits at a time, you can learn to see things *exactly as they are*, in the artist's mode of seeing.

To create a drawing in this way, you must follow each step as Edwards lays them out. If you perform the steps out of order, the result may be unsatisfying.

Keep in mind that if you are explaining an unusual or specialized process, you may need to define special terms. In any how-to process paragraph, you will need to specify the materials or tools needed to carry out the process. In most cases, this information should come right after the topic sentence so that the reader will be fully prepared to complete the process.

Providing Transition for Process Paragraphs

Process writing places events in time order. Therefore, transitional expressions that signal that order help your reader. See the list below for transitions useful in a process paragraph.

ESL Note
See "Strive for Clarity,"
page 556, for more
on the importance
of coherent writing.

Transitional Expressions for Process Writing

Beginning	*Continuing*			*Ending*
begin by	as soon as	second step, etc.	until	finally
initially	next	then	while	last

**COMPREHENSION
AND PRACTICE
8.2**

Considering Carefully Divided Steps and Linear Order

1. Read the following paragraph from Carla Stephens's "Drownproofing," in which she explains how to teach children a technique that even nonswimmers can use to stay afloat:

> When teaching your children, it's advisable to stand with them in shoulder-deep water. Have them bend forward to practice the breathing and arm movements. If they swallow water, be patient and encourage them to try again. Once they're comfortable with the procedure, move into deeper water near the side of the pool to coordinate the floating, breathing and body movements. Water just deep enough for them to go under is sufficient. Remember, all movements should be easy and relaxed.

On a separate sheet of paper, make a list of the steps involved in teaching children this technique. On the lines that follow, briefly explain how the presentation of steps acknowledges that the reader will be teaching children.

the paragraph has no transitional expressions but still you can understand the steps.

2. On the lines that follow, briefly explain why Stephens has used strict linear order to present this process.

she uses the order the steps occur

CHALLENGE 8.1 **Considering Purpose in Process Paragraphs**

collaboration

This chapter features several sample process paragraphs. The names of the authors of these paragraphs, with the appropriate page numbers, are listed below. Working with a classmate, take another look at the paragraphs. Then, on the lines below the names, list the primary purpose and any secondary purposes for each paragraph.

1. Richard Ferber, page 102

_____

_____

_____

2. James F. Shepherd, page 102

_____

_____

_____

3. Simon Winchester, pages 103–104

_____

_____

_____

4. Bettly Edwards, page 104

_____

_____

_____

FOR FURTHER EXPLORATION Process

1. Select one of the following topics. Then, using one of the strategies that you practiced in Chapter 2, prewrite on that topic. Concentrate on the steps involved in the process:

   - how to braid hair in a particular style
   - how an accident occurred
   - how to make a turn on a snowboard
   - how to make an online financial transfer

2. This chapter features several sample paragraphs:

   - a procedure for parents to follow to streamline the bedtime ritual (Richard Ferber, page 102)
   - steps to take to work on improved concentration and performance (James F. Shepherd, page 102)
   - an explanation of the process followed to create an elaborate project (Simon Winchester, pages 103–104)
   - the process to follow in order to complete an art or craft project (Betty Edwards, page 104)

For this assignment, think of a process or procedure you understand that is similar to these. After completing some prewriting, identify and express your focus in a clear topic sentence. Isolate the ideas that do the best job of explaining the process or procedure to your reader, using the material in this chapter to guide you. Then create a paragraph of at least seven to ten sentences.

DISCOVERING CONNECTIONS Process

For this assignment, look at the photo and respond to one of the following questions (or another that the photo inspires). Then, referring to the information in this chapter as a guide, write a paragraph of at least seven to ten sentences. As you write, concentrate on expressing the process in simple, logical steps, with the appropriate use of the imperative mood and linear order.

A. The history of Stonehenge, the enormous monolithic ruin in Amesbury, England, some ninety miles west of London, is estimated to extend back to 3000 B.C. As you imagine it, how would a group of people, without the benefit of any of the construction equipment available today, erect such a massive structure?

B. By anyone's estimation, this undertaking had to have been extraordinary, seemingly beyond the abilities and resources of the people who built it. What process do you follow when you face a task that seems almost beyond your capabilities?

✓ PROCESS PARAGRAPH CHECKLIST

☐ Does the topic sentence clearly state the procedure or technique to be presented?

☐ Does it use the imperative mood (*you*)?

☐ Is the process divided into simple, logical steps? Do you feel any step should be further subdivided to make it easier for the reader to perform the process? Put a ✓ next to any step that needs to be divided.

☐ Are the steps presented in linear order? Underline any step that is out of linear order, and then draw a line to the spot in the paragraph where it actually belongs.

☐ In your judgment, what is the best part of this paragraph? Explain.

☐ Which detail or example would be even better if it were expanded? Why?

RECAP   Process

Key Terms in This Chapter	Definitions
process	the writing technique that explains how to do something or how something occurs Three types of process writing include 1. *process analysis* (how something is done or occurs) 2. *process narrative* (how you did something) 3. *a set of instructions* (how to do something)
imperative mood	designating verb usage that expresses commands or direct address The subject of the sentence in the imperative mood is understood as the reader (*you*) rather than stated directly. EXAMPLE (*You*) Move your books and papers into the other room, please.
linear order	an arrangement of steps in the order of their occurrence

Writing a Process Paragraph

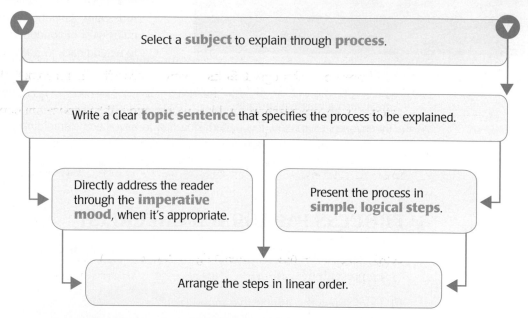

Select a **subject** to explain through **process**.

Write a clear **topic sentence** that specifies the process to be explained.

Directly address the reader through the **imperative mood**, when it's appropriate.

Present the process in **simple, logical steps**.

Arrange the steps in linear order.

Using Odyssey Online with MyWritingLab

For more practice with process analysis, go to www.mywritinglab.com.

CHAPTER 9
Definition

GETTING STARTED ...

 Q Even though my topic is a little complex and abstract, I have a good understanding of it. But how do I present its meaning so that another person will understand it the way I do?

 A To convey your understanding of a topic—the *meaning* that you understand or have assigned to something—use *definition*. Definition establishes borders or distinctions of meaning for a reader, enabling you to seize control of important concepts in your writing, interpreting and translating them for your audience. When you define, you identify the essence of your subject in a topic sentence and then supply supporting sentences that elaborate on and illustrate it.

Overview: Making Meaning Crystal Clear

No matter what your topic is, your job is to communicate your ideas about that topic clearly and precisely. Through **definition**, you can specify the meanings of actions, ideas, places, and things. Beyond the classroom, you could use definition to write mission statements for organizations and businesses and public service announcements about free screenings for sleep disorders.

Navigating This Chapter This chapter will explore the basic requirements for writing an effective definition paragraph:

- providing a topic sentence that highlights the term to be defined
- understanding the elements of an effective definition
- recognizing all the possible meanings of the term defined
- enhancing definition through synonyms, negation, and etymology

Providing a Topic Sentence That Highlights the Term to Be Defined

An effective definition paragraph begins with a topic sentence that highlights the term to be defined. In fact, the topic sentence of a definition paragraph is often a brief definition itself. For example, if you were defining your view of what an *optimist* is, you might begin this way:

EXAMPLE An optimist is a person who sees good even in the worst situations and believes that, somehow, things will always work out for the best.

Read this paragraph from "Weasel Words" by William Lutz, in which he discusses how some businesses twist the meaning of the word *new*:

> *What makes a product "new"?* Some products have been around for a long time, yet every once in a while you discover that they are being advertised as "new." Well, an advertiser can call a product new if there has been "a material functional change" in the product. What is "a material functional change," you ask? Good question. In fact, it's such a good question it's being asked all the time. It's up to the manufacturer to prove that the product has undergone such a change. And if the manufacturer isn't challenged on the change, then there's no one to stop it. Moreover, the change does not have to be an improvement in the product. One manufacturer added artificial lemon scent to a cleaning product and called it "new and improved," even though the product did not clean any better than without the lemon scent. The manufacturer defended the use of the word "new" on the grounds that the artificial scent changed the chemical formula of the product and therefore constituted "a material functional change."

The topic sentence, expressed in question form and shown in italics clearly identifies the term to be defined—*new*—and suggests that the answer isn't as obvious as one might think. The supporting sentences provide examples of how unscrupulous companies label items as new even when the difference between old and new formulations is minimal.

Understanding the Pattern of an Effective Definition

A dictionary definition follows a simple pattern. It first identifies the general class to which the term belongs. Then it gives the special, or distinguishing, characteristics that set the word apart.

EXAMPLE   ┌─── class ───┐   ┌─── distinguished characteristics ───────┐
A flash drive is a *computer device* that *enables a user to store large amounts of information on a unit smaller than a pack of gum*.

Paragraphs that define should generally follow this **pattern of an effective definition.** However, most definition paragraphs require greater elaboration. Especially with abstract subjects such as fear, you will need to include personal interpretation or experience. For such words, in addition to class and distinguishing characteristics, you should also provide specific, concrete examples and details for support.

Note the elements of definition in the following paragraph from "The Search for Marvin Gardens" by writer John McPhee. In this article, he discusses the classic board game *Monopoly* and the actual by-ways of Atlantic City, New Jersey, the names of which make up the blocks on the game board:

> Marvin Gardens is the one color-block Monopoly property that is not in Atlantic City. It is a suburb within a suburb, secluded. It is a planned compound of seventy-two handsome houses set on curvilinear private streets under yews and cedars, poplars and willows. The compound was built around 1920, in

Margate, New Jersey, and consists of solid buildings of stucco, brick, and wood, with slate roofs, tile roofs, multi-mullioned porches, Giraldic towers, and Spanish grilles. Marvin Gardens, the ultimate outwash of Monopoly, is a citadel and sanctuary of the middle class.

The elements of an effective definition are at work here. The opening sentence indicates that, unlike the other locales on the *Monopoly* game board, Marvin Gardens isn't actually in Atlantic City, New Jersey. The next two sentences specify the distinguishing characteristics of this area. Marvin Gardens is a small, planned compound of seventy-two houses on tree-lined private streets in a suburb near Atlantic City. The other sentences then provide additional specific details, including the name of the city that is home to Marvin Gardens. Together this information leads to a complete picture of this small neighborhood made famous by a simple board game.

COMPREHENSION AND PRACTICE

9.1

Considering Topic Sentences and the Elements of Definition

1. Look at this paragraph from Robert Jourdain's book *Music, the Brain, and Ecstasy: How Music Captures Our Imagination* in which he offers a definition of the musical scale:

   Like the scale found at the bottom of a road map, a musical scale provides units of measure, but for pitch space rather than geographical space. The basic unit is called a *half-step* (or a *semitone*). Every key along a piano keyboard represents a half-step. From C to C-sharp is a half-step, and so is from E to F. In the scale system we're accustomed to in the West, there are twelve half-steps (and twelve piano keys) in any octave, say, from middle C to the C above.

   On the lines that follow, briefly explain how the topic sentence contributes to the description of a *musical scale*.

   _____

   _____

   _____

   _____

2. On a separate sheet of paper, explain the role that the elements of an effective definition play in Jourdain's paragraph.

3. In each sentence of definition below, underline the word that is being defined. Then circle the class to which the word belongs, and double underline the distinguishing characteristics that set it apart. Use the example as a guide.

EXAMPLE

A diplomat is a government representative who conducts relationships involving trade, treaties, and other official business with the government of another nation.

a. A gecko is a tropical lizard with soft skin, a short, stout body, large head, and suction pads on its feet.

b. A democracy is a form of government in which the people hold ruling power through elected officials.

c. The nuclear family is a social unit that consists of parents and the children they raise.

Recognizing the Full Effect of the Term Defined

Preparing an effective definition paragraph may also mean taking into account all the possible meanings for the term you are defining. To do this, you need to consider both the **denotation**, or literal meaning of the word, and its **connotations**— all the associations that also come with the word.

For example, the denotation of *clever* is its literal meaning, *quick-witted* and *intelligent.* To call a child clever is a compliment. However, to call a politician or a criminal clever might imply something negative, such as the person's ability to manipulate or take advantage of others. Keep these kinds of connotations in mind when you are writing a definition paragraph.

Consider the following paragraph from Esther Dyson's article "Cyberspace: If You Don't Love It, Leave It" in which she offers another way to define *cyberspace:*

> In the same way, you could think of cyberspace as a giant and unbounded world of virtual real estate. Some property is privately owned and rented out; other property is common land; some places are suitable for children, and others are best avoided by all but the kinkiest citizens. Unfortunately, it's those places that are now capturing the popular imagination: places that offer bomb-making instructions, pornography, advice on how to procure stolen credit cards. They make cyberspace sound like a nasty place.

In this paragraph, Dyson takes the term *cyberspace* and makes it more concrete for the reader by comparing it to a more familiar concept, *real estate.* Her definition works well in part because of what people understand real estate to mean. As she indicates, people *denotatively* think of real estate in terms of property that is owned, rented, or shared. But, people also *connotatively* think of real estate as something valuable, something that can be a source of pride when it is well-maintained and a source of annoyance and fear when it isn't. Through this use of denotation and connotation, Dyson emphasizes that the virtual real estate has the same attributes and qualities as its actual equivalent. As a result, *cyberspace* as a concept is a bit easier to understand.

Enhancing Definition through Synonyms, Negation, and Etymology

As you develop a definition paragraph, these additional strategies are also useful: *synonyms, negation,* and *etymology.*

Synonyms are words that hold a similar meaning. Using a synonym to explain a term is a great way to add clarification to the meaning you are providing. If you are explaining that your best friend is *naïve,* noting that by *naïve* you mean *unsophisticated* will prepare your reader for the other supporting examples and details to follow.

In some cases, you may find that the best way to define something is to explain what it *isn't,* a technique called **negation.** By writing that *intelligence* isn't merely the knowledge of a great volume of facts, you also suggest that being intelligent involves much more, such as understanding the significance of and connections among these facts.

You may also occasionally find a word's origin and historical development—its **etymology**—useful. The etymology of a word is generally available in any collegiate dictionary, although an unabridged print or online dictionary such as *Oxford English Dictionary (OED)* is the best place to find extensive etymological information. If you've ever wondered, for example, whether the world is slanted against left-handed people, consider the etymology of two words, *gauche* and *adroit. Gauche* is defined as "lacking tact or social graces." It comes from a French word, *gauche,* which means *left. Adroit* is defined as "deft and skillful," and it too is derived from a French word, *droit,* which indicates *right.* What is gained by an examination of the etymology of these two words is the implication that left-handed people are somehow awkward or unrefined, whereas right-handed people are capable and proficient.

Consider this paragraph from *Thereby Hangs a Tale: Stories of Curious Word Origins* by Charles Earle Funk:

> The Greek *schole,* which was the original source of *school,* once meant just the opposite from what the schoolboy of today thinks of that institution. It meant vacation, leisure, rest. The education of a Greek boy was by private teachers in reading, writing, arithmetic, singing, and gymnastics. But no man ever considered his education to be completed. His leisure time was spent in listening to the discussions of learned men, and thus this product of leisure, this use of one's spare time came also to be called *schole.* Eventually the Greeks used the term for the lectures or discussions themselves, and ultimately it included as well the place wherein the instruction was given. It was the latter sense, which descended to English use.

Here, by turning to the surprising etymology of the common word *school,* Funk adds another dimension of meaning.

Providing Transition for Definition Paragraphs

One way to ensure that the point you are making is clear for your reader is to supply transition. With definition writing, you may find the following transitional expressions useful:

ESL Note
See "Strive for Clarity," page 556, for more on the importance of coherent writing.

Transitional Expressions for Definition Writing

accordingly	in addition	in other words	on the whole	therefore
indeed	in fact	in the same way	specifically	thus

COMPREHENSION AND PRACTICE

9.2

Considering Denotation, Connotation, and Other Aspects of Definition

1. Read this paragraph from Francine Prose's "Gossip":

> I'm even fond of the word [gossip], its etymology, its origins in the Anglo-Saxon term "godsibbe" for god-parent, relative, its meaning widening by the Renaissance to include friends, cronies and later what one does with one's cronies. One gossips. Paring away its less flattering modern connotations, we discover a kind of synonym for connection, for community, and this, it seems to me, is the primary function of gossip. It maps out ties, reminds us of what sort of people we know and what manner of lives they lead, confirms our sense of who we are, how we live and where we have come from. The roots of the grapevine are inextricably entwined with our own. Who knows how much of our sense of the world has reached us on its branches, how often, as babies, we dropped off to sleep to the rhythms of family gossip? I've often thought that gossip's bad name might be cleared by calling it "oral tradition"; for what, after all, is an oral tradition but the stories of other lives, other eras, legends from a time when human traffic with spirits and gods was considered fit material for gossipy speculation.

On the following lines, briefly explain what you think Prose means in the third sentence when she refers to the "less flattering modern connotations" of gossip.

_____

_____

_____

2. Take another look at the explanations of denotation, connotation, etymology, and synonyms that appear on the previous pages. Then, on a separate sheet of paper, explain the role they play in the impact of Prose's paragraph.

CHALLENGE 9.1 **Considering Purpose in Definition Paragraphs**

collaboration

This chapter features several sample definition paragraphs. The names of the authors of these paragraphs, with the appropriate page numbers, are listed below. Working with a classmate, take another look at the paragraphs. Then, on the lines below the names, list the primary purpose and any secondary purposes for each paragraph.

1. William Lutz, page 110

_____

_____

_____

_____

2. John McPhee, pages 110–111

_____

_____

_____

_____

3. Esther Dyson, page 112

_____

_____

_____

_____

4. Charles Earle Funk, page 113

_____

_____

_____

_____

FOR FURTHER EXPLORATION Definition

1. Select one of the following topics. Then, relying on one of the strategies that you practiced in Chapter 2, prewrite on that topic. Focus on the qualities of the term.

   - conscience
   - an effective mentor or coach
   - a sports, music, dance, computer, or religious fanatic
   - a perfect date

2. This chapter features several sample paragraphs:

   - an explanation of the deliberate misuse of a word (William Lutz, page 110)
   - a source for a name of a ordinary object, in this case, part of a board game (John McPhee, pages 110–111)
   - an explanation of a real space or area that can be difficult to comprehend (Esther Dyson, page 112)
   - the background and origin of a commonly understood word (Charles Earle Funk, page 113)

For this assignment, consider a concept, object, situation, word, or phrase similar to the ones discussed in these paragraphs. Then prewrite on this topic. Once you have identified a specific focus and strong supporting ideas, create a paragraph of at least seven to ten sentences in which you use definition to help your reader share your understanding of the subject. Use the material in this chapter to guide you.

DISCOVERING CONNECTIONS   Definition

For this assignment, consider the photograph and answer one of the following questions, or another that the photo inspires. Using the information in this chapter to guide you, write a paragraph of at least seven to ten sentences in which you employ definition to identify the special qualities of your topic. As you develop your paragraph, make sure that you take into account the elements of an effective definition and the full meaning of the term and make appropriate use of synonyms, etymology, and negation.

A. The Great Wall of China, running more than 4,000 miles from east to west across China, is often described as a wonder of the world. In your view, what characteristics or elements are necessary for something to qualify as a wonder of the world?

B. When it comes to a vacation or trip of some kind, many people would term China an exotic destination. When you use or hear the word *exotic,* what does it mean to you? What special aspects or features do you expect in relation to the term?

✓ DEFINITION PARAGRAPH CHECKLIST

- ☐ Does the topic sentence highlight the term to be defined?

- ☐ Does it include the elements of an effective definition? What are they?

- ☐ Does it take into consideration both the denotation and connotations of

- ☐ the term?

- ☐ Are any examples or details too general or too abstract to be effective? Underline it and suggest a concrete example that might be used instead.

- ☐ Have appropriate uses been made of synonyms, negation, and etymology?

- ☐ In your judgment, what is the best part of this paragraph? Explain.

- ☐ Which detail or example would be even better if it were expanded? Why?

RECAP Definition

Key Terms in This Chapter	Definitions
definition	the writing technique used to specify the meanings of both concrete and abstract objects, ideas, events, or persons
pattern of an effective definition	two-step method of defining by first identifying the general class to which the term belongs and then listing its distinguishing characteristics
	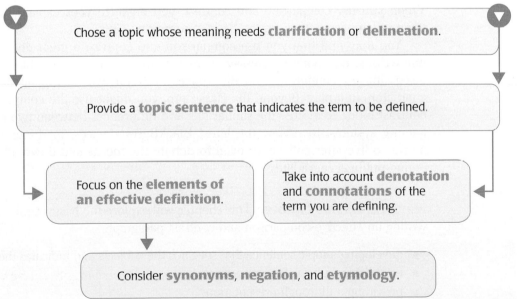
denotation	the direct, specific meaning of a word, as listed in the dictionary
connotations	the additional, subjective meanings a word suggests, deriving from the associations or emotional overtones it has
synonym	a word that has a meaning similar to another
negation	a technique of definition that involves explaining what a subject is not
etymology	the record of a word's origin and historical development

Writing a Definition Paragraph

Chose a topic whose meaning needs **clarification** or **delineation**.

Provide a **topic sentence** that indicates the term to be defined.

Focus on the **elements of an effective definition**.

Take into account **denotation** and **connotations** of the term you are defining.

Consider **synonyms**, **negation**, and **etymology**.

 **Using Odyssey Online with MyWritingLab**
For more practice with definition, go to www.mywritinglab.com.

CHAPTER 10

Comparison and Contrast

GETTING STARTED ...

Q I want to write about two subjects that have similarities and differences. What's the best way for me to do this?

A Use the *comparison and contrast* mode. Through comparison and contrast, you clarify the subjects by matching them or pitting one against the other. Include a topic sentence that expresses your subjects and the focus—on comparison or contrast. Then lay out a clear basis for comparison or contrast and arrange your supporting ideas so that they have the most impact on your reader. That's all there is to it.

Overview: Expressing Similarities and Differences

Because we often make decisions after considering alternatives, mastering the writing technique that examines alternatives, **comparison and contrast**, is important. To compare is to examine *similarities;* to contrast is to examine *differences.* When you use comparison and contrast, you organize your explanation of one thing relative to another, on the basis of common points.

You may find that you use comparison and contrast a great deal in academic writing, especially with essay examinations. This pattern might be ideal for discussing the similarities and differences between two eras in history or two characters in a play. Beyond the classroom, you might use the comparison and contrast mode to discuss the similarities and differences between two electronic gaming systems, to review the latest BlackBerry devices, to discuss the best places to live after college, or even to debate the merits and downfalls of competing political candidates.

Navigating This Chapter This chapter will explore the basic requirements for writing an effective comparison and contrast paragraph:

- developing a topic sentence that specifies the subjects and indicates the focus
- establishing a basis for comparison
- providing a thorough presentation
- arranging ideas effectively

Providing a Topic Sentence That Specifies Both Subjects and Indicates the Focus

The topic sentence of a comparison and contrast paragraph specifies the two subjects to be examined. It also indicates whether the focus is on similarities or differences.

Take a look at this paragraph from Mary Pipher's *Reviving Ophelia:*

> *Analysis of classroom videos shows that boys receive more classroom attention and detailed instruction than girls.* They are called on more often than girls and are asked more abstract, open-ended, and complex questions. Boys are more likely to be praised for academics and intellectual work, while girls are more likely to be praised for their clothing, behaving properly, and obeying rules. Boys are likely to be criticized for their behavior, while girls are criticized for intellectual inadequacy. The message to boys tends to be: "You're smart, if you would just settle down and get to work." The message to girls is often: "Perhaps you're just not good at this. You've followed the rules and haven't succeeded."

Pipher's topic sentence (shown in italics) indicates her subject and her focus—the contrast in levels and types of attention that boys and girls receive in the classroom. The supporting sentences then follow through on that contrast. They discuss differences in questions, praise, criticism, and underlying messages that male and female students receive in the typical U.S. classroom.

Establishing Your Basis for Comparison

Whenever you use comparison and contrast, you need to establish your **basis for comparison.** In other words, once you have chosen your subjects and your focus, you must specify the characteristics or elements you are going to examine.

For example, in a paragraph examining two brands of laptop computers, you might examine *purchase price, screen size, operating system,* and *ease of use.* Once you have established this basis of comparison, the next step is to discuss each brand in relation to these features. To be sure you include comparable information for both brands on every point, you may find it helpful to construct a planning chart first.

	Computer 1	Computer 2
Price		
Screen size		
Operating system		
Ease of use		

Look at this paragraph by N. L. Gage and David C. Berliner, which contrasts experienced physicists with newcomers to the field:

> How do expert physicists differ from novices? One difference is that experts take more time than novices in studying a problem. But once they start to work, they solve problems faster than novices do. The experts also seem more often than novices to construct an abstract representation of the problems in their minds. That is, in their working memory they hold mental representations of the blocks, pulleys, inclined planes, levers, or whatever they need to solve a problem. Expert physicists also tend to classify new problems more frequently. They may decide a problem is a type-X problem, to be solved by using the laws of inclined planes. Or they may see the problem as belonging to

the type that deals with forces, pulleys, and blocks, which are always solvable by using some variation of Newton's second law, F = MA (Force = Mass x Acceleration).

As you can see, the basis for comparison is clear. Expert physicists differ from novices in terms of how much time they spend solving problems and how they study, visualize, and classify problems.

COMPREHENSION AND PRACTICE

10.1

Consider Topic Sentences and a Clear Basis for Comparison

1. Read the following paragraph from *Language and the Sexes* by Francine Frank and Frank Ashen:

> Consider the following claim: Women and men don't speak the same. Admittedly, in the United States of America, most people speak English. But they speak it differently, and the differences between women's and men's speech go beyond the variations in regional speech which we call dialects. Everybody knows that men and women *sound* different when they speak. Women have high-pitched voices, which we may sometimes find to be shrill. They speak rapidly and often sound "emotional." Men, on the other hand, have deep resonant voices; they speak more slowly than women. It is true that children of both sexes sound more or less alike, but when boys' voices change at puberty, the differences become clearcut. In matters of usage, women's speech tends to be more polite and more "grammatical" than that of men.

On the following lines, briefly explain the relationship between the topic sentence and the supporting sentences that follow it.

_____

_____

_____

_____

2. On the lines that follow, list the ideas that represent the basis for comparison in this paragraph.

_____

_____

_____

_____

3. In the eighth sentence, Frank and Ashen include details about children's voices. On a separate sheet of paper, explain why you think they included this information in a discussion otherwise devoted to adults.

Providing a Thorough and Specific Presentation

To develop an effective comparison and contrast paragraph, you need to examine the subjects fully. Of course, no rule sets an automatic number of points of comparison you should establish. Common sense indicates, however, that the more thoroughly you examine the subjects, the more likely your reader will understand your point. Therefore, regardless of the number of points you are discussing about your subjects, present them in full detail.

Consider this paragraph from Amy Tan's "Mother Tongue," in which she discusses the diction she uses to talk about her own writing:

> Recently, I was made keenly aware of the different Englishes I do use. I was giving a talk to a large group of people, the same talk I had already given to half a dozen other groups. The nature of the talk was about my writing, my life, and my book, *The Joy Luck Club.* The talk was going along well enough, until I remembered one major difference that made the whole talk sound wrong. My mother was in the room. And it was perhaps the first time she had heard me give a lengthy speech, using the kind of English I have never used with her. I was saying things like "The intersection of memory upon imagination" and "There is an aspect of my fiction that relates to thus-and-thus"—a speech filled with carefully wrought grammatical phrases, burdened, it suddenly seemed to me, with nominalized forms, past perfect tenses, conditional phrases, all the forms of standard English that I had learned in school and through books, the forms of English I did not use at home with my mother.

Here, Tan specifies in great detail the characteristics that mark the language she uses as a professional writer discussing her craft. As she notes, this formal speech differs considerably from the English she customarily uses in informal conversations with her mother.

Arranging Your Ideas Effectively

When you write a comparison and contrast paragraph, you can choose between two organizational plans. The first alternative, the **block format**, examines all the elements of subject A and then all the same elements in the same order for subject B. Imagine, for example, you were writing a paragraph about two online social networking sites. If you used the block format, you would first examine one site in terms of privacy settings, ease of use, and popularity. Then you would examine the same criteria in the same order for the second site. Here is an example of a paragraph from an astronomy textbook by Jay M. Pasachoff:

> Venus and the Earth are sister planets: their sizes, masses, and densities are about the same. But they are as different from each other as the wicked sisters were from Cinderella. The Earth is lush; it has oceans and rainstorms of water, an atmosphere containing oxygen, and creatures swimming in the sea, flying in the air, and walking on the ground. On the other hand, Venus is a hot, foreboding planet with temperatures constantly over 750 K (900°F), a planet on which life seems unlikely to develop. Why is Venus like that? How did these harsh conditions come about? Can it happen to us here on Earth?

This paragraph is arranged in the block method. First, the writer discusses various characteristics of Earth, and then he notes the contrasting characteristics of Venus.

The other method of arrangement is the **alternating format**. When you follow this method, you switch back and forth between subjects as you examine each point. With the paragraph about two online social networking sites, you would first discuss how private you can make your profile on site 1 and then how private you can do so on site 2. Next you would explain how easy to use site, 1 is and then how easy to use site 2 is, and so on.

Note the organizational plan of this paragraph from "Dazzled in Disneyland," an article by Aubrey Menen:

> There are two kinds of legends: with one sort we can get inside them; with the other we are always spectators. I suppose there can be no American male who has not, at some time in his life, found himself alone in the countryside and explored Tom Sawyer island, or fought Indians, or crept on his belly up to a paleface fort. But nobody, I think, at any age plays Water Rat and Toad, or goes into Mole's house, or plays Prince Charming or Cinderella (unless driven to it by sentimental elders). These stories are too complete to have room for the outsider. We would know what to say to Pinocchio if we met him, or the Three Ugly Sisters. But we do not imagine ourselves being these people. A lesser man than Disney would not realize this. But here Tom Sawyer's island is big enough for children to play on; and Pinocchio's village is so small there is not even room in its streets to put one's foot. Once again Disney shows himself a master of the use of proportion.

As you can see, this paragraph is arranged in the alternating format. First Menen discusses the type of fantasies that one participates in, such as the story of Tom Sawyer. Then, for contrast, he brings in imaginings associated with children's stories like *The Wind in the Willows* and Cinderella in which one is a spectator. Then he discusses the size of Tom Sawyer's Island in Disneyland and contrasts it with the size of Pinocchio's village.

For information on using these formats in an essay, see "Using Comparison and Contrast to Develop an Essay" on page 205 in Chapter 15.

Providing Transition for Comparison and Contrast Paragraphs

Transitional expressions are a great help to readers as they follow your organizational plan. A paragraph of comparison will, of course, use different sorts of transitions than a paragraph of contrast. The list below shows some of the transitional expressions you will find useful for each of these techniques.

ESL Note
See "Strive for Clarity,"
page 556, for more
on the importance of
coherent writing.

Transitional Expressions for Comparison and Contrast Writing

Contrast		*Comparison*	
although	in contrast	also	just as
but	on the other hand	both, neither	like
however	unlike	in the same way	similarly

COMPREHENSION AND PRACTICE 10.2 | **Considering a Thorough Presentation and an Effective Arrangement**

1. Consider this paragraph from Elizabeth Wong's "To Be an All-American Girl," in which she discusses cultural differences she experienced as a child:

> The language was a source of embarrassment. More times than not, I had tried to disassociate myself from the nagging loud voice that followed me wherever I wandered in the nearby American supermarket outside Chinatown. The voice belonged to my grandmother, a fragile woman in her seventies who could outshout the best of the street vendors. Her humor was raunchy, her Chinese rhythmless, patternless. It was quick, it was loud, it was unbeautiful. It was not like the quiet, lilting romance of French or the gentle refinement of the American South. Chinese sounded pedestrian. Public.

In your view, does Wong discuss enough detail in terms of Chinese versus the languages she preferred, or would you include additional information? Use the lines that follow for your answer.

_____

_____

_____

_____

2. On a separate sheet of paper, identify the organizational plan used in this paragraph. Explain also whether or not you think the order was a good choice and what leads you to this conclusion.

CHALLENGE 10.1 | **Considering Purpose in Comparison and Contrast Paragraphs**

collaboration

This chapter features several sample comparison and contrast paragraphs. The names of the authors of these paragraphs, with the appropriate page numbers, are listed below. Working with a classmate, take another look at the paragraphs. Then, on the lines below the names, list the primary purpose and any secondary purposes for each paragraph.

1. Mary Pipher, page 119

_____

_____

_____

2. N. L. Gage and David C. Berliner, pages 119–120

_____

_____

_____

3. Amy Tan, page 121

_____

_____

_____

4. Jay M. Pasachoff, page 121

_____

_____

_____

5. Aubrey Menen, page 122

_____

_____

_____

FOR FURTHER EXPLORATION Comparison and Contrast

1. Select one of the following topic pairs. Then, using one of the strategies that you practiced in Chapter 2, prewrite on that topic pair. Focus on the similarities and differences between the two people, places, or items.

   - two computer game systems
   - two aunts, uncles, or cousins
   - advertisements for two brands of the same kind of product
   - the way you reacted to a situation in the past and the way you would react now

2. This chapter features several sample paragraphs:

   - a discussion of how males and females are treated in the classroom (Mary Pipher, page 119)
   - an explanation of how experts handle things versus how newcomers perform (N. L. Gage and David C. Berliner, pages 119–120)
   - a discussion of the ways someone speaks to different audiences (Amy Tan, page 121)

- an examination of two places, one close and familiar, the other far away and mysterious or unknown (Jay M. Pasachoff, page 121)
- a discussion of two types of fantasies from childhood (Aubrey Menen, page 122)

For this assignment, think of related subjects similar in some way to those presented in these paragraphs. After prewriting, identify your focus and isolate strong supporting examples and details. Then create a paragraph of at least seven to ten sentences in which you use comparison and contrast to make your point about your subjects. Refer to the material in this chapter as a guide.

DISCOVERING CONNECTIONS Comparison and Contrast

For this assignment, consider this photo and address one of the following questions, or another that the photo inspires. Using the information in this chapter to guide you, write a paragraph of at least seven to ten sentences in which you use comparison and contrast to evaluate the subjects you are examining. As you write, make sure to establish a basis for your comparison and contrast, provide a thorough presentation, and arrange the information effectively.

A. The photo features a slum in the foreground and skyscrapers in the background. In what main ways do you imagine that people living in one area differ from those living in the other? Despite the economic disparities, what do you think the people living in these two distinct areas might have in common?

B. The scene in the picture might be described as *before* and *after,* with the skyscrapers representing progress. Is progress always a good thing, or can you think of a situation that was better in the past than it is now? In what ways was the situation better then than it is now?

✓COMPARISON AND CONTRAST PARAGRAPH CHECKLIST

☐ Does the topic sentence specify the subjects and indicate the focus?

☐ Does the paragraph establish a basis for comparison? Make sure that each characteristic or element is discussed in equal detail for each subject.

☐ Is the presentation thorough? Write *amplify* above any point that should be discussed in greater detail.

☐ Are the ideas arranged effectively? Would the paragraph be more effective if the ideas were arranged differently or if a different format were used? Explain.

☐   In your judgment, what is the best part of this paragraph? Explain.

☐   Which detail or example would be even better if it were expanded? Why?

RECAP   Comparison and Contrast

Key Terms in This Chapter	Definitions
comparison and contrast	the writing technique that examines similarities and differences between subjects *Comparison* may be used to develop similarities between subjects; *contrast,* to develop differences.
basis for comparison	the aspects, characteristics, or elements to be examined for both subjects in a paragraph of comparison and contrast
block format	a method of arranging elements for comparison and contrast in which all ideas about one subject are presented first, followed by all ideas about the second subject
alternating format	a method of arranging elements for comparison and contrast in which each of the elements or characteristics is discussed for both subjects on a point-by-point basis

Writing a Comparison and Contrast Paragraph

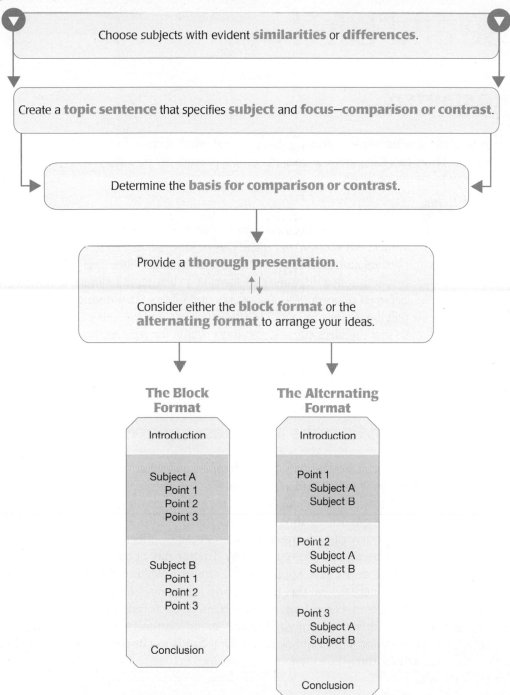

Choose subjects with evident **similarities** or **differences**.

Create a **topic sentence** that specifies **subject** and **focus—comparison or contrast**.

Determine the **basis for comparison or contrast**.

Provide a **thorough presentation**.

Consider either the **block format** or the **alternating format** to arrange your ideas.

The Block Format

Introduction

Subject A
Point 1
Point 2
Point 3

Subject B
Point 1
Point 2
Point 3

Conclusion

The Alternating Format

Introduction

Point 1
Subject A
Subject B

Point 2
Subject A
Subject B

Point 3
Subject A
Subject B

Conclusion

Using Odyssey Online with MyWritingLab

For more practice with comparison and contrast, go to
www.mywritinglab.com.

CHAPTER 11
Cause and Effect

GETTING STARTED ...

Q I need to explain what made a situation happen and what occurred as a result of it. How can I explain the reasons and outcomes so that they make sense to someone else?

A Whenever you want to explain the *why*—whether suspected or proven—that leads up to or stems from a particular event, the organizing strategy that answers your needs is *cause and effect*. This mode enables you to examine the often complex relationships between an event or experience and what led up to it or resulted from it. Identify your focus in a clear topic sentence and then distinguish between direct and related causes and effects. At the same time, avoid oversimplifying your cause and effect relationships and be sure to arrange the paragraph so that the ideas come across most clearly for your reader.

Overview: Explaining Reasons and Consequences

When you explain why things happen and what occurs when they do, the mode you use is **cause and effect**. *Cause* is the *reason* something occurred; *effect* is the *result* of what occurred. Nothing happens without a reason or without some kind of consequence, so in writing, you rarely find one without the other. Often, however, your writing focuses on either cause or effect.

A paragraph explaining why Twitter has become so popular would call for a cause and effect approach. So would a writing dealing with the results of a slight increase in the temperature of oceans and one explaining the recent increase in certain antibiotic-resistant bacterial infections. Beyond the classroom, this mode might feature in an annual report discussing a company's growth or a grant proposal seeking funds to convert a former mill to a series of artists' lofts.

Navigating This Chapter This chapter will explore the basic requirements for writing an effective cause and effect paragraph:

- providing a topic sentence that focuses on either cause or effect
- distinguishing between direct and related causes and effects
- avoiding oversimplification of causes and effects
- providing an effective arrangement

Providing a Topic Sentence That Focuses on Cause or Effect

Make sure the topic sentence clarifies whether the focus of your writing will be on cause or on effect. Consider the following paragraph by writer Alice Walker from her essay "Looking for Zora":

> *There are times—and finding Zora Hurston's grave was one of them—when normal responses of grief, horror, and so on do not make sense because they bear no real relation to the depth of the emotion one feels.* It was impossible for me to cry when I saw the field full of weeds where Zora is. Partly this is because I have come to know Zora through her books and she was not a teary sort of person herself; but partly, too, it is because there is a point at which even grief feels absurd. And at this point, laughter gushes up to retrieve sanity.

The topic sentence (shown in italics) specifies that the paragraph will focus on cause. It states that Walker's reaction to seeing the unmarked and untended grave of African-American writer Zora Neale Hurston did not match her profound sadness. The supporting sentences then specify why she reacted as she did.

Distinguishing between Direct and Related Causes and Effects

Some causes and effects are more directly connected than others. For example, the primary cause of an automobile accident might be bad weather. However, excessive speed and lack of experience on the part of the driver may be contributing factors. You must distinguish between **direct causes** and **effects** and **related** ones so that you don't overstate a particular cause and effect relationship.

You must also make sure not to confuse cause and effect with **coincidence,** which refers to events, ideas, or experiences that occur at the same time but purely by accident. For example, that the power went off in your next door neighbor's apartment while you were using your hair dryer doesn't mean that one event caused the other.

In this brief excerpt from *Tuesdays with Morrie: An Old Man, a Young Man, and Life's Greatest Lesson,* writer Mitch Albom spells out the direct causes and effects of the amyotrophic lateral sclerosis (ALS), commonly called Lou Gehrig's disease, that is destroying Professor Morrie Schwartz's entire neurological system:

> ALS is like a lit candle: it melts your nerves and leaves your body a pile of wax. Often, it begins with the legs and works its way up. You lose control of your thigh muscles, so that you cannot support yourself standing. You lose control of your trunk muscles, so that you cannot sit up straight. By the end, if you are still alive, you are breathing through a tube in a hole in your throat, while your soul, perfectly awake, is imprisoned inside a limp husk, perhaps able to blink, or cluck a tongue, like something from a science fiction movie, the man frozen inside his own flesh. This takes no more than five years from the day you contract the disease.

His opening sentence specifies the cause—that ALS patients become increasingly paralyzed because the condition essentially destroys nerves. Then the other sentences detail the effects, which occur over a brief, five-year period. The disease first hits the lower extremities and travels up. As it does, patients can no longer control their movements. Eventually, it paralyzes all muscles, including the diaphragm, which enables breathing, leaving the patient helpless but completely aware.

COMPREHENSION AND PRACTICE

11.1

Considering Topic Sentences and Cause and Effect Relationships

1. Consider this well-constructed cause and effect paragraph from *The Autobiography of Malcolm X,* written by Malcolm X and Alex Haley:

> I was so fascinated that I went on—I copied the dictionary's next page. And the same experience came when I studied that. With every succeeding page, I also learned of people and places and events from history. Actually the dictionary is like a miniature encyclopedia. Finally the dictionary's A section had filled a whole tablet—and I went on into the B's. That was the way I started copying what eventually became the entire dictionary. I went a lot faster after so much practice helped me pick up handwriting speed. Between what I wrote in my tablet, and writing letters, during the rest of my time in prison I would guess I wrote a million words.

On the lines that follow, briefly explain the connection between the topic sentence and the supporting sentences.

_____

_____

_____

_____

2. Use the following lines to identify whether the focus in the paragraph is on cause or on effect and what in the paragraph makes you think this.

_____

_____

_____

_____

3. On a separate sheet of paper, explain whether you think the cause and effect relationship Malcolm X and Alex Haley outline in this paragraph is direct or related and upon what information you base your conclusion.

Avoiding Oversimplification of Causes and Effects

When you write about causes and effects, be sure to avoid **oversimplification** of either one. Rarely does an event or situation have a single cause or a single effect.

Think of a serious problem such as juvenile delinquency. If you were to state that children whose parents are lenient will end up as juvenile delinquents, you would be *oversimplifying* a situation that is quite complex. Certainly a lack of discipline in childhood can contribute to bad behavior later in life. But to claim that one situation automatically leads to the other would not be accurate. Other outcomes are possible. (We all know people who were raised in undisciplined environments but who became solid citizens. We all also know individuals who had strict upbringings but still ended up in trouble.)

This paragraph, from Steven Pinker's *Words and Rules,* discusses why identifying the exact pronunciation of a word in English at a particular time in history is difficult:

> We can never say for sure what the pronunciation of a given word at a given time actually was. Just as there are regional accents today (London, Boston, Texas, and so on), there were regional varieties of English centuries ago; indeed, many more of them, because people did not move around as much as we do, did not send their children to melting-pot schools, and had no dictionaries to consult. Also, the written record is haphazard. Most words and pronunciations were in use long before the first literate person chanced to write them down, and many others went to the grave along with their speakers.

As you can see, tracing the exact pronunciation of an English word throughout the history of the language is not a simple matter. To illustrate the difficulty, Pinker provides several reasons for the complexity.

Providing an Effective Arrangement

Regardless of whether the focus of your paragraph is on cause or effect, you should consider the best way to provide the supporting information. For example, chronological order would be useful in a paragraph that discusses the *causes* of acid rain, which are both gradual and cumulative. Spatial order would be the best way to arrange a paragraph on the *effect* of a water leak in an apartment: the collapse of a portion of the living-room ceiling, stains across the wall below it, and warping of the hardwood floor.

With many subjects, however, you will probably find that emphatic order—beginning with a strong example and building to more serious examples—the best choice. Take a look at this paragraph from *Concepts of Chemical Dependency,* in which Harold E. Doweiko uses emphatic order to arrange some of the effects of addiction:

> At this point in the continuum, the person demonstrates the classic addiction syndrome. Multiple social, legal, financial, occupational, and personal problems become worse. The person also will demonstrate various medical complications associated with chemical abuse and may be near death as a result of chronic addiction. This individual is clearly addicted beyond any shadow of a doubt in the mind of an outside observer. It should be noted, however, that the addicted individual may try to rationalize away or deny problems associated with his or her alcohol or drug use even at this late stage. More than one elderly alcoholic, for example, has tried to explain away an abnormal liver function as being the aftermath of a childhood illness.

First, addiction leads the individual to ignore worsening problems that disrupt every aspect of the person's life. Worse, addiction leads the abuser to ignore health concerns—some potentially deadly—resulting from substance abuse. Worst of all, addiction leads to serious self-delusion: that substance abuse has nothing to do with health problems, despite clear evidence to the contrary.

Providing Transition for Cause and Effect Paragraphs

Remember—transitional phrases will help you to clarify which of your supporting statements express causes and which express effects. Here is a list of appropriate transitional words:

ESL Note
See "Strive for Clarity,"
page 556, for more on
the importance of
coherent writing.

Transitional Expressions for Cause and Effect Writing

Cause		Effect	
because	since	as a result	if
cause	so that	consequently	therefore
reason	unless	effect	thus

COMPREHENSION AND PRACTICE 11.2

Considering Complex Cause and Effect Relationships and Effective Arrangement

1. Read the following paragraph from *The Western Heritage* in which Donald Kagan, Steven Ozment, and Frank M. Turner discuss the economic aftermath of the Black Death in Europe:

As the number of farm laborers decreased, their wages increased and those of skilled artisans soared. Many serfs now chose to commute their labor services by money payments or to abandon the farm altogether and pursue more interesting and rewarding jobs in skilled craft industries in the cities. Agricultural prices fell because of lowered demand, and the price of luxury and manufactured goods—the work of skilled artisans—rose. The noble landowners suffered the greatest decline in power from this new state of affairs. They were forced to pay more for finished products and for farm labor but received a smaller return on their agricultural produce. Everywhere their rents were in steady decline after the plague.

In your view, how well does this paragraph explain the relationship between the Black Death and the economic changes that resulted from it? On a separate sheet of paper, evaluate the effectiveness of the paragraph, supporting your answer with specific details and examples from the paragraph.

2. On the lines below, identify the order followed in this paragraph and explain what in the paragraph leads you to this conclusion.

_____

_____

_____

CHALLENGE 11.1 **Considering Purpose in Cause and Effect Paragraphs**

This chapter features several sample cause and effect paragraphs. The names of the authors of these paragraphs, with the appropriate page numbers, are listed below. Working with a classmate, take another look at the paragraphs. Then, on the lines below the names, list the primary purpose and any secondary purposes for each paragraph.

collaboration

1. Alice Walker, page 129

_____

_____

_____

2. Mitch Albom, page 129

_____

_____

_____

3. Steven Pinker, page 131

_____

_____

_____

4. Harold E. Dowciko, page 131

_____

_____

_____

FOR FURTHER EXPLORATION Cause and Effect

1. Select one of the following topics. Then, following one of the strategies that you practiced in Chapter 2, complete a prewriting on that topic.

   - the appeal of blogs, message boards, or social networking sites
   - lack of consumer confidence in a company or product
   - parental pressure for better performance in the classroom or on the playing field
   - a belief in a religious, ethnic, sexual, or racial stereotype

2. This chapter features several sample paragraphs:

- The feelings after a long, involved task has been completed (Alice Walker, page 129).
- The results stemming from a terminal illness (Mitch Albom, page 129)
- What causes people to communicate or express themselves in different ways (Steven Pinker, page 131)
- The consequences of dangerous or self-destructive behavior (Harold E. Doweiko, page 131)

For this assignment, consider a connection or relationship you have experienced, witnessed, or learned about similar to those indicated and explained in these paragraphs. After prewriting on this subject, identify a focus and then create a paragraph of at least seven to ten sentences that makes the connection or relationship clear for your reader. Refer to the material in this chapter as you write.

DISCOVERING CONNECTIONS Cause and Effect

For this assignment, take a look at the photo and focus on one of the following questions, or another that the picture inspires. Using the information in this chapter to guide you, write a paragraph of at least seven to ten sentences in which you use cause and effect to explain your topic. As you develop your paragraph, be sure to recognize the differences between direct and related causes and effects, to avoid oversimplification, and to provide an effective arrangement.

A. The ice floe in the picture appears to be shrinking, yet the penguins remain. Now compare this image to how some people, whether in personal situations or natural disasters, sometimes wait too long to abandon circumstances that will likely only worsen. Why do you think people often refuse to face the truth? Give some examples from recent current events or from your life to help support your response.

B. If the climate changes seen in the last few years continue, penguins and hundreds of other creatures will have to adapt to survive. Have you ever had to make a significant change in the way you work, behave, or think? Describe what led you to change. How has this change affected your life?

✓ CAUSE AND EFFECT PARAGRAPH CHECKLIST

☐ Does the topic sentence focus on either cause or effect?

☐ Does the paragraph distinguish between direct and related causes and effects? Underline any details that seem like coincidences rather than true causes or effects.

☐ Does the writer provide a sufficient number of causes or effects to support the main idea? If you feel more specific details are required, write, "I'd like to know more about ———" in the margin next to the appropriate sentence or passage.

☐ Is the supporting material effectively arranged? Suggest any changes in the margin of the paper.

☐ In your judgment, what is the best part of the paragraph? Explain.

☐ Which detail or example would be even better if it were expanded? Why?

RECAP   Cause and Effect

Key Terms in This Chapter	Definitions
cause and effect	the writing technique that explains why things happen **(cause)** and what occurs when they do **(effect)**
direct causes	primary or main reasons
direct effects	primary or principal results
related causes or effects	contributing reasons or results
coincidence	events, ideas, or experiences that occur by accident at the same time
oversimplification	error in reasoning that causes one to overlook the complexity in a cause and effect relationship
	EXAMPLE "She doesn't want a career because her mother was never home when she was a child."

Writing a Cause and Effect Paragraph

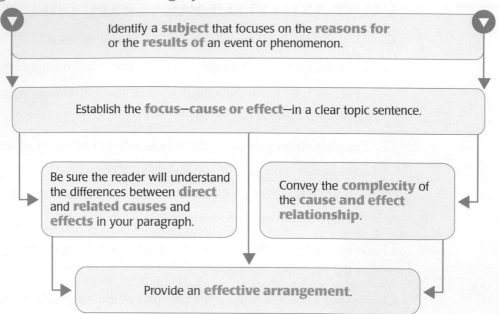

Identify a **subject** that focuses on the **reasons for** or the **results of** an event or phenomenon.

Establish the **focus—cause or effect—**in a clear topic sentence.

Be sure the reader will understand the differences between **direct** and **related causes** and **effects** in your paragraph.

Convey the **complexity** of the **cause and effect relationship**.

Provide an **effective arrangement**.

Using Odyssey Online with MyWritingLab

For more practice with cause and effect, go to www.mywritinglab.com.

CHAPTER 12
Division and Classification

GETTING STARTED ...

 Q I've chosen a pretty complicated topic to write about, involving a number of aspects and elements. How can I simplify it and present it in manageable parts.

 A The secret is to *analyze* the subject—to scrutinize its components to gain a better understanding of the whole topic—through *division* and *classification*. Whether your subject calls for a separation into parts (division) or an arrangement of elements into smaller groups (classification), this organization strategy makes it easy for your reader to understand the complicated issue you are presenting. Just identify the basis of your analysis through a solid topic sentence, establish a consistent method of analysis, and focus on distinct and complete groupings, and you'll be fine.

Overview: Analyzing the Whole in Terms of the Parts

Division and *classification* helps you simplify complex subjects in your writing so that you can communicate them clearly to a reader. Although division and classification are separate processes, they are usually discussed together and often appear together in writing. Both processes involve *analysis*, looking at something large or complex by breaking it down into parts. **Division** refers to the separation of a subject into component parts. **Classification** refers to the arrangement of component parts into groups on the basis of some principle or characteristic.

Division and classification would dominate in a paragraph about exercise programs available at your gym, including weight training, aerobic programs, and core exercises. Beyond the classroom, you would use division and classification for an effective sales presentation and focus on the pitch, product demonstration, summary of benefits, and close.

Navigating This Chapter This chapter will explore the basic requirements for writing an effective division or classification paragraph:

- providing a topic sentence that defines the scope of the discussion and indicates an emphasis on either division or classification
- establishing a logical method of analysis
- maintaining a consistent presentation
- using distinct and complete groupings

Specifying Scope and Emphasis through a Topic Sentence

The topic sentence specifies the scope of the subject that the writer will examine. It also often indicates whether the emphasis in the paragraph will be on division or classification.

A typical topic sentence for a classification paragraph will name the large group to be divided and then specify the *basis of classification.* This is the principle or characteristic used for making subdivisions or *classes.* The topic sentence may also name the classes, as in the following example:

EXAMPLE

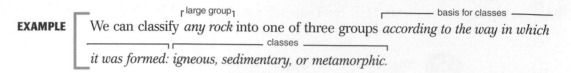

We can classify *any rock* into one of three groups *according to the way in which it was formed:* igneous, sedimentary, or metamorphic.

Take a look at this paragraph from William Zinsser's *American Places: A Writer's Pilgrimage to 15 of This Country's Most Visited and Cherished Sites,* in which he discusses Niagara Falls:

> *One misconception I brought to Niagara Falls was that it consisted of two sets of falls, which had to be viewed separately.* I would have to see the American falls first then go over to the Canadian side to see their falls, which, everyone said, were better. But nature hadn't done anything so officious, as I found when the shuttle bus from the Buffalo airport stopped and I got out and walked, half running, down a path marked FALLS. The sign was hardly necessary; I could hear that I was going in the right direction.

Here the topic sentence (shown in italics) identifies the subject—Niagara Falls. It also specifies the paragraph's focus: that this natural wonder is actually one enormous water fall, not two. The supporting sentences then use division to explain the way people often divide Niagara into the American Falls and the Canadian Horseshoe Falls, at the same time indicating that such a division isn't accurate.

Establishing a Logical Method of Analysis

Whether your focus is division or classification, you need to establish a logical method of analyzing the group or subject you choose. Any subject can be presented in a variety of ways. You need to choose divisions or categories that will enable your reader to understand your subject.

Imagine that you are writing about e-commerce—doing business on the Internet. You could approach this broad topic from a number of directions. One paragraph could focus on common uses of the Internet as one category: to sell handmade products, to do personal banking, and to purchase various goods. Another category could focus on the types of businesses found on the Internet: grocery services, gasoline sales programs, personal counseling centers, and pet food delivery services. To make your categories clear to your readers, be sure to include examples of the individual transactions and businesses you identify.

Consider this paragraph from "Risk" by Paul Roberts, in which he discusses the kinds of dangerous outdoor activities that Americans are seeking:

> Risky business has never been more popular. Mountain climbing is among America's fastest growing sports. Extreme skiing—in which skiers descend cliff-like runs by dropping from ledge to snow-covered ledge—is drawing wider interest. Sports like paragliding and cliff-parachuting are marching into the recreational mainstream while the adventure-travel business, which often mixes activities like climbing or river rafting with wildlife safaris, has grown into a multimillion-dollar industry. "Forget the beach," declared *Newsweek* last year. "We're hot for mountain biking, river running, climbing, and bungee jumping."

The method of analysis that Roberts employs here is clear and logical. He identifies his general subject as "risky business," and then he uses classification to identify the various kinds of activities: extreme skiing, paragliding, cliff-parachuting, river rafting, mountain biking, mountain climbing, and bungee jumping.

COMPREHENSION AND PRACTICE 12.1

Considering Topic Sentences and a Logical Method of Analysis

1. Take a look at this paragraph about reinforcement from a psychology textbook by Zick Rubin, Letitia Anne Peplau, and Peter Salovey:

> Reinforcement is the process of using rewards—or reinforcers—to strengthen particular responses. A reinforcer is any event that strengthens the response it follows—that is, that increases the likelihood of that response occurring again. One of the most important challenges for anyone trying to teach something to an animal or person is to figure out just what things are reinforcing to that individual. Some things, such as food, water, and affection, seem to be naturally reinforcing; these are called *primary reinforcers*. Other things or events become reinforcing as a result of their association with primary reinforcers; these are called *secondary reinforcers*. Secondary reinforcers play a big part in shaping our behavior. Think of all the behaviors we engage in to earn awards, pats on the back, and grades. We have learned that the awards, pats, and grades are rewarding because they tend to go along with other more basic rewards, such as affection and esteem.

On the lines that follow, briefly explain how the topic sentence establishes the focus of the paragraph and prepares the reader for the rest of the discussion.

_____

_____

_____

2. The topic sentence in this paragraph offers a brief definition. By opening their paragraph this way, how have Rubin, Peplau, and Salovey addressed the needs of their reader? Use the following lines for your answer.

_____

_____

3. Analyze the method of analysis that Rubin, Peplau, and Salovey use to discuss reinforcement. Then on a separate sheet of paper, indicate whether, in your view, the method is logical, identifying what in the paragraph leads you to your conclusion.

Maintaining a Consistent Presentation

As you decide on the focus of your division or classification paragraph, you also need to maintain a **consistent presentation,** which involves divisions or classes established on a set basis, with no unrelated categories.

Imagine you were writing a paragraph about your expenses. You would be likely to discuss such items as *rent, food, clothing, savings,* and *entertainment.* You wouldn't discuss an upcoming raise or an expected tax return because these are *sources of income,* not *expenses.*

Take a look at this well-constructed classification paragraph from E. B. White's *Here is New York* about different ways that people who come into contact with New York City classify this metropolis:

> There are roughly three New Yorks. There is, first, the New York of the man or woman who was born here, who takes the city for granted and accepts its size and its turbulence as natural and inevitable. Second, there is the New York of the commuter—the city that is devoured by locusts each day and spat out each night. Third, there is the New York of the person who was born somewhere else and came to New York in the quest of something. Of these three trembling cities the greatest is the last—the city of final destination. It is this third city that accounts for New York's high-strung disposition, its poetical deportment, its dedication to the arts, and its incomparable achievements.

As you can see, the paragraph offers three different classifications of the city and then explains each type in relation to the other two. The result is a passage that is consistent in its presentation.

Using Distinct and Complete Groupings

As you develop a division and classification paragraph, you also need to use **distinct and complete groupings.** When a grouping is *distinct,* it is clearly distinguished from other groupings. When it is *complete,* it is expressed in full detail.

Imagine that you are writing a paragraph that focuses on the people who attend your community theater. If you were to divide these people into only two groups—family members of the cast and other people from the community—the second category would be too general and therefore incomplete. In fact, *other people from the community* might be composed of several groups: senior citizens, invited city officials, high school students, families with young children, and so forth. None of these groupings overlap; each one has a distinctive set of members. In order to make your analysis complete, you would want to be sure that these categories do not overlook anyone who attends the plays.

Consider the way this paragraph from "Cellular Divide," an article about stem cell research by Sharon Begley, discusses types of cells:

> The cells that make up days-old embryos embody a world of potential. Four days after fertilization, the embryo is a hollow ball of cells called a blastocyst. Cells in the outer layer are destined to become the placenta. Those in the inner layer have not yet decided what they will be when they grow up: they are "pluripotent," able to differentiate into any of the 220 cell types that make up a human body, from the kidney, heart and liver to the skin, neuronal and pancreatic. These are the famous embryonic stem cells. For a few short days they are blank slates waiting for destiny (or the complex interplay of genes and biochemistry) to write their future.

In this paragraph, Begley ensures that her groupings are distinct and complete. To do so, she divides the types of cells constituting a human embryo in the first days after conception into two groups. The first group includes those on the outer layer, which become the placenta. The other group is made up of the *stem cells:* the undifferentiated cells that will become one of the 220 human cell types.

Providing Transition for Division and Classification Paragraphs

Certain words and phrases will help you to stress the divisions or classifications you establish in your paragraph. The list below gives you some possibilities.

ESL Note
See "Strive for Clarity," page 556, for more on the importance of coherent writing.

Transitional Expressions That Show Division or Classification

can be categorized (classified)	the first type (kind), second type, etc.
can be divided	the last category

COMPREHENSION AND PRACTICE 12.2

Considering Consistency in Presentation and Distinct and Complete Groupings

1. Read the following paragraph from *Gifts Differing* by Isabel Briggs Myers and Peter B. Myers, in which they discuss how people perceive the world around them:

> Of the two very different kinds of perception, sensing is the direct perception of realities through sight, hearing, touch, taste, and smell. Sensing is needed for pursuing or even casually observing hard facts; it is equally essential to enjoying the moment of a sunrise, the crash of surf on a beach, the exhilaration of speed, and the smooth workings of one's body. Intuition is the indirect perception of things beyond the reach of the senses, such as meanings, relationships, and possibilities. It translates words into meaning and meaning into words whenever people read, write, talk, or listen; people use intuition when they invite the unknown into their conscious minds or wait expectantly for a possibility, a solution, or

an inspiration. Intuition works best for seeing how situations might be handled. A thought that starts "I wonder if" is probably intuition, and the thought "Aha!" indicates that intuition has brought to mind something enlightening and delightful.

On the lines that follow, identify the components that Myers and Myers include, and then explain whether you think the paragraph maintains the focus on these subjects only.

_____

_____

_____

2. On the following lines, briefly explain how the examples and details that the Myerses supply help to keep the divisions distinct and complete.

_____

_____

_____

CHALLENGE 12.1   **Considering Purpose in Division and Classification Paragraphs**

collaboration

This chapter features several sample division and classification paragraphs. The names of the authors of these paragraphs, with the appropriate page numbers, are listed below. Working with a classmate, take another look at the paragraphs. Then, on the lines below the names, list the primary purpose and any secondary purposes for each paragraph.

1. William Zinsser, page 138

_____

_____

_____

2. Paul Roberts, page 139

_____

_____

_____

3. E. B. White, page 140

_____

_____

_____

4. Sharon Begley, page 141

_____

_____

_____

FOR FURTHER EXPLORATION Division and Classification

1. Consider one of the following topics:

   - levels of dishonesty
   - kinds of shoppers that you might see during busy shopping seasons
   - categories of comedy
   - services the federal government provides that benefit the average citizen

   After prewriting on the subject using one of the strategies you practiced in Chapter 2, identify a specific focus and then write a paragraph of at least seven to ten sentences in which you use division and classification to analyze your subject. Use the material in this chapter to guide you.

2. This chapter features several sample paragraphs:

   - an analysis that shows that what has traditionally been thought of as different or separate is actually the same (William Zinsser, page 138)
   - an explanation of the types of popular leisure-time activities (Paul Roberts, page 139)
   - an explanation of classifications of a big city (E. B. White, page 140)
   - a discussion of the way things evolve, grow, or change (Sharon Begley, page 141)

   For this assignment, think of a complex subject from your own background or experiences similar in some way to those discussed in these paragraphs. After prewriting on this topic, identify a focus and then create a paragraph of at least seven to ten sentences in which you use division and classification to make your subject clear for your reader. Use the material in this chapter to guide you.

collaboration

3. Exchange your paragraph with a classmate. Evaluate the paragraph you receive using the division and classification paragraph checklist below. Write your comments on a separate sheet of paper, and then return the paragraph and your assessment to the writer.

4. Using your reader's comments to guide you, revise your paragraph.

DISCOVERING CONNECTIONS Division and Classification

For this assignment, consider this image and one of the following questions, or another that the picture inspires. Using the information in this chapter to guide you, write a paragraph of at least seven to ten sentences in which you employ division and classification to examine your topic in detail. As you create your paragraph, concentrate on key factors such as a logical method of analysis, a consistent presentation, and distinct and complete groupings.

A. Based on the details in the picture, how would you classify the contents in each of the bins? If your neighborhood supports recycling programs, describe the local recycling process and how people generally respond to it.

B. Recycling is just a small contribution to the larger effort of rescuing the environment from long-term damage and abuse. What activities currently threaten the environment? In what ways can we help make a difference?

✓ DIVISION AND CLASSIFICATION PARAGRAPH CHECKLIST

☐ Does the topic sentence define the scope of the discussion and indicate an emphasis on either division or classification?

☐ Is a logical, consistent method of analysis maintained throughout?

☐ Should any details or examples be further subdivided? If so, underline them.

☐ Are the elements used distinct and complete? If you think any of the material needs to be made clearer or more specific, write, "I'd like to know more about _____" in the margin next to it.

☐ In your judgment, what is the best part of this paragraph? Explain.

☐ Which detail or example would be even better if it were expanded? Why?

RECAP Division and Classification

Key Terms in This Chapter	Definitions
division and classification	writing techniques used to break down a subject **(division)** or group ideas **(classification)** for analysis so that the subject is easier to grasp
consistent presentation	using the same principle of division or classification for all the parts of a topic under discussion and providing parallel elements of description or analysis for each
distinct and complete groupings	categories for classification or division that are clearly distinguished from others and expressed in full detail

Writing a Division or Classification Paragraph

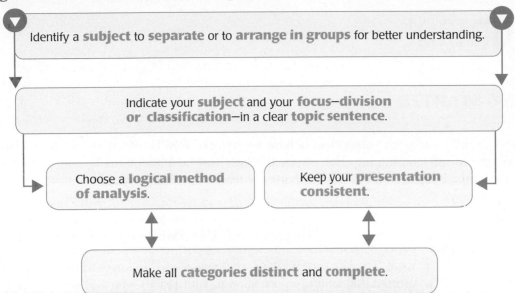

Identify a **subject** to **separate** or to **arrange in groups** for better understanding.

Indicate your **subject** and your **focus**—**division or classification**—in a clear **topic sentence**.

Choose a **logical method of analysis**.

Keep your **presentation consistent**.

Make all **categories distinct** and **complete**.

Using Odyssey Online with MyWritingLab

For more practice with division and classification, go to www.mywritinglab.com.

CHAPTER 13
Argument

GETTING STARTED ...

Q I feel strongly about my subject and believe my point of view is reasonable and worth considering. But what's the best way to present my stand on this subject so that I can persuade my reader to consider what I have to say?

A When you set out to persuade your reader, you are writing an *argument* paper, which demonstrates your support, criticism, or understanding of some issue. The key is to think of what *you* needed to know to be convinced. If you present that kind of information to your reader, you will be well on your way to success. Be sure to recognize the relationship between fact and opinion and to avoid any errors in logic. At the same time, employ an appropriate tone and arrange your supporting examples in emphatic order. Doing these things will give you the best chance of persuading your reader.

Overview: Understanding Persuasion

An argument differs from the modes presented in the last eight chapters. **Argument** is not a mode but an aim or **purpose**. With argument, you use a variety of modes to *persuade* your reader to accept a point of view.

A paragraph asserting that the United States needs tighter gun control would be an argument. So would one maintaining that ownership of pit bulls, hybrid wolf dogs, and other aggressive dog breeds should be restricted. Beyond the classroom, an entry on an online forum urging a restriction of motorized vehicles in wildlife preserves would be an argument, as would an endorsement letter urging individuals to vote for a specific candidate for city mayor.

Navigating This Chapter This chapter will explore the basic requirements for writing an effective argument:

- expressing a clear stance on the issue in a topic sentence
- providing sufficient support
- using a tone that is reasonable and convincing
- avoiding errors in logic
- arranging your support in emphatic order

Providing a Topic Sentence That Expresses a Clear Stance on the Issue

The topic sentence should clearly state the **stance** you are taking on the issue. In other words, it should indicate whether you are *in favor of* or *against* the point being raised. For example, imagine you were writing a paragraph about a National Health Care program to provide health insurance for all U.S. citizens. If you were writing to support this initiative, you might write a topic sentence like this:

EXAMPLE
> The federal government owes it to its citizens to establish a National Health Care program.

But if you were writing to oppose a National Health Care program, you might write a topic sentence like this one:

EXAMPLE
> A National Health Care program covering all citizens is a luxury that the United States simply can't afford.

Consider the stance set forth by the topic sentence, shown here in italics, in this paragraph about a proposal to require uniforms for public school students:

> *A policy that requires public school students to wear uniforms would be a bad idea for several reasons.* First of all, no style of clothing looks good on everyone. In their pre-teen and teen years, students are especially sensitive about their appearance, and having to wear clothing that doesn't fit them well will do little to help their fragile self-esteems. In addition, uniforms are expensive, and students would need to have at least two complete sets of uniforms to allow for laundering. Of course, since most students aren't likely to wear their uniforms after school, parents also have to purchase everyday clothes like jeans, shirts, and skirts, adding significantly to the amount they must spend on clothes. During the school year, students may outgrow their uniforms or the clothing may just wear out, increasing the cost for some families. Most important, a policy requiring students to wear uniforms ignores the rights of families to make clothing decisions that are best for them. Certainly schools should be able to restrict clothing that features obscene or objectionable slogans or that exposes too much skin. But making all students dress the same says that individuality is less important than conformity. The world already has too many followers.

In this paragraph, the topic sentence presents a clear direction for the reader. Both the issue and the writer's stance are explicitly stated: students in public schools should not be required to wear uniforms. As a result, the reader is prepared for the supporting sentences that follow.

Developing Sufficient Support through Sound Reasons

No absolute guideline exists about the amount of information needed to develop a sound argument. Think of a subject about which you are undecided: How much support would you need to see before *you* would accept that position? You would probably require several solid supporting details and examples before you would be convinced. Your reader demands the same of you when you write. As a general rule, include at least three reasons, or *points*, to support your stance.

As you develop your reasons with details and examples, keep in mind the difference between *fact* and *opinion*. A **fact** is a verifiable truth. That driving on icy roads is dangerous is a fact. There is no room for discussion. An **opinion**, however, is a belief. It may be founded on impressions, experiences, or a person's base of knowledge. When you say that city officials' failure to treat icy roads during a recent storm means that they don't care about the danger, that's an opinion. The validity of an opinion depends on how well it is supported by facts. Therefore, incorporate facts as often as possible to support your examples.

To help develop your argument, first list points that support your position. Next, list points that someone holding the opposite point of view might raise. The first list of points will form the framework for your argument. The second list allows you to address opposing points, which you can refute completely or turn to your advantage.

Imagine that you are against a proposal to establish English as the official national language of the United States, and you plan to write about that. Here are two lists of ideas you've generated about the subject, one against the proposal and one supporting it.

Against the proposal

- The United States was founded so all could enjoy freedom, regardless of background.
- When we force people to reject their heritage, we all lose.
- The proposal discriminates against immigrants—it's prejudice.
- Learning a new language is too difficult a burden for many old people.
- English-language classes aren't readily available, especially for working people.
- If we become English-speaking only, some people won't be able to work, adding to welfare lists.

In favor of the proposal

- It saves money on things like bilingual education and government forms that now have to be printed in several languages.
- If people want to live here, they should learn to speak English.
- The majority rules.
- Some jobs are advertised only for people who can speak another language besides English. Native speakers shouldn't lose out on jobs because they can't speak another language.

The points you've developed to oppose the proposal are valid, so you could feel comfortable including any of them in your writing.

In addition, you could also adapt and use a couple of the points from the list in favor of the proposal. Your thought process might go something like this: Yes, it's true that printing government forms in multiple languages and providing bilingual education cost taxpayers money. But a prosperous nation such as the United States should put people's needs ahead of dollar signs. And, yes, people who become permanent residents of the United States should learn English, but not because a law mandates it. Clearly, knowing the primary language of the United States opens up economic doors, making life easier overall. Rather than punishing people for not knowing English, our government should more aggressively educate newcomers concerning how speaking English will benefit them.

Now here's an argument paragraph that might result from the material on the lists:

> A law making English the official national language of the United States would be a terrible mistake. For one thing, such a law would discriminate against immigrants. The United States was established on the principle of freedom for all, regardless of background, and it was settled and made great by immigrants. It's unfair to make the newest groups coming to the United States face a greater burden than earlier groups of immigrants faced. Certainly, people should learn English because knowing the main language of the country provides many economic and social benefits. But mastering English isn't that easy, especially if the people are older. Also, except in major cities, language classes aren't always readily available, particularly at convenient hours for people who work. In addition, if we become an English-only nation, some immigrants who don't speak English will be unable to get jobs. Rather than working to support themselves, they will be forced to turn to welfare. But most of all, when we force people to abandon their own language, we are also suggesting that they abandon their culture. Our society has evolved as it has because of the positive contributions of so many groups. When we discourage a group from contributing, we all lose.

As you can see, points from the list opposing the proposal to make English the official national language of the United States dominate in this paragraph. In addition, some points from the list in favor of the proposal have been refuted and added to the other points. The result is an effective argument paragraph.

When you use information from another document or individual to support your argument, you must **document** the source of that information. Doing this will help you *avoid plagiarism*, discussed in Chapter 4 (see pages 64–65) and in Chapter 14 (page 182). In some of the argument paragraphs you will write, you can acknowledge your sources in a simple, in-text explanation: "According to a recent report in *U.S. News and World Report*, the number of college students selecting computer science as their major has increased for the seventh straight year."

In many cases, especially with longer, more formal assignments, you will need to provide more specific documentation for your sources. You'll need to include such details as the author's name, the title of the work, the publisher, the date of publication, the pages involved, and so on. Always ask which style of formal documentation your instructor prefers.

You will probably find that your instructors want you to use one of two common systems. One is the Modern Language Association (MLA) method, generally called for with assignments in English or other humanities disciplines. The other is the American Psychological Association (APA) method, generally appropriate for assignments in education, the social sciences, and the natural and physical sciences. Chapter 15 (pages 214–218) provides brief examples of both systems and more complete information is available in the reference section of your college library. You can also turn to this book's accompanying Web site, Odyssey Online with MyWritingLab.

COMPREHENSION AND PRACTICE

Considering Topic Sentences and Sufficient Valid Support

13.1

1. Read the following paragraph about a controversial aspect of adoption:

> Adopted children should be able to read through their sealed adoption files and make contact with their biological parents if they choose. Many adoptees feel that something is missing in their lives. They feel an emotional gap that can only be filled by learning more about their biological parents. Also, adoptees should have the same rights as everyone else to learn about their heritage, race, and ethnicity. Most people consider this kind of knowledge important. If their adoption records remain sealed, how can adoptees gain a full understanding of their own background? However, the most important reason for unsealing adoption records is medical. Researchers have proven that many diseases and medical conditions, such as diabetes and heart disease, tend to run in families. Therefore, without a full medical history of their biological relatives, some adoptees may actually be at medical risk.

What is the connection here between the topic sentence and the rest of the sentences in the paragraph? Use the lines that follow for your answer.

_____

_____

_____

_____

2. Evaluate this paragraph in terms of valid support. On a separate sheet of paper, indicate if you think there are enough reasons to convince a reader that the point of view is reasonable. In addition, indicate if any of the supporting examples should be expanded and explain why.

3. On a separate sheet of paper, list three facts with which you are familiar, leaving a couple of lines blank beneath each fact. Then, below each fact, write an opinion about that fact. Use the example below as a guide.

EXAMPLES

Fact: The incumbent mayor defeated her opponent by only 150 votes, less than 1 percent of the people who went to the polls.

Opinion: The mayor's narrow victory indicates that voters are fed up with her quarreling with the president of the city council.

Using a Reasonable, Convincing Tone

Another factor that will affect your reader's acceptance of your point of view is your **tone**, the attitude you express about your subject. If your tone is sarcastic, superior, or patronizing, you may alienate a reader who might otherwise be swayed to agree with your point of view. On the other hand, if your tone is sincere and respectful, you'll enhance the chance that your point of view will be favorably received.

One way to make your writing reasonable and convincing is by avoiding **absolute** terms. For instance, it is better to say that people without survival suits *rarely* stay alive more than a few minutes in the frigid winter waters of the North Atlantic rather than to say they *never* do. Here is a list of more moderate terms that you can substitute for absolute language:

Absolute Word	*Moderate Substitute*
all	most
always	frequently
every	many
never	rarely

Also, avoid personally attacking or insulting opponents of your argument (see Argument *ad hominem,* page 152). With an emotionally charged subject like gun control, for example, it's easy to understand how sentences such as these might appear in an early draft:

> Most people who buy handguns do so for personal protection. *However, a person would have to be stupid not to know* that handguns are statistically more likely to be stolen or to cause accidental injury than to be used effectively for protection.

The message in these sentences is valid, but the name-calling is insulting to both the opponents of the writer's position and the readers who are merely poorly informed about this issue.

Now, consider this version of the sentences:

> Most people who buy handguns do so for personal protection. *However, many people are unaware* that handguns are statistically more likely to be stolen or to cause accidental injury than to be used effectively for protection.

The message is the same in the second version, but the simple change in phrasing eliminates inflammatory name-calling. Instead, the writer is providing information in an objective tone that is much more likely to make poorly informed readers want to learn more about the issue.

Using Sound Logic

To persuade a reader, an argument must feature logical reasoning leading to a valid conclusion. You can establish such a *line of reasoning* by engaging in one of two reasoning processes: induction or deduction. Although the goal of these two reasoning processes is the same, they approach the subject from opposite directions.

With **induction**, you move from a series of specific instances or pieces of evidence to a general conclusion. Physicians employ inductive reasoning in diagnosing an illness. For example, a dermatologist might conclude that a patient's skin rash is a form of eczema because every other rash like this one that she has examined has proven to be eczema.

An answer reached in this way involves an *inductive leap.* Although this diagnosis is a reasonable conclusion based on the evidence, it isn't the only possible valid explanation. The rash may closely resemble eczema, but it may actually be the result of another condition. The more specific instances backing it up, however, the more likely the conclusion is sound.

Deduction, in contrast, involves reasoning from a general statement to a specific conclusion. Say, for example, you know that flat, low-lying inland areas are especially vulnerable to tornadoes. You also know that your cousin lives in a flat, low-lying inland area. You could therefore conclude that your cousin's neighborhood is a likely target for tornadoes.

Use of sound logic will strengthen your argument. Faulty logic or **logical fallacies,** like those described in the following table, will weaken it.

Avoid Logical Fallacies

Fallacy	Examples of Fallacious Logic	Instead Use Sound Logic
Argument ad hominem (Latin for "argument to the man")		
Attacking the person	That editorial writer criticizes the entertainment business for its portrayal of the American family, yet she is divorced herself.	Respond to the opposing positions.
Bandwagon approach		
Urging acceptance because "everybody does it"	Everyone wants the City Council to institute new zoning requirements.	Cite objective, qualified authorities or statistics.
Begging the question		
Assuming as fact what must be proven	NASA's call for increased funding in these hard times is more proof that these scientists care about nothing but their pet programs.	Provide relevant, documented evidence.
Circular reasoning		
Restating your opinion and calling it a reason	That car is the best choice because, compared to the competition, it is superior.	Give real reasons.
Creating a red herring		
Diverting attention to an unimportant point	Senator Hogg says that genetic engineering is too much like playing God, but she isn't even responsible enough to file her campaign finance reports on time.	Provide compelling evidence.
Either/or reasoning		
Suggesting only two alternatives when many possibilities exist	If we don't institute statewide testing in high schools, we will face another generation of poorly educated students.	Explore all relevant possibilities.

Avoid Logical Fallacies *(continued)*

Fallacy	Examples of Fallacious Logic	Instead Use Sound Logic
Hasty generalization Making an assumption based on insufficient evidence	I've used that medicine for two days and my cough is still not gone, so it's obvious that the pills aren't working.	Base conclusions on many objective facts.
***Non sequitur* (Latin for "it does not follow")** Coming to an incorrect conclusion in relation to the evidence	Homeless people don't have permanent places to live, so it's obvious that they have no pride.	Think through relationships using logic.
Oversimplification Wrongfully reducing a complex subject	Using solar energy will eliminate all our energy problems.	State all important aspects; admit inconsistencies.
***Post hoc, ergo propter hoc* (Latin for "after this, therefore because of this")** Assuming a cause-effect relationship between two things that occurred by coincidence	The killer had just eaten at a fast-food restaurant, so something in the food must have triggered his aggression.	Check your thinking for irrational statements.

Find the logical fallacy in this paragraph about a proposal to reclassify alcoholism as a social problem or condition rather than a disease:

> Government officials should not be allowed to reclassify alcoholism as a social problem rather than a disease. One of the principal reasons that alcoholism is so difficult to treat is that people tend to deny that they have a drinking problem. If alcoholism is viewed as it once was, not as an illness but as a moral weakness, some people who desperately need treatment may not seek it because of this stigma. Worse, reclassifying alcoholism as a social problem may increase the sense of worthlessness that many alcoholics feel. How can they develop the kind of confidence and self-esteem they need to deal with their problem when society says that their alcoholism is all their own fault? Worst of all, reclassification would mean that health insurers would no longer have to pay when people undergo treatment for alcohol dependency. Everybody knows that insurance companies have no compassion for people. Most people can't afford to pay for this valuable treatment out of pocket, and, as a result, will go without treatment. For these reasons, government officials should not reclassify alcoholism as a social problem.

As you probably noted, the weakness in logic appears in the seventh sentence: *Everybody knows that insurance companies have no compassion for people.* This error is an example of the *bandwagon approach*—the reader should accept the point merely because "everybody" believes it. But no evidence supports the idea that insurance companies are heartless or that such a belief is universally accepted, so this sentence must be eliminated in order to maintain the validity of the point of view expressed in the paragraph.

Arranging Your Support in Emphatic Order

Most often, writers arrange ideas in an argument paragraph in emphatic order. Using *emphatic order* means arranging your details and examples in such a way that each point builds in greater importance. Presented this way, the reasons compel your reader to continue on. (Emphatic order is discussed at length on pages 54–55.) Your initial point should be lively enough to spark and hold your reader's interest and to begin cultivating acceptance of your point of view. Each point should grow increasingly stronger so that your argument builds to a forceful, convincing conclusion.

Consider the order of the reasons in the following paragraph about keeping animals in captivity and forcing them to perform for humans:

> We humans don't have the right to capture animals and force them to perform for our pleasure in circuses, zoos, or aquatic parks. First of all, even under the best of circumstances, the environments in which these animals are kept differ vastly from what they would enjoy in the wild. For example, in their natural environments, animals like killer whales, polar bears, and dolphins cover territories that measure hundreds of miles. In captivity, they are held in compounds that are a fraction of that size. Receiving regular meals doesn't seem like a fair trade for this loss of freedom to roam. In addition, creatures such as elephants, great apes, and other primates are highly social and accustomed to living in large groups. But most animals in captivity live in far smaller groups, depriving them of the wider interaction they would enjoy in the wild. Worst of all, when we force animals to perform for us, we fail to respect their native intelligence, grace, and dignity. Instead, we allow them to be subjected to long hours of training to make them behave in ways that are simply not normal for these highly intelligent animals. That's what people should think when they see an elephant standing on a tiny stool or a dolphin dancing on its tail across a pool.

As you can see, the supporting sentences follow emphatic order. The initial reason—that the environments in zoos, circuses, and aquatic parks are considerably different from and considerably smaller than the ones in the wild—is strong. It is a compelling reason to support the idea that keeping animals in captivity to perform for people's pleasure is wrong. The second point—that these animals are often kept in isolation—is even stronger. Depriving animals accustomed to living in groups the comfort of others seems especially cruel. But the final point—forcing animals to endure training so they will behave in ways that they don't in the wild—is strongest of all. Forcing animals to perform in this fashion goes against their nature. Their behaviors are shaped simply for our pleasure. This final point is a suitable conclusion to the paragraph.

Providing Transition for Argument Paragraphs

Transitional phrases can help guide your readers through your line of reasoning and highlight the emphatic order. The list below gives some of these transitions.

ESL Note
See "Strive for Clarity,"
page 556, for more
on the importance of
coherent writing.

Transitional Expressions for Argument

To Establish Reasons	*To Answer the Opposition*	*To Conclude*
first (second, third, etc.)	some may say	therefore
most important	on the other hand	thus

COMPREHENSION AND PRACTICE 13.2

Considering Tone, Logic, and Order

1. Read the following paragraph about roadside memorials to the victims of auto accidents:

> Cities and towns should enforce ordinances against unauthorized roadside memorials put up following fatal traffic accidents. As well intentioned as the people who create these displays may be, these memorials don't belong on our streets and highways. For one thing, they force everyone to deal with the tragedy, including those who don't know the victim or the circumstances of the accident. It makes a sad situation even more depressing and turns what should be a private matter into a public spectacle. Worse, the displays quickly become shabby-looking. The flowers wilt, the ribbons get dirty and fade, and the notes and cards disintegrate and blow away. The result is just an eyesore. But worst of all, these memorials can become traffic hazards themselves. They can be major distractions, drawing the eyes of drivers who should be watching the road. Streets and highways are simply not appropriate spots for memorials to victims of traffic accidents, and city and state officials should always remove them.

   How would you describe the tone in this paragraph? What in the paragraph leads you to this conclusion? Use the lines that follow to respond briefly to these questions.

   _____

   _____

   _____

   _____

   _____

2. Assess the order of the supporting examples as they are currently presented. On the lines that follow, indicate whether you would leave the examples ranked as they are or change the order, briefly explaining your reasoning.

   _____

   _____

   _____

   _____

   _____

3. Turn again to the list of logical fallacies on pages 152–153. Select three of the types of fallacies, and, on a separate sheet of paper, write an additional example sentence for each, using the current example as a guide.

CHALLENGE 13.1   **Considering Additional Purposes in Argument Paragraphs**

collaboration

This chapter features several sample argument paragraphs. The specific points of these paragraphs, with the appropriate page numbers, are listed below. Because they are argument paragraphs, their primary purpose is obviously to persuade. Working with a classmate, take another look at the paragraphs. Then, on the lines below the specific points, list the secondary purposes for each paragraph.

1. Requiring public school children to wear uniforms, page 147

_____

_____

_____

2. Objecting to making English the official language of the United States, page 149

_____

_____

_____

3. Reclassifying alcoholism as social problem or condition rather than a disease, page 153

_____

_____

_____

4. Prohibiting the captivity and forced performance of animals, page 154

_____

_____

_____

FOR FURTHER EXPLORATION Argument

1. Consider the following topics and then choose the one with which you most strongly agree or disagree.

   - All public places, including parks and beaches, should be smoke-free zones.
   - College students should have to pass competency examinations in writing, critical thinking, and mathematics before receiving their degrees.
   - Police should be able to search cars without a warrant if they suspect someone has an illegal weapon.

- All college students should be required to perform thirty hours of community service as part of their graduation requirements.

Following one of the strategies that you practiced in Chapter 2, prewrite on the subject you have chosen, developing evidence for your stand on the issue. Then write a paragraph of at least seven to ten sentences that expresses and supports your point of view.

2. This chapter features several sample paragraphs:

- Imposing a requirement on a group (page 147)
- Changing an aspect of life for people living in the United States (page 149)
- Modifying a rule that will affect medical treatment (page 153)
- Addressing the rights of animals (page 154)

For this assignment, consider a topic like one of these. Review the paragraphs if necessary, choose the area you are most interested in exploring, and prewrite on this subject. Once you have identified your stand on the subject, develop supporting examples and details that you rank in emphatic order. Then develop a paragraph of at least seven to ten sentences that effectively supports your point of view, using the material in this chapter to direct you.

collaboration

3. Exchange your paragraph with a classmate. Evaluate the paragraph you receive, using the argument paragraph checklist on the next page. Write your comments on a separate sheet of paper, and then return the paragraph and your assessment to the writer.

4. Using your reader's comments to guide you, revise your paragraph.

DISCOVERING CONNECTIONS Argument

For this assignment, consider the photo and address one of the following questions or another that it inspires. Using the information in this chapter to guide you, write a paragraph of at least seven to ten sentences in which you take a stand on your subject and persuade your reader. As you develop your paragraph, make sure you supply sufficient support, use an appropriate tone, avoid errors in logic, and arrange your ideas effectively.

A. Geishas are women in Japan who are specially trained to entertain and serve as hostesses, especially for men. Some might argue that the existence of women fulfilling ancient social roles, regardless of culture, hurts the chances for women in general to be treated as equals in social and business settings. What do you think?

B. The women in the picture are dressed and made up the same way. In society at large, many people would assert that complete uniformity in terms of appearance, reasoning, behavior, attitude, and so on, is not a good thing. In your view, what is the best way to encourage individuality without destroying the basic level of coherence that keeps society functioning?

✔**ARGUMENT PARAGRAPH CHECKLIST**

☐ Does the topic sentence clarify the writer's stance on the issue?

☐ Are there sufficient examples and details to support the stance?

☐ Is the tone reasonable, sincere, and serious? Put a ✔ next to any places where you see a problem in tone.

☐ Is the presentation logical? Underline and label any logical fallacies.

☐ Is the material effectively arranged in emphatic order or some other method of arrangement? Explain.

☐ In your judgment, what is the best part of this paragraph? Explain.

☐ Which detail or example would be even better if it were expanded? Why?

RECAP Argument

Key Terms in This Chapter	Definitions
argument	writing that seeks to persuade a reader to accept the writer's point of view
purpose	the aim or intent in a piece of writing
stance	the position taken on a subject—the writer's opinion
fact	a verifiable truth
	EXAMPLE The city is in the process of tearing down several historic buildings.
opinion	a belief based on impressions, experiences, or a knowledge base. In argument, opinions must be backed up by facts.
	EXAMPLE The city should be trying to preserve historic buildings instead of tearing them down.
documentation	the process of acknowledging the source of supporting information taken from another document or individual
tone	the attitude you express about your subject
absolute term	a word or phrase that indicates a single and exclusive meaning
induction	a system of reasoning that moves from specific examples to a general conclusion
deduction	a system of reasoning that moves from general premises to a specific conclusion
logical fallacies	common errors in reasoning: argument *ad hominem;* bandwagon approach; begging the question; circular reasoning; creating a red herring; either/or reasoning; hasty generalization; *non sequitur;* oversimplification; *post hoc, ergo propter hoc*

Writing an Argument Paragraph

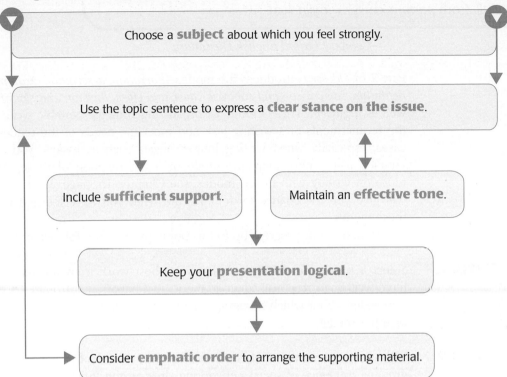

Choose a **subject** about which you feel strongly.

Use the topic sentence to express a **clear stance on the issue**.

Include **sufficient support**.

Maintain an **effective tone**.

Keep your **presentation logical**.

Consider **emphatic order** to arrange the supporting material.

Using Odyssey Online with MyWritingLab

For more practice with argument, go to www.mywritinglab.com.

PORTFOLIO 2

> **portfolio • noun** (pl. **portfolios**) ... **2** a set of pieces of creative work intended to demonstrate a person's ability. ORIGIN Italian *portafogli,* from *portare* 'carry' + *foglio* 'leaf'.

—Compact Oxford English Dictionary

Part 2 of *Odyssey* introduces the modes—*narration, description, example, process, definition, comparison and contrast, cause and effect, division and classification*—as well as *argument.* These modes, or organizing strategies, enable writers to fulfill the requirements of a writing task and meet the needs of the reader. In some cases, especially when writing longer pieces such as essays, you might find yourself using more than one mode or a combination of these modes. (For more on writing with mixed modes, see Chapter 15, page 214.) This portfolio will give you the chance to demonstrate what you have learned about using these modes.

To mark your progress up to this point, prepare the following portfolio:

BEST WORK

Select a paragraph that you feel is your best work from the paragraphs you have written in response to assignments in Chapters 5 through 13. If you are undecided about which paragraph is best, feel free to consult with a classmate or other reader.

ESSAY ANSWER

The sample paragraph that concludes the first section of the book discusses the growing influence of social networking sites on the Internet. Reread this paragraph (pages 69–70) and then write a brief answer (about 200 words) to one of the following essay questions:

- This paragraph discusses several different social networking sites. How do you feel about such sites? In what ways do these sites influence your daily life? You will probably find narration, example, cause and effect, among other modes, useful as you answer this question.

- For some people, the time they spend on social networking sites such as Facebook is time lost from things they need to do. It's just a form of *work avoidance,* a behavior that most of us engage in from time to time when we face tasks that hold little interest for us. What triggers work avoidance for you? What have you found to be the best diversion to distract you from what you don't want to do? Why? You will probably want to turn to example, comparison and contrast, and process, among other modes, as well as the elements of argument to answer this question.

TIMED WRITING

TIMED WRITING

In thirty minutes, complete a writing of at least 200 words in response to one of the following essay questions:

- Use ONE of the modes to explore the topic of a party. For example, use *narration* to tell the story of a particularly memorable party from your past, story or use *description* to bring the scene to life again. What was the reason for the party or what happened as a result? Use *cause and effect* to examine it. What type of party was it? How did it differ from other types of parties you've attended? Use *division and classification* to explain the distinctions or *example* to illustrate them. Use *process* to spell out the planning that took place. Use *definition* to note the key characteristics or elements that made it good. Was it much worse—or better—than a similar party you attended earlier? Then use *comparison and contrast* to discuss it.

- Suppose the local school district has banned all birthday parties in the kindergarten classes to make sure that children whose birthdays occur during school vacations don't feel slighted. Is this a good idea or a bad idea? Why do you feel this way? Use *argument* to present your point of view on this subject.

REFLECTION   One of the many interesting things about writing is that not everyone deals with or reacts to the process the same way. Some people dislike prewriting because they find it stressful to get started. Others do fine with prewriting but dislike revising because it sometimes feels like this stage never ends. It's really a matter of working styles and personal interests.

People react differently to the modes, preferring some to others. How about you? Which mode do you feel most comfortable with? Why do you think you prefer this mode to others? And which mode do you find most difficult? What about this strategy makes it unappealing to you?

In a paragraph of seven to ten sentences, address these questions.

PART 3

Moving On to the Essay

CHAPTER 14
Developing an Essay

 While I'm comfortable writing a paragraph, writing a multiparagraph piece, an *essay,* intimidates me. It seems like such a big job. What can I do to feel more comfortable with essay writing?

 First, relax. Once you relax, you are likely to find that you enjoy essay writing more because the process, which is the same as writing a paragraph, liberates you—you can explore subjects more thoroughly because your scope is larger and you have many more blanks to fill in. The secret to successful essay writing is to *provide specific details and examples*—lots of them.

Overview: Understanding the Essay

Up to this point, you have focused on writing paragraphs as a way to develop your skills. But as a college student and as a professional beyond the classroom, you will often be asked to prepare longer, more complex pieces of writing. For many college assignments, you will be asked to prepare an **essay,** a multiparagraph writing. An essay covers a subject in thorough detail, exploring multiple facets and angles, something that is simply not possible in a single paragraph.

Make no mistake about it: what you have already learned about writing paragraphs is crucial to your success with essay writing. Paragraphs are the building blocks of essays. Furthermore, the basic process for writing a paragraph—prewriting, composing, and revising—is the same for writing an essay.

Navigating This Chapter In this chapter you will learn what you need to know about writing an essay, including:

- the structure of an essay
- the stages of essay writing: prewriting, composing, and revising
- the importance of the thesis
- the importance of meeting your reader's needs
- the role of the introduction and conclusion

Understanding the Structure of an Essay

An essay consists of three parts: an introduction, a body, and a conclusion.

The Introduction

The **introduction** of an effective essay is usually a single paragraph that indicates the subject and direction of the paper. This paragraph sparks the interest of the reader and compels that reader to continue reading. The most important part of the introduction is the **thesis**, the element that specifies the subject and focus of the entire essay.

The Body

The **body** of an essay is the series of paragraphs that support and illustrate the thesis. The number of paragraphs to include in the body depends on your focus and direction, but the minimum number is three.

In the **five-paragraph essay**, the body consists of three paragraphs. Each discusses in detail one of the three points that are identified in the introduction and reiterated in the conclusion—giving us a total of five paragraphs. The five-paragraph essay may prove particularly useful for completing timed writing assignments such as essay examinations and writing assessments. (See Chapter 16 for a more complete discussion of the five-paragraph essay.)

An essay, however, is not restricted to five paragraphs, especially if it consists of 500 to 700 words; in this case, the body can consist of four to ten paragraphs, depending on the length of the paragraphs themselves. Regardless of the number of paragraphs, however, each paragraph must contain a clear topic sentence and supporting details, all relating to the thesis.

The Conclusion

The **conclusion** of an essay, usually a paragraph, strengthens the overall message expressed by the thesis and the supporting examples and details. The conclusion brings the essay to a logical and appropriate end, summing up the *significance* of the essay. Although most conclusions don't introduce new ideas, sometimes they raise issues that readers may want to pursue.

The figure on the next page shows the structure of a five-paragraph essay. Notice that the introduction and conclusion appear larger than the other paragraphs. That's because the introduction contains the thesis—the main point—and the conclusion restates or reemphasizes it. Notice also that the arrows between paragraphs point in both directions, signifying that the paragraphs relate to each other as well as to the thesis.

Examining the Process of Writing an Essay

ESL Note
See "Writing Essays" on pages 556–557.

To write an essay, you follow the same general process that you would to write a paragraph: *prewriting, composing,* and *revising.* The difference is that with an essay, you explore the subject in far greater detail.

During prewriting, you generate the ideas you'll need to complete your essay. In Chapter 2, you discovered which prewriting technique—or combination of techniques—you prefer to use to develop examples and details about a subject. While developing an essay, you also develop a manageable focus, which you then express in a sentence called the **thesis**.

Your draft thesis is your bridge from prewriting to composing. When you compose, you turn your attention to your most promising prewriting ideas, the ones that offer the strongest support, explanation, or illustration for your thesis. Your job is to convey the message of each point clearly in complete sentences, which are then arranged into the paragraphs that form the introduction, body, and conclusion. Ultimately, your essay should address the needs of your reader. The following figure shows the structure of a five-paragraph essay:

The Structure of an Essay

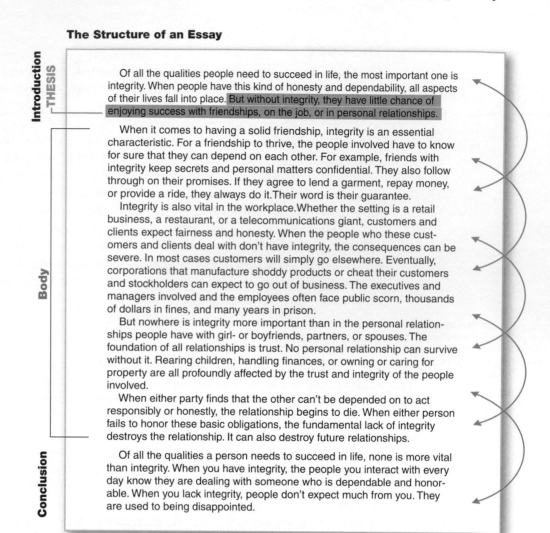

After you've completed your first draft, you revise—you refine and polish your draft. First, *reassess* the essay's *unity, coherence,* and *use of language.* Then *redraft* to address any problem spots. Finally, *edit* to eliminate any remaining errors. The figure on the next page illustrates the process of writing an essay.

As the two-way arrows in the visual show, the essay writing process often requires you to repeat some steps. In other words, the process is *recursive.* If, for example, you find during the revising stage that one or more of the paragraphs need additional detail, you simply return to prewriting to generate new information. You then move to composing to turn the new ideas into correct, reader-centered sentences. Finally, you edit this newly generated material to make sure that it is expressed correctly.

Imagine that you have to write an essay of 500 to 700 words. Of the topics suggested, you choose *superstition,* a subject that you have always found interesting. Now it's time to work through the writing process to create an essay that is as thorough, complete, correct, and effective as possible.

The Process of Writing an Essay

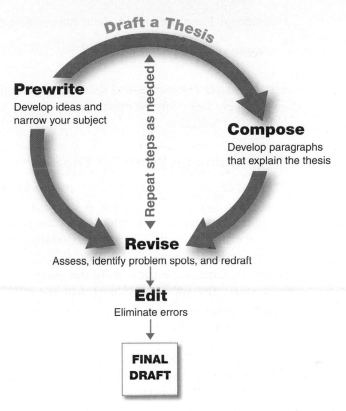

Prewriting: Generating Ideas and Identifying a Manageable Focus

ESL Note
See "Unity," page 555,
for more on the impor-
tance of keeping your
writing focused; "Think
about Audience
Expectations," page 556,
for more about the
needs of your audience;
and "Strive for Clarity,"
page 556, for more
on the importance of
keeping your writing
clear.

Take a look at the following freewriting on the subject of superstition:

> Superstitions—I love this topic. People can be so crazy about what makes
> you have good luck or bad luck. What to do and what to avoid. How about
> good luck charms? Coins, lucky item of clothing. Black cats? Old wives' tales?
> Break a mirror—bad luck, throwing salt over your shoulder. My aunt Irene—
> green was her unlucky color—nothing green in her house— just not rational!
> Walking under a ladder—why do people say that is unlucky? Athletes a lot
> have weird routines. A special number of bounces, rituals on the field with bat
> or gloves—. Just crazy—why would any of that help? Lottery tickets—some
> people think a particular kind of ticket is lucky and others are unlucky. I

always get stuck in line behind people getting lottery tickets—such a waste of

money! I read an article about how some people think that there are special

lucky slot machines at casinos!

The highlighted examples and details represent the most promising ideas and suggest a likely focus for the essay: the frequency of common kinds of superstitious beliefs and behaviors.

Developing an Effective Thesis

Think of the thesis as a signpost in sentence form that lets the reader know what is to come in the rest of the paper. A topic sentence states the main idea of a single paragraph, but a thesis statement states the main idea of the *entire* essay.

An effective thesis, like an effective topic sentence, is generally composed of two parts: a *subject* and the *writer's attitude about* or *reaction to* that subject. This structure clarifies the purpose of the essay and establishes the reader's expectation about the way the subject will be discussed. For example, if you were writing an essay about a recent phenomenon in communication, your thesis might look like this:

EFFECTIVE THESIS

——— subject ——— ——— attitude or opinion ———
The micro-blogging tool known as Twitter has truly captured the attention of

millions of Internet users.

This thesis is effective because it features both a subject and an attitude or opinion about that subject. In addition, it indicates that the primary purpose of the piece is informative and that the rest of the paper will likely provide examples of the growing influence of Twitter.

One way to remember what a good thesis *is* is to remember what a thesis *isn't.* An effective thesis is *not*

- an *announcement* of your intent, featuring words like *I plan, I intend,* or *This paper concerns,* because these expressions merely repeat what you should make obvious with your thesis.

INEFFECTIVE THESIS I want to talk about the growing interest in Twitter.

- a *statement of fact,* because a fact is a verifiable truth, leaving no room for discussion or debate:

INEFFECTIVE THESIS Twitter users respond in a maximum of 140 characters to the question, "What are you doing now?"

- a *title,* since a title is not usually a sentence and is generally intended to provide only a broad hint of the subject of your essay:

INEFFECTIVE THESIS [Twitter: TMI (Too Much Information)

With these guidelines in mind, here's a thesis for an essay on superstition:

EFFECTIVE THESIS [Superstitions, irrational ideas or concepts related to good or bad fortune, play a larger role in the world around us than most people realize.

This thesis expresses a specific subject and an attitude or opinion about that subject. It also clearly states what will follow in the body and conclusion of the essay.

COMPREHENSION AND PRACTICE
14.1

Revising Ineffective Theses

Turn each of the following sentences or titles into an effective thesis. Use the example as a guide.

EXAMPLE [The Apartment Where I Grew Up

Although I grew up in a tiny, run-down apartment, I have many good memories of the days I spent playing there.

1. I plan to show that having a good educational experience in kindergarten can have an enormous impact on a child's self-image.

_____

_____

_____

2. Tabloids like the *National Enquirer* sell millions of copies a week.

_____

_____

_____

3. The Ideal Occupation

_____

_____

_____

4. Manatees are large aquatic mammals that live within the intercoastal water-ways of Florida.

_____

_____

_____

5. I want to show that law enforcement officials should not unfairly target young drivers.

_____

_____

_____

CHALLENGE 14.1   Developing Support for a Thesis

1. Review again the following thesis for an essay:

EXAMPLE   The micro-blogging tool known as Twitter has truly captured the attention of millions of Internet users.

collaboration

Make a list on a separate sheet of paper of several details and examples that could be used to support this thesis.

2. Working with a classmate, choose one of the ineffective theses on the subject of Twitter (pages 168–169), convert it into an effective thesis, and identify at least three ideas that could be used to support the thesis.

Composing

Once you have developed a draft thesis, you move to the *composing* stage, during which you create a complete first-draft essay. Return to the supporting examples and details that you highlighted as the most promising for development, and identify the ones that offer the best support for the thesis you have developed. Then group related ideas together. When restated more completely, in correct sentence form, the ideas in these groups will become the basis for the supporting paragraphs of your essay. Here again is the thesis on superstition:

Superstitions, irrational ideas or concepts related to good or bad fortune, play a larger role in the world around us than most people realize.

And here are the ideas that were highlighted in the freewriting, with related ideas grouped together:

good luck charms

- coins

- lucky item of clothing

old wives' tales/advice

- black cats?

- break a mirror—bad luck

- throwing salt over your shoulder

- walking under a ladder

athletes—rituals

- a special number of bounces

- rituals on the field with bats or gloves

Once you have grouped together your best prewriting material, the next step is to express it more completely and clearly, using additional details, examples, and illustrations. Remember that your goal is to create an essay that will make sense to somebody else. Since you know a great deal about most of the subjects you will write about, you might incorrectly conclude that your reader has the same background and frame of reference as you do. Therefore, always keep your reader's needs in mind and the essay *reader centered.* The secret to meeting your reader's needs is to think of yourself *before* you learned what you know about the subject. What specific examples and details did you need to know before you fully understood the subject yourself? Supply the answers to this question, and you'll be on your way.

Creating an Effective Introduction and Conclusion

An essay contains two important paragraphs that perform specialized functions: the introduction and the conclusion. The introduction contains the thesis, engages the reader, and previews the structure of the essay. The conclusion summarizes the point of the essay, restating the significance of the ideas while bringing the paper to a logical and appropriate end.

Introduction   You can develop an effective introduction in several ways. One technique is to draw a reader's attention and interest by using an **anecdote**—a brief, entertaining story that emphasizes the thesis—as was done in this introduction to an essay about identity theft:

> Every Friday afternoon, my aunt would make it a point to log into her bank's Web site to make sure that her paycheck had been safely deposited. But this payday was like no other. When she logged into the site, she discovered that both her checking and savings accounts were empty—over $10,000 gone without a trace. After five minutes on the phone, my aunt learned the meaning of a new term: identify theft.

Another technique is to include specific facts or statistics that emphasize the relevance of the thesis for the reader:

EXAMPLE

How common a crime is identify theft? According to statistics compiled by groups like the Better Business Bureau and the Federal Trade Commission, more than 13 million Americans have been victims of identity theft (http://www.privacyrights.org/ar/idtheftsurveys.htm).

Still another approach is to begin the introduction with a relevant or well-known saying, axiom, or quotation:

EXAMPLE

The person who first made the statement, "You don't know what you have until you lose it" certainly wasn't thinking of identity theft, but millions of victims of this crime now recognize the truth of those ten simple words.

An additional option is to begin with a **rhetorical question.** This type of question is designed not to be answered, but to provoke thought or discussion:

EXAMPLE

What must it be like to go online to pay some bills, only to discover that all your money—checking account, savings account, every penny you have—has vanished?

Some other introductory techniques, used alone or in combination with other approaches, include

- comparing or contrasting your subject with another subject
- providing a reference to a well-known work of literature, popular culture subject, song, and so on
- including appropriate historical background
- offering a broad view of the subject leading to a narrow point about it
- presenting a definition, of the subject itself or of some aspect of it

The placement of the thesis will depend on your intent and your reader's needs. Making it the first or second sentence of your introduction immediately identifies the point of your essay. Putting it toward or at the end, however, can sustain and prolong interest, drawing your reader further into your subject. Regardless of where you place the thesis, keep in mind that your introduction should always suggest the direction the essay will take.

ESL Note
See "Reinforce Your Point with a Concluding Paragraph," page 557, for more on preparing an effective conclusion.

Conclusion The conclusion is the writer's last word on the subject, a final thought or a question for the reader to consider. In general, conclusions don't present new information in detail. The place to develop new thoughts and ideas fully is the body, not the conclusion.

As with an introduction, how you choose to conclude your essay should depend upon the particular situation. In many cases, you may find that referring back to the introduction will be the way to go. Embodying the point of the paper in an anecdote is another good technique. Asking and answering a relevant question or providing a pertinent quotation can also work just as effectively. Simply stated, whatever technique helps you bring the essay to an effective close is the correct choice for that essay.

COMPREHENSION AND PRACTICE 14.2

Understanding Techniques for Introductions and Conclusions

1. Of the listed techniques available to use in introductions or conclusions (pages 171–172), which do you find most interesting? Why?

_____

_____

_____

2. On a separate sheet of paper, briefly explain which you think you would find easier to write for an essay, an introduction or a conclusion, and why.

Understanding the Relationship between Topic Sentences and the Thesis As Chapter 3, "Composing: Creating a Draft," indicated, the main sentence in any paragraph is called the *topic sentence*. Because an essay is a multiparagraph writing, it contains several topic sentences, each of which is directly connected to the thesis.

Here is the thesis from a paper about honesty in the United States:

EXAMPLE In the United States today, it seems as if people don't care about honesty and lawful behavior anymore.

This thesis indicates that the rest of the essay will deal with examples of dishonesty or illegal behavior. The figure on page 174 illustrates the relationship between the thesis and the topic sentences of this essay. As the figure shows, each topic sentence deals with some form of dishonesty or unlawful behavior. In terms of the relationship between the thesis and these topic sentences, *dishonesty or unlawful behavior* represents the *common thread,* the element that all the paragraphs share. The thesis indicates that honesty is no longer valued. Each topic sentence directly supports, illustrates, or explains this thesis by presenting a different aspect of dishonesty. The conclusion then restates the significance of the thesis—that in all areas of life, society no longer values honesty as it once did.

Developing a Solid First Draft Once you have organized selected details into a list like the one on page 171, then it's time to develop a solid **first draft** of the essay. Using your categorized groups of prewriting ideas and examples as a foundation, you should be able to compose an introduction, body, and conclusion. Remember—this version of your essay doesn't have to be perfect. You'll still have a chance to address remaining problem spots during the revising stage.

The first complete version, the **rough draft**, is for your eyes only. Prepare this draft on a computer so that you can take advantage of the various spelling and grammar tools. Always double- or triple-space your draft so that when you

The Relationship between Topic Sentences and the Thesis

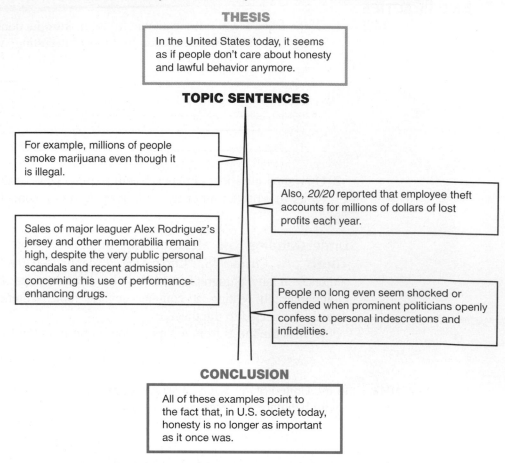

THESIS

In the United States today, it seems as if people don't care about honesty and lawful behavior anymore.

TOPIC SENTENCES

For example, millions of people smoke marijuana even though it is illegal.

Also, *20/20* reported that employee theft accounts for millions of dollars of lost profits each year.

Sales of major leaguer Alex Rodriguez's jersey and other memorabilia remain high, despite the very public personal scandals and recent admission concerning his use of performance-enhancing drugs.

People no long even seem shocked or offended when prominent politicians openly confess to personal indescretions and infidelities.

CONCLUSION

All of these examples point to the fact that, in U.S. society today, honesty is no longer as important as it once was.

print the document, you will have room to add any corrections by hand. Step away from the draft before taking another look at it. Then, review and correct it for obvious errors in form or awkward spots. You want this version to be clean and readable—this draft, your first, is the one that you'll share with another reader.

At some point during the composing process, you will also need to develop a title for your essay. Start with a **working title**, just a general name that reminds you of your main focus. Then, once you complete your first draft, you can refine the title. There is no magic formula for the perfect title. Sometimes a key phrase from the essay will do the job. Other times, a play on words of some kind—a pun, for instance, or a tweaking or inversion of an easily recognizable name or saying—will work. Since the purpose of the title is to heighten curiosity about the essay, be sure to select a phrasing that will intrigue or tantalize your reader—but remember that it should relate to the point of your essay as well.

Here is the *first draft* of the essay on superstitions:

Superstitions

(1) Superstitions, irrational ideas or concepts related to good or bad

fortune, play a larger role in the world around us than most people realize. Common groups of superstitions involve objects that can bring good luck, behaviors that can influence luck, and actions that can cause bad luck.

(2) The belief in good luck charms is one of the best-known superstitions. For some people, the good luck charm is a special item. For others, the good luck charm is more traditional. Casinos take advantage of people's belief in luck.

(3) Other well-known superstitions are sayings passed down from generation to generation. For instance, from childhood, people are often told that throwing salt over their shoulders will bring good luck and that breaking a mirror will bring bad luck. Old wives' tales warn us not to walk under a ladder and not to let a black cat cross our paths. Of course, no evidence exists that any of these things cause bad luck, but people often follow these directions, just to be sure.

(4) Many people believe that performing certain rituals can provide good luck. Sometimes a basketball player will bounce the ball a certain number of times. Some baseball players perform strange rituals with their gloves or bats. Regardless of the particular actions, the players perform them because they believe they will bring them good luck.

(5) Exactly why people believe in these irrational superstitions is difficult to understand. In any case, when you notice people holding a special object, performing some little ritual, or following some old directive, wish them luck.

This first draft contains the basics: a thesis, prewriting ideas expressed in sentence form, and paragraphs arranged into an introduction, body, and conclusion. At this point, however, it is in a limited and rough form. Before it fulfills the promise that it holds, it needs to be reexamined and reworked. In other words, it needs to be revised.

CHALLENGE 14.2   Relating Thesis and Topic Sentences

collaboration

1. Take another look at the first draft of the essay about superstition on pages 174–175. On a separate sheet of paper, list the topic sentence of each paragraph.

2. Working with a classmate, discuss the relationship between the thesis, the topic sentences in the body, and the topic sentence in the conclusion. Then create a figure like the one about honesty on page 174.

Revising

Once you have completed a draft of your essay, it is a good idea to take a day or so break from it. This way, you will bring a rested and refreshed eye to the final stage of the writing process: *revising.* When you revise, you *refine* and then *polish* your draft. You follow the same steps to revise an essay as you follow to revise a paragraph: *reassess, redraft,* and *edit.*

Reassessing   When you *reassess,* you reexamine the essay for the following:

- *Unity*—all examples and details must be directly connected
- *Coherence*—all the material must have clear transitions, be expressed in standard English, and be arranged in a logical order
- *Effective language*—all ideas must be specific and concise

ESL Note
See "Unity," page 555, for more on the importance of ensuring that all the information you include is directly connected to your main idea.

Revising for Unity   In a successful essay, all the elements work together to support the thesis. When you reassess for unity, make sure that each component is directly connected to your main idea. Sometimes, an entire paragraph is not connected to the thesis. In other cases, individual sentences within a paragraph are not connected to the topic sentence. Both cases distract the reader from your main point.

Look again, for example, at paragraph 2 of the first-draft essay on superstition:

> The belief in good luck charms is one of the best-known superstitions. For some people, the good luck charm is a special item. For others, the good luck charm is more traditional. Casinos take advantage of people's belief in luck.

As the topic sentence indicates, the main point of the paragraph concerns common kinds of superstitions. The second and third sentences of the paragraph refer to examples of superstitions (although in their current form, the examples are too general to be wholly effective). But the fourth sentence goes off in a different direction, disrupting the unity of the paragraph. To maintain unity, this sentence needs to be eliminated.

ESL Note
See "Strive for Clarity," page 556, for more on the importance of keeping your writing coherent.

Revising for Coherence   In an effective essay, when one idea flows smoothly to the next, it is *coherent.* To achieve coherence, (1) provide adequate *transitions* between paragraphs and between sentences and (2) *organize* your ideas in a logical order.

Transitions   As Chapter 4, "Refining and Polishing Your Draft," showed, transitions help establish a smooth flow of ideas. Both *synonyms* and *common transitional expressions* help show relationships among your ideas. (See pages 48–49 for lists of transitions.) When you reassess a draft, carefully identify any instances where the flow between sentences or paragraphs should be improved, and make sure ideas follow logically from one to the other.

Consider again the paragraph about ritualized behavior on the part of athletes from the first draft essay about superstition:

> Many people believe that performing certain rituals can provide good luck. Sometimes a basketball player will bounce the ball a certain number of times. Some baseball players perform strange rituals with their gloves or bats. Regardless of the particular actions, the players perform them because they believe they will bring them good luck.

This paragraph contains good information. Right now, however, the paragraph is choppy and doesn't flow smoothly for two reasons: (1) the information itself is not as complete and detailed as it could be, and (2) the paragraph lacks transitions.

Now look at the final draft of the same paragraph. Notice how much better this paragraph is, thanks to the additional details (in italics) and transitions (in boldface):

> **In addition to lucky objects,** many people believe that performing certain rituals can provide good luck. *Consider professional athletes, for example.* Sometimes a basketball player will bounce the ball a certain number of times— *no more, no less—before shooting a foul shot.* **Also,** some baseball players *while waiting for a pitch will adjust their equipment, from batting helmet to wristbands to gloves, always in the same order.* Regardless of the particular actions, the players perform them because they believe they will bring them good luck.

Proper Organization   As we've established, a successful, *coherent* essay uses transitions; it also uses proper organization. Chapter 4 discussed several methods of establishing order:

1. *Chronological order*   arranging events on the basis of order of occurrence

2. *Spatial order*   arranging descriptive details on the basis of their physical relationship with each other

3. *Emphatic order*   arranging points according to their importance

When you reassess a draft for organization, make sure the reader can easily follow it. If the essay is arranged chronologically, check that the sequence of events is presented in the order in which each event actually occurred. If the essay is arranged spatially, make sure that the reader is able to visualize the scene. If the essay is arranged emphatically, ensure that it sustains the reader's interest and effectively accentuates the thesis.

In the essay on superstitions, the thesis suggests that superstitions play a greater part in life than people may realize. Therefore, to most effectively convey this point, the writer uses emphatic order—moving from strong to stronger to strongest supporting ideas.

But that's not exactly how it worked out in the first draft. For instance, many individuals keep lucky items, so identifying this group first makes sense (paragraph 2). But, not everyone knows that some professional athletes perform rituals on the field or court (paragraph 4), and more people than not have been exposed to common, superstitious sayings since childhood (paragraph 3). Since the point of the essay is to convey how superstitions play a greater role in our lives than we realize, presenting the discussion about sayings, proverbs, and adages as the final, most emphatic, point would make more sense.

Revising for Effective Language   In a successful essay, the language captures the meaning the writer intends. When you reassess a draft, look for and replace any vague, general, or unclear language with specific and concise terms. To re-create the experience or clarify your point, **amplify**—include additional specific examples or details.

Consider again the first-draft paragraph about good luck charms:

> The belief in good luck charms is one of the best-known superstitions. For some people, the good luck charm is a special item. For others, the good luck charm is more traditional. Casinos take advantage of people's belief in luck.

This paragraph fails to create a clear picture for the reader for two reasons: (1) the language is vague and general and (2) it offers little support. For example, the second and third sentences define good luck charms as being either *special* or *more traditional*. But what does this mean? Remember: a writer's job is not merely to tell something, but to *show* through specific details and examples what the writer intends. To improve this draft paragraph, the writer needs to amplify.

Now consider this version from the final draft, with the changes shown in italics:

> The belief in good luck charms is one of the best-known superstitions. *Many people keep special objects that they believe will somehow keep them safe or provide an extra edge.* For some people, the good luck charm is a special item, *like a particular "lucky" shirt or key chain with a special symbol of some kind attached.* For others, the good luck charm is more traditional, *something like a rabbit's foot or four-leaf clover. Even though it's completely irrational, many people seem to derive comfort by keeping these lucky charms with them wherever they go.*

ESL Note
See "Confusing Words,"
page 553, for a discus-
sion of words that may
present particular prob-
lems for you.

As you can see, this version is far more effective, thanks to the more specific lan-guage and added details. For example, the new second sentence now explains why people keep lucky charms, and then the two sentences that follow specify the types of lucky charms that people keep. Finally, the disruptive, unrelated sentence about casinos from the first draft has been eliminated and replaced with a directly related sentence about the power that some people ascribe to special objects.

Seeking Help from an Objective Reader In addition to reassessing your draft yourself, it's always a good idea to get feedback from an objective reader. Choose someone who will respond honestly and intelligently to your work. Your reader will find the following reader assessment checklist useful in responding to your first draft.

ESL Note
See "Think about
Audience Expectations,"
page 556, for addi-
tional details about ad-
dressing the needs of
the reader.

✓READER ASSESSMENT CHECKLIST

☐ Do you understand the point I am making? Does my thesis statement clearly state the topic along with my perspective on it? (thesis)

☐ Do I stick to that point all the way through? Does the topic sentence of each paragraph relate to the thesis? (unity)

☐ Are all my ideas and examples clearly connected and easy to follow? (coherence)

☐ Are the words I've used specific and concise? (effective language)

☐ Are my introduction and conclusion effective?

☐ What changes do you think I should make?

Here are a reader's comments in reaction to the first-draft essay on superstitions:

> I learned a lot from your paper—it's already good. You have a clear thesis, and the paragraphs in the body are all connected to it. The introduction let me know where you were going with this topic, and the conclusion repeated it. The best feature is the topic. I am really interested in superstitions myself. I think a couple of things would make your paper even better. I was wondering if you thought about changing the order of the last two sets of examples so the ideas build up even more. I was a little confused about the casino stuff—I'm not sure I could see a clear connection. But my biggest suggestion is that you give some more examples of superstitions and rituals. The stuff you have included is really interesting, and as I read I wanted to know even more. I think if you expand your discussion, your paper would be outstanding.

With these kinds of suggestions, you are prepared to move to the next step: redrafting.

**COMPREHENSION
AND PRACTICE
14.3**

Understanding Effective Revision

1. Of the questions making up the reader assessment checklist on page 179, which do you find easiest to answer? Why?

_____

_____

_____

2. Why is it a good idea to give yourself a break between the composing and revising stages of writing?

_____

_____

_____

3. How can an objective reader help you improve your essay?

_____

_____

_____

Redrafting   When you redraft, you need to rethink your essay, considering the best way to bring the scene or situation into even better focus. Redrafting involves addressing any problem spots in unity, coherence, logical order, and specific language identified by you or your objective reader. As Chapter 4 (pages 62–63) outlines, redrafting is different every time you write. Sometimes you will have to make changes and adjustments in several areas, and other times you will need to concentrate to a greater degree on one particular area.

Often you'll need to change the wording of a detail or example so that your reader can better visualize or understand it. You'll find that clarifying your ideas in this way will be worth the extra work. Your essay will better express what you want to say as a result.

You will also likely need to provide additional, specific examples and details to support your ideas and fill any gaps (amplify). Such transitional expressions as *for example* and *for instance* are helpful to you in this regard (see Chapter 3, page 38). They remind you to supply a specific supporting example, and they cue your reader that a specific illustration will follow. With redrafting, your ultimate goal is always the same: to do everything you can to communicate your ideas fully to your reader.

Editing: Eliminating Errors   The final step in revising an essay is *editing*, which you accomplish through careful *proofreading*. Remember that good content alone won't make an essay effective. It must also be free from errors in standard written English—grammar and usage, spelling, and punctuation. These kinds of errors are serious because they distract your reader from your message.

When you edit, use the following proofreading checklist, which lists several of the most common writing problems, to identify specific weaknesses in your essay. Next to each listing is the abbreviation commonly used to identify this error. The inside back cover of this book includes a more complete list of errors and abbreviations.

✓ PROOFREADING CHECKLIST

☐ Have I eliminated all sentence fragments? *(frag)*

  (See Chapter 18 for more on sentence fragments.)

☐ Have I eliminated all comma splices? *(cs)*

  (See Chapter 20 for more on comma splices.)

☐ Have I eliminated all run-on sentences? *(rs)*

  (See Chapter 20 for more on run-on sentences.)

☐ Is the spelling *(sp)* correct throughout?

  (See Chapter 29 for more on spelling.)

☐ Is the verb tense *(t)* correct throughout?

  (See Chapters 22, 23, and 24 for more on verb tense.)

☐ Do all subjects agree with their verbs? *(subj/verb agr)*

  (See Chapters 21 and 25 for more on subject–verb agreement.)

☐ Do all pronouns agree with their antecedents? *(pro/ant agr)*

  (See Chapter 26 for more on pronoun–antecedent agreement.)

When it comes to your own essay, you may find that you have no problems with some of the items on the list. At the same time, your paper may contain weaknesses not covered on the list. The best thing to do is adapt the list so that it covers your own particular problem spots. Use your adapted proofreading checklist every time you write, regardless of whether it's an essay, a term paper, or a letter.

Another proven technique to eliminate errors in form is to team up with a classmate. Neither you nor your proofreading partner will be especially familiar with the essay you are examining, so you will each be better prepared to find any remaining errors in that document.

Also, take full advantage of your word processor's spell checking or style checking features, but keep in mind that a computer doesn't reason the way a human does—despite advances in software. As Chapter 4 explains (page 66), if you write *desert* when you actually mean *dessert,* the computer may not discover this oversight because *desert* is a correctly spelled word. Furthermore, these computer programs aren't always reliable with matters of subject-verb agreement and sentence fragments. They may mistakenly reason that a noun or pronoun serving as an object of a preposition near the verb is the subject. Or, they may identify an imperative sentence as a fragment because the subject is implied rather than stated. Therefore, do not rely solely on these tools. Always proofread your paper one more time to make sure that all errors have been caught and corrected.

Finally, make it a point to be well rested whenever you edit. Fatigue combined with familiarity with what you have written can make it easy to overlook errors.

Understanding Plagiarism—and How to Avoid It

In Chapter 4 (pages 64–65) you were introduced to the crime of **plagiarism**, using someone else's work—published or unpublished words, ideas, or illustrations—without giving the creator of that work sufficient credit. Some academic plagiarism happens unintentionally, as identifying whether you've actually plagiarized something can sometimes be difficult. But, however honestly unintended, if you commit an act of plagiarism, you must face the consequences.

The key to avoiding plagiarism is to acknowledge, or document, your sources. **Documentation** involves providing essential information about the source of the material—information that would enable readers to find the material for themselves, if they so choose. It tells the reader (1) which ideas are the writer's, (2) which ideas are someone else's, (3) where the writer got the facts and other information, and (4) how reliable the sources are.

While the **fair use doctrine** allows writers to legally use a limited amount of another's work in their own papers and books, responsible writers still take care to accurately and clearly credit the source for *every* use of another's material. Failing to do this is the same as claiming all the material to be yours; in essence, you are lying. This act is a serious breach of scholarly ethics whose possible consequences are a failing grade or disciplinary action ranging from suspension to expulsion. A record of such action can adversely affect professional opportunities in the future as well as graduate school admission. Academic professionals can face public disgrace or even be forced out of a position. In the business world, plagiarism leads to distrust and can significantly damage one's career. You must therefore understand what plagiarism is, learn how to discern whether you have actually plagiarized, and document every source. For more on how to properly document sources, see "Acknowledging Your Sources" on pages 214–218 of Chapter 15.

Examining the Final Draft

Here is the final draft of the essay on superstition. The various changes in the essay have been highlighted, and the annotations accompanying the text point out how revision transformed a good first draft into something far better:

1. The title is more specific and therefore more effective.
2. Instead of two sentences, this final-draft version includes four. In this amplified form, the introduction provides a more complete direction for the reader.

1.
Superstitions: The Irrational Beliefs That Influence Our Behavior

Superstitions, irrational ideas or concepts related to good or bad fortune, play a larger role in the world around us than most people
2.
realize. Cultures all over the world hold beliefs that doing or possessing certain things can bring them good luck or cause them bad luck. People here in the United States are no different. Common groups of

3. A new sentence that indicates a rationale for belief in the power of good luck charms has been added.

4. Specific details about what constitutes a special item and a traditional good luck charm have been supplied.

5. The sentence about casinos that disrupted paragraph unity in the first draft has been eliminated and replaced with a directly related sentence reiterating the power that some people attribute to special objects.

6. The additional transition improves the flow between paragraphs as well as within the paragraph.

7. Details and examples, expressed in effective language, now make the rituals that some professional athletes perform on the field or court specific and clear for the reader.

8. The added transition emphasizes emphatic order.

9. Clarification of the forms and general theme of this kind of folklore and additional, specific examples of this kind of superstitious belief make this paragraph, and, as a result, the entire essay, much more effective.

3.
superstitions in daily evidence in the U.S. involve objects that can bring good luck, behaviors that can influence luck, and actions that can cause bad luck.

The belief in good luck charms is one of the best-known
4.
superstitions. Many people keep special objects that they believe will somehow keep them safe or provide an extra edge. For some people,
4.
the good luck charm is a special item, like a particular "lucky" shirt or key chain with a special symbol of some kind attached. For others, the
4.
good luck charm is more traditional, something like a rabbit's foot or
5.
four-leaf clover. Even though it's completely irrational, many people seem to derive comfort by keeping these lucky charms with them wherever they go.
6.
In addition to lucky objects, many people believe that performing
6.
certain rituals can provide good luck. Consider professional athletes, for example. Sometimes a basketball player will bounce the ball a certain
7.
number of times—no more, no less—before shooting a foul shot. Also,
7.
some baseball players while waiting for a pitch will adjust their equipment, from batting helmet to wristbands to gloves, always in the same order. Regardless of the particular actions, the players perform them because they believe they will bring them good luck.
8.   9.
Perhaps the best-known superstitions are proverbs, axioms, and sayings to ward off bad luck passed down from generation to generation. For instance, from childhood, people are often told that throwing salt over their shoulders will bring good luck and that breaking a mirror will bring bad luck. Old wives' tales warn us not to
9.
walk under a ladder, not to open an umbrella inside a house, and not
9.
to let a black cat cross our paths. Other sayings warn that putting a hat on a bed or shoes on a table will certainly bring bad luck. Of course,

no evidence exists that any of these things cause bad luck, but

people often follow these directions, just to be sure.

    Exactly why people believe in these irrational superstitions is
                                10.
difficult to understand. Maybe it is because life in general is so

uncertain. In any case, when you notice people holding a special

object, performing some little ritual, or following some old directive,
                               10.
wish them luck. They need it, or at least they think they do.

10. The two additional sentences help the conclusion reemphasize the significance of the points made in the introduction and body of the essay.

As the annotations show, developing this final draft involved making a significant number of changes. The point here is that writing isn't a one-shot process. Often you will find that you need to work through several drafts before your essay is as effective as it could be.

If you compare the first draft of this essay with the final draft, one thing is obvious: Revision works, as the following instructor's comments indicate:

Congratulations—this revision is excellent. You have improved the paper in so many ways. The new supporting examples make your point about the frequency and influence of superstitions much clearer. Your introduction is much more detailed and effective—it really prepares the reader for the rest of the essay. You've also adjusted your presentation to take full advantage of emphatic order. In each paragraph, you've made sure to include solid examples and plenty of transitions. And your conclusion does a great job of encapsulating the significance of your essay. You should definitely include a clean copy of this essay in your portfolio. You should also submit it to be included in the class anthology that we will be putting together at the end of the course. And I'll be glad to take another look at it if you decide to revise it again. As we've discussed in class, an essay isn't restricted to five paragraphs. Perhaps you can come up with another aspect or two about superstitions to discuss.

CHALLENGE 14.3 **Evaluating a First-Draft Essay**

collaboration

1. Read the following first-draft essay on home shopping. Then, working with a classmate, answer the questions that follow on a separate sheet of paper.

The Home Shopping Phenomenon

(1) Home shopping has become a popular alternative for busy shoppers.

(2) There are a couple of different home shopping networks on cable television. All the shows seem to work the same, a host introduces the product, describes it, and posts the price. Then a phone number and Web address are flashed. You can get a good deal on collectibles and sports memorabilia.

(3) The home shopping networks sells designer clothing, including outerwear and shoes. Occasionally, a fashion designer comes on to discuss the clothing while fashion models walk around displaying them.

(4) Celebrities come on to sell her own brands of fragrances or jewelry. Cheap rings, bracelets, or necklaces can cause allergic reactions. The celebrities chat with the hosts and encourage viewers to buy.

(5) What makes it all especially convenient is that you never have to leave your couch to shop. When you see what you want on the screen, you dial the 1-800 number or go to the posted Web site, give a credit card number, and the item is on its way to your door. No crowded mall parking lots, no long lines at the registers.

(6) In today's fast-paced world, it's often hard to find time to go out shopping, especially during the holiday season.

a. Evaluate the introduction and conclusion. In what way would you suggest they be changed?

b. Which paragraph in this draft supplies the best support for the thesis? Explain why.

c. Turn again to the reader assessment checklist (page 179) and the proofreading checklist (page 181), and use them to assess and edit this first draft. On a separate sheet of paper, make a list of problem spots and errors that need to be addressed.

2. Imagine that the writer has asked you to write a critique in which you indicate (a) what is good in the essay and (b) what still needs work. On a separate sheet of paper, write a paragraph of seven to ten sentences analyzing the essay.

FOR FURTHER EXPLORATION Writing an Essay

1. Focus on one of the following topics. Use the prewriting technique—or combination of techniques—that you prefer to generate some preliminary ideas while considering what purposes you might fulfill as you write about the topic:

- a school, work, or national issue that you think receives too much attention
- an item that you would like to pass on to a child or grandchild some day
- a change that you feel would improve life in your city or town
- your biggest complaint about working or communicating on the Internet

2. Evaluate your prewriting material; identify a focus and potential supporting ideas, details, and examples; and create a draft essay of at least five paragraphs. Use the material in this chapter, especially the sample essay about superstition (pages 182–184), to guide you as you develop your essay.

collaboration

3. Exchange your draft with a classmate. Using the material in this chapter as a guide, evaluate the draft essay you receive, considering unity, coherence, and effective language. Proofread carefully, and use the abbreviations in the proofreading checklist and on the inside back cover of this book to identify any errors you see in the essay you receive. Return the essay to the writer, along with a written response along the lines of the sample peer response on page 179.

4. Create a final draft, addressing any problems your writing partner identified.

DISCOVERING CONNECTIONS Writing an Essay

For this assignment, consider one of these questions or another that the picture inspires. Using the information in this chapter to guide you, create an essay of 500–700 words that examines your topic in full detail. Make sure you supply an introduction that includes a clear thesis, plenty of supporting examples and details, and a concluding paragraph that restates the significance of what you have told your reader.

A. Does the picture of the East Indian dancers make you think of a special occasion? What was the event? Why were you involved? What was the most significant or memorable part?

B. Thanks to television and media exposure, dance in a variety of forms—break dancing, fusion dancing, line dancing, ballroom dancing, and so on—is a hot topic. What is your best—or worst—dance experience? When did it occur? Who else was involved? Why did the experience create such an impression on you?

RECAP   Developing an Essay

Key Terms in This Chapter	Definitions
essay	a multiparagraph writing that deals more extensively with a subject than a paragraph does
introduction	a paragraph that opens an essay, providing a clear thesis and engaging the reader
body	the series of paragraphs that provide support and illustration for a thesis

Key Terms in This Chapter	Definitions
five-paragraph essay	an essay form, especially useful with some timed writing situations, that features an introduction presenting three main points, a body containing three paragraphs discussing those three points, and a conclusion restating the significance of those three points
conclusion	a paragraph that closes the essay, summarizing the essay's point and bringing the essay to a logical and appropriate end
thesis	the sentence in the introduction that specifies the main subject of the essay and the writer's attitude or position on it
anecdote	a brief, entertaining story, often used to make a point An anecdote may be used effectively in an introduction or a conclusion.
rhetorical question	a question designed not to be answered, but to provoke thought or discussion A rhetorical question may be used effectively in an introduction to engage readers.
first draft	an initial version of a piece of writing with the most obvious errors corrected
rough draft	the first version of a piece of writing that has yet to be evaluated for errors
working title	a general label you assign to a piece of writing early on to indicate the major focus
amplifying	the process of providing additional specific details and examples
plagiarism	appropriating someone else's work
documentation	acknowledging sources of adapted material in accordance with a recognized system such as that of the Modern Language Association (MLA)
fair use doctrine	ruling governing the amount of another's work that can be included in a document

The Process of Writing an Essay

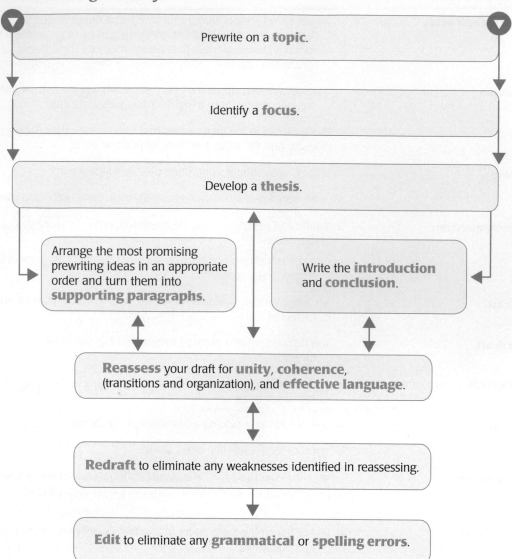

Prewrite on a **topic**.

Identify a **focus**.

Develop a **thesis**.

Arrange the most promising prewriting ideas in an appropriate order and turn them into **supporting paragraphs**.

Write the **introduction** and **conclusion**.

Reassess your draft for **unity**, **coherence**, (transitions and organization), and **effective language**.

Redraft to eliminate any weaknesses identified in reassessing.

Edit to eliminate any **grammatical** or **spelling errors**.

Using Odyssey Online with MyWritingLab

For more practice developing an essay, go to www.mywritinglab.com.

CHAPTER 15
Examining Types of Essays

GETTING STARTED ...

 Q I'm sure I will be writing essays on a variety of subjects. Will what I've learned so far about writing different kinds of paragraphs help me write essays?

 A Absolutely. Everything you've learned about the writing process and the characteristics of the different modes or organizing strategies for paragraphs is just as valid for writing essays. Rely on the skills you have developed so far, and you will be able to write effective essays that meet the needs of your reader.

Overview: Understanding How to Use the Modes to Develop Essays

Effective writing fulfills a purpose while communicating the writer's ideas. Chapters 5 through 12 showed how to use the various **modes** or organizing strategies to develop paragraphs: *narration, description, example, process, definition, comparison and contrast, cause and effect,* and *division and classification.* Chapter 13 explained that *argument* differs from the modes because it is a **purpose** or aim, not a mode.

Chapters 14 introduced the essay, explaining how this type of writing differs from a paragraph. Probably the most significant difference is in scope. When you write an essay, you deal with a subject in far greater detail than you can with a single paragraph. To write an essay, you actually use a number of modes in combination, but one mode will always dominate. You'll probably be especially aware of the interaction among multiple modes when you are writing an argument essay. With argument, you use whatever combination of modes does the best job of persuading your reader to accept the point you are presenting.

Navigating This Chapter In this chapter, you will learn how to use the modes to write the following types of essays:

- narration
- description
- example
- process
- definition
- comparison and contrast
- cause and effect
- division and classification
- argument (mixed modes)

The Relationship between Your Purpose and the Modes

Understanding the connection between your purpose and the modes is crucial. As Chapter 1 explained, people write to fulfill one of three purposes: to *inform,* to *entertain,* or to *persuade.* The modes are your means to fulfill the purpose you choose. In most essays, one mode will dominate, with other modes providing additional support.

Open your favorite magazine, and read a few of the articles. Perhaps one article reports recent findings about fat consumption and heart disease. In this case, the writer's primary purpose is to *inform* readers about the data linking diet and heart disease. Another article humorously discusses people's seeming addiction to reality television. In this case, the writer's primary purpose is to *entertain.* Of course, not all writing that entertains is intended to make you laugh. For example, a story about a small town raising money to send a promising young musician to college might not be funny, but it would entertain you. Finally, the primary purpose of an article asserting that nuclear power plant construction should be halted until safety concerns are addressed would be to *persuade.*

Look closely at the articles, and you will also see the modes in action. For example, the article about the scientific research might feature *cause and effect* as its primary mode to link coronary disease to diet. It might also feature such modes as *example* to develop specific case studies and *definition* to explain the terms used in the article.

The essay about people's love for reality television might have *division and classification* as a primary mode to explain the various subcategories of reality TV that people enjoy. It might also include such modes as *description* to capture scenes from the shows being discussed and *narration* to discuss the actions of the participants.

The essay about nuclear power plants might feature *example* as the primary mode to illustrate the dangers at specific nuclear power plants. It might also feature *process* to show how nuclear power plants generate electricity. In addition, it might include *cause and effect* to show how radiation leakage could affect nearby residents' health. Finally, it might include *description* to show in vivid terms the destruction that could result from a nuclear accident.

Most essay assignments will call for one particular mode to dominate. Remember, though, that you will actually use a combination of modes to fulfill your purpose, something you'll perhaps be most aware of when you deal with an argument essay. The rest of this chapter will examine ways to use the modes to develop essays.

Using Narration to Develop an Essay

As Chapter 5 explained, writing that relates a series of events is *narration.* For example, if you were writing a paper about your first day at a new job, narration would be a natural choice. Like narrative paragraphs, **narrative essays** are usually arranged in *chronological order.* In addition, narrative writing is often presented from the *first person point of view* (using *I, me, my*), although it may be written in the *third person* (using *he, she, her, him, they*). In order to be effective, a narrative essay must also be *unified* and include plenty of specific details for support.

Examining a Narrative Essay

Take a look at this narrative essay about the first day at a new job:

Lost and Confused: My First Day in the Hospital Halls

(1) Any change is difficult to handle. Beginning a new job is no different, especially when the new job involves more responsibility than the last one. My first day as a dietary aide at City Hospital was such an ordeal, I don't think I'll ever forget it. By the end of that first workday, I was so frustrated and embarrassed that I never wanted to return.

(2) Here's how it all began. At 6:45 on that first morning, half an hour before my shift officially started, I entered the imposing building and headed to the first floor, where the kitchen and cafeteria are located. In spite of my nervousness, I found my time card and punched in. I then introduced myself to the woman sitting at the desk next to the time clock and asked her where I should go next. She told me to report to Mr. Javits in the kitchen.

(3) Just as I was beginning to think I would make it through the day, I met Mr. Javits, and I became convinced that I wouldn't. First, he looked at me and yelled, "Who the hell are you?" After I explained that I was a new dietary aide, he quickly assigned me to set up and deliver morning meals to the entire cardiac unit. Mr. Javits warned me that any mistake in preparation or delivery of the meals could have serious consequences for the patients. By the time he finished talking, my shirt was soaking wet.

(4) My first round of deliveries was a disaster. The cardiac unit was being renovated, and the painting crew had removed the room numbers. I figured that once I identified one room, I would be able to find the rest easily. The rooms weren't arranged sequentially, however, so I had to personally identify all the patients and go through their menu choices with them. As a result, I fell behind schedule at each room. I began to know what salmon must feel like as they try to swim upstream.

(5) The worst was yet to come. When I returned to the cafeteria with the trays, Mr. Javits was waiting for me. He began yelling and demanding to know where I had been. As I pointed to the notice on the wall announcing the renovation of the cardiac floor, I accidentally bumped Mr. Javits's hand and spilled his cup of coffee over the front of his uniform. At this point, I felt that the end of the day would never come.

(6) The lunch shift was almost as bad as the breakfast shift. This time, Mr. Javits assigned me to the orthopedic area. To distribute the meals, I had to travel the length of the hospital and take two different sets of elevators. By the time I collected the trays and returned them to the cafeteria, I was late again. My shift was scheduled to end at 2:30, and it was almost 3 p.m. Fortunately, Mr. Javits had already left.

(7) After this kind of start, it is hard to believe that I soon became an expert on the hospital. Within a couple of days, I knew my way around the building. After a month, Mr. Javits even put me in charge of training new workers. I also found out that most of my co-workers had had similar experiences on their first day working in the hospital cafeteria. Like me, they had been completely intimidated at the prospect of something new.

CHALLENGE 15.1   **Analyzing the Sample Narrative Essay**

Refer to the sample narrative essay, "Lost and Confused" on page 191 to answer each question.

collaboration

1. Reread the introduction of the essay. Underline the thesis.

2. Underline the topic sentences of paragraphs 2 through 6. In an essay, each topic sentence relates back to the thesis, but it also serves as a building block for its own main idea. Work with a classmate to analyze the role of these sentences. On a separate sheet of paper, explain (a) how each topic sentence in the essay is related to the thesis and (b) how each one is developed through its supporting information.

3. On the same sheet, list transitional expressions that help establish the sequence of events.

FOR FURTHER EXPLORATION Narrative Essay

1. Using the essay on page 191 to guide you, write a narrative essay of about 500 words on your first day at a new job or on one of the following topics:

   - a good childhood playground experience
   - an experience with severe weather
   - an embarrassing incident
   - a time when you witnessed someone's kindness

collaboration

2. Exchange your draft with a classmate. Evaluate the essay you receive using the narrative essay checklist on page 193. Write your answers on a separate sheet of paper, and then return the essay and your assessment to the writer.

3. Using your reader's comments to guide you, revise and redraft your narrative essay.

DISCOVERING CONNECTIONS 15.1 Narrative Essay

For this assignment, consider this photo. Using the preceding discussion on narration as a guide, write an essay of about 500 words in response to one of the accompanying questions or another that the photo inspires. Remember to pay close attention to chronological order, thorough development, and appropriate point of view.

A. This photo shows people walking across a rope bridge in a rain forest in Vietnam. The view from the bridge must be spectacular. What is the single most spectacular view you have ever encountered? What were the circumstances that brought you to this place?

B. The people in the picture are walking forward into the fog, without looking back at all. Can you recall a time when you made a clean break from something, leaving the past behind while moving forward into unknown territory? What were you leaving? Why were you moving on? In doing so, did you make the correct decision?

✓ NARRATIVE ESSAY CHECKLIST

ESL Note
See "Think about Audience Expectations," page 556, for more information about the needs of the audience, and "Strive for Clarity," page 556, for more on the importance of keeping your writing coherent.

☐ Does the introduction set the scene for the sequence of events to follow?

☐ Is *first person* or *third person* point of view used consistently?

☐ Does the paper follow chronological order? If a flashback has been used, has the switch in time been made clear for the reader?

☐ Is the essay unified, with all supporting ideas and examples related to the main idea? Circle any material that isn't unified.

☐ Are there enough specific details and examples to guide the reader? Put an * next to any spot that you'd like to know more about.

☐ In your judgment, what is the best part of this essay? Explain.

Using Description to Develop an Essay

Writing that uses words to paint a picture of a scene, individual, or experience is *descriptive* (see Chapter 6). Effective description emphasizes specific sensory details, as it would in an essay about an unusual experience. **Descriptive essays** often combine both *objective* description (observable details and sensations) and *subjective* description (the impressions that the details and sensations create within the writer). In addition, descriptive writing often uses *spatial order* to organize details for the reader.

Examining a Descriptive Essay

Take a look at this descriptive essay about a childhood vacation:

Niagara Falls, Up Close and Personal

(1) As I was growing up, my parents both worked long hours at their jobs to provide for my brothers and me. But they didn't settle for just the basics of food and clothing. Even though it meant many hours of overtime to pay for it, they made sure that each summer, during the last week of June, we went somewhere on vacation. I have great memories of trips to beaches, amusement parks, and national parks. But the vacation I remember best was the trip to Niagara Falls when I was 12. The Falls were awesome to look at, but the morning that we went on the Cave of the Winds tour and walked under the Falls is what made the trip so amazing.

(2) When we arrived at Goat Island, a small island separating the American and Canadian Falls, I don't think any of us knew what to expect. The entrance to the Cave of the Winds tour is a stone building that looks like a miniature castle. Once my father paid the entrance fee, we went inside where we had to change into huge yellow hooded raincoats and weird fabric shoes. Then we got on an elevator that took us down about 170 feet to the base of the Falls.

(3) When we stepped off the elevator, the air was filled with the roar of the water rushing over the nearby Bridal Veil Falls, a small strand of waterfall between the Canadian and American Falls. Our guide told us to follow her and warned us to stay together. Then we headed over to a wooden walkway that led from the base of the falls up over enormous boulders to a point where a huge torrent of water poured down. At that point was an area called the Hurricane Deck, where visitors could stand to feel the power of Niagara Falls pour down on them.

(4) As we got closer to the falls, the air was so filled with mist that rainbows were everywhere. The crowd in front of me looked like a series of yellow blobs. The thundering of the Falls was so loud that the only way to be heard was to shout, even to the people right next to me. The stairs leading up to the Hurricane Deck were wet and slippery, so I had to hold onto the railing to keep from falling as I passed people coming back down. Standing on the Hurricane Deck itself felt like being under ten streaming fire hoses. I squinted up at the crest of the falls, but all I could see was Niagara's relentless green and white waters blotting out the blue of a beautiful June sky. In the entrance building, I had felt ridiculous putting on a raincoat and booties. "How wet could you get on a little walk?" I had asked myself. Now, with my feet drenched and the hood of my soaking wet coat tied tightly around my face, I understood why rain gear was required.

(5) Anyone who has ever seen Niagara Falls knows it's impossible not to be awed by the extraordinary beauty and intense power of this natural wonder. Day and night, crowds of people stand at the American and Canadian Falls, quietly gazing at millions and millions of gallons of water passing over the edge to crash on the rocks far below. Thanks to our experience on the Cave of the Winds tour, my family and I were able to go one step further and feel a bit of that water pour over us.

CHALLENGE 15.2   **Analyzing the Sample Descriptive Essay**

Refer to the sample descriptive essay "Niagara Falls, Up Close and Personal" on pages 193–194 to answer each question.

1. Reread the introduction of the essay. Underline the thesis.

collaboration

2. Working with a classmate, analyze paragraphs 2 through 4 of the essay. On a separate piece of paper, explain how each one supports the thesis. Rate these three paragraphs according to how effectively they use description:
1 = very effectively; 2 = somewhat effectively; 3 = not effectively.

collaboration

3. Working with the same classmate, examine each sentence of description in paragraphs 2 through 4. Make a list of all subjective details and all objective details as well as points in the essay where spatial order is employed.

FOR FURTHER EXPLORATION Descriptive Essay

1. Using the sample descriptive essay to guide you, write an essay of about 500 words on an unusual experience of your own or on one of the following topics:

- the best-looking person you have ever met
- an accident scene

- the feeling of physical exhaustion
- a vivid dream

collaboration

2. Exchange your draft with a classmate. Evaluate the essay you receive using the descriptive essay checklist below. Write your answers on a separate sheet of paper, and then return the essay and your assessment to the writer.

3. Using your reader's comments to guide you, complete the final draft of your descriptive essay.

DISCOVERING CONNECTIONS 15.2 Descriptive Essay

For this assignment, consider the following photo. Using the discussion on the descriptive essay to guide you, write an essay of about 500 words in response to one of the accompanying questions or another that the photo inspires. Make sure you consider such key aspects as sensory details, objective and subjective description, and spatial order.

A. Sports fans can always be counted on to cheer enthusiastically for their favorite team or heckle mercilessly the opposing team. Look closely at the details in this photograph. How would you characterize the attitude and behavior of these fans? What evidence from the photo supports your claim? Using concrete language to support your view, describe what moment you feel has been captured in this photo.

B. Have you ever participated in a public event that inspired deep emotions? What was that event? What did you feel? What was the most memorable moment you experienced?

ESL Note
See "Think about Audience Expectations," page 556, for more information about the needs of the audience, and "Strive for Clarity," page 556, for more on the importance of keeping your writing coherent.

✓ DESCRIPTIVE ESSAY CHECKLIST

☐ Does the introduction engage the reader? Does the thesis prepare the reader for the event to be described?

☐ Does the essay include effective use of both objective and subjective description?

☐ Are the paragraphs arranged so that the reader can picture the scene being painted? Explain.

☐ Does each paragraph feature a number of specific, concrete sensory details to support the thesis?

☐ In your judgment, what is the best part of this essay? Explain.

☐ Which detail or example would be even better if it were expanded? Why?

Using Example to Develop an Essay

As Chapter 7 discussed, *example* uses specific instances to illustrate, clarify, or back up some point you've made. An **example essay** would be a natural choice to discuss tattooing. When you write an essay that relies heavily on this technique, make sure that the examples you include are *relevant* and *specific*. In addition, *amplify*—provide enough examples to develop your main idea fully. Don't forget to take advantage of the transitional expressions *for instance* and *for example* to alert your reader that a specific example is to follow. Finally, pay close attention to how you arrange the examples you include so that they have the maximum effect on your reader. Depending on the focus of your essay, you may find *chronological* and *emphatic order* particularly useful.

Examining an Example Essay

Consider the following example essay on tattooing:

Making Their Marks: The Popularity of Tattooing

(1) Many people seem content enough to go through life looking like everybody else. But for others, nothing seems more important than distinguishing how they look from the rest of society. Some set themselves apart by how they dress. Others show their individuality by how they wear their hair. Today, some people with an independent streak have found another way to make themselves stand out from the crowd. These people are choosing tattooing, an ancient form of body art that is among the most popular trends of the past decade.

(2) The history of decorating the body in this way goes back thousands of years. Originally, members of a tribe would undergo elaborate tattooing or scarring to signify membership in the group. For example, natives of some islands in the South Pacific would tattoo their faces with intricate designs, while ancient tribes in other lands would cut parts of their bodies to leave scars in particular designs.

(3) For much of the recent past, tattoos held little appeal for the average person. Indeed, they were largely associated with groups such as bikers and sailors. In fact, until fairly recently, tattooing wasn't even legal in many states. The only way for people who wanted a tattoo to get one was to find an illegal tattoo parlor or travel to a country where tattooing was legal. Either way, they endured great pain and risked infection and public disapproval just to decorate their skin.

(4) All that has changed today, however. For one thing, tattooing is now legal in many areas throughout the country. In addition, tattoo parlors are licensed and inspected regularly to make sure they are sanitary. The instruments are sterilized, in many cases using the same technology that purifies dental instruments.

(5) But the biggest change is the clientele who seek tattoos. Today it isn't just an occasional outlaw walking into a tattoo parlor looking to cover a bicep with a skull or anchor or someone's name. Now the waiting room at the tattoo parlor is often crowded with plenty of ordinary people. That outlaw has to get in line with nurses, college students, stockbrokers, and mothers, all looking for something that will mark them as different from the rest of the crowd.

(6) Nobody knows how long the current interest in tattooing will last. Right now, though, the number of people with colorful skin decorations seems to be on the increase. It looks like none of the new tattoo parlors will be closing any time soon.

CHALLENGE 15.3   Analyzing the Sample Example Essay

Refer to the sample example essay "Making Their Marks" on page 196 to answer each question.

1. Reread the introduction. Underline the thesis, and consider where it appears in the paragraph. On a separate sheet of paper, explain if you agree with its placement in the paragraph or would suggest moving it to another point. Explain your reasoning.

2. On a separate sheet of paper, make a list of the examples, paragraph by paragraph, and identify which example you find strongest or most compelling, and why you feel this way.

collaboration

3. Both chronological and emphatic order are used in this essay. Working with a classmate, decide which order dominates and what in the essay leads you to this conclusion.

FOR FURTHER EXPLORATION Example Essay

1. Using the example essay to guide you, write an essay of about 500 words on a popular activity or on one of the following topics:

   - good role models
   - distinctive styles of dress
   - entertaining advertisements on television, radio, or the Internet
   - bad social habits

collaboration

2. Exchange your draft with a classmate. Evaluate the essay you receive using the example essay checklist on page 198. Write your answers on a separate sheet of paper, and then return the essay and your assessment to the writer.

3. Using your reader's comments to guide you, complete the final draft of your example essay.

DISCOVERING CONNECTIONS 15.3 Example Essay

For this assignment, consider this photo. Using the information from the example discussion to guide you, write an essay of about 500 words in response to one of the accompanying questions or another that the photo inspires. As you develop your essay, be sure that the examples you include are specific and relevant and that the organization is appropriate for the focus of the essay.

A. *American Idol* is just one example of the slew of reality television shows that have captured audiences in both the United States and Great Britain. What are some others that you watch or are at least familiar with? What is it about these kinds of shows that catch the interest of the viewing public?

B. Reality television is a trend like any other. In fashion, for instance, the trend could be cowboy boots and skinny jeans. What other trends—in television, fashion, technology, music, and so forth—have caught the public's eye in the last two years? Why do you think they have garnered so much attention?

✔ EXAMPLE ESSAY CHECKLIST

ESL Note
See "Think about Audience Expectations," page 556, for more information about the needs of the audience, and "Strive for Clarity," page 556, for more on the importance of keeping your writing coherent.

☐ Does the introduction spell out the concept or principle to be illustrated?

☐ Are all the examples directly connected to the thesis? Put a ✔ next to any example that you feel is not relevant.

☐ Are all the examples specific? Put an * next to any example that you feel needs to be made more specific.

☐ Are there enough examples to support the thesis? Write *for example* or *for instance* next to any passage that you think could use another example.

☐ Are the examples effectively arranged? Make a note next to any example you think should be moved to a different place.

☐ In your judgment, what is the best part of this essay? Explain.

☐ Which example would be even better if it were expanded? Why?

Using Process to Develop an Essay

Chapter 8 introduced *process*, the writing technique used to explain how to do something, how something occurs or is done, or how you did something. For instance, an essay explaining how to windsurf would clearly be a **process essay**. When you are explaining how to do something, you should use the *imperative mood* to address the reader directly. The imperative mood is usually not appropriate for other types of process writing. For example, if you were writing an essay explaining how acid rain affects the environment or an essay detailing how you investigated your family history to create a family tree, you would not address the reader directly. Many process essays are organized in linear order, using transitional words such as *first, next, then, afterward,* and so on. Be sure that each step describes a small and manageable part of the task, and that you warn your reader about any particularly difficult or potentially confusing steps.

Examining a Process Essay

Consider this essay, which explains the basis steps involved in windsurfing:

Ride Like the Wind: Windsurfing Basics

(1) Are you the kind of person who quickly becomes bored sitting on a beach or lying in the sand? If so, then windsurfing may be your answer to true fun in the sun. The brightly colored sails of windsurfers speeding across the water are familiar sights to many regular beachgoers. Maybe you have

daydreamed about being the person out there maneuvering that sail. If so, you can do more than imagine it. You can begin your personal journey across the waves by following a few basic steps.

(2) At many beach areas and resorts, windsurfer rentals are available. In some cases, inexpensive beginner lessons are available, always a good idea. But if lessons aren't a possibility for you, you can still get a genuine feel for this extreme sport on your own. Be sure to tell the rental agent that you are a beginner so that you end up with an appropriate board and a sail size between 4.5 and 6.0 meters, depending on your size and weight. The larger the sail, the more difficult it will be for you to maneuver, so smaller is probably better than larger, at least for your first try.

(3) Once you are at the water's edge and ready to begin sailing, you need to attach the sail by locking it into the universal joint on the board. Lay the sail across the board so that it is floating on the surface of the water opposite to you. With the sail attached, pull the board into water about thigh deep and position it so that it is perpendicular to the wind. Straight into the wind, the board will simply stall. Keep the front of the board to your right, and the mast, the long pole to which the sail is attached, on the side opposite you. Climb onto the board and place your feet on either side of the point where the mast and the sail join the board. Bend slightly at the knees and slowly pull on the rubberized cord attached to the mast and sail until you can reach the mast with your right hand. Grab the mast just below the boom, which is the bar extending across the sail on both sides. This position is called neutral. At the same time, look around you to orient yourself to the shore and the horizon to make sure you don't end up beached or, worse, on your way out to deep water.

(4) Now you are ready to go for your first ride. Still holding the mast in your right hand, slowly take a step toward the rear of the board. Place your left foot sideways and centered a comfortable distance back and your right foot facing straight, with your toes just about touching the base of the mast. Keep your weight on your back foot, at this point your left. Grab the boom lightly with your left hand, between six inches and a foot out from the mast. As the sail catches the wind, use the mast to steer, straight to travel straight, back to move to the right, and front to move to the left. Use the boom to control speed, pushing or pulling it slightly to catch the wind while using your body weight to counteract the pull of the wind.

(5) At the end of your run, you will need to turn the board to return to your starting point. To turn the board, step back to the neutral position—your feet on either side of the mast. Lower the sail, moving it toward the rear of the board. As you do, the board will begin to turn. Continue to guide the sail across the back of the board while stepping around the mast until you are again in the neutral position. Stop to orient yourself again to the shore and the horizon, use the rubberized cord to raise the mast and sail, and grab it with your left hand. Step back, placing your right foot in the center of the board a comfortable distance back and your left foot facing forward, toes almost touching the base of the mast. Grab the boom about six inches to a foot from the mast and set off, using the mast to steer and the boom for speed.

(6) Unless you are a world-class athlete, expect to start and stop and to fall off the board plenty of times. At the same time, expect to have plenty of fun. Stick with it and, before too long, you'll be the one speeding across the water while daydreamers on the beach watch.

CHALLENGE 15.4   **Analyzing the Sample Process Essay**

Refer to the sample process essay "Ride Like the Wind" on pages 198–199 to answer each question.

collaboration

1. Working with a classmate, find and underline the thesis in the introduction.

2. What are the steps of windsurfing? List them in order on a separate sheet of paper, along with the transitional expressions used to establish order in the essay.

collaboration

3. With your classmate, evaluate each step in the process. Do you need more information about any steps? What questions would you ask the writer to get the information you need?

FOR FURTHER EXPLORATION Process Essay

1. Using the sample process essay to guide you, write your own essay of about 500 words: that tells how to perform some sporting or outdoor activity. If you prefer, write on one of the following topics:

   • how to open a Facebook account and set up a page
   • how to teach a child to tie a shoe
   • how a thunderstorm, tornado, or tsunami occurs
   • how you conducted a study or experiment

collaboration

2. Exchange your draft with a classmate. Evaluate the essay you receive using the process essay checklist on page 201. Write your answers on a separate sheet of paper, and then return the essay and your assessment to the writer.

3. Using your reader's comments to guide you, complete the final draft of your essay.

DISCOVERING CONNECTIONS 15.4 Process Essay

For this assignment, consider this photo. Using the information from the process discussion to guide you, write an essay of about 500 words in response to one of the accompanying questions or another that the photo it inspires. As you write, concentrate on expressing the process in simple, logical steps, with the appropriate use of the imperative mood and linear order.

A. The Grand Canyon underwent a major, yet slow geologic process in order for it to become the natural wonder it is today. What other processes can you think of—in nature, in the arts, in school, or at work—that generally occur slowly, but usually produce amazing results? Describe the steps of this process with as much detail and precision as possible.

B. The Grand Canyon is clearly one of the most magnificent places on earth. If you were going on vacation there or to another U.S. National Park, what process would you follow to make such a trip as satisfying as possible?

✓ PROCESS ESSAY CHECKLIST

ESL Note
See "Think about Audience Expectations," page 556, for more information about the needs of the audience, and "Strive for Clarity," page 556, for more on the importance of keeping your writing coherent.

☐ Does the introduction identify the procedure or technique to be presented?

☐ Is the reader addressed directly through the imperative mood (*you*)? Is it appropriate for this essay? Why?

☐ Are the steps presented in linear order? Underline any step that is out of order, and then draw an arrow to the spot in the essay where it actually belongs.

☐ Is each step simple and clear? Put a ✓ next to any step that you think should be divided or explained further.

☐ In your judgment, what is the best part of this essay? Explain.

☐ Which detail or example would be even better if it were expanded? Why?

Using Definition to Develop an Essay

Chapter 9 introduced *definition,* the writing technique used to identify the essential characteristics or qualities of an object, location, or individual. An essay focusing on a common slogan or expression, for example, would rely heavily on definition. To write a **definition essay**, you need to recognize the *elements of an effective definition:* The term is placed in its appropriate class and then differentiated from the other elements in its class. In general, you should provide a *working definition* in the introduction and then build an *extended definition* throughout the body of the paper. This is done by supplying *clear, specific,* and *detailed* examples and illustrations. At the same time, take into consideration both the *denotation,* the literal meaning of the term, and its *connotations,* additional subjective or emotional impacts it will have on readers. Also, don't be afraid to turn to synonyms, negation, and etymology—a word's origin and historical development—as a way to enhance the definition. In addition, you should present the material you include in an order that enhances understanding.

Examining a Definition Essay

Consider the following five-paragraph essay, which provides a personal definition for living *green:*

The Simple Life

(1) I have to be honest. When I first heard terms like *being green, the green revolution,* and *living the green way,* I wasn't sure what to think. But after considering discussions about green issues in my environmental studies

class as well as articles in newspapers and magazines, on the television news, and on a number of blogs, I have an answer. For me, living a green life is a combination of common sense and restraint that involves keeping things simple and being efficient regarding the products I buy and use and the energy I consume.

(2) To be green in terms of the purchases I make, I am now more deliberate in my choices. When I shop for fresh fruits and vegetables, for example, I do my best to buy locally grown produce, and I go to local restaurants that do the same. That way, I am helping in my own small way to reduce environmental impacts from the transportation of goods. For everyday and hang around clothes, I check out a couple of second hand stores near my house. The clothes are still in great shape, and they are available at a fraction of the original price, plus there is no extra shipping or packaging involved. I also check out eBay and Craigslist, and if I buy anything, I use the U.S. Postal Service for delivery. The Postal Service delivers mail to my house six days a week anyway, so these purchases create no additional need for transportation. Finally, I try to resist peer pressure and not buy something new just because everyone else has. My cell phone is the one I received for free when I signed up, and I've had the same iPod for four years. Why should I upgrade and add to the enormous and growing pile of electronic waste when the devices I have meet all my needs?

(3) Being green also means being efficient in how I manage and carry out my life. For instance, I make it a point to recycle thoroughly. I use the bins the city has provided for all my clean paper, plastic, and glass. I also recycle the ink cartridges from my printer. An added bonus for acting responsibly is that, in exchange, many retailers, including Staples, offer rebates or reduced prices on new printer ink. When I shop for groceries, I use my own fabric bags, so I don't use any additional plastic or paper bags. In addition, I bought a filter for the faucet in my house and a reusable stainless steel bottle for water, eliminating the many plastic bottles that I used to send to the landfill. In terms of food preparation, I try to cook no more than will be eaten as a meal and as leftovers, reducing the amount of food waste that goes into the trash.

(4) But the thing that I consider the most important aspect of living a green life involves my use of energy. There is no question: if the U.S. is going to become more energy independent and improve the quality of the environment, we all have to be more attentive to how we use, and often waste, energy. Therefore, I now pay a lot more attention to how to conserve. I still drive my car when necessary, but I try to plan things out so that I can use less gas by combining trips and errands. When a destination is close, I walk or ride my bike, and I also make it a point to use public transportation as often as I can. There is talk that the city will soon start a bus run from my neighborhood to campus. Once that's in place, I'll take the bus to school, and there will be one less car adding to congestion and pollution on city streets. Although it was a little expensive, I replaced all the light bulbs in my apartment with energy efficient compact fluorescent bulbs. Rebates helped with the cost, and the promise of longer bulb life should help me break even in a year or so. Out of sheer laziness, I used to leave my computer on all day and my phone and iPod chargers plugged in until

my environmental professor pointed out that doing so is like leaving a faucet dripping all day long. I also got serious about the most basic strategy to reduce energy consumption at home: I began switching off the lights whenever I left a room. They are all simple, common sense steps leading to a green life.

(5) Stepping into a green life has been much easier than I could have imagined. It's really all about intention and moderation. I buy only what I need when I need it, and I keep it local when I can. I handle what I have carefully, reuse it when I can, and dispose of it responsibly when it's no longer useful. Finally, I do my best to limit the natural resources I use and carbon emissions created as a result. It's that simple.

CHALLENGE 15.5   **Analyzing the Sample Definition Essay**

Refer to the sample definition essay "The Simple Life" on pages 201–203 to answer each question.

collaboration

1. Find and underline the thesis in the first paragraph. On a separate sheet of paper, write the term that is defined and the writer's working definition of it.

2. Working with a classmate, analyze paragraphs 2 through 4. First, underline the topic sentence in each. Then study the way each topic sentence is developed. On your paper, summarize the way each paragraph develops or extends the definition.

3. As the first sentence of the fourth paragraph suggests, the primary means of organization is emphatic order. Do you agree with the current arrangement of the body of the essay, or would you suggest that one or more of the supporting paragraphs be reordered? On a separate sheet of paper, explain your reasoning.

FOR FURTHER EXPLORATION Definition Essay

1. Using the sample essay that starts on page 201 to guide you, write an essay of about 500 words defining a common saying, tagline, or buzzword or on one of the following topics:

   - real maturity
   - a serious slacker
   - a major slob
   - true courage

collaboration

2. Exchange your draft with a classmate. Evaluate the essay you receive using the definition essay checklist on page 204. Write your answers on a separate sheet of paper, and then return the essay and your assessment to the writer.

3. Using your reader's comments to guide you, complete the final draft of your definition essay.

DISCOVERING CONNECTIONS 15.5 Definition Essay

For this assignment, consider this photo. Using the information from the definition discussion to guide you, write an essay of about 500 words in response to one of the accompanying questions or another that the photo inspires. As you develop your essay, make sure you have taken into account the elements of an effective definition and the full meaning of the term and made appropriate use of synonyms, etymology, and negation.

A. How do you feel about the attempts made to beautify the camel? Are the attempts successful? When it comes to an animal, what does beautiful even mean?

B. The Bedouin, nomadic tribes who live in the deserts of North Africa and the Middle East, still depend on camels for transportation. They live a lifestyle that some describe as *timeless*. What does timeless mean to you?

✓ DEFINITION ESSAY CHECKLIST

ESL Note
See "Think about Audience Expectations," page 556, for more information about the needs of the audience, and "Strive for Clarity," page 556, for more on the importance of keeping your writing coherent.

☐ Does the introduction introduce the term or principle to be defined?

☐ Does the essay begin with a working definition and then develop an extended definition?

☐ Does the extended definition reflect both the denotations and connotations of the term and draw on synonyms, negation, or etymology?

☐ Are the supporting details and examples clear and specific? If you find any that are too general or too abstract, suggest a way to clarify or sharpen them.

☐ Are the supporting paragraphs effectively arranged in an appropriate order? Explain.

☐ In your judgment, what is the best part of this essay? Explain.

☐ Which detail or example would be even better if it were expanded? Why?

Using Comparison and Contrast to Develop an Essay

The writing technique that focuses on examining alternatives is called *comparison and contrast* (see Chapter 10). *Comparison* means examining similarities, and *contrast* means examining differences. For example, an essay evaluating distance-learning classes versus traditional versions would call for comparison and contrast. In your college courses, you will often be called on to explain how two people, objects, or phenomena are alike or how they are different. With most comparison and contrast essays, restrict your focus to *two subjects* that have some common ground. In addition, be sure you have an adequately developed *basis of comparison* using at least three points.

To arrange a **comparison and contrast essay**, use either a *block format* or an *alternating format*. For the block format, include a thesis in your introduction, and then present the first point, the second point, the third point, and so on, for Subject A. Afterward, examine the first point, the second point, and the third point for Subject B.

For the alternating format, examine the two subjects at the same time. In other words, after the introduction, address the first point for Subject A and Subject B, then the second point for Subject A and Subject B, then the third point for Subject A and Subject B, and so on. This method is helpful for longer papers. It may be hard for a reader to keep all the points for Subject A in mind while reading the second half of such a paper. See page 127 for illustrations of both the block and alternating formats.

Examining a Comparison and Contrast Essay

Here's a five-paragraph comparison and contrast essay that contrasts distance-learning classes with traditional college classes.

Distance Learning versus Traditional Classes: Things You Should Consider

(1) Today, college students have an option for learning that their counterparts a decade ago did not. This innovation is called *distance learning,* and it involves doing a significant amount of classwork—in many cases, all of it—independently, usually through the Internet. Unlike students in a traditional college course, distance-learning students don't go to class at a set time for a presentation or a face-to-face discussion with classmates. Instead, they log onto their computers at their own convenience and go online for a virtual course. Distance learning has continued to grow over the last ten years, with some institutions like the University of Phoenix operating without even having a traditional campus. If you are tempted by the idea of sitting in front of your computer screen instead of walking into a classroom, you should consider a few things that I learned the hard way with my first distance-learning experience.

(2) The first thing to keep in mind with distance learning is the need for greater-than-average time management. With a traditional history class that meets two or three times a week, a good deal of your time is already managed for you. The instructor monitors daily attendance, so you are more inclined to be in class and to keep up with your work in case you are called on or face a surprise quiz. Also, when instructors make adjustments in deadlines to match the pace of the discussions or add an assignment that isn't on the syllabus, you know about it right away because you are sitting in the classroom. All of these things help students stay current with their work. When you take a course online, you have to make time management a major priority. In many cases, you can log in to the class at any time. For example, every week I would plan to do the work for my distance-learning class on Thursday evening, but often other things would come up. On at least three occasions, I was called into work. As a result, I found myself truly struggling to keep up

with the class. So the first lesson is this: if you choose a distance-learning class, set up a strict work schedule and stick to it.

(3) The second thing to keep in mind is how different the total learning experience is likely to be. In a traditional literature class, for instance, a significant part of the learning experience is the give and take among students and instructor in response to the work being discussed. Somebody raises a point, the instructor offers an interpretation, another student reacts, and so on. Such interactions can't be planned or, in many cases, replicated. They are spontaneous—and very valuable. In a distance-learning version of the same class, these kinds of moments won't necessarily occur. Even with carefully arranged discussion boards and course chat rooms, the conversations are less immediate and perhaps less vibrant. I found it harder to become involved in online discussions because the back-and-forth exchanges were often slightly delayed as people formulated what they wanted to say and then typed or texted their responses. Also, I realized how much I depend on tone of voice and body language in evaluating what my classmates are saying. So if you choose a distance-learning course, you will need to adjust your expectations in terms of class interactions.

(4) But maybe the most important point to keep in mind about distance-learning classes is the amount of time and work involved. When you sign up for a traditional class, you know from your previous educational experiences that the course involves work in class and out of class. In many college courses, you will need to devote two hours of out-of-class work for each hour you spend in class. For a three-credit course like Introduction to Marketing, the total commitment of time—class time plus homework—is nine hours a week. But with distance-learning options, it's easy to forget that you need to allow for the full time. Despite some deceptive television and Internet advertisements, a legitimate distance-learning course doesn't involve less work than a traditional course. In fact, if you aren't experienced with working on the computer, you may need to devote even more time. Even if you are an Internet whiz, remember that while the system of delivery in a distance-learning class is different, the work is the same. As I learned, it's not easier, just different.

(5) At some point before you graduate from college, you may consider choosing distance learning to complete a course. Distance learning offers a number of advantages, including flexibility to do your work when it's convenient for you. But to succeed in a distance-learning class, you need to pay close attention to time management and to be prepared for a different learning experience. Most of all, however, remember the biggest lesson that I learned: a distance-learning course involves the same amount of work as a traditional version.

CHALLENGE 15.6 **Analyzing the Sample Comparison and Contrast Essay**

Refer to the sample comparison and contrast essay "Distance Learning versus Traditional Classes" on pages 205–206 to answer each question.

1. In the introduction, what point is made about distance learning versus traditional classes? What does the introduction tell you about the purpose of this essay? Write your answers on a separate sheet of paper.

collaboration

2. Working with a classmate, analyze paragraphs 2 through 4. What basis of comparison is used to examine the two types of classes? List the basis of comparison on your paper.

collaboration

3. Still working with a classmate, identify the format used to arrange this essay. On your paper, prepare a diagram like the one on page 127 in Chapter 10 to illustrate the organizational plan.

FOR FURTHER EXPLORATION Comparison and Contrast Essay

1. Using the essay just presented to guide you, write a comparison or contrast essay of about 500 words on the educational experiences you have had thus far versus those you had in another setting—high school, the military, at home. Or, select one of the following topics:

   - life in two different countries, cities, towns, or regions
   - love and infatuation
   - two musical groups, professional athletes, or political leaders
   - MySpace versus Facebook

collaboration

2. Exchange your draft with a classmate. Evaluate the essay you receive using the comparison and contrast essay checklist on page 208. Write your answers on a separate sheet of paper, and then return the essay and your assessment to the writer.

3. Using your reader's comments to guide you, complete the final draft of your comparison or contrast essay.

DISCOVERING CONNECTIONS 15.6 Comparison and Contrast Essay

For this assignment, consider this photo. Using the information from the comparison and contrast discussion to guide you, write an essay of about 500 words in response to one of the accompanying questions or another that the photo inspires. As you write, make sure to establish a basis for comparison, provide a thorough presentation, and arrange the information effectively.

A. Two distinctly different types of buildings are featured in this photo. Just beyond the waters of the fountain in the forefront of the picture is a 71-foot-tall steel and glass pyramid designed in 1985 by Chinese-born American architect I. M. Pei. Behind the pyramid is a small section of the Louvre, an enormous palace in Paris, France—now a museum housing some of the world's greatest works of art—constructed between 1546 and 1878. Which do you see as more beautiful? What elements of the structure you have chosen make it stand out in comparison to the other?

B. A number of visitors, many of them no doubt sightseers waiting to enter the Louvre, appear near the pyramid. From the experiences you have had as a tourist and as a resident in your city or town, how do visitors differ from the people who actually reside in a place?

✓ COMPARISON AND CONTRAST ESSAY CHECKLIST

ESL Note
See "Think about Audience Expectations," page 556, for more information about the needs of the audience, and "Strive for Clarity," page 556, for more on the importance of keeping your writing coherent.

☐ Does the introduction specify the essay's focus and the subjects to be compared or contrasted?

☐ Does the essay concentrate on two subjects?

☐ Is a basis for comparison established and followed? Make sure that each characteristic or element is discussed in detail for each subject. Put a ✓ at any point where an element or characteristic is missing, and write *amplify* above any point that should be discussed in greater detail.

☐ Has the block format or the alternating format been used to arrange the paragraphs? Would the essay be more effective if it were arranged differently, for example, using block format instead of alternating format or vice versa?

☐ In your judgment, what is the best part of this essay? Explain.

☐ Which detail or example would be even better if it were expanded? Why?

Using Cause and Effect to Develop an Essay

Cause and effect is the writing technique you use to focus on what led to something or what happened as a result (see Chapter 11). Cause is *why* something occurred, and effect is the *outcome* or *consequence* of an occurrence. An extended writing in which you discuss how a new job has changed your life would be a cause and effect essay.

For a **cause and effect essay**, remember that most events or experiences have *more than one* cause and *more than one* effect. Therefore, don't oversimplify. Furthermore, be sure that any cause and effect relationships you suggest aren't actually *coincidences*—events that occur close to the same time by accident. Finally, arrange the various causes or effects you present in a logical order.

Examining a Cause and Effect Essay

Look at this essay about the various consequences of advancing to a more responsible job:

More Than a Promotion

(1) When I was about ten years old, I spent two weeks at my cousin's house just outside of Chicago. One day we went into the city with my aunt to see the department store that she managed. She showed us around the store

and then took us up to her office. I sat quietly watching her make phone calls and instruct her staff on what she wanted done that day. After half an hour, I knew I wanted to do just what she did for a living when I grew up. Six months ago, I got my chance to fulfill my dream when I was made the night and weekend manager at a large drug store. Almost overnight, I went from simply doing my job as a part-time clerk to keeping the ten people I supervise happy and productive. The many changes my promotion has brought about have definitely made me a different person.

(2) One way the promotion has changed my life is financial. When I was a clerk, I worked twenty hours a week at $11 an hour with no benefits. After taxes, my weekly pay was about $165. As a manager, I work at least forty hours a week for a take-home salary of almost $600 a week, and I have full insurance coverage. Since I've become a manager, I have been able to buy a car and save money on a regular basis. With a little luck, I should be able to afford to move out of my mother's house and into my own apartment in six months or so.

(3) My new responsibilities have also helped build up my self-confidence. At first, I almost didn't take the job because I wasn't sure I could handle the responsibility. My supervisor convinced me to take it by telling me that she wouldn't have recommended me if she didn't feel I was capable. After the first few weeks on the job, I found out something about myself that I had never realized. Not only am I able to handle responsibilities such as motivating other workers, setting work schedules, and doing the payroll, but I am actually good at all these things. Because of these successes, I'm more confident whenever I face a new task.

(4) Taking the promotion has also meant I had to grow up a lot. For one thing, I had to learn to budget my personal time. As a manager, I work almost twice as many hours as I did when I was a clerk. Furthermore, managers often have to attend meetings at night or on weekends and do paperwork at home. No longer do I have time to ride around with my friends. I also can no longer do things like call in sick when I just don't feel like working. A clerk might be able to get away with that, but a manager can't. Managers are paid to be responsible.

(5) I've also had to adjust to a new relationship with the people I supervise. Before, I was one of them, but now I'm their boss. I have to make decisions about such things as who has to work Friday and Saturday nights and who gets extra hours when business is good. In addition, I have to evaluate them every four months to see who gets merit raises and who doesn't. Some of the people I was friendliest with when I was a clerk barely talk to me now because I won't play favorites when it comes to schedules and raises. I sometimes feel guilty when I have to give someone a bad evaluation for job performance or lack of punctuality. I know that when I was a clerk, I sometimes was lazy and showed up late or left a few minutes early. But I'm a manager now, and I have a responsibility to make sure that my company is getting its money's worth.

(6) I've been a manager for six months now, and I can honestly say that I enjoy the job far more than I ever expected to. I like earning more money, and the idea that people are willing to put their trust in me has made me more confident overall. I also like the fact that I've learned to take responsibility. I know that, overall, this job has helped to make me a better person.

CHALLENGE 15.7   **Analyzing the Sample Cause and Effect Essay**

Refer to the sample cause and effect essay "More Than a Promotion" on pages 208–209 to answer each question.

1. What event is the focus of this cause and effect essay? Does the essay explore the causes for this event or the consequences of it? Write your answers on a separate sheet of paper.

collaboration

2. Working with a classmate, analyze paragraphs 2 through 5 of the essay. First, underline the topic sentence of each paragraph. Then, on your paper, write the specific changes that occurred in the writer's life.

collaboration

3. Imagine that the focus of this essay was on causes, not effects. Consider the causes of the promotion—diligence at work, a positive attitude, natural leadership ability, and a supervisor's confidence. Working with a class-mate, write a cause and effect paragraph that focuses on these causes. (Remember—your thesis should state the effect and reveal that you will explore the causes.)

FOR FURTHER EXPLORATION Cause and Effect Essay

1. Using the essay "More Than a Promotion" to guide you, write an essay of about 500 words concerning a change in employment, schools, or personal relationships. If you prefer, choose one of the following topics:

   - plagiarizing another person's work
   - the appeal of an activity, style of clothing, or type of music
   - your choice of academic major
   - an insulting comment

collaboration

2. Exchange your draft with a classmate. Evaluate the essay you receive using the cause and effect essay checklist on page 211. Write your answers on a separate sheet of pa-per, and then return the essay and your assessment to the writer.

3. Using your reader's comments to guide you, complete the final draft of your cause and effect essay.

DISCOVERING CONNECTIONS 15.7 Cause and Effect Essay

For this assignment, consider the following photo. Using the information from the cause and effect discussion to guide you, write an essay of about 500 words in response to one of the accompanying questions or another that the photo inspires. As you develop your essay, be sure to recognize the differences between direct and related causes and effects, avoid over-simplification, and provide an effective arrangement.

A. Natural habitats such as the subtropical wetlands in Florida's Everglades contain some of the most unusual animal and plant life in the United States. Unfortunately, various factors, including global climate change, have led to the endangerment of

some of those species such as the manatee, pictured here. Consider what you already understand about global climate change, and supplement your knowledge by doing a little research. Then discuss how even slight shifts in weather patterns or temperatures can endanger the very survival of creatures like the manatee.

B.   Think of your daily routines: how often do you get into your car to drive when you could easily walk, ride your bike, or take public transportation? When you wash the dishes, do you let the water run, or do you use only what you need to soap and then rinse? How many plastic bags do you come home with after a single grocery store trip? Consider how your own daily activities and actions affect the quality of the environment we all share. If you made changes in your daily routine so that you were living a more environmentally aware existence, how would this adjustment affect your life in terms of convenience and personal comfort?

✓CAUSE AND EFFECT ESSAY CHECKLIST

ESL Note
See "Think about Audience Expectations," page 556, for more information about the needs of the audience, and "Strive for Clarity," page 556, for more on the Importance of keeping your writing coherent.

☐ Does the introduction indicate a focus on either cause or effect?

☐ Are the cause and effect relationships supported with enough examples and details to avoid oversimplification? If you feel more specific details are required, write, "I'd like to know more about _____" in the margin next to the insufficiently explored passage.

☐ Does the essay distinguish between direct and related causes and effects? Underline any details that seem like coincidences rather than true causes or effects.

☐ Are the supporting paragraphs effectively arranged in a logical order?

☐ In your judgment, what is the best part of this essay? Explain.

☐ Which detail or example would be even better if it were expanded? Why?

Using Division and Classification to Develop an Essay

To analyze a complex subject, use **division and classification** as explained in Chapter 12. *Division* is the separation of a subject into its component parts. *Classification* is the arrangement of the subcategories into groups on the basis of common characteristics or principles. An essay in which you discuss types of televised sports would use both division and classification. When you write a division and classification essay, make sure to choose a *logical method of analysis* so that your reader can understand the basis for your examination. In addition, make sure you keep your *presentation consistent*, with divisions or classifications that are *clearly related.* At the same time, keep your groupings *distinct* and *complete*—that is, distinguished from others and expressed in full detail.

Examining a Division and Classification Essay

Look at this essay about the various types of televised sports:

Television: The Sports Fan's Paradise

(1) One of the most popular activities in the country is watching sports. Most sports fans would prefer to attend games in person, but cost and other life responsibilities keep most people from attending more than a few games a year. Fortunately, for sports fans, network television and cable outlets make it possible to watch some kind of sporting activity on a daily basis. Most of the sports available on television for fans to enjoy can be grouped in four basic categories.

(2) The first group is probably the type that has been featured on television the longest: major league professional sports. This group includes Major League baseball, NFL football, NBA basketball, and NHL hockey. More recently, WNBA basketball and Major League soccer have also enjoyed wide exposure. Fans love these games because of long-standing rivalries between teams and the opportunity to see a sport's elite players.

(3) Another category that draws fans includes individual sports like golf and tennis. These sports, unlike the major league group, have no organized leagues or seasons. Instead, fans have the chance to see the stars of these sports compete all year long in both national and international competitions.

(4) College sports represent another group of televised sporting events. This category of sports remains among the most watched, especially football and basketball games. The various Bowl Games at the end of the football season and the NCAA March Madness basketball tournament games are among the ratings leaders each year.

(5) The fourth group is one that has grown in popularity over the past ten years. This category might be termed alternative sports. These sports, which once appeared only on such sports cable stations as ESPN and ESPN2, have gradually become more mainstream. Events such as the World's Strongest Man contests, bodybuilding events, and Ultimate Frisbee games now often appear for wider audiences to enjoy. The events that have attracted the most attention in this group are various extreme sports featured in competitions like the X-Games. These competitions feature stunt BMX biking and skateboarding events as well as such innovations as street luge.

(6) Certainly, there are other popular sporting events besides those in these categories. NASCAR racing, bowling, Summer and Winter Olympics, and skating competitions all draw big television audiences. But these four categories do include the sports that American fans find most captivating, at least for now. Stay tuned.

CHALLENGE 15.8 **Analyzing the Sample Division and Classification Essay**

Refer to the sample division and classification essay "Television: The Sports Fan's Paradise," above, to answer each question.

1. Find and underline the thesis statement in the first paragraph. Then, on a separate sheet of paper, list the essay's subject and the classes into which it is divided.

collaboration

2. Find and underline the topic sentences of paragraphs 2 through 5. Working with a classmate, analyze these paragraphs. On your paper, name each class of televised sports and describe the characteristics of each type that is discussed.

collaboration

3. Working with a classmate, identify another category of televised sports or subdivide one of the existing categories. Then write a paragraph that illustrates or explains this new classification.

FOR FURTHER EXPLORATION Division and Classification Essay

1. Using the essay on televised sports to guide you, write a division and classification essay of about 500 words on types of movies or sitcoms, or on one of the following topics:

- categories of popular music
- dining opportunities in your city or town
- elements of a winning team
- types of video game consoles

collaboration

2. Exchange your draft with a classmate. Evaluate the essay you receive using the division and classification essay checklist on page 214. Write your answers on a separate sheet of paper, and then return the essay and your assessment to the writer.

3. Using your reader's comments to guide you, complete the final draft of your essay.

DISCOVERING CONNECTIONS 15.8 Division and Classification Essay

For this assignment, consider this photo. Using the information from the division and classification discussion to guide you, write an essay of about 500 words in response to one of the accompanying questions or another that the photo inspires. As you create your essay, concentrate on key factors such as a logical method of analysis, a consistent presentation, and distinct and complete groupings.

A. The world of Hollywood is all about division and classification: from the A-list stars to the B-list stars; from the actors and actresses to the paparazzi. What message do you think this kind of classification sends to the stars, to the people who want to take their pictures and interview them, and to the people who live for celebrity gossip?

B. When you look at this photo, what do you notice first? Are your eyes drawn to the figure in the center or to the figures in the foreground? What elements in the photo enable the photographer to manipulate and divide your attention in this way? How do the different aspects of the photo combine to create an effective image?

✓ DIVISION AND CLASSIFICATION ESSAY CHECKLIST

ESL Note
See "Think about
Audience Expectations,"
page 556, for more
information about the
needs of the audience,
and "Strive for Clarity,"
page 556, for more
on the importance of
keeping your writing
coherent.

☐ Does the introduction specify the focus of the discussion and indicate an emphasis on either division or classification?

☐ Are the elements distinct and complete? If you think any divisions or classifications need to be subdivided further to make them clearer or more specific, write, "I'd like to know more about _____" in the margin next to them.

☐ Does the essay feature a logical, consistent method of analysis throughout?

☐ Are the supporting paragraphs presented in an effective order?

☐ In your judgment, what is the best part of this essay? Explain.

☐ Which detail or example would be even better if it were expanded? Why?

Writing an Argument Essay: Using Mixed Modes

When you write an **argument essay**—an essay that attempts to *persuade*—you must make your stance on the issue clear in the introduction and supply at least three strong reasons in the body that will encourage your reader to agree with you. As you write, adopt a reasonable tone, avoiding an emotional or condescending tone. In general, use qualifying terms such as *most, rarely,* and *frequently* rather than absolute ones such as *all, never,* and *always.* In addition, make sure to follow a logical line of reasoning and avoid errors in logic known as *logical fallacies.* See the list of logical fallacies on pages 152–153. Finally, be sure to arrange your points in a logical order, such as order of importance.

Imagine, for example, that you were writing an essay about enrolling children as young as three into intensive tutoring or academic programs, or in high-pressured athletics, dance, or musical training. You are opposed to this concept, so your purpose is to persuade your reader that no matter how well intentioned parents may be, forcing very young children to undertake this high-pressured lifestyle can have serious consequences.

To fulfill this aim, you'll employ several modes, including *classification* to spell out the wide variety of intensive programs available and *definition* to clarify the kinds of pressure and stress children may experience. You might also turn to *example* to illustrate the kinds of activities children will miss out on because they're too busy being tutored or trained. *Cause and effect* will help you discuss the negative physical effects that result from overscheduling a child. Remember—since your ultimate goal when writing an argument essay is to convince your reader to accept your point, be sure to use an effective combination of modes to help you make your case.

Acknowledging Your Sources

Because the focus of an argument essay is generally controversial—and likely complicated—you may want to buttress your argument with support from experts. Whenever you incorporate expert opinion into your paper, you must always acknowledge your sources in two places: in the body of the paper and in a list at the end of the paper. The list provides your readers with a complete citation for each of your sources. Failing to acknowledge or document your sources is the same as claiming the opinions you've gathered to be your own—an act of *plagiarism*. (For more on understanding plagiarism and how to avoid it, see Chapter 14, page 182.)

Expert opinion may be collected in a number of ways. For example, let's say you decided to research the negative effects of overscheduling young children. You attended a class presentation given by a child psychologist, heard a podcast, and read an online or print article that supports your argument. To incorporate this information into your essay, you may do so in the following forms (note that the original source appears in abbreviated form in parentheses at the end of the borrowed material):

- a **direct quotation**:

    A 2007 *Wall Street Journal* article, "Helping Overbooked Kids Cut Back," makes the same point: "But the trend has gone too far, the American Academy of Pediatrics said in January in the journal *Pediatrics*; kids need more time for free play and family togetherness" (Shellenbarger).

- a **paraphrase**:

    A podcast of a 2002 NPR series on children made the point that overscheduled children often miss out on other, less-structured possibilities for learning while also dealing with increased pressure from parents to perform (Stamberg).

- a **summary**:

    In a recent guest lecture here on campus, a child psychologist who has worked for years with preschool children emphasized that he is convinced that the harm in terms of stress and frustration that very young children experience from intensive study and practice is far greater than any benefit they could gain (Kyd).

A sample list of citations could look like this:

Works Cited

Kyd, Peter. PSY 52.04—Child Psychology. B-213. Brayton Hills College, Springfield, MT. 25 Oct. 2010. Guest lecture.

Shellenbarger, Sue. "Helping Overbooked Kids Cut Back." *Wall Street Journal.* Wall Street Journal Online, 17 May 2007. Web. 11 Nov. 2010.

Stamberg, Susan. "Overscheduled Kids." *Morning Edition*. National Public Radio. 3 Sept. 2002. Podcast. 11 Nov. 2010.

While several methods of documentation exist, most instructors will ask you to follow either the **Modern Language Association (MLA)** system or the **American Psychological Association (APA)** system. The sample list of Works Cited you see above follows the MLA style.

MLA Format   Imagine that you want to include a direct quotation to support your own writing. The first place to acknowledge your source is immediately after the information you have included. At that point, insert a set of parentheses containing the author's last name. If you are following MLA style, you also include the page number, as these examples show:

MLA parenthetical citation

From a book

Nelle Harper Lee, author of *To Kill a Mockingbird*, and Truman Capote, author of *Breakfast at Tiffany's* and *In Cold Blood*, were friends from childhood who felt closely connected on a number of levels. Their relative affluence in comparison to most of the people in their hometown of Monroeville, Alabama, was one thing that bound them together as different from others. "This can be interpreted as Nelle and Truman thinking they were better than everybody else. In their defense, Monroeville during the Depression in the 1930s was not much to be above. The cultural index, or standard of living, in the South at the end of the 1920s was already the lowest in the nation" (Shields 44).

From a newspaper, magazine, or other periodical

Researchers have long understood the physiology of pain. What remains unclear is why pain becomes a long-term issue for some but not for others. "Scientists don't know why some people develop chronic problems after injuries while others continue on with no pain. It is nearly impossible to answer the question on a wide scale; pain simply has too many causes" (Carmichael 43).

Instead of quoting, you could include the same information in the form of a paraphrase. To do so, you express *in your own words* the points raised in the direct quotation. You don't use quotation marks, but you do acknowledge your source in exactly the same way: the author's last name and page number immediately following the paraphrase. You do the same if you use a summary.

The second place that you must acknowledge your source is at the end of your paper, in a section called *Works Cited*, as these examples show. All titles and subtitles of full-length works such as books, reference works, newspapers, magazines, journals, DVDs, and CDs are italicized. Article and song titles are set in quotation marks. Note that the second (and each subsequent) line of each entry is indented. Also, the latest MLA guidelines ask that you indicate whether the source is a *Print* or *Web* document.

Works Cited

For a book

Shields, Charles J. *Mockingbird: A Portrait of Harper Lee*. New York: Henry Holt,

2006. Print.

For a newspaper, magazine, or other periodical

Carmichael, Mary. "The Changing Science of Pain." *Newsweek* 4 June 2007:

40–47. Print.

APA Format   If you use the APA method, you record the information in the text of your paper in a slightly different way—the author's last name plus the *year of publication, preceded by a comma,* rather than a page number—as these examples show:

APA parenthetical citation

From a book

Nelle Harper Lee, author of *To Kill a Mockingbird*, and Truman Capote, author of *Breakfast at Tiffany's* and *In Cold Blood*, were friends from childhood who felt closely connected on a number of levels. Their relative affluence in comparison to most of the people in their hometown of Monroeville, Alabama, was one thing that bound them together as different from others. "This can be interpreted as Nelle and Truman thinking they were better than everybody else. In their defense, Monroeville during the Depression in the 1930s was not much to be above. The cultural index, or standard of living, in the South at the end of the 1920s was already the lowest in the nation" (Shields, 2006).

For a newspaper, magazine, or other periodical

Researchers have long understood the physiology of pain. What remains unclear is why pain becomes a long-term issue for some but not for others. "Scientists don't know why some people develop chronic problems after injuries while others continue on with no pain. It is nearly impossible to answer the question on a wide scale; pain simply has too many causes" (Carmichael, 2007).

You must provide the same information—the author's last name, a comma, and the year of publication—following a paraphrase or summary.

Your list of citations at the end of the paper should appear under the title *References,* and will look slightly different from the MLA style's Works Cited listing. While you italicize the titles of books, reference works, and government documents, you capitalize only proper nouns and the first words of the title and subtitle. All titles and subtitles of journals and magazines are also italicized, but follow the *standard* rules of capitalization rather than the APA style of book title capitalization.

Initials rather than first names are used for author names, and the name is followed by the date of publication, in parentheses, plus a period.

Note also that no quotation marks are used to signify the title of periodical article. Again, make sure to indent the second line (and any subsequent lines) of each entry.

References

For a book

Shields, C. J. (2006). *Mockingbird: A portrait of Harper Lee*. New York: Henry

Holt and Company.

From a newspaper, magazine, or other periodical

Carmichael, M. (2007, June 4). The changing science of pain. *Newsweek*,

40–47.

If you have questions or need additional guidance on MLA, APA, or other systems of documentation, see the reference section of your college or university library, which also offers complete explanations and thorough illustrations of how to acknowledge other sources of information, including audio and video presentations, pamphlets, Internet articles, DVDs, interviews, and so on. Your college or university writing or tutoring center will have information and guidelines about documentation as well. Finally, be sure to visit the MLA and APA Web sites and MyWritingLab for even further assistance. Remember: Always acknowledge your sources. Plagiarism is never acceptable—never!

Examining an Argument Essay

Look at this argument essay about South African sprinter Oscar Pistorius's quest to be allowed to compete in international events, including the Olympics.

Oscar Pistorius: The Race for Fairness in International Competition

(1) In March 2007, South African sprinter Oscar Pistorius finished second in the 400 meter run in South Africa's national track and field championship. His time of 46.56 was just a few fractions of a second over Olympic qualifying standards, and it ranked him among his country's best performers in this event. His 2007 performance in the 200 meters was also just short of the Olympic qualifying time. But a number of critics tried unsuccessfully to keep Pistorius from attempting to quality for the 2008 Beijing Olympics, arguing that he had an unfair advantage. The irony in this charge is that Pistorius is a double amputee. His deformed lower legs were removed before his first birthday, and he runs on sleek carbon fiber prosthetic limbs called Cheetahs. Critics of the decision to allow him to compete with able-bodied athletes should accept that his prosthetics give him no advantage and that advances in equipment and training are enjoyed by all. Most of all, they should accept that allowing him to compete is a matter of basic fairness. If Oscar Pistorius is fast enough to run with the world's best, then he should be allowed to compete in any meet, including the Olympics.

(2) For one thing, it's hard to imagine that having no lower legs could be any kind of advantage for a runner. His prosthetic devices—the J-shaped

Cheetahs—have no muscles or joints. They contain no motors or drivers of any kind. Pistorius still has to do the work, using the muscles in his upper legs and hips to power himself forward. Some people argue that he actually has to work harder than able-bodied runners because "… unlike other sprinters who push off with their upper and lower legs and stay low coming out of the blocks, Pistorius essentially has to stand straight up out of the blocks and start generating power almost exclusively with his hips" (Epstein). In other words, he has to take his natural athletic ability and push it to its limits and beyond. He is just doing what all champions must do to succeed.

(3) Critics who claim that Pistorius is benefiting from the kind of technological advance that the Cheetahs represent conveniently overlook the fact that science and technology have affected all athletes in some way. Their uniforms, their shoes, even the surfaces they run and play on are vastly different from and vastly superior to those of the past. For the 2008 Olympics, for instance, Nike introduced Flywire, running spikes weighing a mere ounce per shoe, a startling 41 percent lighter than any previous spikes (Hochman). Injuries that once ended athletic careers can be surgically repaired today, with specialized rehabilitation making the area stronger than it was before the injury. Today's training and dietary regimens are all based on the best scientific data around. It's not fair to single out Pistorius when technological advances of some kind play such a big role in the performance of all top athletes.

(4) Most important of all, Pistorius should be allowed to compete in any meet he qualifies for because he has earned that chance. The truth is that the majority of today's elite amateur athletes are amateurs in name only. Unlike amateurs of years gone by who immediately forfeited amateur status if they accepted money for their performances, today's top amateurs live in a different world entirely. For example, American superstar sprinter Tyson Gay is sponsored by sporting gear giant Adidas (David) and receives generous financial support so that he can devote his days to working out and perfecting his skills in order to remain among the best in the world. Pistorius has proven that he can compete in this arena, and he should not be disqualified because he has found a way to overcome a physical disability.

(5) From the simplest schoolyard games to the Olympics, athletic competition is supposed to be about people pushing themselves to their limits against the rest of the field. Those people who want to keep Oscar Pistorius from taking part in national and international competitions because he wears prosthetic legs are wrong. Instead of trying to block his participation, they should welcome it. He is an extraordinary athlete who through his own hard work has earned the right to compete with the best in the world.

Works Cited

David, Chelan. "Olympic Aspirations." *Apparel Magazine: Technology & Business*

   Insight—From Concept to Consumer (1 Aug. 2008): n. pag. Web. 24 Oct. 2010.

Epstein, David. "Pistorius' Victory Is Inspirational—and Controversial." S.I.Com

   (17 May 2008): n. pag. Web. 23 Oct. 2010.

Hochman, Paul. "High-Tech Gear for Olympic Athletes." *Fast Company* (20 June 2008): n. pag. Web. 24 Oct. 2010.

CHALLENGE 15.9   **Analyzing the Sample Argument Essay**

Refer to the sample argument essay "Oscar Pistorius" on pages 218–219 to answer each question.

1. Find the thesis statement in the first paragraph and underline it. Then, on a separate sheet of paper, explain how the other sentences in the introduction draw the reader's attention to the subject.

collaboration

2. Working with a classmate, analyze the paragraphs in the body of the essay. Make a list of the different modes that the writer has used to try to make the case that Oscar Pistorius should be allowed to compete in any international competition, including the Olympics, for which he has run a qualifying time.

collaboration

3. Analyze the support given for each reason. Which is most convincing to you? Which reason is least convincing? Working with a classmate, brainstorm further support for this reason (or develop an alternative reason) and revise or replace this paragraph.

FOR FURTHER EXPLORATION Argument Essay

1. Using the essay on Oscar Pistorius as a guide, write an argument essay of about 500 words taking a stance on whether athletes should be banned from their sports if they have taken performance-enhancing drugs. If you prefer, choose one of the following topics instead, and write an argument essay in which you support or refute it.

   - Public higher education should be free for all students who qualify academically.
   - State governments should institute competency testing for all prospective teachers.
   - Bike riders, in-line skaters, and skateboarders should be required by law to wear helmets.
   - People convicted of drunk driving should be forced to have special license plates indicating their crime.

collaboration

2. Exchange your draft with a classmate. Evaluate the essay you receive using the argument essay checklist on page 221. Write your answers on a separate sheet of paper, and then return the essay and your assessment to the writer.

3. Using your reader's comments to guide you, complete the final draft of your argument essay.

DISCOVERING CONNECTIONS 15.9 Argument Essay

For this assignment, consider the following photo. Using the information from the argument discussion to guide you, write an essay of about 500 words in response to one of the accompanying questions or another that the photo inspires. As you develop your essay, make sure you supply sufficient support, use an appropriate tone, avoid errors in logic, and arrange your ideas effectively. Use the combination of modes that most effectively persuades your reader to accept your point of view.

A. This collection of trash represents only a fraction of what is abandoned by climbers on the trek up Mt. Everest. Certainly this image is an extreme example of a problem that plagues cities and towns across the United States, where everything from major appliances and furniture to tires to bottles, cans, and paper cups are just tossed along the roadside or into waterways. What penalties should officials impose to punish those who care so little about the environment we all share?

B. Extreme sports like mountain climbing are dangerous enterprises. Every year here in the United States, extreme sports enthusiasts are lost, injured, or stranded, requiring extensive—and expensive—search and rescue operations. Should the rescued individual have to reimburse the government for the cost of his or her rescue? Or are these kinds of rescues part of what the money we pay in taxes should already be covering?

✓ ARGUMENT ESSAY CHECKLIST

ESL Note
See "Think about Audience Expectations," page 556, for more information about the needs of the audience, and "Strive for Clarity," page 556, for more on the importance of keeping your writing coherent.

☐ Does the introduction clarify the writer's stance on the issue?

☐ Are there at least three reasons, properly documented if necessary, to support the stance?

☐ Is the tone throughout the essay respectful and concerned? Put a ✓ next to any sentence in which the tone seems inappropriate.

☐ Is the presentation logical? Underline any errors in logic.

☐ Does the essay feature qualifying terms rather than absolute ones when appropriate?

☐ Are the supporting paragraphs effectively presented in emphatic order or some other method of arrangement? Explain.

☐ In your judgment, what is the best part of this essay? Explain.

☐ Which detail or example would be even better if it were expanded? Why?

RECAP Examining Types of Essays

Key Terms in This Chapter	Definitions
modes	organizing strategies to develop paragraphs and essays
purpose	your intent or aim when you write
narrative essay	a multiparagraph writing that relates a sequence of events in story fashion
descriptive essay	a multiparagraph writing that uses concrete, sensory language to recreate a scene, situation, or individual
example essay	a multiparagraph writing that uses specific instances to illustrate, clarify, or back up a thesis
process essay	a multiparagraph writing that spells out how to do something, how something is done, or how you did something
definition essay	a multiparagraph writing that specifies the characteristics or elements of some object, location, or individual
comparison and contrast essay	a multiparagraph writing that examines similarities and differences between two or more subjects
cause and effect essay	a multiparagraph writing that considers reasons leading to some situation or condition or the outcomes or consequences of an event or phenomenon
division and classification essay	a multiparagraph writing that analyzes a complex subject either by separating it into its component parts or by grouping its parts into categories
argument essay	a multiparagraph writing that takes a firm stand on an issue and then attempts to convince readers to agree with that stand
MLA system of documentation	the Modern Language Association's method of acknowledging sources
APA system of documentation	the American Psychological Association's method of acknowledging sources

The Relationship between the Purpose of an Essay and the Modes

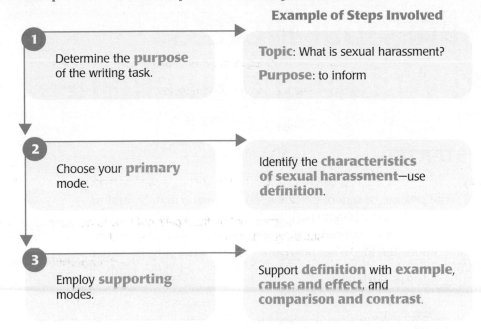

Example of Steps Involved

1 Determine the **purpose** of the writing task.

Topic: What is sexual harassment?

Purpose: to inform

2 Choose your **primary** mode.

Identify the **characteristics of sexual harassment**—use **definition**.

3 Employ **supporting** modes.

Support **definition** with **example**, **cause and effect**, and **comparison and contrast**.

Using Odyssey Online with MyWritingLab

For more practice examining types of essays, to go www.mywritinglab.com.

CHAPTER 16
Adjusting Your Process: Timed Writing and Summaries

GETTING STARTED ...

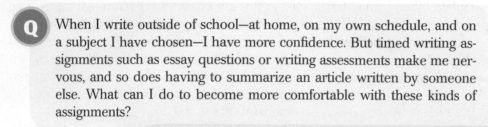

Q When I write outside of school—at home, on my own schedule, and on a subject I have chosen—I have more confidence. But timed writing assignments such as essay questions or writing assessments make me nervous, and so does having to summarize an article written by someone else. What can I do to become more comfortable with these kinds of assignments?

A Pressure doesn't have to paralyze you. First, you need to recognize exactly what you need to do and under what time and length limitations you need to work. Then set your sights on doing the best work you are capable of doing *under these circumstances.* Your work won't be as polished as it would be if you had ample time to draft and revise, but that doesn't mean it won't be good.

Overview: Understanding How to Deal with the Pressure of Timed Writing

With rare exceptions, people in any field—sports, business, music, medicine, law, engineering, education—do their best work when they have time to think through a task, to *plan, concentrate,* and *reexamine* it. As the previous chapters illustrate, following this strategy helps you produce your best writing.

But sometimes people must *adapt* the process they normally follow so that they can perform effectively in less-than-ideal conditions. A journalist, for example, must be prepared to deviate from a planned series of questions if the interview takes an interesting turn and the deadline is looming. An athlete on the field or court must make immediate adjustments if someone misses a shot or commits a foul. An actor must be ready to ad-lib if another actor "drops a page," leaving out crucial dialogue. An EMT must be prepared to treat the victim of an auto accident in the vehicle if the person is trapped. In each of these cases, the situations give these people little choice. If they don't adapt, they won't succeed.

With writing, you will also occasionally need to adapt your standard process. For instance, when answering a timed essay question and completing a timed writing assessment, you must carefully consider how many minutes to devote to each part of the writing process before your time runs out. When preparing a summary, you will need to work in a different direction. Instead of developing your own ideas in full detail, you need to reduce someone else's to their essence.

Navigating This Chapter This chapter discusses strategies that will lead you to success whenever you must:

- answer essay questions
- complete a writing assessment
- prepare a summary

Answering an Essay Question Effectively

An **essay question** calls for a clear, concise, multiparagraph response within a limited period of time. The process is no different from the process you use to complete other writing tasks. Your goal is the same: to work through the writing process and to communicate to your reader what you know about the question.

You may not believe it, but an essay question can be *easier* to answer than multiple-choice or short-answer questions. Nonessay kinds of questions focus on single bits of information, so they sometimes end up quizzing you on what you *don't know.* But essay questions give you the chance to show what you *do know,* to demonstrate in detail what you understand about the subject.

To develop an effective strategy for writing a successful essay answer, follow three simple steps: *preparation, anticipation,* and *rehearsal.* As the figure on page 226 shows, the three steps are closely connected. Preparation gives you the foundation for the rest of the process, and anticipation gears you up for rehearsal.

Preparation

The best way to *prepare* yourself to answer essay questions is to apply yourself in your coursework. Learn the information you will need during an exam by (1) reading actively and (2) taking effective classroom notes.

✓ STEPS TO ACTIVE READING

☐ Read the introduction and conclusion for an overview of the material.

☐ Preview all headings and subheadings in the selection, highlighting any main ideas.

☐ Read any *charts, boxed areas,* or *lists* for summaries of important information.

☐ Highlight or underline information you judge to be important—*specific* names, dates, distances, conditions, and so on.

☐ Look for any *definitions* and information presented *in order* (*first, second, third,* and so on), and identify *transitional expressions* and words such as *important, crucial,* and *vital* that signal important material will follow.

☐ Write any points that you feel are especially important in the *margin* or in your *notebook.*

☐ Use the material you have highlighted or underlined to prepare a *summary,* a greatly reduced version of the original material,

(continued)

expressed in your own words. (A discussion of summary writing appears later in this chapter.)

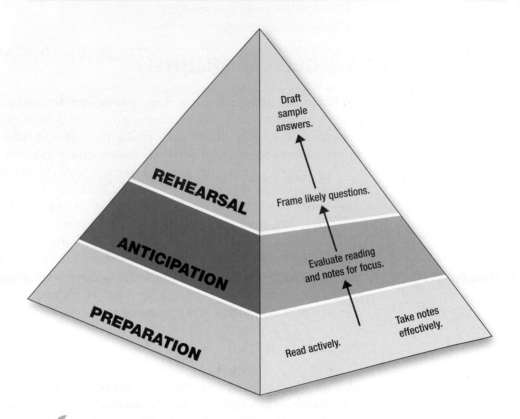

✔ STEPS TO EFFECTIVE NOTE-TAKING

☐ Concentrate on recording information that you are unsure of or that is new to you.

☐ Assume that any material your instructor puts on the board is important.

☐ Listen for words such as *important, vital, crucial,* and so on. These words signal key concepts.

☐ Focus on definitions and material the instructor repeats or presents in sequence *(first, second, third).*

☐ Keep your notes as neat and orderly as possible.

☐ If you are writing them by hand, record the notes on every other line so that you always have room to add information. If you are using a laptop, double- or triple-space so that you can read and edit your notes easily.

☐ Use abbreviations or your own personal shorthand system.

☐ Reread your notes an hour or so after the class is over and flesh out, clarify, and tie together the information.

☐ Write a summary, interpretation, or analysis of the material.

Anticipation

In addition to learning your course material, think strategically about an upcoming essay exam. Begin by evaluating your notes and readings to identify the topics your instructor might use for essay questions.

✓ STEPS TO ANTICIPATING WHAT MAY BE ON AN ESSAY EXAM

☐ Concentrate on the ideas you've identified as important in your reading.

☐ Note the focus of any questions or checklists your instructor has provided or discussed.

☐ Review your classroom notes, paying particular attention to material that your instructor described as *important, crucial, vital,* and so on, or repeated more than once.

☐ Discuss important ideas with your classmates. This kind of discussion will help you clarify your own thinking, and it may provide additional perspectives on those ideas.

Rehearsal

Once you have identified the information you feel is likely to be included on the examination, you should *rehearse.* In this context, rehearsal means creating several **practice questions,** the type of queries that might appear on an exam, and then drafting answers to them.

Drawing Up a Practice Question   Imagine that you are studying for an essay exam in your introductory psychology class. Over the past two weeks, you've discussed a great many topics in relation to the sensation of pain. From your notes and reading, you have identified the psychological factors involved in the perception and management of pain as the likely focus of essay questions.

With this focus identified, you create the following practice question, intended to be answered within a maximum of 20 minutes:

> Research in the area of pain management suggests that psychological factors are involved in the perception of pain. What three psychological factors influence pain perception? Provide a concrete example for each factor. Also, what are three treatments commonly used to manage pain? Again, provide a concrete example for each treatment, explaining why the treatment works.

With an actual exam, you must first identify exactly what the essay question is asking you to do. Even though you have developed the sample question yourself, you should follow the same strategy. That way, each practice session will mirror the process you will follow during an exam.

In this case, the question asks you to supply a total of *six* points, with a specific example of each. *Three* of the points must be psychological factors, and *three* must be common treatments. With this information identified, you are ready to move to the next step: answering a practice question.

Developing a Sample Essay Answer   As indicated earlier, you have set a time limit of 20 minutes to develop an effective answer, so you need to get to work. Incidentally, with such a tight time constraint, don't expect your writing to be perfect. Perfection takes hours, not minutes. Instead, plan to do the best writing you can under those circumstances. Concentrate on making your answer *complete* in terms of *content* and *correct* in terms of *form*.

Here are the steps you should follow when answering an essay question. The time estimate is based on the 20 minutes set aside to develop an effective answer:

Prewriting
(5 minutes or so)

- Read the question thoroughly, making sure you understand what is expected.
- On a piece of scrap paper, the back of the exam sheet, or the inside cover of the exam book, use the technique you like best for developing preliminary information that will address the question.
- Identify the most promising ideas and the direction you want to follow with your answer.

Composing
(10 minutes or so)

- Write a sentence—your *thesis*—that expresses the direction you want to take by restating or responding to the question.
- Express your most promising preliminary ideas in sentence form. List your most important ideas first, in case you run out of time.
- Write on every other line so that you'll have room to add information or make changes or corrections later.

Revising
(5 minutes or so)

- Reevaluate what you've written, making sure you have addressed the question.
- Proofread, concentrating on the particular errors you are prone to.
- Make any last-minute corrections or additions by drawing a line through the material to be deleted and placing a caret (^) below the line and inserting the new material immediately above it.

EXAMPLE

                                                        a person's culture.
A second factor that influences pain is ~~different cultures~~.
                                                            ^

Here again is the essay question:

> Research in the area of pain management suggests that psychological factors are involved in the perception of pain. What three psychological factors influence pain perception? Provide a concrete example for each factor. Also, what are three treatments commonly used to manage pain? Again, provide a concrete example for each treatment, explaining why the treatment works.

Now, here are the prewriting ideas you've generated in response to the question:

> OK, 3 psy. factors? 1. anxiety, like worrying about a date making a headache worse 2. culture, your culture tells you how to react, like men not

complaining 3. experience with pain, the pain you have from an injury or from having a baby makes you expect to have the same pain or more the second time. Now 3 effective treatments? 1. acupuncture is used to treat things like headaches-works by releasing endorphins 2. medication-pain killers like percodan following surgery work by keeping Substance P from being released-the result is euphoria 3. cognitive therapy, learning new ways to deal with pain. Instead of saying "I can't stand this pain," tell yourself "the pain is only temporary"-works because people feel more in control

As you can see, the prewriting material includes the six points the question calls for. Now you need to express your focus—the *thesis*. In this case, you can simply restate the main idea of the question, that psychological factors play a role in both the perception and treatment of pain:

> Research shows that psychological factors are involved in pain perception and treatment.

At this point, convert your promising prewriting ideas into correct sentences that support or illustrate your thesis. Always take a moment to identify the best order to present the material. The question itself provides a *scaffolding*, indicating how you should arrange your supporting ideas. For example, the essay question about pain asks first about perception and second about treatment. Therefore, it makes sense to present your points in that order. Once you have completed your answer, take a few moments to reevaluate what you have written. Does it actually answer the question? Finally, proofread and neatly make any last-minute corrections.

Here is the resulting answer, with annotations pointing out the key features.

ESL Note
See "Sentence Basics,"
pages 543–544;
"Agreement," pages
546–548; "Confusing
Verb Forms," pages
549–551; "Spelling,"
page 552; "Other
Common Grammar
Problems," pages
552–554; and "Revise
to Correct Errors,"
page 557, for more
on dealing with errors
in form.

Clear thesis expressing the main idea

Research shows that psychological factors are involved in pain perception and treatment. (One factor)

First psychological factor with an example

that will make pain worse is anxiety. For example, if you have a headache and feel anxiety that the headache will prevent you from going on a date, the headache is likely to hurt even more than it originally

Note correction

did. A (second factor) that influences pain is different ^a person's culture.

Second psychological factor with an example

cultures. Different cultures have different rules about how people should react to pain. For example, some cultures believe that men should not complain about pain. A man from this type of culture might feel severe pain but still not see a doctor because he

Third psychological factor with an example

doesn't want to seem unmanly. A (third factor) that is involved in pain perception is past experience. If a woman has a lot of pain when her first baby is born, she is likely to expect a lot of pain when her second baby is born. This expectation, based on past experience, is likely to make the pain worst because you experience what you expect to experience.

worse

Note correction

Three types of pain treatments are acupuncture, medication, and cognitive therapy. (Acupuncture) involves inserting small needles into the body to lessen pain. For instance, if you get migraines, you might go for acupuncture in order to lessen the pain. It is thought that acupuncture works by closing gates and releasing endorphins. (Medication) involves taking drugs to stop the pain. If you have surgery, you might take percodan. It is thought that medications work by blocking the release of Substance P and creating euphoria. (Cognitive therapy) involves learning new ways to interpret pain. For example, the person with back pain might be taught to think, "This pain is only temporary" instead of "I can't stand this pain." It is thought that cognitive therapy lessens pain by increasing the person's sense of control.

First pain treatment with an example

Second pain treatment with an example

Third pain treatment with an example

As you can see, this process led to an effective answer that directly addresses the question. It identifies and illustrates three psychological factors related to pain perception and three methods to treat pain. The points are presented in sentence form and arranged in a logical order. In short, the answer is simple, clear, complete, and correct, exactly what you need to get the best grade possible on your essay examination.

COMPREHENSION AND PRACTICE

16.1   **Focusing on Answering Essay Questions**

1. On the following lines, explain the advantages you have with essay questions that you don't have with multiple-choice or fill-in-the-blank questions.

_____

_____

_____

2. On the lines below, briefly explain what you find most difficult about answering essay questions and why you think you experience this difficulty.

_____

_____

_____

3. Choose a print or online article of about 1,000 words or a passage of that length in one of your textbooks. Actively read the document, following the guidelines for active reading (pages 225–226).

CHALLENGE 16.1   Developing and Answering Essay Questions

1. Imagine that you are preparing for an essay examination in one of your courses. Go through the reading you have done for the course as well as your relevant classroom notes. On a separate sheet of paper, list the key information that appears in both your reading and your notes.

2. From this list of material, develop three essay questions. Write each question on a separate sheet of paper.

TIMED WRITING

3. Prepare answers of 200 to 300 words for each question. You have 20 minutes per answer. Write each answer immediately under the appropriate question.

collaboration

4. Exchange your questions and answers with a classmate. Evaluate the material you receive, using the essay answer checklist below. Return the answer and your assessment to the writer.

5. Correct the problem spots your reader has identified in your answers.

✓ ESSAY ANSWER CHECKLIST

☐ Does the essay answer directly address the question being asked? Make a note in the margin next to any point that does not relate to the question.

☐ Should any section of the answer be amplified? Put a ✓ next to the section that needs more explanation.

☐ Are there any mistakes in spelling or usage? Circle any errors.

Completing a Writing Assessment Effectively

U.S. college students today face a number of challenges that their counterparts a decade ago generally did not. For example, an increasing number of institutions have mandatory *entrance* and *exit assessments*. Students must complete these tests to be admitted to a particular course or to receive credit for it. In many cases, these evaluations require that a student write something in accordance with specific guidelines on a particular topic, often within a given time period.

To succeed with this kind of **writing assessment**, you do many of the same things you do when you answer an essay question.

✓ STEPS TO COMPLETING A WRITING ASSESSMENT

☐ Be realistic. Don't expect to write a perfect paper. Concentrate instead on making it the best paper possible *under the circumstances*. Your job is to write an essay that proves your overall competence.

☐ Make sure you understand exactly what the assessment is asking you to do. Carefully examine the topic and any accompanying information before you begin developing ideas. Underline or write down key words and phrases from the assignment that suggest the direction or focus you are expected to take.

> **ESL Note**
> See "Unity," page 555, for more on the importance of keeping your writing focused; "Think about Audience Expectations," page 556, for more information about the needs of the audience; and "Strive for Clarity," page 556, for more on the importance of keeping all timed writing assignments complete and correct.

☐ Manage your time. Once you know how much time you will have, divide the writing process up accordingly. For instance, if you have 50 minutes total, devote approximately 10 minutes to prewriting and approximately 25 minutes to composing. You will then have at least 10 minutes to revise.

☐ Make sure that the document is as complete and correct as possible *under the circumstances*. Check for an introduction with a clear thesis, several body paragraphs supporting that thesis, and a conclusion that closes the paper effectively. Make any last-minute corrections or additions neatly, just as you would with answers to essay questions.

Understanding the Five-Paragraph Essay

Because you are working such a tight time line, you may want to consider using a format called the **five-paragraph essay**. With this format, you use the thesis to specify three main points relative to the topic. Then, in the next three paragraphs—the body of the essay—you discuss each subtopic, one per paragraph. Finally, you add a conclusion that restates the significance of the thesis and the supporting points.

The sample essay shown from prewriting to final draft in Chapter 14, "Superstitions: The Irrational Beliefs That Influence Our Behavior," is a five-paragraph essay. So are several of the essays in Chapter 15, including "Oscar Pistorius: The Race for Fairness" (pages 218–220), shown below in outline form. The outline illustrates the arrangement of the typical five-paragraph essay:

Oscar Pistorius: The Race for Fairness

Introduction:

Reason (1) His prosthetics give him no advantage.

Reason (2) Advances in equipment and training are enjoyed by all.

Reason (3) Allowing him to compete is a matter of basic fairness.

+

Thesis: If Oscar Pistorius is fast enough to run with the world's best, then he should be allowed to compete in any meet, including the Olympics.

Paragraph 2:

His prosthetics give him no advantage. + Additional specific details and explanation.

Paragraph 3:

Advances in equipment and training are enjoyed by all. + Additional specific details and explanation.

Paragraph 4:

Allowing him to compete is a matter of basic fairness. + Additional specific details and explanation.

Conclusion:

Athletic competition is a matter of people pushing themselves to their limits. It is unfair, illogical, and mean-spirited to deny Oscar Pistorius the right to compete with his peers.

Examining a Sample Writing Assessment

Writing assessments appear in a variety of forms. One common type presents a brief excerpt accompanied by a specific writing assignment related to the passage. Here's an example of this type of assessment:

Exit Assessment

Name _____

Student ID Number _____

Date _____

Read the following passage and then write an essay of 300 to 500 words on one of the options that follow the excerpt. Use the pages attached to this sheet. You have 50 minutes to complete all work. Your essay will be judged on its overall effectiveness. Therefore, try to develop a writing that features

- a clear thesis
- solid supporting examples, effectively arranged
- appropriate, specific language
- correct usage, spelling, and punctuation

Assignment

Consider this excerpt from Isabel Briggs Myers's *Taking Type into Account in Education:*

> Children in all the grades should be given maximum opportunity to learn the things that have meaning and interest for them in terms of their own kind of perception and their own kind of judgment. To the extent that they are given this opportunity, they gain not only in interest but in application and intelligence as well. People of any age, from six to sixty, apply themselves with greater vigor to the task at hand when they are interested. People of any age are more intelligent when they are interested than when they are bored.

Now choose *one* of the following options and develop a writing that responds to it:

Option A: Based on Briggs Myers's statement and your own experiences with school, what specific changes would you suggest to make sure that every school becomes the kind of place where more learning takes place?

Option B: In this passage, Briggs Myers uses the word *interest* several times to emphasize how important this element is to success in learning and in life. Consider the examples Briggs Myers provides along with what you've seen, read, and experienced. Then give your view of the types of interest or curiosity that can lead to success in school and the world beyond.

The guidelines provided indicate that the maximum amount of time available to complete the writing is 50 minutes, so it's important to get to work immediately. When an assessment assignment offers more than one possibility, the first step is to select the option that holds the most appeal. Then spend about 10 minutes doing some prewriting.

Here, for example, is some brainstorming in response to Option B:

> Different kinds of curiosity lead people to success
>
> - Curiosity about the world
>
>   kids want to learn about clouds and rain,
>
>   about plants and animals
>
>   about where they come from
>
>   helps them understand their relationship with the rest of the world
>
> - Curious about their families
>
>   what about their history
>
>   any famous ancestors?
>
> - Interest in letters and numbers
>
>   in school kids are curious about letters and numbers
>
>   understand them, words and math suddenly make sense—like magic
>
> - Curiosity about what jobs involve
>
>   what their parents do for jobs
>
>   what other kinds of workers do, what equipment they use leads
>
>   them to careers
>
> Thesis: The types of interest that most help to foster success
>
> include curiosity about nature, about letters and numbers, and about
>
> the work world.

With prewriting material generated, the next step is to use the most promising ideas to create a draft. Under these time constraints, about 20 minutes is available. As with any essay, an assessment essay should include an introduction, several body paragraphs, and a conclusion. The introduction should restate the significance of the assignment itself and include a clear thesis. The body paragraphs should explain and support that thesis, and the conclusion should reemphasize the point being made in the essay. Then, once the draft is complete, the remaining time can be used to revise, making any last-minute corrections or additions.

Here is the assessment essay that results from this process, with annotations to illustrate the key points:

In this excerpt from <u>Taking Type into Account in Education</u>, Isabel Briggs Myers discusses what children need in order to develop fully. She believes that keeping children interested in what they are doing is the secret to success. In my view, the types of interest that foster success include (curiosity about nature,)① (about letters and numbers,)③ and (about the work world.)②

Thesis indicating three key points about the topic

From the time they are able to speak, children ask questions about the world around them. They are clearly interested in all aspects of their world. They want to know where clouds come from, why sometimes it's cold and sometimes it's not, and why dogs and cats don't get along. As they learn the answers, they ask more questions. Life is confusing. If people are going to succeed, they need to be able to understand their environment. With each round of questions and answers, children begin to be able to make sense of the world around them. This curiosity drives them toward success.

Discussion of point ①, with examples

Note corrections

Note addition

Curiosity about letters and numbers is also crucial ② if children are going to succeed in school and in the world outside school. Before children they can read, write, and calculate, letters and numbers must seem like some kind of magic. But once they learn how letters form words and how numbers are added and subtracted to solve problems, the mystery is solved. Suddenly they can understand what a book or sales receipt means. When this interest is stimulated, they are developing the foundation for a life of success.

Discussion of point ②, with examples

Note correction

Note addition

③
A third type of interest that will lead to success

Discussion of point ③, with examples

is a curiosity about the world of work. It starts when

kids ask their parents about their jobs. As they are

For example, from day to day, they see police officers, pediatricians,

growing up, they also observe other people at work. Then

teachers, construction workers, etc. doing their jobs.

they are introduced to other occupations in school,

Note addition

learning about the tools and specialized equipment

involved. These experiences draw children to consider

different career possibilities. Once they become

interested in a particular field, they have a reason to

concentrate more in school. As a result, their prospects

for future success are enhanced.

Conclusion with a sentence recapping the three points

Many things influence whether children eventually

succeed in life. One of those things is making sure that

                              curious

children remain curiosity. In particular, (maintaining ①

their interest in their environment,) (in language and ②

mathematics,) and (in different career possibilities) gives ③

them the best chance for future success.

Note correction

This writing assessment essay is effective for several reasons. For one thing, the introduction directly addresses the assignment and contains a clear thesis. For another thing, the body contains several supporting ideas expressed in detail. Finally, it has a conclusion that reemphasizes the points made in the essay.

As the annotations indicate, this assessment essay follows the format of the five-paragraph essay presented earlier. If the time available permits, however, always feel free to include more than three points about your subject. Think of three as the minimum number of points you need to present, and you'll be all set.

COMPREHENSION AND PRACTICE 16.2

Focusing on Writing Assessments

1. Regardless of the task involved, what happens to you when a strict deadline for completion is imposed? Use the lines below to explain your reaction.

_____

_____

_____

2. Take another look at the annotated five-paragraph essay on superstition (pages 182–184). On the lines below, explain how the introduction of the essay prepares the reader for the body to follow.

_____

_____

_____

3. On the following lines, briefly explain the relationship between good time management and success with a timed writing assessment.

_____

_____

_____

CHALLENGE 16.2   **Completing a Writing Assessment**

TIMED WRITING

1. Here again is **Option A** of the sample exit assessment provided earlier:

Based on Briggs Myers's statement and your own experiences with school, what specific changes would you suggest to make sure that every school becomes the kind of place where more learning takes place?

Now take 50 minutes to complete an assessment essay that responds to this option.

collaboration

2. Exchange your completed assessment essay with a classmate. Evaluate the essay you receive, using the writing assessment checklist below. Return the essay and your evaluation to the writer.

3. Correct any problem spots your reader has identified.

✔ WRITING ASSESSMENT CHECKLIST

ESL Note
See "Writing Paragraphs," pages 555–556, for more on paragraph development, and "Reinforce Your Point with a Concluding Paragraph," page 557, for more on preparing an effective conclusion.

- ☐ Does the introduction have a clear thesis that directly addresses the topic or scenario assigned in the assessment? Write a brief note in the margin if you think the introduction is off target.

- ☐ Do all the paragraphs provide specific support for the thesis? Put a ✔ next to any paragraph that doesn't offer support.

- ☐ Does the conclusion restate the significance of what has been presented? Write a brief note in the margin next to the conclusion, if you think it doesn't bring the assessment to an effective close.

- ☐ Are there mistakes in spelling or usage? Circle any errors.

Writing an Effective Summary

As part of your studies, you will often have to take some document, identify the key points in it, and then express them in a greatly reduced form. The resulting writing is called a **summary**. In some fields, a summary is called an *abstract* or *précis*. Depending on the length of the document itself, a summary may be as little as 5 to 10 percent the length of the original. You therefore need to focus on only the most important or significant points in the original. That way, you will produce a document that expresses the essence of the original.

As with an essay answer and a writing assessment, an effective summary is the product of the following series of steps. Use this process, and you'll find writing a summary much easier:

✓ STEPS TO WRITING AN EFFECTIVE SUMMARY

1. Read the original document *actively*.

   a. Examine the title, introduction, headings and subheadings, conclusion, and other features designed to indicate the key points in the writing.

   b. Reread the writing, highlighting key ideas.

      ☐ Note any **signal words** emphasizing importance, for example, *crucial, vital, significant, prominent, extraordinary.*

      ☐ Note any charts, boxed information, or lists as well as specific names, dates, distances, amounts, conditions, and statistics representing what the writer considers important.

2. Make a list of the key ideas you've identified.

   a. Express these ideas in your own words. Consult a dictionary for any word in the original that is unfamiliar to you so that you express its meaning correctly.

   b. Write out these ideas in complete sentence form.

3. Eliminate the *least* essential ideas from your preliminary list.

   a. Avoid more than one reference to the same point.

   b. Trim or discard lengthy examples and explanations.

   c. Cut any material taken from footnotes.

4. Use the sentences you have written to create a draft summary.

   a. Include enough information so that the summary makes sense for someone who has not read the original.

   b. Present the material in your summary in the same order as in the original document.

(continued)

c. Unless instructed otherwise, don't include your own opinion of the original.

d. Provide transition wherever it is needed so that your draft seems like a coherent paragraph and not just a list of sentences.

5. Revise your draft summary. Make sure that
   a. the summary makes sense independent of the original.
   b. you have supplied sufficient transition.
   c. you have eliminated any of your own commentary on the original.
   d. you have eliminated any errors.

6. Acknowledge your source, using an appropriate system of documentation (see Chapter 15, pages 214–218).

Examining the Process of Preparing a Summary

Take a look at the following brief excerpt from *Environmental Issues: An Introduction to Sustainability,* 3rd ed., an environmental studies textbook by Robert L. McConnell and Daniel C. Abel:

How Do We Use Minerals

Human societies have exploited mineral deposits for thousands of years. Attempts to determine the span of time over which the Greek epic poems *The Illiad* and *The Odyssey* were written focused on the poet's mention of iron and bronze—an alloy of copper and tin—in weaponry.

The U.S. Geological Survey publishes an annual Minerals Yearbook, tracking the production and use of nearly ninety mineral commodities from "abrasives" to "zirconium." You can access information on minerals there at http://minerals.usgs.gov/minerals/.

During the past century and a half, steel has been manufactured by alloying various elements with iron to provide the characteristics exhibited by steel varieties. Stainless steel, for example, contains a thin surface layer of nickel and/or chromium. Cobalt is used to impart heat resistance to steel products, especially the engines of high-speed jet aircraft and rockets. The weapons of modern warfare have placed great demands on such relatively rare metals as cobalt, chromium, and molybdenum.

Demand for metals for weaponry means that many nations, like the United States, are dependent on other nations for their entire supply of these commodities.

An effective summary begins with the identification of the most essential information. Here again is the above passage, with important details highlighted and less essential material crossed out:

Human societies have exploited mineral deposits for thousands of years. ~~Attempts to determine the span of time over which the~~ Greek epic poems *The Illiad* and *The Odyssey* ~~were written focused on the poet's~~ mention of iron and bronze ~~—an alloy of copper and tin—~~ in weaponry.

~~The U.S. Geological Survey publishes an annual Minerals Yearbook, tracking the production and use of nearly ninety mineral commodities from "abrasives" to "zirconium." You can access information on minerals there at http://minerals.usgs.gov/minerals/.~~

~~During the~~ past century and a half, steel has been manufactured by alloying various elements with iron ~~to provide the characteristics exhibited by steel varieties~~. Stainless steel, for example, contains a thin surface layer of nickel and/or chromium. Cobalt ~~is used to~~ impart heat resistance to steel products, especially the ~~engines of high-speed jet aircraft and rockets. The~~ weapons of modern warfare ~~have placed~~ great demands ~~on such~~ relatively rare metals ~~as cobalt, chromium, and molybdenum.~~

~~Demand for metals for weaponry means that~~ many nations, like the United States, are dependent on other nations for ~~their entire supply of~~ these commodities.

The less significant information has been crossed out and the key ideas high-lighted, providing the basis for the following summary:

Summary: How Do We Use Minerals

Human have exploited mineral deposits for thousands of years. The ancient Greek epic poems *The Illiad* and *The Odyssey* mention weapons of iron and bronze. For over 150 years, steel has been manufactured by alloying other elements with iron. For example, stainless steel has a thin surface layer of nickel and/or chromium. Cobalt imparts heat resistance to steel products. Relatively rare metals are in demand for weapons of modern warfare, and many nations, like the United States, depend on other nations for these commodities.

Work Cited

McConnell, Robert L., and Daniel C. Abel. *Environmental Issues: An Introduction to Sustainability.* 3rd ed. New York: Pearson Education, 2008. Print.

This summary reduces the 180-word passage to 84 words—a little more than 45 percent of the original—while still capturing and communicating the main points of the complete version. Notice that the summary is followed by an acknowledgment of the document from which the summary was created, in correct MLA form. Remember—when you take or adapt information from another text, always acknowledge your source.

COMPREHENSION AND PRACTICE 16.3

Focusing on Summarizing

1. On the following lines, briefly explain how reading actively can help you begin the process of developing a summary.

_____

_____

_____

_____

2. In your view, why is providing transition important in preparing a summary? Use the following lines for your answer.

_____

_____

3. In general, which do you find more difficult, identifying essential information in a document or expressing that information? On a separate sheet of paper, identify the task you find harder and explain why.

CHALLENGE 16.3   Developing an Effective Summary

1. Make a copy of a passage of approximately 500 words from a print or online article, or book. Following the guidelines presented in this chapter, create a summary on a separate sheet of paper that is no more than half the length of the original.

collaboration

2. Exchange the passage you used as well as your draft summary with a classmate. Read the passage you receive, and then on a separate sheet of paper evaluate your partner's summary, using the summary checklist below. Return the passage and draft summary, along with your notes, to your reader.

3. Using your partner's comments to guide you, revise your summary.

✓ SUMMARY CHECKLIST

☐ Is the main point of the summary clear? Write a brief note in the margin near the beginning of the summary if you think the main point should be stated more directly.

☐ Is there any portion that you think could be reduced or eliminated without making the summary less effective? Put a ✓ next to any section that could be trimmed or cut.

☐ Is there sufficient transition throughout? Put an * next to any spot that could use some transition.

QUICK STUDY   **Student Example**

This chapter focuses on three common applications of writing. Two involve dealing with the pressure of time. The third involves condensing something without losing the essence of the original. Here is a paragraph on a related subject—an experience when a shortage of time led to a serious mistake:

> One day last month, I almost got killed as a result of trying to beat the clock.
>
> I had come home from school at 3 P.M. to do some reading for one of my classes
>
> before heading to work at the supermarket at 5:30. I sat in my big comfortable

living room chair to read, and unfortunately I quickly fell asleep. When I awoke, it was 5:13, which gave me only 17 minutes for a trip that usually takes at least 20. I ran to my car, started it up, and raced down the road much faster than the 35 mph posted for the route. But my luck ran out when I reached an intersection a couple of miles from the store. Suddenly, a truck started to cross the road in front of me. I jammed on my brakes, swerved to the right, and went across the sidewalk and into a vacant lot behind it, where I finally came to a stop in a huge cloud of dust. For the next 30 seconds or so, I sat there shaking as I thought about how close I came to hitting that truck broadside. From that day on, no matter how late I am, I just take it slow. The next time I might not be so fortunate.

First complete the following activities in response to this paragraph:

1. On the following lines, explain how the details in the body of this paragraph help to support the main idea expressed in the topic sentence.

   _____

   _____

   _____

2. On a separate sheet of paper, evaluate this paragraph. Identify what you see as the strongest point and explain why. Also, if you think some area should be developed more fully, indicate and explain that as well.

3. Using the material in this chapter to guide you, provide a brief summary (two-sentence maximum) on the lines that follow of the experience discussed in this paragraph.

   _____

   _____

   _____

Now explore the topic in writing. You can respond, as the paragraph above does, to an instance when you had to deal with the pressure of time, or you can respond to one of these other topics related to the focus of this chapter:

- a plea to change the way testing is done in schools
- the best tip you have for improving time management

- what you would keep if you had to eliminate 90 percent of your possessions
- something in your life or in the world at large that would be better if it were greatly reduced or condensed

1. Prewrite on the subject you have chosen, identifying a focus and several key ideas, and then complete a draft paragraph of at least seven to ten sentences.

collaboration

2. Exchange your draft with a classmate. Evaluate the paragraph you receive. If you discover any weaknesses in content or form, make a note in the margin and then return the paper to the writer.

3. Consider the comments and corrections your reader has made and create a final draft of your paragraph.

RECAP Adjusting Your Process: Timed Writing and Summaries

Key Terms in This Chapter	Definitions
essay question	a specific writing assignment given as part of an examination that calls for a clear, concise, multiparagraph response within a limited period of time.
practice question	an essay question that a student creates to rehearse for an exam Formulate practice questions by identifying key topics in readings and notes.
writing assessment	a writing assignment, often administered with strict time limits, required to qualify for or complete a course or level of education
five-paragraph essay	a format that involves an introductory paragraph introducing three aspects of a subject, a three-paragraph body discussing each of these aspects, and a conclusion recapping these points
summary	a greatly reduced version of a document that effectively captures and communicates the essence of the original. sometimes called an *abstract* or *précis*
signal words	language that emphasizes importance: *crucial, vital, significant, prominent, extraordinary*

The Process of Preparing for an Essay Exam

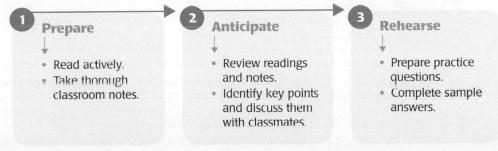

1 Prepare
- Read actively.
- Take thorough classroom notes.

2 Anticipate
- Review readings and notes.
- Identify key points and discuss them with classmates.

3 Rehearse
- Prepare practice questions.
- Complete sample answers.

The Process of Creating a Summary

1 **Actively read the original document.**

- Note title, the introduction, any headings, and conclusion.
- Reread, highlighting key ideas.
  - Note signal words.
  - Note charts, boxed information, and lists.
  - Note statistics and specific names, dates, amounts, and distances.

2 **List the key ideas.**

- Express them in your own words.
- Write them in sentences.

3 **Edit the list to reflect only the most essential information.**

- Eliminate multiple references.
- Cut lengthy examples and supplemental information.

4 **Use the sentences you have written to create a draft summary.**

- Make the summary coherent and complete, using necessary transitions.
- Don't include your own opinion.

5 **Revise the draft.**

- Does it make independent sense?
- Is it free from any commentary?
- Is there enough transition?
- Are there any remaining errors?

Using Odyssey Online with MyWritingLab

For more practice with timed writing and summaries, go to
www.mywritinglab.com.

> **portfolio • noun** (pl. **portfolios**)...**2** a set of pieces of creative work intended to demonstrate a person's ability. ORIGIN Italian *portafogli*, from *portare* 'carry' + *foglio* 'leaf'.

—Compact Oxford English Dictionary

This portfolio offers you the opportunity to demonstrate what you have learned about writing essays (Chapters 14 and 15) and fulfilling specific writing assignments—answering essay questions, completing writing assessments, and creating a summary (Chapter 16). To mark your progress up to this point, prepare the following portfolio:

BEST WORK Select your best piece from assignments completed for this section. If you can't decide which of your documents is superior to the others, seek the opinion of a classmate or another reader.

ESSAY ANSWER Read the following two essay questions, choose one, and provide an answer of around 300 to 400 words.

1. Reread the essay about South African sprinter Oscar Pistorius, whose performances have sparked controversy because he runs on prosthetic legs (pages 218–220).

   - Summarize in two or three sentences the essay's point of view.
   - Offer your stand on the following issues, remembering what you have learned about argument. You will probably find example, process, cause and effect, and description especially useful to support your point of view.

      - Where should officials draw the line in terms of devices, equipment, or enhancements for athletes? For example, should long-distance runners be allowed to use shoes with tiny springs in the soles that absorb shock and offer a bit more lift?
      - A procedure that replaces a damaged ligament in the elbow with a ligament from another part of the body is already fairly commonplace among professional baseball players. Should doctors be allowed to perform this kind of surgery as a way to add double or triple the effectiveness of an athlete's arm or leg? Why or why not?

2. The incidence of life-threatening obesity, especially among the young, is at a level that some physicians have called *epidemic*. Yet, the one place that everybody should have the opportunity to participate—physical education classes in elementary, middle, and high school—continues to be under attack. Some local and state education officials argue that with pressures associated with meeting mandated standards in academics, schools can no longer afford to devote time and money to physical education. And many students argue that in a world where young people often choose computer games over traditional sports, gym classes are no longer relevant. Take a stand on this issue yourself: Do you think physical education classes should be continued, adapted in some way, or done away with? Apply what you have learned about writing an argument essay. You will probably find example, cause and effect, description, and narration useful in terms of supporting your point of view.

Take a close look at this picture. Then in 30 minutes, provide an essay response to one of the following assignments.

- Think critically about the image. What is happening here? The legs of a person appear in the right forefront of the picture. What do you think is wrong with this individual? Why aren't the other people paying any attention to him or her? Do the looks on the faces of the people walking forward indicate anything significant? Choose one or more of these questions, and analyze the photograph.

- Consider the scene captured in the photo. Does it make you think of an experience you have had yourself or a situation you witnessed? How did you and others react? What was the outcome? Knowing what you know now, would you have acted in a different way? Describe the episode in detail and explain the significance of the experience.

REFLECTION   While they share the same process, writing a paragraph and writing an essay are very different tasks. Address this issue in writing. First summarize in two or three sentences how you approach writing an essay versus writing a paragraph. Then in a paragraph of seven to ten sentences, focus on one advantage of exploring a subject in an essay versus doing so in a single paragraph, and why you find this aspect a positive thing.

PART 4

Developing Sentence Sense

CHAPTER 17
The Sentence

GETTING STARTED ...

Q I've completed some prewriting on my subject and developed a focus. I feel confident that my ideas are good, but how do I make sure that I express my focus and supporting ideas in proper sentence form?

A You need to check for the basic components of a sentence in each unit you write. Make sure that each verb has a subject and that the resulting unit expresses a complete thought. There is no other way to ensure that your reader will understand your ideas the way you do.

Overview: Understanding Sentence Basics

Learning to recognize and construct complete sentences is crucial to your success as a writer. For a group of words to be a **sentence**, it must contain a *verb* and *subject* and express a complete thought. The verb represents the action or condition presented. The subject is the doer of the action or the person, place, thing, or idea that is under discussion. Keep in mind that many of the sentences you write will have more than one subject–verb unit. But to qualify as a sentence, a group of words must have at least one subject–verb unit that makes independent sense.

Navigating This Chapter In this chapter, you will discover how to identify and use:

- action verbs, linking verbs, helping verbs, verb phrases, and compound verbs
- simple subjects, complete subjects, and compound subjects
- types and classes of sentences

Understanding Verbs

By definition, a **verb** is a word that shows action or establishes a link between the subject and another word that renames or describes it. In most English sentences, the subject precedes the verb. However, when you're identifying the components in a sentence, first look for the verb. Without a verb, there would be no subject.

A verb that describes what the subject did, does, or might do is called an **action verb**:

EXAMPLES Mischa *sang* six songs at the party last night.

We *enjoyed* her performance.

250

Not all verbs are action verbs, however. **Linking verbs** join or *link* the subject and a word that identifies or describes it, indicating a state of being. Linking verbs include all forms of the verb *to be*. Several action verbs are classified as linking verbs whenever they imply a connection rather than show an action:

Common Linking Verbs	Verbs That Can Serve as Linking Verbs		
forms of *to be* (*am, is, was, were, will be, might have been*, etc.)	feel become appear	look taste smell	grow sound stay

EXAMPLES

In high school, Sun Yee *was* a member of the Student Council.

Gregory *seems* happy with his choice.

ESL Note
See "Sentence Basics," pages 543–544, for more on the use of linking verbs.

Was is a linking verb because it connects *Sun Yee* with a word that identifies her: *member*. The linking verb *seems* links *Gregory* with the descriptive word *happy*.

To identify the verb in a sentence, try asking yourself *what word describes action or shows a connection between two things?* Sometimes the verb in a sentence is composed of more than one word. These verbs may be either verb phrases or compound verbs. A **verb phrase** is a *main verb* plus a *helping verb,* as the italicized words in the following examples show:

EXAMPLES

helping main
verb verb
Ronny *is managing* the office.

helping main
verb verb
They *had bought* several sweaters last month.

Here's a list of common helping verbs:

Common Helping Verbs

am	being	do	have	must	were
are	can	does	is	shall	will
be	could	had	may	should	would
been	did	has	might	was	

A **compound verb** consists of two or more verbs connected by *and* or *or* that share the same subject. Look at the italicized verbs in the following examples:

EXAMPLES

During the rainstorm, the house lights *blinked* and *flickered.*

Uncle Tony *was, is,* and always *will be* a Red Sox fan.

COMPREHENSION AND PRACTICE

Identifying Verbs

17.1 Underline the verbs in the following sentences. In the space above each, label the verb *A* (action) or *L* (linking). Some verbs will be verb phrases, so make sure that you have underlined both the helping and main verbs. Use the example to guide you.

A

EXAMPLE Attitudes toward technology in education <u>have changed</u> in recent years.

(1) In February 2008, an amazing new source of information about the earth's creatures and plant life became available on the Internet. (2) This resource, *The Encyclopedia of Life,* is an ongoing compilation of information about all the world's organisms, including microscopic creatures. (3) A broad array of scientists, software engineers, computer specialists, and philanthropic organizations joined forces to establish this one-of-a-kind database, accessible online at eol.org. (4) A major objective of this ambitious project is the development of a catalog of the nearly two million known species of life. (5) The completion of *The Encyclopedia of Life* will take ten full years. (6) Over this decade, scientists will add information about the estimated millions of undiscovered life forms. (7) Eventually, *The Encyclopedia of Life* will be comparable to about 300 million pages of information. (8) A conservative estimate of the total cost for all of this work is $100 million. (9) With this enormous amount of information available online, scientists in the field will be able to check their discoveries against the entire database. (10) For the general public, *The Encyclopedia of Life* will provide quick and complete answers about earth's complex ecosystems.

COMPREHENSION AND PRACTICE

Using Verbs in Your Writing

17.2 Choose ten of the following verbs, verb phrases, and compound verbs. Use them to write ten sentences on a separate sheet of paper.

pass and dribble	has found	records	opens
scurries	decays	celebrated	protested
had called	are discussing	jogs	have thought
have moved	study or fail	mix	triumphed

CHALLENGE 17.1 **Identifying and Evaluating Verbs in an Essay**

1. Choose a passage of ten sentences from one of the readings in Part 7 or from a newspaper or magazine article or a section of one of your other textbooks. Make a copy of the passage, and underline all the verbs.

2. Label as action or linking the verbs you have underlined. Also label all verb phrases and compound verbs.

collaboration

3. Exchange your passage with a classmate. On the passage you receive, indicate which action verb is the most effective. In the margin of the paper, briefly explain why.

Recognizing Subjects

ESL Note
See "Word Order," pages 545–546, for more on the placement of subjects.

In addition to a verb, the second component required for a group of words to be a sentence is a **subject.** In a sentence, the subject is the word that performs the verb's action or is the focus of discussion. It is either a **noun,** a word that names a person, place, thing, or idea, or a **pronoun,** a word that substitutes for a noun. Finding a subject is easy. First, find the verb, and then ask yourself *who or what is doing what is being discussed?* The word that answers the question is the subject.

Take a moment to identify the verbs and the subjects in the following sentences:

EXAMPLES

The sales representative asked several preliminary questions.

The bus will be late because of the accident downtown.

In the first example, the verb is *asked.* Now ask *who or what asked several preliminary questions?* The subject is *sales representative.* In the second example, the verb is *will be.* Ask *who or what will be late because of the accident downtown?* The subject is *bus.*

Most sentences contain both a simple subject and a complete subject. The **simple subject** is an individual word that identifies who or what is doing the action or being discussed. The **complete subject** is that simple subject plus any words or phrases that describe or modify it, indicating *which one, how many,* or *what kind.*

In the sentences below, both the verbs and complete subjects are identified. Find the simple subject of each sentence.

EXAMPLES

———————————————— complete subject ————————————————
Inexpensive phones with full keyboards, high-quality cameras, and Internet capability
——— verb ———
were introduced several years ago.

————————— complete subject —————————┐┌ verb ┐
An apartment in those rehabilitated mill buildings offers an affordable option for

working families.

ESL Note
See "Agreement," pages 546–548, for more about matching subjects and verbs correctly and "Prepositions," page 554, for more on prepositional phrases.

The simple subject is the specific word the rest of the sentence is discussing. In the first sentence, the simple subject is *phones.* In the second sentence, it is *apartment.*

Being able to identify the simple subject is important because the verb must *agree with* or match the simple subject. Modifiers in the complete subject can mislead you into selecting the wrong verb form, especially if the words are in a **prepositional phrase.** A prepositional phrase begins with a *preposition* and ends with a noun or pronoun called the *object of the preposition*. The preposition *relates* this object to another word in the sentence, often by indicating location, direction, or time. Here is a list of common prepositions:

Common Prepositions

about	behind	during	on	to
above	below	except	onto	toward
across	beneath	for	out	under
after	beside	from	outside	underneath
against	besides	in	over	unlike
along	between	inside	past	until
among	beyond	into	since	up
around	but (except)	like	than	upon
as	by	near	through	with
at	despite	of	throughout	within
before	down	off	till	without

When the object of the preposition comes right before the verb, as it does in these two sentences, you may be tempted to make the verb agree with this object rather than with the actual simple subject. Remember, however, that *an object can't be a subject.* Therefore, when you are checking subject–verb agreement, don't be distracted by any prepositional phrases.

Consider again the preceding examples, this time with the prepositional phrases crossed out:

EXAMPLES

prepositional phrase

Inexpensive phones with full keyboards, high-quality cameras, and Internet capability were introduced several years ago.

prepositional phrase

An apartment in those rehabilitated mill buildings offers an affordable option for working families.

With the prepositional phrases crossed out, it's easier to find the actual simple subjects. In the first sentence, the subject is the plural noun *phones,* not the singular object of the preposition, *capability.* In the second, the subject is the singular noun *apartment,* not the plural object of the preposition, *buildings.* (For more about subject–verb agreement, see Chapter 21.)

Sometimes a **compound subject** answers the question *who or what is doing the action or being discussed?* Compound subjects consist of two or more nouns or pronouns, usually connected by *and* or *or.* These subjects may cause confusion for writers, who must decide whether the subject is singular or plural.

EXAMPLES

Dana or Rebekka shuts off the computers in the office after 5 P.M.

Squirrels, birds, and opossums live in the trees and shrubs behind the cafeteria.

ESL Note
See "Sentence Basics," pages 543–544, for more on the use of the imperative mood.

In the first sentence, the verb is *shuts,* and the answer to the question *who or what shuts?* is the compound subject *Dana or Rebekka. Or* implies a choice. Only one person shuts off the computers, so the verb is singular. In the second sentence, the verb is *live,* and the answer to the question *who or what live?* is the compound subject *squirrels, birds, and opossums. And* implies addition, making the subject plural. All these animals live in the trees and shrubs, so the verb is plural.

As Chapter 8, "Process," explains, with the *imperative mood* or *command,* the subject is *understood* rather than explicitly stated. When you write, "Place your shoes in plastic bags before packing them in your suitcase," the subject isn't actually expressed. Yet, it is obvious that you are saying, "*You* place your shoes in plastic bags before packing them in your suitcase." In other words, the subject is *understood* to be *you.*

COMPREHENSION AND PRACTICE

17.3

Distinguishing between the Simple and the Complete Subject

Underline the complete subject and circle the simple subject in the sentences below. Remember—the simple subject is the specific noun or pronoun that is doing the action or being discussed. Use the example as a guide.

EXAMPLE   The (crowd) in the streets waited impatiently for the beginning of the fireworks display.

(1) Sports championships on television attract huge viewing audiences.

(2) The NCAA Final Four Basketball tournament in March is one good example.

(3) Serious fans of professional tennis can cheer for their favorite players in the popular Wimbledon tournament during July. (4) The glitzy Super Bowl with its hours of pregame shows attracts the most armchair quarterbacks all year. (5) However, the traditional favorite of many sports fans is still October's World Series.

COMPREHENSION AND PRACTICE

17.4

Identifying the Principal Parts of Compound Subjects

Each sentence in the following paragraph has a compound subject. Underline these compound subjects and then circle the principal parts—the simple subjects—making up the compound sentence, as the example shows.

EXAMPLE   Ceiling (fans) and window (fans) can help cool a room and avoid the high cost of air conditioning.

(1) My brothers and sisters, our friends, and I used to treat the Greene Schoolyard in our old neighborhood as our personal playground. (2) My best friend Benni and I would have a jump rope contest near the front door of the school every afternoon. (3) My sister Linna or one of the older girls would be the contest judge. (4) Around back, my older brothers Tomas and Ramon had drawn a big chalked square on the brick wall for speed ball games. (5) During speed ball, a form of baseball, the older boys and a few of the girls would pitch a rubber ball against the square. (6) A chalk mark on the ball or a smudge in the square was evidence of a strike. (7) Late summer and early spring marked football and soccer season. (8) The narrow lawn at the side of the building and the dirt yard behind it were perfect fields for these sports. (9) Every afternoon after school, my brother James and one of the other big kids would divide up the rest of us into two teams. (10) The lawn, the dirt yard, and the rest of the schoolyard are all gone now, with two big additions to the school filling that space.

CHALLENGE 17.2   **Using Compound Subjects in Your Writing**

1. Below is a list of compound subjects. Choose ten of these subjects, and on a separate piece of paper, write a sentence using each one. Add modifiers if you wish.

heat and humidity	a shovel or rake
swimming or sailing	soccer and football
red meat, eggs, and cheese	travel and tourism
hardcovers or paperbacks	AT&T or Verizon
wind and rain	my father and mother
winning or losing	breakfast and lunch

collaboration

2. Exchange sentences with a classmate. Underline the verbs in each sentence and then return the draft to its writer. Check your sentences to be sure each has a correct verb. If not, revise your sentences to make them correct and complete.

Understanding Sentence Types and Classifications

There are four different types of sentences: declarative, interrogative, imperative, and exclamatory. Each type serves a specific purpose.

Declarative sentences make statements:

EXAMPLE   Today's major appliances use considerably less energy.

Interrogative sentences present direct questions:

EXAMPLE   When are you planning to switch Internet providers?

Imperative sentences express commands or requests.

EXAMPLE   Make sure to log off after using the computers in the Learning Resources Center.

Note that the subject of an imperative sentence is "you understood," that is, it is implied or understood to be the person receiving the command.

Exclamatory sentences express strong excitement or emotion and are always followed by an exclamation point:

EXAMPLE   I can't believe I won!

Sentences can also be classified according to the number and types of clauses (subject–verb units) the sentences contain. The four different classifications include the simple, compound, complex, and compound-complex.

Simple sentences consist of a single main clause:

EXAMPLE   *In many ways, Xbox 360 is the most versatile game system available today.*

Compound sentences consist of two or more main clauses connected by a coordinating conjunction or a semicolon:

EXAMPLES   *The wind was blowing fiercely, and we were pelted with hail the size of golf balls.*

                 The wind was blowing fiercely; we were pelted with hail the size of golf balls.

Complex sentences consist of one main clause and one or more subordinate clauses:

EXAMPLES

After the movie began, *the people in the back of the theater finally quieted down.*

The artist **who illustrated that new graphic novel** *had no formal training.*

Compound-complex sentences consist of two or more main clauses connected by a coordinating conjunction and one or more subordinate clauses.

EXAMPLE

The restaurant **where we originally planned to go** *was closed,* and *the second place* **where we stopped** *had a 45-minute wait for a table.*

To ensure that your writing is successful, use the combination of types and classes that most effectively communicate your ideas.

QUICK STUDY   Student Example

This chapter examines the components necessary to present something in complete form. Here is a paragraph on a related subject—two concepts that belong together:

Confidence is an important personal quality, but it should always be accompanied by common sense. For example, no matter how confident people feel before an exam, they would be foolish not to study or at least review the material before the test. The same thing is true for athletic activities. It's one thing to be confident about swimming a long distance in a pool or completing a difficult climb on a climbing wall. At the same time, it would be silly not to recognize that swimming in the open water and climbing an actual cliff are much more dangerous. Police officers, firefighters, and others in high-risk occupations depend on a mixture of confidence and common sense. Confidence enables them to act quickly and decisively, but common sense helps to keep them from ignoring their training and taking a step that could put them or somebody else in unnecessary danger. In every aspect of life, then, the secret is to maintain a balance between confidence and common sense.

First complete the following activities in response to this paragraph:

1. On the following lines, briefly explain how the topic sentence prepares the reader for the discussion in this paragraph.

_____

_____

_____

2. In your view, which sentence provides the strongest support for the topic sentence? On a separate sheet of paper, write that sentence, underlining all verbs and circling all subjects, using the material in this chapter to guide you. Then explain why you think this sentence offers the strongest support.

3. Do you agree with the order of the examples in this paragraph or would you recommend a different arrangement? Use the lines below to explain your reasoning.

_____

_____

_____

Now explore the topic in writing. As the preceding paragraph does, you can discuss two ideas or people that in your view shouldn't be separated, or choose one of these other topics related to the focus of this chapter:

- what in your view is vital to feeling complete as a person
- the elements necessary for a group or team to function effectively
- how to avoid misunderstanding what was said in a conversation
- an action you wish you had taken in response to some problem you faced

4. Prewrite on the subject you have chosen, identifying a focus and several key ideas, and then complete a draft paragraph of at least seven to ten sentences.

collaboration

5. Exchange your draft with a classmate. Evaluate the paragraph you receive. If you discover any problem spots, especially in terms of complete sentences, make a note in the margin and then return the paper to the writer.

6. Consider the comments and corrections your reader has made and create a final draft of your paragraph.

CHAPTER QUICK CHECK   Sentence Basics

In each sentence in the following passage, identify all subjects and verbs. Underline each complete subject, and then circle each simple subject. With any compound subjects, circle each of the simple subjects within it. Double underline all verbs, verb phrases, and compound verbs. Put an X in front of any sentence in the imperative mood. Use the example to guide you.

EXAMPLE

The (lawyer) with her briefcase and her (client) with a small notebook <u>had been</u>

<u>stopped and searched</u> by the police officer at the door.

(1) Because of a recent technological development, a complete book can be produced in a matter of minutes. (2) Experts in this field refer to this innovation as Print on Demand or POD and believe strongly in its future. (3) With this technology, books and other documents are digitized and stored in electronic form. (4) Individual customers and small businesses can then select books and print them up right in the bookstore. (5) As a result of this development, the problem of out-of-print books should be greatly reduced or completely eliminated. (6) In electronic form, a book will never go out of print or be out of stock. (7) Major publishers of commercial and academic books can now publish smaller batches of books and save money as a result. (8) Think of the possibilities. (9) For instance, without a contract, novelists, short story writers, and poets have few publishing opportunities. (10) Through Web-based POD companies like Lulu, iUniverse, and Xlibris, these people can fulfill their publishing dreams and distribute their work themselves.

SUMMARY EXERCISE   Sentence Basics

In each sentence in the following passage, identify all subjects and verbs. Underline each complete subject, and then circle each simple subject. With any compound subjects, circle each of the simple subjects within it. Double underline all verbs, verb phrases, and compound verbs. Put an X in front of any sentence in the imperative mood.

(1) Honor students are not always the smartest students in class. (2) They probably organize, plan, and prepare the most effectively, however.

(3) Organized students purchase necessary tools for their classes.

(4) The items and equipment at the top of their shopping list might include

an assignment notebook and calendar, highlighters, and folders. (5) A pocket dictionary and a flash drive are other useful tools.

(6) In just about every case, successful students with job or family commitments have scheduled manageable study time in advance. (7) They have analyzed their time needs for study and balanced their schedules. (8) Of course, study schedules must be flexible and realistic. (9) Emergencies can happen and may interrupt work on assignments. (10) Therefore, a list of assignments and due dates is an excellent planning tool. (11) Less serious students do the fun, easy assignments first. (12) Successful students, however, complete the assignments in a logical order. (13) They tackle challenges a step at a time.

(14) Preparation also leads to good grades. (15) One good study technique is called prereading. (16) Savvy students preview the textbook materials before the lecture. (17) Introductions. chapter highlights, and review sections often emphasize key points. (18) Successful students read assignments on time, but they also take good class notes and anticipate test questions. (19) This preparation before the day of a test repays them with good scores as well as better learning.

(20) Good grades are within your reach. (21) Make effective study habits your number one priority.

FOR FURTHER EXPLORATION Sentence Basics

1. Focus on one of the following topics. Using the prewriting technique—or combination of techniques—best suited to your style, examine the possibilities that the subject holds and consider what purposes you might fulfill as you write:

   - the habits or behavior of sloppy people
   - the story behind a private or family joke
   - a famous vacation destination
   - a chore or task at home or work that you find particularly frustrating

2. Evaluate your prewriting material, identify a focus, and work your way through the rest of the writing process to create a draft essay of at least 500 words on this subject.

collaboration

3. Exchange your draft with a classmate. Check the draft you receive for weaknesses, especially errors in subject–verb usage. Mark any word groups from which a subject or a verb is missing, using the material in this chapter as a guide, and then return the draft to the writer.

4. Revise your essay, correcting any errors in subject–verb usage or other problems discovered by your reader.

RECAP   The Sentence

Key Terms in This Chapter	Definitions
sentence	a series of words containing a subject and verb and expressing a complete thought
verb	a word or words that describe the action or the condition of the subject
action verb	a word or words expressing action completed by the subject **EXAMPLE** Marcel *held* the door for his sister.
linking verb	a word or words connecting the subject with other words that identify or describe it The most common linking verbs are the forms of *to be.* **EXAMPLE** Kathyrn *is* an excellent athlete.
verb phrase	a main verb plus one or more helping verbs **EXAMPLE** Karen *has been taking* dancing lessons for five years.
compound verb	two or more verbs connected by a conjunction and relating to the same subject **EXAMPLE** Shannon *cooked* and *served* the meal.
subject	the noun or pronoun that is the doer of the action or the focus of the verb Find the subject by answering the question *who or what is doing the action or being discussed?* **EXAMPLE** *Paul* enjoyed the party.
noun	a word that names a person, place, or thing **EXAMPLE** The *river* overflowed its banks.
pronoun	a word that substitutes for a noun **EXAMPLE** *He* loves to tell ghost stories.
simple subject	the noun or pronoun that answers the question *who or what is doing the action or being discussed?*

Key Terms in This Chapter	Definitions
complete subject	the simple subject plus any words or phrases that describe or modify it EXAMPLE The *books on that shelf* are best-sellers.
prepositional phrase	a group of words beginning with a preposition and ending with a noun or pronoun that is the object of the preposition The subject of a sentence can *never* be in a prepositional phrase. EXAMPLE The clothes *on the floor* are dirty.
compound subject	two or more nouns or pronouns connected by a conjunction and acting as the subject for the same verb EXAMPLE Our wonderful *friends* and our dear *neighbors* collected money to help us after the fire.
declarative sentence	makes a statement EXAMPLE It is so nice to see the sun again.
interrogative sentence	presents direct questions EXAMPLE Will it rain again tomorrow?
imperative sentence	expresses a demand or request EXAMPLE Stop fighting right now!
exclamatory sentence	expresses strong excitement or emotion EXAMPLE I can't believe I won the lottery!
simple sentence	a single main clause EXAMPLE I love dessert.
compound sentence	two or more main clauses connected by a coordinating conjunction or semicolon EXAMPLE *Lisette drove for the first time in ten years*, and *she didn't crash into anything.*
complex sentence	one main clause and one or more subordinate clauses EXAMPLE **After the sitter changed Josiah's diaper,** *he managed to fall back asleep.*
compound-complex sentence	two or more main clauses connected by a coordinating conjunction and one or more subordinate clauses EXAMPLE *Clara first chose a sweater* **that was made of both wool and silk,** *but she ultimately changed her mind.*

The Basic Elements of a Sentence

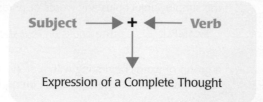

Subject ⟶ **+** ⟵ Verb

Expression of a Complete Thought

Using Odyssey Online with MyWritingLab

For more practice with sentences, go to www.mywritinglab.com.

CHAPTER 18
Fragments

GETTING STARTED ...

 Q I know a sentence fragment is a serious writing error, but I'm not sure why. What is it about a fragment that makes it such a big deal?

 A Think of the name of the error—*fragment.* A sentence fragment is a big deal because it is only a portion of a sentence—*incomplete communication.* To keep your writing free of sentence fragments, focus on what makes a sentence a sentence. Make sure that each unit you write contains a subject and a verb and expresses a complete thought. Do this every time, and your writing will be fragment-free.

Overview: Recognizing and Writing Complete Sentences

To communicate your full meaning to your reader, you need to express your good ideas in correct sentence form. That means you must avoid **sentence fragments,** units that lack a verb or a subject or fail to express a complete thought to the reader. Sentence fragments are serious errors that do not communicate ideas fully and therefore fail to convey your intended meaning to your reader.

Navigating This Chapter In this chapter, you will learn how to avoid and correct fragments created by:

- omitting a subject or a verb
- mistaking a phrase for a sentence
- mistaking a subordinate clause for a sentence
- mistaking an appositive for a sentence

Correcting Fragments with Missing Subjects or Verbs

ESL Note
See "Sentence Basics" on pages 543–544.

As the previous chapter shows, to be a sentence, a group of words must contain a verb and subject. When you are checking your own sentences, first identify the verb. If you cannot find an action or linking verb, the group of words is a fragment, as in the following:

FRAGMENT The use of acupuncture to treat rheumatoid arthritis.

There is no verb here, only a noun and its modifiers, so this group of words is a fragment. To change it to a sentence, add a verb to complete the thought.

REVISED The use of acupuncture to treat rheumatoid arthritis *shows* the growing influence of alternative medicine.

ESL Note
See "Word Order,"
pages 545–546, for
more on the use of
verbals (words
ending in *-ing* or *-ed*).

Sometimes a group of words has a word that could serve as a subject and a word or group of words that seems to be a verb, but in fact this group of words is a **verbal**, a verb form that can't communicate a complete action or meaning, as in the following:

FRAGMENTS The front-end manager *looking* for volunteers for an overtime shift.

Daisy *spoken* to Charlie an hour before the accident.

Eddie *to run* the Chicago Marathon again.

All three groups of words are fragments because they contain verbals (italicized)—looking, spoken, to run—not verbs. To make them into sentences, substitute the verbals with true verbs:

SENTENCES The front-end manager *looked* for volunteers for an overtime shift.

or

The front-end manager *is looking* for volunteers for an overtime shift.

SENTENCES Daisy *spoke* to Charlie an hour before the accident.

or

Daisy *had spoken* to Charlie an hour before the accident.

SENTENCES Eddie *ran* the Chicago Marathon again.

or

Eddie *will run* the Chicago Marathon again.

See Part 5, "Understanding Subjects and Verbs," for more on using verbs correctly.

Even if a group of words has a verb, it's not a sentence unless it also has a subject, the word or group of words that answers the question *who or what is doing the action or being discussed?* If no word answers the question, then there is no subject, and the group of words is a fragment, as in the following:

FRAGMENT Told Stephen's boss about Stephen's excellent computer skills.

This group of words is not a sentence. There is a verb—*told*—but if you ask *who or what told*, there is no answer.

To correct this fragment, simply add a subject:

SENTENCE

────── subject ──────
Professor Tessier told Stephen's boss about Stephen's excellent computer skills.

COMPREHENSION AND PRACTICE

18.1

Identifying and Correcting Fragments with Missing Subjects and Verbs

The following passage contains several fragments that lack either a subject or a verb. In some cases, units contain a verbal instead of a verb. Put a + in front of any sentence that is correct. Underline each fragment, and then correct each by adding a subject or a verb above the appropriate spot and a ^ below it. Cross out any words that should be revised or eliminated. Use the example to guide you.

EXAMPLE

The food in the cooler had
^
~~Had~~ to be thrown out because of contamination.

(1) A few weeks ago, I visited a wonderful place, a newly opened butterfly sanctuary. (2) The sanctuary itself a large closed area within a larger building. (3) In this area, flowering plants are arranged in a number of small garden settings. (4) Several paths running across the sanctuary for easy access to the entire area. (5) The butterflies in a completely safe environment, with no predators of any kind. (6) As a result, they to fly around and feed freely. (7) Can walk right up to brightly colored butterflies for a close look at their delicate features and distinct wing patterns. (8) Sometimes, butterflies on people's clothing. (9) Above the exit, a sign asks people to check themselves to avoid accidentally taking butterflies out the door upon leaving. (10) Was truly a unique experience.

CHALLENGE 18.1   **Writing Supporting Sentences for a Paragraph**

collaboration

1. Working with a classmate, compose a paragraph of at least seven to ten sentences to support one of the topic sentences listed below.
   a. Knowledge of a second language is important in today's global economy.
   b. Today's computer games are often too violent for children younger than twelve years old.

2. Exchange your sentences with another writing team. Check the paper you receive for fragments. Write *frag* in the margin beside each fragment you find. Return the paper to its writers. Make any corrections needed to your paper.

Correcting Phrase Fragments

A *phrase* is a group of two or more related words that lacks a subject–verb unit. As the previous chapter indicated, two common types of phrases are verb phrases (page 251) and *prepositional phrases* (pages 253–254). When a phrase is left to stand alone, it is a **phrase fragment.**

FRAGMENTS

Will soon be sleeping. *(Verb phrase)*

Inside the house. *(Prepositional phrase)*

Both examples lack a subject–verb combination, so both are fragments.

To turn these phrases into complete sentences, you need to supply the missing elements, as these versions show:

SENTENCES

┌── subject ──┐
My grandfather will soon be sleeping.
┌subject┐┌verb┐
Daryl left his jacket inside the house.

COMPREHENSION AND PRACTICE

18.2

Identifying and Correcting Phrase Fragments

The following passage contains several fragments resulting from phrases used incorrectly as sentences. Underline these fragments. Then, on a separate piece of paper, rewrite the paragraph, turning the fragments into sentences. Use the example to guide you.

EXAMPLE

Under the porch.

The frightened kitten hid under the porch.

(1) Being a musician demands a lot of dedication. (2) Have to practice hours daily. (3) Some musicians keep an unusual schedule. (4) Until the early morning hours. (5) Then they sleep until the afternoon. (6) Family life becomes difficult. (7) With this work schedule. (8) Sometimes musicians face weeks without employment. (9) Through all this, musicians keep playing. (10) Have a need to bring the joy of music to their audiences.

Correcting Subordinate Clause Fragments

ESL Note
See "Agreement," pages 546–548, for more about clauses.

Even if a group of words contains a subject and a verb, it is still a fragment if it does not express a complete thought. A **subordinate clause fragment**, for example, contains a subject and a verb, but it cannot stand on its own. Subordinate clauses are introduced by either *subordinating conjunctions* or *relative pronouns*.

Common Subordinating Conjunctions

after	before	since	when
although	even though	so that	whenever
as	if	than	where
as if	in order that	though	wherever
as soon as	once	unless	whether
because	rather than	until	while

Relative Pronouns

that	who
what	whom
which	whose

The function of a subordinate clause is to explain or describe another portion of the sentence. It is called *subordinate* because it depends on a **main clause**, the primary subject–verb unit of the sentence, to make complete sense. In fact, subordinate clauses are sometimes called *dependent clauses*, as in the following:

FRAGMENTS

After the *EMTs arrived.*

That *Michaela saw* outside the bus station.

Both examples have subjects and verbs, but neither one expresses a complete thought. Each leaves the reader waiting for more information.

To correct this type of fragment, you have a couple of choices. You could add or delete words so that the clause makes sense on its own:

SENTENCES

The EMTs arrived within minutes of receiving the emergency call.

Michaela saw Theo outside the bus station.

In the first sentence, *after* has been deleted, and *within minutes of receiving the emergency call* has been added. In the second sentence, *That* has been deleted, and *Theo* has been added. Both groups of words now express complete thoughts.

You can also choose to correct this type of fragment by adding a main clause to the subordinate clause to express a complete thought:

SENTENCES

After the EMTs arrived, *they began treating the injured people immediately.*

The car that Michaela saw outside the bus station *was broken down.*

In both cases, the combination of clauses expresses a complete thought.

COMPREHENSION AND PRACTICE

18.3

Identifying and Correcting Subordinate Clause Fragments

The following passage contains several subordinate clause fragments. Underline these fragments. Then, on a separate piece of paper, rewrite the paragraph, turning the fragments into sentences. Use the example as a guide.

EXAMPLE

Even though the new movie had received poor reviews. The crowd waiting to see it was huge.

Even though the new movie had received poor reviews, the crowd waiting to see it was huge.

(1) Sometime in the near future, your pockets or purse may no longer jingle the same way. (2) Because the penny may soon disappear from use. (3) Although not everyone agrees with their stance. (4) Some merchants and retail groups are asking the government to eliminate this coin. (5) In their view, the penny, which now costs more than a cent to manufacture, no longer serves a useful purpose. (6) That it had served over its long history. (7) These critics complain about the nuisance factor of dealing with all those pennies. (8) Unless the purchase is for an even amount of money. (9) Every cash transaction involves the use of several pennies. (10) According to people pushing to eliminate the penny, a better plan is to round off all final prices to denominations ending in 5 or 10.

COMPREHENSION AND PRACTICE

18.4

Rewriting Subordinate Clauses as Sentences

On a separate sheet of paper, turn the following subordinate clauses into sentences by adding a main clause. Check your work for correct use of capitals and punctuation. Use the example to guide you.

EXAMPLE

even though the class had ended

The students continued their discussion, even though the class had ended.

1. who plans to ride to the game on the team bus

2. whenever a false alarm is sounded

3. which hung on a chain around her neck

4. although it won two Academy Awards

5. since it wasn't my fault

collaboration

CHALLENGE 18.2 **Analyzing and Completing Sentences**

1. Exchange the sentences that you have written for Comprehension and Practice 18.4, above, with a classmate. Check the sentences you receive to ensure that they are now sentences. Put a ✓ next to any unit that you think is still a fragment, suggest a way to turn the fragment into a sentence, and return the sentences to your classmate.

2. Consider any changes your classmate has suggested, and make any necessary corrections to your own sentences.

Correcting Appositive Fragments

An **appositive** is a word or group of words that renames or explains another noun or pronoun. Some appositives contain subjects and verbs, but like subordinate clauses, appositives don't express complete thoughts on their own, as in the following:

FRAGMENTS

The spot where my *car had broken* down.

A talent *she* usually *kept* hidden.

Both groups of words have subjects and verbs, but neither expresses a complete thought.

To eliminate this kind of fragment, you can change and adjust the order of the words to express a complete thought:

SENTENCES

My *car had broken* down at that spot.

She usually *kept* that talent hidden.

You can also join the fragment with a main clause so that it expresses a complete thought:

SENTENCES

Fortunately, a car dealership was on the corner, the spot where my car had broken down. (*The appositive now focuses on* corner.)

Tami entertained the crowd by singing, a talent she usually kept hidden. (*The appositive now modifies* singing.)

COMPREHENSION AND PRACTICE

18.5

Identifying and Correcting Appositive Fragments

The following passage contains several appositive fragments. Underline these fragments. Then, on a separate piece of paper, turn those fragments into complete sentences. Use the example to guide you.

EXAMPLE

A task that frustrates him.

Tim had to balance his checkbook, a task that frustrates him.

(1) Last summer, I worked as a nanny. (2) The best temporary job I ever had. (3) My duties included dressing, feeding, and entertaining two children. (4) The nicest, most well-behaved kids I have ever known. (5) They enjoyed the zoo, the beach, and the park. (6) Just a few of the places I took them. (7) They were always excited, no matter what we did. (8) They especially liked the school playground. (9) A place that was always nearly deserted in the summer. (10) I was sorry to see that summer end.

COMPREHENSION AND PRACTICE 18.6

Rewriting Appositives Correctly as Sentences

On a separate sheet of paper, turn each of the following appositives into a sentence by adding a main clause containing a word for the appositive to rename or explain. Use the example to guide you.

EXAMPLE

a park on the outskirts of the city

Evergreen Acres, a park on the outskirts of the city, is the best place to view the comet.

1. the quietest person in the office

2. the most influential musician of the decade

3. a dangerous intersection for pedestrians

4. the best seat in the auditorium

5. a required course in my major

CHALLENGE 18.3 Working with Subordinate Clauses and Appositives

1. Read one of the essays in Part 7, a newspaper or magazine article, or a chapter in one of your other textbooks. Find at least three subordinate clauses and at least two appositives. On a separate piece of paper, write the sentences that contain these elements.

collaboration

2. Exchange your sentences with a classmate. Take a look at the sentences you receive and, on a separate sheet of paper, briefly explain the relationship between the independent and dependent clauses.

QUICK STUDY   **Student Example**

This chapter focuses on the problems that result from incomplete information. Here is a paragraph on a related subject—something that didn't make sense until it was viewed from a different perspective:

Until I began my job as a server at a restaurant. I never understood the importance of learning how to work well with others. When I was a little kid. I always preferred to play and do things by myself, so I never enjoyed doing any group work in school. It didn't make any difference whether my group was solving a math problem, working on an art project, or completing a research assignment. I always secretly felt that I could have done the work faster and more effectively on my own. But now that I am part of a crew at the restaurant, I know how important working as a team is. For example, the other servers and I depend on the hostess to manage the flow of diners, and she depends on us to be fast, efficient, and courteous. The kitchen staff depends on us to record the orders accurately, and we depend on them to prepare each order correctly and get them out quickly to keep the customers satisfied. If anybody on the team messes up. The mistake affects all of us. Unhappy customers don't leave good tips, and sometimes they don't come back. Because of the experiences I have at this job. I finally appreciate the value of working as a team.

First complete the following activities in response to this paragraph:

1. Two brief passages in this paragraph are highlighted. Evaluate these sections for sentence fragments. On a separate sheet of paper, turn any fragments into correct sentences, using the material in this chapter to help you correct them.

2. On the following lines, briefly explain how the sentences in the body of the paragraph connect and support the main idea of the paragraph.

_____

_____

_____

3. The paragraph relies largely on comparison and contrast to tell this story. In your view, which of the two periods of time contrasted is stronger and more effective, the discussion of the past or the discussion of the present? On the lines below, identify and briefly explain your choice.

_____

_____

_____

Now explore the topic in writing. You could discuss some idea or concept that you didn't understand until you viewed it as part of a larger issue like the paragraph above does. You might also choose one of these subjects related to the subject matter of this chapter:

- how a group you are or were a part of changed when someone else joined it
- how some aspect of life would be different if a part or element of it were removed
- a situation in which something small or seemingly insignificant became a major disruption
- what did or could happen if someone acts without fully understanding the consequences

collaboration

4. Exchange your draft with a classmate. Evaluate the paragraph you receive. If you discover any problem spots, especially sentence fragments, make a note in the margin and then return the paper to the writer.

5. Consider the comments and corrections your reader has made and create a final draft of your paragraph.

CHAPTER QUICK CHECK Fragments

Underline the fragments in the following passage. Then, on a separate sheet of paper, revise the passage by correcting the fragments, using the techniques you practiced in this chapter. Remember that fragments can be corrected in a variety of ways.

(1) The Vietnam Veterans' Memorial, one of the best-known U.S. monuments, has had a controversial history. (2) After the government announced their plans for a memorial to honor Vietnam combat casualties. (3) A number

of architects submitted designs for consideration. (4) A blue ribbon selection committee. (5) Chose a design by a young Asian-American woman, Maya Lin. (6) Lin's plans called for a wedge-shaped black, polished-granite wall. (7) With the names of the war dead inscribed in rows across its surface. (8) Although some people immediately praised Lin's design. (9) One critic described it as a "black scar in the earth." (10) Despite this rocky beginning, the Memorial among the most visited of all the historical sites in Washington, D.C.

SUMMARY EXERCISE Fragments

Underline the fragments in the following essay. Then, on a separate piece of paper, revise the essay by correcting the fragments, using the techniques you practiced in this chapter. Remember that fragments can be corrected in a variety of ways.

(1) One of today's most popular and influential comic performers is Stephen Colbert. (2) The host of Comedy Central's hit show, *The Colbert Report.* (3) From its first broadcast in 2005, *The Colbert Report* almost immediately becoming one of the cable network's highest rated shows.

(4) Colbert, the youngest of eleven children, is a native of Charleston, South Carolina. (5) When he was ten years old. (6) His father, an administrator at the Medical University of South Carolina, and two of his brothers were killed in a plane crash. (7) Following this tragedy and his family's subsequent relocation to another Charleston neighborhood, found it difficult to relate to or maintain interest in the things kids his age found appealing. (8) He became interested in drama and performing in high school, eventually studying acting at Northwestern University.

(9) In 1997, after experiencing some success as a performer and as a freelance writer and script consultant for a number of other shows, including *Saturday Night Live.* (10) Colbert joined Comedy Central's *The Daily Show* (11) For nine years, he appeared regularly on the show as a correspondent, offering satiric commentary on events in the news.

(12) On *The Colbert Report,* Colbert the role of a pompous, clueless politically conservative pundit and commentator. (13) Within a matter of weeks of the first broadcast, the show and Colbert began to attract national attention. (14) For instance, *truthiness,* a word Colbert coined in 2005 to name a belief based not on any facts but on a gut reaction, quickly started to appear in newspapers and other media.

(15) Recognizing that much of his audience is young and technologically savvy. (16) He once encouraged his viewers to edit an entry on elephants on Wikipedia to include incorrect details, leading to a crash of its servers. (17) In 2009, Colbert's fans, at his urging, made him the top vote-getter in NASA's online contest to name a new room in the International Space Station.

(18) To bring greater attention to the U.S. troops still serving in Iraq. (19) Colbert brought his show to the soldiers in 2009, even having his trademark carefully coifed hair shaved off on camera. (20) During the same time, he also served as guest editor of an edition of *Newsweek* magazine, a clear sign that Colbert's impact on the public consciousness has far exceeded the reaches of cable television.

FOR FURTHER EXPLORATION Fragments

1. Focus on one of the following topics, using the prewriting technique—or combination of techniques—that you prefer to generate some preliminary ideas, and consider what purposes you might fulfill as you write about it:

   - an e-mail or text message that you sent or received by accident
   - the wisdom of little children
   - the behavior of tourists
   - rule or law you would like to see changed

2. Evaluate your prewriting material, identify a focus, and work your way through the rest of the writing process to create a draft essay of at least 500 words on this subject.

collaboration

3. Exchange your draft with a classmate. Check the draft you receive for weaknesses, especially sentence fragments, using the material in this chapter as a guide. Underline any fragments and then return the draft to the writer.

4. Revise your essay, correcting any fragments or other problems discovered by your reader.

RECAP　Fragments

Key Terms in This Chapter	Definitions
sentence fragment	a group of words that fails to express a complete thought because it lacks a subject, a verb, or other needed words **EXAMPLE**　Although they tried not to laugh [not a complete thought]
verbal	a verb form that is used as another part of speech and therefore doesn't communicate a complete action or meaning A verbal cannot substitute for a verb in a sentence. **EXAMPLE**　*Running* down the stairs
phrase fragment	a group of two or more related words that lacks a subject–verb unit, used incorrectly as a sentence **VERB PHRASE**　Are looking **PREPOSITIONAL PHRASE**　About time
subordinate clause fragment	a group of words that contains a subject and a verb but does not express a complete thought A subordinate clause must be joined to a main clause to express a complete thought. **EXAMPLE**　That had struck the coast
main clause	the primary subject–verb unit of a sentence **EXAMPLE**　*The hurricane* that had struck the coast *was not expected*.
appositive	a word or group of words that renames or explains a noun or pronoun next to it An appositive must be connected to a main clause to express a complete thought. **EXAMPLE**　A retired police officer

Eliminating Fragments

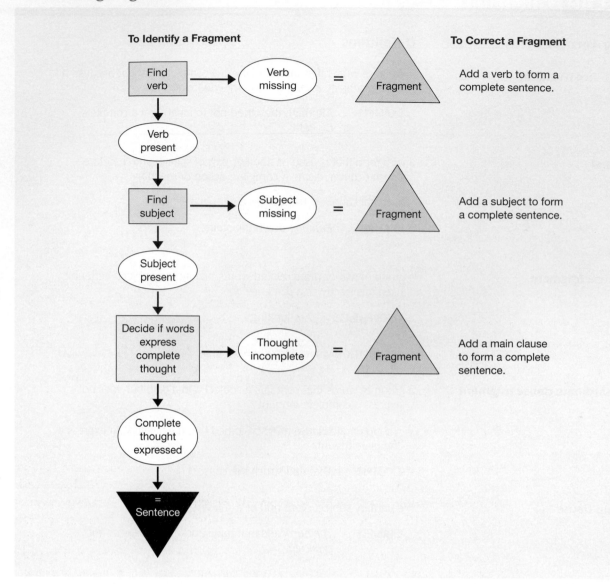

Using Odyssey Online with MyWritingLab

For more practice with fragments, go to www.mywritinglab.com.

CHAPTER 19
Subordination and Coordination

GETTING STARTED ...

 Q Some of my sentences are really short, and I don't want my writing to seem stiff or choppy. Is there something I can do so that my sentences are fuller and more interesting?

 A One way to enliven your writing is to improve the flow by combining short sentences. To create an equal balance between sentences that have about the same significance, use *coordination* and connect sentences with a *coordinating conjunction* such as *and* or with a semicolon. To indicate that one short sentence depends on another to communicate your full meaning, use *subordination* and connect sentences with a *subordinating conjunction* such as *because*. Both methods will help keep your writing interesting and highly readable.

Overview: Combining Clauses for Sentence Diversity

When you write, as the previous two chapters detailed, you must express your ideas in complete sentence form. A sentence that contains a single subject–verb unit and expresses a complete thought is called a *simple sentence*. However, writing that consists of only simple sentences will sound choppy or monotonous. You can emphasize some ideas through *subordination*—combining an idea in a main clause with an idea in a *subordinate clause*. The subordinate clause depends on the main clause to make sense. Alternatively, you can join ideas through *coordination*—linking two main clauses (or simple sentences) with a semicolon or a coordinating conjunction and comma.

Navigating This Chapter In this chapter, you will learn to:

- identify and use simple and complex sentences to express your ideas with variety
- use subordinating conjunctions to connect and show relationships between clauses
- use relative pronouns to introduce subordinate clauses that describe a noun or pronoun
- use a coordinating conjunction and a comma, a semicolon, or a semicolon and a conjunctive adverb to create a compound sentence

Using Subordination

To use **subordination** effectively, you need to understand the difference between a simple sentence and a complex sentence. A **simple sentence** consists of only one subject–verb unit or *clause*, as this example shows:

SIMPLE SENTENCE

⌐subject⌐   ⌐ verb ⌐
The *reporter* on the scene *detailed* the degree of damage.

ESL Note
See "Agreement," pages 546–548, for more on the use of subordinate clauses.

As a writer, you will also rely on **complex sentences,** which combine a main, or independent, clause and a **subordinate,** or dependent, **clause.** As Chapter 18 illustrates, subordinate clauses are introduced by either **subordinating conjunctions** such as *although, because, if, until,* and *when* or **relative pronouns** such as *that, what, which,* and *who.* (See page 269 for a complete list of common subordinating conjunctions and relative pronouns.)

If you join a simple sentence and a subordinate clause in a complex sentence, the simple sentence becomes the **main clause,** as this example shows:

COMPLEX SENTENCE

——————— main clause ——————— ⌐— subordinate clause ——
The reporter on the scene detailed the degree of damage where the explosion had occurred.

In a complex sentence, you may also place the subordinate clause before the main clause. In this case, a comma is needed before the conjunction. No matter where it is placed, the main clause of a complex sentence contains the most important idea.

Subordinating conjunctions do more than connect clauses. They also indicate the *relationship* between the two clauses in terms of time, purpose, result, condition, or cause. Consider the following complex sentences:

EXAMPLE

——————— main clause ——————— ⌐———— subordinate clause ————
My car insurance increased $500 this year *because* I received a speeding ticket.

EXAMPLE

————— subordinate clause ————— ⌐——— main clause ———
If Linda concentrates on her studies, she could earn a scholarship.

In the first sentence, *because* indicates that the first occurrence—the increase in insurance rates—is the result of the second occurrence. In the second, *if* suggests under what condition Linda will earn a scholarship.

Relative pronouns are used to introduce subordinate clauses that either *describe* a noun or *specify* a noun or pronoun in the sentence. Look at the following sentences, with the subordinate clauses italicized:

EXAMPLES

Any person *who provides encouragement and emotional support* is a true friend.

Food *that is low in fat* is better for a healthy heart.

In the first sentence, the relative pronoun *who* introduces the subordinate clause specifying what kind of person qualifies as a true friend. In the second, the relative pronoun *that* indicates which type of food is heart healthy.

COMPREHENSION AND PRACTICE 19.1

Combining Simple Sentences to Create Complex Sentences

The following paragraph is composed of simple sentences. On a separate piece of paper, rewrite the paragraph, joining ideas to create complex sentences. Use subordinating conjunctions and relative pronouns to introduce subordinate clauses. (Refer to the lists on page 269.) Be sure that the ideas you want to emphasize are in the main clauses of your new sentences. You may decide to leave some simple sentences just as they are for variety. Be sure you use punctuation and capitals correctly.

(1) I have made running a top priority in my daily routine. (2) I run a three mile loop in the park. (3) The park is near my apartment. (4) My run is important to me for many reasons. (5) First, this workout helps me deal with stressful situations. (6) These may come up at work. (7) I have many responsibilities, including preparing the work schedule for all workers. (8) Some mornings it is cold or raining. (9) I refuse to give up the most important hour of my day. (10) All in all, my morning run is an invigorating way to start my day.

CHALLENGE 19.1

Evaluating Your Use of Subordination

collaboration

1. Exchange with a classmate the paragraph you revised in Comprehension and Practice 19.1. On a separate sheet of paper, make a list of changes that you made that are different from the changes your classmate made, noting which sentences remain as simple sentences and which were turned into complex sentences.

collaboration

2. Working with your classmate, discuss your evaluations, and then choose the sentences that you both agree are most effective.

Using Coordination

Another way to join related ideas is to use **coordination**. This is a technique for connecting two or more sentences to give each one equal emphasis. The resulting sentence is called a **compound sentence**.

Achieving Coordination by Using Coordinating Conjunctions

The most common way to create a compound sentence is to connect simple sentences with a **coordinating conjunction** and a comma. The coordinating conjunction in a compound sentence shows the relationship between the equally important subject–verb units that it joins. These units are called **independent clauses** because each clause is essentially a simple sentence that can stand on its own. Here is a list of the coordinating conjunctions.

Coordinating Conjunctions

and	for	or	yet
but	nor	so	

Coordination cannot be used to join clauses that could not function on their own as complete sentences. However, you may use coordinating conjunctions to join complex sentences to simple ones and to join complex sentences to one another. In addition, you may use coordinating conjunctions to create a compound-complex sentence—a compound sentence containing at least one dependent clause.

Using coordination can help you eliminate choppiness from your writing. Consider these two pairs of sentences:

CHOPPY

> The heavy rain flooded the streets. Lightning started two small fires.
>
> The toddler started to fall from the top step. A woman coming up the stairs managed to steady him.

As they are now, these two sets of sentences sound choppy. Now consider the same pairs of sentences when a conjunction and comma are used to join each pair of sentences:

COMBINED

> The heavy rain flooded the streets, *and* lightning started two small fires.
>
> The toddler started to fall from the top step, *but* a woman coming up the stairs managed to steady him.

These compound sentences are more fluid than the sets of simple sentences. The coordinating conjunctions clearly show how the two ideas within each subject–verb pair are related.

COMPREHENSION AND PRACTICE

19.2

Using Coordination

Fill in the blanks, adding a clause that is related to the existing clause before or after the coordinating conjunction. Use the example as a guide.

EXAMPLE

> The basketball game was tied, **so** _____
>
> *the coach left the starting five on the court.* _____

1. The restaurant that I wanted to go to was closed, **so** _____

_____

2. _____

    nor was the coffee shop open down the street.

3. Our stomachs were growling, **so** _____

_____

4. The wait at the bus stop was long, **but** _____

_____

5. _____

    or I would have fainted from hunger.

Achieving Coordination by Using Semicolons

ESL Note
See "Punctuation,"
pages 554–555, for
more on the correct use
of semicolons.

Another way to achieve coordination is to use a *semicolon* (;) to connect independent clauses. A semicolon has the same power to connect as a coordinating conjunction with a comma but makes the connection more direct. Chapter 31, "Other Punctuation and Capitalization," provides much more information about the use of semicolons.

Consider the two versions of the following sentence:

EXAMPLES

The day had been long and hot, *and* all I wanted to do was take a shower.

The day had been long and hot; all I wanted to do was take a shower.

In the first version, the coordinating conjunction *and* simply connects the two clauses. In the second version, however, the semicolon joins the two ideas directly, stressing that the relationship between them is so close and obvious no conjunction is needed.

In addition to using a semicolon alone, you can add a twist to this technique by including a **conjunctive adverb** after the semicolon. Take a look at the following list of conjunctive adverbs:

Common Conjunctive Adverbs

also	however	similarly
besides	instead	still
consequently	meanwhile	then
finally	moreover	therefore
furthermore	nevertheless	thus

Conjunctive adverbs *suggest a relationship* between two thoughts, as the following compound sentences show:

EXAMPLES

In-line skating is great exercise; *furthermore*, it's great fun.

I had planned to get to work early; *however*, two accidents on the highway delayed me for 45 minutes.

Neither *furthermore* nor *however* is used to connect the sentences. The semicolon does that. Note that this technique requires two punctuation marks: a semicolon *before* the conjunctive adverb and a comma *after* it.

COMPREHENSION AND PRACTICE

19.3

Combining Sentences Using Conjunctive Adverbs and Semicolons

Complete each sentence by adding a conjunctive adverb and an independent clause after the semicolon. Use the list of conjunctive adverbs on page 283. Don't forget a comma after the conjunctive adverb. Use the example as a guide.

EXAMPLE

The waiting room at the clinic was crowded; _____

however, I decided to stay until the doctor was available.

1. Washington, D.C.'s Metro system is clean and efficient; _____

   _____

2. The wheels on the subway cars are made of special material that reduces noise; _____

   _____

3. Last year a record number of visitors used the system; _____

   _____

4. The New York subway system is quite different; _____

   _____

5. New Yorkers often choose the bus over the subway; _____

   _____

COMPREHENSION AND PRACTICE

19.4

Using Coordination and Subordination

The paragraph below contains simple sentences. Decide where it can be improved through coordination and subordination. Then rewrite the new version on a separate piece of paper. Use all the methods you have practiced in this chapter to create compound and complex sentences. You may decide to leave some sentences as they are. Use the example as a guide.

EXAMPLE

Many people try to avoid taking Statistics I. It is a difficult course.

Many people try to avoid taking Statistics I because it is a difficult course.

(1) Asthma is a chronic, dangerous lung condition. (2) It can be treated. (3) The causes of asthma are increasing. (4) More and more people suffer from asthma every year. (5) Asthma attacks can be triggered by air pollution, dust, a cold, and even exercise. (6) During an asthma attack, bronchial tubes in the lungs get irritated and constrict. (7) Patients cough, wheeze, and struggle to breathe as a result. (8) Asthma sufferers can lead normal lives. (9) They need proper medication and medical supervision. (10) They also need to understand and avoid the conditions that trigger their asthma attacks.

CHALLENGE 19.2 Evaluating Your Sentence-Combining Techniques

collaboration

1. Share the paragraph you revised in Comprehension and Practice 19.4 with a classmate, and compare the choices you each made to combine ideas. In your discussion, answer the following questions:

   - What options did you use for achieving coordination?
   - Where did you use subordination?
   - Why did you make the changes that you did?
   - Where is your revision different from your partner's?
   - Which ideas did you leave expressed as simple sentences? Why?

collaboration

2. Working together, create a final draft of the paragraph that includes the versions of the sentences that you both agree are most effective.

QUICK STUDY **Student Example**

This chapter focuses on creating relationships between elements. Here is a paragraph on a related subject—the meaning or importance of being independent:

My most important personal goal is to become more financially independent. I had my daughter. I had to move out of my mother's place and apply for financial assistance from the state. Now I live in a subsidized apartment. I receive health care and vouchers for food. I truly appreciate all this help. I hate the way I have to live. I want to have a job so that I can rent my own place and take care of all the expenses for both of us. I want to be the one who pays the bills. I want to be the one in charge. That's the main reason I'm here taking courses. Without a

college degree, I'll never be able to develop financial independence. I hope to
get into the Radiologic Technology Program. I can become an X-ray and ultra-
sound technician. With a job in this field, I can finally achieve my goal and be
self-supporting.

First complete the following activities in response to this paragraph:

1. Take a look at the brief highlighted passages in this paragraph. Consider how
   the passages might benefit from coordination or subordination. Then, on a
   separate sheet of paper, improve the sentences through coordination or subordination. Use the material in this chapter to guide you.

2. In your view, which of the details in the paragraph offer the strongest support
   for the topic sentence? On the following lines, identify the example and explain your choice.

   _____

   _____

   _____

   _____

3. If you were going to make any suggestions for developing this paragraph
   more fully, what area or areas would you identify and why? Use the lines below for your answer.

   _____

   _____

   _____

   _____

Now explore this general idea in writing. Prewrite on the subject you have chosen,
identifying a focus and several key ideas, and then complete a draft paragraph of
at least seven to ten sentences. As the preceding paragraph does, you could examine the importance of or ways to develop independence. You might also choose
one of these subjects:

- the most important relationship you have known or experienced
- what it means to be genuinely equal
- guidelines for being an effective supervisor or superior
- an experience during which working together with someone did not work out
  as planned

collaboration

4. Exchange your draft with a classmate. Evaluate the paragraph you receive. If you discover any weaknesses, especially any spots where subordination or coordination would improve the flow of the writing, make a note in the margin and then return the paper to the writer.

5. Consider the comments and corrections your reader has made and create a final draft of your paragraph.

CHAPTER QUICK CHECK Subordination and Coordination

The writing below is composed of simple sentences. On a separate sheet of paper, revise it by combining sentences to emphasize ideas, to show connections among ideas, and to make the writing smooth. Use the methods you have practiced in this chapter to create complex or compound sentences. In some cases, you may decide to leave a particular sentence as it is.

(1) Memory is a fascinating subject. (2) Scientists continue to study different aspects of this mental capability. (3) One area of continued focus is the connection between aging and a weakening of memory processes. (4) The ability to remember seems to diminish with age. (5) This point may be true to some extent. (6) People of all ages sometimes forget where they have parked their cars or left their keys. (7) Current research points to lack of attention rather than some problem in the brain as the cause of some memory lapses. (8) The desire to suppress traumatic recollections accounts for others. (9) In their recollections, trauma victims often innocently include untrue or inaccurate details or events. (10) Courts are now having to rethink their attitudes about the accuracy of eyewitness reports of crimes.

SUMMARY EXERCISE Subordination and Coordination

The writing below is composed of simple sentences. On a separate piece of paper, revise it by combining sentences to emphasize ideas, to show connections among ideas, and to make the writing smooth. Use the methods you have practiced in this chapter to create complex or compound sentences. In some cases, you may decide to leave a particular sentence as it is.

(1) Important documents in our nation's history are housed in the National Archives in Washington, D.C. (2) Many of the documents are old and fragile. (3) They are carefully protected from further deterioration. (4) Many people see these documents. (5) They are impressed both by their importance and by the care taken to preserve them for the future.

(6) The Constitution, signed by representatives of twelve of the original states in 1787, is housed in the Archives. (7) It is only four pages long. (8) The Constitution contains the foundation of our democratic system. (9) Visitors can see two pages of this famous document. (10) They are housed in bronze and glass cases. (11) The cases are filled with helium gas to preserve the old parchment.

(12) The Archives also displays the Declaration of Independence and the Bill of Rights. (13) The Declaration of Independence, written primarily by Thomas Jefferson, was adopted on July 4, 1776. (14) The Bill of Rights was ratified more than two hundred years ago. (15) Citizens, judges, and scholars still discuss it today. (16) This document speaks about freedom of the press, freedom of religion, freedom of speech, and the right to bear arms. (17) These are still controversial issues today.

(18) All of these documents are stored every night in a special vault. (19) The bronze and glass cases are lowered electronically to the bottom of a vault. (20) It is twenty-two feet below the ground.

FOR FURTHER EXPLORATION Subordination and Coordination

1. Focus on one of the following topics. Use the prewriting technique—or combination of techniques—that fits your style of working to come up with some preliminary ideas while also considering the purposes you might fulfill in writing about the topic:

   - how to maintain a healthful diet
   - the responsibilities and dangers of credit cards
   - problems with the U.S. criminal justice system
   - your dreams for the future

2. Evaluate your prewriting material, identify a focus, and work your way through the rest of the writing process to create a draft essay of at least 500 words on this subject.

collaboration

3. Exchange your draft with a classmate. Check the draft you receive for any problems, especially spots where coordination and subordination would improve the writing, using the material in this chapter as a guide. Put a checkmark next to any problem you identify, with a note in the margin explaining your reasoning. Then return the draft to the writer.

4. Revise your essay, correcting any fragments or other problems discovered by your reader.

RECAP Subordination and Coordination

Key Terms in This Chapter	Definitions
subordination	a way to combine unequal ideas, giving emphasis to one and making the other dependent upon the former
simple sentence	a sentence consisting of a subject and a verb and their modifiers EXAMPLE A mouse had eaten a hole in the bag of popcorn.
complex sentence	a sentence consisting of a main clause and a subordinate clause
subordinate clause	a subject–verb unit that doesn't express a complete thought; also called a *dependent clause* Subordinate clauses are introduced by *subordinating conjunctions* or *relative pronouns*.

Key Terms in This Chapter	Definitions
subordinating conjunction	one of a group of connecting words used at the beginning of a subordinate clause to join it to an independent clause: *after, although, as, as if, as soon as, because, before, even though, if, in order that, once, rather than, since, so that, than, though, unless, until, when, whenever, wherever, whether, while* The subordinating conjunction expresses the relationship between the two clauses. **EXAMPLE** The downtown flooded *because* we had torrential rains.
relative pronoun	one of a group of words used to introduce subordinate clauses that describe or specify a noun or pronoun in a main clause: *that, what, which, who, whom, whose* **EXAMPLE** An author *whose* work I admire is Jamaica Kincaid.
main clause	a subject–verb unit that can stand on its own but is combined with another subject–verb unit A main clause is an *independent clause.*
coordination	the combining of independent clauses of equal importance into *compound sentences* to eliminate choppiness and repetition
compound sentence	a sentence containing two or more independent clauses joined by a connector: (1) a *coordinating conjunction* and a comma, (2) a *semicolon,* or (3) a semicolon plus a *conjunctive adverb*
coordinating conjunction	one of a set of joining words used to connect words or ideas of equal rank: *and, but, for, nor, or, so, yet*
independent clause	a clause with a subject and a verb that can stand alone as a sentence A compound sentence consists of two or more independent clauses joined by a connector. **EXAMPLE** *Spring is on the way*, and *the temperature is rising.*
conjunctive adverb	one of a group of words used with a connector to link ideas by showing how they are related: *also, besides, consequently, finally, furthermore, however, instead, meanwhile, moreover, nevertheless, similarly, still, then, therefore, thus* A conjunctive adverb cannot connect simple sentences itself but does emphasize the connection provided by semicolons. A conjunctive adverb requires a comma after it when used with a semicolon connecting simple sentences. **EXAMPLE** Cheetahs are an endangered species; *however,* many cheetahs were born at zoos last year.

Structure of a Complex Sentence

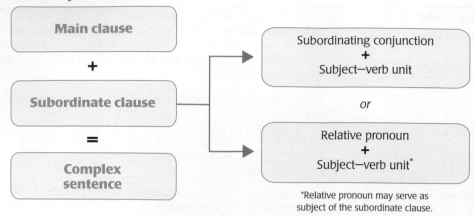

Main clause

+

Subordinate clause → Subordinating conjunction + Subject–verb unit

or

Relative pronoun + Subject–verb unit*

=

Complex sentence

*Relative pronoun may serve as subject of the subordinate clause.

Structure of a Compound Sentence

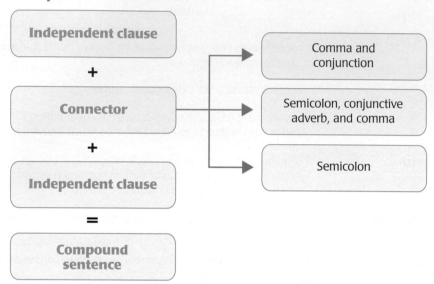

Independent clause

+

Connector → Comma and conjunction

→ Semicolon, conjunctive adverb, and comma

→ Semicolon

+

Independent clause

=

Compound sentence

Using Odyssey Online with MyWritingLab

For more practice with subordination and coordination, go to
www.mywritinglab.com.

Chapter 20
Comma Splices and Run-on Sentences

GETTING STARTED ...

 Q I know I have good ideas on my subject, so I'm happy about that. But I'm concerned that I might be running one idea into the next. What's the best way for me to avoid comma splices or run-on sentences?

 A You are right to be concerned—because such errors tell your reader that you aren't sure where one of your ideas ends and the next begins. To avoid comma splices and run-on sentences, evaluate your writing for all subject–verb units that express a complete thought. Then ask yourself: Do I want to connect these two sentences or keep them separate? If you want to connect them, use a conjunction with a comma in front of it or a semicolon. If you want to separate them, place a period—or an exclamation point or question mark—between the two sentences. That's all there is to it.

Overview: Understanding Comma Splices and Run-on Sentences

Combining sentences is one proven way to improve the flow of a piece of writing. But this technique can be tricky, often leading to two of the more serious—and more frequent—sentence errors: the **comma splice** and the **run-on sentence**. A comma splice is an error in which sentences are incorrectly connected by a comma, a mark of punctuation that *can't connect*. A run-on sentence is an error in which two sentences are run together without proper punctuation or an appropriate connector between them. Avoiding these two sentence errors is a two-step process. First you must recognize them and then you must choose the best of several techniques to eliminate them.

Navigating This Chapter In this chapter, you will learn how to recognize and avoid comma splices and run-on sentences. You will practice correcting these errors by using:

- a coordinating conjunction and a comma
- a subordinating conjunction
- a semicolon (or a semicolon and a conjunctive adverb)
- a period

Identifying Comma Splices and Run-on Sentences

The first step in correcting comma splices and run-on sentences is to identify them. Start by locating the subjects and verbs in your sentences. Then check if you have properly joined or properly separated two subject–verb units.

Take a look at these examples:

COMMA SPLICE

The *flashlight flickered* out, the *batteries were* obviously dead.

RUN-ON SENTENCE

My car *horn is* broken again *I have replaced* it twice already.

ESL Note
See "Sentence Basics" on pages 543–544 and "Punctuation" on pages 554–555.

As the italicized words show, both examples contain two subject–verb units, each of which could stand as a simple sentence itself. In the first example, a comma appears between the two units. But *commas can't connect,* so this example is a comma splice. In the second example, nothing appears between the two subject–verb units. Instead, the first unit just *runs into* the second, which is why this type of error is called a run-on sentence, or simply a run-on.

Avoiding Comma Splices by Recognizing the Functions of the Comma

Understanding what commas do is one way to avoid making comma splices. When you write, you use commas in the following ways:

- To indicate the pause between clauses connected by conjunctions

EXAMPLE The door was closed, but it wasn't locked.

- To separate items in a series

EXAMPLE We looked for the missing ring around the apartment, in the backyard, and in the car.

- To set off introductory material

EXAMPLE With the additional memory, the computer performed much faster.

- To set off elements that interrupt sentence flow

EXAMPLE Showing up early on your first day, for instance, is a great way to impress a new boss.

- To set off direct quotations

EXAMPLE   "I'm just not interested in that class," Vincente explained.

- To fulfill several other purposes, including

    setting off the salutation of a personal letter (Dear Zelda,)

    setting off the parts of dates from the rest of the sentence (March 31, 1982, was the day Jacqueline was born.)

    setting off parts of addresses (His last permanent address was 44 Bogle Street, East Ridge, NM 34268.)

    indicating thousands within numbers (3,211 or 3,211,000)

    setting off a name when you address someone directly (I want you to know, Marilyn, that you have made a tremendous impact on this office.)

If you use commas for these purposes only, you decrease your chances of making a comma splice. For a more complete discussion and additional examples of proper comma use, see Chapter 30, "Commas."

COMPREHENSION AND PRACTICE 20.1

Recognizing Comma Splices and Run-ons

The following paragraph contains several comma splices and run-on sentences. To identify them, first underline every subject and circle every verb. Put an * in front of any comma splice or run-on, and insert a / where one sentence should end and the next should begin. Use the example to guide you.

EXAMPLE   * <u>Jennifer</u> <u>missed</u> class again today,/this is the fifth time <u>she</u> (has been) absent this month.

(1) Over the past decade or so, youth sports leagues in the United States have been the focus of much attention, the behavior of adult fans and parents is the primary reason for this concern. (2) Too often, the adults in charge or in the stands seem to forget the purpose of these leagues. (3) Video evidence of outrageous behavior appears with disturbing frequency on the evening news a quick search on YouTube will also produce numerous video clips. (4) On the screen, parents can be seen yelling and interrupting games and practices, the language is usually not suitable for a family audience. (5) Meanwhile, the players and the rest of the crowd observe this scene with

a mixture of amazement and embarrassment. (6) In some cases, the confrontations actually lead to physical violence among parents or between a parent and a coach or a referee. (7) During one tragic incident, a parent physically attacked a hockey coach, the coach died as a result. (8) The parent was ultimately convicted of manslaughter and sentenced to six to ten years in prison. (9) Clearly, reform is necessary some people have suggested a ban on adult spectators as a solution to the problem. (10) The purpose of these leagues is to give children the chance for fun, adults should not interfere in any way.

CHALLENGE 20.1   **Checking for Comma Splices and Run-ons in Your Writing**

collaboration

1. Make a copy of a paragraph or essay that you are working on and exchange it with a classmate.

2. On the paper you receive, underline the subjects and verbs in each sentence. If you discover any comma splices or run-ons, mark these errors. Return the draft to the writer.

3. Evaluate your classmate's corrections, and make any necessary changes to your own paper.

Correcting Comma Splices and Run-ons by Using Coordinating Conjunctions

One way to correct comma splices and run-on sentences is to use a coordinating conjunction such as *and, but,* and *or* between independent clauses. (See page 282 for a complete listing of coordinating conjunctions.) Besides providing connection, these conjunctions help you eliminate choppiness and repetition, as in the following:

> **COMMA SPLICE** The clock is more than 100 years old, *yet* it keeps perfect time.
>
> **RUN-ON** Karen does volunteer work at an extended-care facility, *and* she also has a weekend job.

In the first sentence, *yet* provides the connection and shows opposition between ideas. In the second, a comma plus *and* link the two clauses; *and* suggests addition of ideas. The sentences now flow better, and, more important, they are now correct. By the way, as the examples above show, always include a comma *before* a conjunction used to connect simple sentences.

COMPREHENSION AND PRACTICE 20.2

Using Coordinating Conjunctions to Correct Comma Splices and Run-on Sentences

Several of the numbered items in the following paragraph are either run-on sentences or comma splices. Put an * in front of any comma splice or run-on sentence. If the item is a run-on, put a / between the independent clauses. Then above the /, add a comma and the coordinating conjunction (*and, or, but, for, nor, so,* or *yet*) that best connects the thoughts in the independent clauses. If the item is a comma splice, simply insert a / and an appropriate coordinating conjunction between the clauses. Use the examples to guide you.

EXAMPLES

I had completed my art project on time/ I forgot to bring it.
, but

Annie has black hair,/it curls naturally.
and

(1) In national politics today, money talks candidates can't expect to win without enormous financial backing. (2) In fact, it isn't unusual for a congressional campaign to cost each candidate several million dollars or more. (3) Most people simply can't afford to pay for a campaign alone, they must count on donations. (4) Of course, incumbents have a great advantage over challengers in terms of fund-raising. (5) Challengers may have great enthusiasm and even greater ideas and plans, they have no power and no influence. (6) Incumbents already have experience and contacts lobbyists and corporations are more willing to contribute to them. (7) They are confident that their donations will pay off the incumbents will act on their behalf after reelection. (8) Meanwhile, the voting public becomes increasingly disillusioned and distrustful of the system. (9) Americans deserve a system that leads to the election of the best candidate, not the one with the biggest campaign chest. (10) Our campaign finance system has to change, incumbents will have little motivation to put the needs of the average citizen above the interests of huge corporations.

COMPREHENSION AND PRACTICE 20.3

Using Coordinating Conjunctions to Correct Comma Splices and Run-on Sentences

The following paragraph contains several comma splices and run-on sentences. Put an * in front of any comma splice or run-on sentence. Then put a / between independent clauses. Choose an appropriate coordinating conjunction from the list below and insert it above where one sentence should end and the next should begin. Don't forget to add a comma if it isn't already there. Use the example to guide you.

and	nor
but	so
for	yet
or	

EXAMPLE   The officer was clearly lying*, yet* the judge allowed his testimony.

(1) A new bakery and coffee shop in my neighborhood has been open for only three weeks already business seems excellent. (2) The shop is called the Stafford Road Stop it sells a wide variety of bagels, muffins, doughnuts, and other pastries. (3) The shop is located right across the street from a Metro stop, many of the patrons stop by on their way into the downtown area. (4) The shop itself is bright and clean, with a large display case and ten small tables, each with two chairs in front of it. (5) A counter with stools is against the front wall patrons can enjoy their food while looking at the busy street scene outside. (6) The staff doesn't hesitate to ask customers about their favorite selections they frequently inquire about the need for new products. (7) According to the owner, the shop will have your favorite baked goods on hand the staff will add them to the menu. (8) She also prides herself on her coffee, patrons can choose from several types, including at least two types of decaffeinated coffee. (9) The quality of all her products is excellent, the prices are reasonable. (10) All in all, the Stafford Road Stop shows every sign of becoming a success story.

CHALLENGE 20.2   **Working with Coordinating Conjunctions**

1. Consider again the list of seven coordinating conjunctions in Comprehension and Practice 20.3. Then, on a separate sheet of paper, write seven compound sentences, the first using *and* to connect the clauses, the second using *but,* and so on.

collaboration

2. Exchange your sentences with a classmate. On the paper you receive, check to make sure the sentences are correct. Then, at the bottom of the page, briefly explain in which sentence the conjunction is most effectively used and why.

Correcting Comma Splices and Run-ons by Using Subordinating Conjunctions

Another way to eliminate comma splices and run-on sentences is to add a subordinating conjunction such as *after, because, if,* or *unless* to connect clauses. (See page 269 for a complete listing of subordinating conjunctions.) As Chapter 19 showed, subordinating conjunctions indicate a relationship between the ideas they connect. Consider the following examples:

Because oil

COMMA SPLICE   ~~Oil~~ from the leaking barge fouled the water for over 20 square miles, more than

1,000 birds were killed.

even though

RUN-ON   On Wednesday afternoon, the needed items were still not here ʌ they promised to

deliver them by Tuesday.

In the first example, *because* joins two ideas related by cause and effect: The death of the birds *resulted from* an oil spill. In the second example, *even though* links the ideas and also indicates the relationship between them: Items were not delivered *despite the fact that* they had been promised.

COMPREHENSION AND PRACTICE 20.4

Using Subordinating Conjunctions to Correct Comma Splices and Run-on Sentences

Each numbered item in the following paragraph is either a run-on sentence or a comma splice. First, put a / between the independent clauses. Then add one of the subordinating conjunctions listed below to show a relationship between the clauses. In some cases, more than one correct answer is possible. With a comma splice, you'll need to add only the subordinating conjunction, but with a run-on sentence, you'll need to add a comma as well as the conjunctive adverb. Use the example as a guide.

after	before
although	since
because	when

Before the

EXAMPLE   ~~The~~ police arrived,/traffic was backed up for three miles.

(1) I started work I never saw the importance of knowing a second language.

(2) Having bilingual workers is important, the needs of all customers can be met.

(3) I thought about it knowledge of a second language seemed like a great idea

for me. (4) I am training to be a paralegal, I will have to deal with people from a wide variety of backgrounds. (5) I know more than one language a law office will be more interested in hiring me.

Using Subordinating Conjunctions to Correct Comma Splices and Run-on Sentences

In the following paragraph, put an * in front of each comma splice and run-on sentence. Then choose an appropriate subordinating conjunction (*because, since, even though, when, although,* or *so that*), and insert it in the proper place above the line to make the sentence correct. Make sure to add a comma if one is needed. Use the example to guide you.

EXAMPLE

$$\quad\quad\quad\quad\quad\quad\quad\quad\quad\quad\quad\quad\quad\quad\quad\quad\quad because$$
*They were late leaving the campground ^ they had to wait for Gil and Sheila.

(1) Some people are counted as unemployed or underemployed by the government, they actually have an income. (2) They are part of the "underground economy." (3) Most people in this situation work for cash they can hide their income from government agencies. (4) In most cases, they charge substantially less their salary is tax free. (5) Sometimes these workers are amateurs just picking up a little extra cash on the weekends or nights. (6) They don't want to declare their earnings, the extra income might raise their overall tax burden. (7) Sometimes trained specialists and union artisans join the underground economy they are between jobs or laid off. (8) Many members of the underground economy have no other means of support, though. (9) They work below the minimum wage they would have no employment otherwise. (10) The underground economy continues to thrive, the government has tried to control it.

CHALLENGE 20.3   **Working with Subordinating Conjunctions**

1. Subordinating conjunctions connect clauses whether they appear between clauses or at the beginning of the sentence. Here again are the six subordinating conjunctions you worked with in Comprehension and Practice 20.4:

after	before
although	since
because	when

On a separate sheet of paper, write six complex sentences in which you use a conjunction to connect subject–verb units, the first using *after*, the second using *before*, and so on.

collaboration

2. Exchange your sentences with a classmate. Choose three of your classmate's sentences and reverse the order of the clauses. Decide which version of the sentence you think is more effective and why. Then discuss your analysis with the writer.

Correcting Comma Splices and Run-ons by Using Semicolons

A semicolon (;) has the same power to connect simple sentences that a conjunction preceded by a comma has. Using a semicolon to provide the link between sentences also enables you to emphasize the connection between the units, adding another dimension to your meaning, as these examples, with corrections, show:

COMMA SPLICE | The campus bookstore has extended its operating hours/students will now be able to shop until 7 P.M.

RUN-ON | The guest speaker waited for questions from the class nobody said a word.

ESL Note
See "Punctuation," pages 554–555, for more about the proper use of semicolons.

In the first example, the clause about the change in store hours is now properly joined to the clause explaining the advantage that students will enjoy. In the second example, the clause explaining the speaker's expectation is connected by a semicolon to the clause describing the class's lack of response.

To clarify the relationship between the clauses, you can use a conjunctive adverb (*also, besides, furthermore, instead, however, moreover, then, therefore,* etc.) with a semicolon. (See page 283 for a complete list of conjunctive adverbs.) Consider these examples:

EXAMPLES | The suit was expensive; *however,* it was very well made.

The band abruptly left the stage; *meanwhile,* two technicians began to check the sound system.

In each example, the semicolon joins the ideas, and the conjunctive adverb clarifies why the ideas are linked. Notice that a comma is needed after each of these conjunctive adverbs.

**COMPREHENSION
AND PRACTICE
20.6**

Using Semicolons to Correct Comma Splices and Run-on Sentences

Each numbered item in the following paragraph is either a comma splice or a run-on sentence. First, put a / between the independent clauses. Then insert a semicolon, alone or with an appropriate conjunctive adverb, to connect the clauses. If you add a conjunctive adverb, write it followed by a comma above the point where the first clause ends and the second begins. (A complete list of conjunctive adverbs appears on page 283.) Use the examples to guide you.

EXAMPLE   At first, the puppy wouldn't come out from behind the chair/Caitlyn eventually
coaxed it out with a doggie biscuit.

or

At first, the puppy wouldn't come out from behind the chair/ *; however,* Caitlyn eventually
coaxed it out with a doggie biscuit.

(1) The city is sponsoring its first Summer Arts Festival the goal is to have such a festival mark the beginning of each season. (2) The Summer Arts Festival will take place under a large tent in Wachusetts Park, the other three festivals will be held in the Historical Center Annex downtown. (3) Visual and performance artists in the surrounding area have been invited to take part, vendors selling everything from ethnic food to specialty clothing to craft items will set up booths. (4) The city's tourist board has hired a company specializing in such events to coordinate the festival various city officials have remained closely involved in the planning. (5) Everyone involved is hoping for a big success at this first festival the city has stated its determination to provide support for a one-year cycle regardless of attendance at the initial event.

COMPREHENSION
AND PRACTICE
20.7

Using Semicolons with Conjunctive Adverbs to Correct Comma Splices and Run-on Sentences

The following passage contains a number of comma splices and run-on sentences. Put an* in front of each. Correct them by using a semicolon and one of the conjunctive adverbs listed below, as the example illustrates.

also	meanwhile	then
consequently	moreover	therefore
furthermore	nevertheless	thus

EXAMPLE   The heavy rains destroyed the old earthen dam *; therefore,* the mayor was forced to declare a state of emergency.

(1) Today, even inexpensive cell phones have high-quality digital cameras, many have video capability. (2) On most smartphones, the cameras even include features like autofocus, brightness control, and autoflash, the pictures are high resolution as a result of superior megapixel density. (3) The images can be moved to a tiny media card and then transferred to a computer through the USB port for just a small fee per transaction, the photos and videos can be directly e-mailed from the phone to a computer. (4) Through computer programs like iPhoto and Adobe Photoshop, these phone pictures can be cleaned up, resized, and enhanced in a variety of ways. (5) A number of photo apps can be downloaded directly to the phone, users can adjust their photos right on the phone itself before transferring them to a computer. (6) With a few easy steps, a person can download these images to illustrate his or her Facebook or MySpace profile they can easily be combined with music and text for a truly personal portrait. (7) Photo and video capability has made the average cell phone user a potential action photographer and videographer. (8) Sites like YouTube make uploading video clips almost effortless people around the world are able to post funny incidents or staged stunts filmed on their phones. (9) Images of accidents, natural disasters, and so on, that might ordinarily never have been seen by the public have been captured by cell phone. (10) It's unlikely that cell phone pictures and videos will ever replace news cameras, they are playing an increasingly significant role on the national level, frequently appearing as part of network and cable news broadcasts.

CHALLENGE 20.4 Working with Semicolons and Conjunctive Adverbs

collaboration

1. For Comprehension and Practice 20.6, you made some choices about how to connect clauses in a paragraph by using either a semicolon or a semicolon and a conjunctive adverb. Make a copy of your corrected version of Comprehension and Practice 20.6, and exchange it with a classmate.

collaboration

2. Compare your changes with the ones your classmate has made. Discuss your choices with your classmate and together decide which version is more effective.

Correcting Comma Splices and Run-ons by Using Periods

Another way to correct comma splices and run-on sentences is to use a period between the subject–verb units to create separate sentences. This option isn't a good idea if the simple sentences are short because it may make your writing seem choppy. If the sentences are fairly long, however, using a period to create separate sentences may be the best solution, as these examples show:

COMMA SPLICE

Larry plans to earn his two-year degree in Business Administration and
        . He
Marketing,/he then will enroll at the university to earn his undergraduate

degree.

RUN-ON

For over a decade, superstar sisters Serena and Venus Williams have brought
        . Their
genuine excitement back to women's tennis their matches, especially some of the

epic battles against each other, have been ratings blockbusters.

ESL Note
See "Punctuation,"
pages 554–555, for
more about the proper
use of end punctuation.

You could certainly eliminate these errors by using a conjunction and a comma or a semicolon. The sentences that would result would be a bit long, however, and long sentences can be difficult to follow. Therefore, using a period to create separate simple sentences is a better choice. When you use this option to correct run-on sentences and comma splices, remember to capitalize the first word of the second sentence.

**COMPREHENSION
AND PRACTICE
20.8**

Using a Period to Separate the Units

In this paragraph, using a period to separate the independent clauses is probably the best option because the clauses are long. Put a / between the clauses, and then insert a period to eliminate the run-on sentence or comma splice. Start the first word of a new sentence with a capital letter. Use the example to guide you.

EXAMPLE

By noontime on opening day, the line leading into the stadium was already a
        . Inside,
quarter of a mile long inside,/10,000 people had already taken their seats, waiting for the first ball to be thrown out.

(1) The recent hurricane changed the entire landscape at Gooseberry

Beach, fortunately, only a few of the houses along the edge of the beach

suffered from the effects of severe erosion. (2) The most severely damaged

house was owned by Mr. Lionel Partridge, one of the oldest residents of the community, the storm ripped off the front of the house, sending all his belongings into the churning ocean. (3) The contour of the beach itself showed the most dramatic change of all, the dunes separating the beach from the road were completely flattened. (4) Foundations of several homes destroyed by earlier hurricanes were visible again they had been buried for more than 25 years. (5) Even with the changes, Gooseberry Beach is still beautiful, the whole experience should remind everyone of the tremendous power of nature.

COMPREHENSION AND PRACTICE

Working with a Period to Separate the Units

20.9   The following paragraph contains several comma splices and run-on sentences. Put an * in front of any comma splice or run-on sentence. Then put a / between the independent clauses. Insert a period where the first sentence should end, and then start the word that begins the second sentence with a capital letter. Use the example to guide you.

EXAMPLE

*The landscapers spent the afternoon digging up the dead sod/~~the~~ . The grass had been completely destroyed by grubs.

(1) Max's first experience with a credit card was not a good one, even at age twenty-one, he wasn't ready for the responsibility. (2) Five years ago, he filled out an application for a credit card at his favorite clothing store. (3) A week later, the card came in the mail his troubles began at that point. (4) His original plan was to buy one item a week, he would then pay off the entire bill at the end of the month. (5) For the first two months, he had no trouble keeping up with the payments as a result, Max decided to buy more things. (6) However, his bill for the third month was more than $800, and he had put aside only $200. (7) Max panicked and didn't pay the bill, for the next two months he received the same bill, plus a finance charge. (8) A few weeks later, Max received a letter from the credit department of the store, it instructed him to call the department. (9) He was scared and ashamed, and he ignored that

letter. (10) Shortly after that, Max received a letter threatening him with legal action after that warning, he began to make payments again, and he cut up his credit card.

Student Example

This chapter discusses the importance of recognizing the logical limits, the beginnings and ends, of the ideas you express. Consider this paragraph on a related topic, an experience that marked the end of a period or stage of life:

The death of my grandmother is the event that marks my passage from child to adult. I was 15 at the time, and up to that point I had never had anyone with whom I was close die. My grandmother was a very important figure in my life, she lived on the third floor in our house, and my brothers and I spent part of every day under her supervision. She didn't exactly spoil us she just dealt with us and our behavior more patiently than our parents. For example, if we refused to share our toys or get along, my grandmother would simply send us to separate rooms until we calmed down and were ready to cooperate. Our parents would have screamed at us and punished us first and asked questions later. I can't count the number of times over the years that I would bring friends up to her apartment and she would slap some Toll House cookies in her oven or made us pancakes. I knew that I could always depend on her. She was so full of life and so healthy that her death from a massive heart attack at home one August morning was a huge shock to everyone. That day was the first time I saw any of her children—my aunts and uncles and my mother—cry as they stopped by our house after hearing the news. It was also the first time that I understood that there is no such thing as always you should never take anything, or anyone, for granted. I knew then that I was no longer a child I was an adult and my life would never be as simple as it was when my grandmother was alive.

1. Several sentences in this paragraph are highlighted. Evaluate these sections for problems with comma splices and run-on sentences. Put a / where one sentence should end and the next one should begin. Then, on a separate sheet of paper, correct the errors, using one of the methods outlined in this chapter to eliminate them.

2. Of all the details included in this paragraph, which do you think is the strongest? Why? Use the following lines for your answer.

_____

_____

_____

_____

3. The focus of this paragraph is the passage from childhood to adulthood. Take another look at the paragraph and then, on the lines below, explain in a sentence or so what you think the writer means by adulthood:

_____

_____

_____

_____

Now explore the topic in writing. Like the preceding paragraph, you could discuss an experience that marked the end of some period in your life or the beginning of another. Or you might choose one of these subjects related to the subject matter of this chapter:

- a place or thing from your childhood to which you still feel a strong connection
- the difficulties of beginning something new
- a time when you accidentally missed a signal or failed to make a connection
- the key limits that parents should impose on their children

collaboration

4. Exchange your draft with a classmate. Evaluate the paragraph you receive. If you discover any errors, especially comma splices or run-on sentences, make a note in the margin and then return the paper to the writer.

5. Consider the comments and corrections your reader has made and create a final draft of your paragraph.

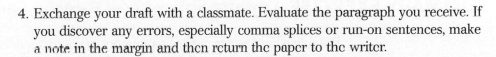

CHAPTER QUICK CHECK Comma Splices and Run-on Sentences

The following passage contains a number of comma splices and run-on sentences. First, identify these errors by putting an * in front of each one. Then, using the various techniques discussed in this chapter, correct the errors. In some cases, more than one solution is possible.

(1) Urban myths about scientific or medical matters are among the most persistent types on the Internet. (2) One group of myths involves suffering and sometimes death for people, they have been exposed to exotic poisons or flesh-eating bacteria. (3) The twists in the stories involve how the afflictions were contracted these victims allegedly were infected from contact with everyday items like vending machines and pay phones. (4) Everybody is exposed to such common objects the stories seem vaguely possible. (5) Some of the myths involve rare, deadly insects or spiders in public restrooms, fast-food restaurants, and convenience stores, the bite of these creatures causes paralysis or death. (6) Of course, these insects or creatures either don't actually exist or don't pose a threat to humans, people still believe in them. (7) In one persistent myth, a pet owner flushes a baby alligator down a toilet in a big city like New York or Chicago the alligator eventually grows to gargantuan size in the sewer system below. (8) In some myths, the U.S. government or some sinister force adds a dangerous drug or compound to prepared foods in some cases a particular brand is actually named. (9) This kind of hoax can cause widespread damage to an innocent manufacturer by ruining its reputation. (10) The nature of the Internet guarantees the fast spread of any new rumors millions of people hear and pass on the latest hoax in a matter of minutes.

SUMMARY EXERCISE Comma Splices and Run-on Sentences

The following passage contains a number of comma splices and run-on sentences. First, identify these errors by putting an * in front of each one. Then, using the various techniques discussed in this chapter, correct the errors. In some cases, more than one solution is possible.

(1) In the neighborhood where I grew up, there was an old, abandoned house. (2) According to all the kids in the neighborhood, it was haunted I didn't believe them. (3) At age eleven, I finally explored that house with my two best friends, I have always regretted this adventure.

(4) The house was located across the street from our school it seemed to call to us every time we passed it. (5) Jack and Nickie wanted to break in, I kept talking them out of it. (6) Finally, I could resist no longer we made our plans to enter the haunted house on the following Saturday night.

(7) At eight o'clock that evening, we met in my backyard I had told my mother we were going to play basketball under the lights at nearby Pulaski Park. (8) We often played at night, she wasn't suspicious. (9) We left my yard quickly and headed off to the house for the big break-in.

(10) We had spent a few days planning our caper, so we had come well prepared. (11) Nickie brought a hammer and a crowbar Jack took his father's big flashlight. (12) I brought a screwdriver and a pair of pliers we wanted to be prepared for every possibility.

(13) Twenty minutes later, we reached the house it was pitch dark and very quiet. (14) We went around back and entered through the cellar door the lock was badly rusted, so we had to pry only a little with the crowbar. (15) Once inside, we crept down the stairs to the dirt cellar it was dark and clammy. (16) Jack shined his light around the cellar everything was covered with dust and cobwebs. (17) We never made it upstairs the floorboards squeaked, and we ran out at lightning speed.

(18) We ran two blocks before stopping none of us had ever been so scared in our whole lives. (19) We all headed home and agreed not to tell anyone else. (20) I've kept the secret I don't know if Nickie or Jack ever told.

FOR FURTHER EXPLORATION Comma Splices and Run-on Sentences

1. Focus on one of the following topics. Using the prewriting technique—or combination of techniques—best suited to your style, explore the possibilities that the subject holds and consider what purposes you might fulfill as you write:

   - the most effective advertisement radio, Internet, television, or print—you've ever been exposed to
   - the one environmental or social issue that never receives the attention it deserves
   - the advantages—or consequences—of being popular
   - what, if anything, should be done to restrict objectionable material on television

2. Evaluate your prewriting material, identify a focus, and work your way through the rest of the writing process to create a draft essay of at least 500 words on this subject.

collaboration

3. Exchange your draft with a classmate. Check the draft you receive for weaknesses, looking in particular for comma splices and run-on sentences. Mark these errors with CS (for comma splice) and RS (for run-on sentence), using the material in this chapter as a guide, and then return the draft to the writer.

4. Revise your essay, correcting any comma splices and run-on sentences or other problems discovered by your reader.

RECAP   Comma Splices and Run-on Sentences

Key Terms in This Chapter	Definitions
comma splice	an error in which sentences are incorrectly connected by a comma
	EXAMPLE The storm dumped four inches of rain across the region, / several cities and towns suffered heavy flooding.
run-on sentence	an error in which two sentences are run together with no punctuation or connectors
	EXAMPLE James forgot his wallet at home / he didn't realize it until he arrived at the register.

To Identify Comma Splices and Run-on Sentences

Identify all subject–verb units.

↓

Establish whether the clauses can stand alone.

Four Ways to Correct Comma Splices and Run-on Sentences

1 **Subject–verb unit** + **Connector** + **Subject–verb unit**

↓

Comma and coordinating conjunction

2 **Subject–verb unit** + **Connector** + **Subject–verb unit**

↓

Subordinating conjunction

or

Connector + **Subject–verb unit and *comma*** + **Subject–verb unit**

↓

Subordinating conjunction

3 **Subject–verb unit** + **Connector** + **Subject–verb unit**

↓

Semicolon

or

Subject–verb unit + **Connector** + **Subject–verb unit**

↓

Semicolon and conjunctive adverb and comma

4 **Subject–verb unit** + **Separator** + **Subject–verb unit,**
beginning with a capital letter

↓

Period or other appropriate end punctuation

Using Odyssey Online with MyWritingLab

For more practice with comma splices and run-on sentences, go to
www.mywritinglab.com.

PORTFOLIO 4

portfolio • noun (pl. **portfolios**) ... **2** a set of pieces of creative work intended to demonstrate a person's ability. ORIGIN Italian *portafogli,* from *portare* 'carry' + *foglio* 'leaf'.

—*Compact Oxford English Dictionary*

This portfolio allows you to demonstrate what you have learned about the basic unit of writing—the sentence. You can measure your knowledge of the essential elements of a correct sentence (Chapter 17); test how well you can recognize and correct a sentence fragment (Chapter 18); practice combining clauses to produce more fluid and effective sentences (Chapter 19); and spend time identifying and correcting comma splices and run-on sentences (Chapter 20). To mark your progress up to this point, prepare the following portfolio:

BEST WORK   Select your best work from assignments completed for this section. Feel free to check with a classmate or other reader if you aren't sure which one of these assignments ranks as your best.

ESSAY ANSWER   A newspaper contains the news of the day and much more. This statement is true today—and it was true fifty years ago, as this assignment will show you. To prepare for this assignment, take a walk to your college library and head to the reference desk to find out where databases or microfilm of old newspapers are kept. Locate a newspaper published fifty years before your birthday. Plan to spend thirty minutes to an hour examining the paper and taking notes on things that catch your interest, including the day's leading stories, prices for common products, places or means of entertainment, cost of real estate, medical care, and so on. Then, using the notes you've taken, prepare an answer of about 200 words to one of the following essay questions:

- Now that you have read through a newspaper from fifty years ago, you can see that the world has changed to a remarkable degree. What is the single biggest change that has occurred from that time to now? Why do you feel this way?

- The newspaper you read carries the month and day of your birthday, but the year is fifty years previous. From what you have read, what do you think the day-to-day life of your counterpart of the past was like? Use examples from your notes as support.

TIMED WRITING   First, read what may be the shortest short story ever written, attributed to a giant of American literature, Ernest Hemingway:

For sale: baby shoes, never worn.

310

TIMED WRITING

Now in thirty minutes, complete a writing of around 200 to 300 words on one of the following topics:

- What type of story do you think these six words suggest? For instance, the story says that the shoes have never been worn, but it doesn't say why. What is the most—or least—likely reason they were never worn? Furthermore, why would the owners of the shoes sell them? Finally, does it matter that they are "baby shoes"? Explain your reasoning in detail.

- This story is an example of *flash fiction*—a piece of fiction that runs less than 500 words. At only six words, this story is an extreme example of this type of writing, and it is a fair question to ask whether it is long enough to be considered an entire story. What do you think? In your judgment, does this passage contain enough of the elements needed to make it an effective piece of fiction? What about the story leads you to this conclusion?

REFLECTION   For your reader to gain a full understanding of what you mean, you need to express your ideas in complete sentence form. But as the chapters in this part of *Odyssey* illustrate, correct sentences can be more difficult to create than you might think. Sentence fragments, comma splices, and run-on sentences are all serious sentence errors, and they are all fairly common, too. Now that you have spent some time concentrating on these problems, write a paragraph of seven to ten sentences in which you identify the particular sentence error that troubles you the most and why you think you struggle more with it than with the other two.

PART **5**

Understanding Subjects and Verbs

CHAPTER 21
Subject–Verb Agreement

GETTING STARTED ...

 Q When I go over what I've written, I'm not always sure that my subjects and verbs fit together. What should I do to make sure that my subjects and verbs always match up?

 A First, the good news is that, for the most part, errors involving **subject–verb agreement** occur in only the present tense. This means your job is easier than you might think. First, isolate each verb and its subject. Once you've done this, double-check the verb ending, making sure you've used a singular form for a singular subject and a plural form for a plural subject. It's as easy as that.

Overview: Understanding Subject–Verb Agreement

When two parties, either companies or individuals, plan a joint enterprise, they draw up an *agreement,* a document outlining the details of their relationship. That way, both parties know the roles they will play to ensure that everything runs smoothly. In writing, agreement refers to the relationship between the subject and verb. Each subject must agree in *number* with its verb in order for your sentences to run smoothly. Number refers to the *quantity* or *amount* the word indicates, either *singular,* meaning one, or *plural,* meaning more than one. Singular subjects call for singular verb forms, and plural subjects call for plural verb forms. Maintaining subject–verb agreement is essential because subjects and verbs communicate your sentences' basic meaning.

Navigating This Chapter In this chapter, you will learn how to recognize and avoid the following errors in subject–verb agreement:

- problems when the subject follows the verb
- problems when words come between subjects and verbs
- problems with indefinite pronouns
- problems from other causes, including compound subjects; collective nouns; singular nouns ending in -*s;* and words referring to measurements, money, time, and weight

Avoiding Agreement Errors When the Subject Follows the Verb

ESL Note
See "Sentence Basics" on pages 543–544 and "Agreement" on pages 546–548.

The secret to avoiding errors in *subject–verb agreement* is to identify the subject. As Chapter 17, "The Sentence," explains, ask yourself *who or what is doing the action or being discussed?* The answer to that question is the subject.

In the majority of the sentences you write, the subject comes before the verb, as these examples show:

EXAMPLES

┌──────subject──────┐ ┌─verb─┐
Volunteer relief workers provide a valuable service at the scenes of fires, accidents, and natural disasters.

┌─subject─┐┌verb┐
The *Internet puts* the world at a person's fingertips.

But not all sentences follow this pattern. In some sentences, the subject appears after the verb. One type of sentence in which the subject follows the verb is a question:

EXAMPLES

verb ┌──────subject──────┐ ┌verb┐
Do division supervisors attend weekly planning meetings?

verb subject ┌──verb──┐
Will ESPN broadcast the X-Games again?

In sentences beginning with *there* or *here,* subjects also follow the verb. *There* and *here* are adverbs, and only a noun or pronoun can be the subject of a sentence. Take a look at these examples:

EXAMPLES

┌verb┐ ┌subject┐
There *are* several new *signs* near the new highway exit.

┌─verb─┐ ┌─subject─┐
Here *comes* the guest *speaker* on the subject of health care reform.

In the first sentence, *signs* is the subject, even though it follows the verb *are.* In the second sentence, the subject is *speaker,* even though it follows the verb *comes.*

Whenever possible, you should restate these kinds of sentences to eliminate the *there* or *here* beginning, which will make the sentences more direct, as these improved versions show:

EXAMPLES

┌subject┐ ┌─verb─┐
Several new *signs* now *appear* near the new highway exit.

┌─subject─┐ ┌verb┐
The guest *speaker* on the subject of health care reform just *arrived.*

COMPREHENSION AND PRACTICE 21.1

Maintaining Agreement When Subjects Follow the Verb

Each of the sentences in the following paragraph contains a pair of verbs in parentheses. First, find and underline the subject with which the verb must agree. Then circle the verb that agrees with that subject, using the example to guide you.

EXAMPLE
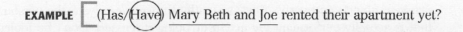
(Has/Have) Mary Beth and Joe rented their apartment yet?

(1) (Doesn't/Don't) people know how easy it is to register as a bone marrow donor? (2) According to recent news articles, there (is/are) a shortage of bone marrow donors. (3) It's too bad, because here (is/are) a wonderful opportunity to help save someone's life, and people are missing out on it because of misconceptions about the procedure itself. (4) First, there (is/are) a blood test. (5) (Is/Are) there a simpler form of testing available? (6) Once a blood sample is taken, there (is/are) some sophisticated tests done at a special lab, and the results are entered into a special bone-marrow-donor registry. (7) Here (is/are) the point at which everyone waits for a match between someone in need of a transplant and a potential donor. (8) Once a match is identified and the donor is notified, there (is/are) a few simple steps during which marrow is extracted from the donor's hip. (9) For the donor, the good news is that there (is/are) very little discomfort. (10) (Does/Do) people have to know any more than this to get involved?

CHALLENGE 21.1 **Examining Subjects and Verbs in Your Writing**

1. Comprehension and Practice 21.1 discusses bone marrow donation. What is your own attitude about bone marrow or organ donation? Are you listed as a donor? Do you know someone who has donated or who has been the recipient of a donation? Address this issue in a paragraph of seven to ten sentences, using present tense verbs only.

collaboration

2. Exchange your paragraph with a classmate. On the paper you receive, identify the subjects and verbs by underlining the subjects and circling the verbs. Put a ✓ next to any sentence that contains an error in subject–verb agreement. When you are finished, return the paragraph to your classmate.

3. Evaluate the corrections your classmate suggested, and make any necessary changes.

Avoiding Agreement Errors When Words Come between the Subject and Verb

Often, problems with subject–verb agreement occur because of the words you use *between* subjects and verbs. Always identify the *simple subject*—the person or thing that is actually performing the action or being discussed. Don't be fooled by the noun closest to the verb, which may not actually be the subject.

In some cases, what comes between a subject and verb is a *prepositional phrase*, which begins with a preposition and ends with a noun or pronoun serving as its object (see Chapter 17). Common prepositions include *about, against, around, behind, beneath, by, down, during, inside, out, through, to, up, within,* and *without.* Take a look at the following sentence, in which a prepositional phrase comes between the subject and the verb:

EXAMPLE

```
                    prepositional
        subject┐ ┌──  phrase  ──┐ ┌verb
```
The spare tire *under the tools* was flat.

The noun closest to the verb is *tools.* But tools is the object of the preposition, and *an object can't be a subject.* The verb must agree with the actual subject, *tire.* Chapters 4 and 14 explain how computer grammar and style programs often miss these errors or offer incorrect advice, so be sure to take the time to ensure that you have indeed identified the correct subject.

Other times, a subject and its verb are separated by a *subordinate clause,* a subject–verb unit introduced by a subordinating conjunction or relative pronoun (see Chapter 19). Common subordinating conjunctions include *after, although, because, if, since, unless, until, when, whether,* and *while.* Common relative pronouns include *that, which, who,* and *whose.* Here is a sentence in which the subject and verb are separated by a subordinate clause:

EXAMPLE

```
┌─subject─┐ ┌──────── subordinate clause ───────┐ ┌verb─┐
```
Students *who have computer network experience* enjoy great job prospects.

ESL Note
See "Agreement," pages 546–548, for more on the use of subordinate clauses.

In this sentence, the verb agrees in number with the actual subject, *students,* not with the word closest to the verb, *experience.*

COMPREHENSION AND PRACTICE

21.2

Identifying Subjects Separated from Verbs by Other Words

For each sentence in the following passage, identify the verbs and subjects, underlining the verbs and circling the subjects. This task will be easier if you cross out any words that come between subject and verb, as the example shows.

EXAMPLE

On some days, the (crowd) ~~in the cafeteria lining up for lunch~~ reaches the back of the building.

(1) Nintendo, home to the Super Mario Brothers, has again captured the imaginations of video gamers everywhere with its revolutionary game console, Wii. (2) Nintendo's system, with its innovative wireless remote controllers,

makes the playing experience vastly different from other systems. (3) Players interested in tennis or golf, for example, simply swing the "Wiimote" like an actual racquet or club. (4) Typically, two players, each holding a Wiimote, stand in front of a television screen or computer monitor to compete against each other. (5) Numerous interactive activities, for example, a fitness system with a special responsive exercise mat, guarantee something for everyone.

COMPREHENSION AND PRACTICE 21.3

Maintaining Agreement with Subjects Separated from Verbs by Other Words

Each of the sentences in the following passage contains a pair of verbs in parentheses. First, find and underline the subject with which the verb must agree. Then circle the verb that agrees with the subject you have underlined, as the example shows.

EXAMPLE

The burners on the stove, which are now covered with drips of paint from the ceiling, (needs/need) to be replaced soon.

(1) A good general contractor who can perform a wide variety of tasks (remains/remain) a rare individual. (2) Too often, people needing work done (enters/enter) the process with uncertainty and trepidation. (3) Stories about unscrupulous contractors doing inferior work (does/do) nothing to reassure them. (4) But my friend Lou Ledoux, who started his contracting company after doing carpentry work part time for years, (qualifies/qualify) as that rare individual. (5) Lou, who does both new construction and general repairs, (does/do) no advertising. (6) Nevertheless, his schedule, particularly during the good-weather months, (remains/remain) full. (7) That's because people, especially those operating on a strict budget, (needs/need) a contractor who is skilled, dependable, and honest. (8) Nobody who has seen the quality of one of his finished projects (has/have) any doubts about Lou's ability. (9) The needs of the client (represents/represent) Lou's top priority. (10) But Lou's calm demeanor regardless of any complications (impresses/impress) people most of all.

Avoiding Agreement Errors with Indefinite Pronouns

Indefinite pronouns are used to refer to general rather than specific people and things, for instance, the indefinite *somebody* rather than the specific *Bill,* the indefinite *anything* rather than the specific *a burrito.* See pages 387 and 392–393 in Chapter 26, for a further discussion and a complete list of indefinite pronouns.

Some indefinite pronouns are singular, some are plural, and a few are singular or plural depending on how you use them. Of these words, *another, anybody, anyone, anything, each, either, everybody, everyone, everything, much, neither, nobody, no one, nothing, one, somebody, someone,* and *something* are singular and call for singular verb forms:

EXAMPLES

Nobody wants to deal with stress on a daily basis.

Someone has to find the owner of that puppy.

Both, few, many, and *several* are always plural and call for plural verb forms:

EXAMPLES

Both of the apartments *look* well maintained.

Many of the hundred people attending the presentation now *want* to participate in the training program.

All, any, more, most, none, and *some* are either singular or plural depending on the word they refer to in the sentence. With one of these pronouns, check the word it refers to. If that word is singular, choose a singular form of the verb; if it is plural, choose a plural form of the verb, as these examples show:

EXAMPLES

All her *enthusiasm* suddenly *disappears* at the thought of rehearsing.

All their *books are* missing.

COMPREHENSION AND PRACTICE

21.4

Maintaining Agreement with Indefinite Pronouns

Underline the verbs in the following sentences. Then fill in the blank in each sentence with an appropriate indefinite pronoun from the list below. In some cases, you may need to use the same pronoun more than once.

anyone	everyone	no one	none	some	most

EXAMPLE

Of the new medications available to combat asthma, _____*some*_____ have proven to be especially effective.

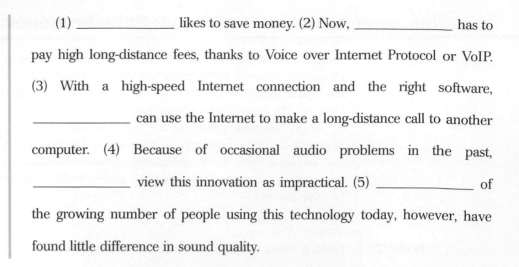

(1) _____ likes to save money. (2) Now, _____ has to pay high long-distance fees, thanks to Voice over Internet Protocol or VoIP. (3) With a high-speed Internet connection and the right software, _____ can use the Internet to make a long-distance call to another computer. (4) Because of occasional audio problems in the past, _____ view this innovation as impractical. (5) _____ of the growing number of people using this technology today, however, have found little difference in sound quality.

COMPREHENSION AND PRACTICE 21.5

Identifying Correct Agreement with Indefinite Pronouns

For each sentence in the following passage, identify the subject by underlining it. Then circle the verb that agrees with that subject from the pair of verbs in parentheses. Use the example to guide you.

EXAMPLE <u>Nobody</u> in the office ((has)/have) a personal parking space.

(1) Springfield, like most medium-sized cities, (has/have) several major neighborhoods. (2) The east end of the city is called "the Flint," and nobody (seems/seem) to know the origin of the name. (3) Many of the people living in the Flint (traces/trace) their heritage to Canada. (4) Everyone who lives in the south end of the city (refer/refers) to this neighborhood as "Maplewood." (5) Some of the larger homes in this part of the city (displays/display) the elegance of the Victorian Age. (6) The neighborhood in the center of the city is called "Below the Hill," and many of the young professionals working in the city (lives/live) here. (7) This part of the city is undergoing a rejuvenation, and everyone (has/have) been rushing to buy and restore the brownstone buildings that line the streets. (8) "The Highlands" and "the Lowlands" in the hilly north end of the city are the other two neighborhoods, and everybody in the city (enjoys/enjoy) the beauty of these two areas. (9) Both (has/have) tree-lined streets and large homes with big yards. (10) Each also (features/feature) a clear view of the Springfield River.

CHALLENGE 21.2 **Writing Sentences Using Indefinite Pronouns That Can Be Either Singular or Plural**

Here again is the list of indefinite pronouns that are either singular or plural depending on what they refer to:

all	any	more
most	none	some

collaboration

Working with a classmate, write two sentences for each, one in which the word refers to a singular subject and one in which the word refers to a plural subject.

Avoiding Agreement Errors from Other Causes

The following situations can also create confusion as you make decisions about subject–verb agreement.

When the Subject Is Compound

Not all subjects are individual words (see Chapter 17). Many are *compound subjects:* more than one noun or pronoun connected in most cases by *and* or *or.* Compound subjects connected by *and* are almost always plural. The exceptions are subjects that are commonly thought of as one, such as *peanut butter and jelly, peace and quiet, bacon and eggs,* and *rock and roll.*

EXAMPLE   A *headache* and a *bruise* on her arm *were* the only indications that Margarita had been in an accident.

[label: plural] *[label: plural verb form]*

If the two subjects are singular and connected by *or,* use a singular form of the verb:

EXAMPLE   A *doughnut* or a *muffin is* not going to help anyone on a diet.

[label: singular] *[label: singular verb form]*

But if the subjects are both plural, use a plural form of the verb:

EXAMPLE   *Doughnuts* or *muffins are* not going to help anyone on a diet.

[label: plural] *[label: plural verb form]*

When the compound subject consists of one singular word and one plural word connected by *or,* make the verb agree with the subject closest to it:

EXAMPLE   The *supervisor* or the *workers are* responsible for the decreased level of production.

[label: singular] *[label: plural]* *[label: plural verb form]*

Workers is closer to the verb, so the correct verb choice is the form that agrees with *workers.*

When the Subject Is a Collective Noun or Is Introduced by a Cue Word

Collective nouns are words that name *groups* of items or people. Common collective nouns include *audience, class, committee, faculty, flock, herd, jury, swarm,* and *team.* (See Chapter 25 for more on collective nouns.) Collective nouns are singular, so they call for singular verb forms:

EXAMPLE
singular
singular⌐ ⌐verb form⌐
This year's *team has won* twenty-five games so far.

In some cases, certain words, called *cue words,* help you to identify whether a subject is singular or plural. Common singular cue words include *a, an, another, each, either, every, neither,* and *one.* A subject introduced by one of these words will be singular and call for a singular verb form:

EXAMPLE
⌐singular
singular
⌐verb form
Neither sales representative *recalls* the meeting.

Common plural cue words include *all, both, few, many, several,* and *some.* Subjects introduced by these words call for a plural verb form:

EXAMPLE
⌐plural
plural
⌐verb form
Few great novels ever *make* good movies.

When the Subject Is a Singular Word Ending in *-s,* a Word Referring to an Amount, or a Word That Has the Same Singular and Plural Form

ESL Note
See "Agreement," pages 546–548, for more on the use of words indicating an amount.

Certain words that end in *-s* may look plural, but they are actually singular and call for singular verb forms. Common words in this category include *economics, ethics, mathematics, measles, mumps, news, physics,* and *politics.*

EXAMPLE
singular
⌐singular⌐ ⌐verb form
Physics appears to be growing in popularity in schools across the nation.

Nouns used to refer to measurements, money, time, and weight can also cause some confusion in terms of subject–verb agreement. These words may seem plural, but because they are used to refer to the entire amount as one unit, they are actually singular and call for singular verb forms:

EXAMPLE
singular
⌐——singular——⌐ ⌐verb form
Fifty dollars is ~~much~~ more than any ticket is worth.

Finally, with certain words such as *antelope, deer, fish,* and *species,* use either a singular or a plural form of the verb depending on whether you mean one or more than one:

EXAMPLES
singular
singular ⌐⌐verb form⌐
That *moose has broken* out of its holding area.

singular
⌐plural⌐ ⌐verb form
Those *moose look* so peaceful as they stand together.

COMPREHENSION AND PRACTICE 21.6

Maintaining Agreement with Compound Subjects

Each of the sentences in the following passage includes a pair of verbs in parentheses. First underline the compound subject, and then circle the verb that agrees with that subject. Use the example to guide you.

EXAMPLE

Even after working all afternoon, David and Bobbie still (has/have) not been able to start the car.

(1) In today's modern world, eye specialists and patients looking to improve their eyesight (has/have) a number of alternatives available. (2) Today, style and comfort (do/does) not have to be sacrificed, thanks to the advent of low-cost designer frames. (3) For those wanting to do without glasses altogether, daily-wear contact lenses or extended-care contact lenses (remains/remain) the most common options. (4) Bifocal contacts and contacts that reshape the lens (is/are) recent innovations in this field. (5) Also, conventional Lasik surgery and custom Lasik procedures (enables/enable) people with vision problems to go without glasses or contacts, making these surgical alternatives an increasingly popular choice among the young and physically active.

COMPREHENSION AND PRACTICE 21.7

Maintaining Agreement with Collective Nouns, with Singular Words Ending in -s, and with Words Referring to Amounts

Each of the following sentences contains the infinitive of a verb (for example, *to* + a simple form of the verb—*to speak*) in parentheses. Identify the subject of the verb by underlining it, and then write the proper *present tense* form of the verb on the line provided. Remember—the story is told in the present, so use present tense forms only. Use the example as a guide.

EXAMPLE

The audience (to be) _____*is*_____ clearly enjoying the concert.

(1) The committee in charge of selecting the Youth Center's Volunteer of the Year (to have) _____ an important job. (2) A nominating team of five committee members first (to select) _____ five semifinalists from the many nominations. (3) In most years, 50 to 100 nominations (to

be) _____ not unusual. (4) The ethics of the situation (to require) _____ careful, objective scrutiny of the nominations. (5) That's because politics often (to play) _____ a part in the nominating process, with companies and organizations lobbying for the opportunity to broadcast the activities of one of their employees to thousands of people across the state. (6) Economics (to do) _____ not come into play, however, because no monetary reward is attached to the award. (7) After the initial selections are made, an hour (to pass) _____ while the team ranks the candidates in ten categories on a 1–5 scale. (8) Ultimately, simple mathematics in the form of the highest composite score (to determine) _____ the winner. (9) Despite efforts to keep the results secret until the annual recognition banquet, news often (to spread) _____ among the rest of the committee. (10) On the night of the recognition banquet, as the audience (to applaud) _____ the winner, the committee sits back and enjoys what its hard work has brought about.

CHALLENGE 21.3 Revising to Achieve Subject–Verb Agreement

collaboration

Working with a classmate, help the writer of the following Letter to the Editor eliminate the errors in subject–verb agreement. Cross out the wrong verb form and write the correct one above it. Some sentences are correct as they are.

Dear Editor:

(1) Right now, few members of the City Council appears to be taking the city's traffic problems seriously. (2) Thirty minutes are clearly an unreasonable amount of time to spend stuck in downtown traffic. (3) Under the worst circumstances, drivers should be able to complete this two-mile drive in half that time. (4) The streets blocked off to make the pedestrian mall five years ago represents the main impediment to improving the flow of traffic. (5) As a result, anyone who

travels on the downtown streets have to take a series of narrow one-way streets in order to get around the mall. (6) When buses or a tractor trailer enter the area, traffic slows down even more than usual. (7) Even the blue-ribbon committee that originally lobbied in favor of the pedestrian mall to bring more consumers downtown want it removed. (8) Of course, eliminating the pedestrian mall will cost money, and so most members of the council seems hesitant to vote in favor of the change. (9) But each of our elected officials have a responsibility to act in the best interest of the citizens. (10) There is many voters who are watching carefully and will make sure that the councilors who won't act will be out of a job.

QUICK STUDY Student Example

This chapter focuses on issues of agreement. Here's a paragraph on a related subject—a strategy to persuade people:

One of the best ways to convince someone to accept your ideas are to discuss your point of view calmly and rationally. People don't always react when someone yell and scream about an issue. This lack of response don't necessarily mean that they agree, however. Some people may not respond because they are trying to avoid an ugly scene, and others may just be uncomfortable or afraid to be around an angry person. But when you discuss a subject rationally, people usually listen. In many cases, people will be more inclined to sign your petition, go along with your plans for the weekend, or reconsider their stand on an issue because of your calm, positive approach to the subject. Today, there is too many people who try to persuade others by being loud and obnoxious. In my view, a respectful tone and positive attitude represents the best strategy to win people over to your side.

Now complete the following activities:

1. Several sentences in this paragraph are highlighted. Evaluate these sections for errors in subject–verb agreement. On a separate sheet of paper, rewrite sentences containing errors, using the material in this chapter to help you correct them.

2. In your view, does the topic sentence of this paragraph prepare the reader for the discussion that follows in the body of the paragraph? What leads you to this conclusion? Use the following lines for your answer.

_____

_____

_____

_____

3. This paragraph exemplifies a piece of persuasive writing: an *argument* paragraph. (See Chapter 13 for more on argument.) Does this paragraph manage to persuade you that the approach it describes is a good way to convince others? On a separate sheet of paper, explain your reaction, identifying what you see as its strengths and its weaknesses.

Now explore the topic in writing. You could focus, as the paragraph above does, on some strategy or technique to improve personal communications or relationships. Or you might choose one of the following instead:

- a time that you experienced or witnessed a disagreement
- a complaint you have about a product or service that didn't live up to its guarantee
- why compromising can often be so hard
- what people need in order to be compatible

collaboration

4. Exchange your draft with a classmate. Evaluate the paragraph you receive. If you discover any problem spots, especially errors in subject–verb agreement, make a note in the margin and then return the paper to the writer.

5. Consider the comments and corrections your reader has made and create a final draft of your paragraph.

CHAPTER QUICK CHECK Mastering Subject–Verb Agreement

The following passage contains the various kinds of errors in subject–verb agreement discussed in this chapter. Consider again the ways to correct these errors illustrated in this chapter. Then identify errors in agreement, crossing them out and writing the correct verb form above the incorrect one, as the example shows:

EXAMPLE Several of my friends from my old neighborhood still ~~plays~~ *play* basketball together

two nights a week in the City League.

(1) Speed and convenience seems to be what most customers are looking for when they go shopping. (2) Because everyone, especially those who have demanding work schedules, want to spend less time in line, more and more retailers have adopted a new check-out system. (3) Under this system, a customer with fewer than 20 items go to a self-service area. (4) In this area, there is 15 stations, each with a computer screen and a small platform containing an electronic scanner. (5) The steps involved in the process requires no special training. (6) All of the instructions appears on the computer screen. (7) The UPC code, printed on all items, are the key to the process. (8) This series of vertical bars and numbers indicate the name and price of the item. (9) The customer runs the UPC code of each item in front of the scanner, and an electronic tone and visual image on the screen tells the customer that the sale has been recorded. (10) A team of three workers monitor the 15 check-out stations, ready to address any problems customers encounter.

SUMMARY EXERCISE Mastering Subject–Verb Agreement

The following passage contains the various kinds of errors in subject–verb agreement discussed in this chapter. Consider again the ways to correct these errors illustrated in this chapter. Then identify errors in agreement, crossing them out and writing the correct verb form above the incorrect one.

(1) For today's consumers, there is many choices available in terms of laptop computers. (2) Thanks to price cuts by most major manufacturers, anybody wanting to be freed from bulky desktop computers are able to do so. (3) Lightning-fast processors and Wi-Fi capability makes today's notebook computers highly popular with a broad spectrum of people, especially students.

(4) The latest class of notebook computers cost far less than ever before. (5) With the first laptops, $3,000 were considered a bargain-basement price. (6) Right now, a laptop with ten times as much memory and many more built-in

features, including CD and DVD players and burners, run in the range of $1,500.

(7) In the past few years alone, there has been enhancements almost beyond belief. (8) With the first generation of laptops, for example, short battery life and small screen size was bothersome. (9) Today, however, most laptops enjoys more robust batteries and bright, easy-to-read screens. (10) Weight, even for the sleekest of the early laptops, were also a serious concern. (11) Now, four pounds are considered heavy for many of these powerhouse portables, with some weighing in at under two pounds. (12) In addition, built-in DVD players, often as powerful as those in a home video system, allows users to watch movies on their computer screen. (13) All these changes has been welcomed by the growing number of laptop owners.

(14) Here, in simple terms, are the biggest improvement in today's notebook computers: speed of processing. (15) For many of the early laptops, *sluggish* and *anemic* is the best words to describe their processing performance. (16) But the newest generation of Pentium chips power many of the latest group of laptops. (17) As a result, even some of the most complex functions takes a fraction of the time once required.

(18) In today's fast-paced world, there is many reasons to choose a laptop. (19) The freedom to work in a variety of settings, however, probably rank right at the top. (20) After all, for many computer owners today, a restaurant or coffee shop with an Internet hotspot have become the place of choice to work, play interactive computer games, and stay in constant touch with the world.

FOR FURTHER EXPLORATION Subject–Verb Agreement

1. Focus on one of the following topics, using the prewriting technique—or combination of techniques—that you prefer to generate some preliminary ideas, considering what purposes you might fulfill as you write about it:

   • ways that government—local, state, or federal—unnecessarily intrudes on the life of citizens

- the reason people gossip or the consequences that can result when they do
- how to reduce bad behavior on the streets and highways
- an occasion when you said exactly the wrong thing

2. Evaluate your prewriting material, identify a focus, and work your way through the rest of the writing process to create a draft essay of at least 500 words on this subject.

collaboration

3. Exchange your draft with a classmate. Check the draft you receive for weaknesses, paying particular attention to subject–verb agreement. Circle any subjects and verbs that don't agree, using the material in this chapter as a guide, and then return the draft to the writer.

4. Revise your essay, correcting any errors in subject–verb agreement or other problems discovered by your reader.

RECAP Subject–Verb Agreement

Key Terms in This Chapter	Definitions
subject–verb agreement	a state in which the subject and verb agree in number Use a singular form of a verb with a singular subject. Use a plural form of a verb with a plural subject.

Ways to Maintain Agreement

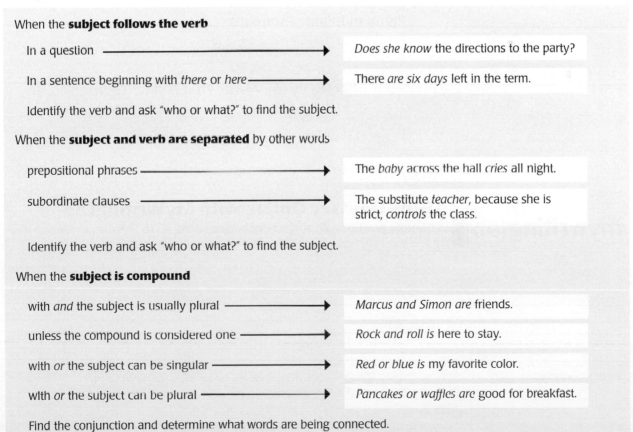

When the **subject follows the verb**

In a question ⟶ *Does she know* the directions to the party?

In a sentence beginning with *there* or *here* ⟶ There *are six days* left in the term.

Identify the verb and ask "who or what?" to find the subject.

When the **subject and verb are separated** by other words

prepositional phrases ⟶ The *baby* across the hall *cries* all night.

subordinate clauses ⟶ The substitute *teacher*, because she is strict, *controls* the class.

Identify the verb and ask "who or what?" to find the subject.

When the **subject is compound**

with *and* the subject is usually plural ⟶ *Marcus and Simon are* friends.

unless the compound is considered one ⟶ *Rock and roll is* here to stay.

with *or* the subject can be singular ⟶ *Red or blue is* my favorite color.

with *or* the subject can be plural ⟶ *Pancakes or waffles are* good for breakfast.

Find the conjunction and determine what words are being connected.

Ways to Maintain Agreement (*Continued*)

When the **subject is an indefinite pronoun**

singular ⟶ *Everyone is* late today.

plural ⟶ *Both* of my grandparents *are* immigrants.

Use singular verbs with singular pronouns and plural verbs with plural pronouns.

When the **subject is a collective noun or a singular noun ending in -s**

collective noun ⟶ The *jury returns* today.

singular noun ending in -s ⟶ The *news follows* my favorite comedy.

If the subject is a unit, use a singular verb.

Singular Indefinite Pronouns

another	each	everything	nobody	somebody
anybody	either	neither	nothing	someone
anyone	everybody	no one	one	something
anything	everyone			

Plural Indefinite Pronouns

both	few	many	several

Indefinite Pronouns Affected by the Words That Follow Them

all	more	none
any	most	some

Using Odyssey Online with MyWritingLab

For more practice with subject–verb agreement, go to www.mywritinglab.com.

CHAPTER 22
Basic Tenses for Regular Verbs

GETTING STARTED ...

 Q One aspect of writing that I have trouble with is verb use, especially choosing the right verb ending. I often mix them up, adding a *-d* or an *-ed* to the end of a verb or putting *will* in front of one for no good reason. Is there any technique or strategy that can help me avoid making mistakes in verb tense while I am working on a draft?

A Working with verbs in English can be confusing because of the various verb tenses. But these specialized forms enable you to capture just the right time period for each situation. To avoid a lot of frustration while working with verb tenses, stop periodically to check for any incorrect switches in verb tense.

Overview: Understanding Tense

ESL Note
See "Agreement" on pages 546–548.

To a writer, no words hold more importance than verbs. Verbs convey action or link elements in a statement. Through verbs, you communicate about people, events, concepts, or possibilities. They also indicate the *past, present,* or *future.* This time element is called **verb tense.** You indicate a change in verb tense by changing the form. Most verbs in English are regular—you convert their present form to past and future tenses in consistent ways.

Navigating This Chapter In this chapter, you will discover how to use the following for regular verbs:

- the present tense to describe a fact, an action, or a situation that is happening now or that happens habitually
- the future tense to describe an action or situation that hasn't occurred yet
- the past tense to describe an action or situation that has already occurred
- the past participle and perfect tenses to describe an action or situation that either was completed in the past or will be completed in the future

Using the Simple Present, Simple Future, and Simple Past Tenses

The **present tense** signifies a fact, action, or situation that is happening *at the moment* or that happens habitually. For regular verbs, the simple present tense is the basic form of the verb, the one you would use in the simplest "I" statement: I laugh, I jump.

What makes the present tense a little confusing is that its form changes depending on the subject. If the subject is *singular,* meaning *one* person or thing, then the verb ends in *-s* or *-es.* If the subject is plural (or the singular *I*), the verb has no *-s.*

EXAMPLES

All day long, that dog *digs* holes in the yard.

Most children *enjoy* a magic show.

The subject in the first example is singular (*dog*), so the verb ends in *-s: digs.* In the second example, the plural subject *children* calls for a verb without an *-s* ending: *enjoy.* The exceptions to this guideline are the pronouns *I* and *you.* Even though *I* is singular, you don't add an *-s* to the present tense verb when *I* is the subject:

EXAMPLE

I *play* basketball every weekend.

You also don't add an *-s* to a present tense verb when *you* is the subject, even when it is singular:

EXAMPLE

You always *clean* your apartment on Saturday.

The simple **future tense** conveys an action or relationship *that hasn't occurred yet.* For regular verbs, the future tense for both singular and plural subjects is formed by adding *will* to the basic form of the verb. No *-s* or *-es* is necessary.

EXAMPLE

The actors *will prepare* for the play. The director *will coach* them.

ESL Note
See "Agreement," pages 546–548, and "Confusing Verb Forms," pages 549–551, for more on using present tense regular verbs properly.

The simple **past tense** indicates an action or situation *that has already occurred.* For regular verbs, the simple past tense is formed by adding *-ed* to the basic verb form. If the verb ends in *-e,* only a *-d* is added. For some regular verbs that end in *-y,* or with a single consonant preceded by a single vowel, forming the past tense requires a little more work. You must either change the last letter or add a letter before you add the *-d* or *-ed* ending. Chapter 29, "Spelling" discusses ways to deal with these verbs. Again, the simple past tense is the same for both singular and plural subjects.

EXAMPLES

Cynthia *answered* many questions in botany class.

Several dozen applicants *responded* to our ad for an assistant manager.

How to Form Simple Tenses for Regular Verbs (Example verb–*call*)

	Simple Present Tense (Use the basic form of the verb, adding -*s* or -*es* for singular subjects except *I* and *you*.)	**Simple Past Tense** (Use the basic form of the verb plus -*d* or -*ed*.)	**Simple Future Tense** (Use the basic form of the verb plus *will*.)
Basic or "I" form	I *call* friends in the evening.	I *called* friends last night.	I *will call* friends tomorrow evening.
Singular	Ami *calls* friends in the evening.	Ami *called* friends last night.	Ami *will call* friends tomorrow evening.
Plural	Joe and Estella *call* friends in the evening.	Joe and Estella *called* friends last night.	Joe and Estella *will call* friends tomorrow evening.

For more on the use of present tense verbs, see Chapter 21, "Subject–Verb Agreement."

COMPREHENSION AND PRACTICE

Working with Future Tense Verbs

22.1 Complete the following sentences by adding a completing thought containing a future tense verb. Use the example to guide you.

EXAMPLE When the warm weather arrives, *the campus will look beautiful*.

1. When the election results are finally tabulated, _____

   _____

2. After Albert shaves his moustache and cuts his hair, _____

   _____

3. As soon as the semester is over, _____

   _____

4. Once the jury reaches a verdict, _____

   _____

5. When the parade is over, the city's public works department _____

   _____

COMPREHENSION AND PRACTICE

Using Past Tense Verbs to Complete Sentences

22.2 Use the following list of basic verbs to complete the paragraph below. Make all verbs past tense by adding *-d* or *-ed.* Answers will vary. Sample answers are shown.

purchase	line	wash	measure	redecorate
brush	fold	pick	start	place

(1) Last weekend, my friend Kathy _____ the living room in her apartment by wallpapering. (2) First, she _____ the walls to find out how much wallpaper to buy. (3) Then she _____ the paper, along with a kit containing several wallpapering tools. (4) She also _____ up two containers of premixed wallpaper paste. (5) She then _____ down the walls to make sure the surface was clean. (6) Once the walls dried, she _____ to hang the wallpaper. (7) After cutting a strip of paper to the correct length, she _____ paste onto the back of the paper. (8) Next, she _____ the strip of paper in half and carried it from the table to the wall. (9) She unfolded the paper and _____ and its top edge against the ceiling. (10) She then _____ up the right side of the paper against the guideline she had drawn to ensure that the paper was straight.

Using the Perfect Tenses

Writers use the **past participle** to form additional tenses: *past perfect, present perfect,* and *future perfect.* All of the **perfect tenses** are formed by adding a helping verb to the past participle of a verb. For regular verbs, the past participle is the same as the simple past tense: the basic verb form plus *-d* or *-ed.*

This chapter discusses perfect tense verbs that use *has, have,* or *had* as helping verbs. Chapter 24 discusses progressive tense verbs that use *am, is, was,* and *were* as helping verbs.

To form the perfect tenses for regular verbs, use the helping verbs shown below:

ESL Note
See "Confusing Verb Forms," pages 549–551, for more on using *has* and "Agreement," pages 546–548, for more on the proper use of perfect tenses.

Perfect Tense	=	Helping Verb	+	Past Participle	Example
Past perfect		had		walked	I *had walked.*
Present perfect		has, have		walked	I *have walked.*
Future perfect		will have		walked	I *will have walked.*

Perfect tense verbs cover time in a slightly different way than simple past, present, and future tenses do.

- The *past perfect tense* expresses action completed in the past before some other past action or event. (Jim *had bought* Nikki's birthday gift before they broke up.)
- The *present perfect tense* expresses action completed at some indefinite period in the past, or action that began in the past and is still going on. (Jim *has bought* me a birthday gift every year since 1998.)
- The *future perfect tense* expresses actions that will be completed in the future before some other future event or action. Note that this tense requires the word *will* before the helping verb. (By August, Jim *will have bought* all his Christmas gifts.)

Take a look at the time line below, which shows the relationship of all the tenses discussed in this chapter.

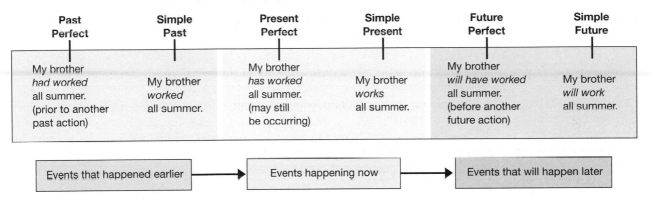

COMPREHENSION AND PRACTICE

Working with the Perfect Tenses

22.3   On another sheet of paper, rewrite the following sentences, changing the present tense verb to either the present perfect, past perfect, or future perfect form and indicate the tense you have used in parentheses. In some cases, more than one tense can be used. Use the example to guide you.

EXAMPLE   Josh earns all of his tuition money.

Josh will have earned all of his tuition money. (future perfect)

1. The blue jay eats the blueberries on the ground below the bush.
2. The pie chills in the refrigerator at least two hours before dinner.
3. Bryan asks his friend for help with algebra.
4. The meteorologist forecasts a stormy weekend.
5. Dan states his preferences for vacation before anyone else.

CHALLENGE 22.1   **Writing with the Perfect Tenses**

1. Write a paragraph of at least seven to ten sentences about the changes from one season to another in your part of the country. Use at least one perfect tense verb in each sentence.

collaboration

2. Exchange your writing with a classmate. On the paper you receive, underline the perfect tense verbs and label them *PaP* for the past perfect tense, *PP* for the present perfect tense, and *FP* for the future perfect tense. Then return the paragraph to the writer.

3. Check to see whether the labels your classmate has supplied are accurate, and relabel any incorrect ones.

QUICK STUDY   Student Example

This chapter discusses the aspect of writing that deals with time. Consider the following paragraph on a related subject—how the passing of time affects people:

> Time definitely *appears* to flow at different speeds depending on what is going on in life. When you are waiting for something to begin, the clock seems to be just barely moving. For example, when children are waiting for a birthday party or the end of school, the hours *become* days. The same thing is true when teenagers *have planned* a special date or parents and grandparents are waiting for the birth of a child. But the opposite is often true once the special event *has concluded*. The long-awaited party, vacation, or date *has flashed* by, and in the blink of an eye, the tiny infant *has become* a toddler. The same people who *wanted* time to speed by now wish they could make the clock stop so they can enjoy the experience. Yet, if another special event is a few weeks off, they *will want* the hands of the clock to start spinning forward again. Of course, all this concern about speeding up or slowing down time is silly because time *runs* at the same speed no matter how much people *desire* to control it

First, complete the following activities in response to this paragraph:

1. Several of the verbs in this paragraph are *italicized*. Above each verb, identify its tense, using the material in this chapter to guide you. Then, on a separate sheet of paper, briefly explain why you think these forms of verbs have been used rather than other tenses.

2. On the following lines, briefly explain how the concluding sentence relates to the main idea expressed in the topic sentence and brings the paragraph to a logical close.

_____

_____

_____

_____

3. The organizing strategy of example plays a big role in this paragraph. In your view, which of the examples supplied does the best job of supporting and illustrating the main point of this paragraph? What about the example makes it particularly effective? Use the lines that follow for your answer.

_____

_____

_____

_____

Now explore the topic in writing. As the paragraph on page 336 does, you could concentrate on how the passing of time affects you. You might instead focus on one of these topics related to the subject matter of this chapter:

- time that you spent on something that you now wish you hadn't
- the hardest part about managing personal time
- a moment that is frozen in time for you
- the best time of life

collaboration

4. Exchange your draft with a classmate. Evaluate the paragraph you receive. If you discover any problem spots, especially in the use of simple and perfect verb tenses, circle the errors, and then return the paper to the writer.

5. Consider the comments and corrections your reader has made and create a final draft of your paragraph.

CHAPTER QUICK CHECK Working with Basic Verb Tenses

For each italicized verb in the following passage, identify the tense, using the labels listed below.

Pr = present tense   *Pa* = past tense   *F* = future tense
PP = present perfect tense   *PaP* = past perfect tense   *FP* = future perfect tense

(1) Quincy Jones *ranks* as one of the true giants in American popular music. (2) Born in 1933 on Chicago's South Side and raised in Seattle, Jones *knew* from age 11 that he *loved* music. (3) During his more than 50-year career in music, "Q," as he *is* known to his friends, *has affected* popular music to a profound degree. (4) Early in his career Jones *had worked* with such musical giants as Dizzy Gillespie, Count Basie, Duke Ellington, Frank Sinatra, and Sarah Vaughan. (5) As a producer, arranger, and conductor, Jones *has put* his mark on the work of a number of rock and roll artists, including Ray Charles, Diana Ross, and Stevie Wonder. (6) In the 1970s, he *suffered* two brain aneurysms that *left* him with a metal plate in his head, but he *refused* to let them slow him down. (7) In fact, in 1982, Jones *stepped* back into the spotlight as the producer of pop star Michael Jackson's *Thriller*, one of the best-selling recordings of all time, and more recently, he *has worked* with a number of rap artists, as well. (8) In addition to his work in the music studio, Jones *has enjoyed* great success in a number of other areas. (9) For instance, in 1961, Jones *became* the vice president of Mercury Records, the first African American to serve in such a capacity, and he *is* co-founder of *Vibe* magazine. (10) His induction into the American Academy of Arts & Sciences *is* a fitting acknowledgment for someone who certainly *will continue* to influence popular music.

SUMMARY EXERCISE Working with Basic Verb Tenses

For each italicized verb in the following passage, identify the tense, using the labels listed below.

Pr = present tense	*F* = future tense	*Pa* = past tense
PP = present perfect tense	*PaP* = past perfect tense	*FP* = future perfect tense

(1) Recent research on the human brain *offers* us a number of interesting findings about the "wiring" of this fascinating organ. (2) Scientists are now

theorizing that, before your birth, your brain *programmed* itself. (3) It *dedicated* large numbers of nerve cells to performing basic functions. (4) However, it *reserved* even more nerve cells for specialized functions that help you learn about the world. (5) These findings *add* great significance to the way we *treat* children. (6) We now believe that a child's neurons *will thrive* with appropriate stimulation. (7) Without direct stimulation and use, however, these nerve cells *will wither* away.

(8) This research *will encourage* parents and teachers to change some of our old views about learning. (9) For one thing, the findings *suggest* that there are certain peak periods of opportunity for learning. (10) They *indicate* that children will make the greatest strides in learning mathematics between birth and four years. (11) The same thing *appears* to be true for learning music. (12) Parents who *had played* simple number games and *had introduced* their children to music during this period *saw* impressive results.

(13) The findings also *urge* us to examine how we *have treated* language. (14) Children *learn* language most easily from birth to age ten. (15) The first few years of life *matter* most. (16) It now *appears* likely that those infants and toddlers who master language quickly *have heard* more words than other children. (17) In addition, children who *have listened* to many words before they reach age two *will have developed* large vocabularies by the time they reach adulthood.

(18) If these preliminary findings *prove* to be true, parents and schools *will want* to make some serious adjustments. (19) For one thing, teachers *will expect* parents to be much more involved at home, since a great deal of valuable learning time occurs before children attend school. (20) In addition, schools *will arrange* to offer instruction in a second language much earlier, perhaps as early as the first few grades.

FOR FURTHER EXPLORATION Regular Verb Tenses

1. Focus on the following topics. Use the prewriting technique—or combination of techniques—that fits your style of working to come up with some preliminary ideas, while also considering the purposes you might fulfill in writing about the topic:

   - the reluctance of many people to take personal responsibility
   - the causes or consequences of pollution
   - the impact of the entertainment industry on average people
   - what should not be shown on commercial television and why

2. Evaluate your prewriting materials, identify a focus, and work your way through the rest of the writing process to create a draft essay of at least 500 words on this subject.

collaboration

3. Exchange your draft with a classmate. Check the draft you receive for weaknesses, paying particular attention to the use of simple and perfect verb tenses. Circle any errors, using the material in this chapter as a guide, and then return the draft to the writer.

4. Revise your essay, correcting any errors in verb use or other problems discovered by your reader.

RECAP Basic Tenses for Regular Verbs

Key Terms in This Chapter	Definitions
verb tense	the form of a verb that tells when the action or situation occurs, either in the present, future, or past
present tense	the basic form of the verb signifying a fact, action, or situation that is occurring now or habitually Many singular present tense verbs end in -s or -es. **EXAMPLE** My son *cleans* our apartment on the weekend. **EXAMPLE** He *ignores* the dust during the week.
future tense	the form of the verb signifying a future action or state of being; the basic verb plus *will* **EXAMPLE** This weekend he *will wash* the kitchen floor.
past tense	the form of the verb signifying an action or state of being that has already occurred; the basic form of the verb plus -d or -ed **EXAMPLE** He *shopped* for groceries on Saturday.
past participle	for regular verbs, a form created by adding -d or -ed to the basic form Use the past participle with a helping verb to form the perfect tenses. **EXAMPLE** Martha *had ended* the relationship months ago.

Key Terms in This Chapter	Definitions
perfect tenses	verb tenses formed by adding some form of *to have* to the past participle of another verb
	Perfect tenses express actions that are complete with reference to another indicated time.
	EXAMPLE We *have shared* the work this way for a few months.
	EXAMPLE I *had finished* the rest of the chores earlier.
	EXAMPLE We *will have succeeded* in sharing responsibilities.

Forming the Basic Tenses for Regular Verbs

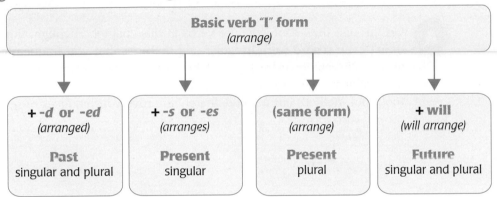

Basic verb "I" form
(arrange)

+ *-d* or *-ed* (arranged)	+ *-s* or *-es* (arranges)	(same form) (arrange)	+ *will* (will arrange)
Past singular and plural	**Present** singular	**Present** plural	**Future** singular and plural

Forming the Perfect Tenses for Regular Verbs

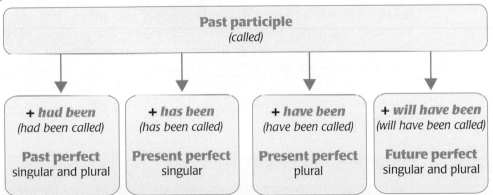

Past participle
(called)

+ *had been* (had been called)	+ *has been* (has been called)	+ *have been* (have been called)	+ *will have been* (will have been called)
Past perfect singular and plural	**Present perfect** singular	**Present perfect** plural	**Future perfect** singular and plural

Using Odyssey Online with MyWritingLab

For more practice with basic tenses for regular verbs, go to www.mywritinglab.com.

CHAPTER 23
Irregular Verbs and Frequently Confused Verbs

GETTING STARTED...

 Q *Irregular verbs,* the onés that don't follow the rules, give me trouble, as do a few others such as *can* and *could* and *will* and *would.* What should I do to keep them all straight?

 A Go through the list of irregular verbs in this chapter. Highlight the ones you didn't even realize were irregular and the ones that you frequently confuse, and make your own list of problem verbs. Add the forms of *can* and *could* and *will* and *would* to the list and then memorize the list. It's not an easy or foolproof method, but it will definitely improve your chances of selecting the proper verb form.

Overview: Understanding Irregular Verbs and Other Verb Problems

As Chapter 22 pointed out, making the past and past participle forms for regular verbs is easy and predictable. You simply add either *-d* or *-ed* to the end of the basic verb form: *create–created, talk–talked.* The problem, of course, is that forming the past or past participle is not predictable for all verbs. These **irregular verbs** are most likely to confuse writers. The verb *to be* is perhaps the most troublesome of these irregular verbs because it has so many forms. Other verbs that give writers trouble are the confusing pairs *can* and *could* and *will* and *would.*

Navigating This Chapter In this chapter, you will learn how to:

- form the present, past, and past participle forms of common irregular verbs
- work effectively with forms of *to be*
- choose correctly between *can* and *could* and between *will* and *would*

Identifying Irregular Verbs

The verbs in the following list are all irregular. As Chapter 22 indicates, the past participle form (the third column below) is used with a helping verb to form a perfect or progressive tense verb.

Irregular Verb Forms

ESL Note
See "Confusing Verb Forms," pages 549–551, for more on using irregular verbs properly.

Present Tense	Past Tense	Past Participle (+ a helping verb = perfect or progressive tense)
am/is/are	was/were	been
arise	arose	arisen
awaken	awoke, awaked	awoke, awaked
become	became	become
begin	began	begun
bend	bent	bent
bind	bound	bound
bite	bit	bitten, bit
bleed	bled	bled
blow	blew	blown
break	broke	broken
bring	brought	brought
build	built	built
burn	burned, burnt	burned, burnt
burst	burst	burst
buy	bought	bought
catch	caught	caught
choose	chose	chosen
cling	clung	clung
come	came	come
cost	cost	cost
creep	crept	crept
cut	cut	cut
deal	dealt	dealt
dig	dug	dug
dive	dived, dove	dived
do/does	did	done
draw	drew	drawn
dream	dreamed, dreamt	dreamed, dreamt
drink	drank	drunk
drive	drove	driven
eat	ate	eaten
fall	fell	fallen
feed	fed	fed
feel	felt	felt
fight	fought	fought
find	found	found
flee	fled	fled
fling	flung	flung
fly	flew	flown
forbid	forbade, forbad	forbidden
forget	forgot	forgotten, forgot
freeze	froze	frozen

(continued)

Irregular Verb Forms *(continued)*

Present Tense	Past Tense	Past Participle (+ a helping verb = perfect or progressive tense)
get	got	got, gotten
give	gave	given
go/goes	went	gone
grind	ground	ground
grow	grew	grown
hang	hung	hung
hang (execute)	hanged	hanged
have/has	had	had
hear	heard	heard
hide	hid	hidden, hid
hold	held	held
hurt	hurt	hurt
keep	kept	kept
kneel	knelt, kneeled	knelt, kneeled
knit	knit, knitted	knit, knitted
know	knew	known
lay	laid	laid
lead	led	led
leap	leaped, leapt	leaped, leapt
leave	left	left
lend	lent	lent
let	let	let
lie	lay	lain
light	lighted, lit	lighted, lit
lose	lost	lost
make	made	made
mean	meant	meant
meet	met	met
mistake	mistook	mistaken
pay	paid	paid
plead	pleaded, pled	pleaded, pled
prove	proved	proved, proven
put	put	put
quit	quit	quit
raise	raised	raised
read	read	read
ride	rode	ridden
ring	rang	rung
rise	rose	risen
run	ran	run
say	said	said
see	saw	seen
seek	sought	sought

Irregular Verb Forms *(continued)*

Present Tense	Past Tense	Past Participle (+ a helping verb = perfect or progressive tense)
sell	sold	sold
send	sent	sent
set	set	set
sew	sewed	sewn, sewed
shake	shook	shaken
shine	shone, shined	shone, shined
shine (polish)	shined	shined
shoot	shot	shot
show	showed	shown, showed
shrink	shrank, shrunk	shrunk, shrunken
shut	shut	shut
sing	sang	sung
sit	sat	sat
sleep	slept	slept
slide	slid	slid
sling	slung	slung
slink	slunk, slinked	slunk, slinked
sow	sowed	sown, sowed
speak	spoke	spoken
speed	sped, speeded	sped, speeded
spend	spent	spent
spit	spit, spat	spit, spat
spring	sprang, sprung	sprung
stand	stood	stood
steal	stole	stolen
stick	stuck	stuck
sting	stung	stung
stink	stank, stunk	stunk
stride	strode	stridden
strike	struck	struck, stricken
string	strung	strung
strive	strived, strove	striven, strived
swear	swore	sworn
sweat	sweat, sweated	sweat, sweated
swell	swelled	swelled, swollen
swim	swam	swum
swing	swung	swung
take	took	taken
teach	taught	taught
tear	tore	torn
tell	told	told
think	thought	thought
throw	threw	thrown
understand	understood	understood

(continued)

Irregular Verb Forms *(continued)*

Present Tense	Past Tense	Past Participle (+ a helping verb = perfect or progressive tense)
wake	woke, waked	woken, waked, woke
wear	wore	worn
weave	wove, weaved	woven, weaved
weep	wept	wept
win	won	won
wind	wound	wound
wring	wrung	wrung
write	wrote	written

As the table shows, the past and past participle forms of irregular verbs are often different. Consider these examples:

EXAMPLES

The windows in the building *shook* each time the furnace started up.

The front picture window *had shaken* so much that it actually cracked.

Because of their unpredictability, irregular verbs in all their forms must be memorized. As you learn the irregular verb forms, keep two things in mind: (1) You *don't* use a helping verb with the past tense, and (2) You *must* use a helping verb with the past participle.

COMPREHENSION AND PRACTICE 23.1

Using Irregular Verbs in Your Writing

On a separate sheet of paper, write three related sentences for each of the irregular verbs listed below: one each for the present tense, the past tense, and the past participle forms. Remember—the past participle requires a helping verb to form a perfect tense verb. Use the examples to guide you.

EXAMPLES

Kathy and John always <u>hear</u> the noise from the Fourth of July fireworks.

Last night, they also <u>heard</u> the oohs and ahhs of the crowd.

In previous years, Kathy and John <u>have heard</u> the band as well as the fireworks.

1. keep	3. sleep	5. freeze	7. write	9. raise
2. bite	4. shake	6. speak	8. become	10. stand

COMPREHENSION AND PRACTICE 23.2

Using Irregular Verbs Correctly

The following passage calls for past tense. Each sentence contains a present tense verb in parentheses. Write the correct past form of this verb on the line that follows. Use the form that the context calls for; include a helping verb if necessary. In some cases, more than one correct answer is possible. Use the example to guide you.

EXAMPLE   When I was growing up, I always (do)___*did*___ my assigned chores as quickly as I could.

(1) Blue Man Group (begin) _____ as a kind of musical and theatrical "happening" in New York City in 1987. (2) The original Blue Men, Matt Goldman, Phil Stanton, and Chris Wink, (know) _____ they had a hit on their hands, both in terms of the stage show and the hard-driving music backing the action on stage. (3) They (bring) _____ such energy and fun to their performance that word rapidly spread about the production. (4) In fact, the original shows (become) _____ so popular that Blue Man troupes were established in several other cities, including Boston, Chicago, Orlando, and Las Vegas. (5) A Grammy nomination for their original music (prove) _____ that they are more than just three pretty, blue faces.

CHALLENGE 23.1 Revising the Tense of a Paragraph

1. Ten verbs are listed below. On a separate sheet of paper, use at least five of these verbs in the present tense to write a paragraph of at least seven to ten sentences that concerns preparing a meal or dining out.

feed	eat
give	sit
make	grind
see	bring
break	forget

collaboration

2. Exchange your work with a classmate. On a separate sheet of paper, rewrite the paragraph you receive, changing the tense of each verb to either the past or the past perfect form. Consult the list of irregular verbs (pages 343–346) as necessary. Return the paragraph to the writer.

3. Check the version of your paragraph prepared by your classmate to make sure that the verbs have been correctly changed. Make any necessary corrections.

Working with Forms of *To Be*

The most irregular of the irregular verbs is the verb **to be.** It is the only verb that uses different forms for different persons in the past tense. However, memorizing the various forms of *to be* is not that difficult because many forms do *not* change when the subject changes.

Look at the table on page 348, which shows the most common forms of the verb *to be:*

Common Forms of the Verb *To Be*

When the subject is ...	the present tense is ...	the past tense is ...	the future tense is ...	the past participle is ...
I	am	was	will be	been
he, she, *or* it	is	was	will be	been
we, you, *or* they	are	were	will be	been

ESL NOTE
See "Sentence Basics," pages 543–544; "Word Order," pages 545–546; and "Confusing Verb Forms," pages 549–551, for more on the correct use of forms of *to be*.

As you can see, *will be* and *been* are used with *all* subjects, although different helping verbs are needed for *been*.

To simplify your understanding of *to be*, concentrate on those forms that *do* change, as this version of the same table shows:

When the subject is ...	the present tense is ...	the past tense is ...	Examples
I	am	was	I *am* tired tonight. I *was* more energetic yesterday.
he, she, *or* it	is	was	He *is* late for his dental appointment. She *was* early for her guitar lesson.
we, you, *or* they	are	were	You *are* the best friend I've ever had. They *were* childhood sweethearts before they were married.

If you keep these forms straight, you'll have far fewer problems using *to be*.

In addition, keep in mind two rules when you are using forms of *to be*.

1. Never use *been* without *has, have,* or *had:*

EXAMPLES
          have been
For some time, we *been looking for a house.*

          had been
Just a year earlier, that superstar comedian *been a complete unknown.*

2. Never use *be* by itself as the verb in a sentence:

EXAMPLES
    are
We *be* proud of your achievement.
    are
You *be* the reason for this celebration.

Although you may hear these rules broken in informal speech, such usages are not acceptable for the writing you will do in college and the workplace.

COMPREHENSION AND PRACTICE

Correcting Errors in the Forms of To Be

23.3   In the following paragraph, correct the errors in the use of *be* and *been*. Cross out the error, and write the verb correctly above it, as the example shows.

EXAMPLE
is
Mary ~~be~~ the most experienced worker in the office.

(1) With all the injuries suffered in professional boxing each year, it be hard to understand why we allow the sport to continue. (2) Nevertheless, boxing is still legal, and it been causing permanent damage to many fighters every year. (3) The brutality of boxing been no longer reserved for men only, either. (4) A few years ago, the first professional bouts between female boxers been broadcast. (5) Regardless of the sex of the combatants, the impact of a punch be unbelievably damaging. (6) Fighters be often lifted off their feet when they been hit. (7) The physical **state** of former heavyweight champion Muhammad Ali was the greatest argument that boxing should be banned. (8) At the beginning of his career, Ali been among the most articulate people in the world of sports. (9) Now he be barely able to speak. (10) Ours are a civilized society, so why do we allow this brutality to continue?

CHALLENGE 23.2   Explaining Problem Verbs

1. From your own experiences, from conversations you have overheard, and from dialogue you have heard in movies or on television or radio, what would you say is the most frequent problem people have with the use of a form of the verb *to be*? Write a paragraph of seven to ten sentences in which you identify the problem and offer specific examples of the error.

collaboration

2. Exchange your paragraph with a classmate. Below the paragraph you receive, write a sentence or two explaining why you think people have difficulty with this use of a form of *to be*.

Choosing between *Can* and *Could* and between *Will* and *Would*

Beginning writers often have trouble choosing between **can** and **could** as helping verbs. These two verbs both mean *to be able to*. *Can* is used to indicate the present tense, and *could* is used to indicate the past tense:

EXAMPLES ⌈ At this moment, no one in the conference *can beat* our relay team.

⌊ Last season, no one in the conference *could beat* our relay team.

Sometimes *could* is also used to indicate a *possibility* or *hope* of doing something:

EXAMPLE ⌈ Our competitors wish they *could beat* our relay team.

Beginning writers also have trouble deciding between the helping verbs **will** and **would**. Although both verbs are used to indicate the future, each links the future with a different period of time.

Look at the following versions of the same sentence, with the verbs italicized:

present
⌈ tense ⌉
EXAMPLES ⌈ Monica *thinks* that she *will major* in computer programming.

past
⌈tense⌉
⌊ Monica *thought* that she *would major* in computer programming.

The first sentence says that *right now,* Monica intends to focus on computer programming in the future. The second sentence indicates that *at an earlier time,* she had intended to study computer programming.

In some instances, *would* is also used to indicate a *hope* or *possibility* rather than a certainty, as this sentence shows:

EXAMPLE ⌈ Many people *would* be able to save if they budgeted carefully.

**COMPREHENSION
AND PRACTICE
23.4**

Correcting Errors in the Use of *Can* and *Could* and *Will* and *Would*

The following passage contains a number of errors in the use of *can* and *could* and *will* and *would.* Correct the errors by crossing out the incorrect word and writing the correct word above it. If a sentence is correct as written, write *OK* above it. Use the example as a guide.

will
EXAMPLE ⌈ I don't know if I ~~would~~ be available to begin work on Monday.

(1) Burn victims will face a far more difficult recovery if it were not for the development of artificial skin. (2) The Food and Drug Administration (FDA) in 2001 approved an artificial skin that can be used in grafting procedures. (3) Up until then, patients can expect attempts at skin grafting to fail more often than not. (4) When a person is severely burned, in many cases only the outer layer of skin would grow back. (5) If the skin graft fails to attach itself to healthy tissue, the procedure would fail. (6) So, before artificial skin

became available, the best that burn patients can hope for was a reduction in the number of failures. (7) Each time a graft failed, the surgeon will harvest a new graft and begin the procedure again. (8) Each time, infection will be a major threat, endangering the health of the patient, whose immune system was already weakened. (9) The collagen material in this artificial skin, which provides an anchor for the graft, would eventually break down and be absorbed by the body. (10) Researchers are now examining ways to grow genetically engineered skin on the collagen mesh before grafting it so that infection would no longer be such a possibility.

CHALLENGE 23.3 **Analyzing Correct *Can/Could* and *Will/Would* Choices**

1. Imagine that you have been asked to explain the difference between *can* and *could* and between *will* and *would* to a group of middle school students. Do some prewriting to develop some ideas to help you with this explanation.

2. Using your prewriting notes, work with a classmate to write a paragraph of at least seven to ten sentences that focuses on the differences between *can* and *could* and *will* and *would*. Make sure to provide examples of correct and incorrect usage for each word.

collaboration

QUICK STUDY   Student Example

This chapter focuses on elements that don't always match normal standards. Take a look at this paragraph on a related subject, someone you know or have met who doesn't conform:

When I hear the word *nonconformist,* the first person I think of is Billy Hardy, a kid who gone to my high school. Billy always find a way to stand out from everyone else. For example, one time during senior year, he shown up with his hair dyed several different colors. A couple of weeks later, after everybody was used to this style, he arranged it in dread locks. A week after that he shaved his head, which lead to a suspension because the vice principal said he looked like a skinhead. It was a ridiculous move because Billy was actually a very mellow, accepting person with friends from every group in the school. He just laughed about the suspension and enjoyed the three days off from school. Also, even though he could play sports better than most kids in gym class, he will not go out for the athletic teams because he think that kind of competition was a waste of time. Instead, he would rode his mountain bike out to the state reservation and go hiking by himself. In addition, he was probably the smartest kid I have ever met, but he rejected pressure from teachers and administrators to take his studies more seriously. For instance, when he had took the SATs, he earned the highest score in the school, but he wouldn't even go to the award ceremony for the top scorers. He said that high SAT scores didn't mean he was better than anyone else. I have never meet anyone as original as Billy Hardy, and I doubt I ever would.

First complete the following activities in response to this paragraph:

1. Several of the irregular verbs in this paragraph are highlighted. Above the verb, write the version of the verb that you think should be used. Then check your answers against the lists supplied in this chapter to see if you have chosen properly.

2. In this paragraph, the organizing strategy of definition plays a significant role. On the lines below, briefly explain how the examples and details in the body of the paragraph contribute to the definition of *nonconformist*.

   _____

   _____

   _____

3. The paragraph features three main supporting ideas, one about appearance, one about sports, and one about academic performance. Do you agree with the current arrangement, or would you have set up the examples differently? On a separate sheet of paper, discuss your opinion of the order of the supporting material, explaining your reasoning.

Now explore the topic in writing. Like the paragraph on pages 351–352, you could discuss someone who qualifies as a nonconformist, or you might focus on one of these subjects related to the subject matter of this chapter:

- an item that isn't up to date or doesn't match what most people have but that you still use or rely on
- why conformity can sometimes be a problem
- an occasion at work, school, or home when what you expected to happen or to experience was radically different from normal
- how to fight the pressure to be just like everyone else

collaboration

4. Exchange your draft with a classmate. Evaluate the paragraph you receive. If you discover any errors, especially in the use of irregular verbs, make a note in the margin and then return the paper to the writer.

5. Consider the comments and corrections your reader has made and create a final draft of your paragraph.

CHAPTER QUICK CHECK Eliminating Problems with Irregular Verbs and *Can* and *Could* and *Will* and *Would*

Proofread the following sentences, and revise any errors you find in the use of irregular verbs *can* and *could* or *will* and *would.* Cross out the incorrect word or words, and write a correct version above it, as the example shows. If a sentence is correct as written, write *OK* above it. In some cases, more than one answer is possible.

EXAMPLE   The fifteen-year-old driver had ~~drank~~ *had drunk* an entire six-pack of beer before he stole my car and crashed it.

(1) Thanks to the wonders of modern technology, the old-fashioned treasure hunt be now a brand-new game. (2) This modern variation of an old activity is called *Geocaching, Geo* for geography and *cache* for something hidden, and it has grew in popularity in the past couple of years. (3) Right now, across the world, thousands of "stashes," generally plastic containers filled with inexpensive trinkets, have been hidden and are waiting to be discovered. (4) The sport was created by a man in Oregon who think of a way to use the formerly classified radio signals from a network of government navigational satellites to explore for "buried treasure." (5) To participate in Geocaching, participants need a computer, a compass, and a hand-held Global Positioning System, or GPS. (6) Participants first went to geocaching.com, a Web site listing the longitude and latitude of caches in a particular area. (7) Players then took these coordinates and enter them into the GPS unit. (8) The GPS device taps into the satellite system, which sends players to within thirty-five feet of the stash. (9) Once participants have this information, they could use hints provided on the Web site to do some old-fashioned detective work and find

where in that thirty-five-foot radius the stash is hidden. (10) Once participants found a particular stash, they often remove one object, replace it with another, record their success on the Web site, and start some research for their next adventure.

SUMMARY EXERCISE Eliminating Problems with Irregular Verbs and *Can* and *Could* and *Will* and *Would*

Proofread the following sentences, and revise any errors you find in the use of irregular verbs *can* and *could* or *will* and *would*. Cross out the incorrect word or words, and write a correct version above it. If a sentence is correct as written, write *OK* above it. In some cases, more than one answer is possible. Some answers may vary.

(1) Today, you could send a greeting card for just about any occasion or person either by traditional mail or electronically. (2) There be plenty of cards for standard events such as birthdays, weddings, and so on, which are available from such online stores as bluemountain.com and egreeting.com, as well as from Websites of such traditional retailers as Hallmark. (3) What is surprising is the range of holidays, occasions, and special needs and concerns addressed through greeting cards.

(4) If you have had no luck in buying the perfect birthday present for someone, you can find a card that apologizes for your failure. (5) You can also bought birthday cards for every variety of relative you can imagine. (6) For example, if you want to get a card created specifically for great-grandmothers or stepsons, you could find one.

(7) In addition to the cards commemorating traditional events such as Thanksgiving, Christmas, Hanukkah, and Valentine's Day, you would find cards for special occasions such as St. Patrick's Day and Halloween. (8) The list continues to grow, too. (9) For example, cards celebrating Kwanzaa recently been added to stores across the nation.

(10) If your boss just gave birth, you don't need to worry. (11) There be cards to mark the occasion. (12) You can chosen between pink ones for girls and blue ones for boys. (13) Do you need a card to apologize to your old friend for not writing sooner? (14) Just check the racks or Web sites, and you could find one.

(15) These cards isn't just for family and close friends, either. (16) They came in different levels of familiarity. (17) For example, if you need a sympathy card for someone you barely known, one is available. (18) There even been greeting cards for ex-spouses and ex-in-laws.

(19) Whether you like humor, sentimentality, or inspirational messages, you would discover a greeting card that suits you. (20) Just head to the nearest card store or go online, and plan to spend some enjoyable time reading over the possibilities.

FOR FURTHER EXPLORATION Irregular Verbs

1. Focus on one of the following topics. Using the prewriting technique—or combination of techniques—best suited to your style, explore the possibilities that the subject holds, and consider what purposes you might fulfill as you write:

   - the difficulty of getting in or staying in shape
   - misconceptions about life in a big city or a small town
   - why rude behavior seems to be increasing
   - whose tweets you follow, or why you have no interest in Twitter

2. Evaluate your prewriting material, identify a focus, and work your way through the rest of the writing process to create a draft essay of at least 500 words on the subject.

collaboration

3. Exchange your draft with a classmate. Check the draft you receive for weaknesses, looking in particular for errors in irregular verb use. Circle any incorrect verbs and write the correct version above it, using the material in this chapter as a guide, and then return the draft to the writer.

4. Revise your essay, correcting any errors in irregular verb use or other problems discovered by your reader.

RECAP Irregular Verbs and Frequently Confused Verbs

Key Terms in This Chapter	Definitions
irregular verbs	verbs that do not form their past tense and past participle in typical ways

Strategies for Learning Irregular Verb Forms: Grouping by Pattern

	Present	Past	Past Participle
All tenses use the same form	let	let	let
	burst	burst	burst
Past tense and past participle use the same form	feel	felt	felt
	mean	meant	meant
In each tense, one letter changes	ring	rang	rung
	drink	drank	drunk
In past tense, one letter changes; in past participle, one letter is added	throw	threw	thrown
	blow	blew	blown

to be	the most challenging irregular verb for writers
	Always use *has, have,* or *had* with *been.*
	Never use *be* alone as a verb.
	Follow the chart below for tenses of *to be.*

Common Forms of the Verb *To Be*

When the subject is …	the present tense is …	the past tense is …	the future tense is …	the past participle is …
I	am	was	will be	been
he, she, *or* it	is	was	will be	been
we, you, *or* they	are	were	will be	been

Verb Pairs Often Confused

can/could	helping verbs that mean *to be able to*
	Use *can* to show present tense.

EXAMPLE	Jayson *can* win the contest.

Use *could* to show past tense, or the possibility or hope of being able to do something.

EXAMPLE	If I *could* sing, I'd join the chorus immediately.

will/would	helping verbs that indicate the future Use *will* to point to the future from the *present*.
	EXAMPLE Howard promises he *will* return before midnight.
	Use *would* to point to the future from the *past* and to indicate a hope or possibility.
	EXAMPLE Howard promised he *would* return before midnight.

Using Odyssey Online with MyWritingLab

For more practice with irregular verbs and frequently confused verbs, go to www.mywritinglab.com.

CHAPTER 24
Passive Voice, Additional Tenses, and Maintaining Consistency in Tense

GETTING STARTED ...

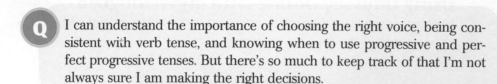

Q I can understand the importance of choosing the right voice, being consistent with verb tense, and knowing when to use progressive and perfect progressive tenses. But there's so much to keep track of that I'm not always sure I am making the right decisions.

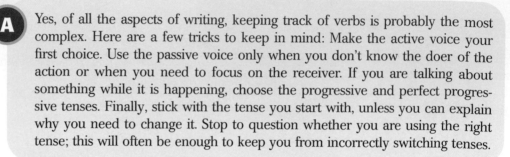

A Yes, of all the aspects of writing, keeping track of verbs is probably the most complex. Here are a few tricks to keep in mind: Make the active voice your first choice. Use the passive voice only when you don't know the doer of the action or when you need to focus on the receiver. If you are talking about something while it is happening, choose the progressive and perfect progressive tenses. Finally, stick with the tense you start with, unless you can explain why you need to change it. Stop to question whether you are using the right tense; this will often be enough to keep you from incorrectly switching tenses.

Overview: Understanding Additional Elements of Verb Use

To work effectively with verbs, you need to do more than master the basic and perfect tenses for regular and irregular verbs. As a writer, you also need to consider the differences between active and passive voice. In addition, you need to learn how to deal with the progressive and perfect progressive tenses. And finally, you need to understand the importance of being consistent in verb tense in a piece of writing.

Navigating This Chapter In this chapter, you will learn how to:

- form the passive and active voices and learn when each is appropriate
- form and use the progressive and perfect progressive tenses correctly
- maintain consistency in verb tense

Forming the Passive and Active Voice

When you combine the past participle form of a verb with a form of *to be,* such as *am, is, was,* or *were,* you are using the **passive voice.** In a sentence with a passive voice verb, the subject *receives* the action:

PASSIVE

┌─ subject ─┐ ┌─verb─┐
Madeleine was told the good news about her promotion by the manager of the production team.

┌── subject ──┐ ┌── verb ──┐
Several *improvements were made* in the customer service area by David.

In most cases, you should choose the active voice because it makes your writing sound more direct, powerful, and concise. In addition, the active voice establishes responsibility for an action. With a verb in the **active voice**, the subject *performs* the action and is the *focus* of the sentence.

ACTIVE

┌─subject─┐   ┌verb┐
The *manager* of the production team *told* Madeleine the good news about her promotion.

┌subject┐┌verb┐
David made several improvements in the customer service area.

ESL Note
See "Sentence Basics," pages 543–544, for more on correct subjects and verbs.

In general, make the active voice your first choice, reserving the passive voice for situations in which it is appropriate. For instance, the passive voice fits when you are discussing actions in which the actor is unknown or emphasizing the receiver of some action, as this example demonstrates:

EFFECTIVE
PASSIVE VOICE

┌─subject─┐ ┌── verb ──┐
The stolen *necklace was returned;* no questions were asked.

COMPREHENSION
AND PRACTICE
24.1

Identifying Passive and Active Voice

Underline the simple subjects and verbs in the following sentences. Watch for compound subjects and verbs and compound sentences. Label active voice verbs with an *A* and passive voice verbs with a *P*. Remember—if the subject receives the action, the sentence is in the passive voice. Use the example to guide you.

EXAMPLE

P
During the police chase, several <u>shots</u> <u>were fired</u>.

(1) Last month, my roommate Trey and I held a yard sale to get rid of our unwanted things. (2) During the week before the sale, the items for sale were all identified. (3) We spent several nights deciding on prices and putting little tags on each item. (4) We also placed a small ad in the community newsletter and on Craigslist, and we posted signs throughout the neighborhood. (5) By 9 A.M. on the Saturday of our sale, our treasures were piled on tables in front of the apartment house. (6) People started arriving by 10. (7) For the next

two hours, every item was handled, but not one thing was bought. (8) At 2 P.M., Trey and I called off our sale. (9) Then everything was carried upstairs where it was originally found. (10) Finally, by 7 P.M. the apartment was straightened out, and we laughed about our short careers as entrepreneurs.

CHALLENGE 24.1   Analyzing the Effect of Active and Passive Voice

1. Rewrite the paragraph from Comprehension and Practice 24.1 on pages 359–360 in two ways. In one version, use every verb in the active voice; in the other, make every verb passive. Use a separate sheet of paper for your paragraphs.

collaboration

2. Working with a classmate, evaluate both versions of the paragraph, and then answer the following questions:
   a. Who or what is the subject in each sentence?
   b. Who or what should be emphasized in each sentence?
   c. Which version of each sentence do you think is most effective? Why?

Using the Progressive and Perfect Progressive Tenses

In addition to using the basic tenses, you also need to master the progressive and perfect progressive tenses.

ESL Note
See "Agreement," pages 546–548, and "Confusing Verb Forms," pages 549–551, for more on forming progressive tenses.

The Progressive Tenses

The simple and perfect tenses that you learned about in Chapters 22 and 23 also have **progressive** forms to indicate ongoing action. For the simple past, present, and future, progressive tenses are formed by adding a form of *to be* to the **present participle** (the *-ing* form) of a verb.

Progressive Tense =	*Form of To Be* +	*Present Participle*	*Example*
Present progressive	am, are, is	going	I *am going.*
Past progressive	was, were	going	I *was going.*
Future progressive	will be	going	I *will be going.*

- The *present progressive tense* indicates something that is currently ongoing. (I *am taking* piano lessons.)
- The *past progressive tense* indicates something that was ongoing in the past. (She *was serving* an internship while she attended the university.)
- The *future progressive tense* indicates something that will be ongoing in the future. (They *will be showing* slides continuously throughout the open house.)

ESL Note
See "Confusing Verb Forms," pages 549–551, for more on the correct use of *has.*

The Perfect Progressive Tenses

You form the **perfect progressive tenses** by using the *-ing* form of a verb with *have been, has been, had been,* or *will have been.*

Perfect Progressive Tense	= Helping Verb +	Present Participle	Example
Present perfect progressive	has been, have been	studying	She *has been studying.*
Past perfect progressive	had been	studying	She *had been studying.*
Future perfect progressive	will have been	studying	She *will have been studying.*

- The *present perfect progressive tense* indicates an action that began in the past and is still ongoing. (Our membership *has been growing* steadily for five years.)
- The *past perfect progressive tense* indicates an action that had been happening in the past but that stopped before the present. (Until 1996, our membership *had been growing.*)
- The *future perfect progressive tense* indicates an action that will be ongoing in the future but that will end before something else begins. (By 2012 our membership *will have been growing* for six straight years.)

Remember—all of these tenses allow you to express actions in time with great precision. It is much more important to learn how to use them than it is to be able to name them or even identify them. When you do the exercises below, refer back to this section if you get confused about the correct tense.

COMPREHENSION AND PRACTICE 24.2

Recognizing the Progressive and Perfect Progressive Tenses

In the sentences below, underline the progressive and perfect progressive tense verbs. Then, in the space above the line, label those verbs, as the example shows. Use the following abbreviations to label the verbs.

PPr = present progressive   *PPPr* = present perfect progressive

PaPr = past progressive   *PaPPr* = past perfect progressive

FPr = future progressive   *FPPr* = future perfect progressive

EXAMPLE   Lately, I have been spending all my spare time surfing the Internet.
                         PPPr

(1) As a result of my government class, I am becoming a news junkie. (2) In the first week of this class, we had been discussing current affairs. (3) One morning, the instructor was lecturing on the role played by the media in all news events. (4) I had already been considering a subscription to *Newsweek*, so I decided to follow through. (5) Within a couple weeks, I was

also scanning two or three newspapers online every day. (6) The more I read, the more I have been noticing the different ways print reporters present the news. (7) My television viewing habits have been changing, too. (8) Now instead of watching sitcoms or some prime-time dramas, I find that I am turning on CNN every night. (9) In addition, I have been watching other all-news stations like MSNBC, Fox News, and CNBC. (10) I will soon be declaring a major, and my new interest in the news is leading me to consider history, government, and pre-law.

COMPREHENSION AND PRACTICE

Using the Present Progressive Tense

24.3 For each sentence below, change the present tense verb in parentheses to a progressive tense verb. Write the correct verb form in the blank space, as the example shows.

EXAMPLE   My sister (watches) _____*is watching*_____ *Nightline* now.

(1) Right now at work, I (take) _____ a safety course. (2) The instructor (try) _____ hard to make the class interesting, and I think she (succeed) _____. (3) At this point, we (evaluate) _____ our work environment to make sure our building is as safe as possible. (4) In fact, two of my co-workers (create) _____ a crisis management plan. (5) In particular, they (concentrate) _____ on ensuring that everyone in the building knows exactly where to go in the case of fire. (6) Also, the course (cover) _____ basic first aid techniques. (7) For example, we (learn) _____ how to recognize things like shock, complications from diabetes, and allergic reactions. (8) In addition, we (review) _____ how to help someone who (choke) _____ by using the Heimlich maneuver. (9) Most important of all, everybody (learn) _____ how to perform CPR. (10) So far, all the people on my crew feel that we (gain) _____ a truly valuable education.

CHALLENGE 24.2   Working with Verb Tenses in Your Writing

1. Choose two verbs from the list of irregular verbs on pages 343–346 and two regular verbs. Write three sentences for each, using verbs in the progressive and perfect progressive tenses.

collaboration

2. Exchange your writing with a classmate. On the paper you receive, underline the verbs and label them as either progressive (*P*) or perfect progressive (*PP*). Then return the sentences to the writer.

Maintaining Consistency in Tense

ESL Note
See "Agreement," pages 546–548, for more on maintaining consistency in tense.

In addition to choosing the correct tense for your sentence context, you must use that tense *consistently*. To maintain **consistency in tense**, use a logical pattern for your verb choices, and avoid switching carelessly from one tense to another. Actions or situations occurring at the present time call for the present tense. If they happened earlier, the past tense is needed, and if they have not yet happened, then the future tense is called for.

It's important to use a consistent time frame within a paragraph and especially within a sentence. To write about past events, use the past tense; don't switch, without good reason, to the present or the future. Use present tense verbs to write about events occurring now and on a regular basis.

PAST TENSE	The pitcher ~~stands~~ *stood* on the mound and *stared* at the batter.
PRESENT TENSE	The pitcher *stands* on the mound and ~~stared~~ *stares* at the batter.

The tense you choose will depend upon the context of your writing. You must make the choice that is most logical to help readers understand the thoughts or events you are writing about.

COMPREHENSION AND PRACTICE
24.4

Keeping Verb Tense Consistent

Several sentences in the following passage suffer from inconsistency in verb tense. Cross out each error, and write the correct verb form above it. Use the example as a guide.

EXAMPLE
As I walked along Main Street, suddenly I ~~see~~ *saw* my friend Kelly with somebody I didn't recognize.

(1) One of the most unusual places I've seen is Clarkin Caverns. (2) Even though we go there almost nine years ago, I still remember what a strange and wonderful place it is. (3) The last time I am there, I first have to go into a small ticket center. (4) Once there were enough people to make up a group, a guide

walks us to an extra large elevator, which quickly lowers us about sixty feet beneath the surface of the earth. (5) When I stepped out of the elevator, I am amazed at what I saw. (6) All around me were beautiful rock formations, and as the group walks around, the guide talked about the cavern. (7) She explains the differences between *stalactites,* which "grow" down from the roof of the cavern, and *stalagmites,* which "grow" up from the ground. (8) As we walked, I keep looking all around, because I was afraid a bat was going to fly down and get caught in my hair. (9) At the end of the tour, our guide puts out the lights for a minute so we can experience total darkness. (10) It is so dark that I can't even see my hands in front of me; never had a place felt peaceful and spooky at the same time.

CHALLENGE 24.3 **Analyzing the Effect of Inconsistent Tense**

1. Reread the paragraph in Comprehension and Practice 24.4 in its original (uncorrected) form, and then write a brief paragraph in which you explain the effect that the inconsistent verb tense has on your ability to understand the story.

collaboration

2. Exchange your assessment of the inconsistent verb tense with a classmate, and compare your evaluations. Then, working together, decide which of the tense switches creates the most confusion, and write a two- or three-sentence passage identifying the problem and explaining why you think this switch causes the most difficulty for a reader.

QUICK STUDY **Student Example**

This chapter discusses different aspects of action and consistency. Take a look at the following paragraph on a related subject—how someone reacted to an awkward or unpleasant situation:

> The thing I remember on my first trip to an airport was how gracefully the woman behind the airline counter reacted to some irate customers. The weather that morning was terrible, and no planes could take off for a few hours because of the thick fog. My own flight wasn't supposed to leave until 2 P.M., so I just sat at the gate and hoped the weather would improve by then.

From nine to noon, customer after customer went up to the attendant to ask about the status of their flights. No matter how agitated or angry the people were, all their questions were answered by the woman calmly and politely. She told them that the entire airport was fogged in and promised to do her best to reschedule them once the weather improved. The worst customer was a man about forty years old, dressed in shorts and a brightly flowered shirt. This obnoxious man had been complaining loudly to everyone around him. When the counter was reached by him, he began yelling at the attendant and pounding on the counter. He said he had been planning this trip for a year and demanded that she immediately put him, his wife, and their two children on a plane so they could catch their connecting flight to Disney World. His wife and kids just stood there. They were staring at the floor, obviously totally embarrassed by this unnecessary scene. Now whenever I am thinking of yelling at someone, I think of how ridiculous that man looked and try to react as coolly and calmly as that attendant did.

First complete the following activities in response to this paragraph:

1. A number of subjects and verbs in this paragraph are highlighted. Using the material in this chapter to guide you, label any highlighted progressive (P) and perfect progressive verbs (PP). Also, identify any highlighted active (Act) and passive (Pass) voice verbs, and then, on a separate sheet of paper, change the sentences containing awkward passive voice verbs so that they are in the active voice, as the examples in the chapter illustrate.

2. On the following lines, briefly explain the main point as expressed in the topic sentence and describe how the information in the body of the paragraph supports this main idea.

_____

_____

_____

_____

3. Reread the paragraph and, on a separate sheet of paper, list all the verbs that are in the active voice. How do these active voice verbs affect the impact of the paragraph? Use the lines below for your answer.

_____

_____

_____

_____

Now explore the topic in writing. As the paragraph on pages 364–365 does, you could concentrate on witnessing public rudeness. You might also focus on one of these topics related to the subject matter of this chapter:

- a time when you regret not taking action
- whether Amazon's new e-book reader, the Kindle, will replace printed books
- a gift that keeps on giving
- actions people can take to improve their lives

collaboration

4. Exchange your draft with a classmate. Evaluate the paragraph you receive. If you discover any problem spots, especially concerning voice, tense, and consistency, circle the errors and then return the paper to the writer.

5. Consider the comments and corrections your reader has made and create a final draft of your paragraph.

CHAPTER QUICK CHECK Mastering Voice, Progressive and Perfect Progressive Tenses, and Consistency in Verb Tense

The following passage contains a number of the errors and weaknesses in verb use outlined in this chapter. Using the various examples throughout the chapter to guide you, identify problems with voice, tense, and consistency. Cross out the incorrect form, and write the correct form above it, as the example shows. In some cases, more than one correct answer is possible.

EXAMPLE

entered
After Karen and Eddie ~~enter~~ the plane, they quickly stored their carry-on luggage and took their seats.

(1) Car-sharing programs, popular for some time in Europe and Canada, are gain converts in such U.S. cities as San Francisco, New York, Washington, D.C., and Boulder, Colorado. (2) Soon, organizers had been establishing car-sharing groups in several other major U.S. cities, including Columbus, Ohio,

and Santa Barbara, California. (3) These kinds of programs benefit both the individuals involved and the cities in which they operated. (4) After all, when several people will be sharing rather than owning cars exclusively, fewer cars clog busy city streets. (5) To join a group, a yearly fee is paid by participants in the range of $200 to $500. (6) In return, members were able to use cars owned by the organization for a fee in the range of $2.00 to $8.00 an hour. (7) The yearly fee covered registration, insurance, and maintenance costs, so members are generally responsible for only a small mileage charge, if anything. (8) When they had been going to need a car, members call or log into the organization's Web site and make a reservation. (9) Then a car is picked up by the users at one of several lots around the city. (10) When users are done with the car, they simply returned it to the same site, turn in the keys, and head for home, free from the headaches that car owners face.

SUMMARY EXERCISE Mastering Voice, Progressive and Perfect Progressive Tenses, and Consistency in Verb Tense

The following passage contains a number of the errors in verb use outlined in this chapter. Using the various examples throughout the chapter to guide you, identify errors in voice, tense, and consistency. Cross out the incorrect form, and write the correct form above it. In some cases, more than one correct answer is possible.

(1) I often wish I spend more time reading as a child. (2) If more reading has been done by me, I wouldn't now feel so embarrassed and frustrated every time I sat down to read.

(3) When I start elementary school, I missed almost half of first grade because of illness. (4) While all my classmates are learning the basics of reading, I was at home in bed. (5) In spite of this, at the end of the year, I am promoted anyway, and my difficulties began.

(6) I never misbehaved in class, so breaks were always given to me by my teachers. (7) When I read aloud, if I hesitate over a word, my teacher would say it for me. (8) As a result, I become very good at pretending to be able to read.

(9) Although I was fall further behind each year, I keep getting promoted. (10) When courses were failed by me, I went to summer school. (11) Even though I attended summer classes, I am still not learning anything.

(12) In my senior year of high school, I have earned straight D's for the first term, except for English, which I will be failing. (13) Because she is concerned about me, my English teacher arranged for me to take a reading test. (14) When the test was finished by me, I discovered that I am not even reading on the sixth-grade level. (15) My teacher gets me a special reading tutor, and after working hard the rest of the year, I am able to read well enough to graduate with my class.

(16) When I am thinking about college, however, all my shame and frustration returned. (17) I failed the college's reading placement test, and a remedial reading course had to be taken by me. (18) I will be determined not to lose this chance to make something of myself, so I work as hard as I could.

(19) I'm proud to say that by the end of that course, I am reading better than any of the other students in the class. (20) I still felt insecure about my ability, so I was planning to keep working to change my attitude.

FOR FURTHER EXPLORATION Voice, Tense, and Consistency

1. Focus on one of the following topics, using the prewriting technique—or combination of techniques—that you prefer to generate ideas, considering what purposes you might fulfill as you write:

   - an effective way to deal with a demanding or difficult person
   - the hottest, coldest, or most uncomfortable day you can ever remember
   - the easiest academic subject
   - the most important personal quality

2. Evaluate your prewriting material, identify a focus, and work your way through the rest of the writing process to create a draft essay of at least 500 words on this subject.

collaboration

3. Exchange your draft with a classmate. Check the draft you receive for weaknesses, paying particular attention to voice, tense, and consistency. Circle any errors, using the material in this chapter as a guide, and then return the draft to the writer.

4. Revise your essay, correcting any errors in verb use or other problems discovered by your reader.

RECAP Passive Voice, Additional Tenses, and Maintaining Consistency in Tense

Key Terms in This Chapter	Definitions
passive voice	a characteristic of sentences in which the subject receives the action of the verb
	EXAMPLE　　Her bicycle was stolen.
active voice	a characteristic of sentences in which the subject does or is responsible for the action
	EXAMPLE　　A photographer took a picture of the scene.
progressive tenses	forms of a verb created by combining some form of *to be* with the present participle of another verb
	Progressive forms express ongoing actions or situations.
	EXAMPLE　　Anne and Michael *are talking* about buying a house.
	EXAMPLE　　Louis *was reading* in the library.
	EXAMPLE　　Laura *will be wallpapering* her room soon.
present participle	formed by adding *-ing* to the basic form of regular and irregular verbs
	EXAMPLE　　play*ing;* ris*ing*
perfect progressive tenses	forms of a verb created by combining some form of *to have* with the present participle of another verb
	Perfect progressive forms express actions or situations that occur over a period of time.
	EXAMPLE　　Anne and Michael *have been talking* about buying a house.
	EXAMPLE　　Louis *had been reading* in the library.
	EXAMPLE　　By 8 P.M., Laura *will have been wallpapering* her room for five hours.

Key Terms in This Chapter	Definitions
consistency in tense	refers to a logical pattern for the verbs within a sentence, paragraph, or essay Consistency requires avoiding careless mixing of verb tenses and maintaining a unified time frame within a piece of writing.

INCONSISTENT	I *answer* all the questions that were asked.
CONSISTENT	I *answered* all the questions that were asked.

Forming the Progressive Tenses

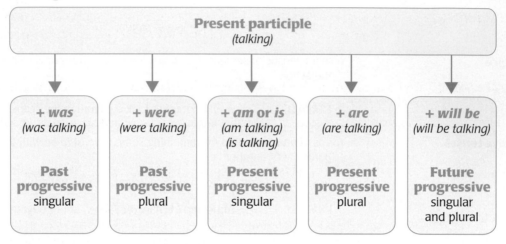

Present participle *(talking)*				
+ was *(was talking)* **Past progressive** singular	**+ were** *(were talking)* **Past progressive** plural	**+ am or is** *(am talking)* *(is talking)* **Present progressive** singular	**+ are** *(are talking)* **Present progressive** plural	**+ will be** *(will be talking)* **Future progressive** singular and plural

Forming the Perfect Progressive Tenses

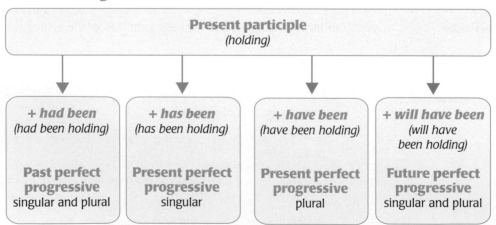

Present participle *(holding)*			
+ had been *(had been holding)* **Past perfect progressive** singular and plural	**+ has been** *(has been holding)* **Present perfect progressive** singular	**+ have been** *(have been holding)* **Present perfect progressive** plural	**+ will have been** *(will have been holding)* **Future perfect progressive** singular and plural

Using Odyssey Online with MyWritingLab

For more practice with passive voice, additional tenses, and maintaining consistency in tense, go to www.mywritinglab.com.

> **portfolio • noun** (pl. **portfolios**) … **2** a set of pieces of creative work intended to demonstrate a person's ability. ORIGIN Italian *portafogli,* from *portare* 'carry' + *foglio* 'leaf'.

—*Compact Oxford English Dictionary*

This portfolio allows you to demonstrate what you have learned about different aspects of verb use. In many ways, verbs are the hubs of all sentences, the words that identify the actions, meanings, or connections between and among the other words. Take this opportunity to practice subject–verb agreement (Chapter 21) as well as to identify the different forms of regular verbs (Chapter 22) and irregular verbs (Chapter 23). You can also test your comprehension and skills related to active and passive voice and the importance of consistency in verb tense. To mark your progress up to this point, prepare the following portfolio:

BEST WORK Select your best work from the assignments completed for this section. Check with a classmate or other reader if you aren't sure which of these assignments is your best work.

ESSAY ANSWER Read the following opening paragraphs from a March 27, 1964, article in the *New York Times* concerning a crime that had occurred on March 14. To this day, more than forty-five years later, the circumstances of this crime almost defy belief:

Thirty-Eight Who Saw Murder Didn't Call the Police
By Martin Gansberg

For more than half an hour 38 respectable, law-abiding citizens in Queens watched a killer stalk and stab a woman in three separate attacks in Kew Gardens.

Twice their chatter and the sudden glow of their bedroom lights interrupted him and frightened him off. Each time he returned, sought her out, and stabbed her again. Not one person telephoned the police during the assault; one witness called after the woman was dead.

Now choose one of the following essay questions and prepare a 200- to 300-word answer.

- As this article points out, Kitty Genovese was the victim of a horrible crime, made all the more terrible because no one came to her aid. Her assailant left and returned three times over a thirty-five-minute period, inflicting a total of seventeen stab wounds, yet none of the neighbors who heard her cries helped her or called the police until after she was dead. The real question here is, why didn't they help? Offer your theory as to why none of Kitty Genovese's neighbors did anything to help her in the early morning hours of March 14, 1964.

- While we often hear or read stories of strangers who have gone to the aid of someone in need, there are other cases where bystanders do nothing, refusing to get involved in any way. Do you think people who observe a crime and don't help the victim or call the authorities should face criminal charges themselves? Explain your position thoroughly, backing up your answer with several specific examples.

TIMED WRITING

TIMED WRITING

Consider this definition of an *artifact*:

> an object made by a human being, typically an item of cultural or historical interest

Go through your belongings and identify an item that fits in this category. Then in thirty minutes, complete a writing of around 200 to 300 words on one of the following topics:

- Explain the function or usefulness of your artifact to a reader who is unfamiliar with it. You'll probably find what you learned about definition (Chapter 9), cause and effect (Chapter 11), process (Chapter 8), comparison and contrast (Chapter 10), and description (Chapter 6) especially helpful in creating your writing.

- Explain the personal connection or significance your artifact has for you to a reader who is unfamiliar with it. You'll probably find what you learned about narration (Chapter 5), example (Chapter 7), description (Chapter 6), and comparison and contrast (Chapter 10) especially useful in creating your writing.

REFLECTION

Working with verbs, as the four chapters in Part 5 of *Odyssey* demonstrate, can be complicated and confusing for a number of reasons. You have to make sure that the verbs you use are appropriate matches for your subjects. You need to be aware of all the forms and tenses of verbs, which is especially difficult when they are irregular. On top of all that, you need to choose wisely between active and passive voice and to be consistent in terms of verb tense. So, of all these potential difficulties, which one gives you the most trouble? Write a paragraph of seven to ten sentences in which you specify this aspect of verb use and explain why you find it so hard to keep straight. Discuss at least one example of a mistake you have made in one of your paragraphs or essays.

PART 6

Keeping Your Writing Correct

CHAPTER 25

Nouns: Working Effectively with Words That Name

GETTING STARTED...

 Q I rely a lot on words that name people, places, and things—nouns. What can I do to make sure I use these words correctly?

 A Nouns play a significant role in your writing. For the most part, working with nouns is fairly straightforward. The *number* of the noun—whether it is singular or plural—probably causes the most frequent problems. As long as you make sure to use the correct singular or plural form and to recognize any cue words that signal number, you should be fine.

Overview: Understanding Nouns

To understand and keep straight all the elements and aspects of the world around us, we name them with words called **nouns.** Nouns are classified into two groups. *Common nouns* name a nonspecific person or thing—*a police officer, a continent, a short story.* **Proper nouns** name a particular person or thing—*Officer Donna Boyd, Asia, "Everyday Use"*—and are always introduced by a capital letter. More important, nouns have two forms. *Singular nouns* name individual people or things; *plural nouns* name several people or things. Correct noun form can be tricky, so mastering this aspect of noun use is crucial to your success as a writer.

Navigating This Chapter In this chapter, you will learn how to:

- turn a singular noun into a plural one
- recognize singular nouns that end in *-s*
- use collective nouns effectively
- use cue words to identify the number of a noun

Reviewing the Function and Form of Nouns

Nouns are the most versatile part of speech in English. Although writers don't generally think about all of them when they write, nouns can perform six different functions in a sentence:

- Nouns can serve as a *subject* of a sentence, as this example shows:

┌subject┐
EXAMPLE   Many small *farms* have gone out of business in the past decade.

ESL Note
See "Agreement," pages
546–548, for more on
nouns as subjects.

- Nouns can also serve as a **predicate nominative,** the word that answers "Who or What?" *after* a linking verb (such as *is* or *was*), as this example shows:

predicate
┌nominative
EXAMPLE   Kevin was the *goalie* for the varsity soccer team.

- In addition, nouns can serve as a **direct object,** the word that answers "Whom or What?" *after* an action verb, as this example shows:

direct
┌object┐
EXAMPLE   Karen mailed the *letter* at the campus mail center.

- Nouns can serve as an **indirect object** as well, the word that answers "To Whom or For Whom?" or "To What or For What?" *after* an action verb, as this example shows:

indirect
┌ object ┐
EXAMPLE   The pharmacist gave the *customer* a brochure explaining the drug's side effects.

- Nouns can also serve as the *object of a preposition,* the word that follows a preposition and completes a *prepositional phrase,* as this example shows:

object of the
┌ preposition
EXAMPLE   The coat in the *closet* originally cost $200.

- Finally, nouns can serve as an **appositive,** a word that helps explain or illustrate another noun, as this example shows:

appositive┐
EXAMPLE   The child clutched her favorite *toy,* a small stuffed *kitten.*

Regardless of a noun's function, you must select the proper form—singular or plural—for each situation. Fortunately, changing nouns from singular to plural is generally easy. To make most nouns plural, simply add -*s* to the singular form:

Singular	*Plural*
cup	cup**s**
decision	decision**s**
flower	flower**s**

Some nouns form their plurals in other ways. For example, most words that end in *-ch, -sh, -x,* or *-s* form their plurals by adding *-es:*

Singular	Plural
brush	brush**es**
mix	mix**es**
pass	pass**es**
watch	watch**es**

For words that end in a *-y* preceded by a consonant, form the plural by changing the *-y* to *-i* and adding *-es:*

Singular	Plural
candy	cand**ies**
enemy	enem**ies**
eulogy	eulog**ies**
mystery	myster**ies**

Certain words that end in *-f* or *-fe* form their plurals by changing the ending to *-ves:*

Singular	Plural
half	hal**ves**
leaf	lea**ves**
shelf	shel**ves**
wife	wi**ves**

Combined or *hyphenated* words form their plurals by adding *-s* to the main word:

Singular	Plural
attorney-at-law	attorney**s**-at-law
brother-in-law	brother**s**-in-law
maid of honor	maid**s** of honor
runner-up	runner**s**-up

Some common words form their plurals by changing letters within the word:

Singular	Plural
foot	f**ee**t
man	m**e**n
mouse	m**ice**
tooth	t**ee**th

Some words have the same singular and plural forms:

Singular	Plural
deer	**deer**
rice	**rice**
sheep	**sheep**
species	**species**

In addition, some words that end in *-o* form their plurals by adding *-s: sopranos* and *pros*. Other words that end in *-o* form their plurals by adding *-es: tomatoes* and *heroes*. Some words from foreign languages form their plurals in keeping with their original language: *analysis/analyses* and *crisis/crises*.

If you have a question about the plural form of a noun, a dictionary should be your first stop. It gives the plural ending after the singular form if the noun forms its plural in an irregular way.

COMPREHENSION AND PRACTICE

25.1

Identifying the Function of Nouns

In each of the following sentences, a noun is underlined. Using the discussion of the function of nouns on page 375 to guide you, write the function of each under-lined noun above it, as the example shows:

predicate nominative

EXAMPLE The manager of the club was once a professional <u>dancer</u> herself.

(1) Rock guitarist Carlos Santana has enjoyed a remarkable <u>career</u> in music that has now spanned five decades. (2) Santana first came into national <u>prominence</u> at the original Woodstock music festival with his capti-vating performance before the half million fans in attendance. (3) From that point, his <u>infusion</u> of Latin and Afro-Cuban flavors into a rock rhythm caught the ears of America. (4) *Santana,* his 1969 debut <u>album</u>, and *Abraxas,* his 1970 multiple platinum follow-up album, produced several hit songs. (5) Some of these songs, including "Evil Ways," "Black Magic Woman," and *"Oye Como Va,"* are still favorite <u>selections</u> on radio stations across the country. (6) Throughout the <u>years</u> that followed, Santana contin-ued recording and performing, using the opportunity to remind the world of the need for peace, tolerance, and compassion. (7) In 1998, Santana's <u>accomplishments</u> were recognized by his peers when he was inducted into the Rock and Roll Hall of Fame. (8) In 1999, Santana's star rose once again with *Supernatural,* his 36th <u>album</u>. (9) *Supernatural* earned the <u>guitarist</u> nine Grammys and to date has sold well in excess of 10 million copies. (10) Santana's follow-up album, *Shaman,* released in 2002, is another

collaborative <u>effort</u>, matching the master guitarist with a wide variety of artists, including opera legend Placido Domingo.

CHALLENGE 25.1   **Recognizing the Function of Nouns**

collaboration

1. Copy two consecutive paragraphs from one of the reading selections in Part 7, from a newspaper, magazine, or online article; or from another of your textbooks. Make a list on a separate sheet of paper of each noun in the passage and the function it is serving.

2. Exchange your paragraphs and the list of nouns with a classmate. Check the paragraphs and the list you receive and put a ✓ next to any noun for which an incorrect function has been listed. Return the material to your classmate.

3. Evaluate any potential problems your reader has identified and make any necessary changes.

Considering Singular Nouns Ending in -s, Collective Nouns, and Cue Words

Although most nouns are made plural by adding -s, not all nouns that end in -s are plural. Words that fall in this category include the following:

Singular Words That End in -s

economics	mathematics	mumps	physics	statistics
ethics	measles	news	politics	

ESL Note
See "Agreement," pages 546–548, for more on the correct use of collective nouns.

Because these words end in -s, it's easy to choose the incorrect verb form when one of these nouns is the subject. Remember—these words are singular and therefore call for singular verb forms. See Chapter 21, "Subject–Verb Agreement," for more information.

Collective nouns are words that stand for *groups* of items or individuals. Here is a list of common collective nouns:

Common Collective Nouns

audience	faculty	group	populace
class	family	herd	school
committee	flock	jury	team
congregation	government	office	tribe

Even though they represent a number of people or things, collective nouns are singular in form. In most cases, a collective noun used as a subject requires a singular form of the verb, as the following sentences illustrate:

EXAMPLES

The *jury wants* to see a copy of the trial transcript.

The *faculty looks* forward to meeting the incoming students.

You should also become familiar with the following **cue words.** When they precede the subject, they alert you that it is singular and therefore calls for a singular verb.

Common Singular Cue Words

ESL Note
See "Articles," pages 551–552, for more on the correct use of articles.

a, an	every
another	neither
each	one
either	

EXAMPLES

Every student *needs* a notebook to use as a journal.

Either book *is* a good choice as a gift.

Also be aware of the following words. When they precede the subject, they cue you that it is plural and therefore calls for a plural verb.

Common Plural Cue Words

all	many
both	several
few	some

EXAMPLES

Many children *are* actually afraid of clowns.

Several stray cats *live* in my neighborhood.

COMPREHENSION AND PRACTICE

25.2

Using Collective Nouns and Verbs Correctly

Complete the following sentences by adding a present tense verb with modifiers. Underline the collective noun or cue word in the first part of the sentence to help you choose the correct present tense verb. Use the example to guide you.

EXAMPLE

The herd of cows *heads for the barn like clockwork at 5 P.M.*

1. Every time we try to eat outdoors, a swarm of wasps _____

_____

2. Each month, the congregation at that church _____

_____

3. Few chairs in the waiting room _____

_____

4. Neither winner of the tri-state lottery _____

_____

5. Many students enrolled at this college _____

_____

6. The audience at the opening night performance of most plays usually _____

_____

7. By next year, the team of twenty scientists _____

_____

8. Many art museums throughout the country _____

_____

9. Every year, the activities committee at the neighborhood center _____

_____

10. Another sign encouraging government officials _____

_____

CHALLENGE 25.2 **Writing Sentences Using Singular Words Ending in -s and Cue Words**

1. On a separate sheet of paper, write a sentence for each of the following words in which the word is the subject of a present tense verb. Review the examples in Chapter 21, "Subject–Verb Agreement," if you need further guidance:

economics	audience	government	statistics	jury
mathematics	committee	news	politics	audience

collaboration

2. Exchange your list of sentences with a classmate. Check the sentences you receive to make sure the words have been used correctly and then return the sentences to the writer.

QUICK STUDY   **Student Example**

This chapter focuses on the means of identification and naming things. Consider the following paragraph, which focuses on a related subject, the name that would be perfect for a new model of an item, in this case, a new brand of sneakers designed for the basketball court:

A great brand name for a newly designed pair of sneakers for basketball would be "Showtime." This title is perfect because of the way basketball is played today at all levels in the United States. Coaches used to teach their players fundamentals like passing, ball-handling, setting up a play, and playing tight defense. But that's not the way it is anymore. Now basketball isn't so much about being part of a team but about being an individual player. The goal for most players now seems to be to become a star, the flashier the better. ESPN and network broadcasts show the performances of top NBA players, the heroes of basketball. But these broadcasts have given fans the wrong idea about the way the game should be played. Of course, kids are the most impressionable fans of all. Naturally, they imitate the outrageous shots and trash-talking style they've seen instead of concentrating on learning how to pass or to wait for the best shot. They want to play the way that their heroes play on television. As a result, basketball today has become as much a show as a game, so that makes "Showtime" the ideal name for a new brand of basketball sneakers.

First complete the following activities in response to this paragraph:

1. Four sentences in the preceding paragraph are highlighted. First, circle all the nouns in these sentences. Then, using the material on page 375 to guide you, write above each noun the function it is serving, either *subject* (S), *direct object* (DO), *indirect object* (IO), *object of the preposition* (OP), *predicate nominative* (PN), or *appositive* (A).

2. Writing of any type is effective when it communicates a clear message to a reader. In your view, what role do the various nouns in this paragraph play in

helping an audience understand the point being made? Use the lines below for your answer.

_____

_____

_____

3. Assess the final sentence of the paragraph. Then, on the lines below, briefly explain whether you think it serves as an effective concluding sentence and why.

_____

_____

_____

_____

Now explore the topic in writing. You could discuss the name you would give a new model or version of a car or some other product and why, as the paragraph above does. You might also concentrate on one of these subjects related to the subject matter of this chapter:

- a place you wish you had never visited
- a cue or hint that you missed or misunderstood, leading to a social disaster
- an idea, belief, or concept that many people find difficult to understand
- the story behind a first name or nickname, either your own or that of someone you know

collaboration

4. Exchange your draft with a classmate. Evaluate the paragraph you receive. If you discover any errors, especially with forms of irregular and collective nouns and with singular nouns ending in -s, circle them and write the correct form above each incorrect one. Then return the paper to the writer.

5. Consider the comments and corrections your reader has made and create a final draft of your paragraph.

CHAPTER QUICK CHECK Working with Nouns

Each sentence in the following passage contains an error in noun or cue word use. First review the discussion of the number of nouns, collective nouns, and cue words. Then correct each error by crossing out the incorrect word and writing the correct form above it, as the example shows.

EXAMPLE   It took me over an hour to install the new ~~shelfs~~. *shelves*

(1) Storys of computer hackers appear frequently in the news because of the ingenious ways that these computer whizzes manipulate computer programs and networks. (2) Often, the articles discuss such actions as illegal entrys into classified government networks, the release of computer viruses, or the theft of credit card numbers. (3) But each hackers argue that they are being unfairly accused of such crimes. (4) They say that the problem isn't with hackers but with a group of computer vandals and thiefs called *crackers*. (5) True hackers aren't interested in using computers to create serious worrys or problems for others. (6) Even when a few hacker break into some network, they do so for the thrill of doing it, not to cause trouble. (7) With crackers, however, the motivationes are quite different. (8) Some crackers use their considerable computer abilitys to break into a network and corrupt or destroy files, often costing the affected organizations thousands and thousands of dollars. (9) Others intentionally commit illegal acts such as pirating software, making free long-distance calls, or obtaining supposedly "secure" information on individuals and companys. (10) Hackers, who take pride in their knowledge and skilles, object to being lumped together with a group that misuses their expertise.

SUMMARY EXERCISE Working with Nouns

Each sentence in the following passage contains an error in noun or cue word use. First review the discussion of the number of nouns, collective nouns, and cue words. Then correct each error by crossing out the incorrect word and writing the correct form above it. In some cases, more than one answer may be possible.

(1) Because of advances in technology, every educators feel that cursive writing is fast becoming a thing of the past. (2) At one time, good penmanship was considered one of the most important signes of professionalism. (3) Even today, many people still view handwriting styles as indicationes of individuality

and maturity. (4) Now, however, with many emphasis on using computers for writing, the art of handwriting is losing its status.

(5) At one time, all student was taught handwriting as a separate subject in school. (6) In each cases, handwriting teachers were chosen because their own writing was considered excellent. (7) Students learned cursive by first practicing different strokes and ovales that they copied from handwriting books. (8) Once these beginneres had mastered the various shapes, they would begin work on actual letters and numbers. (9) The childs were then graded on the precision and accuracy of their handwriting.

(10) In every schools today, however, nobody seems concerned about handwriting instruction. (11) According to a recent article, a typical elementary school classes spends very little time on handwriting. (12) Apparently, the various other educational crisies that must be handled in the classroom take priority over handwriting.

(13) Not everyone is concerned that those dayes are a thing of the past in some regions. (14) In fact, many people see this change as one of the many journeyes students must follow to become part of the electronic age. (15) In some elementary schools today, as soon as children learn the alphabet, a team of teachers show them how to use a computer. (16) They quickly learn to write all their storys electronically, using a keyboard. (17) Some proponents of the change say that in the future, the only scenarioes that will call for handwriting will be taking notes in class, completing written tests, or writing signatures.

(18) Cursive writing of one sort or another has been around for centurys, so no one should seriously expect it to disappear. (19) In fact, good argumentes can be made to ensure that it doesn't. (20) Probably the best solution is to teach students handwriting and word processing so that they can take advantage of both wayes of recording their ideas.

FOR FURTHER EXPLORATION Nouns

1. Focus on one of the following topics. Use the prewriting technique—or combination of techniques—that fits your style of working to come up with some preliminary ideas while also considering the purposes you might fulfill in writing about the topic:

   - a cultural or family tradition that you know well
   - how influential you think fate is in life
   - how you would prepare if you knew a catastrophic storm were going to hit your community in twelve hours
   - specific changes you think public high school administrators could make to radically improve students' motivation and performance

2. Evaluate your prewriting material, identify a focus, and work your way through the rest of the writing process to create a draft essay of at least 500 words on this subject.

collaboration

3. Exchange your draft with a classmate. Check the draft you receive for weaknesses, checking in particular for problems with irregular and collective nouns and with singular nouns ending in -s. Circle any incorrect forms, using the material in this chapter to guide you, and write the correct form above each incorrect one. Then return the paper to the writer.

4. Revise your essay, correcting any errors in irregular verb use or other problems discovered by your reader.

RECAP Nouns

Key Terms in This Chapter	Definitions
noun	a word that names a person, place, thing, or idea Form plural nouns by adding -s or following spelling guidelines.
proper noun	a noun introduced by a capital letter that names a specific person or thing
predicate nominative	a word that answers "Who or What?" *after* a linking verb
direct object	a word that answers "Whom or What?" *after* an action verb
indirect object	a word that answers "To Whom or For Whom?" or "To What or For What?" *after* an action verb
appositive	a word that helps to explain or illustrate another noun
collective noun	a noun that stands for a group of items or individuals Collective nouns are singular in form, and generally call for the singular form of the verb. **EXAMPLE** The *team* is about to win the tournament.
cue word	a word such as *another* or *both* that indicates the number of a noun

Using Odyssey Online with MyWritingLab

For more practice with nouns, go to www.mywritinglab.com.

CHAPTER 26

Pronouns: Understanding Case, Clear Pronoun–Antecedent Agreement, and Nonsexist Pronoun Usage

GETTING STARTED ...

 Q When I write, I often use pronouns, but I'm not always sure I am using the correct ones. Why does working with pronouns seem so confusing?

 A Pronouns can be confusing. For instance, *personal* pronouns have different forms depending on whether they serve as a subject or an object or indicate possession. Some *indefinite* pronouns can be singular, plural, or either. Each time you use pronouns in your writing, try to remember these characteristics. This information will make working with pronouns easier.

Overview: Choosing the Correct Pronoun

Pronouns, which are a kind of verbal shorthand, substitute for nouns. They provide brief, easily recognizable alternatives for nouns, thus adding variety to your language. Pronouns include *personal pronouns, indefinite pronouns, demonstrative pronouns, reflexive/intensive pronouns, relative pronouns,* and *interrogative pronouns.* To work effectively with pronouns, you must consider the form, or *case,* of personal pronouns and *number* and *gender* with indefinite pronouns. You also need to make sure that the pronouns and the words they refer to, called **antecedents,** match or agree. Otherwise, the people, places, things, and ideas being referred to won't be clear for your reader.

Navigating This Chapter In this chapter, you will learn how to:

- recognize the types of pronouns
- understand the cases of personal pronouns
- identify number and gender with indefinite pronouns
- ensure that pronouns and antecedents agree in number and gender

Examining Pronoun Types

ESL Note
See "Sentence Basics,"
pages 543–544, for
more on the proper use
of pronouns.

Pronouns, which we use as alternatives to nouns, can be grouped in several classes:

- **personal pronouns**, which refer to *specific* people, places, things, and ideas

I, me, my, mine	we, us, our, ours
you, your, yours	she, he, her, him, hers, his
it, its, their, theirs	

- **indefinite pronouns**, which refer to *general* persons and things

all	each	little	nobody	others
another	either	many	none	several
any	everybody	more	no one	some
anybody	everyone	most	nothing	somebody
anyone	everything	much	one	someone
anything	few	neither	other	something
both				

- **demonstrative pronouns**, which point out *particular* people or things referred to

this	that
these	those

- **reflexive/intensive pronouns**, which add emphasis to antecedents

myself	ourselves
yourself	yourselves
himself, herself, itself	themselves
oneself	

- **relative pronouns**, which introduce dependent clauses, called *relative clauses*, within a sentence

who	which
whom	that
whose	

- **interrogative pronouns**, which begin questions

Who … ?	Whom … ?	Whose … ?
Whoever … ?	Whomever … ?	Which … ?
Whichever … ?	What … ?	Whatever … ?

Although working with pronouns is fairly straightforward, two issues can cause potential confusion. The first issue is *case*—deciding which of the three forms of a personal pronoun is called for in a particular situation. The second issue is *number*—determining whether the word the pronoun refers to, the *antecedent*, is singular or plural.

Understanding and Applying Pronoun Case

Among the pronouns that you use most often as a writer are the *personal pronouns*, which point out *particular* people, places, things, and ideas. As the table shows, personal pronouns have three separate forms, or *cases: subjective, objective,* and *possessive.*

Personal Pronouns

	Subjective	Objective	Possessive
First person	I, we	me, us	my, mine, our, ours
Second person	you	you	your, yours
Third person	she, he, it, they	her, him, it, them	her, hers, his, its, their, theirs

ESL Note
See "Agreement,"
pages 546–548, for
more on subject–verb
agreement.

Use the *subjective* case pronouns as *subjects* of sentences and as *predicate nominatives*.

EXAMPLES
subject
We were stuck in traffic for over an hour.

predicate nominative
The winner of the math team competition was *she*.

Use the objective case pronouns as *objects;* objects receive the action of the verb (as *direct objects* or *indirect objects*) or are governed by a preposition (as *objects of prepositions*).

EXAMPLES
indirect object / direct object
In the final inning, the pitcher threw *him* four straight *balls*.

preposition / object of the preposition
All the trees *around them* looked the same to the lost children.

See pages 253–254 for a discussion of prepositional phrases.

Use possessive pronouns to show ownership.

EXAMPLES
Your class has been canceled for today.

Her friends were planning a surprise birthday party.

To avoid problems with personal pronouns, keep a few points in mind:

- *An objective pronoun can never serve as a subject.*

The exceptions are *you* and *it,* which can serve as either subjects or objects. *Her, him, me, us,* and *them* are never subjects. Be careful when you are writing sentences with compound subjects linked by *and* or *or.* Make sure that each word in the compound subject could be used alone with the verb in the sentence.

EXAMPLES

Muriel, Billy, and ~~her~~ she *are taking a drawing course together.*

Either the hostess or I ~~me~~ *will seat the guests at the reception.*

- *A subjective pronoun can never serve as an object.*

Errors in the use of objective case also tend to occur in compound objects. Again, try using each element in the compound object alone to see if it can serve as an object.

EXAMPLES

The boss had to make a choice between *Joe* and ~~he~~ him.

My mother could not remember whether Grandpa taught *my uncle* or ~~she~~ her to drive first.

Finally, do not confuse the possessive pronoun *its* with the contraction for *it is* (*it's*). *Its* needs no apostrophe because the word is already possessive. To avoid this error, try inserting *it is* whenever you want to use *its.* If *it is* fits, use *it is* or the contraction *it's.* If *it is* doesn't fit, use the possessive form, *its.*

EXAMPLES

It's
~~Its~~ too late to go to the movies now.

its
The owl flew to ~~it's~~ nest.

COMPREHENSION AND PRACTICE

Using Personal Pronouns and Identifying Pronoun Case

26.1 In the following passage, underline all personal pronouns. Write an *S* above subjective pronouns, an *O* above objective pronouns, and a *P* above possessive pronouns, as the example shows. Use the table of personal pronouns on page 388 for guidance.

EXAMPLE

   S   O   S   P
I wanted to show him how important he was in my life.

    (1) Every Monday when we were in elementary school, my sister and I used to go to the municipal library downtown. (2) It was almost three miles from our apartment, and our parents didn't want us to walk all that way. (3) So after school, Laura and I would go to the bus stop a block away and wait for the downtown bus to pick us up. (4) Because we were so young, riding the bus

was an adventure for us. (5) We were always a little nervous until the driver gave us back our bus passes with new holes punched in them. (6) When we finally reached the library, she and I would go right to the shelves to look for books to take home. (7) It was a challenge to see which one of us could find books that would impress the head librarian more. (8) Adventure stories were my favorite, so I always ended up with a pile of them. (9) My sister wasn't as lucky because the library didn't have as many of her favorites—science fiction—in its collection. (10) As we were leaving, the head librarian would always say, in his formal, bass tone, "Be careful going home, girls, and take care of the books because they belong to all of us."

CHALLENGE 26.1 **Evaluating the Use of Personal Pronouns**

1. Choose a passage of about 300 words from one of your writings; one of the readings in Part 7; one of your other textbooks; or a newspaper, magazine, or online article. Copy three sentences, one containing a subjective pronoun, one containing an objective pronoun, and one containing a possessive pronoun, and label the pronouns.

collaboration

2. Exchange your sentences with a classmate. Assess the sentences you receive, put a ✓ next to any mislabeled pronoun, and then return the sentences to your classmate.

3. Reevaluate any pronoun that your classmate has identified as incorrectly labeled.

Maintaining Agreement in Number

A pronoun must agree with its antecedent in *number:* Both must be singular, or both must be plural. Use singular pronouns to refer to singular antecedents and plural pronouns to refer to plural antecedents.

EXAMPLES

singular   singular
⌐antecedent   ⌐antecedent

Rachael dropped *her* book bag to the floor with a crash.

plural   plural
⌐antecedent   ⌐pronoun

The *students* in health class volunteered *their* time to run the blood drive.

The use of *collective nouns* such as *class, herd, jury,* and *team* can cause confusion in pronoun–antecedent agreement. Remember that collective nouns represent groups of people or things but are generally considered singular, so they call for singular pronouns (see pages 378–379).

plural
┌ antecedent ┐

plural
┌ pronoun

EXAMPLE ⎡ Last night, the Ordinance *Committee* closed *its* meeting, in violation of the Open
Meetings Act.

COMPREHENSION AND PRACTICE

Maintaining Pronoun–Antecedent Agreement

26.2 Each of the following sentences contains a pair of pronouns in parentheses. For each sentence, underline the antecedent, and circle the correct pronoun. Use the example as a guide.

EXAMPLE ⎡ Five <u>children</u> had misplaced (his or her, (their)) books.

(1) Last week, several employees of P. A. Cummings International Airport were hospitalized after experiencing nausea and tingling in (his or her, their) arms. (2) When an airport official was first contacted by the media, (she, they) refused to comment. (3) Instead, the official scheduled a news conference for the next morning, saying (she, they) would respond to questions at that time. (4) Meanwhile, state environmental officials studied the airline terminal to see if (he, they) could discover the cause of the illness. (5) The officials first tested the air to see if (it, they) contained carbon monoxide. (6) After that test proved negative, the chemicals used to clean the carpet were checked to see if (it, they) could have caused the illness. (7) The officials discovered that maintenance workers had used too much cleaning solution when (he, they) cleaned one portion of carpeting on the previous evening. (8) The excess solvent dried to a powder behind the ticket counter, and when the employees walked across that area, (his, their) shoes released the chemical. (9) The employees then breathed in the powder, and (it, they) made them ill. (10) At the news conference, the director of the airport announced that (she, they) would have the carpet in that terminal replaced immediately.

CHALLENGE 26.2 Maintaining Agreement with Collective Nouns

1. Here is a list of collective nouns. On a separate sheet of paper, write a sentence using each collective noun as an antecedent for an appropriate

pronoun. Underline both the collective noun and the pronoun that refers to it, as this example shows:

EXAMPLE

The union has ordered a strike if it can't get management to authorize a wage increase.

| association | committee | crowd | gang | mob |
| club | company | family | group | audience |

collaboration

2. Exchange your sentences with a classmate. Evaluate the sentences you receive, putting a ✓ in front of any sentence in which the pronoun doesn't agree with the collective noun to which it refers, and then return the sentences to the writer.

3. Consider what your classmate has noted and make any necessary changes in your sentences.

Maintaining Agreement with Indefinite Pronouns

Indefinite pronouns refer to someone or something general. For instance, the pronoun *somebody* could refer to one of any number of people, and the indefinite pronoun *anything* could refer to one of any number of items or events. The following indefinite pronouns are always singular:

Singular Indefinite Pronouns

another	each	everything	nobody	other
anybody	either	little	no one	somebody
anyone	everybody	much	nothing	someone
anything	everyone	neither	one	something

Singular indefinite pronouns call for singular verbs. In addition, they must be referred to by singular pronouns (*he, him, his, she, her, hers, it, its*).

EXAMPLES

Everyone standing in line to pay a fine *looks* unhappy.

Anyone who wants to compete in the drama festival must memorize *his* or *her* lines by Friday.

The following indefinite pronouns are always plural:

Plural Indefinite Pronouns

both	others
few	several
many	

EXAMPLES

Several of the students *have* started a rowing club.

The officials gave high scores to *both* dancers for *their* originality.

Some indefinite pronouns are either singular or plural, depending on the word to which they refer:

Indefinite Pronouns Affected by the Words That Follow Them

all	more	none
any	most	some

When you encounter one of these pronouns, check the word to which it refers. If that word is singular, choose a singular form of the verb, and if it is plural, choose a plural form of the verb.

EXAMPLES

           plural   plural
        ┌antecedent   ┌ verb ┐

Some of the *shirts* on sale *were* damaged.

          singular   singular
       ┌antecedent   ┌ verb

All of the *soil* at that construction site *is* contaminated with chemicals.

When an indefinite pronoun is the antecedent for another pronoun, maintaining agreement can be tricky. To avoid making an error in pronoun–antecedent agreement in this situation, first isolate the two pronouns and then check to see if they are both singular or both plural. If they don't match up, you can either change one of the pronouns or replace the indefinite pronoun with a definite noun so that the pronoun and its antecedent agree, as these examples show:

SINGULAR ANTECEDENT

Anyone needing more information about financial aid should bring *their* ~~their~~ [*his or her*] questions to the Financial Aid Office.

or

PLURAL ANTECEDENT

[*Students*] ~~*Anyone*~~ needing more information about financial aid should bring *their* questions to the Financial Aid Office.

PLURAL ANTECEDENT

All of the parents understood the relief that ~~*his or her*~~ [*their*] children felt when the test was postponed.

or

SINGULAR ANTECEDENT

[*Each*] ~~*All*~~ of the parents understood the relief that *his* or *her* children felt when the test was postponed.

COMPREHENSION AND PRACTICE

26.3

Selecting Indefinite Pronouns for Correct Agreement

In each of the following sentences, underline the verb(s) that must match the missing word. Then fill in the blank in each sentence with an appropriate indefinite pronoun from the list below. You may use the same pronoun more than once. Use the example to guide you.

few	everyone	some
somebody	all	many
nobody	no one	none

EXAMPLE *Many* of the delegates <u>have</u> never before <u>attended</u> a political convention.

(1) _____ hopes that he or she will do the right thing when faced with a crisis. (2) But the truth is that _____ knows for certain how he or she would react. (3) Not _____ is able to play the role of a hero. (4) _____ of us experience a kind of paralysis in crisis situations, _____ sick, or pass out. (5) Faced with the same crisis, _____ of us is likely to react in exactly the same way.

COMPREHENSION AND PRACTICE 26.4

Correcting Errors in Agreement with Indefinite Pronouns

Each sentence in the following passage contains an error in agreement with an indefinite pronoun. Cross out each error, and then write the correct pronoun above it. Change the verb if necessary. More than one answer may be possible, as the example shows.

EXAMPLE

his or her
Anybody could improve ~~their~~ grades by working harder.

or

Most students
~~Anybody~~ could improve their grades by working harder.

(1) Sometimes it's easy to get the impression that nobody wants to get involved in helping their neighbors. (2) News accounts regularly appear, for example, relating how one individual took advantage of their power or money to make life difficult for other people. (3) As a result, many begin to change his or her attitudes, becoming increasingly cynical. (4) After a while, residents begin to wonder if help is available in his or her city. (5) However, a restaurant owner in my town has proven that not everyone is apathetic about what happens in their neighborhood. (6) This woman serves holiday dinners for free to all in the surrounding area who otherwise couldn't afford to pay for his or her

meals. (7) Several of the city's most prominent citizens sacrifice time with his or her family to serve these dinners to people experiencing hard times. (8) Many of the employees of the restaurant also volunteer his or her time free of charge to serve the meals. (9) In addition, each of the servers contributes their tips from the prior week to pay for gift packages of clothing and blankets for those seeking a meal. (10) What's especially noteworthy is that everyone involved is trying to help their community.

CHALLENGE 26.3 **Maintaining Agreement with Indefinite Pronouns in Your Writing**

collaboration

As you now know, the indefinite pronouns *all, any, more, most, none,* and *some* are either singular or plural depending on the word following them. Working with a classmate, write two sentences for each of these indefinite pronouns, using each one first as a singular antecedent and then as a plural antecedent.

Maintaining Agreement with Demonstrative and Reflexive or Intensive Pronouns

You may occasionally experience difficulties in maintaining pronoun–antecedent agreement with *demonstrative pronouns,* which point out a particular person or thing.

Demonstrative Pronouns

Singular	*Plural*
this	these
that	those

As the list indicates, two demonstrative pronouns are singular (*this* and *that*), and two are plural (*these* and *those*). *This* and *these* point out things that are near or point to things in the future. *That* and *those* point out things that are farther away or point to things in the past.

When you use a demonstrative pronoun to begin a sentence in a paragraph or essay, you may be referring to the antecedent in the previous sentence. In these cases, check for any errors in pronoun–antecedent agreement by identifying that antecedent. If the antecedent is singular, use *this* or *that;* if it is plural, use *these* or *those.*

EXAMPLE ┌─── antecedent ───┐
There have been *four major accidents* near the park entrance.

Those have
~~*That has*~~ caused the city to install warning signs.

EXAMPLE

The Civic Improvement League is donating $15,000 to establish an

├── antecedent ──┤

This

urban entrepreneur's scholarship at the college. ~~These~~ will be given to students

majoring in marketing or accounting.

Often writers add a clarifying word to the demonstrative pronoun to make the reference more precise. In this case, the demonstrative pronoun then becomes a *demonstrative adjective,* as in the following versions of the sentences that appear above:

demonstrative   clarifying
adjective   word

antecedent ┐

EXAMPLES

There have been four major *accidents* near the park entrance. *Those crashes*

have caused the city to install warning signs.

The Civic Improvement League is donating $15,000 to establish an urban

┌─ antecedent ─┐   demonstrative adjective ┐ ┌ clarifying word

entrepreneur's *scholarship* at the college. *This award* will be given to students

majoring in marketing or accounting.

Another potential problem in maintaining pronoun–antecedent agreement involves the use of *reflexive* or *intensive pronouns,* which are used to emphasize the words to which they refer.

Reflexive or Intensive Pronoun Forms

myself	oneself
yourself	ourselves
himself, herself	yourselves
itself	themselves

Don't use reflexive or intensive pronouns in a sentence unless you have included the word to which the pronoun refers. Reflexive or intensive pronouns may not be used as subjects.

REFLEXIVE

The capsized sailboat righted itself. [*To direct verb's action back to subject*]

INTENSIVE

The president himself will testify. [*To emphasize*]

If these pronouns are used incorrectly as subjects, replace the reflexive or intensive form with a personal pronoun that suits the situation.

EXAMPLE

I

Connie and ~~myself~~ did most of the work on that presentation.

COMPREHENSION AND PRACTICE

26.5

Maintaining Agreement with Demonstrative Pronouns

Each sentence in the following passage contains an error in pronoun–antecedent agreement involving demonstrative pronouns. In each sentence, cross out the incorrect demonstrative pronoun, and above it write one that matches the antecedent. If necessary, turn the demonstrative pronoun into a demonstrative adjective and add a clarifying word. Use the example to guide you.

EXAMPLE

this OR *this incident*

During a storm, a huge tree fell across the power lines, and ~~these~~ caused a major power outage.

(1) Yesterday, the Red Cross held a blood drive on campus, and these proved to be a big success. (2) At most drives the Red Cross runs, around thirty to forty people donate, and those is considered good. (3) At this drive, however, more than a hundred donors showed up, and these was beyond anyone's hope. (4) Many participants were donating for the first time, and in the beginning these complicated work a little for the officials. (5) Some newcomers were visibly nervous, and these seemed to affect the mood of others waiting in line. (6) To help settle everyone down, the Red Cross workers spoke directly with that appearing especially anxious. (7) They explained the steps involved, while stressing the simplicity and safety of that. (8) After the first few newcomers donated blood without a problem, that people behind them in line began to relax. (9) Those made all the difference, and the time passed more quickly and pleasantly for everyone involved. (10) Those was such a success that the Red Cross plans to schedule another drive for the end of the semester.

COMPREHENSION AND PRACTICE

26.6

Using Reflexive and Intensive Pronoun Forms Correctly

Fill in the blanks in the following sentences with an appropriate reflexive or intensive pronoun form from the list on page 396. Use the example as a guide.

EXAMPLE

After waiting at the register for five minutes, the woman finally decided to check the price _herself_.

1. I will be picking you up at the airport _____.

2. The participants _____ criticized the organizers of the natural healing seminar most harshly.

3. At the end of this semester, perhaps you will decide to major in business _____.

4. After several hours, the storm finally blew _____ out.

5. Rather than wait for the city crew to arrive, we cleaned up the field _____.

Maintaining Agreement with *That, Who,* and *Which* Clauses

Clauses introduced by a *relative pronoun—that, who,* or *which*—may also create problems with pronoun–antecedent agreement. If the antecedent that the clause describes is singular, then the verb in the clause must be singular. If the antecedent of the clause is plural, then the verb must also be plural.

EXAMPLES

singular
⌐antecedent⌐ *sells*
The *store that sell* baked goods at half price is always crowded.
⌐—— plural antecedent ——⌐ *allow*
The *special parking stickers, which ~~allows~~* a student to park in the campus garage, may be purchased in the bookstore.

COMPREHENSION AND PRACTICE 26.7

Maintaining Agreement with *That, Who,* and *Which* Clauses

The italicized clauses in the following paragraph contain errors in agreement. Circle the antecedent, and then correct the error by crossing out the incorrect verb and writing the correct one above it. Use the example to guide you.

EXAMPLE

was
The (firefighter) *who ~~were~~ involved in the rescue* received a citation for bravery.

(1) Most people *who was questioned in a recent survey* felt that their memories weren't as sharp as they'd like. (2) These respondents, *who was between the ages of forty-five and sixty-five,* felt that their memories had weakened. (3) For example, their ability to match a name with a face, *which a few years earlier were strong,* now seemed far less reliable. (4) Also, the details of meetings or public gatherings *that in the past was easy to keep straight* now seemed fuzzier. (5) To these people, these memory lapses, *which was really upsetting,*

seemed to be signs of old age. (6) Like many of the beliefs about aging, however, some of the issues *that is associated with growing older* are more stereotype than fact. (7) According to many experts consulted, the kinds of memory problems *that was reported* aren't necessarily related to age. (8) Genuine memory deficits, *which involves serious and sometimes permanent loss of recognition of otherwise familiar people and places,* affect many segments of society. (9) In fact, anyone *who experience a sudden memory loss,* regardless of age, should see a doctor immediately. (10) True memory problems, *which fortunately is not common,* could be a symptom of serious neurological problems or drug interactions.

COMPREHENSION AND PRACTICE 26.8

Identifying and Correcting Agreement Problems with *That, Who,* and *Which* Clauses

The following passage contains several errors in agreement with *that, who,* and *which* clauses. Cross out any incorrect verb, and write the correct verb above it. If a sentence does not contain an error, write *OK* above it. Use the example as a guide.

EXAMPLE

ride

Because of the crowd, many people who usually ~~rides~~ the 8 A.M. crosstown bus had to wait for the 8:30 bus.

(1) I attended a great workshop that were held at school the other day. (2) A speaker who work in the counseling center on campus presented the workshop. (3) The program, which was called "How to Build an Effective Personal Relationship," attracted about twenty participants, both male and female. (4) She first discussed several common misconceptions that people has about love. (5) For example, "love conquers all," a concept that are believed by many people, isn't always true. (6) In some cases, a person can have so many problems that love alone isn't enough to maintain a relationship. (7) She also disproved the naive idea that there is only one right person in the world for each of us. (8) Then she showed how people who thinks the right partner will be the salvation for all their problems in life are setting themselves

up for disappointment. (9) All of us who was participating in the session were impressed because we all had fantasies like those she described. (10) I'm looking forward to the follow-up session, which are scheduled for next Friday.

Keeping the Relationship between Pronoun and Antecedent Clear

To help your reader understand your meaning, you must also make the relationship between the pronoun and the antecedent clear. Look at this sentence:

AMBIGUOUS *Ed* and *Bill* had a fight, and *he* broke *his* nose.

The problem with this sentence is obvious. It does not make clear who did what to whom. The simplest way to correct this type of error is to restate the sentence completely to eliminate the ambiguity, as this version shows:

REVISED During their fight, *Ed* broke *Bill's* nose.

COMPREHENSION AND PRACTICE 26.9

Identifying the Pronoun–Antecedent Relationship

In each of the following sentences, a pronoun is italicized. Circle the antecedent for each of these pronouns, and draw an arrow from the pronoun to the antecedent, as the example shows. Remember—the antecedent to the pronoun may be in a different sentence.

EXAMPLE The (lock) on the suitcase was broken, so I asked my uncle to fix *it*.

(1) Although voice mail has become almost unavoidable over the past few years, many people don't like *it*. (2) *They* prefer the human touch that voice mail can't supply. (3) When people have a question, all *they* want to do is talk to an actual person. (4) But many voice-mail systems force callers to follow a complicated series of commands, and *they* also often include a dizzying array of options. (5) With some voice-mail systems, if callers hit the wrong buttons, *they* can be disconnected and have to call back. (6) Even if people manage to reach the proper extension, *they* may not be out of the voice-mail loop yet. (7) If the individual at that extension is away or using the system to screen

calls, *he or she* will not answer the call personally. (8) A recording will instruct the caller to leave a message, and then *it* will indicate which buttons to press to approve the message. (9) If the caller pushes the wrong buttons, some systems delete the message, and then *they* ask the caller to go through the entire process again. (10) For the average person, such a system often increases the frustration *it* is meant to eliminate.

COMPREHENSION AND PRACTICE 26.10

Correcting Unclear or Ambiguous Pronoun References

Each sentence below contains an unclear or ambiguous relationship between a pronoun and an antecedent. Circle the unclear or ambiguous pronoun. On another sheet of paper, revise the sentence to clarify the relationship. There may be more than one way to correct each sentence. Use the example to guide you.

EXAMPLE

When the vase she threw hit the window, (it) shattered.

The window shattered when the vase she threw hit it.

or

When the vase she threw hit the window, the window shattered.

(1) Last week's accident downtown involving a bus and a tanker truck caused major structural damage to a highway overpass, and it is still being investigated. (2) Heavy rain was falling and the truck was reportedly exceeding the speed limit, and that may have contributed to the accident. (3) Also, that stretch of Whipple Avenue bends sharply and there are no stop signs along the way, and that didn't help the situation either. (4) When the tanker collided with the bus, it burst into flames. (5) The bus then hit a curb, and the driver couldn't handle it. (6) The bus wasn't carrying passengers at the time, and it was an older model, so that may have made the bus less stable. (7) The bus also hit a light pole, and it was badly damaged. (8) The cab and the tanker broke apart, and then it slammed into the side of the overpass. (9) Traffic was snarled and a crowd gathered on the sidewalk, and that created problems at

rush hour. (10) The pavement under the overpass is badly gouged and the concrete over the entrance of the overpass is crumbling, and that is expected to be repaired within a month.

CHALLENGE 26.4   Writing with Clear Pronoun–Antecedent Agreement

1. Write a sentence to precede each of the sentences provided below. Make sure to include an antecedent that matches the pronoun that begins the provided sentence. If necessary, add a clarifying word to those pronouns. Use the example to guide you.

Yesterday, Diane reminded me of the time the two of us locked ourselves

out of the office.

That ^story still makes me laugh.

a. _____

_____

She left the scene of the accident before the police arrived.

b. _____

_____

It caused the restaurant to be closed for an entire week.

c. _____

_____

That gift means I won't have to take out a loan to attend classes next semester.

d. _____

_____

That agreement was the solution everyone was hoping for.

e. _____

_____

That development left us with the rest of the afternoon to straighten everything out.

collaboration

2. Exchange your sentences with a classmate. Evaluate the sentences you receive for pronoun–antecedent agreement. Put a ✓ in front of any sentence in which you believe the agreement is not clear and return it to the writer.

3. Make any necessary changes in your sentences.

Avoiding Problems with Gender in Pronoun–Antecedent Agreement

Gender refers to whether a word is masculine or feminine. Making sure that pronouns agree in gender is usually much easier than making them agree in number. In English, inanimate objects and ideas don't have masculine or feminine forms as they do in languages such as Spanish and French.

With personal pronouns, identifying gender is easy. *I, me, we, you,* and *your* can be either feminine or masculine. Likewise, the plural pronouns *they, them, their,* and *themselves* apply to both genders. The personal pronoun *it* refers to objects only. In fact, you need to worry about gender only with third person pronouns: *she, her, hers, he, him,* and *his.* To correct errors in agreement with any of these words, change the pronoun so that it matches the gender of the word to which it refers:

EXAMPLES

Mother Teresa devoted *his* [her] life to helping the poor in India.

As the man turned to leave, a ticket fell out of *her* [his] coat.

When you use pronouns, you should also eliminate any accidental *sexism* in your writing. **Sexist language,** as the National Organization for Women (NOW) and the National Council of Teachers of English (NCTE) have been pointing out since the 1970s, is language that inappropriately designates gender. The word *foreman,* for instance, suggests that only a man can direct a group of workers.

Words have tremendous power. When you use words like *chairman, salesman,* or *mailman,* you send out the message that only males should conduct meetings, sell things, or deliver mail. The proper way to deal with these words is to make them gender-neutral, that is, with references to neither sex: *supervisor, chairperson, salesperson,* and *mail carrier.*

You must also be concerned with sexism when you use singular indefinite pronouns such as *anybody, someone,* or *everybody.* These words can be either masculine or feminine. It was once acceptable to use *he, him, himself,* and *his* to represent both sexes when using a singular indefinite pronoun. Today, however, this usage is considered sexist, so you should either use pronouns of both genders or rewrite the sentence to make both your pronoun and your antecedent plural.

If you choose the first option, you can connect a feminine and a masculine pronoun with *or* to refer to the indefinite pronoun: *he or she, him or her,* and *his or her,* rather than *he, him,* and *his.* Reverse the pairs if you prefer: *she or he, her or him, her or his.*

EXAMPLE

Everybody should be prepared to do *her or his* best.

The other option is to make both pronoun and antecedent plural. This method is generally a better choice. It eliminates sexism and eliminates the possibility of making an error in gender agreement, as this version shows:

EXAMPLE *People* should be prepared to do *their* best.

COMPREHENSION AND PRACTICE

Avoiding Problems with Gender in Pronoun–Antecedent Agreement

26.11 In the following passage, identify errors in pronoun gender and uses of sexist language. Cross out each error you find, and write the correction above it in the space provided between the lines. More than one correct answer may be possible. Use the example as a guide.

EXAMPLE

People who ride motorcycles *their helmets*
~~Anyone who rides a motorcycle~~ should wear ~~his helmet~~, even on short trips.

or

her or his
Anyone who rides a motorcycle should wear ~~his~~ helmet, even on short trips.

(1) My ambition is to finish school and begin a career in the business world. (2) My first step will be sales because a good salesman can earn a great salary and help her company at the same time. (3) Of course, to be effective, a salesman has to develop contacts in the firms with which he deals. (4) To do this, a salesman has to make regular rounds and get to know as many people as possible in the companies she visits. (5) For example, when a salesman visits a company, he should first visit the foreman to find out what her needs are. (6) Succeeding as part of the sales force is just the first step in my career plans. (7) Eventually, I hope to work my way up to chief executive officer, or even chairman of the board of directors. (8) An effective chairman can make money for herself and his corporation by ensuring that the managers are doing a good job. (9) Everybody has her own management strategies, but I feel the best strategy is to make sure that people are treated fairly and paid according to their efforts. (10) With these kinds of simple ideas, anybody should be able to make his mark in the business world.

COMPREHENSION AND PRACTICE

26.12

Avoiding Sexist Language

Here is a list of sexist words. In the spaces provided, write a neutral, nonsexist alternative for each one. Make sure you don't substitute another equally sexist word in its place. For instance, don't replace *stewardess* with *steward*. Instead, use *flight attendant*. Then, on a separate sheet of paper, compose a sentence using each of your substitutions.

fireman _____   actor _____

congressman _____   anchorwoman _____

mankind _____   businessman _____

weatherman _____   policewoman _____

CHALLENGE 26.5   **Evaluating Sexist Language and Nonsexist Alternatives**

collaboration

1. Make a copy of the last two paragraphs or essays that you have written, and exchange them with a classmate. Read the paragraphs or essays you receive, and make a list of any words you think are sexist.

collaboration

2. Working with this same classmate, examine the lists you have made, and make a new list in which you offer nonsexist versions of these words. Then, together compose a paragraph of seven to ten sentences in which you discuss the ways that sexist language may affect people.

QUICK STUDY   ## Student Example

This chapter concerns matters of making reference, showing ownership, and substituting one thing for another. Take a look at the following paragraph on a related subject. What comes to mind when you think back to some place or event in your life?

Whenever I drive by the elementary school I attended, I think of my Aunt Amelia. Aunt Mil, as everyone in my family called her, was actually my mother's aunt, and she never married or had kids of her own. When my sisters and I were little, my mother had to be at work by 7 A.M., so she couldn't get us ready for school. To help my mother, Aunt Mil would come to our apartment at 6:30 every school morning, just before my mother left for work. Mom would wake us up, kiss us, and head for work, warning us to behave for Aunt Mil. In front of my mother, Aunt Mil would always sound tough, but as soon as my mother was outside, Aunt Mil would start spoiling us. On many days, she would let us pick what we wanted to have for breakfast, even if it meant cooking us pancakes or French toast. After making us promise not to tell our mother, she would also give us a couple of dollars to buy candy on our way home from school. Whenever our mother had to work overtime, Aunt Mil would come back to our apartment in the afternoon and start supper for us. She followed this routine with us until I started high school. By this time, she was almost 80, and her diabetes had become so severe that she could barely walk. When I was in my junior year, she had a stroke and died, and I miss her to this day. Every time I see my old school, I think of Aunt Mil and smile.

First complete the following activities in response to this paragraph:

1. Three of the sentences in this paragraph are highlighted. Circle all the pronouns. Then above each pronoun, write its antecedent, using the material in this chapter to guide you.

2. As Chapter 4 notes (pages 48–50), providing transition is crucial in keeping your writing coherent, and using pronouns is one of the means of providing transition. On a separate sheet of paper, explain how the pronouns in this paragraph make it easy for readers to follow the story and see the connection between ideas.

3. On the following lines, briefly explain which example in the paragraph provides the best evidence that Aunt Mil was a memorable individual and why you feel this way.

_____

_____

_____

_____

_____

Now explore the topic in writing. As the paragraph above does, you could discuss a person, place, or thing that is connected in some way to a specific locale or event. You might also focus on one of these topics related to the subject matter of this chapter:

- a word or phrase that you use with someone close to you that others don't necessarily understand the same way

- a situation that could change drastically depending on the circumstances
- something you own about which you feel great pride
- a time at work or school during which you behaved differently because a substitute was in charge

collaboration

4. Exchange your draft with a classmate. Evaluate the paragraph you receive. If you discover any problem spots, especially in the use of pronouns, circle the errors, write the correct form above the incorrect one, and then return the paper to the writer.

5. Consider the comments and corrections your reader has made and create a final draft of your paragraph.

CHAPTER QUICK CHECK Working with Pronouns

Proofread the following essay for problems with pronoun–antecedent agreement; agreement with *who, that,* and *which* clauses; and sexist language. Eliminate the problems by crossing out the incorrect word and writing a more effective choice above it. If a sentence is correct as written, write *OK* above it. In some cases, more than one solution is possible. Use the example to guide you.

EXAMPLE

The DVD player was out of stock, so I asked for a rain check in order to pur-

chase it at the same price when ~~they~~ *it* came in.

(1) A recent development, which are called face-recognition technology, is being hailed as a way to track and identify criminals. (2) With face-recognition systems, computers record images of faces and then convert it into another form. (3) That can come from a variety of sources, including pictures taken of large groups of people at sports stadiums or busy city streets. (4) The face-recognition programs then isolate each person in the picture and carefully create an individual blueprint or map of their faces. (5) To do so, the software focuses on somebody's unique features, such as their cheekbones, jaw shape and line, and eye shape, size, and location to each other. (6) The system converts this information into a computer code and stores them in a database. (7) In the case of a crime, law enforcement officials can use the system to match these images to others taken by surveillance cameras in stores, banks, government buildings, and airports. (8) Spokesmen for face-recognition companies claim that these systems are nearly foolproof. (9) Some civil liberties

organizations disagree, however, citing independent testing that show these systems to be only 60 to 70 percent accurate. (10) In addition, these groups warn of potential legal fallout, because no one in the pictures taken in public areas has given permission for their images to be used and stored.

SUMMARY EXERCISE Working with Pronouns

Proofread the following essay for problems with pronoun–antecedent agreement; agreement in *who, that,* and *which* clauses; and sexist language. Eliminate the problems by crossing out the incorrect word and writing a more effective choice above it. If a sentence is correct as written, write *OK* above it. In some cases, more than one solution is possible.

(1) I am godmother to my brother's five-year-old twins, a boy and a girl, and I recently went to the toy store to buy him or her birthday presents. (2) Unfortunately, the expedition turned out to be a depressing experience. (3) I discovered that a person can find plenty of toys, but they will find that most of them are unbelievably expensive or inappropriate for young children.

(4) First, I went to the game aisle. (5) With the exception of Candyland, Cootie, and a few other simple games that the twins already own, all the board games were too complicated or too expensive. (6) There were plenty of computer games, but I couldn't afford to buy the game unit themselves. (7) Also, the one game that seemed as if it would be suitable for children their age was beyond my price range. (8) One of the salesmen said that she had just reordered that particular game because they were so popular.

(9) My niece and nephew also wanted some action figures. (10) Anybody who has their own children or has ever baby-sat knows how much kids enjoy pretending. (11) James and Jenna are no different. (12) Both of them enjoy playing his or her own special roles and pretending to have super powers.

(13) However, their favorite characters, which changes colors when dunked in water, cost over $35 each. (14) That amazed me.

(15) Even more amazing and sickening was the number of realistic-looking guns and war toys in the store. (16) Why would anyone want to spend a lot of money so their children could pretend to kill each other? (17) The huge arsenal I observed, however, made it seem as if almost everybody wants to buy their children a toy machine gun.

(18) By the time I finished shopping, I was much sadder and poorer than I had been on the way in. (19) My godchildren loved his or her cards and toys, and that helped me feel better. (20) However, after spending an afternoon seeing what kinds of toys are out there, I'm glad I don't have to make that choices for my own children yet.

FOR FURTHER EXPLORATION Pronouns

1. Focus on one of the following topics. Using the prewriting technique—or combination of techniques—best suited to your style, explore the possibilities that the subject holds and consider what purposes you might fulfill as you write:

   - the advantages—or disadvantages—of fame
   - a time when you witnessed someone you know act in an uncharacteristic way
   - why you think people sometimes give up when they still have a chance of achiev-ing a goal
   - the relationship between respect in the classroom and student behavior

2. Evaluate your prewriting material, identify a focus, and work your way through the rest of the writing process to create a draft essay of at least 500 words on this subject.

collaboration

3. Exchange your draft with a classmate. Check the draft you receive for weaknesses, pay-ing particular attention to the use of pronouns. Circle any errors, using the material in this chapter as a guide, and then return the draft to the writer.

4. Revise your essay, correcting any errors in pronoun use or other problems discovered by your reader.

RECAP Pronouns

Key Terms in This Chapter	Definitions
pronoun	a word used in place of a noun

> **EXAMPLE**   Georgie picked up a *rock* and threw *it* at the abandoned house.

antecedent	the word or words to which a pronoun refers

Singular antecedents call for singular pronouns; plural antecedents call for plural pronouns.

> **EXAMPLE**   The little *girl* dropped *her* hat.

Indefinite pronoun antecedents must agree with their pronouns.

> **EXAMPLE**   *Everyone* who has a coupon will receive 25 percent off *her or his* purchase.

personal pronoun	a pronoun that specifies a particular person, place, thing, or idea

Personal pronouns have three separate forms, or cases, to show person.

Personal Pronouns

	Subjective Case	Objective Case	Possessive Case
First person	I, we	me, us	my, mine, our, ours
Second person	you	you	your, yours
Third person	she, he, it, they	her, him, it, them	her, hers, his, its, their, theirs

indefinite pronoun	a pronoun used to refer to someone or something in general

Singular Indefinite Pronouns

another	each	everything	nobody	other
anybody	either	little	no one	somebody
anyone	everybody	much	nothing	someone
anything	everyone	neither	one	something

Plural Indefinite Pronouns

both	others
few	several
many	

Indefinite Pronouns Affected by the Words That Follow Them

all	more	none
any	most	some

Key Terms in This Chapter	Definitions
demonstrative pronoun	singular: *this, that* plural: *these, those* If a demonstrative pronoun begins a sentence, find the antecedent in the preceding sentence. A demonstrative pronoun placed next to a noun is then called a *demonstrative adjective.* EXAMPLE Some clothes in *that* box are damaged. *Those* should be mended.
reflexive/intensive pronoun	a combination of a personal pronoun with *-self* or *-selves: myself, yourself, himself, herself, itself, ourselves, yourselves, themselves* Reflexive or intensive pronouns are used for emphasis (Ginny *herself* paid for the repair) or to direct the action of the verb back to the subject (Peter threw *himself* across the saddle).
relative pronoun	*that, who, which, whom, whose* A relative pronoun introduces a clause that describes an antecedent; the verb in the clause must agree with the antecedent. EXAMPLE The *attorney* who *is* addressing my class this morning graduated from this college.
interrogative pronoun	What … ? Whatever … ? Which … ? Whichever … ? Who … ? Whoever … ? Whom … ? Whomever … ? Whose … ? An interrogative pronoun introduces a question. EXAMPLE *What* is the problem?
gender	refers to whether a word is masculine or feminine Pronouns must match the gender of their antecedents.
sexist language	language that inappropriately excludes one gender Try using plural antecedents and pronouns instead. EXAMPLE *All bicyclists* using the municipal bike path must wear *their* helmets.

Using Odyssey Online with MyWritingLab

For more practice with pronouns, go to www.mywritinglab.com.

CHAPTER 27

Adjectives, Adverbs, and Other Modifiers: Using Descriptive and Modifying Words Effectively

GETTING STARTED ...

 In my head, my ideas always seem vivid and bright, but when I actually write them down, they sometimes seem vague or lifeless. What can I do to make these ideas as interesting and alive on paper as they are in my mind?

 Adjectives and *adverbs* are the answers you are looking for. These words *modify* or describe other words. When you use adjectives and adverbs correctly and effectively, they make the words they are modifying—and your writing in general—clearer and more specific. To avoid errors in their use, concentrate on choosing the correct form for comparisons and the proper placement of modifiers. Make sure you avoid using two negatives—such as *no, never,* and *not*—in the same subject–verb unit.

Overview: Understanding the Roles of Adjectives and Adverbs

Nouns and pronouns name people and things, and verbs show the action or situations in which those people and things are involved. But writing comprised only of nouns and verbs would not effectively communicate your ideas to your reader. To add precision and color to your writing, you need to include **modifiers,** words that *describe* or *limit* other words in a sentence. **Adjectives** modify nouns or pronouns, and **adverbs** modify verbs, adjectives, and other adverbs. Both adjectives and adverbs are useful for making comparisons and expressing negation. If you look back at the paragraphs and essays you have written so far, you'll discover that you've used many adjectives and adverbs. You'll also see that they inject life into your writing, so it's important to master their use.

Navigating This Chapter In this chapter, you will learn how to:

- use the positive, comparative, and superlative forms of adjectives and adverbs
- distinguish between commonly confused adjectives and adverbs
- avoid dangling and misplaced modifiers
- avoid double negatives

Understanding the Positive Forms of Adjectives and Adverbs

Adjectives and adverbs have three forms: positive, comparative, and superlative. The **positive form** of an adjective describes a noun or pronoun without making a comparison. It tells the reader *how many, what kind,* or *which one.*

EXAMPLE | The *small* dog is *fierce.*

ESL Note
See "Sentence Basics," pages 543–544, and "Word Order," pages 545–546, for more on the correct placement of adjectives and adverbs.

In this sentence, the adjective *small* tells *which* dog and the adjective *fierce* describes *what kind* of dog.

The positive form of an adverb describes a verb, an adjective, or another adverb without making a comparison. It tells the reader *how, when, where,* or *to what extent.*

EXAMPLE | *Finally,* the child spoke *quietly* to the nurse.

In this sentence, the adverb *finally* tells *when,* and the adverb *quietly* describes *how* the child spoke.

COMPREHENSION AND PRACTICE
27.1

Identifying Adjectives and Adverbs

In the passage below, circle the positive form of the adjectives and underline the positive form of the adverbs. Use the example to guide you.

EXAMPLE | Chika often organizes (athletic) activities for the children in her neighborhood.

(1) Last Saturday, my friends and I went for a quick lunch at the Granite Café, a new deli near the college. (2) The restaurant is located in a building that was once the office of the Mill City Granite Works. (3) The building itself is constructed of massive slabs of granite that were actually quarried at the Mill City Granite Works. (4) The deep cavity from when the quarry closed fifty years ago gradually filled with water, so the building is all that remains of this once highly successful business. (5) The city was planning to demolish the run-down building before the café owners bought and rehabilitated it. (6) The owners, Lynette and her brother Kevin, think that the historical significance of the building will probably help attract customers. (7) At noontime on Saturday, Marcel, Shelly, Kathryn, and I first picked a large table near the window. (8) Then we examined the extensive menu to decide on our meals.

(9) We quickly chose from the full array of sandwiches and homemade soups.

(10) The final bill for the four of us was $25, which was a real bargain.

Creating Comparative and Superlative Forms of Adjectives and Adverbs

The **comparative form** of an adjective or an adverb is used to discuss *two* things in relation to each other.

ADJECTIVE This new graphics program is *more complex* than the one I used last year.

ADVERB The nursery school students play *longer* than the first graders.

In the first sentence, the adjective *more complex* compares one computer program with another. In the second sentence, the adverb *longer* compares the extent to which two groups of children play.

The **superlative form** of an adjective or an adverb is used to discuss *more than two* things in relation to each other.

ADJECTIVE This store has the *lowest* prices for name-brand clothes as well as household appliances.

ADVERB Of all the young women in the chorus, Eleanor was the one who danced the *most gracefully*.

In the first sentence, the adjective *lowest* compares the prices of many stores. In the second sentence, the adverb *most gracefully* compares the style of many dancers.

For adjectives and adverbs of one syllable, create the comparative by adding *-er*, and create the superlative by adding *-est* to the end of the positive form of the word.

Positive	*Comparative*	*Superlative*
dark	dark**er**	dark**est**
high	high**er**	high**est**
far	farth**er**	farth**est**
hard	hard**er**	hard**est**

For adjectives and adverbs of more than two syllables, place *more* in front of the word for the comparative or *most* in front of the word for the superlative.

Positive	*Comparative*	*Superlative*
ridiculous	**more** ridiculous	**most** ridiculous
intelligent	**more** intelligent	**most** intelligent
remarkably	**more** remarkably	**most** remarkably
unfortunately	**more** unfortunately	**most** unfortunately

If the adjective or adverb is *two* syllables, which of these two methods should you use? The answer depends on the word. Some two-syllable words take an *-er* or *-est* ending:

Positive	*Comparative*	*Superlative*
early	earli**er**	earli**est**
angry	angri**er**	angri**est**
lazy	lazi**er**	lazi**est**
funny	funni**er**	funni**est**

Other two-syllable words require that you use *more* or *most* before them:

Positive	*Comparative*	*Superlative*
private	**more** private	**most** private
slowly	**more** slowly	**most** slowly
careful	**more** careful	**most** careful
safely	**more** safely	**most** safely

ESL Note
See "Articles," pages 551–552, for the use of articles with the superlative form.

To avoid errors, look up two-syllable adjectives and adverbs in the dictionary. In addition to definitions, a dictionary gives the correct spelling for adjectives and adverbs that form their comparative and superlative forms by adding *-er* or *-est*. If no *-er* or *-est* forms are listed, then use *more* and *most*.

Regardless of the number of syllables, never use both *more* and *-er* or both *most* and *-est* with the same adjective or adverb. Expressions like *more faster* and *most completest* are always wrong.

Some adjectives and adverbs form their comparative and superlative forms in irregular ways:

Positive	*Comparative*	*Superlative*
bad (adjective)	worse	worst
badly (adverb)	worse	worst
good (adjective)	better	best
well (adverb)	better	best
little	less	least
much	more	most

As you can see, two pairs of words on this list share the same comparative and superlative forms. However, these similar words have different functions. *Bad* and *good* are adjectives used to identify *what kind* of people, places, ideas, or things a writer is discussing. *Well* and *badly* are adverbs used to explain *how* something was done.

COMPREHENSION AND PRACTICE

27.2

Using Comparative and Superlative Forms Correctly

Each sentence in the following paragraph contains an incorrect positive, comparative, or superlative adjective or adverb. Cross out the incorrect form, and write the correct form above it, as the example shows.

fastest

EXAMPLE Barbaro was the ~~most fast~~ racehorse I had ever seen.

(1) My friend Laura wants to be a singer, and she already sings more well than most professionals. (2) She has the most sweet voice I've ever heard. (3) She even does a great job with the National Anthem, which most singers claim is the more difficult song around. (4) Her sound is like Beyoncé's except Laura's voice is more deep. (5) Laura is so talented that she tried out for a local talent show when she had the flu, had the worse audition of her life, and still won a place in the show. (6) A local agent who manages Laura says that her abilities are improving quicklier than those of his other singers. (7) Even though it's most difficult now than it was ten years ago for an unknown singer to get a recording contract, Laura has been sending "demo" CDs all over the country. (8) She figures that at worse, all the music companies will turn her down, and she will have wasted a few dollars. (9) Meanwhile, she is attending college, which has made her parents more happy than they were when she announced that she wanted to be a professional singer. (10) Right now the more frustrating thing of all for Laura is finding time both to study and to practice.

Working with Confusing Pairs of Adjectives and Adverbs

Some words have both adjective and adverb forms. Choosing the right form can be confusing for writers. The list below contains the most commonly confused pairs of adjectives and adverbs:

ESL Note
See "Confusing Words," pages 549–551, for more on other potentially confusing modifiers.

Adjective	*Adverb*
awful	awfully
bad	badly
good	well
poor	poorly
quick	quickly
quiet	quietly
real	really

Deciding between *good* and *well* and between *bad* and *badly* probably causes the most headaches for writers. *Good* and *bad* describe a person or thing, whereas *well* and *badly* describe how something is done. In other words, you can say that a person is a *good* public speaker or a *bad* public speaker, but you must say that this individual speaks *well* or speaks *badly*.

Consider the following examples:

EXAMPLES

Shannon is a *good* chef.

Elie cooks *well.*

In the first sentence, the adjective *good* tells *what kind* of chef Shannon is. In the second, the adverb *well* acts describes *how* Elie cooks.

COMPREHENSION AND PRACTICE 27.3

Correcting Errors in the Use of Confusing Adjectives and Adverbs

The following sentences contain errors in the use of adjectives and adverbs. Cross out any incorrect form, and then write the correct form above it. If a sentence is correct as written, write *OK* above it. Use the example to guide you.

EXAMPLE

The dog ran out from between the two cars so ~~quick~~ ^{quickly} that the driver couldn't avoid hitting it.

(1) For years, I needed eyeglasses bad, but I didn't know it. (2) In grade school, I performed poor on any test that required me to read the blackboard. (3) At first, my teachers thought I was being lazy and that I could do good if I paid more attention in class. (4) Then my third-grade teacher sent me for a vision test, and the doctor said I was awful nearsighted. (5) I was real afraid I'd have to wear glasses like my grandfather's, with ugly frames. (6) As it turned out, my glasses didn't look so badly, and the difference they made in my life was unbelievable. (7) Until I got glasses, I was used to sitting quiet in the back of the room, participating only when forced to. (8) After I got my glasses, all that changed quick. (9) When I could see every word on the board well, all I wanted to do was make up for lost time. (10) Although I still received a few poorly test scores, school became a more happy experience for me.

CHALLENGE 27.1   **Using Confusing Pairs of Adjectives and Adverbs in Your Writing**

1. Write topic sentences for three paragraphs. Include in each sentence an adjective or adverb from the list of confusing pairs on page 416.

collaboration

2. Working with a classmate, consider the topic sentences you have written and select the one that you both believe has the most promise. Working together, compose a paragraph of seven to ten sentences. Include plenty of adjectives and adverbs to make your writing colorful and precise.

Avoiding Dangling and Misplaced Modifiers

ESL Note
See "Word Order," pages 545–546, for more on avoiding dangling and misplaced modifiers.

As you saw in Chapter 24, the present participle, or *-ing* form of a verb, can be combined with a helping verb to form a verb in the progressive tense. Without a helping verb, this form can't act as the verb in a sentence. When it describes another word or phrase, it is called a **participle,** as these examples show:

EXAMPLES

Yelling angrily, Dion left the room.

The teacher tried to quiet the *laughing* children.

In the first sentence, the participle *Yelling* is describing the proper noun *Dion.* In the second sentence, the participle *laughing* is describing the noun *children.*

Using participles can help you combine ideas and eliminate choppiness in your writing. Consider these sentences, none of which uses participles.

EXAMPLES

The telephone service workers had coffee in the small restaurant. They took a break from work.

The teenaged girl behind the counter polished the glass pastry cabinets. She whistled softly.

Although the sentences in each example are correct, they are choppy. By changing one of the sentences to a dependent clause beginning with a participle and making a few other changes in wording, you can combine these sentences:

EXAMPLES

Taking a break from work, the telephone service *workers* had coffee in the small restaurant.

Whistling softly, the teenaged *girl* behind the counter polished the glass pastry cabinets.

In the first example, the participle and the words that follow it, *Taking a break from work,* now describe *workers.* In the second example, the participle and the words that follow it, *Whistling softly,* now describe *girl.*

When you use a participle, be sure to place it near the word it describes in a sentence. Otherwise, your readers may not understand what word it is describing. Consider these examples:

FAULTY

Hanging from the ceiling, Jacob saw the new lamp.

Looking for her dress, the cat suddenly jumped onto Janet's back.

The participle in the first sentence is *Hanging*. Right now, however, the sentence suggests that it is *Jacob* and not the new lamp that is *hanging* from the ceiling. This type of error, which occurs when a modifier is placed near a word that it does not modify rather than near the word it does, is called a **misplaced modifier.** The participle in the second sentence is *Looking*. At this point, the sentence indicates that *Janet's cat* was *looking* for a dress. This type of error, which occurs when a modifier has no word that it can logically modify, is called a **dangling modifier.**

Avoiding these types of errors is simple. Always check any sentence in which you have included a participle to make sure the modifier is describing the correct word. If there is an error, you can correct it by putting the participle next to the word it modifies or by changing the wording of the sentence:

CORRECTED

Hanging from the ceiling, the new lamp caught Jacob's eye.

or

Jacob saw the new lamp *hanging* from the ceiling.

CORRECTED

Looking for her dress, Janet suddenly felt her cat jump onto her back.

or

As Janet was looking for her dress, her cat suddenly jumped onto her back.

Not all misplaced modifiers involve participles. Any modifier, whether it is an individual word or a group of words, is a misplaced modifier if it suggests a relationship between words when no such relationship does or could exist. Consider these examples:

MISPLACED

As a young child, my great-grandfather often took my sister to the park.

The new sales representative sold the portable stereo to the woman *with the built-in compact disc player.*

The modifiers in these two sentences are obviously misplaced because the resulting sentences just don't make sense. A person can't be a young child and a great-grandfather at the same time. And people don't have stereo components in their bodies.

Avoid these kinds of misplaced modifiers by restating parts of the sentence or rearranging the order of the sentence so that the modifiers are next to the words they modify, as these corrected versions show:

CORRECTED

As a young child, my sister often went to the park with my great-grandfather.

The new sales representative sold the portable stereo with the built-in compact disc player to the woman.

COMPREHENSION AND PRACTICE

27.4

Identifying Participles

Each sentence in the following paragraph contains a participle. Underline the participle and the word it describes. Draw a line connecting the two elements, as the example shows.

EXAMPLE | Staring at the map, Gracie tried to determine where she was.

(1) Entering a convenience store downtown last week, my brother Joe knew something was wrong. (2) Trying to figure out what the problem was, he looked around the store. (3) Picking up a few items and talking, two older women walked from the back of the store. (4) Waiting for them to finish their shopping, Joe looked around the rest of the store. (5) Standing behind the counter, the clerk seemed particularly nervous. (6) Turning around, Joe saw a figure all in black, with sunglasses and a baseball cap pulled low. (7) Quickly striding toward the register, this man appeared to reach for something under his jacket. (8) Pretending he couldn't find what he wanted, Joe inched toward the door. (9) Driving by the store at that moment, a police car caught his attention. (10) Responding to Joe's yells for help, the officers headed into the store in time to stop the robbery.

COMPREHENSION AND PRACTICE 27.5

Identifying and Correcting Dangling and Misplaced Modifiers

Each of the following sentences contains a dangling or misplaced modifier. First, underline the dangling or misplaced modifier. Then, on a separate piece of paper, restate or rearrange each sentence so that the modifiers are describing the correct words. More than one correct answer is possible. Use the example as a guide.

EXAMPLE | Flying around the lamp, the child was fascinated by the moth.

CORRECTED | Flying around the lamp, the moth fascinated the child.

or

The child was fascinated by the moth flying around the lamp.

(1) Expecting nothing but a normal day, the discovery Jennifer made one late spring afternoon changed her outlook for the summer. (2) She had been applying for a job for a month requiring computer skills. (3) Having taken a course in computer applications, spreadsheets and PowerPoint presentations were among her areas of expertise. (4) Sending out applications to several companies downtown, her hopes were that one of these places would come

through for her. (5) But the hopes seemed distant after three weeks looking for a good job. (6) Everything changed when lying under her refrigerator, Jennifer found a letter that she had dropped the previous day. (7) When she read the letter, she broke into a smile, informing her that she had been offered a job for the summer. (8) Shaking, the phone seemed to move as she called to accept the job. (9) As a prospective employee, her supervisor, Ms. Tally, told Jennifer about the various duties involved. (10) Hanging up the phone, her smile of happiness grew even broader.

CHALLENGE 27.2   Using Participles to Combine Sentences

collaboration

Working with a classmate, combine the following simple sentences to eliminate choppiness by changing one of the sentences into a participial phrase. Use the example as a guide.

EXAMPLE   Reggie was reading a novel. He was sitting on the couch.

Sitting on the couch, Reggie was reading a novel.

1. The protesters were marching in front of the factory. They were carrying signs.

_____

_____

_____

2. The scholarship winner waved in acknowledgment. She smiled at her grandmother.

_____

_____

_____

3. Jeremy and Jackie enjoyed the reflection of the stars on the water. They sat on a bench overlooking the harbor.

_____

_____

_____

_____

4. The skateboarders took advantage of the empty streets on the holiday afternoon. They practiced in front of City Hall Plaza.

_____

_____

_____

_____

5. The crowd at the comedy club laughed uncontrollably at the comedian. They came alive when she began her routine.

_____

_____

_____

_____

Avoiding Double Negatives

ESL Note
See "Double Negatives," page 552, for more on avoiding double negatives.

Expressing negation can also cause problems for writers. _No, never, nowhere, nobody, nothing, no one,_ and _none_ are all used to express the idea of _no_. Adverbs like _scarcely, hardly,_ and _barely_—as well as _not,_ the adverb used to create _contractions_ (such as _did + not = didn't_)—also express negation.

When two of these negative words are used in the same sentence, they form what is called a **double negative.** Double negatives are never acceptable in college or professional writing. To avoid double negatives in your writing, check your sentences to make sure you have only one negative in each.

Correcting a double negative is easy: simply eliminate one of the negative words or change it to a positive form. Note the negatives in the examples below as well as the methods used to correct the errors.

EXAMPLE   Although my feet are very narrow, I have ~~not~~ had no trouble finding reasonable work shoes.

or

                                                              any
Although my feet are very narrow, I have not had ~~no~~ trouble finding reasonable work shoes.

EXAMPLE   The firefighters couldn't do nothing to stop the forest fire.

or

                            anything
The firefighters couldn't do ~~nothing~~ to stop the forest fire.

As corrected, each of these sentences expresses the point originally intended, but now does so with a single negative.

COMPREHENSION AND PRACTICE

Avoiding Double Negatives

27.6   In the following paragraph, circle the correct words in parentheses, avoiding double negatives. Use the material above and the following example as a guide.

EXAMPLE   Madeleine and David don't plan to travel ((anywhere), nowhere) special this summer.

(1) Even though I don't know (anything, nothing) about professional sports, I enjoy going to see a professional baseball game once in a while. (2) In fact, I never turn down (any, no) invitation to see the Mud Hens. (3) This minor league team has not had (any, no) problem attracting crowds since it opened its new stadium five years ago. (4) The design of the stadium is a major factor, since the place has (any, no) obstructed-view seats. (5) I have never heard (anybody, nobody) who has attended a game there say a negative thing about the place. (6) In addition, the food services provider doesn't have (any, no) items for sale that cost more than $3, and this provider often publishes discount food tickets in the paper. (7) As a result, even big families don't have (any, no) problem enjoying a few snacks during the game. (8) On game nights,

when my cousin can't get (anybody, nobody) from work to drive him to the park, I drive and he buys me a ticket. (9) At most games, the crowd is large, and you can't find (any, no) empty seats behind home plate. (10) Unfortunately, it seems as if every time I go to a game, the team has (any, no) luck and ends up losing.

Identifying and Correcting Double Negatives

Some of the sentences in the paragraph below contain double negatives. Put an * in front of any sentence containing a double negative, and then rewrite the sentence on a separate sheet of paper. More than one correct version is possible. Use the example as a guide.

EXAMPLE

*She wouldn't never leave town without contacting me first.

She would never leave town without contacting me first.

or

She wouldn't leave town without contacting me first.

(1) Bad habits are a plague not only for the offenders but also for the victims of the offending behavior. (2) For instance, many people who swear in public probably don't intend to offend nobody. (3) However, even if these people don't mean nothing by it, their bad habit can frighten, anger, or depress listeners. (4) Another bad habit many people share is not listening fully to those who are talking to them. (5) These offenders engage you in conversation, ask you a question, and then do not pay no attention as you try to answer. (6) There is not hardly anything more frustrating than trying to communicate with someone whose mind has moved on to other things. (7) The worst habit of all is gossiping about others. (8) Gossiping is particularly unfair because the people being discussed are not around to say nothing to defend themselves. (9) They never have no chance to confront the people talking about them. (10) Unfortunately, I am guilty of all these bad habits myself, so I don't have the right to lecture nobody else.

CHALLENGE 27.3   Building an Argument for Using Standard English

1. Although some people use double negatives in casual speech, these errors aren't acceptable in college or professional writing. Imagine you have been asked to address a class of sixth graders on the subject of using proper language in writing and speaking. On a separate sheet of paper, list at least four reasons you would give to explain why double negatives and other nonstandard forms (*ain't, we be,* and so on) are unacceptable in writing.

collaboration

2. Working with a classmate, compare your lists, identify the four strongest reasons, and then create a paragraph of between seven and ten sentences that could be handed out to sixth-grade students as a guide for writing.

QUICK STUDY   Student Example

This chapter focuses on ways of enhancing, labeling, or ranking ideas, individuals, actions, and so on. Consider this paragraph on a related subject, something that at this point the writer doesn't do well and would like to do better:

> One thing that I wish is that I didn't swim so bad. I first learned to swim at the YMCA during a school vacation when I was in the fifth grade. During that week, the instructor taught us how to float and do a few basic strokes and kicks. By the end of the week, I was able to stay afloat and paddle around a little. But I'm embarrassed to say that fifteen years later, I still swim poor. I hate not being a more competenter swimmer because it has kept me from doing things that I'd really like to try. For example, last year a bunch of my friends went on a trip to do some snorkeling. Worrying that they would think I was afraid of the water. an excuse about having other plans was all I could think of. Now the same group is planning to try windsurfing, and I would really like to go along on the trip, but I just don't have no confidence when I am in the water. If I could only find a class for adults that would teach swimming basics, I know that I could overcome this fear. I don't want to be a competitive swimmer. I just want to be in water over my head without feeling like I'm about to drown.

First complete the following activities in response to this paragraph:

1. Five of the sentences in the above paragraph are highlighted. Evaluate these sentences for mistakes in the use of adjectives and adverbs, dangling or misplaced modifiers, and double negatives, using the material in this chapter as a

guide. Circle any errors and then, on a separate sheet of paper, rewrite the sentences to eliminate the mistakes.

2. On the lines below, briefly explain how the order in which this paragraph is arranged helps to make it easier for a reader to understand the point being made.

_____

_____

_____

3. The paragraph discusses several reactions the writer has experienced, including feeling fearful, embarrassed, and unconfident. Choose one of these sensations and then, on a separate sheet of paper, write a brief paragraph in which you explain what experiencing that sensation feels like.

Now explore the topic in writing. As the paragraph above does, you could focus on something that you don't do especially well but that you would like to do better. Or you might turn your attention to one of these topics related to the subject matter of this chapter:

• something—a room or apartment, a car, an outfit, and so on—that you completely transformed
• a time when you discovered that something didn't match the description you had been given
• the best—or worst—movie, concert, or artistic or athletic performance you've ever seen
• how to enhance or improve your social life

collaboration

4. Exchange your draft with a classmate. Evaluate the paragraph you receive. Look for any problems, especially with the use of adjectives and adverbs, including misplaced and dangling modifiers and double negatives. Circle any errors, write corrected versions above them, and then return the paper to the writer.

5. Consider the comments and corrections your reader has made and create a final draft of your paragraph.

CHAPTER QUICK CHECK Working with Adjectives and Adverbs

The following passage contains errors involving double negatives, incorrect forms of adjectives and adverbs, and misplaced modifiers. Cross out each error and write the correct form above it. For misplaced modifiers, you may need to insert new words or cross out an entire clause and rewrite it. Also, there may be more than one way to correct the double negatives. Use the example to guide you.

EXAMPLE Greg's new digital phone is ~~more~~ smaller than Krystall's.

(1) One of the compellingist literary voices of the current age is Jamaica Kincaid. (2) Best known for her beautiful coming-of-age novel *Annie John*, published in 1983, the Caribbean island of Antigua is where Kincaid was born. (3) Not experiencing no happiness or fulfillment while growing up, she decided to abandon Antigua and head to the United States. (4) She left her home at age seventeen in the Caribbean, and she traveled to New York City, where she became an *au pair*, a live-in babysitter. (5) After attending colleges in New York and New Hampshire but not earning no degree, she began her professional writing career. (6) She had also changed her name from Elaine Potter Richardson by this time to Jamaica Kincaid. (7) During the mid-1970s, Kincaid was writing so good that she began to attract attention for her work in several periodicals, particularly the *New Yorker*. (8) After viewing her writing, the publisher quick invited her to join the staff of this influential magazine, and she remained associated with the periodical for twenty years. (9) Kincaid is considered to be one of the most superbest postcolonial writers, artists whose writing concerns countries formerly under the control of the British Empire. (10) In works like *Annie John, Lucy, The Autobiography of My Mother*, and *Mr. Potter*, Kincaid explores a number of real intense and sensitive themes, including alienation, isolation, and mother-daughter relationships.

SUMMARY EXERCISE Working with Adjectives and Adverbs

The following passage contains errors involving double negatives, incorrect forms of adjectives and adverbs, and misplaced modifiers. Cross out each error, and write the correct form above it. For misplaced modifiers, you may need to insert new words or cross out an entire clause and rewrite it. Also, there may be more than one way to correct the double negatives.

(1) I didn't never think my life would improve when a 24-hour supermarket opened in my neighborhood, but I was in for a pleasant surprise. (2) I have never been no believer that bigger always means more better. (3) Also, the idea of grocery shopping at midnight seemed awful strange to me, but I decided to give it a try.

(4) I was real surprised to see how few people had the same idea. (5) When I drove into the parking lot at midnight, I saw a smallest number of cars. (6) Filling the aisles, the produce section had a small crowd. (7) They were thumping melons, inspecting heads of lettuce, and picking apples just as they would if the sun were shining its most bright.

(8) I quick discovered the appeal of shopping at night. (9) First of all, there weren't hardly any customers at midnight, so it was more simple to maneuver in the aisles. (10) Also, I didn't have to fight no crowds, so I felt more freer to examine the selection of items at my leisure.

(11) The store seemed calmest, too. (12) Speaking more quiet than they do during the day, I found the workers more pleasanter. (13) Even the checkout area was awful still. (14) The most loud sound was the beep of the computer scanners.

(15) Best of all, there wasn't no long wait in line to check out and pay for my groceries. (16) Normally, I am squeezed in between people who apparently don't have no limits on their grocery budgets. (17) Imagine my delight when I found I could check out quick, without the normal ten-minute wait in line.

(18) Leaving the parking lot, I felt that this shopping trip was a positive experience. (19) I liked going about my shopping quiet and calm, without being bothered by other shoppers. (20) The only problem was that the next day, I was more sleepier than usual.

FOR FURTHER EXPLORATION Adjectives and Adverbs

1. Focus on one of the following topics, using the prewriting technique—or combination of techniques—that you prefer to generate ideas. Consider what purposes you might fulfill as you write:

   - ways that modern technology rules your life
   - the best way to spend a first date
   - the ideal place to live
   - techniques you have found to stretch a dollar

2. Evaluate your prewriting material, identify a focus, and work your way through the rest of the writing process to create a draft essay of at least 500 words on this subject.

collaboration

3. Exchange your draft with a classmate. Check the draft you receive for weaknesses, checking in particular for errors in the use of adjectives and adverbs, including misplaced and dangling modifiers and double negatives. Circle any mistakes and, using the material in this chapter to guide you, indicate the correct version above the error. Return the paper to the writer.

4. Revise your essay, correcting any errors in modifier use or other problems discovered by your reader.

RECAP   Adjectives, Adverbs, and Other Modifiers

Key Terms in This Chapter	Definitions
modifier	a word that describes or limits other words in a sentence
adjective	a word that describes a noun or pronoun An adjective answers the question *which one, how many,* or *what kind?*
adverb	a word that describes a verb, adjective, or another adverb An adverb tells *how, when, where, to what extent,* or *how much.*
positive form	the form of an adjective or adverb that describes a noun or pronoun without making a comparison EXAMPLE tall, poorly
comparative form	the form of an adjective or adverb used to compare two things EXAMPLE **more** handsome, lovel**ier**
superlative form	the form of an adjective or adverb used to compare more than two things EXAMPLE **most** remarkable, slow**est**
participle	a verb form that functions as an adjective in a sentence EXAMPLE *Singing sweetly,* the nightingale darted from tree to tree. Use participles when combining sentences and to eliminate choppiness.
misplaced modifier	a modifier placed near a word that it does not modify Place a participle near the word or words it describes in a sentence.
dangling modifier	a modifier with no word that it can logically modify
double negative	an incorrect construction using two negative words in the same unit of ideas EXAMPLE *Nobody* should bring *nothing* flammable. (anything) Negative words include *no, not, never, nowhere, nobody, nothing, no one, none, scarcely, hardly, barely.*

Guidelines for Adjective and Adverb Forms

Type of Word	Positive	Comparative	Superlative
One-syllable word	*brave*	positive form + *-er braver*	positive form + *-est bravest*
Words of three or more syllables	*enjoyable*	*more* + positive form **more** *enjoyable*	*most* + positive form **most** *enjoyable*
Some two-syllable words	*funny*	change *-y* to *-i* + *-er funnier*	change *-y* to *-i* + *-est funniest*
Other two-syllable words	*famous*	*more* + positive form **more** *famous*	*most* + positive form **most** *famous*

Commonly Confused Adjectives and Adverbs

Positive	Comparative	Superlative
bad (adjective)	worse	worst
badly (adverb)	worse	worst
good (adjective)	better	best
well (adverb)	better	best
little	less	least
much	more	most

Using Odyssey Online with MyWritingLab
For more practice with adjectives and adverbs, go to
www.mywritinglab.com.

CHAPTER 28
Parallelism: Presenting Related Items in a Similar Form

GETTING STARTED ...

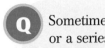

Sometimes I seem to get tripped up when I am presenting ideas in pairs or a series. When I'm done, the sentence sometimes sounds funny, as if the ideas I put together don't "fit" with each other. What am I doing wrong?

You are struggling with something called *parallelism,* the technique used to make related ideas flow together. For ideas to be parallel, they must follow the same basic form or structure. To maintain parallelism, focus on conjunctions because they are the words that form connections. Check any items connected by conjunctions, especially *and, or,* and *but,* and then use the first item in the series as a pattern for the other items.

Overview: Balancing Ideas in Your Writing

Multiple births are often newsworthy events. You have probably seen media coverage or a photo in the newspaper of triplets or quadruplets, all dressed in matching outfits. When it comes to presenting a series of items in your writing, this is the image you should keep in mind. All related ideas should look the same—be parallel. Maintaining **parallelism** means presenting any series of ideas, whether individual words or groups of words, in the same form. Faulty parallelism causes your reader to focus on the items that don't match rather than on the good ideas being presented. Therefore, it's important to spend some time mastering this aspect of writing.

Navigating This Chapter In this chapter, you will discover how to maintain parallelism:

- with words in a series
- with phrases
- with words linked by correlative conjunctions such as *either/or*

Maintaining Parallelism with Words in a Series

ESL Note
See "Word Order,"
pages 545–546, for
more on presenting
items in a series, and
"Agreement," pages
546–548, for more on
presenting verbs in a
series.

When you use words in a series, all the words should have the same grammatical structure. Generally, coordinating conjunctions (*and, but, for, nor, or, so,* and *yet*) are used to join the words. To maintain parallelism, keep two points in mind:

1. *Connect only similar parts of speech.* Join nouns with nouns, verbs with verbs, adjectives with adjectives, and so forth. Do not connect a verb with an adjective, a noun with an adverb, and so forth.

2. *Do not connect individual words in a series to phrases or clauses.* Keep the structure of the series, as well as the number of words in it, parallel.

EXAMPLES

Steve Martin is an actor, a comedian, and ~~he writes plays~~. *a playwright*

The weather this summer has been hot, rainy, and ~~a steam bath~~. *steamy*

COMPREHENSION AND PRACTICE 28.1

Using Parallel Words in a Series

Complete each statement with a word that maintains the parallel structure of the sentence. Use the example as a guide.

EXAMPLE

The antique painting was dusty, scratched, and *faded* .

(1) How can you tell whether someone is telling the truth or a _____? (2) This question has stymied everyone, including parents, spouses, and _____, as long as there has been a civilized society. (3) Existing polygraph tests measure truthfulness on the basis of such signs of anxiety as increased perspiration and _____. (4) But polygraph results are not considered reliable because not everyone reacts to tragedy, adversity, or _____ in the same way. (5) Some people react by shaking, sweating, and _____, while others simply become seemingly emotionless. (6) Also, complicating the issue is that outright lies, denial, and _____ are all types of dishonesty, but people don't judge them all the same way. (7) Brain research makes it possible to tell if a person's statement is trustworthy or _____. (8) To find out whether brain activity will signal when someone is being truthful or _____, neuroscience researchers used an MRI to measure brain activity of eighteen

volunteers. (9) The volunteers were given a specific playing card—for example, the jack of hearts or the _____—and told to lie when a computer correctly identified the card. (10) The MRI results showed different levels of brain activity depending on whether the person was telling the truth or _____.

COMPREHENSION AND PRACTICE
28.2

Maintaining Parallel Structure with Words in a Series

Each sentence in the following passage contains an error in parallelism. Cross out the errors, and, when necessary, write the correct version above the faulty one. You can correct some sentences by simply eliminating words. In some cases, more than one correct answer is possible. Use the example as a guide.

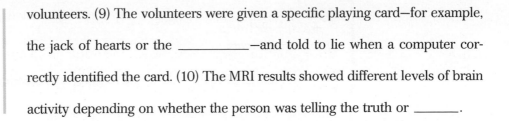

EXAMPLE

become irritable

Every time I try to stop smoking, I gain weight, get headaches, or ~~irritability takes over~~.

(1) I know from experience that employers in the twenty-first century want employees who are intelligent, enthusiastic, and they want them to be well educated. (2) After my military service, I missed out on a number of good jobs because the employers said I lacked technical experience or post-secondary education was needed by me. (3) After a year of looking for a desirable job, I became discouraged, angry, and I was depressed. (4) Now I am in college, working in the computer lab and computer science is being studied by me. (5) As a result, I will have some specific knowledge, confidence, and I will also have experience to offer an employer.

Maintaining Parallelism with Phrases

Phrases connected by *and* or *or* must also follow parallel structure. A phrase is a group of words that acts as a single word. Common types of phrases include prepositional phrases, *-ing* phrases, and *to* + *verb* phrases. It's correct to connect prepositional phrases with other prepositional phrases or *to* + *verb* phrases with other *to* + *verb* phrases. To correct errors that join nonparallel phrases, all you have to do is change the incorrect phrase to match the others, as these examples show:

EXAMPLES

throughout the entire city

The explosion affected people living *near the house, around the neighborhood, and* ~~the entire city was involved~~.

> When she's not in art class, she is busy *sketching animals, painting nature scenes, drawing portraits*
> or *to draw portraits*.
>
>   *to decorate*
> My grandmother always loved *to knit sweaters and decorating handkerchiefs*.

COMPREHENSION AND PRACTICE 28.3

Using Parallel Structure with Phrases

Circle all coordinating conjunctions in the sentences below. Then underline any phrases connected by coordinating conjunctions. If the connected phrases are not expressed in parallel form, change one so that it matches those to which it is connected. More than one correct answer may be possible. Use the example as a guide.

EXAMPLE

> The car crashed through the fence, across the yard, and it went into the pool.

(1) Until I was ten years old, I was frequently in trouble for breaking windows, beating up other kids, and to bother old people in my neighborhood. (2) I had a terrible attitude, whether I was at school, on the street, or I was home, until I joined the Agnes Kidd Memorial Boys and Girls Club. (3) The staff at the Club taught me to respect others, to help those less able, and respecting other people's property. (4) Within a month, I became a different person at home, around the neighborhood, and to spend time with in school. (5) I had been having trouble with math and reading was troublesome for me, so I spent time with a tutor from the after-school program at the Club. (6) Because of the staff's influence, I began to become more attentive to my younger sisters and doing my chores without being reminded. (7) Before long I was bringing home good report cards, making new friends, and I was feeling more confident. (8) I am determined to repay the staff for their help with my attitude and they helped me with school. (9) To do so, I intend to study hard in college and earn my degree in elementary education with a minor in physical education. (10) Then I can begin working with children in a community center or maybe to get a job in an elementary school.

COMPREHENSION AND PRACTICE

Keeping Phrases Parallel

28.4 The sentences in the following passage contain errors in parallelism of phrases. Cross out these errors, and then provide correct versions above the faulty ones if necessary. In some cases, you can correct the sentence simply by eliminating words. More than one correct answer may be possible with some sentences. Use the example to guide you.

EXAMPLE

Elaine looked for her lost credit card under the bed, behind the bureau, and ~~she even looked~~ in her old pocketbook.

(1) Yesterday, a guest speaker in my sociology class gave an outstanding lecture on stereotypes, urban myths, and on preconceived notions about life in a small town. (2) In high school and when I had presentations in other college classes, I had never gained much from these kinds of presentations. (3) However, when the class began, I quickly discovered that whether he was discussing the video, asking questions, or he related a personal experience, the speaker had my complete attention. (4) After his lecture, the speaker led a discussion on ways to broaden knowledge and eliminating stereotypical reasoning about rural life. (5) I left that classroom with a different perspective on life in the country and my attitude about guest speakers was new on guest speakers.

CHALLENGE 28.1 **Analyzing Parallelism in Literature**

1. Read the following excerpt, which makes great use of parallelism, from John Steinbeck's *The Grapes of Wrath.* This powerful novel details the struggle of the Joads, a family who traveled west during the Great Depression in a vain search for work, security, and dignity. In this passage, Steinbeck describes one source of anguish for starving families like the Joads, who were forced to stand idly by while agribusinesses, bent on controlling prices, destroyed surplus food.

The people come with nets to fish for potatoes in the river, and the guards hold them back; they come in rattling cars to get the dumped oranges, but the kerosene is sprayed. And they stand still and watch the potatoes float by, listen to the screaming pigs being killed in a ditch and covered with quick-lime, watch the mountains of oranges slop down to a putrefying ooze; and in the eyes of the people there is failure; and in the eyes of the hungry there is a growing wrath. In the souls of the people the grapes of wrath are filling and growing heavy, growing heavy for the vintage.

collaboration

2. Working with a classmate, underline the parallel elements you find in this passage. Then write a paragraph of seven to ten sentences in which you explain how the parallel structure helps you understand the point that Steinbeck is making.

Maintaining Parallelism When Using Correlative Conjunctions

You must also be careful to maintain parallelism when you use the following word pairs, called **correlative conjunctions,** to connect items:

both/and   not only/but also
either/or   whether/or
neither/nor

These pairs indicate two possibilities, alternatives, conditions, and so on. The words or phrases that these pairs connect must be parallel. To eliminate faulty parallelism in this kind of construction, make the second item match the first, as these examples show:

EXAMPLES

I tried to sneak into the club *by both trying the back door and ~~I showed~~ the guard a* *fake ID.* ^{showing}

The salesclerk was *neither polite nor ~~did she work efficiently~~.* ^{efficient}

COMPREHENSION AND PRACTICE 28.5

Maintaining Parallelism with Units Connected by Correlative Conjunctions

Complete the following sentences by filling in the blanks with words or phrases that complete the thought and maintain sentence parallelism. Use the example as a guide.

EXAMPLE

By the time I get to the shower in the morning, either all the hot water is used up or _____all the towels are missing_____ .

1. The fire at my neighbor's apartment last Christmas was terrifying not only for

   my friend but also _____.

2. The fire started when one of her house guests either dropped a cigarette on a

   chair or _____.

3. Regardless of the cause, the damage was heavy, not only to the apartment itself

   but also _____.

4. When I looked out the window on the night of the fire, the roof was not only

   smoking but also _____.

5. At first I couldn't tell whether the smoke was coming from her apartment or

   _____.

6. By the time the fire department arrived, both the front doorway and

_____ were engulfed in flames.

7. Whether she was suffering from smoke inhalation or _____

_____, my neighbor was hospi-

talized for three days.

8. Neither my family nor _____ could sleep until we

knew that she and her guests were all right.

9. Fortunately, my neighbor was able to collect insurance money and _____

_____ .

10. Since then, she doesn't allow smoking in her apartment, so anyone wanting to

smoke either steps out on the balcony or _____

_____ .

CHALLENGE 28.2   Using Parallelism Correctly

1. One element in each of the following groups is not parallel. Cross out the
nonparallel element, and revise it to make it parallel. Then, on a separate
sheet of paper, write a sentence using each item.

   a. both a midterm and we must write three papers

   b. either a situation comedy or to watch a talk show

   c. near the cafeteria, the gym, and beside the administration building

   d. dribbling, pass, and shoot

   e. not only interesting but it was funny, too

   f. whether it is during the summer or the winter is when it occurs

   g. playing video games, the Internet is used, and watching DVDs

   h. across the street and she went up the stairs

   i. to know the answer but being afraid to volunteer in class

   j. both the person making the complaint and the person who was accused

collaboration

2. Exchange your sentences with a classmate. Evaluate the sentences you receive to make sure that all errors in parallelism have been corrected. Put a ✓

above any element that you believe is still not parallel, and then return the sentences to the writer.

QUICK STUDY   **Student Example**

This chapter deals with similarities and differences in related elements. Consider the following paragraph on a related subject, how family life today differs from family life years ago:

> Family life today differs greatly from family life forty or fifty years ago in terms of size, family makeup, and how the family spends time together. Forty or fifty years ago, families seemed larger, many times having three or more children. Sometimes other relatives like grandparents, there were cousins, too, or aunts and uncles lived in the same household. Today, households seem smaller. Extended family members generally live on their own, either in their own homes or they live in apartments or assisted living centers. Most families today also have fewer children. In my neighborhood, for example, most of the families have two or three children, and in my high school class only two kids had more than two siblings. Another difference is that forty or fifty years ago, many families had two parents living in the same house, and usually only one of those parents worked outside the home. Today, single-parent families are more common, and in families with two parents living in the same home, both often have jobs. Forty or fifty years ago, families used to spend their time together differently, too. If they had a television, it was probably one set that the entire household had to share, which often meant they watched shows together, and there was probably one phone in the house for everyone to share. Today, many families have two or more televisions, often with full cable, so different family members can watch television without spending time together or to be in the same room with each other. If they also have computer game systems, Internet access, and individual cell phones, family members spend time using this technology rather than interacting with each other. I am happy I am living

in today's modern world, but I also have to admit that today's families don't enjoy the same degree of togetherness that families forty or fifty years ago did.

First complete the following activities in response to this paragraph:

1. Four of the sentences in this paragraph are highlighted. Evaluate these sentences for errors in parallelism, using the material in this chapter to guide you. Circle the errors and then, on a separate sheet of paper, rewrite the sentences correctly.

2. The organizing strategy of comparison and contrast plays a significant role in this paragraph. (See Chapter 10 for more on comparison and contrast.) On the lines that follow, briefly explain how using comparison and contrast makes the subject easier for the reader to understand.

_____

_____

_____

_____

_____

3. What do you think of the way the examples are arranged in this paragraph? Do you agree with the current order, or would you suggest rearranging them? Use the following lines to identify your standpoint and your reasoning.

_____

_____

_____

_____

_____

Now explore the topic in writing. As the paragraph above does, you could concentrate on some issue associated with family relations or family life. You might also focus on one of these topics related to the subject matter of this chapter:

- what you think (or _know_ from experience) it is like to be a twin or triplet
- a group you know or are part of that is like a family
- the person in your family that you most resemble in terms of personality, physical appearance, and so on
- a time you heard something—a rumor about a friend, an offer for a product, and so one—that just didn't sound right

collaboration

4. Exchange your draft with a classmate. Evaluate the paragraph you receive. If you discover any problem spots, especially with parallelism, circle the errors and then return the paper to the writer.

5. Consider the comments and corrections your reader has made and create a final draft of your paragraph.

CHAPTER QUICK CHECK Maintaining Parallelism

Check the sentences in the following passage for the types of errors in parallelism described in this chapter. Cross out each incorrect form, and write any correction in the space above it. In some cases, more than one correct answer is possible. If a sentence is correct as written, write *OK* above it.

(1) Some engineers are beginning to experiment with a surprising material for building new structures and to renovate old ones: cardboard. (2) Of course, cardboard has been around for a long time, but until recently almost nobody thought it would be any good as a primary structural component in houses and to be used in other buildings. (3) Most people think of how easy it is to tear up a cardboard gift box or poking a hole in a cardboard shipping container, and they rule out other uses for this product. (4) As they see it, cardboard is too weak, flimsy, and it is insubstantial to be used for serious building projects. (5) But structural engineers have discovered that when it is properly prepared and treated, cardboard can be both durable and it is also surprisingly strong. (6) Cardboard is, after all, made from recycled paper, which means that it is actually composed of processed wood. (7) When it has been tightly compressed, coated with water-resistant chemicals, and it has been manufactured for different lengths and widths, cardboard has proven to be both strong and resilient. (8) In fact, some structural engineers in England demonstrated the strength of cardboard by designing and they built a cardboard bridge that they then drove a car across. (9) In addition, engineers recently constructed a school building that, except for the concrete foundation, they used glass windows, and roof framing, is largely made of treated cardboard. (10) The school building stands as proof that whether the cardboard is

a small gift box or a large shipping container is made from cardboard, it may have another life that most of us have never considered.

SUMMARY EXERCISE Maintaining Parallelism

Check the sentences in the following passage for the types of errors in parallelism described in this chapter. Cross out each incorrect form, and write your correction in the space above. In some cases, more than one correct answer is possible. If a sentence is correct as written, write *OK* above it.

(1) Alcohol abuse is one of the most misunderstood problems in the world. (2) Even though researchers have shown that alcoholism is a disease, many people still think that it's a sign of a defect, weakness, or the person is lazy. (3) As a result, many individuals suffering from this disease are more likely to hide the problem than seeking treatment.

(4) In the United States, drinking is treated as sexy, glamorous, and you can look macho. (5) For example, television commercials for alcohol show beautiful bars filled with attractive models, sports stars, or some are celebrities, all having fun. (6) People are encouraged to think that they can be like those glamorous, famous people if they drink.

(7) However, for many, drinking is neither glamorous nor it is not special; instead, their genetic makeup means that drinking is as dangerous for them as to play Russian roulette. (8) Without even being aware of it, they become dependent on alcohol, and their patterns of living can change, too. (9) As time passes, they need to drink more and more alcohol to function. (10) Without alcohol, both their bodies and their mental state of being go through excruciating symptoms of withdrawal.

(11) Alcoholism is a disease of denial, and many individuals suffering from it are unable to admit they have a problem. (12) In some cases, they lose their families, their jobs, their friends, and their self-respect is gone before they

finally admit that they are addicted. (13) Unfortunately, some alcoholics choose to die rather than acknowledging that they have a problem.

(14) Those who do accept that they are addicted can begin recovery with a treatment program. (15) They can go into a detoxification center, they might go to a public treatment center, or a private substance abuse clinic. (16) With professional care, they undergo withdrawal from alcohol and also receiving counseling to understand why they feel the need to drink. (17) For recovering alcoholics, Alcoholics Anonymous provides a support group; they can draw strength from others who are taking steps to overcome their addiction and put their lives back together.

(18) Most of us think of addiction as a problem with drugs such as cocaine, methamphetamines, or heroin are making a comeback. (19) However, the most common addicts do not stick needles in their arms or are swallowing pills; they abuse alcohol. (20) If more of us were aware that alcohol abuse affects people without regard for age, race, people of both sexes or religion, then perhaps fewer would start down that road to alcohol addiction.

FOR FURTHER EXPLORATION Parallelism

1. Focus on one of the following topics. Use the prewriting technique—or combination of techniques—that fits your style of working to come up with some preliminary ideas while also considering the purposes you might fulfill in writing about the topic:

   - what the expression *The American Dream* means to you
   - the invention or innovation that has had the greatest transformative effect on the world
   - a situation during which you experienced a strong case of déjà vu
   - the worst kind of dishonesty

2. Evaluate your prewriting material, identify a focus, and work your way through the rest of the writing process to create a draft essay of at least 500 words on this subject.

collaboration

3. Exchange your draft with a classmate. Check the draft you receive for weaknesses, checking in particular for any errors in parallelism. Circle any errors, using the material in this chapter as a guide, and then return the draft to the writer.

4. Revise your essay, correcting any errors in parallelism or other problems discovered by your reader.

RECAP Parallelism

Key Terms in This Chapter	Definition
parallelism	a way of creating structural balance in writing by expressing similar or related ideas in similar form
	Individual words that are connected by a conjunction should be parallel.
	EXAMPLE That car is *old* and *rusty*.
	Phrases that are connected by a conjunction should be parallel.
	EXAMPLE She looked *in the closet* and *under the bed*.
	Words that follow pairs of correlative conjunctions should be parallel.
	EXAMPLE *Neither* the police *nor* the insurance adjuster could identify the cause of the accident.
correlative conjunction	conjunctions used in pairs (like *both/and* and *either/or*) to connect items

The Basic of Parallelism

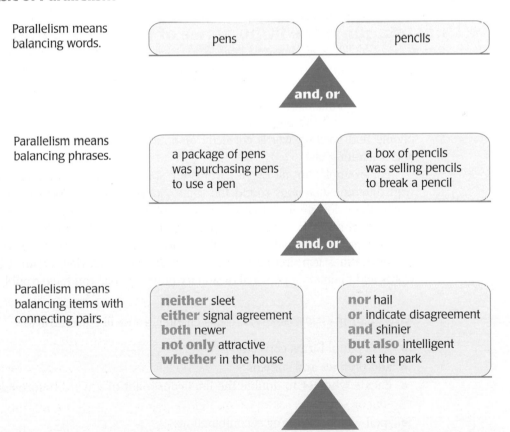

Parallelism means balancing words.

pens   pencils

and, or

Parallelism means balancing phrases.

a package of pens
was purchasing pens
to use a pen

a box of pencils
was selling pencils
to break a pencil

and, or

Parallelism means balancing items with connecting pairs.

neither sleet
either signal agreement
both newer
not only attractive
whether in the house

nor hail
or indicate disagreement
and shinier
but also intelligent
or at the park

Using Odyssey Online with MyWritingLab

For more practice with parallelism, go to www.mywritinglab.com.

CHAPTER 29
Spelling: Focusing on Correctness

GETTING STARTED ...

 No matter how hard I try to learn the rules, I still seem to have trouble with spelling. Why is the spelling of the English we use here in the United States so hard to master, and what can I do to become a better speller?

English has been drawn from a number of other languages, so it's no surprise that you find spelling challenging. Exceptions to the spelling rules are common, and it's these exceptions—not the rules themselves—that give people the most difficulty. To continue to improve as a speller, keep a list of the words that *in particular* give you trouble. Every time you write, use this list to check your draft. Before long, you will find that your spelling is getting better and that you notice errors more easily.

Overview: Understanding the Importance of Correct Spelling

ESL Note
See "Spelling" on page 552.

Spelling *always* counts, as any experienced writer will tell you. Errors in spelling are often the most obvious flaws in writing. Make no mistake about it—some people simply don't have much difficulty with spelling, so for them spelling errors almost jump off the page. For others, however, the story is quite different. These people find spelling words correctly or noticing misspellings to be an enormous and frustrating task.

For example, not all English words are spelled as they sound, and some words with different meanings sound the same. Some words conform to spelling rules, while others deviate from them. But as complicated as spelling is, readers *always* expect correct spelling, and any misspelled words can spoil the effect of an otherwise excellent paper. Fortunately, a number of techniques can help you become a better speller. Besides learning basic spelling rules, you can review commonly confused words and maintain a personal dictionary of words that you have trouble spelling.

Navigating This Chapter In this chapter, you will learn how to:

- spell plural forms correctly
- add prefixes and suffixes
- decide whether to double the final consonant of a word before adding *-ing* or *-ed*
- spell words with *ie* or *ei* combinations
- choose correctly among *-sede, -ceed,* and *-cede,* and other endings that sound alike
- deal with commonly confused words
- master the most commonly misspelled words

Basic Rules for Forming Plurals

As Chapter 25 illustrated, the most basic rule for forming plurals is to add *-s* to the singular forms:

book　books　　　computer　computer**s**　　　banana　banana**s**

However, there are numerous exceptions to this basic rule, as the following guidelines show.

Nouns that end in *-ch, -sh, -x,* or *-s*　For nouns that end in *-ch, -sh, -x,* or *-s,* form the plural by adding an *-es:*

porch　porch**es**　　　fox　fox**es**　　　lash　lash**es**

Nouns that end in *-y*　The plural for most nouns ending in *-y* depends on the letter preceding the *-y.* If that letter is a vowel (*a, e, i, o, u*), simply add *-s:*

delay　delay**s**　　　key　key**s**　　　tray　tray**s**

If the letter before the *-y* is a consonant, change the *-y* to *-i* and add *-es:*

worry　worr**ies**　　　duty　dut**ies**　　　sky　sk**ies**

Nouns that end in *-o*　For nouns that end in *-o,* look at the preceding letter to decide whether to add *-s* or *-es.* If the letter preceding the final *-o* is a *vowel,* simply add *-s:*

radio　radio**s**　　　stereo　stereo**s**　　　trio　trio**s**

If the letter before the *-o* is a *consonant,* you usually add an *-es:*

potato　potato**es**　　　echo　echo**es**　　　veto　veto**es**

Exceptions　Nouns referring to music, such as *altos, falsettos, solos,* and *sopranos,* do not obey this rule. In addition, with a few nouns ending in *-o* preceded by a consonant, you may add either *-s* or *-es:*

cargo　cargo**s** *or* cargo**es**　　　motto　motto**s** *or* motto**es**
zero　zero**s** *or* zero**es**

Words that end in *-f* or *-fe*　Learn which plurals end in *-fs* or *-fes* and which ones must change to *-ves.* Some nouns that end in *-f* or *-fe* form plurals with a simple *-s:*

safe　safe**s**　　　belief　belief**s**　　　chief　chief**s**

For others, however, you must change the *-f* to *-ves:*

thief　thie**ves**　　　knife　kni**ves**　　　wife　wi**ves**

For some nouns, two forms are acceptable:

scarf   scarf**s** *or* scar**ves**   hoof hoof**s** *or* hoo**ves**

dwarf   dwarf**s** *or* dwar**ves**

If you are in doubt about how to form the plural for one of these words, check a dictionary to find the proper spelling.

Nouns with Latin endings   Make nouns with Latin endings plural in keeping with the original language:

alumnus   alumn**i**   crisis   cris**es**

For some of these nouns, however, it is also acceptable to add *-s* or *-es* to form the plural:

appendix   appendi**xes** *or* append**ices**

memorandum   memorand**a** *or* memorand**ums**

index   inde**xes** *or* indi**ces**

Hyphenated or combined nouns   For hyphenated and combined nouns, form the plural by adding *-s* to the main word:

sister**s**-in-law   leftover**s**   attorney**s** general

Irregular plurals   With some common words, form the plural by *changing letters within the word or adding letters to the end:*

man   men   foot   **feet**   louse   lice   child   child**ren**

Nouns with the same singular and plural forms   A few common words have the same form whether they are singular or plural:

one deer   several deer   one sheep   many sheep

one species   five species

Nonword plurals and words discussed as words   For abbreviations, figures, numbers, letters, words discussed as words, and acronyms, form the plural by adding either an *-s* or *-'s* (apostrophe + *-s*). Use the *-'s* with all lowercase letters, with the capital letters *A, I, U,* or any other time when adding the *-s* alone might confuse the reader:

one A   four A**'s**   one i   several i**'s**   one the   many the**'s**

COMPREHENSION AND PRACTICE

Providing the Correct Plural Form of Words

29.1   Following the guidelines on pages 445–446, provide the plural of each italicized word in the following passage. Cross out the singular form, and write the plural above it, as the example shows.

EXAMPLE The *hero* were two *man* who tackled the purse snatcher.
heroes · *men*

(1) Winter seems to bring with it a variety of *illness*, and this past winter was one of the worst *season* in a long time for *family* with young *child*. (2) I am a single parent of two *son*, both under five *year* old and both with *allergy*. (3) Last month, both *boy* had *bout* with *cold* or *infection*. (4) It was hard for me to see my two *baby* suffer. (5) There were many *night* when I was still counting *sheep* at 2 or 3 A.M. (6) One morning, after staying up with them most of the night, I awoke with *pain* in my chest. (7) It felt as though ten *knife* were cutting into my *lung*. (8) Finally, I called one of my *sister-in-law* and asked her to take me to the clinic. (9) The doctor diagnosed double pneumonia, which kept me out of *class* for two *week*. (10) I've never been one to fantasize about *superhero*, but there were certainly *time* last winter when I dreamed of being rescued.

CHALLENGE 29.1   Working with Plural Nouns

1. On a separate sheet of paper, choose five of the following singular nouns and make them plural. Then write a present tense sentence for each, as this example shows:

EXAMPLE leaf

The **leaves** begin to fall during late September.

attorney-at-law	deer
play	birch
echo	wife
analysis	duty
glass	handkerchief

collaboration

2. Now exchange your sentences with a classmate. In the sentences you receive, check that the plural forms are correct. Also, check to make sure that the proper verb form is used. Note any problems and then return the paper to the writer. Correct any problems your writing partner has identified.

Basic Rules for Prefixes and Suffixes

You can change the form and meaning of many words by adding *prefixes* and *suffixes* to them. A **prefix** is a unit such as *un-*, *dis-*, *mis-*, or *semi-* added to the beginning of a word. A **suffix** is a unit such as *-ness*, *-ing*, or *-ous* added to the end of a word.

Prefixes   When you add a prefix to a word, do not change the spelling of the word:

believable   **un**believable   obey   **dis**obey

understand   **mis**understand

Suffixes -*ly* and -*ness*   In most cases, simply add *-ly* or *-ness* without changing the spelling of the original word:

real   real**ly**   faithful   faithful**ness**   usual   usual**ly**

For words with more than one syllable that end in *-y*, you change the *-y* to *-i* before you add *-ly* or *-ness:*

lonely   lonel**iness**   easy   eas**ily**   silly   sill**iness**

Exception   When you add *-ly* to *true*, you drop the final *-e: truly.*

Suffixes for words ending in -*e*   For words ending in *-e*, drop the final *-e* when adding a suffix beginning with a vowel:

cope   cop**ing**   disapprove   disapprov**al**   fame   fam**ous**

Keep the final *-e* if the suffix begins with a consonant:

care   care**ful**   arrange   arrange**ment**   safe   safe**ty**

Exceptions   With words such as *mile*, *peace*, and *notice*, you keep the final *-e* when you add suffixes beginning with a vowel: mile*age*, peace*able*, notice*able*. Drop the final *-e* of such words as *whole*, *argue*, and *judge* when you add a suffix beginning with a consonant: whol*ly*, argu*ment*, judg*ment*.

Suffixes for words ending in -*y*   For words ending in *-y* preceded by a consonant, change the *-y* to *-i* before you add the suffix, unless the suffix itself begins with *-i* as with *-ing:*

bury   bur**ied**   simplify   simpl**ified**   *but*   hurry   hurry**ing**

Doubling the final consonant when adding a suffix   For one-syllable words that end in a *single* consonant preceded by a *single* vowel, *double the final consonant* before adding a suffix beginning with a vowel:

plan   plan**ned**   slip   slip**ping**   flat   flat**ten**

However, if the final consonant is preceded by *another consonant* or by *more than one vowel,* do not double the final consonant. Just add the suffix beginning with a vowel:

wash   wash**ing**   stoop   stoop**ed**   fail   fail**ure**

Multisyllable words ending with a vowel–consonant pattern must be pronounced to identify which syllable is emphasized or *accented.* If the accent is on the *final syllable,* double the final consonant before adding the suffix:

begín   begin**ning**   commit   commit**ted**   contról control**lable**

If the accent is *not* on the last syllable, just add the suffix:

bénefit   benefit**ed**   prófit   profit**able**   súffer   suffer**ing**

COMPREHENSION AND PRACTICE

Adding Suffixes to Words

29.2 Complete each sentence in the following passage by combining the word and suffix in parentheses. Refer to the guidelines on pages 448–449 for help. Use the example as a guide.

EXAMPLE   When it comes to (happy + ness) ____*happiness*____, Jerome has more than his share.

(1) When I was growing up, I wanted to take piano lessons, but my parents could never afford to make the (arrange + ments) _____. (2) Year after year, I would listen wistfully to my favorite songs, (hope + ing) _____ my parents could work out a way to pay for lessons. (3) I knew we didn't have much money to spare, so I never questioned their (judge + ment) _____. (4) If they (true + ly) _____ felt we couldn't afford it, I understood. (5) I didn't want to cause any (argue + ments) _____ between them. (6) At the same time, I was (whole + ly) _____ convinced that I could be a good pianist if I got the chance. (7) When it came to my schoolwork, I learned (easy + ly) _____, and I was sure that music would be no different. (8) It wasn't that I wanted to become (fame + ous) _____ or anything; I just wanted a chance to learn to play the piano. (9) (Final + ly) _____, last year, I was able to put aside enough money from my own job to start piano

lessons. (10) Now, one afternoon a week, I travel to a small office downtown,

and I (happy + ly) _____ indulge in my long-awaited lessons.

Deciding Whether to Double the Final Letter

Each sentence in the following passage contains a word and a suffix in parentheses. Decide whether to double the final letter of the word before adding the suffix. Write the correct spelling of each word on the line provided. Use the example as a guide.

EXAMPLE

On my Caribbean vacation, I went (snorkel + ing) ___*snorkeling*___ among brilliantly colored reefs and tropical fish.

(1) I'll never forget the day when I finally (stop + ed) _____

smoking. (2) For years, my mother had been (beg + ing) _____ me to quit.

(3) Even though I was only thirty, I found activities like (run + ing) _____

almost impossible. (4) Nonetheless, it wasn't until I visited my grandfather in

the hospital that I finally (realize + ed) _____ the damage I was doing

to myself. (5) My grandfather had been a heavy smoker for fifty years, and

now he was (suffer + ing) _____ from emphysema and lung cancer.

(6) He and my grandmother had looked forward to his retirement so they

could spend their time (travel + ing) _____. (7) His sickness

meant that they had done all that hoping and (plan + ing) _____ for

nothing. (8) As I walked out of the hospital, I threw my pack of cigarettes

in the trash, and I haven't (pick + ed) _____ up a cigarette since.

(9) (Occasional + ly) _____, I think of Gramps. (10) I remember my

(mortal + ity) _____ and am no longer tempted.

The Basic Rule for *ie* or *ei*

The basic rule for words with *ie* or *ei* combinations is this:

I before *e*
Except after *c*
And when sounded like *a*
As in *neighbor* or *weigh*

These common words feature *ie* combinations:

gr**ie**f   bel**ie**ve   f**ie**ld   ach**ie**ve   hyg**ie**ne

And these common words need an *ei* combination:

rec**ei**ve   perc**ei**ve   c**ei**ling   b**ei**ge   fr**ei**ght

Receive, perceive, and *ceiling* call for *ei* because these letters follow *c. Beige* and *freight* call for *ei* because the combination sounds like *a.*

Exceptions   There are a number of exceptions to this rule. For instance, even though the combination doesn't follow *c, e* comes before *i* in the words *either, neither, leisure, seize, their,* and *weird.* And in *species, science,* and *ancient, i* comes before *e* even though the letters follow *c.* Whenever you come across these exceptions in your reading, make a note of them. Later in this chapter, you will learn how to make your own spelling dictionary.

Basic Rules for *-sede, -ceed,* and *-cede,* and Other Endings That Sound Alike

Words that end in *-sede, -ceed,* and *-cede*   Only one word in English ends in *-sede:*

super**sede**

Only three words in English end in *-ceed:*

pro**ceed**   ex**ceed**   suc**ceed**

All other words with this sound end in *-cede:*

pre**cede**   se**cede**   inter**cede**

Have versus of   The correct forms *could've, should've,* and *would've* sound like the incorrect forms *could of, should of,* and *would of.* When it comes to these three verbs, don't trust your ear—always write *could have, should have,* and *would have.* Then, if you still want to use the contraction, change the words in your final draft.

Used to and supposed to   In speaking, we often fail to pronounce the final *-d* in the expressions *used to* and *supposed to.* As a result, these two expressions are frequently misspelled as *use to* and *suppose to.* Always add the final *-d* in *used* or *supposed.*

A lot and all right   Two expressions that commonly appear in writing are *a lot* and *all right.* A common error is to use the nonstandard forms *alot* and *alright.* These forms are not correct, so always use the standard versions, *a lot* and *all right.*

COMPREHENSION AND PRACTICE

Choosing the Correctly Spelled Word

29.4 Circle the correctly spelled word in the sets of parentheses in each of the following sentences. Use the example as a guide.

EXAMPLE   If she doesn't (recieve, (receive)) the money she was awarded by the jury, Mrs. Andreas will have to take her former landlord to court again.

(1) Through recent experience, I have come to (beleive, believe) that the only way a supervisor can earn the respect of workers is to be fair and consistent. (2) When workers see that someone else is allowed (alot, a lot) of leeway as far as work schedules or punctuality, they naturally resent it. (3) I'll (concede, conceed) that a boss should be as flexible and accommodating as possible. (4) But what I experienced last week when I was (suppose to, supposed to) have Friday night off caused me to lose respect for my supervisor. (5) On Thursday, one of my co-workers said that she had to attend a party for her (neice, niece) and needed the night off. (6) My boss didn't even (weigh, wiegh) the consequences, and he agreed and told me I would have to fill her spot on Friday. (7) I angrily responded that I already had plans and that Diane (could of, could've) made the request before the schedule was posted. (8) When my boss finally said it would be (all right, alright) if I worked for only two hours instead of the full four, I agreed, but I wasn't happy about it. (9) I know it's unfair to expect that anyone can (acheive, achieve) a perfect record in terms of pleasing all employees. (10) Still, it's not always easy to be a worker and see problems that never (should of, should've) occurred.

COMPREHENSION AND PRACTICE

Identifying and Correcting Misspelled and Misused Words

29.5 Each of the sentences in the following passage contains at least one misspelled or misused word. Cross out each incorrect form, and write the correct version above it. Use the example as a guide.

EXAMPLE   The caravan proceded at a liesurely pace.
                                     proceeded   leisurely

(1) Although many people have trouble beleiving it, thousands and thousands of adults in the United States cannot read. (2) It's wierd to think of adults being unable to do what schoolchildren can, but many are well behind second graders in reading ability. (3) In my sociology class, a guest speaker from the Adult Literacy Program explained that these people should of been given special help in school but somehow "feli through the cracks." (4) As a result, they never recieved the attention they needed. (5) The speaker explained that some of our friends and nieghbors might fall into this category. (6) In many cases, niether parents nor teachers noticed that these people were having difficulty during the course of growing up, so they did nothing to help. (7) It's amazing that many individuals manage to succede at various jobs despite their lack of literacy. (8) Somehow, they get use to bluffing their way through life. (9) The guest speaker explained that the greatest fear these people have is that someone will percieve that they cannot read. (10) Fortunately, the Adult Literacy Program has a 90 percent success rate, so these people can hope to acheive literacy if they are willing to try.

Dealing with Commonly Confused Words

ESL Note
See "Spelling," page 552, for more on the correct spelling of commonly confused words.

Sometimes, rather than misspelling a word, you wind up using a word that sounds like or reminds you of the word you intended to use. Such mistakes are common for *homonyms*, words that sound the same but have different spellings and meanings. Mistakes also occur with words that, for a number of reasons, people tend to confuse. On the following pages is a list of the frequently confused words.

Commonly Confused Words

Words	Definitions	Examples
accept **except**	to take or receive other than, excluding, but	The family refused to *accept* any financial support. They refused all donations *except* food.
advice **advise**	opinions, suggestions to give suggestions, guide	The counselor tried to provide sound *advice*. To *advise* the man any further, she would need to know more about his finances.
affect **effect**	(verb) to influence, stir the emotions (noun) a result, something brought about by a cause	Exercising definitely *affects* me. One welcome *effect* is an increased energy level.

(continued)

Commonly Confused Words *(continued)*

Words	Definitions	Examples
all ready	everyone or everything prepared	When she returned from jury duty, her work was *all ready* for her to complete.
already	before, previously	She had *already* missed work the week before because of illness.
among	used to refer to a group or to distribution	Kerry stood *among* the crowd of students protesting the newly imposed dress code.
between	used to refer to individual relationships	The principal, standing *between* the superintendent and the mayor, glared at her.
brake	*(noun)* a device to stop; *(verb)* to come to a halt	The driver's foot slipped off the *brake*. He could not *brake* in time to stop for the light.
break	to shatter, pause	He was lucky he didn't *break* his nose when he hit the windshield.
can	to be physically able to	I *can* usually get the new clothes priced and hung up on the display racks in about three hours.
may	to have permission to	*May* I leave once I've completed my work?
choose	to decide or select [present tense]	This semester, Terence will *choose* his own classes for the first time.
chose	decided or selected [past tense]	Last semester, he wasn't sure what classes to take, so his adviser *chose* all his courses.
conscience	inner sense of right and wrong	To live with a guilty *conscience* is a terrible ordeal.
conscious	aware, awake	All day long, you are *conscious* that you've done something wrong.
council	a group formally working together	The city *council* reacted angrily to the charge that the real estate agent had bribed them.
counsel	*(verb)* to give advice; *(noun)* a legal representative	The mayor tried to *counsel* the members to be quiet, but she was unsuccessful.
desert	*(noun)* a dry, arid, sandy place; *(verb)* to abandon	The park was as hot and dry as a *desert*. One by one, the picnickers began to *desert* us and headed straight for the beach.
dessert	the final part of a meal	None of them even bothered with the *dessert* Kathy had made, a delicious blueberry pie.
fewer	refers to items that can be counted	During the last month, I've had *fewer* quizzes in accounting.
less	refers to amounts or quantities that can't be counted	Unfortunately, I've had *less* time to study.
good	used to describe persons, places, things, and ideas	My brother has had *good* results with his used computer.
well	used to specify how something is, was, or would be done	He told me that it has run *well* from the moment he plugged it in.
hear	to listen	I could barely *hear* the music.
here	refers to direction or location	Sit *here,* where the sound is better.

Commonly Confused Words *(continued)*

Words	Definitions	Examples
hole	an empty spot	One of the magazines in the collection has a *hole* in the cover.
whole	complete	But I don't think you should throw out the *whole* set.
its	possessive form of *it*	The kitten kept dunking *its* nose in the milk.
it's	contraction for *it is* and *it has*	*It's* funny to see the kitten with a milk mask.
knew	understood [past tense]	The senator *knew* her constituents well.
new	recent, unused, fresh	She felt that it was time for someone *new* to take a turn.
know	to understand [present tense]	You *know* what the problem is.
no	negative, the opposite of *yes*	The problem is that we get *no* direction from Jerry.
now	at this point	The question *now* is what are we going to do about it?
lay	to put down, spread out	Once you *lay* the chair on its side, disconnect the arms.
lie	to rest or recline	Then *lie* down on the floor and find the seam running up the back of the chair.
lead	to go first, direct [present tense]	Parents should always *lead* their children by example.
	soft metal; graphite [rhymes with *bed*]	The responsibilities of parenthood sometimes feel like a *lead* weight.
led	went first, directed [past tense]	When they are grown, you'll be glad you *led* them well.
loose	not tight, unfastened	*Loose* clothing is better for exercise.
lose	to misplace, fail, not win	If you *lose* the game, don't *lose* your sense of humor.
of	stemming from, connected with or to	Peter is fond *of* late night TV.
off	away from, no longer on	On his day *off*, he sleeps late.
passed	went by [past tense of *pass*]	An ambulance suddenly appeared and *passed* us.
past	time gone by, former time	From *past* experience, I knew that it was heading to Parklane Hospital.
personal	individual, private	The shoplifter had a history of *personal* problems.
personnel	employees, staff	When the security *personnel* took her to the manager's office, she began cursing and kicking.
precede	to come before	One goal of this intervention program is to identify what *precedes* an incident of child abuse.
proceed	to go on	After they study the causes, they *proceed* through the formal process of filing an official complaint.
principal	*(noun)* the head of a school;	In high school, Giselle wanted to get back at the *principal* by ordering ten pizzas in his name.
	(adjective) primary, chief	My *principal* objection to this plan was that we might get caught.
principle	a rule of conduct; a basic truth	One of my *principles* is to avoid needless complications.

(continued)

Commonly Confused Words *(continued)*

Words	Definitions	Examples
quiet	still; silent	After Joanie finished yelling, the room was completely *quiet*.
quite	very; completely	Her friends were *quite* surprised that their party had disturbed her.
than	conjunction, used in comparisons	From a distance, people think John is older *than* his older brother Billy.
then	next, at that time	*Then* they take a closer look and see that Billy has wrinkles and gray hair.
their	the possessive form of *they*	The reporters were ordered to reveal the names of *their* sources to the judge.
there	refers to direction or location	Immediately, the lawyers who were *there* objected.
they're	contraction for *they are*	The reporters will be going to jail because *they're* not going to follow the judge's orders.
threw	tossed, hurled [past tense]	The supervisor accidentally *threw* out the envelope containing the day's receipts for the store.
through	in one side and out the other, from beginning to end	We had to go *through* twenty bags of trash before we found the envelope.
to	in the direction of, toward	Susan and Lai stopped at a gas station for directions *to* the hotel.
	also used to form an infinitive	They needed *to* fill the tank anyway.
too	also, excessively	They bought some snacks for the evening, *too*.
two	more than one, less than three	They had stopped just *two* blocks away from the hotel.
waist	middle part of the body	He constantly worries that his *waist* is getting bigger.
waste	use up needlessly; leftover material	If he'd eat less junk food, he wouldn't *waste* so much time worrying.
weak	not strong, feeble	No matter how much I study, my memory still seems *weak*.
week	seven days	Even after a *week* of study, I still don't know those math theorems.
weather	atmospheric conditions	The *weather* has been unusually mild.
whether	indicating an alternative or question	Scientists are now trying to determine *whether* these warmer temperatures are due to global warming.
were	past tense plural of *are*	My mother and I *were* hoping to drive to Washington, D.C., in April.
we're	contraction for *we are* or *we were*	*We're* going to go in September instead.
where	indicates or raises a question about direction or location	The neighborhood *where* my uncle lives is near the National Zoo.
who	used as a subject	It took us several minutes to discover *who* had started the fight on the floor.
whom	used as an object	Once we cleared the room, we decided which shoes belonged to *whom*.

Commonly Confused Words *(continued)*

Words	Definitions	Examples
who's	contraction for *who is* or *who has*	I'm not sure *who's* supposed to drive.
whose	possessive form of *who*	I don't know *whose* car we will use, either.
your	possessive form of *you*	Sometimes knowing all the rules governing *your* job is not enough.
you're	contraction for *you are*	Once *you're* on the job by yourself, rules don't help much.

COMPREHENSION AND PRACTICE 29.6

Identifying the Correct Word from Pairs of Commonly Confused Words

In each sentence in the following passage, circle the correct word from the pair in parentheses. Use the example to guide you.

EXAMPLE A job can have a profound (affect, ⓔffect) on your whole life.

(1) If I had to (choose, chose) the strangest experience in my (passed, past), it would be the summer I worked third shift at the aluminum barrel factory. (2) I figured I could (lead, led) a beachcomber's life by day and (than, then) go nightclubbing with my friends before my shift started. (3) Quickly, however, I realized that I had planned on everything (accept, except) sleep, and my lack of foresight began to (affect, effect) me. (4) For instance, I always had a tough time drifting (of, off) to sleep because there was no (quiet, quite) around my house during the day. (5) (Their, There) were few days when I could wake up in time to go to the beach, and so my (principal, principle) goal became simply to make it through each week.

COMPREHENSION AND PRACTICE 29.7

Identifying Errors with Commonly Confused Words

Each sentence in the following paragraph contains an error in one of the words from the list of commonly confused words. Cross out the incorrect words and write the correct ones above them, as the example shows.

EXAMPLE   His ~~principle~~ *principal* objection to the job offer was that it involved a two-hour-a-day commute.

(1) I suffered my first serious injury a month ago when I stepped in a whole in the sidewalk. (2) From the moment my right foot touched the edge of the broken sidewalk, I somehow new I was about to hurt myself. (3) I even tried to shift the weight from that foot, but unfortunately I was all ready in the middle of my stride. (4) As I came down on the side of my foot with all my weight, I could almost here the tissue tearing. (5) The pain was overpowering, and I had to sit down in order to remain conscience. (6) Than I took a look at my ankle and became sick to my stomach. (7) It was swollen to at least three times it's normal size. (8) In addition, my entire right leg felt as heavy as a bar of led. (9) Fortunately, their was a phone nearby, so I called my brother for a ride to the hospital. (10) The doctor said it is generally better to brake an ankle than to tear several ligaments as I had.

CHALLENGE 29.2   Using Commonly Confused Words Correctly

1. The sentences in Comprehension and Practice 29.7 contain ten incorrectly used words. For each of these incorrectly used words, write a sentence in which you use the word correctly.

collaboration

2. Exchange the sentences you have written with a classmate. In the sentences you receive, make sure that the words are now used correctly. Note any problem spots and return the sentences to the writer.

Learning the Most Commonly Misspelled Words

In addition to remembering the various spelling rules and their exceptions, you should also keep your own personal spelling dictionary. Make a list, *in alphabetical order,* of words you misspell in your day-to-day writing. Keep this list with your dictionary for handy reference when you write.

A computer file is the best place to maintain your list. Keep a copy on your computer desktop, insert new words in alphabetical order, and print out a new copy. If you handwrite your list, leave two or three lines between words. When you discover a misspelled word in one of your papers, add it on a blank line.

Look through the list of commonly misspelled words that follows and mark the ones that you misspell. Include these words in your personal spelling dictionary.

Commonly Misspelled Words

A

absence	acquired	a lot	answer	assented
academic	acre	although	Antarctic	association
acceptance	across	aluminum	anxious	athlete
accident	actual	always	apologize	attacked
accidentally	actually	amateur	apparatus	attempt
accommodate	address	among	apparent	attendance
accompany	administration	amount	appreciate	attorney
accomplish	advertise	analysis	approach	authority
accumulate	again	analyze	approval	auxiliary
accurate	agreeable	angel	argument	available
accustom	aisle	angle	arrival	awful
ache	alcohol	angry	article	awkward
achieve	all right	anonymous	ascended	
acquaintance				

B

bachelor	bathe	believe	boundaries	bureau
balance	beautiful	benefit	breath	bury
bargain	because	biscuits	breathe	business
basically	beginning	bookkeeping	brilliant	
bath	belief	bottom	Britain	

C

cafeteria	cereal	cocoa	committee	cooperate
calendar	certain	collect	company	cooperation
campaign	change	colonel	comparative	corporation
cannot	characteristic	color	competent	correspondence
careful	cheap	colossal	competitive	courteous
careless	chief	column	conceivable	courtesy
catastrophe	children	comedy	condition	criticize
category	church	comfortable	consistent	curriculum
ceiling	cigarette	commitment	continuous	
cemetery	circuit	committed	convenience	

D

daily	definitely	diameter	discuss	dominate
daughter	definition	diary	disease	doubt
dealt	dependent	different	disgust	dozen
debt	describe	direction	distance	drowned
deceased	description	disappointment	distinction	duplicate
decision	despair	disastrous	distinguish	
defense	despise	discipline	dominant	

E

earliest	emergency	environment	essential	exhausted
efficiency	emphasis	equip	exaggerated	existence
efficient	emphasize	equipment	excellent	experience
eligible	employee	equipped	excessive	extraordinary
embarrass	envelop	especially	excitable	extremely
embarrassment	envelope			

(continued)

Commonly Misspelled Words *(continued)*

F

fallacy	February	fiery	fourth	fulfill
familiar	feminine	foreign	freight	further
fascinate	fictitious	forty	frequent	futile
fatigue				

G

garden	genuine	gracious	guarantee	guest
gauge	ghost	grammar	guardian	guidance
general	government	grateful	guess	gymnasium
generally				

H

handicapped	height	humor	hygiene	hypocrite
handkerchief	hoping	humorous	hypocrisy	

I

illiterate	incidentally	inevitable	intelligence	irresistible
imaginative	incredible	infinite	interest	irreverent
immediately	independent	inquiry	interfere	island
immigrant	indictment	instead	interpret	isle
important				

J

jealousy	jewelry	judgment

K

kitchen	knowledge	knuckles

L

language	leave	lengthen	library	literature
later	legitimate	lesson	license	livelihood
latter	leisure	letter	lieutenant	lounge
laugh	length	liable	lightning	luxury

M

machinery	maintenance	marry	mathematics	mechanical
maintain	marriage	marvelous	measure	medicine
medieval	minute	missile	month	muscle
merchandise	miscellaneous	misspell	morning	mustache
miniature	mischief	mistake	mortgage	mutual
minimum	mischievous	moderate	mountain	mysterious

N

naturally	necessity	nickel	noticeable	nuisance
necessary	negotiate	niece		

O

obedience	occurrence	omit	opportunity	organization
obstacle	official	opinion	oppose	original
occasion	often	opponent	optimism	ought
occurred				

Commonly Misspelled Words *(continued)*

P

pamphlet	perceive	phase	practically	probably
parallel	percentage	phenomenon	precisely	procedure
paralyze	perform	physical	preferred	professor
parentheses	performance	physician	prejudice	protein
participant	permanent	picnic	preparation	psychology
particularly	permitted	piece	presence	publicity
pastime	perseverance	pleasant	pressure	pursuing
patience	personality	politics	primitive	pursuit
peasant	perspiration	possess	priority	
peculiar	persuade	possibility	privilege	

Q

qualified	quantity	quarter	question	questionnaire
quality				

R

readily	recognize	relevant	renewal	resistance
realize	recommendation	relieve	repeat	responsibility
really	reference	remember	repetition	restaurant
reasonably	referring	remembrance	requirement	rhythm
receipt	regretting	reminisce	reservoir	ridiculous
receive	reign	removal	residence	
recipient				

S

salary	sensible	sophisticated	stature	stretch
sandwich	separate	sophomore	statute	subsidize
scenery	sergeant	souvenir	stomach	substantial
schedule	severely	specimen	straight	substitute
scissors	similar	statistics	strategy	subtle
secretary	solemn	statue	strength	sufficient
summarize	surprise	surprising	susceptible	suspicion
superior				

T

technique	thorough	tournament	transferring	tremendous
temperament	thoroughly	tragedy	travel	truly
temperature	through	traitor	traveled	Tuesday
tendency	tomorrow	transfer	treasure	typical
theory	tongue			

U

unanimous	urgent	useful	utensil

(continued)

Commonly Misspelled Words *(continued)*

V

vacancy	valuable	vein	villain	visibility
vacuum	vane	vicinity	violence	visitor
vain	vegetable			

W

| warrant | Wednesday | weird | writing | written |

Y

yesterday

Z

zealous

COMPREHENSION AND PRACTICE

29.8

Identifying and Correcting Commonly Misspelled Words

Each sentence in the following passage contains a misspelled version of a word from the list of commonly misspelled words. Cross out the misspelled word and write the correct version above the incorrect one, as the example shows:

EXAMPLE

Their bank ~~balence~~ *balance* had already dropped below $100.

(1) Today, it seems as if there's more and more corruption in goverment. (2) The newspapers are filled with stories of public officials who have shown incredible lapses in judgement leading to their arrests. (3) For example, a year ago our own mayor was accused of giving a big contract to one of his aquaintances. (4) On another occassion, a state police officer was caught selling drugs he had confiscated. (5) Last Wenesday, a high-ranking official in the Defense Department was accused of demanding kickbacks from the companies that supply military hardware. (6) With the posibility of being caught so strong, you'd think that public officials would not be tempted. (7) Sometimes, you wonder how much inteligence these individuals possess. (8) Personally, I'm discusted with the whole situation. (9) I think that public officials convicted of a crime against the people they are representing should definately be imprisoned. (10) It should be a maximum security prison, too, so that they have to face the embarasment of being known as common criminals.

CHALLENGE 29.3 **Developing Your Own Personal Dictionary**

1. Begin your own personal dictionary by scanning the list of commonly mis-spelled words on pages 459–462. Highlight the twenty that you have the most trouble with. Make a separate list of just these words, in alphabetical order.

collaboration

2. Working with a classmate, compare your lists. If your classmate has included words that you also have difficulty with, add them to your own list.

3. Proofread your class notes for the last two weeks. Identify any words you have misspelled, and add these words to your list to complete your initial ver-sion of your personal dictionary. From this point on, every time you misspell a word in anything you write, revise your personal dictionary so that it will be especially useful when you proofread.

QUICK STUDY **Student Example**

This chapter focuses on rules and their exceptions, on matters of correctness and incorrectness. Take a look at the following paragraph, which focuses on a related subject, an exception to some rule or guideline:

> Nothing is more important to me then telling the truth, yet I think there are times when its exceptable to tell someone a lie. For example, if someone asks what I think about a new hairstyle or outfit, and it doesn't look great, what's the sense in telling the truth? It's too late to change anything, and my negative opinion certainly won't help the person feel any better. In this situa-tion, it's kinder to make a general or neutral statement like, "It's really differ-ent," or, "It's OK," even if it isn't exactly the truth. I also beleive it's sometimes alright to lie by withholding information, as long as the result is not dangerous or hurtful to anyone. For instance, if I know an embarassing story about an aquaintance, and a freind asks me about it, I keep quite unless I have a reason to talk about the incident. Most of the time, the truth is none of anyone else's business and it would just needlessly damage the other person's reputation. I truely think that honesty is the best policy, but when the truth could do more harm than good, it shouldn't be the only policy.

First complete the following activities in response to this paragraph:

1. Four sentences in the above paragraph are highlighted. Evaluate these sentences for misspelled and incorrectly used words. Circle each error and write the correctly spelled version above it.

2. The second sentence contains a rhetorical question, a question that, as Chapter 14 explains, is designed not to be answered but to provoke discussion or thought. Do you think the same idea would be more—or less—effective if it were phrased in statement form instead? Why? Use the lines below for your answer.

_____

_____

_____

_____

_____

3. Asserting, as this paragraph does, that lying is acceptable is a controversial stand. On a separate sheet of paper, assess the supporting examples in the paragraph, explaining whether in your view they offer sufficient support to accept the premise that dishonesty can sometimes be justified and why you feel this way.

Now explore the topic in writing. As the paragraph above does, you could discuss an acceptable reason to ignore a rule or guideline. You might also concentrate on one of these subjects related to the subject matter of this chapter:

- the traffic law you find most difficult to follow
- someone you know who enjoys breaking the rules
- the best way to correct a misunderstanding between friends or family
- the one rule that everyone needs to follow

collaboration

4. Exchange your draft with a classmate. Evaluate the paragraph you receive. If you discover any weaknesses, especially spelling errors or incorrectly used words, circle them and write correctly spelled versions above the incorrect ones. Then return the paper to the writer.

5. Consider the comments and corrections your reader has made and create a final draft of your paragraph.

CHAPTER QUICK CHECK Spelling Skills

The following passage contains numerous misspelled words. Using the various rules and examples in the chapter to guide you, find and cross out errors. Write the correct version above the incorrect one.

(1) Experts continue to discuss the possible affects that television and Internet advertising can have on the viewing public, especially impressionable children. (2) The ads in question are largly for things like fast food and toys, although critics have also pointed to companys that market products like breakfast foods and clothing. (3) Even those who's television watching is fairly limited are exposed to thousands and thousands of commercials in a year, leading to the beleif that commercials can unduly influence kids. (4) Advertisers certainly no that children today have more influence over family purchases then ever before. (5) Another argument critics raise is that commercials for these products and services air most heavily during times when children are sure to veiw them. (6) Their is no doubt, these critics assert, that advertisers make a conscience attempt to convince kids that they must have what is being sold. (7) The sheer volume of advertisements, especially on shows geared too children, is clear evidence of the psycology behind this strategy. (8) Predictably, manufacturers dissagree strongly, claiming its not their intent to mislead or unduly influence anyone. (9) They stress that weather advertising actually effects anyone's behavior has never been positively proven. (10) In addition, they point out that they have a legal right to advertize on television and the Web, regardless of what there opponents might feel about them.

SUMMARY EXERCISE Spelling Skills

The following passage contains numerous misspelled words. Using the various rules and examples in the chapter to guide you, find and cross out errors. Write the correct version above the incorrect one.

(1) Peer pressure is one of the strongest forces people have to face in their lifes. (2) Being excepted is important to most people. (3) When people go against peer pressure, though, they can find it a very lonely expereince.

(4) Many times students missbehave in school because of peer pressure. (5) The influence of this force is particularly noticable in middle and high school classes. (6) If a group of kids in the hallway is making trouble, for example, quite kids will sometimes join in because they don't want the other kids to think they are different. (7) By themselves, these quiet kids would never make any fuss, but if their is a group, peer pressure takes over.

(8) Kids generaly have their first experiences with sex, alcohol, or drugs because of peer pressure. (9) Even though they know they should of re-fused, some young people have been pressured into doing things they weren't ready for. (10) If kids are at a party and someone is drinking or useing drugs, many kids find it hard to resist trying it. (11) They feel that if they don't, the other kids will think they are wierd or childish.

(12) Peer pressure effects people after high school, too. (13) For exam-ple, if people are in class in a college wear hardly anyone asks or answers questions, they may find themselves acting like their classmates. (14) Most people don't want to look like a show-off or teacher's pet in front of their freinds. (15) If most people in a department don't like the boss, the others may hesitate to volunter for any extra work. (16) With this kind of occurence, most people will simply go along with the group because they want to fit in so badly.

(17) Although peer pressure is a strong force, it is one that must be resistted. (18) People have to learn to do what is correct for them, even if it means they won't win everyone's approval. (19) When they procede in this way, they will find that others respect them for who they are. (20) Once people begin behaving in a way that is most authentic for them, they won't waist so much time worrying what others think.

FOR FURTHER EXPLORATION Spelling

1. Focus on one of the following topics. Using the prewriting technique—or combination of techniques—that you are most comfortable with, develop some initial ideas while also considering the purposes you might fulfill in writing about the topic:

   - your first visit to a hospital as a patient or a visitor
   - the appropriateness of vigilante justice
   - an issue or concern associated with organ donation
   - a piece of writing—a poem, a short story, a novel, a play, a blog entry—that caused you to change your thinking on a subject

2. Evaluate your prewriting material, identify a focus, and work your way through the rest of the writing process to create a draft essay of at least 500 words on this subject.

collaboration

3. Exchange your draft with a classmate. Check the draft you receive for problems, in particular, errors in spelling. Circle any incorrectly spelled or misused words, using the material in this chapter to guide you, and write the correct form above the incorrect one. Then return the paper to the writer.

4. Revise your essay, correcting any errors in spelling or other problems discovered by your reader.

RECAP Spelling

Key Terms in This Chapter	Definitions
prefix	letter or letters added to the beginning of a word that change its meaning: *un-, dis-, semi-, re-, il-*
	EXAMPLES **un**able, **il**legible
suffix	letter or letters added to the end of a word that change its meaning: *-ness, -able, -ous, -ly, -er, -ed, -ing*
	EXAMPLES sad**ness**, slow**ly**

Spelling Guidelines for Adding Prefixes and Suffixes

(Check the dictionary for exceptions to these general guidelines.)

To add a prefix	prefix + word (no spelling change)
	dis + approve = **dis**approve
To add *-ly* or *-ness*	word + *-ly* or *-ness* (usually no spelling change)
	clear + ly = clear**ly**
	Change *-y* to *-i* before adding *-ly* or *-ness*
	silly + ness = sill**iness**

To add **-ed**	Change -y to -i before adding -ed
	carry + ed = carr**ied**
To add a suffix that begins with a vowel	Drop -e at the end of a word before adding suffix
	cope + ing = co**ping**
	Double the final consonant if
	• the word has one syllable
	stop + ed = stop**ped**
	• the final consonant is preceded by a single vowel
	hot + est = hot**test**
	• the accent is on the last syllable of a word with two or more syllables
	admit + ing = admit**ting**
To add a suffix that begins with a consonant	Keep -e at the end of the word
	hope + ful = hopeful

Using Odyssey Online with MyWritingLab

For more practice with nouns, go to www.mywritinglab.com.

CHAPTER 30
Commas

GETTING STARTED ...

Q I'm never really sure if I've used enough or too many commas. Why is working with commas so confusing? How can I make sure I am putting them just where they're needed?

A Even experienced writers have difficulty with—and disagreements about—comma use. Comma use can be confusing because of what the mark represents: a pause. In conversation, people pause for a number of reasons—to take a breath, to emphasize a point, to figure out what to say next, and so on. But in writing, not all pauses call for commas. When one thought is over, for example, the pause would actually be a *full stop,* calling for a period—or a question mark or exclamation point. And sometimes no mark of pause is needed because no distinct slowing is actually needed or called for. To help strengthen your understanding of comma use, write seven brief sentences—each to show one use of the comma—on a file on your computer desktop or separate sheet of paper to use as a quick reference.

Overview: Understanding Comma Use

ESL Note
See "Punctuation" on pages 554–555.

With speech, you frequently pause within thoughts to emphasize or clarify some point. With writing, you use the same technique. When you want to signal these pauses within a sentence, the mark of punctuation you will use most often is a **comma.**

Navigating This Chapter In this chapter, you will learn how to use a comma to:

- indicate a pause between two clauses connected by a conjunction
- separate items in a series
- indicate a brief break between introductory material and the main part of the sentence
- set off words, phrases, and clauses that interrupt the flow of a sentence
- set off a direct quotation from the rest of a sentence
- set off elements in certain letter parts, dates, addresses, and numerals
- set off nouns of direct address

Using a Comma between Clauses Connected by Conjunctions

ESL Note
See "Punctuation," pages 554–555, for more on this aspect of comma use.

A comma is used to indicate a pause between clauses connected by a conjunction or a pair of conjunctions.

COMPOUND SENTENCE

    coordinating conjunction
The movie was good, *but* the book was better.

COMPOUND SENTENCE

    correlative conjunction   correlative conjunction
Either the wind blew the campfire *out, or* the ranger put it out.

COMPLEX SENTENCE

    subordinating conjunction
Even though the office was warm, everyone put in a full day's work.

[*Use a comma when the subordinate clause comes first.*]

COMPREHENSION AND PRACTICE

30.1

Working with Commas and Conjunctions

Add a comma, a conjunction, and another clause to complete the following sentences. Review Chapter 19, to remember rules for creating complex and compound sentences and to find lists of subordinating and coordinating conjunctions. Use the example to guide you.

EXAMPLE

    When Jerry misplaced his calculator, he had to buy a new one.

1. _____

   jury duty is part of every citizen's responsibility.

2. Serving on a jury can disrupt a person's life

   _____

3. _____

   prospective jurors are often able to delay serving for a variety of reasons.

4. Being part of the judicial system is interesting

   _____

5. The juror's day at court starts at 8:30 A.M.

   _____

6. _____

   all the jurors are sworn in.

7. Then, the presentations by the lawyers begin

_____

8. In my state, most jurors serve for only a day

_____

9. Jurors may serve for up to a month for trials of capital crimes

_____

10. _____

jurors are sometimes sequestered.

Using Commas to Separate Items in a Series

ESL Note
See "Punctuation,"
pages 554–555, for
more on this aspect of
comma use.

Commas are used to separate three or more items in a series. When only two items are connected by *and, or,* or *but,* no comma is needed.

WORDS IN SERIES Jacqueline spends her summer days *swimming, sailing, sunbathing,* or *sleeping.*

PHRASES IN SERIES *In the fall, in the winter,* and *in the spring,* however, her schoolwork leaves her little time for these activities.

COMPREHENSION AND PRACTICE

Using Commas in a Series

30.2 Fill in the blanks in the following sentences, supplying the items to complete each series. Place commas where necessary. Use the example as guidance.

EXAMPLES The ____city____ and ____county____ cooperate on a recycling program

that requires people to separate ____plastic,____ ____paper,____ and

____glass____ from the rest of their trash.

(1) I work full time on the third shift, so my workday begins at 11 P.M.,

when other people are _____ or _____. (2) The plant

where I work makes plastic items such as _____ _____

and _____. (3) The machines I work with generate a great deal of _____ and _____ so I dress lightly and wear earplugs. (4) In addition to running my machines, I supervise two other workers to make sure they _____ and _____. (5) The factory has a series of small windows near the ceiling, and if I look up from my machine, I can see _____ _____ and _____. (6) After three hours, I take my first break, during which I _____ _____ or _____. (7) When my break is over, I _____ and _____. (8) Before I know it, it's suppertime, so I _____ _____ or _____. (9) During the rest of the shift, I have time to complete my paperwork, including _____ and _____. (10) At 7 A.M., I head home to bed while everybody else is _____ _____ or _____.

Using a Comma to Set Off Introductory Material

Often the main portion of a sentence is introduced by a word, phrase, or clause that indicates a time, place, or condition. If this introductory material consists of *four or more words* or contains a *verbal,* separate it from the rest of the sentence by a comma. (See page 266 for a discussion of verbals.)

EXAMPLE

Within the pile of shredded paper, the mouse nursed three babies.

Yelling and splashing frantically, Courtney drifted away from shore.

Occasionally, you will use a word or brief phrase to introduce a sentence. Use a comma to set off such an introductory element if it helps to emphasize or clarify the main point of the sentence.

EXAMPLES

In fact, the substitute teacher had never even been in the school before.

Soon after, the meeting was interrupted by strange noises.

COMPREHENSION
AND PRACTICE   **Using Commas after Introductory Phrases and Clauses**

30.3   If the introductory phrase in each of the sentences in the following paragraph needs a comma, insert it. If a comma appears where it is not necessary, cross it out. Use the example to direct you.

EXAMPLE   At the major intersection near the entrance of the school,an accident was slowing, down traffic.

(1) After hatching on Florida beaches and crawling off into the surf tiny loggerhead turtle hatchlings begin a journey that will take them across the Atlantic Ocean and back again. (2) Over, a period of several years the baby loggerheads will travel thousands of miles as they swim and ride the warm currents of the Atlantic, feeding and growing. (3) For a number of years no one has been sure of exactly how they managed to navigate such an enormous trip while avoiding the colder waters that would kill them. (4) However research suggests that the answer lies in the innate ability of these creatures to react to natural magnetic fields marking a section of the ocean waters. (5) Called the Atlantic Gyre this area is an oceanwide current of warm water that moves in a clockwise fashion, eastward across the Atlantic, along the coasts of Spain and Africa, and back westward to the east coast of the United States. (6) The turtles, apparently, follow a series of magnetic markers that keep them within the warmer waters that they need to survive. (7) For the study, that led to these findings loggerhead hatchlings were placed in a specially designed saltwater tank. (8) To simulate particular magnetic fields researchers equipped the tank with special copper coils. (9) Then, they outfitted the turtles with a device that would record the direction in which the hatchlings were swimming. (10) As the scientists changed the magnetic fields the baby turtles responded by swimming in a direction that would keep them within the safe warm-water zone in the open ocean.

Using Commas to Set Off Elements That Interrupt Sentence Flow

Sometimes you use commas within a sentence to surround a word, phrase, or clause that interrupts the flow of the sentence. For instance, when a word adds emphasis, provides transition, or renames or illustrates another word in the sentence, use commas to set it off:

EXAMPLES

Our next car, *however,* ran like a top.

The crow, *for example,* is a highly intelligent bird.

We had skybox seats, *the best in the stadium,* for the game.

ESL Note
See "Punctuation," pages 554–555, for more on the use of commas with elements that interrupt sentence flow.

In addition, use commas to set off *nonrestrictive elements,* clauses or phrases that could be left out of a sentence without changing its basic meaning. Nonrestrictive clauses and phrases add extra but nonessential information:

EXAMPLE

┌─────────── nonrestrictive clause ───────────┐
This year's spring weather on Cape Cod, *which is usually calm and warm,* was cool and blustery.

If you were to leave *which is usually calm and warm* out of the sentence, the reader would still understand the main point. The clause is *nonrestrictive.*

Some clauses and phrases are *restrictive,* meaning that your reader needs them to identify or restrict the meaning of the word they modify. Therefore, you don't set them off with commas, as this example shows:

EXAMPLE

┌─────────── nonrestrictive clause ───────────┐
All students *driving vehicles with handicapped plates* may park in the first row of Parking Lot C.

Leave the italicized phrase out of this sentence, and you send the wrong message. Without these words, the sentence says that *all* students may park in a lot that is actually reserved for disabled students only. Therefore, *driving vehicles with handicapped plates* is restrictive, and no commas are used.

COMPREHENSION AND PRACTICE
30.4

Using Commas with Elements That Interrupt Sentence Flow

In the following sentences, insert commas where you think they are needed to set off words from the rest of the sentence. Use the example as a guide.

EXAMPLE

Joie began singing lessons with her neighbor, a former professional, only to discover that she really didn't enjoy studying voice.

(1) A newspaper article about two children which I read in the dentist's office tells an incredible story about parental overprotection. (2) The parents of a three-year-old boy according to the story obtained a restraining order to

keep a three-year-old girl away from their child. (3) They said that their son who attends preschool with the girl is afraid to play in the park because of the girl's aggression. (4) Why didn't the judge who is supposed to temper justice with common sense tell both sets of parents to straighten out the difficulties between their children by themselves? (5) I wonder whether that little boy who has such anxious parents will ever learn to solve problems on his own.

Using Commas to Set Off Direct Quotations

As a writer, you will sometimes want to *quote,* to write down word for word what other people say. When you do so, you let your reader know that the words are a *direct quote* by enclosing the passage in quotation marks (" "). (See Chapter 4, for a discussion of the inclusion of direct quotations in a paper.) You then use a comma to set the direct quote off from the *attribution,* the part that identifies the speaker.

Note the placement of the comma in these three formats incorporating a direct quotation.

1. When the quote is at the beginning of a sentence, insert a comma within the closing quotation mark:

EXAMPLE *"My wallet—it's not in my pocketbook,"* Katlyn said, with an edge of panic in her voice.

2. When the quote is at the end of a sentence, place a comma before the opening quotation mark:

EXAMPLE She said quietly, *"I can't find it anywhere."*

3. When the quote is interrupted in the middle by the attribution, insert a comma within the closing quotation mark of the first portion and a second comma before the opening quotation mark of the second portion:

EXAMPLE *"And I'm sure I had it,"* she cried, *"when we left the mall."*

Recognizing Other Situations in Which Commas Are Needed

In addition to these uses of commas, remember to use a comma

- to set off the salutation of a personal letter (not a business letter): *Dear Monique,*
- to set off the parts of dates from the rest of the sentence: *August 25, 2002,* was a crucial day for my family.

- to set off parts of addresses in a sentence: His last permanent address was *756 Craft Street, Tampa, FL 34268.*
- to indicate thousands within numbers: *9,870* or *9,000,000*
- to set off a name when you address someone directly: I'm telling you, *John,* that you need to save for retirement.

COMPREHENSION AND PRACTICE

Using Commas with Quotation Marks

30.5   In the following paragraph, underline each attribution, and insert commas and quotation marks where needed to separate the attribution from the exact words of the speaker. Use the example as a guide.

EXAMPLE   Then the <u>announcer said</u>,"I'm afraid I have some bad news to report."

(1) Things aren't the way they used to be my Great-Aunt Dot complained the other day. (2) She said I don't mean to complain, but you young people don't seem to have done much to make this world a better place. (3) When I was young she continued my generation worked to improve things around us. (4) She stopped for a minute, shook her head, and said Maybe I'm not being fair. (5) Aunt Dot then asked me outright What do you think of your generation?

(6) When I could see that her concern was genuine, I smiled at her and answered Well, I think my generation is doing all right. (7) I paused for a moment to think and said People my age *do* care about the world around them. (8) Aunt Dot seemed unconvinced, so I asked What about the park clean-up program, the recycling drive, and the March for Justice, all sponsored by high school and college students? (9) As she nodded in agreement, I added Of course, I think your generation did much more, with your dedication to Civil Rights and work to eliminate poverty. (10) She smiled, and I added We will just have to try harder to emulate your generation.

CHALLENGE 30.1   ### Providing Necessary Commas

1. The following letter of application contains no commas. To help this job applicant make a positive impression, proofread the letter and insert commas where they are needed. Put *OK* in front of any unit that doesn't require commas.

325 Whipple Street
East Franklin, MA 02652
December 1 20XX

Ms. Mary Hayes
Director of Human Resources
East Franklin Y.M.C.A.
49 Richmond Street
East Franklin, MA 02650

Dear Ms. Hayes:

I am writing to apply for the part-time position as Assistant to the Director of Youth Services which you have advertised in the *East Franklin Gazette.* Having spent the past three summers as a youth counselor in the "Kids at Work" summer job program here in East Franklin I have the experience enthusiasm and qualifications your position requires.

I have just completed my first year at Bristol Community College where I am majoring in criminal justice. After I receive my degree I plan to work full time with young people either through a social agency or the State Police Outreach Center.

As a counselor for "Kids at Work" I was in charge of twenty teenagers between the ages of fourteen and eighteen which required me to demonstrate both responsibility and leadership. During my first two summers on the job for example I arranged work schedules supervised work activities and taught a job skills seminar. The seminar was so successful that my director made it a permanent part of the summer program. For the past two summers I've also served as senior counselor which means I was in charge of training all new counselors.

In terms of the position of Assistant to the Director of Youth Services I believe my experiences have prepared me well. I would like to discuss my qualifications in greater detail so I respectfully request that you schedule an interview for me. Thank you.

Sincerely

Cosette J. Valjean

Cosette J. Valjean

collaboration

2. Working with a classmate, compare the commas you have added, and, after rechecking the rules, make any necessary changes.

QUICK STUDY **Student Example**

This chapter concerns matters related to pausing between things, keeping them separate, or setting them off for emphasis. Now consider the following paragraph, which concerns an associated topic, the most meaningful quote or proverb you know:

> The most meaningful quotation I have ever heard is this one: "A child's life is like a piece of paper on which every passerby leaves a mark." My middle school English teacher wrote it on the board on the first day of class and I have never forgotten it because I think it is so true. Children can be easily influenced by what they hear and see around them. They believe that what adults in positions of authority like parents or grandparents teachers members of the clergy and so on, do or tell them is correct. For instance if children see adults treating each other with respect or hear those adults tell them they are smart talented and beautiful they accept it as true. But when children witness those same adults behaving badly mistreating others expressing prejudices drinking excessively or using illegal drugs they think that's normal and acceptable too. Even worse when adults call children stupid ugly or worthless telling them that they will never amount to anything children will believe them. If adults just took a moment to consider this proverb fewer children would grow up believing terrible things about themselves and others.

First complete the following activities in response to this paragraph:

1. The paragraph above contains no commas. Using the material in this chapter to guide you, insert commas where they are needed.

2. On the lines below, briefly explain how the concluding sentence emphasizes the connection between the topic sentence and the supporting sentences.

_____

_____

3. The supporting sentences in this paragraph present positive effects that adults can have on children and then present negative effects. On a separate sheet of paper, evaluate this order. Identify whether you agree with the current arrangement or would suggest presenting the negative effects before the positive ones. In either case, explain your reasoning.

Now explore the topic in writing. As the paragraph above does, you could discuss a saying or proverb and why you think it's important. You might also focus on one of these topics related to the subject matter of this chapter:

- a pause or break you took that you now wish you hadn't
- a public figure who deserves to be set off from others
- a time when you had to deal with the separation from a person or place important to you
- examples of interruptions students typically face as they try to study for a test, complete a project, or finish a paper

collaboration

4. Exchange your draft with a classmate. Evaluate the paragraph you receive, looking for problem spots, especially in comma use. Indicate any point where a comma is needed and cross out any unnecessary commas, and then return the paper to the writer.

5. Consider the comments and corrections your reader has made and create a final draft of your paragraph.

CHAPTER QUICK CHECK Comma Use

Add commas where they are needed in the sentences below. Review the functions of commas to help you as you proofread.

(1) If it's true that we tend to overlook the value of things that are right in front of us then there is no better illustration than our lack of attention to estuaries. (2) An estuary is a partially enclosed wetland area where fresh water from rivers streams and other tributaries flows into the ocean, mixing fresh and salt water. (3) Here in the United States San Francisco Bay, Boston Harbor, Tampa Bay, and Puget Sound are all examples of estuarine areas. (4) No one would argue that estuaries are beautiful areas noted for appealing to tourists as well as homeowners but they serve an even more vital role in terms of the environment. (5) As water flows through an estuary for example the

marsh filters out pollutants and sediments, leaving the fresh and salt water cleaner. (6) In addition, the marsh land and various plants help to soak up and divert flood waters prevent erosion and protect property along the shore from damage. (7) Most important of all estuaries provide the perfect habitat for an enormous range of sea life, including migratory birds aquatic plants, crabs, lobsters shellfish, and reptiles. (8) Estuaries are generally protected from tides and ocean waves by sandbars, barrier islands, or reefs so they are ideal areas for reproduction. (9) In fact, 75 percent of the commercial fish catch of the continental United States which is worth some $2 billion is dependent on estuaries. (10) When this fragile ecosystem is destroyed by filling or dredging the results can include such severe consequences as widespread fish kills and unsafe drinking water.

SUMMARY EXERCISE Comma Use

Add commas where they are needed in the sentences below. Review the functions of commas to help you as you proofread.

(1) For those interested in a unique physical activity slacklining may be the perfect answer. (2) This nontraditional sport offers the challenge of rock climbing or surfing and it holds the same kind of counterculture cachet as skateboarding and other extreme sports. (3) Slacklining which involves maintaining balance on strips of nylon webbing loosely strung between two supports has found enthusiasts all over the world.

(4) A pair of rock climbers from the Yosemite Valley California area Jeff Ellington and Adam Grosowsky are credited as the originators of slacklining. (5) According to published accounts the climbers trying to kill time in the early 1980s strung some of their climbing cables and straps a few feet above the ground between anchor points.

(6) After some time spent experimenting they switched to their climbing webbing. (7) They began to balance and then walk along these flat lines which are typically stretched from 30 to 100 feet between two trees or other support points. (8) Other climbers in the Yosemite Valley area gravitated to the activity and interest in slacklining soon began to spread first across the United States and then because of the Internet around the world.

(9) Although it has something in common with tightrope walking slacklining differs significantly from its older cousin which has been around for hundreds of years. (10) The line in slacklining for example is kept loose allowing enthusiasts to bounce or sway. (11) Also unlike the line in tightrope walking which is round the line in slacklining is flat. (12) This difference gives slackliners more stability a key factor in being able to maintain balance and perform tricks.

(13) The most common form of slacklining is called *trickling* sometimes also called *lowlining*. (14) Because the webbing in this form of slacklining is normally fairly low to the ground slackliners can attempt a number of dynamic moves. (15) Common tricks include walking forward and backward bouncing turning and dropping to the knees. (16) More expert slackliners push their bodies to the limit performing flips tandem walks and jumps from one line to another.

(17) For the time being interest in slacklining shows no sign of lessening. (18) In fact other variations of this extreme sport have emerged including *highlining free-style-slacklining* and *rodeo-slacklining*. (19) Because a minimum of equipment is needed to begin a slacklining adventure don't be surprised to see people setting up in a park parking lot or other open area near you. (20) If you ask nicely somebody might even invite you to become a slackliner yourself.

FOR FURTHER EXPLORATION Commas

1. Focus on one of the following topics, using the prewriting technique—or combination of techniques—that you prefer to generate some preliminary ideas, and consider what purposes you might fulfill as you write about it:

   - your favorite place from your childhood
   - ways that creativity appears in day-to-day living
   - why reality television shows are currently so popular
   - a time you witnessed the behavior of or had to deal with a bully

2. Evaluate your prewriting material, identify a focus, and work your way through the rest of the writing process to create a draft essay of at least 500 words on this subject.

collaboration

3. Exchange your draft with a classmate. Check the draft you receive for weaknesses, especially with the use of commas. Using the material in this chapter as a guide, put a ✓ where a comma is needed and cross out any unnecessary commas. Then return the draft to the writer.

4. Revise your essay, correcting any errors with comma use or other problems discovered by your reader.

RECAP Commas

Key Term in This Chapter	Definition
comma	a punctuation mark that indicates a pause within a sentence

Comma Functions

To indicate a pause between two clauses connected by a conjunction

EXAMPLE	She picked up the pen, but then she put it down again.

To separate items in a series

EXAMPLE	Accounting, marketing, and management are all areas that interest me.

To separate an introductory phrase of four or more words from the rest of the sentence

EXAMPLE	Until the end of the race, I'll keep my fingers crossed.

To set off words, phrases, or clauses that interrupt the flow of a sentence

EXAMPLE	The people in the front of the line, those who had camped out all night on the sidewalk, bought the first tickets.

To set a direct quotation off from the rest of the sentence

EXAMPLE	"This course has been wonderful," said Lee-Ann.

To set off the salutation in a personal letter

EXAMPLE	Dear Latisha,

To set off parts of dates and addresses and names of direct address

| EXAMPLE | Will you join us, Tim, on July 14, 2006, at Flying Y Ranch, Casper, Wyoming? |

To indicate thousands within numbers

| EXAMPLE | 6,950 or 1,000,000 |

Using Odyssey Online with MyWritingLab

For more practice with commas, go to www.mywritinglab.com.

CHAPTER 31

Other Punctuation and Capitalization

GETTING STARTED ...

 Sometimes I'm not sure which mark of punctuation fits in a particular situation. I also have trouble with capitalization. I don't capitalize words I should, or I capitalize words that don't need it. There's so much to re-member—what's the best way to develop greater skill in these areas?

 Dealing with punctuation and capitalization can seem confusing because each writing situation requires you to make multiple decisions regarding their use. The good news is that these two aspects of writing are governed by rules, and the rules are fairly straightforward. For the most part, punctu-ation marks are distinct from each other. And whether a word should be capitalized or not depends on where the word appears in the sentence and whether it is a proper or a common noun.

Overview: Maintaining Correctness and Clarity through Punctuation and Capitalization

Think of *punctuation* and *capitalization* as the nuts and bolts of writing, the ele-ments that hold writing together. **Punctuation** involves the use of the various sym-bols that guide your reader through your writing. **Capitalization** involves the use of an uppercase letter at the beginning of a word to make it stand out or clarify its meaning. Like the nuts and bolts that hold the massive girders of a bridge to-gether, these elements of writing play a vital role in communicating your ideas to your reader.

Navigating This Chapter In this chapter, you will learn how to use:

- periods, question marks, and exclamation points to indicate the end of a sentence
- quotation marks to indicate a person's exact words
- apostrophes to indicate ownership or to take the place of letters left out when contractions are formed
- colons to signal important information
- semicolons to emphasize a connection between independent clauses
- parentheses and dashes to signal additional information
- capitalization to emphasize words

Using Periods, Question Marks, and Exclamation Points

To indicate the end of a sentence, use one of three marks of end punctuation. Use a **period** to indicate a stop at the end of a sentence that makes a statement:

EXAMPLE The old man sitting under the tree is my uncle.

Use a **question mark** when a sentence expresses a question directly:

EXAMPLE Where did you park the car?

Use an **exclamation point** when a sentence expresses strong excitement or emotion:

EXAMPLE Watch out for that hot pipe!

ESL Note
See "Punctuation,"
pages 554–555, for
more on the proper use
of end punctuation.

Be careful not to overuse exclamation points. Use them only when you need to demonstrate profound excitement or emotion, not merely to spice up your writing.

COMPREHENSION AND PRACTICE
31.1

Selecting the Correct End Punctuation

The sentences in the following passage all lack end punctuation. In the space provided, write the correct mark of end punctuation for each sentence, as the example shows.

EXAMPLE The technician reported that the computer system wouldn't be repaired for

two weeks _._

(1) Giant dinosaurs may have ruled the earth 100 million years ago, but even the giants among these giants apparently may have had something to fear ___ (2) According to paleontologists, that something was Sarcosuchus imperator, a cousin of the modern-day crocodile that was 40 feet long and weighed a whopping 10 tons ____ (3) The first evidence of this massive creature, a six-foot skull, was found in a desert area of Niger, West Africa, in 1964 by a team of French scientists ___ (4) Subsequent digs in 1997 and 2000 yielded additional skulls and enough other fossilized remains to create a skeleton that is nearly 50 percent complete ___ (5) How fearsome was Sarcosuchus ___ (6) For one thing, its jaws contained more than 100 teeth,

including large numbers that could tear flesh and crush bone ___ (7) This mighty predator had other adaptations that made it especially suited for its life as a river dweller ___ (8) For instance, it had a huge bulbous growth at the end of its snout, which experts believe enhanced its ability to breathe and smell, and its eyes tilted upward ___ (9) As this huge crocodile quietly lurked beneath the surface, almost completely hidden, even the largest dinosaurs of its time would easily be fast food ___ (10) Imagine what a good Hollywood director could do with that lunchtime scene _____

Using Quotation Marks

When you record a person's words exactly as they were said, the resulting material is called a **direct quotation**. Direct quotations must be enclosed in **quotation marks**:

EXAMPLE   The smiling clerk said, "Thank you. Come again."

Notice that the first word of a direct quotation is capitalized and that the end punctuation is placed within the closing quotation mark. Notice also that a comma sets the direct quotation off from the *attribution,* the words that identify the speaker.
    You can also place the direct quotation before the attribution:

EXAMPLE   "Thank you. Come again," the smiling clerk said.

Notice that a comma is still needed to separate the direct quotation from the attribution. In this case, the comma is placed *within* the closing quotation mark. Punctuation of direct quotations is discussed further in Chapter 30, "Commas." In writing, an exchange of direct quotations between two speakers is called **dialogue**. Start a new paragraph each time you switch speakers so that readers can keep track of who is talking.

EXAMPLE   "Marguerite, you know I can't stand the smell of tuna fish," said Brian, pushing the bowl away.
        "But you know it's my favorite food. How could I give it up?" she replied.

When you restate or explain what someone has said, the resulting expression is called an **indirect quotation**. No quotation marks are needed because indirect quotations do not represent a person's exact words.

EXAMPLES   Then the clerk behind the counter thanked us and said that she hoped we'd come again.

The company president said that profits for the third quarter were far lower than she had anticipated.

Quotation marks are also used to set off titles of short documents such as magazine or newspaper articles, book chapters, songs, short stories, and poems:

EXAMPLES

Leon read the fourth chapter, "Your Child's Brain," aloud to Joyce.

Listening to "Unchained Melody" always makes me cry.

COMPREHENSION AND PRACTICE

Distinguishing between Direct and Indirect Quotations

31.2   Some of the sentences below contain indirect quotations, and others contain direct quotations. Insert quotation marks in the space above the direct quotations, as the example shows.

EXAMPLE

"Please check to make sure that you've locked the door," my grandmother said as we left her apartment.

(1) When I walked into the emergency room on the day I cut my head while running, the attendant behind the counter asked me to explain what had happened. (2) I felt myself blush as I said, I ran into the side of a building. (3) He looked up from the desk and asked me to repeat what I had said. (4) I told him again that I had run into a building.

(5) How could that happen? he asked.

(6) A piece of the building was jutting out, and I didn't see it, I explained.

(7) Are you kidding me? he asked, beginning to laugh. (8) I told him that I was serious and that I'd appreciate it if he would lower his voice.

(9) I'm sorry, he said, as he tried to stop laughing. (10) When he finally asked a doctor to examine me, he graciously refrained from laughing as he told her why I needed help.

CHALLENGE 31.1   **Writing Dialogue**

1. On a separate sheet of paper, record a recent exchange between yourself and a friend or family member in dialogue form. Make all sentences direct quotations, and remember to begin a new paragraph every time the speaker changes.

collaboration

2. Exchange your work with a classmate. On the paper you receive, circle any errors you find in the use of end punctuation and quotation marks. Return the paper to the writer.

3. Evaluate the corrections your classmate has made, and make any necessary changes.

Using Apostrophes

Writers use **apostrophes** (') to show possession and form contractions. Make singular nouns possessive by adding an apostrophe and an *-s,* even if the noun ends in *-s:*

EXAMPLE   artist**'s** easel; girl**'s** wallet; business**'s** assets

If the possessive form sounds awkward to you, change it to a prepositional phrase. Rather than writing *Jonas's response,* write *the response of Jonas.*
Make most plural nouns possessive by adding only an apostrophe:

EXAMPLE   artists**'** easels; girls**'** wallets; leopards**'** spots

For plural words that *don't* end in *-s,* form the plural by adding an apostrophe and an *-s:*

EXAMPLE   men**'s** shirts; people**'s** attitudes; children**'s** toys

Pronouns such as *your* and *its* are already possessive, so they don't require an apostrophe. To make indefinite pronouns—such as *anybody, everybody, anyone, everyone,* and *nobody*—possessive, add an apostrophe and an *-s:*

EXAMPLE   everyone**'s** fault; anybody**'s** attention

To make compound subjects possessive, determine whether you are discussing one item that is possessed jointly or separate items owned by each subject. If the subjects jointly possess something, put an apostrophe and an *-s* after the last subject. If each subject possesses his or her own item, then add an apostrophe and an *-s* to each subject:

EXAMPLES   Lenny and Lila**'s** house [*One item jointly owned*]

Lenny**'s** and Lila**'s** paychecks [*Two items separately owned*]

For compound words like *maid of honor* and *father-in-law,* form the possessive by adding an apostrophe and an *-s* to the end of the word. Do the same for names of businesses and corporations that are compound:

EXAMPLE   brother-in-law**'s** car; Lord & Taylor**'s** sale

Apostrophes are also used to form *contractions,* words that you create by combining two words. The apostrophe takes the place of the letters left out when the words are combined.

ESL Note
See "Confusing Verb Forms," page 549–551, for more on the correct use of apostrophes in contractions.

Here is a list of common contractions:

Common Contractions

aren't are not	he's he is, he has	should've should have
can't cannot	I'd I would	that's that is
couldn't could not	I'll I will	they'll they will
didn't did not	I'm I am	they're they are
doesn't does not	isn't is not	who's who is, who has
don't do not	it'll it will	won't will not
hadn't had not	it's it is, it has	you'd you would
hasn't has not	she'd she would	you'll you will
haven't have not	she'll she will	you're you are
he'd he would	she's she is, she has	
he'll he will	shouldn't should not	

Notice that the letters in a contraction follow the same order as they do in the original two words. The exception is *won't*, the contraction for *will not*.

When you write, be sure to distinguish between *it's*, the contraction for *it is* and *it has*, and *its*, the possessive pronoun, which requires no apostrophe.

COMPREHENSION AND PRACTICE

Using Apostrophes

31.3 Each sentence below contains a number of italicized words. Some need an apostrophe to show possession; others can be combined into contractions. Write the appropriate contraction or possessive form above each italicized section, as the example illustrates.

EXAMPLE

> *We'll*   *Franny's*
> *We will* reach *Frannys* house in about twenty-five minutes.

(1) *It is* hard to believe that the local commuter rail station *has not* been replaced yet. (2) *Did not* the *mayors* task force recommend five years ago that the station be knocked down and rebuilt? (3) *I am* surprised that the public safety *commissioners* office has not condemned the structure. (4) After all, the building and the parking lot look as if they *have not* been maintained for ten years, and *that is* a shame. (5) The other stations along the line *are not* any older, and *they are* regularly cleaned and painted. (6) Why *has not* the same attention been given to *Troys* station? (7) Certainly the number of people using the commuter rail *systems* Fast Trax trains from this station *has not* lessened. (8) In fact, *it is* just the opposite, with 10 percent more city residents

deciding that *they will* ride these trains from this station. (9) I *do not* think I am overreacting when I say that city officials *have not* done everything they *should have.* (10) *Is not* our well-being the *citys* first responsibility?

CHALLENGE 31.2 **Using *Its* and *It's* in Your Writing**

1. As you can see from the list of common contractions on page 489, contractions of *it has* and *it is* are written as *it's.* For this Challenge, write ten sentences, five in which you use *its* and five in which you use *it's.* Then recopy the sentences, eliminating all apostrophes.

collaboration

2. Exchange your sentences with a classmate. On the paper you receive, insert apostrophes where they are needed, and return the paper to the writer.

3. Together, evaluate the changes made to both sets of sentences. Check the guidelines on pages 488–489 for any correction about which you disagree.

collaboration

Using Other Marks of Punctuation

Colons

A **colon** calls attention to what comes next. It is used to introduce a formal statement such as an explanation or announcement or a long or formal quotation. It is also used to introduce a list, often in combination with the words *as follows* or *the following.* Study the following examples:

EXAMPLES

Now it was clear why Grandfather had been behaving so strangely: he had suffered a small stroke.

So far, I've test-driven three cars: a Scion X$_b$, a Toyota Yaris, and a Ford Focus.

In the first example, the colon introduces an explanation. In the second example, the colon introduces a list.

Do not use a colon for a list that follows a verb or a preposition.

EXAMPLE

You must bring two pencils, a calculator, and a good eraser.

Colons have other functions, too:

- Use a colon after the salutation of a formal letter *(Dear Ms. Newman:).*
- Use a colon to separate hours and minutes *(10:45),* biblical chapter and verse *(John 4:11),* and the city of publication and the publishing company in bibliographic citations and footnotes *(New York: Pearson Education).*

COMPREHENSION AND PRACTICE

Using Colons

31.4   Insert colons where they are needed in the space above the following sentences. If a sentence is correct, write *OK* above it. Use the example to guide you.

EXAMPLE   My goal was simple : write a play, sell it to Broadway and Hollywood, and become filthy rich.

(1) Today, I had a 330 P.M. appointment with Dr. Smits to ask her permission to enroll in her advanced computer applications course. (2) I had not completed the two course prerequisites CPR 101, Introduction to Computers, and CPR 102, Networking. (3) However, I did have something that I thought might encourage her to add me to her class three years' experience working with computers at my job. (4) My plan was simple explain what systems and software I had used and ask her to substitute my experience for the prerequisites. (5) I arrived early so that I could do the one thing that I hadn't done organize my presentation. (6) By 325, I was well organized, but I was also feeling nervous. (7) If she refused, I would have to do something I considered ridiculous take courses that duplicated all the experience I already had. (8) When she arrived, she quietly listened to my story and quickly gave her answer yes. (9) Thanks to her willingness to credit my work experience, I can start out at the proper level and fill those two spots in my curriculum with other courses that will help me grow as a professional.

Semicolons

ESL Note
See "Punctuation," pages 554–555, for more on the correct use of semicolons.

A **semicolon**, as you saw in Chapter 19 and Chapter 20, has the same power to connect as *and* preceded by a comma. But when you use the semicolon alone, you are saying that the connection between the clauses is so strong that no word is needed to signal it:

EXAMPLE   By ten o'clock, Elaine's car had already been stuck in the snow three times; she just wanted to turn around and head for home.

The semicolon connects the two thoughts and emphasizes the connection between Elaine's experience and her wish to quit.

As Chapter 19 also showed, using a conjunctive adverb with a semicolon is another way to connect clauses. Conjunctive adverbs, which include words such as *however, finally,* and *therefore,* can suggest a relationship between sentences. A conjunctive adverb alone can't connect, though, so you must use a semicolon *before* the conjunctive adverb to connect the clauses:

EXAMPLE David has had plenty of experience as a pipe fitter; *however,* he hasn't done much welding.

The semicolon connects the two clauses, and the conjunctive adverb *however* stresses that David's experience as a pipe fitter doesn't include welding.

COMPREHENSION AND PRACTICE

31.5

Using Semicolons

Many of the sentences in the following paragraph are missing semicolons. In the space above these sentences, insert semicolons where they are needed. Some sentences are correct. Just mark these sentences *OK.* Use the example to direct you.

EXAMPLE Cliff couldn't have been involved in the incident; he was out of town on that day.

(1) Last year, my friend Lani's life was thrown into turmoil she discovered that she had been adopted. (2) This knowledge upset her greatly she felt more confused and insecure than she had ever felt before. (3) After twenty years, she suddenly discovered that she had other biological parents she couldn't understand why her mom and dad hadn't told her before now. (4) For the first time in her life, Lani felt anger and resentment toward her mother and father she felt that she could no longer trust them. (5) Lani's adoptive parents didn't help the situation much they just acted as if nothing had changed. (6) Furthermore, the discovery made her troubled relationship with her brother, her adoptive parents' biological child, much worse. (7) Lani had always felt that she and her brother were very different now she understood why she felt that way. (8) This feeling was replaced by insecurity Lani feared that her parents loved her brother more than her. (9) After a year of counseling, Lani has adjusted she has finally accepted that she was adopted. (10) She understands that her parents had good intentions they simply didn't consider the possible consequences of withholding information.

Parentheses and Dashes

Parentheses enclose information added to a sentence but not vital to it. Added dates, asides, and explanations may be enclosed in parentheses.

EXAMPLES

The people in the car (all wearing seatbelts) escaped injury.

Hypothermia (dangerously low body temperature) threatens the elderly during these cold stretches.

In the first example, the parentheses enclose added information that the reader doesn't actually need to understand the sentence. In the second example, the parentheses enclose the definition of a specialized term.

Dashes are used to set off information that deserves special attention.

EXAMPLES

The murderer turns out to be—but I don't want to spoil the ending for you.

As the winners were announced—the crowd had been waiting more than an hour for this moment—a loud cheer filled the auditorium.

In the first example, the dash indicates an abrupt change in thought and sentence structure. In the second, the dashes set off information that emphasizes the importance of the main idea. Dashes and parentheses are sometimes interchangeable. However, dashes indicate a stronger interruption. Neither mark should be used frequently, or it will lose its effectiveness.

COMPREHENSION AND PRACTICE

Using Parentheses and Dashes

31.6   Some sentences in the following passage need either parentheses or dashes. Correct the sentences by inserting the proper marks of punctuation. In some cases, more than one correct answer is possible. Write *OK* above any sentence that is correctly punctuated. Study the example first.

EXAMPLE

In the back of the arcade (the one on Main Street, not the one on Plymouth

Avenue) police found the missing boy.

(1) Working as an aide in two hospitals St. Jude's and United has proven to me that I want to become a nurse. (2) In the two years that I've worked at these hospitals, I have gotten to know some of the most dedicated people I've ever met. (3) These are people who put their patients before everything even themselves. (4) I've seen some of them stay an hour beyond their shift because a patient took a sudden turn for the worse. (5) In the cardiac intensive

care units at St. Jude's there is one for adults and another for infants I've seen nurses going out of their way to reassure patients and their families. (6) The nurses don't mind because they feel comforting people is an important part of their job. (7) I've even seen them trying to calm the emergency medical technicians EMTs who have had to transport a badly injured person. (8) When you consider the hours and the stress, the pay isn't great around $40,000 a year, but there are other things to be gained. (9) When you can see that you've made someone feel better, you can walk away with a good feeling. (10) Sometimes not as often as you might think you can even help to save lives.

Understanding Capitalization

Capitalization, the practice of using initial capital letters to distinguish words, is governed by basic guidelines for standard use.

- Always capitalize the first word of any sentence:

EXAMPLE The bike was the first thing the thieves took.

- Always capitalize the personal pronoun *I:*

EXAMPLE As far as **I** am concerned, Eileen is the only one of my childhood friends who ever understood me.

- Capitalize *proper names* of individuals or things, including holidays, countries, states, historical periods or events, buildings, monuments, months (but not seasons), days of the week, planets, races, religions, and nationalities:

Marge Hill	**Argentina**	**Lincoln Memorial**	**Valentine's Day**
Renaissance	**May** (but spring)	**Civil War**	**Monday**
Venus	**Islam**	**Chinese**	**Baptist**
Maine (ME)			

- Capitalize words designating family relationships when these words are part of, or a substitute for, a specific name:

EXAMPLE When I was in elementary school, **Aunt Mary** always went with my parents to parent/teacher night.

- Capitalize the first letter of a formal title such as *Doctor, Senator,* or *Mayor* when the title is used with a name:

EXAMPLE   We expect Mayor Keith to call a news conference soon.

- Capitalize words like *Street, Avenue,* and *Boulevard* when these words are part of a specific address:

EXAMPLE   50 Earle Street

- Capitalize geographical regions of the United States and other parts of the world, but not directions:

EXAMPLE   After being stationed in the Far East for three years, I settled in the Midwest on the east side of the Mississippi.

- Capitalize the main words of *specifically* named courses:

EXAMPLE   Introduction to Physics; Ecology of North America; American History I; Writing 101

- Capitalize the names of languages, whether or not they refer to specific academic subjects:

EXAMPLE   Chinese; Khmer; Portuguese

- Capitalize the main words in the titles of books, magazines, newspapers, television shows, songs, articles, poems, movies, and so on. Do not capitalize a preposition or conjunction of fewer than five letters or *a, an,* or *the* unless it is the first word in the title.

EXAMPLE   *The Invisible Man; Rolling Stone; Of Mice and Men;* "A Rose for Emily"

- Capitalize the names of specific brands, companies, clubs, associations, and so on:

EXAMPLE   Mazda Protege; General Electric; National Organization for Women

- Capitalize *acronyms,* words formed from the first letters of several words:

EXAMPLES   MADD (Mothers Against Drunk Driving)

   AIDS (Acquired Immune Deficiency Syndrome)

- Capitalize the first words at the beginning of a letter, known as the *salutation,* and the first word of the ending, called the *complimentary close:*

Common Salutations	*Common Complimentary Closes*
Dear Dr. Lannon:	Sincerely,
Dear Kurtis,	Very truly yours,
Dear Sir or Madam:	Respectfully,

COMPREHENSION AND PRACTICE

Working with Capital and Lowercase Letters

31.7 Circle the correct letter—capital or lowercase—from each set in parentheses. Refer to the guidelines above if you are in doubt. Use the example to direct you.

EXAMPLE (F/f)or any florist, the busiest days of the (Y/y)ear are (V/v)alentine's (D/d)ay and (M/m)other's (D/d)ay.

(1) (P/p)rofessor (G/g)odwin, my instructor for (I/i)ntroduction to (B/b)usiness, always stresses the importance of exhibiting a professional appearance on the job. (2) (O/o)n the first day of (C/c)lass, (P/p)rofessor (G/g)odwin said, "(I/i)f you want (P/p)eople to take you seriously, you must dress as if you belong on the cover of (B/*b)usinessweek.*" (3) (H/h)e urged us to go down to (S/s)outh (M/m)ain (S/s)treet and (W/w)est 53rd (S/s)treet, where (R/r)etail stores like (E/e)ddie (B/b)auer and (S/s)aks (F/f)ifth (A/a)venue and the (C/c)orporate offices for (T/t)imex and (J/j)ohn (H/h)ancock are located. (4) (T/t)here, he said, we would see (M/m)anagers and (E/e)xecutives dressed in (C/c)onservative (B/b)usiness suits. (5) (N/n)one of these (B/b)usinesspeople is dressed in (L/l)evi's (J/j)eans or (N/n)ike (S/s)neakers because all of them know the importance of dressing well on the job.

QUICK STUDY **Student Example**

This chapter discusses signals for beginnings and endings, possessing and condensing, and emphasizing or minimizing. Consider this paragraph on a related subject, the personal possessions the writer would keep if she had to reduce her belongings to what she could fit in a single shoebox:

What would I save if I could keep only one shoebox full of personal be-

longings Most of what I would keep might seem odd to some people First of all, I would keep a coin bank in the shape of a chevrolet corvette, which used to sit on my grandfathers workbench My grandmother gave it to me after my Grandfathers funeral It would take up almost a quarter of the box, but how could I not keep it Every time I look at it, it reminds me of him In addition, I would keep my Godchilds many drawings from when she was in Nursery School They show the two of us doing things together like going to the playground and to the Beach If I fold them up carefully, I'd still have almost half the box available I would fill the rest of the box up with several things One would be a stack of about 100 photos from my childhood showing everything from vacations at disneyworld and yellowstone national park to birthday parties to graduations Then, in the space I had left, I would stick the ticket stubs and wristbands I have saved from all the concerts and sporting events I have ever attended, especially from the first time I saw the chicago cubs play The things I would keep have no monetary value, but I consider them the most valuable things I own because of the memories they hold

First complete the following activities in response to this paragraph:

1. The sentences in the above paragraph have no end punctuation. In addition, there are errors in capitalization and apostrophe use. Insert the proper end punctuation and correct any errors in capitalization and apostrophe use.

2. How does the topic sentence of this paragraph prepare the reader for the discussion that follows in the body and the statement expressed in the closing sentence? Use the lines below for your answer.

_____

_____

_____

3. On a separate sheet of paper, assess the order of presentation of the supporting examples, explain why you think the writer arranged them in this way, and state whether you agree with it and why or why not.

Now explore the topic in writing. As the paragraph above does, you could discuss what you would keep if you had to reduce your belongings to a precious few. Or you might turn your attention to one of these topics related to the subject matter of this chapter:

- something about your personality that you wish you could de-emphasize
- a question for which you have long wanted to find an answer
- the characteristic or feature that distinguishes a family member or friend from the ordinary person
- the most surprising announcement you have ever heard

collaboration

4. Exchange your draft with a classmate. Evaluate the paragraph you receive, looking for any problems, especially in terms of punctuation and capitalization. Circle any errors, write corrected versions above them, and then return the paper to the writer.

5. Consider the comments and corrections your reader has made and create a final draft of your paragraph.

CHAPTER QUICK CHECK Punctuation and Capitalization

The following passage contains numerous errors in the use of end punctuation, quotation marks, apostrophes, colons, semicolons, dashes, parentheses, and lower-case and capital letters. Consult the examples throughout the chapter. Then correct all errors by inserting needed punctuation or by writing corrected letters in the space above, as the example shows.

EXAMPLE

Until last year, my neighbor Pete, who served in vietnam, didnt realize he had been exposed to agent orange during his tour of duty there.

(1) One of the most important steps for job-seekers is to make sure their resumes are widely circulated and reviewed? (2) Thanks to the Internet, people have another way to ensure that the maximum number of employers review their work credentials online resume-posting services. (3) When resumes are posted on the Web, an individuals qualifications can be quickly examined with a few clicks of a computer mouse. (4) The leading global careers site several million hits monthly is Monster.com, which traces its origins to a site called The Monster Board, created in 1994 by Jeff Taylor. (5) In 1999, the Monster Board merged with Online Career Center, and the resulting company eventually became Monster Jobs, which is now based in maynard, massachusetts.

(6) Taylor, who is CEO Chief Executive Officer of the company, came up with the concept for the site while he was an undergraduate at the University of Massachusetts, in Amherst, Massachusetts. (7) In 1999, Taylor gambled on the power of conventional advertising when Monster.com spent $4 million to purchase three 30-second commercials during the super bowl. (8) As a result, Monster began to draw huge numbers of visitors to its site, and Taylor didnt make the mistake that other Internet companies had made after an advertising blitz. (9) As Taylor later started a speech, We're the only Internet site that advertised on the Super Bowl that didn't crash because of added traffic. (10) Not content to leave anything undone, Taylor in 2001 finished up something he had left behind to begin his company the requirements for his college degree.

SUMMARY EXERCISE Punctuation and Capitalization

The following passage contains numerous errors in the use of end punctuation, quotation marks, apostrophes, colons, semicolons, dashes, parentheses, and lower-case and capital letters. Consult the examples throughout the chapter. Then correct all errors by inserting needed punctuation or by writing corrected letters in the space above.

(1) On february 15, 2005, Chad Hurley, Steve Chen, and Jawed Karim began a Media revolution when they registered the following domain name for their start-up company YouTube.com. (2) Born out of a desire to share family videos with relatives across the country, YouTube previewed in May 2005, and in november of the same year, it opened for business? (3) During it's first month of operation, a handful of videos about thirty were exchanged on the Web. (4) Since then, millions of videos have been added, shared, and viewed across the World, with estimates of more than 65,000 new videos being uploaded on a daily basis.

(5) The companys founders were all originally employees of PayPal, the popular online payment service now owned by eBay. (6) The first home of YouTube was actually a small office in san mateo, california. (7) For the financial support needed to get started, hurley, chen, and karim turned to Sequoia Capital this venture capital firm had also helped apple and Google in their early days. (8) Following it's original investment of $3.5 million, Sequoia added another $8 million. (9) Within a year, YouTube was one of the fastest-growing Sites on the Web. (10) According to a 2006 report from Alexa Internet, Inc. a company that tracks Web site traffic, YouTube ranks among the five most frequently visited Web sites.

(11) YouTubes growth has been phenomenal however, it has not been without growing pains. (12) Perhaps the biggest problem the company faced was a charge of violation of Copyright for running content from television shows, commericals, sports programming, concerts, and so on. (13) By 2007, after YouTube was acquired by Google the same company that operates the world's most powerful search engine this issue was pretty much settled. (14) For one thing, powerhouse media outlets like nbc, cbs, espn, and warner music group finally recognized the advantage of having millions of YouTube viewers checking out snippets of their productions.

(15) So what is it that draws so many visitors to YouTube. (16) Jacqueline Wright, 28, of ann arbor, mi, says simply, "I *love* YouTube," explaining that she regularly visits to view material from the world of television, movies, Popular Music, and news. (17) But thats not all that YouTube has made possible it has also enabled people to connect to the rest of the world through the power of video. (18) Whether theyre viewing the antics of others or transmitting some aspect of their own personal lives or the products of their creative energies, they are part of a legitimate Social Network.

(19) YouTube is so entrenched in Modern Culture that it even played a part in the debates leading up to the 2008 Presidential Election. (20) From a small office in california to the Oval Office in washington, dc now that's an extraordinary trip?

FOR FURTHER EXPLORATION Punctuation and Capitalization

1. Focus on one of the following topics. Use the prewriting technique—or combination of techniques—that fits your style of working to come up with some preliminary ideas while also considering the purposes you might fulfill in writing about the topic:

   • the qualities a natural leader possesses
   • a competition or contest you won—or lost
   • two situations that would call for you to speak, dress, or behave differently
   • the importance of understanding one's cultural, ethnic, or religious background

2. Evaluate your prewriting material, identify a focus, and work your way through the rest of the writing process to create a draft essay of at least 500 words on this subject.

collaboration

3. Exchange your draft with a classmate. Check the draft you receive for weaknesses, checking in particular for errors in punctuation and capitalization. Circle any mistakes, using the material in this chapter to guide you, and return the paper to the writer.

4. Revise your essay, correcting any errors in punctuation and capitalization or other problems discovered by your reader.

RECAP Other Punctuation and Capitalization

Key Terms in This Chapter	Definitions
punctuation	a system of symbols that signals starts, stops, and pauses in writing
capitalization	the practice of emphasizing words by beginning them with capital letters
period (.)	an end mark used to indicate the end of a statement
	EXAMPLE I have a dream**.**
question mark (?)	an end mark used to indicate the end of a question
	EXAMPLE Have we met before**?**
exclamation point (!)	an end mark used to indicate the end of an exclamation and to show great feeling
	EXAMPLE Stop**!** That area is mined**!**

Key Terms in This Chapter   Definitions

direct quotation	a record of someone's exact words

> **EXAMPLE**   Peter said, "If you'll wait, I'll go with you."

quotation marks (" ")	marks used to set off someone's exact words
dialogue	an exchange of direct quotations between two or more people, with a new paragraph to mark each change in speakers

> **EXAMPLE**   "I said I wanted to go home at ten," said Joe.
> "Yes, but you didn't specify A.M. or P.M.," said Dianne.

indirect quotation	a restatement of someone else's words

> **EXAMPLE**   Peter asked me to wait and said he'd go with me.

apostrophe (')	a mark used in a noun to show ownership or possession or in a contraction to signify letters left out

To show possession:

add 's to singular nouns   a child**'s** book

add ' to plural nouns   the students' answers

add **'s** to plural nouns that don't end in **-s**   women**'s** concerns

To form contractions:

add ' to show letters omitted from the contraction   haven't

colon (:)	a mark that indicates a pause in a sentence and that introduces a quotation, formal statement, or list

> **EXAMPLE**   The news was good**:** the test results were negative.

semicolon (;)	a connecting mark that separates related independent clauses but emphasizes the connection between them

> **EXAMPLE**   Shelley is dramatic**;** her twin sister is quite shy.

parentheses	marks that enclose nonvital information within a sentence

> **EXAMPLE**   The movie **(**which she saw with her sister**)** made Mavis cry.

dashes	marks that set off information to create emphasis

> **EXAMPLE**   Vincent van Gogh**—**who mutilated his ear**—**was a genius.

Guidelines for Capitalization

The first word in a sentence

> EXAMPLE   **A** light bulb burned out in the kitchen.

The personal pronoun *I* and the proper names of people, things, and places

> EXAMPLE   **S**ean and **I** are going to **T**ulsa on **F**riday.

Words that designate family relationships when they are part of, or a substitute for, a specific name

> EXAMPLE   **U**ncle Rod always calls to check on **G**randma.

Formal titles used with a person's name

> EXAMPLE   **D**r. Dave Feeney has been selected for the award.

Words that are part of a specific address or specific section of a country

> EXAMPLE   Our plant in the **S**outhwest is located at 1411 **L**incoln **W**ay in **T**ucson.

Main words in specific academic subjects, languages, and titles

> EXAMPLE   In my **I**ntroduction to **E**nvironment class, we are reading Rachel Carson's *Silent Spring*.

Brand names, company and association names, and letters of acronyms

> EXAMPLE   My sister works for **AT&T**.

First letters of the salutation and complimentary close of a letter

> EXAMPLE   **D**ear Paul, **Y**ours truly,

Using Odyssey Online with MyWritingLab

For more practice with other punctuation and capitalization, go to www.mywritinglab.com.

> **portfolio** • **noun** (pl. **portfolios**) . . . **2** a set of pieces of creative work intended to demonstrate a person's ability. ORIGIN Italian *portafogli,* from *portare* 'carry' + *foglio* 'leaf'.

—Compact Oxford English Dictionary

This portfolio allows you to demonstrate what you have learned about grammar, usage, and mechanics. Take this opportunity to practice working with four important parts of speech: *nouns, pronouns, adjectives,* and *adverbs* (Chapters 25, 26, and 27). Review your understanding of parallel structure (Chapter 28), and practice some techniques you've learned to improve your spelling (Chapter 29). Test your knowledge of the various functions of the comma (Chapter 30) and other types of punctuation marks (Chapter 31). Also, take this opportunity to apply the rules of capitalization (Chapter 31). To mark your progress up to this point, prepare the following portfolio:

BEST WORK   Select your best work from the assignments completed for this section. If you can't decide which one is best, consult with a classmate or another reader.

ESSAY ANSWER   Following is a painting by Vincent van Gogh titled *Self-Portrait, Dedicated to Paul Gauguin;* it is one of the thirty-five self-portraits van Gogh painted between 1886 and 1889. Study it carefully, and then write a 250- to 300-word answer to one of the essay questions.

- How does van Gogh speak to you in this painting? What do you think he was trying to say about himself, about his circumstances and environment, about his view of the world? What aspects of the painting inform your reaction? Is it van Gogh's use of colors? Or is it his posture, the look on his face, or maybe even the look in his eyes? Respond to the painting, using these questions or some others that come to mind as your starting point.

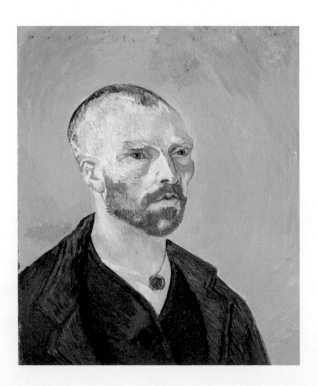

- This painting, like van Gogh's other paintings, is considered a masterpiece of art. Do you agree with this assessment? In your view, does this painting qualify as a masterpiece? Why? What aspects of the painting lead you to your conclusion?

TIMED WRITING

TIMED WRITING

Consider the following quotation:

> Forget the past. No one becomes successful in the past.
> —Anonymous

Now choose one of the following options, and, in thirty minutes, complete a writing of around 300 words in response to the option you have selected. Remember to supply numerous specific supporting examples and details.

- This quotation suggests that to succeed, we should ignore the past. Some people, however, believe that the opposite is true, that our past behavior should be a lesson for improving our lives. Which side of the debate are you on? Why?

- In your view, what is the best formula for success? What leads you to this conclusion?

REFLECTION

Together, the seven chapters that make up Part 6 of *Odyssey* show how much the parts of something—in this case, key parts of speech and applications such as *parallelism, spelling, punctuation,* and *capitalization*—contribute to the effect of the whole. If you have a problem with any of these aspects of writing, your paragraphs and essays will be far less successful than they should be. The reason for this is simple: errors in form distract your reader from the point you are making.

Now react from the standpoint of a reader. Of the errors illustrated in the chapters making up Part 6, which one do you find most distracting? Why do you find this weakness more troubling than the others? Write a paragraph of seven to ten sentences in which you address these questions. Remember—supply plenty of specific supporting examples and details.

PART 7

Connecting: Responding to Reading

Overview: Responding to What You Read

A strong relationship exists between solid reading skills and success in writing, and to get the most out of what you read, you need to approach it actively. When you read **actively,** you respond to the ideas other writers have developed and discover the strategies they have used to express those ideas. This part of the text includes writings by both professional authors and students. After each selection, you will find questions to help you think about and respond to the ideas in the reading. Additional assignments will help you explore the connections between those ideas and your own experiences. The questions will also encourage you to use the various modes in your own writing.

Navigating This Section In this section of the text, you can explore:

- a variety of modes that writers use to fulfill their purposes
- additional subjects for writing
- strategies writers use to express their ideas and experiences

Taking Notes

Just as writing effectively has many benefits, reading actively enables you to get more out of your reading. As a way to improve your reading skills, your instructor may ask you to maintain a response journal in which you record your questions, comments, and responses to what you read.

As you read, *annotate* or make notes in the margins of the pages you are reading or highlight sections for later reference. You might also keep your notes in a computer file. These notes will help you prepare for discussions with your classmates and explore ideas for your own writing assignments.

Active Reading Strategies

Sometimes it is difficult to know what questions to ask and what notes to take. The five guidelines below apply to any reading assignment. They will provide direction and help you focus your responses to the readings.

Review them before you begin to read each selection, and be sure to record your responses as you read.

1. **Establish the context.**
   What's going on? Who is involved? When did it happen? Where? How? Why? These are the questions that news stories generally answer in their opening sentences to establish the *context* for readers. As you read, use these kinds of questions to identify details and examples that establish the context of the reading.

2. **Explore the purpose and modes.**

   As Chapters 5 through 15 explain, writers use modes, or organizing strategies—narration, description, example, process, definition, comparison and contrast, cause and effect, and division and classification—to communicate their ideas to readers. To construct an argument, writers use a combination of these modes. As you read, first determine the author's purpose for writing. Is it to inform, to entertain, or to persuade? What is the dominant mode the author uses to fulfill this purpose? What other modes does the author use, and how are they combined?

3. **Explore the main ideas.**

   As you read, highlight or record in your journal parts of the reading that state the author's thesis. Do the same for evidence that supports that idea. Finally, highlight or record the author's conclusions about the subject.

   Try to identify the main ideas or topic sentences of the paragraphs. Can you trace a common thread, the element that all the paragraphs have in common? Are there sentences or paragraphs that confuse you or sections that you don't understand? Make note of these to discuss with your classmates. Next, identify supporting information that helps you understand the writer's points. What details catch your eye? Why are these effective?

4. **Respond to the ideas.**

   What do you think of the reading? Why do you think the way you do? Do you agree with the ideas the author has expressed? Are you familiar with the context or the ideas making up the foundation of the reading? Does the author present an experience or view of the world that is new to you? Your answers to these questions will help you greatly in understanding the writing. As you talk or write about the piece, you will also be making sense of it. Remember as you read that a good piece of writing touches the reader. When you read, explore what the writer has done to touch you.

5. **Read again.**

   Active reading can be challenging, but it is also rewarding. To fully understand a piece of writing, conduct at least two or three readings of it. You'll no doubt discover some elements or aspects in a second reading that you missed in the first. It is worth your effort to analyze the elements you discover so that you will be able to use a similar approach in your own writing.

Active Reading Illustrated

Here is a brief excerpt from "The Future of TV Sports Is Glowing" by Ted Rose. This article explores and explains how technological innovations have changed the way televised sports are presented. The annotations illustrate the way active reading can help you uncover a writer's meaning and the various techniques that enable the writer to communicate that meaning:

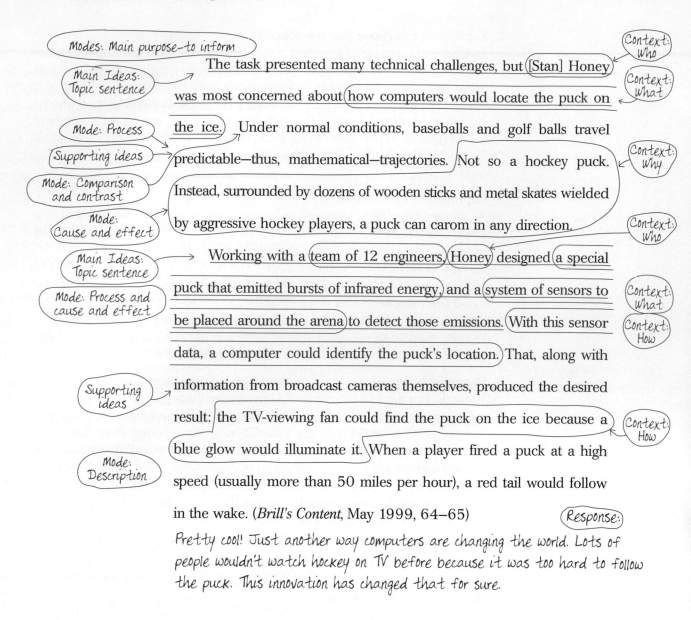

Modes: Main purpose—to inform

Main Ideas: Topic sentence

The task presented many technical challenges, but [Stan] Honey was most concerned about how computers would locate the puck on the ice. Under normal conditions, baseballs and golf balls travel predictable—thus, mathematical—trajectories. Not so a hockey puck. Instead, surrounded by dozens of wooden sticks and metal skates wielded by aggressive hockey players, a puck can carom in any direction.

Context: who
Context: what
Context: why
Context: who

Mode: Process
Supporting ideas
Mode: Comparison and contrast
Mode: Cause and effect

Main Ideas: Topic sentence
Mode: Process and cause and effect

Working with a team of 12 engineers, Honey designed a special puck that emitted bursts of infrared energy, and a system of sensors to be placed around the arena to detect those emissions. With this sensor data, a computer could identify the puck's location. That, along with information from broadcast cameras themselves, produced the desired result: the TV-viewing fan could find the puck on the ice because a blue glow would illuminate it. When a player fired a puck at a high speed (usually more than 50 miles per hour), a red tail would follow in the wake. (*Brill's Content*, May 1999, 64–65)

Context: who
Context: what
Context: How
Context: How

Supporting ideas

Mode: Description

Response:

Pretty cool! Just another way computers are changing the world. Lots of people wouldn't watch hockey on TV before because it was too hard to follow the puck. This innovation has changed that for sure.

As the annotations illustrate, active reading helps you isolate a number of elements of the writing. For instance, it helps you focus on the *context: what* was involved (the development of a hockey puck that would be easier to see on a television screen), *who* was involved (Stan Honey and a team of twelve engineers), and *how* they did it (they built a puck that emits signals and installed sensors throughout the ice rink).

Active reading also enables you to note the purpose (*main* purpose, to *inform; secondary* purpose, to *entertain*) and the various *modes* (*comparison and contrast, process, cause and effect,* and *description*), as well as the *main ideas* (the *topic sentences* and the *supporting sentences*). And the *response* to the reading helps you focus on the significance or meaning of the passage to a more complete degree. When you understand how a writer communicates ideas to a reader, you are better able to communicate your own ideas to your reader. That's why active reading is so important.

5:00 a.m.: Writing as Ritual

Judith Ortiz Cofer

Franklin Professor of English and Creative Writing at the University of Georgia, Judith Ortiz Cofer has won awards and international recognition for her writing, which includes a novel, essays, short stories, and several volumes of poetry. In this selection from The Latin Deli, *a book of prose and poetry, she writes about how she discovered the time she needed to create. In what ways does setting aside time to do something make that activity more important?*

1   An act of will that changed my life from that of a frustrated artist, waiting to have a room of my own and an independent income before getting down to business, to that of a working writer: I decided to get up two hours before my usual time, to set my alarm for 5:00 a.m.

2   When people ask me how I started writing, I find myself describing the urgent need that I felt to work with language as a search; I did not know for a long time what I was looking for. Although I married at nineteen, had a child at twenty-one—all the while going through college and graduate school *and* working part-time—it was not enough. There was something missing in my life that I came close to only when I turned to my writing, when I took a break from my thesis research to write a poem or an idea for a story on the flip side of an index card. It wasn't until I traced this feeling to its source that I discovered both the cause and the answer to my frustration: I needed to write. I showed my first efforts to a woman, a "literary" colleague, who encouraged me to mail them out. One poem was accepted for publication, and I was hooked. This bit of success is really the point where my problem began.

3   Once I finished graduate school, I had no reason to stay at the library that extra hour to write poems. It was 1978. My daughter was five years old and in school during the day while I traveled the county, teaching freshman composition on three different campuses. Afternoons I spent taking her to her ballet, tap, and every other socializing lesson her little heart desired. I composed my lectures on Florida's I-95, and that was all the thinking time I had. Does this sound like the typical superwoman's lament? To me it meant being in a constant state of mild anxiety which I could not really discuss with others. What was I to say to them? I need an hour to start a poem. Will someone please stop the world from spinning so fast?

4   I did not have the privilege of attending a writers' workshop as a beginning writer. I came to writing instinctively, as a dowser finds an underground well. I did not know that I would eventually make a career out of writing books and giving readings of my work. The only models I knew were the unattainable ones: the first famous poet I met was Richard Eberhart, so exalted and venerable that he might as well have been the Pope. All I knew at that time was that at twenty-six years of age I felt spiritually deprived, although I had all the things my women friends found sufficiently fulfilling in a "woman's life" plus more; I was also teaching, which is the only vocation I always knew I had. But I had found poetry, or it had found me, and it was demanding its place in my life.

5   After trying to stay up late at night for a couple of weeks and discovering that there was not enough of me left after a full day of giving to others, I relented and

did this odious thing: I set my alarm for five. The first day I shut it off because I could: I had placed it within arm's reach. The second day I set two clocks, one on my night table, as usual, and one out in the hallway. I had to jump out of bed and run to silence it before my family was awakened and the effort nullified. This is when my morning writing ritual that I follow to this day began. I get up at five and put on a pot of coffee. Then I sit in my rocking chair and read what I did the previous day until the coffee is ready. I take fifteen minutes to drink two cups of coffee while my computer warms up—not that it needs to—I just like to see it glowing in the room where I sit in semidarkness, its screen prompting "ready": ready whenever you are. When I'm ready, I write.

6   Since that first morning in 1978 when I rose in the dark to find myself in a room of my own—with two hours belonging only to me ahead of me, two prime hours when my mind was still filtering my dreams—I have not made or accepted too many excuses for not writing. This apparently ordinary choice, to get up early and to work every day, forced me to come to terms with the discipline of art. I wrote my poems in this manner for nearly ten years before my first book was published. When I decided to give my storytelling impulse full rein and write a novel, I divided my two hours: the first hour for poetry, the second for fiction; two pages minimum per day. Well or badly, I wrote two pages a day for three and one-half years. This is how my novel, *The Line of the Sun,* was finished. If I had waited to have the time, I would still be waiting to write my novel.

7   My life has changed considerably since those early days when I was trying to be everything to everyone. My daughter is eighteen and in college, not a ballerina, Rockette, or horsewoman but a disciplined student and a self-assured young person. Thus I do not regret the endless hours of sitting in tiny chairs at the Rock-Ette Academy of Dance or of breathing the saturated air at the stables as I waited for her. She got out of her activities something like what I got out of getting up in the dark to work: the feeling that you are in control, on the saddle, on your toes. Empowerment is what the emerging artist needs to win for herself. And the initial sense of urgency to create can easily be dissipated because it entails making the one choice many people, especially women, in our society with its emphasis on the "acceptable" priorities, feel selfish about making: taking the time to create, stealing it from yourself if it's the only way.

EXPLORING THE READING THROUGH DISCUSSION

1. What motivated Judith Ortiz Cofer to begin to write poetry?

2. What is the problem to which Cofer refers at the end of the second paragraph? How does she solve her dilemma?

3. What steps does Cofer follow in her writing rituals? List them.

4. What does Cofer create as a result of following her ritual? Does she gain anything else?

5. Cofer uses colons several times in her essay. Find the sentences that include colons. Why do you think she chose to use this punctuation mark when she did? Refer to Chapter 31, "Other Punctuation and Capitalization," as you explore this question.

DEVELOPING VOCABULARY

List any words in this selection that are new to you. Write your understanding of each word from the context. Then look up each word in the dictionary, and write the definition that you think best fits the meaning in this writing.

_____

_____

_____

_____

DISCOVERING CONNECTIONS THROUGH WRITING

1. What steps do you follow in your own writing ritual? Include details to answer your readers' questions about when, where, and why you follow this process.

2. Do you take time to engage in an activity that makes you feel that you "are in control, on the saddle, on your toes"? Describe what you do and what the positive results are.

3. Clearly, writing was a long-term goal for Cofer. It took her nearly ten years to write her first book of poetry and three and one-half years to finish her first novel. Do you have a long-term goal? Explain what your goal is and what steps you are taking to reach it.

Fish Cheeks

Amy Tan

Amy Tan is an acclaimed writer who has explored the relationships between immigrant Chinese mothers and their daughters. Her first novel, The Joy Luck Club *(1989), is based on some of her own experiences. As you read this essay, first published in* Seventeen *magazine, try to understand the feelings of a little girl living in two cultures. How can feeling different from others affect your social interactions?*

1   I fell in love with the minister's son the winter I turned fourteen. He was not Chinese, but as white as Mary in the manger. For Christmas I prayed for this blond-haired boy, Robert, and a slim new American nose.

2   When I found out that my parents had invited the minister's family over for Christmas Eve dinner, I cried. What would Robert think of our shabby Chinese Christmas? What would he think of our noisy Chinese relatives who lacked proper American manners? What terrible disappointment would he feel upon seeing not a roasted turkey and sweet potatoes but Chinese food?

3   On Christmas Eve I saw that my mother had outdone herself in creating a strange menu. She was pulling black veins out of the backs of fleshy prawns. The kitchen was littered with appalling mounds of raw food: A slimy rock cod with bulging eyes that pleaded not be thrown into a pan of hot oil. Tofu, which looked like stacked wedges of

rubbery white sponges. A bowl soaking dried fungus back to life. A plate of squid, their backs crisscrossed with knife markings so they resembled bicycle tires.

4   And then they arrived—the minister's family and all my relatives in a clamor of doorbells and rumpled Christmas packages. Robert grunted hello, and I pretended he was not worthy of existence.

5   Dinner threw me deeper into despair. My relatives licked the ends of their chopsticks and reached across the table, dipping them into the dozen or so plates of food. Robert and his family waited patiently for platters to be passed to them. My relatives murmured with pleasure when my mother brought out the whole steamed fish. Robert grimaced. Then my father poked his chopsticks just below the fish eye and plucked out the soft meat. "Amy, your favorite," he said, offering me the tender fish cheek. I wanted to disappear.

6   At the end of the meal my father leaned back and belched loudly, thanking my mother for her fine cooking. "It's a polite Chinese custom to show you are satisfied," explained my father to our astonished guests. Robert was looking down at his plate with a reddened face. The minister managed to muster up a quiet burp. I was stunned into silence for the rest of the night.

7   After everyone had gone, my mother said to me, "You want to be the same as American girls on the outside." She handed me an early gift. It was a miniskirt in beige tweed. "But inside you must always be Chinese. You must be proud you are different. Your only shame is to have shame."

8   And even though I didn't agree with her then, I knew that she understood how much I had suffered during the evening's dinner. It wasn't until many years later—long after I had gotten over my crush on Robert—that I was able to fully appreciate her lesson and the true purpose behind our particular menu. For Christmas Eve that year, she had chosen all my favorite foods.

EXPLORING THE READING THROUGH DISCUSSION

1. What is the lesson that the author finally appreciates after "many years"? Why didn't she agree with her mother at the time?

2. Compare the responses of the two families to the dinner and briefly summarize how, in general, each family reacted. How did the narrator feel during and after the meal? Why did she feel this way?

3. Tan uses a number of sensory details to describe the Christmas Eve menu. Which of these details do you find most compelling? List it and explain why you selected it.

4. At what point in the essay is Tan's use of transition most effective? What leads you to this conclusion?

5. Do you think "Fish Cheeks" is a good title for this story? Explain your reasoning.

DEVELOPING VOCABULARY

List any words in this selection that are new to you. Write your understanding of each word from the context. Then look up each word in the dictionary, and write the definition that you think best fits the meaning in this writing.

DISCOVERING CONNECTIONS THROUGH WRITING

1. The narrator's mother tells her, "You must be proud you are different. Your only shame is to have shame." What does the mother mean by this? Do you agree? Write about a situation you know or an experience you have had that supports her belief.

2. Have you ever participated in a traditional event or shared a special occasion with friends of another religion or culture as Robert and his family do? How did you feel? What did you learn? Provide plenty of concrete examples in your essay.

3. Write a narrative about a holiday celebration you remember well. In your essay, be sure to use effective description to put your readers at the scene.

iPod World: The End of Society?

Andrew Sullivan

Technology is meant to improve our lives. It helps us save time, communicate quickly, and expand our knowledge of the world around us. In the following essay published in the New York Times Magazine *in 2005, Andrew Sullivan, a native of England and a book author, journalist, and blogger, writes about some of the unintended and negative effects of one popular technology: the iPod. Do you think technology improves our social networking or isolates us from each other and the world?*

1   I was visiting New York City last week and noticed something I'd never thought I'd say about the big city. Yes, nightlife is pretty much dead (and I'm in no way the first to notice that). But daylife—that insane mishmash of yells, chatter, clatter, hustle and chutzpah that makes New York the urban equivalent of methamphetamine—was also a little different. It was just a little quieter. Yes, the suburbanization of Manhattan is now far-gone, its downtown a Disney-like string of malls, riverside parks, and pretty upper-middle-class villages. But there was something else as well. And as I looked across the throngs on the pavements, I began to see why. There were little white wires hanging down from their ears, tucked into pockets or purses or jackets. The eyes were a little vacant. Each was in his or her own little musical world, almost oblivious to the world around them. These are the iPod people.

2   Even without the white wires, you can tell who they are. They walk down the street in their own MP3 cocoon, bumping into others, deaf to small social cues, shutting out anyone not in their bubble. Every now and again, some start unconsciously emitting strange tuneless squawks, like a badly-tuned radio, and their fingers snap or their arms twitch to some strange soundless rhythm. When others say, "Excuse me," there is no response. "Hi." Ditto. It's strange to be among so much people and hear so little. Except that each one is hearing so much.

3   Yes, I might as well fess up. I'm one of them. I witnessed the glaze New York looks through my own glazed pupils, my own white wires peeping out of my eardrums. I joined the cult a few years ago: the sect of the little white box worshipers. Every now

and again, I go to the church—those huge, luminous Apple stores, pews in the rear, the clerics in their monastic uniforms all bustling around, or sitting behind the "Genius Bars," like priests waiting to hear confessions. Others began, like I did, with a Walkman—and then another kind of clunkier MP3 player. But the sleekness of the iPod won me over. Unlike previous models, it actually gave me my entire musical collection to rearrange as I saw fit—on the fly, in my pocket. What was once an occasional musical diversion became a compulsive obsession. Now I have my iTunes in my iMac for my iPod in my iWorld. It's Narcissus' heaven: we've finally put the "i" into Me.

4   And like all addictive cults, it's spreading. There are now 22 million iPod owners in the United States and Apple is now becoming a mass market company for the first time. Walk through any U.S. airport these days, and you will see person after person gliding through the social ether as if on auto-pilot. Get on a subway, and you're surrounded by a bunch of Stepford commuters, all sealed off from each other, staring into mid-space as if anaesthetized by technology. Don't ask, don't tell, don't over-hear, don't observe. Just tune in and tune out. It wouldn't be so worrisome if it weren't part of something even bigger. Americans are beginning to narrowcast their own lives. You get your news from your favorite blogs, the ones that won't challenge your own view of the world. You tune into a paid satellite radio service that also aims directly at a small market—for New Age fanatics, or liberal talk, or Christian rock. Television is all cable. Culture is all subculture. Your cell-phones can receive email feeds of your favorite blogger's latest thoughts—seconds after he has posted them—or sports scores for your own team, or stock quotes of just your portfolio. Technology has given us finally a universe entirely for ourselves—where the serendipity of meeting a new stranger, or hearing a piece of music we would never choose for ourselves, or an opinion that might actually force us to change our mind about something are all effectively banished. Atomization by little white boxes and cell-phones. Society without the social. Others who are chosen—not met at random.

5   Human beings have never lived like this before. Yes, we have always had homes or retreats or places where we went to relax or unwind or shut the world out. But we didn't walk around the world like hermit crabs with our isolation surgically attached. Music in particular was once the preserve of the living room or the concert hall. It was sometimes solitary but it was primarily a shared experience, something that brought people together, gave them the comfort of knowing that others too understood the pleasure of that Brahms symphony or that Beatles album.

6   But music is as atomized now as living is. And it's also secret. That bloke next to you on the bus could be listening to heavy metal or Gregorian chant. You'll never know. And so, bit by bit, you'll never really know him. And by his very white wires, he is indicating he doesn't really want to know you.

7   What do we get from this? The awareness of more music, more often. The chance to slip away for a while from everydayness, to give our lives our own soundtrack, to still the monotony of the commute, to listen more closely and carefully to music that can lift you up and keep you going. We become masters of our own interests, more connected to people like us over the Internet, more instantly in touch with anything we want or need or think we want and think we need. Ever tried a Stairmaster in silence? And why not listen to a Hayden trio while in line at Tesco?

8   But what are we missing? That hilarious shard of an overheard conversation that stays with you all day; the child whose chatter on the sidewalk takes you back to your own early memories; birdsong; weather; accents; the laughter of others; and those thoughts that come not by filling your head with selected diversion, but by allowing your mind to wander aimlessly through the regular background noise of human and mechanical life. External stimulation can crowd out the interior mind. Even

the boredom that we flee from has its uses. We are forced to find our own means to overcome it. And so we enrich our life from within, rather than from the static of white wires.

9   It's hard to give up, though, isn't it? Not so long ago, I was on a trip and realized I had left my iPod behind. Panic. But then something else. I noticed the rhythms of others again, the sound of the airplane, the opinions of the cabby, the small social cues that had been obscured before. I noticed how others related to each other. And I felt just a little bit connected again. And a little more aware. Try it. There's a world out there. And it has a soundtrack all its own.

EXPLORING THE READING THROUGH DISCUSSION

1. Who are the iPod people, according to Andrew Sullivan? What about them and the way they behave makes it easy for you to recognize them?

2. According to Sullivan, in what ways are iPod people like the members of a cult?

3. In your view, what does Sullivan mean when he writes that "Americans are beginning to narrowcast their own lives"?

4. According to Sullivan, what are the positive and negative effects of using iPods?

5. In your own words, explain the meaning of the title of the essay. Do you think the title is effective? Why or why not?

DEVELOPING VOCABULARY

List any words in this selection that are new to you. Write your understanding of each word from the context. Then look up each word in the dictionary, and write the definition that you think best fits the meaning in this writing.

_____

_____

_____

_____

DISCOVERING CONNECTIONS THROUGH WRITING

1. If you own an iPod, write an essay describing the circumstances during which you use it and how your experiences are enhanced thanks to the iPod. If you have deliberately chosen not to own or use an iPod, explain why you reject what so many others have embraced.

2. In the past, music was "primarily a shared experience," writes Sullivan. Write an essay about a time when your enjoyment of music was enhanced because you were hearing it with others.

3. Sullivan, writing about the effects of technology, says it has "given us finally a universe entirely for ourselves." Choose one item of technology that you

regularly use and write about its effects on your own life. Are you more isolated or more connected as a result of this technology? What are the benefits and the drawbacks to using this technology?

Getting Coffee Is Hard to Do

Stanley Fish

Getting a morning cup of coffee is a simple, enjoyable ritual for many people. For Stanley Fish, a distinguished author, educator, and literary scholar, though, it has become a chore. In this essay, first published in the New York Times *in 2007, Fish asks readers to think about the growing self-service trend. Have you ever felt out of place or confused when facing a task that someone else used to do for you?*

1   A coordination problem (a term of art in economics and management) occurs when you have a task to perform, the task has multiple and shifting components, the time for completion is limited, and your performance is affected by the order and sequence of the actions you take. The trick is to manage it so that the components don't bump into each other in ways that produce confusion, frustration, and inefficiency.

2   You will face a coordination problem if you are a general deploying troops, tanks, helicopters, food, tents, and medical supplies, or if you are the CEO of a large company juggling the demands of design, personnel, inventory, and production.

3   And these days, you will face a coordination problem if you want to get a cup of coffee.

4   It used to be that when you wanted a cup of coffee you went into a nondescript place fitted out largely in linoleum, Formica, and neon, sat down at a counter, and, in response to a brisk "What'll you have, dear?" said, "Coffee and a cheese Danish." Twenty seconds later, tops, they arrived, just as you were settling into the sports page.

5   Now it's all wood or concrete floors, lots of earth tones, soft, high-style lighting, open barrels of coffee beans, folk-rock and indie music, photographs of urban landscapes, and copies of *The Onion*. As you walk in, everything is saying, "This is very sophisticated, and you'd better be up to it."

6   It turns out to be hard. First you have to get in line, and you may have one or two people in front of you who are ordering a drink with more parts than an internal combustion engine, something about "double shot," "skinny," "breve," "grande," "aulait" and a lot of other words that never pass my lips. If you are patient and stay in line (no bathroom breaks), you get to put in your order, but then you have to find a place to stand while you wait for it. There is no such place. So you shift your body, first here and then there, trying not to get in the way of those you can't help get in the way of.

7   Finally, the coffee arrives.

8   But then your real problems begin when you turn, holding your prize, and make your way to where the accessories—things you put in, on, and around your coffee—are found. There is a staggering array of them, and the order of their placement seems random in relation to the order of your needs. There is no "right" place to start, so you lunge after one thing and then after another with awkward reaches.

9   Unfortunately, two or three other people are doing the same thing, and each is doing it in a different sequence. So there is an endless round of "excuse me," "no, excuse me," as if you were in an old Steve Martin routine.

10   But no amount of politeness and care is enough. After all, there are so many items to reach for—lids, cup jackets, straws, napkins, stirrers, milk, half and half, water,

sugar, Splenda, the wastepaper basket, spoons. You and your companions may strive for a ballet of courtesy, but what you end up performing is more like bumper cars. It's just a question of what will happen first—getting what you want or spilling the coffee you are trying to balance in one hand on the guy reaching over you.

11   I won't even talk about the problem of finding a seat.

12   And two things add to your pain and trouble. First, it costs a lot, $3 and up. And worst of all, what you're paying for is the privilege of doing the work that should be done by those who take your money. The coffee shop experience is just one instance of the growing practice of shifting the burden of labor to the consumer—gas stations, grocery and drug stores, bagel shops (why should I put on my own cream cheese?), airline check-ins parking lots. It's insert this, swipe that, choose credit or debit, enter your PIN, push the red button, error, start again. At least when you go on a "vacation" that involves working on a ranch, the work is something you've chosen. But none of us has chosen to take over the jobs of those we pay to serve us.

13   Well, it's Sunday morning, and you're probably reading this with a cup of coffee. I hope it was easy to get.

EXPLORING THE READING THROUGH DISCUSSION

1. What do you think is Stanley Fish's primary purpose for writing "Getting Coffee Is Hard to Do," to entertain, inform, or persuade? Explain your reasoning.

2. In the introduction, Fish defines a "coordination problem" that can "produce confusion, frustration, and inefficiency." What specific details and examples does he include in his essay to support his thesis that "these days, you will face a coordination problem if you want to get a cup of coffee"? List the three that you find strongest.

3. As Fish explains it, how would he prefer to get his cup of coffee?

4. In your view, what is Fish's tone, or attitude, in this essay—is he angry, sarcastic, frustrated, or amused about his "pain and trouble"? What details or examples in the essay lead you to this conclusion?

5. In what paragraph does Fish make the best use of specific language? Why do you think this phrasing is so effective?

DEVELOPING VOCABULARY

List any words in this selection that are new to you. Write your understanding of each word from the context. Then look up each word in the dictionary, and write the definition that you think best fits the meaning in this writing.

_____

_____

_____

_____

DISCOVERING CONNECTIONS THROUGH WRITING

1. At the end of his essay, Stanley Fish writes about the "growing practice of shifting the burden of labor to the consumer. . . ." Have you also observed this trend? When have you felt that you were "doing the work that should be done by those who take your money"? Develop a thesis that indicates your attitude about this practice and write an essay to support your idea with specific examples.

2. Have you ever had a job in which your main responsibility was to serve customers? Based on that experience, do you agree with Fish's attitude about getting a cup of coffee or other self-service experiences? Write a response to Stanley Fish. Be sure your tone is clear, and let readers know why you agree or disagree with him.

3. Sometimes, as Fish has described, a seemingly simple process can be very complicated. Write about a process that, on the surface, looks easy but in fact can be challenging. As Fish does in his essay, be sure to describe those challenges as well as the steps in the process.

Back, But Not Home

Maria Muniz

Maria Muniz, a native of Cuba, wrote her essay for the Op-Ed page of the New York Times *in 1979. In recent years, Cuba has been in the news, ever since. Fidel Castro, president of the Caribbean island since 1959, recently became ill and questions arose about Cuba's future leadership. This essay, however, focuses on the thoughts and feelings of a young girl who was brought to a new country, leaving friends and family behind. How will she make this new place her home while still keeping "la Cubana" alive within?*

1   With all the talk about resuming diplomatic relations with Cuba, and with the increasing number of Cuban exiles returning to visit friends and relatives, I'm constantly being asked, "Would you ever go back?" In turn, I have asked myself, "Is there any reason for me to go?" I have had to think long and hard before finding my answer. Yes.

2   I came to the United States with my parents when I was almost five years old. We left behind grandparents, aunts, uncles and several cousins. I grew up in a very middle-class neighborhood in Brooklyn. With one exception, all my friends were Americans. Outside of my family, I do not know many Cubans. I often feel awkward visiting relatives in Miami because it is such a different world. The way of life in Cuban Miami seems very strange to me and I am accused of being too "Americanized." Yet, although I am now an American citizen, whenever anyone has asked me my nationality, I have always and unhesitatingly replied, "Cuban."

3   Outside American, inside Cuban.

4   I recently had a conversation with a man who generally sympathizes with the Castro regime. We talked of Cuban politics and although the discussion was very casual, I felt an old anger welling inside. After 16 years of living an "American" life,

I am still unable to view the revolution with detachment or objectivity. I cannot interpret its results in social, political or economic terms. Too many memories stand in my way.

5   And as I listened to this man talk of the Cuban situation, I began to remember how as a little girl I would wake up crying because I had dreamed of my aunts and grandmothers and I missed them. I remembered my mother's trembling voice and the sad look on her face whenever she spoke to her mother over the phone. I thought of the many letters and photographs that somehow were always lost in transit. And as the conversation continued, I began to remember how difficult it often was to grow up Latina in an American world.

6   It meant going to kindergarten knowing little English. I'd been in this country only a few months and although I understood a good deal of what was said to me, I could not express myself very well. On the first day of school I remember one little girl's saying to the teacher: "But how can we play with her? She's so stupid she can't even talk!" I felt so helpless because inside I was crying, "Don't you know I can understand everything you're saying?" But I did not have words for my thoughts and my inability to communicate terrified me.

7   As I grew a little older, Latina meant being automatically relegated to the slowest reading classes in school. By now my English was fluent, but the teachers would always assume I was somewhat illiterate or slow. I recall one teacher's amazement at discovering I could read and write just as well as her American pupils. Her incredulity astounded me. As a child, I began to realize that Latina would always mean proving I was as good as the others. As I grew older, it became a matter of pride to prove I was better than the others.

8   As an adult I have come to terms with these memories and they don't hurt as much. I don't look or sound very Cuban. I don't speak with an accent and my English is far better than my Spanish. I am beginning my career and look forward to the many possibilities ahead of me.

9   But a persistent little voice is constantly saying, "There's something missing. It's not enough." And this is why when I am now asked, "Do you want to go back?" I say "yes" with conviction.

10   I do not say to Cubans, "It is time to lay aside the hurt and forgive and forget." It is impossible to forget an event that has altered and scarred all our lives so profoundly. But I find I am beginning to care less and less about politics. And I am beginning to remember and care more about the child (and how many others like her) who left her grandma behind. I have to return to Cuba one day because I want to know that little girl better.

11   When I try to review my life during the past 16 years, I almost feel as if I've walked into a theater right in the middle of a movie. And I'm afraid I won't fully understand or enjoy the rest of the movie unless I can see and understand the beginning. And for me, the beginning is Cuba. I don't want to go "home" again; the life and home we all left behind are long gone. My home is here and I am happy. But I need to talk to my family still in Cuba.

12   Like all immigrants, my family and I have had to build a new life from almost nothing. It was often difficult, but I believe the struggle made us strong. Most of my memories are good ones.

13   But I want to preserve and renew my cultural heritage. I want to keep "la Cubana" within me alive. I want to return because the journey back will also mean a journey within. Only then will I see the missing piece.

EXPLORING THE READING THROUGH DISCUSSION

1. As the author explains it, why does she want to return to Cuba someday?

2. When asked about her nationality, Muniz replies that she is "Outside American, inside Cuban." What do you think she means by this answer?

3. What difficulties did the author face "grow[ing] up Latina in an American world"?

4. How is her life as an adult different from her life as a child?

5. What is the main method of organization the author uses in her essay? What in the essay leads you to this conclusion?

DEVELOPING VOCABULARY

List any words in this selection that are new to you. Write your understanding of each word from the context. Then look up each word in the dictionary, and write the definition that you think best fits the meaning in this writing.

_____

_____

_____

_____

DISCOVERING CONNECTIONS THROUGH WRITING

1. As an immigrant, Maria Muniz writes about building a new life in a new country. After years, that new country has become her home, a place where she is happy. Still, she longs to see the family of her original homeland. What does "home" mean to you? Is it a place? Or does the word mean a feeling within or a connection to family? Write about your view of home so that readers understand what makes the word special to you.

2. Muniz writes that when visiting other Cuban Americans, she has been "accused of being too 'Americanized.'" She also, however, wants to "preserve and renew [her] cultural heritage." Have you come to the United States from another country or do you know someone who has? Write about one or more challenges you or your acquaintance has faced in adapting to a new country while honoring and celebrating another cultural heritage.

3. Although not her main focus, throughout her essay Maria Muniz mentions the Cuban revolution and the United States' relationship with Cuba. What do you know about this island nation or "the Castro regime"? Conduct some research, and write a brief essay about what you discover. Be sure to acknowledge the source of your information. Refer to Chapter 15 or your instructor's directions for guidelines.

Words, Good or Bad, Can Echo through a Lifetime

Bob Greene

Language can change lives. That belief is the main point of Bob Greene's article, first published as a column in the Chicago Tribune. *He writes about the power of both spoken and written words to affect people's lives, often not deliberately. How important has someone's praise or criticism been to your own success?*

1   "Are you too stupid to do anything right?"

2   The words—spoken by a woman to a little boy who evidently was her son—were spoken because he had walked away from her. Chastised—these words were said at a volume high enough that all the strangers in the vicinity could hear—the boy, his face blank, his eyes downcast, returned quietly to the woman's side.

3   Not a big moment. Perhaps—not anything that could qualify as abuse or neglect or any of the other unhappy words that have become a part of our national lexicon. Yet small moments sometimes last for a very long time. Small moments sometimes last for eternity.

4   And a few words—words that mean little at the time to the people responsible for them—can have enormous power. "Are you too stupid to do anything right?" Words like that can echo.

5   So can words of the other kind.

6   What makes me think about this is a story I heard recently from a man named Malcolm Dalkoff. He's 48; for the last 24 years he has been a professional writer, most of these years spent in the advertising industry. Here is what he told me:

7   As a boy in Rock Island, Ill., he was terribly insecure and shy. He was quiet, he was scared, he mostly stayed by himself. He had few friends, and no sense of self-confidence.

8   In October of 1965, his English teacher at Rock Island High School—her name was Ruth Brauch—gave the class an assignment. The students had been reading *To Kill a Mockingbird,* by Harper Lee. Mrs. Brauch assigned the class members to write a chapter that would follow the last chapter of the novel. Their own chapter.

9   Malcolm Dalkoff wrote his chapter and turned it in. Today, he cannot recall feeling anything special about the act of writing that chapter, or what grade Mrs. Brauch gave him.

10   What he does remember—what he will never forget—are the four words his teacher wrote in the margins of the paper:

11   "This is good writing."

12   Four words. And they changed his life.

13   "Up until I read those words, I had no idea of who I was or what I was going to be," he said. "After reading her note I went home and wrote a short story, something I had always dreamed of doing but never really believed I could do."

14   Over the rest of that year in school, he wrote many short stories, always bringing them to school for Mrs. Brauch to look at and evaluate. She was encouraging: she was tough: she was honest. "She was just what I needed," Dalkoff said.

15   He was named co-editor of his high school paper: his confidence grew, his horizons broadened, he started off on a successful and fulfilling life. He is convinced that none of this would have happened had that woman not written those four words in the margin of his paper.

16   At his 30th high school reunion in Rock Island, the teachers did not attend—just the returning students, now men and women in middle age. But Dalkoff, back home for reunion weekend, went to Mrs. Brauch's house; she was now retired.

17   And he told her. He told her what her four words had done for him. He told her that because she had given him the confidence to believe that he might be worth something, the confidence to try to be a writer, he had been able to pass that confidence on to the woman who would become his wife, who became a writer herself. He told Mrs. Brauch about a woman who worked in his office—a woman who was working in the evenings toward a high school equivalency diploma—who had come to him for help. She respected him because he was a writer, he said—that is why the woman trying to get her diploma at night turned to him for advice and assistance.

18   Mrs. Brauch was especially moved by that story—the story of helping the young woman. "I think we both realized at that moment that Mrs. Brauch cast an incredibly long shadow," he said.

19   When Dalkoff came to Mrs. Brauch's house, he brought as a gift some books he had especially enjoyed over the years.

20   She said to him, "You shouldn't have."

21   He thought to himself: She's right. It should have been castles.

22   "Are you too stupid to do anything right?"

23   "This is good writing."

24   So few words. And they can last forever. They can change everything.

EXPLORING THE READING THROUGH DISCUSSION

1. In his essay, Bob Greene recalls the story of a man who is convinced that he would not have the life he enjoys if a teacher had "not written those four words in the margin of his paper." In two or three sentences, summarize the power of words as Greene explains it.

2. What do you imagine are the effects of the words that the little boy hears?

3. In what ways did Mrs. Brauch "cast an incredibly long shadow"?

4. Find examples of the author's use of dashes in his essay. Why do you think he selects this punctuation? What other choices could he have made?

5. Do you think the author's final brief paragraphs provide an effective conclusion? Explain.

DEVELOPING VOCABULARY

List any words in this selection that are new to you. Write your understanding of each word from the context. Then look up each word in the dictionary, and write the definition that you think best fits the meaning in this writing.

_____

_____

_____

_____

DISCOVERING CONNECTIONS THROUGH WRITING

1. In your life, what words have been said to you that influenced you, either positively or negatively? Write to explain what effects those words have had.

2. "Small moments sometimes last for eternity." In your experience, what small moment have you later found to be important? Write to tell the story of your experience.

3. A good teacher is defined in this essay as one who is encouraging, tough, and honest. Does this match your definition? Write an essay in which you offer your own definition of a good teacher, a good parent, or a good manager. As you write, focus on three characteristics of that person to help your reader understand your definition.

Love in Culture
Ryoko Kokuba (student)

One challenge of learning a new language is understanding both the denotation and the connotations of words. Knowing and using the best word to express certain meaning is important for writers as well. In her essay, Ryoko Kokuba, a native of Japan, explains how she explored the meaning of the word "love." What words do you use carefully because of the impact of their meaning?

1   When I first heard a girl say, "I love Subway's Italian sandwich," I looked at her twice, wondering why she needed to use the verb "love" for a sandwich. It has been almost a year and a half since I arrived in the U.S. As I am living in this new adventurous life, I often encounter cultural differences in the way that people speak. One of the words, perhaps the most interesting word that I have ever heard, is "love."

2   In the Japanese culture, *Ai,* translated in English as "love," is such a transcendent word that you are not allowed to utter it casually. It's a very emotional and sacred supreme word that you can only share with a significant person in order to express strong affection. *Ai,* at the same time, has a sense of responsibility since it promises the feeling of affection under any circumstance. As a matter of fact, I've almost never used this word hypothetically. It does not mean that I'm a cold person who doesn't know what love is. I, however, intentionally don't use *Ai* because its meaning is so precious that I don't want to devalue it. Another reason for this is the fact that I'm not ready to take the responsibility for saying such a deep word spontaneously.

3   On the other hand, in the American culture I hear the word "love" much more often than when I was in Japan. For example, in school I sometimes witness a young couple exchange the words, "Love you!" and "Love you too" as if it were a frank greeting. Other times, I come across a scene such as the McDonald's commercial, "I'm lovin' it" which shows how people use the word "love" to describe their favorite items, products, colors and other objects.

4   So are these examples indicating that "love" in English is treated much more lightly compared to the Japanese *Ai?* It didn't take too long for me to figure out the answer. Last Christmas when I visited my friend, his father showed me the

most beautiful Christmas present I've ever seen. It was a Christmas present from him to his wife, a poem that he wrote to her:

> I could say so many things about our love
> And what you mean to me
> But it would all add up to those simple words
> I just don't say often enough …
> I'm glad you're my wife, and I love you.

As I read this piece, I could clearly imagine a man who is a hard worker, who always appears to be strong, struggling to express his affection toward his beloved wife. In the way he used the word "love" in this piece, I finally came upon my definition of "love." It was the same "love" that perfectly matches with the nuance of the Japanese *Ai*.

5   Could "love" in English then have as deep a meaning as what it has in Japanese?

6   The more I studied this word, the more puzzled I got. My hand eventually reached out to the *Compact Oxford English Dictionary:*

Love: noun (1) an intense feeling of deep affection. (2) a deep romantic or sexual attachment to someone. (3) a great interest and pleasure in something. (4) a person or thing that one loves Verb: (1) feel love for. (2) like very much. (3) showing love or great care.

After I read the definitions in the dictionary, my great mystery for the use of the word "love" in English was cleared. I realized that my confusion for the use of the word "love" came basically from the cultural difference. For instance, we have a precise word to describe a "romantic or sexual attachment to someone," called *Renai;* if you want to articulate your favor toward certain products or objects, it needs to be called *Aiyou,* and there are more words to describe a penchant. Among these, *Ai* is the strongest word and it specifically indicates only one of the definitions of "love" in the English dictionary, "an intense feeling of deep affection." In contrast, "love" in English could apply to any of these words, which include anything from an individual's favorite objects, to strong affection toward someone.

7   Interestingly, this particular cultural difference in the use of "love" appears in multiple languages. In my current Portuguese class, I've learned that there is a significant rule for using "love": *Amar* for a person and *Adorar* for objects. This rule, which distinguishes the word "love" depending on a subject, is also true in Spanish and the rest of the Romance languages. My professor emphasized this rule in order for us to recognize the significant differences between the uses of "love" in English and in other languages.

8   The way ancient Greek philosophers differentiated the use of love is somewhat similar to what it is in Japanese. They made some distinctions about the word "love" based on different subjects and situations. For instance, *Eros* was used for love in the sensual and romantic way that occurs between a man and a woman. *Filia* indicates the love in friendship and even a couple; *Filia* is love in general. *Agape* is the ultimate and spiritual love that falls into the category of unconditional love such as the affection between God and his beloved ones. *Agape* emphasizes non-benefit and self-sacrifice. Therefore it is used in the Bible as the love to be practiced among people.

9   Having known how other cultures express the sense of affection, the word "love" in English is, in my opinion, the most simplified word that refers to the diversity of different feelings, emotional states and levels of liking. My biggest misunderstanding for this particular word, "love," was caused by my lack of knowledge

of its wide-ranging use. From generic pleasure to interpersonal affection, or from the Subway's Italian sandwich to an intense affection in a man's poem to his wife, all came up to this one special word, "love."

EXPLORING THE READING THROUGH DISCUSSION

1. Do you think, as Ryoko Kokuba did, that the word "love" is used too casually in the United States? Support your answer with specific examples of how you have heard the word used.

2. Take another look at the definition Kokuba offers for the meaning of *Ai*. Now, in your own words, explain the special significance of this Japanese word.

3. What sources of information did Kokuba use to help her understand the various meanings of the word "love"?

4. What do you think are the two most common synonyms for "love" in English? How do these words differ in connotation?

5. Identify at least three of the modes that Kokuba uses in her essay.

DEVELOPING VOCABULARY

List any words in this selection that are new to you. Write your understanding of each word from the context. Then look up each word in the dictionary, and write the definition that you think best fits the meaning in this writing.

_____

_____

_____

_____

DISCOVERING CONNECTIONS THROUGH WRITING

1. Have you studied a second language at some point in your education? Did any words or expressions confuse you? Write an essay in which you discuss what you experienced as you struggled with the confusing words and expressions of this new language.

2. Choose another abstract term—*hope, freedom, excellence, intelligence, creativity, beauty,* and so on—and provide a personal definition of the term. Be sure to avoid vague or general language, instead relying on specific details and examples to support your definition.

3. Kokuba writes about the language in a commercial for a fast-food restaurant. Think of a favorite television commercial or print or Internet advertisement, and write an essay in which you focus on the way that language is employed, being sure to provide multiple supporting examples.

Pride
Stephanie Jezak (student)

Although no magic formula for success exists, certain attributes or traits play significant roles. One of the most important, as Stephanie Jezak asserts in her essay, is pride. In her view, pride grows out of accomplishments, big and small, and motivates people to push onward for even greater success.

1   Pride is one of the most important things people can have in their lives. Without it, people would have a hard time feeling good about themselves. Pride is an inner feeling of achievement or satisfaction. There are many different things that allow a person to feel self respect. There are a few decisions that I am personally very proud of myself for making.

2   My decision to come back to school was nerve wracking. I was nervous because I hadn't been in a school setting in about six years. After I graduated from high school I took a few classes at BCC, but I soon realized I wasn't ready. I was much more interested in going out at night and sleeping in late, and just having fun as most teenagers are. Finally after some encouragement from my boyfriend, and two and a half years at my awful job, I decided it was time. Although very often it's difficult to juggle work and school, I know this will prove to be one of the best decisions I've ever made. The day I graduate will surely be one of my proudest moments because I will have attained one of the most important things in my life, an education.

3   Another decision I am very proud of is my choice to eat a vegetarian diet. This was very important at first. I used to eat meat every day until the day I decided to quit. I had a couple of reasons for becoming a vegetarian; they were based both on health reasons and the treatment of animals. First of all, vegetarian diets are likely to lessen the risk of different types of cancer, and heart disease. And second, I have always sympathized with animals, and since I was young I always wanted to try a meat free diet. It was difficult at that time, however, because my parents bought and prepared all of my meals. Now that I am older I can make decisions on what food I want to put into my body, and hopefully spare the lives of some animals. I have followed a vegetarian diet for two years now, and I am proud to have made this lifestyle change.

4   My decision to exercise is probably the one that I struggle with the most on a day to day basis. All of my other big decisions are sort of habit now. I do it without thinking much about it (go to school, avoid meat). Exercise, however, I have to force myself to do. I can think of a million bad reasons why I shouldn't or don't have to exercise, but there's always a million more good reasons to do it. When I finish doing my work out I feel this tremendous sense of pride that comes only from this particular activity. I also feel a great sense of relief that I'm done and can relax. I've only been exercising now for about three months, but I think it's something I will increasingly be proud of.

5   I feel good about a number of decisions I have made over the last several years. Returning to school has helped me develop a better self-image and prepare me for a meaningful career, and changing my diet and exercise habits has added to the overall quality of my life. But becoming an ex-smoker after nine years has shown me how strong a person I can be, something that gives me great pride.

EXPLORING THE READING THROUGH DISCUSSION

1. Do you agree with Stephanie Jezak about the importance of pride? What do you see as the relationship between pride and self-respect?

2. What are the challenges Stephanie has to face to stick with her decisions? Does dealing with these difficulties increase her sense of pride?

3. Stephanie is most proud of her decision to quit smoking. Do you agree that dealing with this habit is worthy of the value that she assigns it? Explain your reasoning.

4. What role does transition play in the effectiveness of this essay? List three instances where, in your view, transition is especially strong.

5. One role of a conclusion is to restate the significance of what a writer expresses in the introduction and body. In your view, does Stephanie's conclusion fit this description?

DEVELOPING VOCABULARY

List any words in this selection that are new to you. Write your understanding of each word from the context. Then look up each word in the dictionary, and write the definition that you think best fits the meaning in this writing.

_____

_____

_____

_____

DISCOVERING CONNECTIONS THROUGH WRITING

1. What are you proud of doing or what decisions are you proud of making? Write about what has given you that "inner feeling of achievement or satisfaction" that Stephanie discusses.

2. Stephanie takes particular pride in having quit smoking. How about you: did you have a bad habit that you managed to beat? Write an essay in which you explain the process you followed to succeed.

3. As her essay explains, a number of the steps that Stephanie has taken to improve herself have left her with a sense of great pride. But what happens when pride becomes something else—arrogance, perhaps, or intolerance for others? Explain what you think happens to cause people to step over that line and what consequences await those who do.

To Be Free, or Not to Be?

Elizabeth Cabral (student)

While serving her country, Elizabeth Cabral also learned about herself and what she values. Although she writes that she made a mistake, she also realizes that she grew as a result of her decision to enlist in the Army. What criteria are important to you in selecting a career?

1   Everyone makes decisions about who they want to be, what they want to do, and where they want to go in life. Some people work very hard to fulfill their dreams and once that mission is accomplished they realize it was all a very big mistake. I am one of these people. As a little girl, I idolized my uncle. He was strong, he was invincible, he was a Marine, and he was my hero; he could do anything. I knew that when I grew up I wanted to be just like him. I grew up with a love for all the branches of the military because of him. Uncle told me that he wasn't a hero; being a Marine was just a job. When I was 17, I decided to follow my dream of being in the service by enlisting in the United States Army. Being in the military, however, isn't just a job as I found out; being in the military is a way of life.

2   Bright and early Monday morning, most people who have "normal" jobs get up and get ready for work. After hitting the snooze buttons on their alarm clock two or three times, they make their way down to the kitchen where they fix breakfast. They have their morning dose of caffeine, maybe while reading the morning paper headlines or watching the news. They soon scurry to the bathroom to take a "quick" shower so they won't be too late to work. Following the shower, second cup of coffee in hand, these people pick out what they feel like wearing that day. What tie matches what shirt, or if the weather is good enough for the skirt they had in mind. These ordinary people do their hair and make-up the way they want it. Different people have different personalities, and they show who they are by how they present themselves. Saying goodbye to the rest of the family, they scramble to the car and take off to work. They may get stuck in traffic or stop at a local coffee shop on their way to work, which quite possibly may make them late. It does not matter to a lot of these people if they make it in to the office late; as long as no one sees them, tardiness won't matter. If, however, someone does give them a lot of trouble for being late all the time, they can always quit and find a new job. As far as these everyday Joe's and Jane's are concerned there are always employers out there with better benefits or pay looking for employees just like them.

3   On the other hand, my "normal" day started out very different from that of these civilians, whose mundane days were my daydreams. My blaring alarm would jar me awake before the sun had the courage to show itself, at 5:30 Monday morning. As much as I longed to, I had no time to hit the snooze button. I quickly made my bed, in case there was an inspection of our two-man room, which was the dump the Army saw fit to call barracks. My physical training uniform, otherwise known as P.T.'s, was laid out from the night before; I would have to hurry to make it to formation on time. I quickly brushed my teeth and pulled my hair into the tight knot that regulation required my hair to be in. I grabbed a water bottle and ran out the door to where my unit would gather in formation to salute the flag at 0600, stopping only to lock my barracks door. Extra physical training, what we called P.T., was a regular punishment for being late even a minute or two. Excessive tardiness, which could mean five or ten minutes late, could mean an Article 15. An Article 15 was extra work, also known as extra duty, and deduction of a half-month's pay. Being late was not an option, not unless a person was willing to pay the consequences. There was no quitting, either. As a member of the service, I was property

of the United States Government. My family lived half a country away, so there were no good morning or goodbye kisses waiting for me before I left for P.T.

4   After P.T., my unit went to the dining facility to eat breakfast. Egg Beaters, freezer-burnt waffles or pancakes and grits were the usual menu. I wasn't permitted to pick and choose what I wanted to eat; the food was slopped on my plate unceremoniously. After my delightful breakfast, it was time to be released back to the barracks for "personal hygiene." This time was given for a quick shower and for carefully putting on my starch-stiffened uniform, making sure my pant legs and sleeves were more than sufficiently creased and my boots spit shined to regulation. Then it was off to my "job."

5   While civilians do their jobs knowing what time they will get off work because of their set schedule, I got out of work when my sergeant said I could leave. The time was different every day. Civilians' workdays normally last from 9:00 a.m. to 5:00 p.m. On the other hand, my work normally lasted from 0600, known as 6:00 a.m., until 1600, or 4:00 p.m., with breaks for breakfast and lunch. Unlike civilians, I couldn't call out of work for a sick day; my chair on command decided if I was sick enough to stay in bed. There was no such thing as "playing hooky"; if I tried to, an Article 15 would soon follow that choice. Civilians have conferences, office meetings and presentations to break up their workweek; I had weapon, deployment and Middle Eastern cultural training to fill my extra time. On one hand, civilians look forward to having the weekend to themselves to spend with their family. In contrast, I would wonder whether or not I had the 24-hour weekend duty, whether my unit would approve my next leave request, or when would be the next time I would get to see my family.

6   Travel on the job for many civilians usually consists of an all-expense-paid business trip. They will probably stay in a Holiday Inn-like hotel, and eat a continental breakfast in the morning after spending the night relaxing in the hotel pool. These people will probably complain that the rental car the company paid for is too small, in other words saying that their company is too cheap to pay for something worth driving. These trips last days, if not a week, and they will soon safely be back with their loved ones.

7   In contrast, servicemen and -women have a different view of travel. Travel can mean to go home to those they love; usually this time is around the holidays. They share memories with those they love, staying with family if they have the extra room. A different type of travel always hung over my head like a dark cloud. It was what we were training for, deployment. As we were told the date for our upcoming "trip" overseas, I wondered if the next time I saw my family would be the last. It wasn't a far-fetched worry. Regardless of fears, deployment is a reality to those in the service, and fears eventually take the back burner to things that need to get done. There would be no hotels to stay at in Iraq, only makeshift aluminum-walled barracks. There are no car rentals in war-torn parts of the world, only Hummers. A soldier is lucky to have it armored because many are not.

8   Although people may say that soldiers, like myself, signed up for that life, many of us didn't realize exactly what we were signing away in the recruiter's bustling office. It was our freedom and freewill. While some soldiers thrive in that environment, I longed for a civilian life, in a civilian workplace, under civilian rules and freedoms. I wanted to be with those that loved me and that I loved, with the freedom to quit a job or take a day off if need be. Although I struggled under the pressure to be perfect, I learned important lessons on discipline, respect and punctuality that I can take with me into the civilian workplace. Being in the military definitely taught me to appreciate freedom in a new way and to not take the little things in life for granted. I am proud to have done my time in the service; nevertheless I am happy to be a civilian again and to be able to enjoy life like other civilians do.

EXPLORING THE READING THROUGH DISCUSSION

1. What is the thesis of this essay? Briefly explain how the body paragraphs provide effective support for the thesis.

2. Elizabeth Cabral describes a morning routine for most people with civilian jobs. How is your morning routine similar to or different from what she describes?

3. In terms of what Elizabeth presents in her essay, what do you think is the most important difference between military and civilian life?

4. Do you think Elizabeth relies more on the block method, the alternating method, or a combination of both in organizing her essay? How does this organizational method help Elizabeth communicate her message to her readers?

5. In her conclusion, Elizabeth states that her time in the service taught her "to appreciate freedom in a new way and to not take the little things in life for granted." What do you think she has learned?

DEVELOPING VOCABULARY

List any words in this selection that are new to you. Write your understanding of each word from the context. Then look up each word in the dictionary, and write the definition that you think best fits the meaning in this writing.

_____

_____

_____

_____

DISCOVERING CONNECTIONS THROUGH WRITING

1. Once she had fulfilled her childhood dream of joining the military, Elizabeth Cabral realized that becoming a soldier "was all a very big mistake." Write about a time when an expectation or dream became a disappointing reality. Consider using the mode of comparison and contrast to organize your ideas, discussing what you had envisioned versus what the reality actually was.

2. While in the military, Elizabeth learned to become disciplined, respectful, and punctual, all important qualities in the workplace. If you were a supervisor or manager, what personal qualities would you look for when hiring someone? Write an essay in which you detail the characteristics of a good employee. Use emphatic order so that readers will know what quality is most important to you.

3. Have you ever served in the military or known someone who has? Write an essay to compare or contrast that experience with Elizabeth's. As you write, be sure to amplify, spelling out your ideas in full detail.

Fear Not
Greg Andree (student)

Before this student author took a long walk across a dance floor, he considered what fear is and how it can affect us. As you read, ask yourself whether you have experienced each of the fears Greg Andree describes. What is it about some situations that can make us so afraid?

1   I looked across the dance floor; one of the most attractive women I had ever seen sat talking with some friends. She glanced toward me, but I turned away. Was she really looking at me? Why not? I'm a handsome guy. In fact, my mom tells me that all the time. I took a quick look back at her; she was still looking in my direction.

2   Why wouldn't she be looking at me? But she might just be looking at my friend who was sitting near me, or for that matter, she might just be trying to see what time it was (a clock hung just above my head). I could have misinterpreted a look at a clock for a glance in my direction.

3   What was keeping me from just getting up, walking over to her, and asking her to dance? Well, besides the fear of rejection from her and the dread of humiliation in front of her friends and mine, nothing at all.

4   I remember that as a kid I often sat alone in my basement doing my homework. It was the only place in the house I could go to be alone—well, besides the bathroom. If you spent too much time in there, though, people began to talk.

5   As daylight turned to dusk and then to darkness, the basement's shadows seemed to take on a life of their own; sounds that might have been ordinary before now sounded strange and menacing. I decided that this was no longer the ideal place for me to be alone with my thoughts. I got up and started walking slowly toward the steps that led to my family and the safety of their number. I wanted to run but refused to give the monster the satisfaction of knowing that it drove me from my own basement. I had to be brave and fight the panic that was welling up inside me. By the time I reached the stairs, I could feel its hot breath on my neck. I was sure that the creature was about to attack and drag me down into his hidden lair. Before it could, I ran, taking the stairs two at a time. If I could only reach the top, I would be safe.

6   Looking back now, it seems silly, but to a nine-year-old it was life or death. It's the same as when a thirteen-year-old, afraid of not fitting in, does everything within his power to belong. The worst thing in the world to a young teenager is the "problem" of being unique, having special talents or interests that are outside the margins of acceptability to the "popular" kids in school.

7   An example of this, from a boy's perspective, is that you're accepted if you excel in sports but are hopelessly doomed to exile if you are talented in music or art. As we get older, we realize these talents are gifts, not curses, and are grateful for our uniqueness, although knowing this now didn't make it easier then.

8   Now, as a college student, I have other fears. What if I fail in the career I've chosen, if I don't fulfill my dreams? How will I support myself, my family? Someday, if I do prosper in my career, will I look back at my college years and laugh at fears that now seem so enormous? What will my fears be then? Old age, senility, death? I don't really know.

9   What I do know is that no matter who we are or what our station in life is, we all have fears. Some are reasonable and keep us safe from the dangers that surround us constantly, and others are unreasonable and ridiculous, or seem so

to those of us who don't share them. Some make us strive to do better; others keep us from attempting the things we would really like to do. If there's a fear holding you back from accomplishing your dreams, you have two choices: Either find a way to overcome it, or cower in its shadow and learn to live with what could have been.

10   But enough of all that. I was in the middle of one of my adventures. Now, where was I? Never mind, I remember. . . .

11   What should I do? Just sit there and not take the chance, or seize the day as Robin Williams would have said in the movie *Dead Poets Society?* Which is best, to have loved and lost, or, in this case, tried and failed, or to have never tried at all? Finally, I thought of the advice Kevin Kline had given to a young pirate in Gilbert and Sullivan's *Pirates of Penzance:* "Always follow the dictates of your heart, my boy, and chance the consequences."

12   With this in mind, I got to my feet and made my way across the room to where she and her friends were sitting. I stood just a few feet from her. Doing my best Christian Slater imitation, I looked into her eyes and said, "Excuse me, Miss, would you care to dance?" She seemed to think it over for a moment, then took my hand and nodded her approval. "You do understand you'll be dancing with me, right?" I said. She laughed and said that she understood that I was included in the bargain.

13   As we danced, she leaned in close to me, her face inches from mine, and I felt her warm breath caress my cheek. She looked into my eyes and said, "Do you know what time it is? I really couldn't see the clock that well from where I was sitting."

EXPLORING THE READING THROUGH DISCUSSION

1. What is the thesis of this essay? Why do you think the author placed it where he did?

2. What types of fears does Greg Andree describe? Of the fears he discusses, which do you think is the worst? Why?

3. Greg makes the point that some fears "are reasonable and keep us safe from the dangers that surround us constantly, and others are unreasonable and ridiculous." What examples can you think of to support this statement?

4. From Greg's discussion, as he grew older, what did he learn about the things that he had feared?

5. Greg's story begins and ends at a dance. At what point does he shift from the chronological order of his narrative? How does he help readers understand that they are reading a flashback?

DEVELOPING VOCABULARY

List any words in this selection that are new to you. Write your understanding of each word from the context. Then look up each word in the dictionary, and write the definition that you think best fits the meaning in this writing.

_____

_____

DISCOVERING CONNECTIONS THROUGH WRITING

1. Write about a time you were afraid. Help readers understand not only what happened but also how the fear affected you. Did it hold you back in any way, or did it motivate you to find a way to overcome it?

2. "If only I had known then what I know now." Have you ever had this thought? Write an essay in which you detail the circumstances and explain your regrets.

3. Greg quotes a line he heard in a film version of a Gilbert and Sullivan play: "Always follow the dictates of your heart, my boy, and chance the consequences." Do you agree with this advice? Provide specific examples to help your readers understand why you think the way you do.

Nontraditional Jobs
Jennifer Mcelroy (student)

As a student in a vocational-technical high school, Jennifer Mcelroy was given the opportunity to explore several trades and to benefit from work experiences in her chosen field. Her choice, however, surprised nearly everyone. Have you ever worked at a job where your abilities were questioned?

1   Why are certain jobs considered not to be fit for a woman? This is a question that runs through my mind quite often. Graduating from the Automotive Collision Repair shop made me realize that no job should be considered "nontraditional."

2   In 1998, I started my first year of Diman Regional Vocational Technical High School. This school was different to me from any other school I attended because for two weeks I was in academic classes, and for the next two weeks I was in a hands-on working environment which rotated throughout the school year preparing us to go out into the workforce right after graduation.

3   During my first three months at the school I did an exploratory program, exploring many different trades to decide which career best suited me. I chose the Automotive Collision Repair shop because there is nothing I love more than cars and figured I would love to work on them.

4   Before my first week in the shop was up, I was called down along with the only other girl in the shop named Holly to see Mr. Fernandes. He was the freshman guidance counselor who tried to change our minds about our career decision. He tried to get us to switch to Dental Assisting or Health Careers because he felt they were more "girly." He said that he didn't know of any girl that graduated and actually got a job in a body shop. Well, my response to him was even if I didn't get a job doing what I loved, I at least would know more about my hobby.

5   One day during my sophomore year, I had already started to prove that I could do anything a man could do. Kevin, a junior, had been doing body work on a 1992 Chevrolet Cavalier's driver's door. The door had a dent in it and needed

body filler to be put on and sanded to restore the door to its normal shape. After an hour I heard Kevin asking Mr. Tabicas to look over his work, and the next thing I knew I was being called to where they were standing. Mr. Tabicas told Kevin that the door was as wavy as the ocean and he was going to have someone show him how it was supposed to be done. Well, this is where I came into the picture.

6   The first thing I did was use a D.A. to sand the dent and 2 inches around it. Next, I mixed body filler and put it on the dent. After the body filler dried, I sanded the area with 80 grit sand paper until the door was back to its normal shape. The last thing you do before the car is ready to prime and paint is sand it over with 220 grit sand paper.

7   When I finished, everyone in the shop was really impressed, especially Kevin because he had underestimated me before I started working on the door. Kevin said "Congratulations! I really didn't think you could have done the job as well as you did." I said "Thank you, I appreciate it. I bet you won't ever underestimate me again." This made me feel better than ever!

8   Throughout my four years in the Automotive Collision Repair shop I entered every Trade Show we had and maintained straight A's for shop grades. A Trade Show was held annually in the month of January. This was a chance for any students to show off the work they had done. Any student that entered from my shop would have to do some major or minor repair to a car along with two or three other students. The first thing that had to be done was the body work, then preparing the car to be painted, and then completing the paint job. I was always in first or second place. I knew that drove all the men in the shop crazy because I did better than they did.

9   If a student had passing grades in every class during their senior year they were allowed to go to work instead of shop as long as it had something to do with their career. This was called Co-Op, and it gave students the opportunity to make money instead of being in school. Luckily for me, I had started working at Colonial South Chevrolet during my sophomore year. The only problem was that I didn't work in the body shop. I worked in the office, but to my surprise they still let me participate in the program. Actually I was the only person out of the whole senior class to have a job related to the trade.

10   Time flew by so fast and before I knew it I was sitting at graduation rehearsal with my mother and my grandmother. This is where the principal handed out scholarships and the head chair of each shop handed out the outstanding vocational shop student award. I received a scholarship for an essay I had written, which shocked me, but the thing that shocked me the most was hearing my name being called for the Automotive Collision Repair shop's outstanding student! I knew I had done well in the trade but because of all the things I was told I expected one of the men to get the award.

11   When I look back to the day that I entered the Automotive Collision Repair shop, I feel that I was looked at differently than any man that walked in just because of the fact I was a female. This did not in any way make me turn around and walk out. It just made me a stronger person and made me push farther for what I wanted, which was to do really well in this trade and show them I had just as much skill as any man did. I knew I accomplished something.

12   No job should be classified as "nontraditional" for a man or a woman. I hope someday that the word "nontraditional" is erased from everyone's vocabulary because a job is something that needs to be filled by a person. If someone has the knowledge and experience to do what needs to be done, then why it should matter what sex they are?

EXPLORING THE READING THROUGH DISCUSSION

1. Jennifer Mcelroy asks a question in both the introduction and the conclusion. Why do you think she chose this strategy rather than to make her points in declarative sentence form? Do you agree with her approach? Explain your reasoning.

2. Jennifer makes the point that "No job should be classified as 'nontraditional' for a man or a woman." List three vocations or professions that have historically been viewed as appropriate just for women or just for men and explain why such designations are unnecessary and unfair.

3. Why did Jennifer choose Automotive Collision Repair as her trade while at the vocational high school? Do you agree that she made the correct choice?

4. What examples does Jennifer include in her essay to show that she "had just as much skill as any man did" in automotive repair? Which example do you think is the most effective? Why?

5. Of the supporting examples Jennifer provides, which one do you feel is the most specific and concise? Explain your reasoning.

DEVELOPING VOCABULARY

List any words in this selection that are new to you. Write your understanding of each word from the context. Then look up each word in the dictionary, and write the definition that you think best fits the meaning in this writing.

_____

_____

_____

_____

DISCOVERING CONNECTIONS THROUGH WRITING

1. According to Jennifer Mcelroy, meeting the challenges of being a female in a traditionally male trade made her "a stronger person" and made her "push farther for what I wanted, which was to do really well. . . ." Tell the story of a challenge you met at home, work, or school. Include detailed examples to show readers how you succeeded.

2. What career are you interested in pursuing? Write an essay explaining the different reasons that have motivated you to pursue this line of work.

3. Jennifer is proud of her success in repairing a dent on a car door, and she explains the process of how she accomplished the task well. Write an essay in which you discuss a task that you accomplished, explaining the steps you followed and the results that made you proud.

R-E-S-P-E-C-T

Josh Trepanier (student)

Are people becoming increasingly ruder? Are parents shirking their duties to teach good manners? Or is etiquette less important in our fast-paced world? As you read this student's essay, explore your responses to these and other questions that are raised. Why do you think people in general are not more considerate of others?

1   Can you remember a time when men held doors for women and elders, and took off their hats when they were inside? Do you recall the days when youngsters wouldn't dare talk back to their parents or grandparents out of sheer respect? People who do remember those instances must be appalled at the lack of manners in today's society. It is becoming increasingly difficult to find people who still use the simple words *please* and *thank you* on a daily basis. Even "polite society" is no longer very polite. The general level of respect people have for other people has declined rapidly in the past few decades and it will continue to decrease until we teach ourselves and our children otherwise.

2   Who is to blame for the current decline in manners? The place where kids are most disrespectful is usually the place where they learn to be that way—at home. Children are refusing to obey parents more and more every day. Eight years ago, I could have never worn my hat at the dinner table; my mom would have thrown a fit. Nowadays, youngsters sit down to supper with their hats on, while playing hand-held video games, and parents don't blink an eye. Some kids are even allowed to use profane language in front of their parents. Such casual attitudes about disrespect are at the root of the growing problem America is having with unmannered youth. If impoliteness around the household continues to go unnoticed, the rude children will someday turn into rude adults, continuing the current trend of disrespectfulness. Of course, the media have also contributed to the growing problem by portraying the rudeness of our youth in a comical light in many modern family sitcoms.

3   Another way Americans show this loss of manners is in how they treat their elders. The number of senior citizens in nursing homes is on the rise, and I'm sure many of them could be just as well taken care of at home. However, some people don't have the patience and respect they once had for their parents, and a nursing home is becoming an easy alternative for rising numbers of elderly people across the country. Elders are also shown less and less respect on the roads. Older people who drive a little slower than the fast-paced younger drivers are harassed by the honking horns, flashing lights, and hand gestures of more youthful drivers. I'm sure the senior citizens of today are wondering why they don't get the same kind of respect they showed their elders. It is too bad that there isn't a single good reason to give them for the loss of manners Americans seem to suffer from.

4   Teachers across the United States experience the bad etiquette of students on a daily basis. For the most part, it is the high school teachers who see the biggest change in their pupils' attitudes. Teens are no longer afraid to talk back to teachers, which would have resulted in a few whacks from a ruler years ago. Maybe if we give the teachers their rulers back, kids might be a little more careful of what they say during school. The problem is that the instructors hear the disrespectful adolescents and let them get away with being totally ignorant. I suppose it's true that they aren't paid to babysit, but by allowing rude behavior to go unchastised

for so long, teachers have only made their own jobs more irritating. The students will continue to use little or no manners in school until somebody puts an end to the everyday lack of respect they are allowed to show their teachers.

5   Basically, the problem America is now facing is one of neglect. We can no longer afford to ignore our children's bad manners. Had we put a stop to these lax attitudes about manners when they first showed up in kids, the problem most likely wouldn't have become as extreme as it is. We, as a nation, need to recognize and rectify the problems that exist due to the rudeness and disrespect of our youth. Although chivalry may be a thing of the past, I think it's time for courtesy and respect to make a comeback in our society.

EXPLORING THE READING THROUGH DISCUSSION

1. Which sentence serves as the thesis for Josh Trepanier's essay? How does this sentence prepare his reader for the discussion to follow in the body of his essay?

2. Identify the topic sentence in each paragraph, and briefly explain the connection between these topic sentences and Josh's thesis.

3. Do you also consider all the behaviors Josh discusses to be bad manners, or are some of them just adjustments toward informality or simplicity in response to modern life? Explain your reasoning, including specific details and examples.

4. Of all the examples of disrespectful or rude behavior that Josh includes, which one do you personally find most objectionable? Why?

5. Do you agree with the way that Josh presents his examples, or would you suggest that he adjust the order in some way? Explain your reasoning.

DEVELOPING VOCABULARY

List any words in this selection that are new to you. Write your understanding of each word from the context. Then look up each word in the dictionary, and write the definition that you think best fits the meaning in this writing.

_____

_____

_____

_____

DISCOVERING CONNECTIONS THROUGH WRITING

1. It's hard to argue with Josh's view that rudeness and disrespectful behavior are second nature in contemporary society. What is the most outrageous example of rude or disrespectful behavior that you have ever experienced or witnessed? As you write, be sure to amplify in order to paint a complete picture for your reader.

2. According to Josh, teachers need to be stricter concerning student manners in the classroom. If you were a teacher, what specific behaviors do you think you would not allow? Why?

3. Josh writes that "chivalry may be a thing of the past." What is your understanding of that word? Should chivalry be forgotten? Would you like to see it come back? Be sure to provide reasons to support your argument.

Adam

Sarah Martin (student)

As a little girl, Sarah Martin lost her teenage cousin Adam to AIDS. Although she was quite young at the time, his life—and then his death—had a profound effect on her. In this essay, she shares her vivid memories of him from the point of view of a child. In what ways is a young child's understanding of complex, tragic events different from that of adults dealing with the same circumstances?

1   It may not be the very first memory I possess, but the final appearance of my cousin Adam when I was barely four years old has haunted me since his death. A tainted blood transfusion infected him with AIDS when he was much younger, and it took his life at sixteen. I have always wondered why with modern science his death couldn't be prevented.

2   My Great Auntie Jean's house was full of angels: painted angel figurines, sculpted busts and embossed letter openers, jeweled angel sun-catchers hooked on plastic suction cups adhered to the window panes. The watercolor angel lampshades would emit yellow light and illuminate pillars of cigarette smoke in the den. My Great Auntie Jean painted colorful angel shaped ceramics. Wind chimes with great robed sentries to heaven were hung out back in the yard full of stepping-stones and weeds. An angel held a dried up birdbath and grew grayer as I grew taller.

3   My cousin Adam loved to visit her almost as much as I did. I loved to lust after Aunt Suzie's bongo drums that I could never touch. I loved to drink the red berry tea with honey and hunt for Easter eggs under the bushes any time of year. Adam liked to watch TV with my uncles and laugh with them about things I never understood.

4   Adam would pick the raspberries I couldn't reach.

5   "That big, big one at the top!"

6   "This one?"

7   "The *bigger* one!" He would smile down at me and make an effort to reach through the prickly bush and claim my treasure.

8   His sister Julie never liked to be included, so he would amuse me with hide and seek games while she played the coveted bongo drums. Sometimes she would join us out of loneliness and we would all pretend to be adventurers under the dripping air conditioner. On Saturday we would walk the neighborhood and I would be recruited to bring everyone's mail to their front door.

9   Just after kindergarten began, my family threw a big party with all kinds of people at the Elk's club, a fundraiser. I had a basket of ribbons with pins on them. My job was to hand them out to all of Adam's guests. I asked my mother why we were having such a big party for Adam. She told me it was to keep him from getting sick. I thought it was the best idea ever and gave out all the ribbon pins I had to keep Adam from getting sick. He got up on stage and thanked all of his guests

for supporting "the effort" in between short coughing bouts. When he got offstage I looked around for any more ribbons I could give away to keep him from coughing.

10   We were in Great Auntie Jean's yard, standing next to my favorite raspberry bush. Adam was kneeling in front of me. His face was red and splotchy, bumps were all over his skin. His braces glinted silver in the sun; they held his teeth together. Raspy words came from his wide red mouth. His throat looked raw. "I can't play hide and seek with you anymore, Sarah." I wasn't listening. I was too busy scrutinizing how red everything about Adam was.

11   "I'm going away for a while, okay? You'll need to play with Julie instead." His eyes turned red, too and he blinked until it went away.

12   "Let's go play before you go then!" I replied. He laughed at me and picked a big red raspberry from near the clouds.

13   The adults of my family were all grave and quiet for the next few weeks. "Adam is paralyzed on the left side," was whispered over coffee between my aunts and my uncles. What does paralyzed mean? I wondered as I tapped on the bongo drums I was finally allowed to play. His mother cried all the time into her tea. She smoked more cigarettes than my Great Auntie Jean.

14   We stopped hearing about Adam's sickness. We stopped going to Great Auntie Jean's house. I don't remember any funeral being held. I may not have been allowed to go. We had his obituary taped to the fridge until the ink faded and the words disappeared.

EXPLORING THE READING THROUGH DISCUSSION

1. What is your first response to this essay? What details in the writing contribute to your feelings?

2. On the basis of the information that Sarah provides, how would you describe the relationship she had with Adam? Which detail do you think does the best job of exemplifying their relationship? What makes that detail stand out from all the others?

3. Sarah writes her story from the point of view of a child. How does this contribute to the effectiveness of her essay?

4. In several places, Sarah includes dialogue in her essay. Why do you think she chose to include the specific conversations rather than write a summary of what was said?

5. In telling the story of Adam, Sarah relies heavily on description. In your view, what sensory detail creates the most vivid impression? Explain your reasoning.

DEVELOPING VOCABULARY

List any words in this selection that are new to you. Write your understanding of each word from the context. Then look up each word in the dictionary, and write the definition that you think best fits the meaning in this writing.

_____

_____

DISCOVERING CONNECTIONS THROUGH WRITING

1. What's your earliest memory? Write an essay recounting it. You might discuss it from the vantage point of an adult looking back, or you could tell the story, as Sarah Martin does, from the standpoint of a child. Don't forget to provide enough details to give readers a vivid picture of your memory.

2. Sarah's Great Auntie Jean's house was "full of angels." Are you a collector yourself, or do you know someone who is? Write an essay in which you discuss the type and degree of that collection.

3. At the end of her essay, Sarah writes that she has no memory of her cousin's funeral and isn't sure if she was allowed to attend. From the information she includes, it's clear that she was much more aware of the significance of what was happening to her cousin than any adults realized. What do you see as the best strategy to help children deal with the inevitable harsh realities of life such as sickness, violence, and death? Express your stand on this issue clearly, and remember to provide several specific supporting examples.

Tips for ESL Writers

As someone who can speak and write in a language—perhaps two or three—other than English, you are truly fortunate. The knowledge of more than one language gives you a genuine advantage in a multicultural country and in a world in which all major corporations are multinational.

Chances are, you sometimes find becoming a better writer in American English frustrating. When you write in English, you must think about the many possible ways that English differs from your native language, perhaps in terms of sentence structure or word order. In addition, you must focus on the common problems you have with English grammar and usage so that you communicate clearly. The rules for capitalization, articles, spelling, and punctuation can also be very confusing. Most important of all, the logic of paragraphs and essays written in English might be very different from the logical forms of composition in your native language group and culture. To communicate effectively you must learn to use the patterns that English speakers use to understand each other. The following guidelines will help you achieve this goal.

Sentence Basics

- Make sure each sentence has a subject and a verb. If a group of words does not have both, it does not express a complete idea. *See Chapter 17, "The Sentence," and Chapter 18, "Fragments."*

FAULTY
⌐⌐ verb ⌐
Thought of a good idea. *[Subject missing]*

REVISED
⌐subject—verb⌐
You thought of a good idea. *[A statement]*

In writing, the subject can be an implied *you* only if you are making a command. *See the section "Recognizing Subjects" on pages 253–256 in Chapter 17.*

EXAMPLE
⌐subject—verb⌐
[*You*] *Think* of a good idea! *[A command]*

- Make sure that *is* and *are* verbs are linked to a subject. The words *it* and *there* and words describing a location can sometimes be substituted in the normal location of a subject at the beginning of a sentence. In such cases, the actual subject comes after the verb. (Usually, in English, the subject comes *before* the verb.) *See the section "Avoiding Agreement Errors When the Subject Follows the Verb" on pages 314–316 in Chapter 21, "Subject–Verb Agreement," and the* section *"Working with Forms of* To Be" *on pages 347–349 in Chapter 23, "Irregular Verbs and Frequently Confused Verbs."*

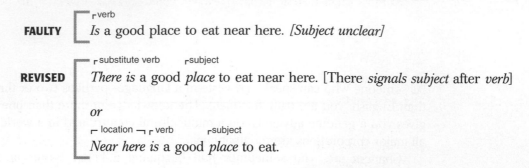

FAULTY   *Is* a good place to eat near here. *[Subject unclear]*

REVISED   *There is* a good *place* to eat near here. [There *signals subject* after *verb*]

or

Near here is a good *place* to eat.

- In English sentences, the word *there* with some form of the verb *to be* is commonly followed by a noun or pronoun, which serves as the subject. The noun or pronoun may have modifiers, or it may be followed by a word or phrase that specifies a place.

EXAMPLES

There will be a new *student entering class today.*

There is *no one here.*

There are three *cars in the lot.*

- The word *it* with the verb *to be* is commonly followed by an adjective, an adjective with a modifier, an identification, or an expression of time, weather, or distance.

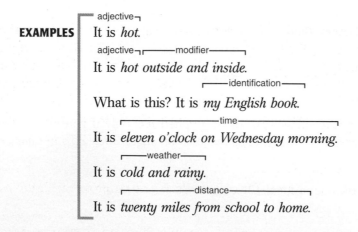

EXAMPLES

It is *hot.*

It is *hot outside and inside.*

What is this? It is *my English book.*

It is *eleven o'clock on Wednesday morning.*

It is *cold and rainy.*

It is *twenty miles from school to home.*

Don't use *there* in these expressions:

FAULTY   *There* is long. *There* has been a long time.

REVISED   *It* is long. *It* has been a long time.

Word Order

- In most English sentences, the subject comes first, followed by the verb.

FAULTY
┌ verb   ┌ subject
Is good the *idea.*

REVISED
subject ┐ ┌ verb
The *idea is* good.

- Adjectives, even a string of adjectives, usually come *before* nouns. *See Chapter 27, "Adjectives, Adverbs, and Other Modifiers: Using Descriptive and Modifying Words Effectively," for more information about adjectives.*

FAULTY
┌ noun   ┌──────── adjectives ────────┐
The *man* is talking—*tall, thin,* and *handsome.*

REVISED
┌──────── adjectives ────────┐ ┌ noun ┐
The *tall, thin, handsome man* is talking.

- Groups of words that modify a noun, however, usually come immediately *after* the noun if they begin with a relative pronoun. *who, whom, whose, which, that,* and so forth.

FAULTY
┌ noun ┐   ┌──────── modifier ────────┐
The *man* is talking *who won the award.*

REVISED
┌ noun ┐ ┌──────── modifier ────────┐
The *man who won the award* is talking.

- In some cases, modifiers with an *-ed* or *-ing* verb form must go after a noun they identify if they add essential identifying information to the sentence. They can appear either immediately before or immediately after a noun to which they add extra information, though. Consider the following examples, in which the *-ed* modifier is necessary to identify *which person. See the section "Avoiding Dangling and Misplaced Modifiers" on pages 418–422 in Chapter 27.*

FAULTY
┌──────── modifier ────────┐   ┌ which person?
Worried about a missing credit card, the store manager met with the *customer.*

REVISED
┌ noun ┐ ┌──────── identifying modifier ────────┐
The store manager met with the *customer worried about a missing credit card.*

Now compare the revised sentence above with the example below, in which the modifier adds extra information.

EXAMPLE
┌──────── modifier ────────┐ ┌ noun ┐
Forgetting his promise, John is talking instead of listening.

- If the modifier is necessary to identify the noun, you don't use commas to separate it from the noun. If the modifier adds information about the noun, but the sentence makes sense without it, then set the modifier off with commas. *See the section "Using Commas to Set Off Elements That Interrupt Sentence Flow" on pages 474–475 in Chapter 30, "Commas."*

EXAMPLE
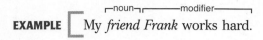
My *friend Frank* works hard.

The modifier is needed to identify which friend, *my friend Frank,* not *my friend Tom,* so no commas are needed.

EXAMPLE
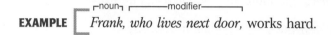
Frank, who lives next door, works hard.

The modifier provides extra information that isn't necessary for the sentence to make sense, so it needs commas.

- Adverbs usually are placed after *to be* verbs (*is/are/was/were*) but before other one-word verbs. *See the section "Understanding the Positive Forms of Adjectives and Adverbs" on pages 413–414 in Chapter 27.*

EXAMPLES

verb ┐┌adverb
They *are often* late.
┌adverb┐┌verb┐
Birds *usually arrive* in the spring.

- Adverbs often go between verbs that have two parts (verb phrases).

EXAMPLE

helping
verb ┐ adverb┐┌verb┐
They *have often arrived* late.

- Pronouns that rename the subject in the same sentence are usually unnecessary and confusing—even when a long modifier separates the subject from the verb. The order of the words in a sentence makes the idea clear.

FAULTY

subject┐┌───modifier────subject┐┌verb┐
The *place* where they studied *it was* old.

REVISED

subject┐┌────modifier────┐┌verb┐
The *place* where they studied *was* old.

Agreement

- Make the subject and verb agree in number. Be especially careful about collective nouns, such as *family* and *class,* and words that specify uncountable things, such as *sugar* and *water. See the section "Considering Singular Nouns Ending in -s, Collective Nouns, and Cue Words" on pages 378–380 in Chapter 25, "Nouns: Working Effectively with Words That Name."*

- You can count *fingers, books,* or *students,* so they are called *count* words. You cannot count *freedom, advice,* or *machinery,* so they are called *noncount* words. Noncount words always take a singular verb and a singular pronoun reference.

noncount   plural   plural
noun   verb   pronoun   plural
                              reference   verb

FAULTY   *Sugar make* the recipe better. *They are* tasty.

noncount   singular   singular
noun   verb   pronoun   singular
                              reference   verb

REVISED   *Sugar makes* the recipe better. *It is* tasty.

- Some words are count with one meaning and noncount with another meaning.

EXAMPLES   Three *chickens are* in the yard. *[Countable animals]*

Chicken is good with white wine. *[Noncountable meat]*

Three pieces of *chicken is* enough. *[Quantity of noncountable meat]*

- As the last example shows, some aspects of noncount words can be measured. You can count the number of *lumps* of sugar, *cups* of milk, *tablespoons* of flour, or *gallons* of water, but you cannot say *ten sugars, three milks, two flours,* and *four waters* as a complete grammatical form. Even though you can number *quantities* like *two pounds, six quarts, three minutes, five dollars,* and *ten gallons,* the "*of* phrase" with the noncount word makes a singular subject, which needs a singular verb *(two pounds of butter is).* You must use a *singular verb* with any quantity of noncount items. *See the sections "Using the Simple Present, Simple Future, and Simple Past Tenses" on pages 331–334 in Chapter 22, "Basic Tenses for Regular Verbs," and "Maintaining Agreement with Indefinite Pronouns" on pages 392–395 in Chapter 26, "Pronouns: Understanding Case, Clear Pronoun–Antecedent Agreement, and Nonsexist Pronoun Usage."*

count
noun

EXAMPLES   Twelve *cups are* necessary because we have twelve guests. [*12 items*]

quantity +   noncount
noun

Two cups of *water is* enough. [*A measurement of a noncount noun*]

noncount   count
noun   noun

Ten *dollars is* enough. [*Amount*] Ten dollar *bills are* enough. [*Number*]

noncount   count
noun   noun

My *luggage is* heavy. [*Amount*] My two *bags are* heavy. [*Number*]

quantity +   noncount
noun

FAULTY   Ten gallons of *gasoline are* all I need.

quantity +   noncount
noun

REVISED   Ten gallons of *gasoline is* all I need.

- Adjectives are *always* singular.

FAULTY the *talls* men; the *six-year-olds* children

REVISED the *tall* men; the *six-year-old* children

- Adjectives that end in *-ing* are active, while adjectives that end in *-ed* are passive. *See the section "Forming the Passive and Active Voice" on pages 358–360 in Chapter 24, "Passive Voice, Additional Tenses, and Maintaining Consistency in Tense."*

EXAMPLE She is *boring*.

This adjective is formed from the active verb. It shows the effect that she has on others—she makes them feel bored.

EXAMPLE She is *bored*.

This adjective is derived from the passive verb. It shows the effect something has on her—something makes her feel bored.

- A single phrase or clause subject takes a singular verb.

FAULTY ┌──phrase as subject──┐ ┌verb   ┌──clause as subject──┐┌verb
Understanding the rules are hard. That they must be followed are clear.

REVISED ┌──phrase as subject──┐ ┌verb   ┌──clause as subject──┐┌verb
Understanding the rules is hard. That they must be followed is clear.

- Verbs presented in a series with commas should agree in tense and form. *See Chapter 28, "Parallelism: Presenting Related Ideas in a Similar Form."*

FAULTY The child *was running, jumped,* and *has skipped.* [*Mixed tense forms*]

REVISED The child *ran, jumped,* and *skipped.* [*All past tense forms*]

- Use the present or present perfect tense, not the future tense, in a subordinate clause indicating time or condition, whose main clause is future tense. *See the section "Maintaining Consistency in Tense" on pages 363–364 in Chapter 24 for more on keeping the tense consistent.*

FAULTY ┌──subordinate clause──┐ ┌main clause┐
After I will do my homework, I will go out.

REVISED ┌──subordinate clause──┐ ┌main clause┐
After I have done my homework, I will go out.

Confusing Verb Forms

Don't omit the *-s* in the third person singular, present tense verb forms. *See the section "Using the Simple Present, Simple Future, and Simple Past Tenses" on pages 331–334 in Chapter 22.*

FAULTY He *come* here every day.

REVISED He *comes* here every day.

- Memorize the irregular verbs. *See the section "Identifying Irregular Verbs" on pages 000–000 in Chapter 23.* Some verb pairs such as the following can be confusing, but remembering which takes an object and which does not will help you tell the difference. The verbs *shine/shone, lie, sit,* and *rise* never have an object; the verbs *shine/shined, lay, set,* and *raise* always have an object:

No Object	*Object*
His shoes shone.	He shined *his shoes.*
She lay in the sun.	She laid *her books* on the floor.
She sat in the chair.	She set *the table* for four.
The sun rises every morning.	They raised *the flag.*

- Use complete passive verb forms; combine a form of *to be* with the past participle of another verb. *See the section "Forming the Passive and Active Voice" on pages 358–360 in Chapter 24.*

FAULTY His work finished.

REVISED His work *was* finished. [*Add form of* to be]

or

He finished his work. [*Transform to active voice*]

- Use *-'s* to make contractions using *is* and *has,* but shorten *has* only when it is a helping verb. To sound more formal, avoid contractions like *she's.* Write *she is* instead.

FAULTY She's some money.

REVISED She has some money.

INFORMAL She's ready to help.

FORMAL She is ready to help.

- When verbs describe a completed mental process (*believe, consider, forget, know, remember, think, understand*), a consistent preference (*drink, swim, eat*), a state of being (*am, appear, have, seem, remember, forget, love*), or a perception (*feel, hear, see, taste*), they can't be progressive. When verbs refer to an incomplete process, they can be progressive. *See the section "Using the Progressive and Perfect Progressive Tenses" on pages 360–363 in Chapter 24.*

EXAMPLES   I *consider* my choice good. [*An already completed decision*]

I *am considering* going. [*A decision-making process not yet complete*]

I *think* he should be president. [*A completed intellectual position*]

I *am thinking* about what to do this summer. [*An incomplete thought process*]

I *drink* coffee. [*A consistent preference*]

I *am drinking* coffee. [*An incomplete action*]

FAULTY   I *am seeing* you. I *am liking* you, but I *am loving* cheeseburgers.

REVISED   I *see* you. I *like* you, but I *love* cheeseburgers.

- *Do* and *make* do not mean the same thing in English. *Do* often refers to action that is mechanical or specific. *Make* often refers to action that is creative or general: The teacher *makes* up the exercise (creative), but the student *does* the exercise (mechanical). However, there is no clear rule explaining the difference. You will just have to memorize their usage.

Mostly Mechanical or Specific	Mostly Creative or General
do the dishes	make the bed
do the homework	make an impression
do the laundry	make progress
do your hair	make up your mind
do (brush) your teeth	make (cook) a meal
do (write) a paper	make (build) a house
do the right thing	make mistakes
do someone a favor	make a speech
do good deeds	make a living
do away with	make arrangements

FAULTY   I have to *make the homework* before I can *do a speech.*

REVISED   I have to *do the homework* before I can *make a speech.*

- *Tell* and *say* do not mean the same thing in English:

tell time	say a prayer
tell a story or a joke	say hello
tell me	say that we should go
tell the difference	say, "Let's go!"

FAULTY ⌈ say me; tell hello; say a joke

REVISED ⌈ tell me; say hello; tell a joke

Articles

Articles (*a, an,* and *the*) can be very confusing in English, so you must pay special attention to them.

- Use *a* before words that begin with consonant sounds and *an* before words that begin with vowel sounds.

  1. *A* and *an* mean the same as *one* or *each:* I want *an* ice cream cone. *[Just one]*

  2. *A* and *an* go with an unidentified member of a class: *A* small dog came toward her, *a* bone in its mouth. *[Some unknown dog, some unknown bone]*

  3. *A* and *an* go with a representative member of a class: You can tell by the way he talks that he is *a* politician.

  4. *A* and *an* go with a noun that places an idea in a larger class: The car is *a* four-wheeled vehicle.

See the section "Considering Singular Nouns Ending in -s, Collective Nouns, and Cue Words" on pages 378–380 in Chapter 25.

- *The* serves many functions:

  1. *The* modifies known people, objects, and ideas: *the* mother of *the* bride, *the* head of *the* household in which he stayed, *the* Copernican theory

  2. *The* goes with superlatives: *the* best, *the* least

  3. *The* goes with rank: *the* first book, *the* third child with this problem

  4. *The* goes with *of* phrases: the way of *the* world

  5. *The* goes with adjective phrases or clauses that limit or identify the noun: *the* topic being discussed.

  6. *The* refers to a class as a whole: *The* giraffe is an African animal.

  7. *The* goes with the names of familiar objects (*the* store) and the names of newspapers (*The Wall Street Journal*), but not the names of most magazines (*Time*).

  8. *The* goes with the names of historical periods (*the* French Revolution), legislative acts (*the* Missouri Compromise), political parties (*the* Democratic Party), branches of government (*the* executive branch), official titles (*the*

President), government bodies (*the* Navy), and organizations (*the* Girl Scouts).

9. *The* goes with rivers (but not lakes), canals, oceans, channels, gulfs, peninsulas, swamps, groups of islands, mountain ranges, hotels, libraries, museums, and geographic regions: *the* Panama Canal, *the* Mississippi River, Lake Superior, *the* Okefenokee Swamp, *the* Hilton, *the* Smithsonian, *the* South.

FAULTY   According to *New York Times,* the Lake Victoria is one of most beautiful lakes in world.

REVISED   According to *the New York Times,* Lake Victoria is one of *the* most beautiful lakes in *the* world.

Spelling

- Follow these steps to avoid common spelling errors:

  1. Don't leave *h* out of *wh* words: *which,* not *wich*

  2. Don't add an *e* to words that start with *s: stupid,* not *estupid*

  3. Don't confuse words that sound alike in English—homonyms—but have different meanings and different spellings:

his/he's (he is)	which/witch	there/their
whether/weather	here/hear	through/threw
advice/advise (noun/verb)	too/to/two	though/thought

  4. Don't confuse grammatical functions because of familiar sound combinations: *whose* or *who's* (*who is*), not *who his*

  5. Don't confuse words that sound similar using your native language's pronunciation patterns but have different meanings and different sounds in English:

this (singular)/these (plural)	chair/share
read/lead	boat/vote
heat/hit	

  See Chapter 29, "Spelling: Focusing on Correctness."

Other Common Grammar Problems

Double Negatives

- Double negatives are not acceptable in English. As in mathematics, two negatives equal a positive. *See the section "Avoiding Double Negatives" on pages 422–425 in Chapter 27.*

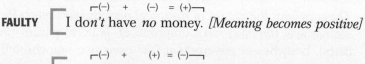

FAULTY   I do*n't* have *no* money. *[Meaning becomes positive]*

REVISED   I do*n't* have *any* money. *[Meaning remains negative]*

Confusing Words

Some key words are confusing:

- *Too* and *very* don't share the same meaning. *Very* is an intensifier that means *extremely* or *excessively*. It emphasizes quantity. *Too* is often negative and critical. It is sometimes attached to a word that goes with an infinitive (*to* + verb) to emphasize negative effects.

EXAMPLES
It is *very* cold, but we can walk to the restaurant. [Very = *intensely*]

It is *too* cold to walk, so we should take a taxi. [Too = *negative*]

FAULTY
He is *very* fat to play on the soccer team.

REVISED
He is *too* fat to play on the soccer team. *[He cannot play soccer because he is quite overweight.]*

- *Hard* can be an adjective or an adverb, but *hardly* is always an adverb meaning *barely, almost none,* or *almost not at all.*

EXAMPLES
adjective—noun
He learned a *hard* lesson. *[A difficult lesson]*
—verb—adverb
He worked *hard.* *[With great effort]*
adverb—verb
He *hardly* worked. *[Barely, almost not at all]*
adverb—verb
Hardly anyone watches black-and-white television. *[Almost no one]*

- *A few* (count) and *a little* (noncount) mean *some,* while *few* and *little* mean *almost none.* The difference is between a positive attitude and a negative attitude.

EXAMPLES
I have *a little* money, so I can lend you some. *[Some, thus positive]*

I have *little* money, so I can't lend you any. *[Almost none, thus negative]*

A few students came, so we were pleased. *[Some, thus positive]*

Few students came, so we were disappointed. *[Almost none, thus negative]*

- *Some* and *any* both mean an indefinite amount. However, *some* is used in positive statements, while *any* is used in negative statements.

EXAMPLES
I have *some* money. *[Positive]*

I *don't* have *any* money. *[Negative]*

- Usually, *well* is an adverb, whereas *good* is an adjective. However, *well* can sometimes be an adjective referring to health. *See the section "Working with Confusing Pairs of Adjectives and Adverbs" on pages 416–418 in Chapter 27.*

EXAMPLES

noun┐ ┌adjective
The *boy* is *good*. *[Well-behaved]*

verb┐┌ adverb
He doesn't feel *well*. *[Poor health]*

noun┐ ┌adjective
The *boy* is *well*. *[Healthy, not sick]*

Prepositions

Prepositions can be very confusing. *See the section "Recognizing Subjects" on pages 253–256 in Chapter 17.*

- Use *on* when one thing touches the surface of another and *in* when one thing encloses another: *on* the desk (on top), *in* the desk (inside a drawer). Also, use *on* if you must step up to board (get *on* a motorcycle/bus/train/large ship), but use *in* if you must step down (get *in* a small boat/car).

- *Since* goes with a specific initial time (*since* 3 P.M.; *since* July 3); *for* goes with duration, a length or period of time (*for* two hours; *for* ten days).

Punctuation

English rules for punctuation differ greatly from those in other languages.

- All sentences have an ending punctuation mark. Statements end with a period (.). Exclamations end with an exclamation point (!). Questions end with a question mark (?). Statements, exclamations, and questions end with only one mark. Avoid multiple punctuation marks at the end of sentences. *See the section "Using Periods, Question Marks, and Exclamation Points" on pages 485–486 in Chapter 31, "Other Punctuation and Capitalization."*

- Do not use commas to connect complete ideas or statements that can stand alone. Instead, use a period and a capital letter, a semicolon, or a comma and a coordinating conjunction. *See Chapter 20, "Comma Splices and Run-on Sentences."*

FAULTY

We finished class, then we got a pizza, later we went to a movie.
[Comma splice]

REVISED

We finished class. Then we got a pizza. Later we went to a movie.
[Separate sentences]

or

We finished class; then we got a pizza; later we went to a movie.
[Clauses joined with semicolons]

or

We finished class, then got a pizza, and later went to a movie.
[Simple sentence with compound verb]

- Commas go before and after a modifying word, phrase, or clause that adds extra information. This means that the sentence can stand alone without the added information. Modifying words, phrases, or clauses that are necessary for identification take no commas. In other words, if the material is crucial to the meaning of the sentence, then do not use commas. *See the section "Using Commas to Set Off Elements That Interrupt Sentence Flow" on pages 474–475 in Chapter 30.*

┌noun┐ ┌──────modifier──────┐
EXAMPLE Never eat beef *that is undercooked.*

Without the modifier, the sentence meaning is changed and incorrect; use no commas.

┌──────noun──────┐ ┌──────modifier──────┐
EXAMPLE Supermarkets, *which we take for granted,* did not even exist a hundred years ago.

Without the modifier, the sentence retains its basic meaning; use commas.

- Semicolons are used to connect independent clauses. They may also be used to separate longer groups of words or lists that already contain commas.

EXAMPLES Cats are lazy; dogs jump around.

Turn in your uniforms on Friday, May 24; Monday, May 27; or Wednesday, May 29.

Writing Paragraphs

Focus on the Needs of Your Audience   Remember that for your paragraph to be effective, it must communicate your ideas simply, clearly, and directly to your reader. Therefore, to meet the needs of your reader, begin with a specific topic sentence to provide direction. Support this topic sentence with several solid supporting examples, and then add a closing sentence that restates the significance of the paragraph

Indentation   Don't use a dash (–) to signal the beginning of a new paragraph. Instead, indent the first line of the paragraph to identify your change of subject or focus. *See the section "Recognizing the Structure of a Paragraph" on pages 27–31 in Chapter 3, "Composing: Creating a Draft."*

Unity   Every sentence in a paragraph should be connected to the same topic, or main idea. In other words, the material should be unified. *See the section "Maintaining Unity" on pages 46–48 in Chapter 4, "Refining and Polishing Your Draft."* If you change direction in the middle of the paragraph to talk about another idea, even if it is related, your teachers may call it a *digression*. Digressions are allowed in some languages, but not in English. One way to avoid digression is to have a plan for organizing your examples. For example, move from most common to least common, or from the familiar to the unfamiliar, or from the least important to the most important.

EXAMPLES

a common traveler's problem in airports

next most common problem

the most common problem

an important study habit for final exams

a more important study habit for final exams

the most important study habit for final exams

Finally, avoid digressions by keeping sentences short and tightly connected. Don't try to put too many unrelated ideas in one sentence or paragraph.

FAULTY The writer warned us about the problem, he said it was very dangerous, he gave us convincing statistics. *[Three separate ideas; comma splice]*

REVISED The writer used convincing statistics to warn about the dangerous problem. *[Ideas are combined and connected.]*

Writing Essays

Think about Audience Expectations   Be businesslike: Go directly to your main idea. Don't try to tell your readers everything. Choose and limit your focus as much as possible. This narrowing of the topic may be much more extreme than you are used to in your native language or culture.

Strive for Clarity   Most North American readers like everything important to be explained; they don't like to have to guess what something means. Thus, you must keep your writing clear and simple. At the same time, be as specific as possible with your ideas. Your readers will want facts, details, and examples, so provide as many as you can. In other words, **amplify**.

Don't try to be too formal, but don't rely too heavily on the pronoun *you*. Doing so will make your writing less specific and clear. Say *who* you mean: the student, the tourist, the opposition. Finally, when you revise your sentences, eliminate extra words and imprecise expressions.

FAULTY   [the group of people who lead the university and decide on policy

REVISED   [the board of governors

Reinforce Your Point with a "Concluding Paragraph"   Never just stop writing. Always conclude with a few final words about your topic. This conclusion can repeat your main idea, but it should also show the significance of what you have said. Try to say how or why your topic is important and worth paying attention to.

Revise to Correct Errors   Proofread before you turn in your paper. When you proofread, watch for the common mistakes discussed above. If possible, have a native speaker in one of your classes or a writing lab look at your paper before you turn it in. *See Chapter 4, "Refining and Polishing Your Draft," Chapter 14, "Developing an Essay," and Chapter 15, "Examining Types of Essays," for guidelines on how to develop and write an essay.*

Credits

Text Credits

Judith Ortiz Cofer, "5:00 a.m.: Writing as Ritual." From *The Latin Deli: Prose & Poetry* by Judith Ortiz Cofer. Copyright 1993 by Judith Ortiz Cofer. Used by permission of the University of Georgia Press.

Amy Tan, "Fish Cheeks." Copyright © 1987 by Amy Tan. First appeared in *Seventeen Magazine.* Reprinted by permission of the author and the Sandra Dijkstra Literary Agency.

Andrew Sullivan, "Society Is Dead. We Have Retreated into the iWorld." Originally published in *The Sunday Times.* Copyright © 2005 by Andrew Sullivan, reprinted with permission of The Wylie Agency LLC.

Stanley Fish, "Getting Coffee Is Hard to Do." From *The New York Times.* August 5, 2007. © 2007, *The New York Times.* All rights reserved. Used by permission and protected by the copyright laws of the United States. The printing, copying, redistribution, or retransmission of the material without express written permission is prohibited.

Maria Muniz, "Back, But Not Home." *The New York Times,* July 13, 1979 (Op-Ed). © 1979, *The New York Times.* Reprinted by permission.

Bob Greene, "Words, Good or Bad, Can Echo through a Lifetime." *The Chicago Tribune,* November 10, 1997. Copyright © 1997 by Tribune Media Services, Inc. All rights reserved. Reprinted with permission.

Ryoko Kokuba, "Love in Culture." Used by permission of the author.

Stephanie Jezak, "Pride." Used by permission of the author.

Elizabeth Cabral, "To Be Free, or Not to Be." Used by permission of the author.

Greg Andree, "Fear Not." Used by permission of the author.

Jennifer Mcelroy, "Non-Traditional Jobs." Used by permission of the author.

Josh Trepanier, "R-E-S-P-E-C-T." Used by permission of the author.

Sarah Martin, "Adam." Used by permission of the author.

Photo Credits

Part opener: © FogStock LLC/Index Stock Imagery, Inc.; **10:** Lonely Planet Images/Getty Images; **24:** Getty Images; **43:** Pedro Armestre/AFP/Getty Images; **71:** Alison Wright/Corbis; **83:** Akiko Aoki/Getty Images; **91:** Gary Yeowell/Getty Images; **99:** Harvey Martin/Peter Arnold; **107:** Daniel Berehulak/Getty Images; **116:** Getty Images; **125:** Juan Pratginestos/Getty Images; **134:** Minden Pictures/Getty Images; **144:** Dougal Waters/Getty Images; **157:** Issei Kato/Reuters/Landov; **186:** Charles & Josette Lenars/Corbis; **192:** Skip Nall/Getty Images; **195:** Altrendo Images/Getty Images; **197:** Photo by Kevin Winter/American Idol 2009/Getty Images for FOX; **200:** Ron Watts/Corbis; **204:** Stephen St. John/National Geographic Image Collection; **207:** Marc Trigalou/Getty Images; **211:** Reinhard Dirscherl/Getty Images; **213:** Pigeon Productions SA/Getty Images; **221:** Devendra M. Singh/AFP/Getty Images; **248:** AFP/Getty Images; **504:** Self Portrait dedicated to Paul Gauguin, 1888 (oil on canvas) by Vincent van Gogh (185390) © Fogg Art Museum, Harvard University Art Museums, USA/Bequest from the Collection of Maurice Wertheim, Class of 1906/The Bridgeman Art Library.

Rhetorical Index

Writers combine rhetorical modes to communicate their ideas in paragraphs and essays. Often, one mode is dominant, and one or more additional modes are used to provide illustration or support. To help you understand the characteristics of each mode, this index lists the paragraphs and essays in the text by chapter. Paragraphs and essays that contain characteristics of more than one mode are listed more than once, under the headings for each of those modes.

Paragraphs and Essays by Mode in Each Chapter

PART ONE Starting Out

1 Ensuring Success in Writing

Example
A successful and, in some cases, controversial innovation, 8
From my experience, 5
A successful and controversial innovation in television, 8

Definition
A successful and controversial innovation, 8
From my experience, 5

Cause and Effect
A successful and controversial innovation in television, 8

3 Composing: Creating a Draft

Narration
The most beautiful sight I ever witnessed, 36
Last year, my aunt was a victim of identify theft, 28

Description
The most beautiful sight I ever witnessed, 36
Last year, my aunt was a victim of identify theft, 28

Example
The most beautiful sight I ever witnessed, 36
Last year, my aunt was a victim of identify theft, 28
Carl Jung's theories about personality types, 38
Connecting: Only a Click Away, 41

Cause and Effect
Connecting: Only a Click Away, 41

4 Refining and Polishing Your Draft

Narration
Getting my driver's license was the most stressful experience, 46
Being called for jury duty, 51
One of my best childhood memories, 52
When I was young, one of my favorite spots, 57
My job last summer as a flagger for a construction company, 58

Description
Getting my driver's license was the most stressful experience, 46
The biggest transformation I have ever seen, 52
When I was young, one of my favorite spots, 57
My job last summer as a flagger for a construction company, 58
The parents of juveniles, 54

Example
Research has led to dramatic changes, 63
Through their own behavior, 46, 76
Everyone who drives or rides in a car, 60
The parents of juveniles, 54

Comparison and Contrast
The biggest transformation I have ever seen, 52

Process
Good time management is the key to success in college, 49
When I want to relax, 50

Cause and Effect
The parents of juveniles, 54
Research has led to dramatic changes, 63

Index

A

a/an, 551
Abel, Daniel C., 240
Absolute terms, 151, 158
Abstracts. *See* Summaries
accept/except, 153
Acronyms, 495
Action verbs, 250, 262
Active reading, 225–226, 508–510.
 See also Reading
Active voice, 359, 369
"Adam" (Martin), 540–541
Addresses, 476, 477, 495
ad hominem argument, 151, 152
Adjectives. *See also* Modifiers
 comparative form of, 414–416,
  429, 430
 confusing, 416–418, 430
 ESL writers and, 548
 explanation of, 412, 429
 positive form of, 413–414,
  429, 430
 superlative form of, 414–416,
  429, 430
Adverbs. *See also* Modifiers
 comparative form of,
  414–416, 429
 confusing, 416–418, 430
 conjunctive, 283–284, 289
 explanation of, 412, 429
 positive form of, 413–414, 429
 superlative form of,
  414–416, 429
advice/advise, 453
affect/effect, 453
Agreement. *See* Pronoun–antecedent
 agreement; Subject–verb
 agreement
Albom, Mitch, 129
all ready/already, 454
all right, 451
a lot, 451
Alternating format
 for comparison and contrast
  essays, 122
 explanation of, 122, 126
*American Places: A Writer's Pilgrimage
 to 15 of This Country's Most
 Visited and Cherished Sites*
 (Zinsser), 138
American Psychological Association
 (APA) method, 149, 216–218, 222

among/between, 454
Amount, agreement in, 322–324
Amplification
 in drafts, 62–63
 in essays, 178, 556
 explanation of, 187
Analysis, logical method of,
 138–141
and, 433
Andree, Greg, 533–534
Anecdotes, 171, 187
Antecedents, 386. *See also*
 Pronoun–antecedent agreement
any/some, 553
APA system of documentation, 149,
 216–218, 222
Apostrophes
 in contractions, 488–489
 explanation of, 488, 502
 with possessive nouns, 488
 use of, 489–490
Appositive fragments, 271, 272
Appositives
 explanation of, 271, 277, 385
 nouns as, 375
Argument writing
 checklists for, 158, 221
 developing support in, 147–150
 emphatic order in, 154
 for essays, 214–221
 examples of, 147, 149–151,
  153–155, 218–219
 explanation of, 146, 158,
  159, 222
 logic in, 151–153
 tone in, 150–151
 topic sentences in, 147
 transitional expressions for, 154
"Aria: A Memoir of a Bilingual
 Childhood" (Rodriguez), 86
Articles, ESL writers and, 551–552
Ashen, Frank, 120
Audience, 555, 556. *See also* Readers
The Autobiography of Malcolm X
 (Malcom X & Haley), 130
Average readers, 5, 11

B

"Back, But Not Home" (Muniz),
 520–521
bad/badly, 416–417
Bandwagon approach, 152

Bauby, Jean-Dominique, 88–89
Begging the question, 152
Begley, Sharon, 141
Berliner, David C., 119–120
between/among, 454
Bird by Bird (Lamott), 77
Block format
 for comparison and contrast essays,
  121–122
 explanation of, 121, 126
Body
 of essays, 165, 186
 of paragraphs, 28, 44
Brainstorming
 example of, 14–15
 explanation of, 14, 24
brake/break, 454
Branching
 example of, 18
 explanation of, 17, 25

C

Cabral, Elizabeth (student),
 530–531
can/could, 349–350, 356
can/may, 454
Capitalization
 explanation of, 484, 494, 501
 guidelines for, 494–496, 503
Carson, Rachel, 95
Case, pronoun, 388–390, 410
Cause and effect writing
 avoiding oversimplification in,
  130–131
 checklists for, 135, 211
 distinguishing between direct and
  related issues in, 129–130
 effective arrangement in,
  131–132
 for essays, 208–211
 examples of, 129–132, 208–209
 explanation of, 129, 135,
  136, 222
 topic sentences in, 129
 transitional expressions for,
  49, 132
Causes
 direct, 129, 135
 explanation of, 128
 related, 129, 135
 transitional expressions for, 132
-cede, 451